Gree
Medi
Britisl
The Instruments and Accoutrements of Ancient Medicine

Ralph Jackson

With contributions from
Susan La Niece, Duncan Hook
and Rebecca Stacey

The British Museum

For Sylvia

Publication supported by

Publishers
The British Museum
Great Russell Street
London WC1B 3DG

Series editor
Sarah Faulks

Greek and Roman Medicine at the British Museum:
The Instruments and Accoutrements of Ancient Medicine
Ralph Jackson

ISBN 9780861592326
ISSN 1747 3640

Front cover: Tombstone of the physician Jason, with a larger-than-life depiction of a cupping vessel at right, symbol of his profession. British Museum, London, 1865,0103.3 (Cat. no. 6.4)

Printed and bound in the UK by 4edge Ltd, Hockley

Papers used by the British Museum are recyclable products made from wood grown in well-managed forests and other controlled sources. The manufacturing processes conform to the environmental regulations of the country of origin.

Contents

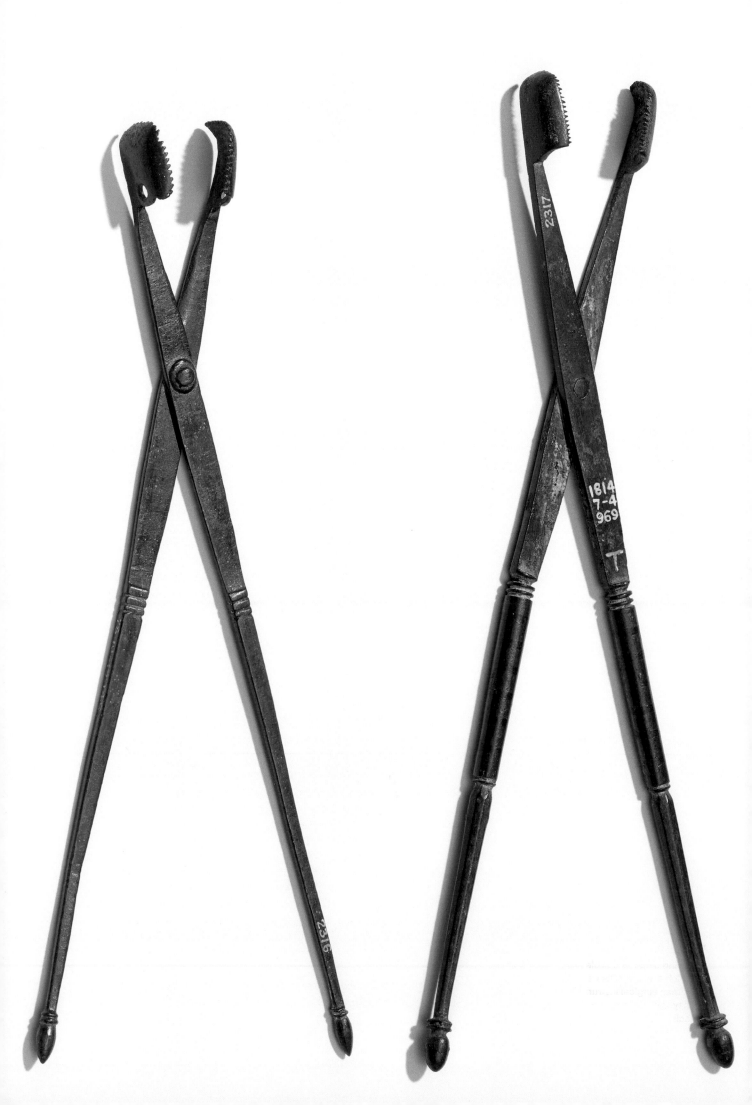

Preface

When I was appointed a curator in the British Museum's Department of Prehistoric and Romano-British Antiquities in 1977 I already had an interest in Roman medicine and it soon became my principal field of research alongside many other curatorial responsibilities. At that time little work was being done on the archaeology of medicine, as opposed to the very considerable research on ancient medical texts. Medical instruments, in particular, were ill-understood, and it was clear that there was considerable scope for investigating and clarifying the Museum's holdings. Many stimulating hours were spent delving into, and researching, the displayed and reserve collections, confirming some of the objects already identified as medical instruments, identifying new ones and rejecting others that were found to be not medical instruments but domestic implements or craft tools.

In tandem with that research I made study trips to examine and record instruments in collections in many other museums in Britain. Further afield I was able to enrich my records through work on collections in several different countries, including the important Vesuvian collections in Pompeii and Naples in 1981, key collections in Germany and Paris in 1985, the very significant collections in Rome and Ostia in 1991 and then, in 1996 and 2001, in Bologna, on the extraordinary medical assemblage of the Rimini *domus* del Chirurgo. In Britain, as in all those other places, I had fruitful discussions with curatorial and academic colleagues, and with medical practitioners, which enabled me to begin to publish the results of my research.

I started with the Museum's set of instruments from Italy, one of the largest sets of medical instruments then known. In publishing it I endeavoured not only to reveal its intrinsic interest, and to place it in the context of other Roman medical finds, but also to integrate the evidence of the instruments with that from the contemporary medical texts (Jackson 1986; Jackson 1987). Subsequently, in a paper in the then new *Journal of Roman Archaeology*, I reviewed current work on Roman medicine and published the first comprehensive illustrated typology of Roman surgical instruments (Jackson 1990a). Also evident at that time was the lack of an up-to-date, accurate and accessible overall account of Roman medicine, a gap I sought to fill with my book *Doctors and Diseases in the Roman Empire* (British Museum Press 1988). Here, too, the integration of historical, epigraphic, scientific and archaeological research underpinned the work, with the aim of achieving a balanced picture of ancient medicine, both for an academic and a lay readership.

In my other projects on medical history in the ancient world I have explored new aspects, focussed on particular subjects or provided general accounts and overviews. A paper on the archaeology of waters and spas (Jackson 1990c) was later re-visited and developed, with an emphasis on the modes of provision and perceived benefits of waters (Jackson 1999). The socio-cultural context for healers in the Roman world and their *modus operandi*, were the subjects of further papers (Jackson 1993; Jackson 1995a; Jackson 2005b; Jackson 2009a; Jackson 2012b), while in others I dealt specifically with surgeons and their instruments (Jackson 1997a; Jackson 2002a; Jackson 2018a). In particular, the opportunity was taken to correlate the results of current research on surgical instruments with the finest written source on the

Facing page: Two uvula forceps (*staphylagra*) (Cat. nos 3.101, 3.100) which exemplify the careful design and fine craftsmanship of many Roman surgical instruments. With their hollow, finely toothed jaws they were used above all in throat operations, especially to facilitate the excision of an elongated uvula

instrumentation of the early Roman Empire, the *On Medicine* (*De medicina*) of Cornelius Celsus (Jackson 1994a).

A continuing research interest has been the identification of instruments developed for surgical specialisms and applied to specific operative techniques which, together with the publication of important finds, new and old, has helped to expand and clarify our understanding of ancient surgery. These include syntheses of all sources of evidence for two of the major areas of ancient medical treatment, eye medicine (Jackson 1996a; Jackson 2013) and bone surgery, including cranial trepanation (Jackson 2002c; Jackson 2005a); detailed accounts of the enigmatic artefacts commonly known as 'oculists' stamps', together with a discussion of their role in ancient healing systems (Jackson 1990b; Jackson 1996b; 2012a); a full treatment of vesical calculus, lithotomy and the instrumentation employed in resolving this painful condition, famously included in the 'Hippocratic Oath' (Jackson 2010); comprehensive studies of bivalve dilators, uvula forceps and the operation for counter-circumcision (Jackson 1991; Jackson 1992; Jackson 2005c); full publication of an important surgical kit from Cyrene (Jackson 2021) and of the very early and idiosyncratic set of instruments in the 'Doctor's Burial' at Stanway (Jackson 1997c; Jackson 2007a; Jackson 2011c) and other important new finds (Jackson 1997b; Jackson 2007b); an in-depth study of the varieties and uses of the most basic of surgical tools, the scalpel (Jackson 2014a); focused analyses of the evidence for the practice of medicine and surgery in Roman London and Britain (Jackson 2008; Jackson 2011a); and reports on the fabulous instrumentation from the *domus* del Chirurgo at Rimini, the largest and most important find, Empire-wide, to date (Jackson 2002b; Jackson 2003; Jackson 2009b; Jackson 2011d; Jackson 2011e).

Throughout, I have worked closely with colleagues in Britain and abroad, especially in Germany, Austria, Belgium, the Netherlands, France, Switzerland, Italy, Greece and the USA. Our research on securely contexted and well-dated finds has defined a diagnostic range of Roman medical instruments, and it is now possible to identify with confidence the many important, but mostly un-contexted, instruments in the British Museum collections. My protracted study of those collections is here combined with the critical work of other British Museum specialists – Susan La Niece, Duncan Hook, Rebecca Stacey, Craig Williams and Saul Peckham – to all of whom I owe unbounded thanks for the detailed scientific examinations and analyses, the finest drawings, and the clearest photographs. It is our hope that this publication will comprise a major contribution to the understanding of ancient surgical instruments, of Greek and Roman surgery and of the history of medicine.

It is impossible to name all of the myriad people who have been involved in my work on this book, but I owe especial thanks to all of the following:

At the British Museum, to Catherine Johns, Don Bailey†, Richard Hobbs, Stephen Crummy, Sam Moorhead, Simon James, Chris Entwistle, Tim Potter†, Jill Cook, Brian Cook†, Dyfri Williams, Lesley Fitton, Ian Jenkins†, Judith Swaddling, Susan Walker, Lucilla Burn, Paul Roberts, Peter Higgs, Thorsten Opper, Alexandra Villing, Ross Thomas†, Kim Overend, Alex Truscott, Tim Chamberlain, Celeste Farge, Charles Arnold, Evelyn Wood, Trevor Coughlan, Keith Lowe, David Hurn, Rosario (Charo) Rovira Guardiola, Elisabeth O'Connell, Nick Reeves, Andrew Burnett, Richard Abdy, Roger Bland, Janet Larkin, Mary Hinton, Mike Cowell, Paul Craddock, Caroline Cartwright, Nigel Meek, Sheridan Bowman, Janet Ambers†, Pippa Pearce, Marilyn Hockey and Robert Anderson.

Beyond the British Museum, my thanks are above all to Ernst Künzl, Larry Bliquez and Vivian Nutton, the kindest and most generous of colleagues over so many decades, to all of whom I owe an enormous debt of gratitude; also to many others who have generously provided information, shared new finds, and discussed important aspects of ancient medicine, including Antje Krug, Klaus-Dietrich Fischer, Jacopo Ortalli, Michel Feugère, Danielle Gourevitch†, Marie-Hélène Marganne, Véronique Dasen, Muriel Pardon-Labonnelie, Jacques Voinot, Paul Janssens†, Lara de Merode, Luciana Rita Angeletti, Valentina Gazzaniga, Carla Serarcangeli, Renato Mariani-Costantini, Gino Fornaciari, Luigi Taborelli, Demetrios Michaelides, Despina Ignatiadou, Maarten Dolmans, Alain Touwaide, Emanuela Appetiti, George Boon†, Nina Crummy, Philip Crummy, Jenny Hall, Angela Wardle, Nick Griffiths, Michael Vickers, Chris Sparey-Green, Lindsay Allason-Jones, Jim Thorn†, Dorothy Thorn†, Bob Arnott, James Longrigg, Helen King, Rebecca Flemming, Philip van der Eijk, John Scarborough†, Roger Tomlin, Mark Hassall, Alan Bowman, Anthony Birley†, John Kirkup, Paul Swain, Spyros Retsas, Ravi Kunzru, Kordula Gostenčnik, Annette Frölich, Peter Clayton, James Ede, Paul Thackray, Nodge Nolan†, Bruno Vanwalscappel, Alexia Morel, Christof Flügel, Gail Boyle, Janette McWilliam, Peter Schertz and Ralf Grüsssinger.

I am especially grateful to Vivian Nutton and to Nina Crummy, both of whom kindly found time to read through a draft of this book. With their deep knowledge and expertise they made many valuable suggestions for its improvement. On the editorial side my most profound thanks go to Sarah Faulks, who combines long experience with a warm, patient, friendly approach and the highest professional standards. That is a formidable combination of skills, and Sarah has been simply the finest editor I could have wished for. I thank, too, Carolyn Jones for immaculate copy-editing and Nicola King for a terrific index. Finally, I reserve my warmest thanks for Sylvia Took, who has shared with me, for many years, the excitement of new finds which continue to illuminate more fully the practice of medicine in the Greco-Roman era. But she has also had to endure the protracted process of this publication, so to Sylvia I owe my greatest debt of all, and I dedicate this book to her.

Chapter 1
Introduction: The British Museum Greek and Roman Medical Collection

Strategies for the preservation of health and for the prevention and treatment of illness and disease have been discerned in the surviving written records and material remains of most societies since earliest times. Compared to the prehistoric past, the evidence for the ancient Greek and Roman periods is comparatively full, though still sparse or lacking in some key areas. The written evidence includes numerous detailed medical texts supplemented by writings commenting on medicine and medical practitioners, while the physical evidence includes the workplaces, homes and memorials of medical practitioners, their medical equipment and *materia medica*, and, via their mortal remains, some of the patients themselves, with traces of their diseases and treatments.

This book focuses on the medical equipment. It includes a full discussion, *comparanda* and catalogue of the principal instruments, implements and utensils of Greek and Roman surgery in the British Museum collection, together with other selected objects in the collection which also shed light on Classical medicine and health-care, both mortal and divine. It comprises mainly objects in the Department of Greece and Rome and the Department of Britain, Europe and Prehistory, together with a small component in the Department of Egypt and Sudan and the Department of Coins and Medals.

Medicine in antiquity had none of the clear-cut divisions that characterise healing systems today, and a diverse range of objects played their part in the prevention or treatment of disease. Not all were designed exclusively for healing or health-preserving roles, and it is important to differentiate the distinctive purpose-made medical and surgical equipment from para-medical and para-surgical implements and utensils which had non-medical applications, too. Central to the British Museum's Greek and Roman medical collection is a very important assemblage of surgical instruments, the great majority of which belong to the period of the Roman Empire. They comprise examples of all the essential tools of ancient surgery, together with several examples of more rarely preserved specialised instruments. They vary from simple (but effective) instruments to examples with elaborate decoration or costly inlays. The collection also includes medical and pharmaceutical implements and utensils, notably scoops and spoons, palettes, jars and drug boxes – some of them still containing traces of *materia medica*.

One very particular aspect of Roman medicine, and one of the few areas of specialisation, was eye medicine. The Museum collection includes a few instruments relating to eye surgery, but also more extensive evidence for the medical treatment of eye conditions, notably the objects known as oculists' stamps or collyrium-stamps, small stone blocks engraved with prescriptions for eye complaints and intended for marking sticks of eye-salves (*collyria*) (**Fig. 1**). The 14 stamps in the British Museum comprise one of the largest collections of these artefacts, which are especially characteristic of the north-west provinces of the Roman Empire. The collyrium-stamps are not the only inscribed material of medical significance. There are also decrees honouring Greek physicians; Roman wooden writing-tablets mentioning doctors, drugs and patients; and a graffito on a

Figure 1 The 14 collyrium-stamps in the British Museum collection (Cat. nos 3.131–44)

pottery bowl fragment recording a veterinary doctor. Perhaps most famous of all is the inscribed tombstone of the doctor Jason, from Athens, showing him in characteristic pose, examining a patient. The other images of healing personnel, primarily the healer gods Asklepios/Aesculapius and Hygieia/Salus, are in a variety of media – stone statuary and sculpture, bronze and terracotta figurines, and engraved gemstones. There are coins and lamps with scenes and images of medical significance, engraved and inscribed amulets, a range of stone, metal and terracotta anatomical votives, representing most of the body parts, and a movingly realistic depiction of disease on a Hellenistic ivory figurine.

These objects entered the British Museum in a number of different ways over a long period of time. There was no policy for the concerted acquisition of medical material. Instead, the Greek and Roman medical collection accumulated naturally as a component of the opportunistic acquisition of worldwide material culture. In consequence, the medical collection, though rich, is somewhat uneven in its coverage. From the very beginning of the Museum there was an interest in things medical – Sir Hans Sloane (1660–1753), whose carefully selected collection comprised the largest and most important of the three founding collections of the Museum in 1753, was a medical practitioner (Wilson 2002, 11–18). So, too, were many collectors and antiquaries of his day, and interest in the history of their profession caused some of them to collect ancient medical objects. The benefactors, donors and vendors, of the 18th and 19th centuries in particular, contributed important artefacts and groups of material to the greatly expanding collection of the British Museum. Two collyrium-stamps (Cat. nos 3.140 and 3.143) and a statuette of Asklepios were acquired as part of the Sloane Bequest. Soon after, in 1772, by means of 'the first parliamentary grant for the augmentation of the Museum

collection' (Walters 1899, xiii), the Museum purchased the large 'first collection of antiquities' amassed by Sir William Hamilton (1730–1803). Unlike Sloane, whose collection was concentrated on natural history, Hamilton, 'a man of the Enlightenment', socially and diplomatically successful as Minister to Naples, formed his collections in Italy at a time when the study of Classical Roman antiquity was being revolutionised (Wilson 2002, 45–8). Mainly concerned with more substantial pieces, his collection nevertheless includes a gold finger-ring with a bust of Asklepios and a bronze figurine showing the god reclining.

More significant for present purposes was the large and wide-ranging collection of Mr Charles Townley (1737–1805), which was acquired by the British Museum after his death. Celebrated principally for its Classical sculpture, it also contained a selection of surgical instruments and objects connected to medicine and health in the Roman era, including several notable pieces: nine engraved gems showing Asklepios and Hygieia, a bronze figurine of Hygieia (Cat. no. 6.33), a fine ivory figurine depicting severe spinal deformity (**Fig. 2**) (Cat. no. 6.10), and a lamp with a satirical scene of surgery (Cat. no. 6.11). The Roman surgical instruments included two scalpel handles, two spring forceps, a fine uvula forceps, a double sharp hook, a needle-holder, a spouted spoon, three scoop probes and three spatula probes (Cat. nos 3.57, 3.74, 3.83, 3.89, 3.100, 3.103, 3.106, 3.115, 3.117, 3.122). Although details of provenance and finding circumstances directly linked to the instruments are lacking there is a record of the acquisition of surgical instruments in an entry in one of Townley's manuscript notebooks of purchases he made: '1777 Rome April 11, Ditto [i.e. Byres] for some antient [sic] chirurgical instruments &c 13 in number' (Mr Brian Cook *in litt.* 1 May 1991). The fact that Townley purchased the instruments from Byres implies they were found in the neighbourhood of Rome or in the city itself. For Townley formed his collection by purchasing from collectors and dealers in Rome, and James Byres, one of a group of rich Englishmen who lived in Rome with rights to excavation at major sites there, was one of his chief sources (Wilson 2002, 46, 65–6).

Another collection formed mainly in Italy was that of the 1st duc de Blacas d'Aulps (1771–1839), former French Ambassador to Naples and to Rome. His son, the 2nd Duke (1815–1866), inherited and enlarged the already formidable collection – it included the fabulous late 4th-century AD Esquiline Treasure – and when he died the British Museum acted quickly to purchase it (Wilson 2002, 151–2). Comprising distinguished sculpture and bronzes, paintings, glass and vases, and an exceptional collection of gems, it also included a large number and range of objects connected to ancient health and healing – seven engraved gems depicting Asklepios and Hygieia (Cat. nos 6.35–7), the marble head from a colossal statue of Asklepios (Cat. no. 6.38), a marble figured relief dedicated to Asklepios, an inscribed marble votive relief (Cat. no. 6.14), and 17 medical instruments (**Fig. 3**) (Cat. nos 3.58–9, 3.61–2, 3.82, 3.87, 3.94–5, 3.102, 3.112–13, 3.128). It is not known which of the Dukes acquired the instruments, where they were found and under what circumstances, but it is probable that they were a set found in or around Naples or Rome, cities in which the 1st Duke had been French Ambassador (see p. 99).

The collection of Mr Charles Roach Smith (1807–1890), another celebrated early acquisition by the Museum, was of a very different nature to that of the Dukes of Blacas. It consisted of over 5,000 objects, mostly of Roman and medieval date and often with precise finding details, painstakingly assembled between the 1830s and 1850s during building and sewage works and dredging of the Thames in London (Kidd 1977). Purchased in 1856, it formed the nucleus of the Museum's burgeoning British collection. Smith was an enthusiastic and vociferous antiquary, but he was, by profession, a pharmacist and appropriately his collection included a samian cup impressed with a collyrium-stamp (Cat. no. 3.145).

Provenance is also the merit of the few objects of medical significance in the part of the collection of Gaulish bronzes of Ambroise Comarmond that the Museum purchased in 1851: 'statuettes and smaller objects found chiefly in the neighbourhood of Lyons'. Two (Cat. nos 3.104, 3.126) have a provenance – Vaison – and the other two (Cat. nos 3.110, 3.147), like the rest of the collection, are likely to have been found in or near Lyon. Similarly, in the collection of Classical antiquities, bequeathed to the Museum in 1856 by Sir William Temple (1788–1856), the three surgical instruments were probably acquired when he was British Minister at Naples, and are likely, therefore, to have come from southern Italy – no find-spot was specified for the two scalpel handles (Cat. nos 3.52 and 3.63), but the forceps is provenanced Ruvo, Puglia (Cat. no. 3.86). Also from Italy – from Rome – is the finely inlaid scalpel handle (Cat. no. 3.68) from the collection of the Italian dealer Count Alessandro Castellani (1823–1883). Important parts of his choice collection, principally of gems, jewellery and sculpture, were purchased by the Museum in 1872 and 1873 and, in addition to the scalpel handle, included a bronze

Figure 2 A Hellenistic ivory figurine depicting a man suffering serious, chronic disease (Cat. no. 6.10)

figurine of Asklepios and a gem engraved with an image of the god. Another notable gem, probably the seal-stone of a specialist in eye medicine, was purchased in 1859 (Cat. no. 6.3), and in 1864 a fine marble statuary group of Asklepios with Telesphorus (Cat. no. 6.42) was acquired by the Museum as part of the collection purchased from Percy Smythe, 8th Viscount Strangford (1825–1869). A year later, following the death of Comte de Pourtalès-Gorgier (1776–1855) and the sale of his collection at auction in Paris, the Museum purchased the already famous Athenian marble tombstone of the doctor Jason, with its vivid scene showing Jason examining a patient (Cat. no. 6.4).

Objects with Asklepian imagery are amongst several notable pieces linked to health and medicine in the collection bequeathed to the Museum by Mr James Woodhouse, who died in 1866. Woodhouse lived in southern Italy and then on Corfu, where he formed a large collection of coins and miscellaneous antiquities, mostly found on Corfu. In addition to a cupping vessel (Cat. no. 3.49), the Museum's only example, Woodhouse had previously given the Museum a coin, minted in Atrax, Thessaly, with the image of a cupping vessel on its reverse (Cat. no. 6.27). As well as a range of probes, one of silver (Cat. Cat. nos 3.114, 3.120), the objects relevant to healing and medicine in his

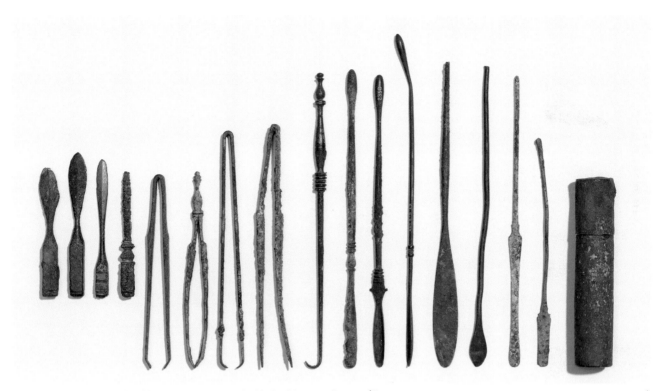

Figure 3 The Roman medical instruments acquired with the Blacas collection (Cat. nos 3.58–9, 3.61–2, 3.82, 3.87, 3.94–5, 3.102, 3.112–13, 3.128)

bequest include a miniature lead ointment pot (Cat. no. 3.130), a lamp with an image of Asklepios on the discus, and a fine terracotta figurine of the god (Cat. no. 6.31). The ointment pot joined another, from Athens (Cat. no. 3.129), that the Museum had acquired in 1842 as part of the Thomas Burgon Collection. Also in 1866 the Museum was presented with a medicine box from Cyrenaica (Cat. no. 3.125) by George Dennis (1814–1898), whose *Cities and Cemeteries of Etruria* had been published by the Museum in 1848. Soon after, in 1870, the Museum purchased the collection of the Rev. John Hutton Pollexfen (1813–1899) of over 800 Colchester antiquities, assembled in the town in the 1850s and 1860s (Jackson 2012c). It included a specialised surgical forceps, new to the Museum collection (Cat. no. 3.99).

The acquisition of the Pollexfen Colection was achieved through the strenuous efforts of Sir Augustus Wollaston Franks (1826–1897) who, 14 years earlier, had enthusiastically encouraged the Museum's purchase of the Roach Smith collection. Keeper of the Department of British and Mediaeval Antiquities and Ethnography from 1866–1896 (declining the Directorship in 1878), Franks was a great polymath, regarded by some as the most important figure in the history of the Museum (Caygill and Cherry 1997; Wilson 2002, 193). As one of Europe's most powerful curator-connoisseurs, he was in touch with numerous collectors and he encouraged many to donate to the British Museum, like General Augustus W.H. Meyrick (1826–1902) who, in 1878, presented his large collection of Asian arms and Egyptian, Greek and Roman antiquities. This 'large collection of small objects' (Walters 1899, xvi) included a significant number and range of medical instruments – five scalpel handles, a uvula forceps, a needle-holder and four spatula probes (Cat. nos 3.53, 3.55, 3.60, 3.70, 3.75, 3.101, 3.107, 3.116, 3.118). They are intrinsically interesting, and the

similarity of the patina of the uvula forceps and needle-holder suggest they may have been found together. Unfortunately, however, all the instruments lack any record of their place and circumstance of discovery as, too, does a collyrium-stamp (Cat. no. 3.142) that Meyrick had evidently acquired from his cousin, Sir Samuel Rush Meyrick at Goodrich Court.

Collyrium-stamps were one of the many classes of material that took the interest of Augustus Franks and he compiled a detailed notebook of them – *List of stamps of Roman oculists* (undated manuscript in Department of Britain, Europe and Prehistory, British Museum). Appropriately, four of the Museum's collyrium-stamps and a scalpel handle (Cat. nos 3.54, 3.131–3, 3.137), all with provenance, were among the many gifts and bequests that Franks made, and a further two collyrium-stamps were acquired (Cat. nos 3.136, 3.141), probably at his prompting, during his long keepership. Around the turn of the century three notable scalpel handles were acquired as individual objects (Cat. nos 3.64–5, 3.76) to join the growing collection of medical instruments, while H.B. Walters included a number of hitherto undocumented instruments in his 1899 catalogue of bronzes, amongst them several scalpel handles and forceps (Cat. nos 3.51–2, 3.56, 3.85) and the fine folding handle for a surgical drill (Cat. no. 3.78) which, lacking any *comparanda*, he included in his section G Miscellaneous Implements, described as 'compasses, working on a hinge' (Walter 1899, 338, no. 2674).

Then, in 1907, a work of fundamental importance to our subject was published, John Stewart Milne's *Surgical Instruments in Greek and Roman Times*. The son of a Hartlepool schoolmaster, Milne was a medical practitioner and surgeon with first-hand experience of the practice of pre-modern medicine. That experience, together with his Classical education, enabled him to write with particular insight into ancient surgery and its instruments, because some of the

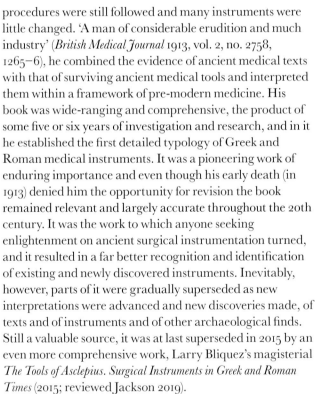

Figure 4 A Roman carnelian gemstone showing a doctor with his patient under the watchful eye of the great healer god Asklepios/ Aesculapius (Cat. no. 6.5). Drawing by Sue Bird

procedures were still followed and many instruments were little changed. 'A man of considerable erudition and much industry' (*British Medical Journal* 1913, vol. 2, no. 2758, 1265–6), he combined the evidence of ancient medical texts with that of surviving ancient medical tools and interpreted them within a framework of pre-modern medicine. His book was wide-ranging and comprehensive, the product of some five or six years of investigation and research, and in it he established the first detailed typology of Greek and Roman medical instruments. It was a pioneering work of enduring importance and even though his early death (in 1913) denied him the opportunity for revision the book remained relevant and largely accurate throughout the 20th century. It was the work to which anyone seeking enlightenment on ancient surgical instrumentation turned, and it resulted in a far better recognition and identification of existing and newly discovered instruments. Inevitably, however, parts of it were gradually superseded as new interpretations were advanced and new discoveries made, of texts and of instruments and of other archaeological finds. Still a valuable source, it was at last superseded in 2015 by an even more comprehensive work, Larry Bliquez's magisterial *The Tools of Asclepius. Surgical Instruments in Greek and Roman Times* (2015; reviewed Jackson 2019).

Milne drew heavily on the medical discoveries at Pompeii and Herculaneum for, in contrast to many of the instruments then in museums and private collections, they provided at least a secure provenance and the *terminus ante quem* of AD 79, if not always a properly recorded context, for numerous medical instruments, some of novel form. Nevertheless, with comparatively few sets or groups of instruments from secure dated contexts at his disposal, he occasionally wrongly attributed a medical application to a number of objects (see, e.g., Bliquez 2015, 4). Those in the British Museum include two iron knives from Orvieto that are not Roman surgical knives but 16th-century table

cutlery (Walters 1899, 2330–1; Milne 1907, 27, pl. 5.1-2; Scarborough 1969, pl. 44, lower left; Bliquez 1981, 12, top left; Victoria and Albert Museum 1979, 4–7, nos 19–20), and two 'bifurcated probes', which are also, in fact, items of cutlery (see Varia, Cat. nos 3.148, 3.150).

In 1908, when the first 'Greek and Roman Life' exhibition was mounted, in order '…to bring together a number of miscellaneous antiquities…. in such a method as illustrates…. the public and private life of the Greeks and Romans' (*Guide to Greek and Roman Life* 1908, vii), 'Medicine and Surgery' was an integral part, as it is today in the Gallery of Greek and Roman Life (Gallery 69). Introducing the 1908 gallery, the guide's author A.H. Smith (*ibid.*) noted 'it is necessary to warn visitors that they must not expect to find the subject in any sense exhaustively treated' and continued 'it is hoped that in course of time further acquisitions may be made with the view of strengthening those portions which may be at present be regarded as inadequate'. That has certainly been the case, and the medical collection is no exception. A finely engraved carnelian seal-stone with a scene of medical examination closely similar to that on the tombstone of Jason was acquired in 1912 (**Fig. 4**) (Cat. no. 6.5); and a steady stream of acquisitions of individual instruments was made in the century that followed Smith's hope, each of which supplemented and helped to deepen the understanding of the Museum's medical collection. Among them was another fine medicine box, acquired in 1921, this time with specific details of its place and circumstance of discovery (Cat. no. 3.124).

In 1920, a selection of some of the instruments discovered at Pompeii and Herculaneum was among a range of copies of bronzes purchased from the Naples Foundry company Chiurazzi/De Angelis. These were copies of specialised, purpose-made surgical tools, types at that time not represented in the Museum collection, and they had been

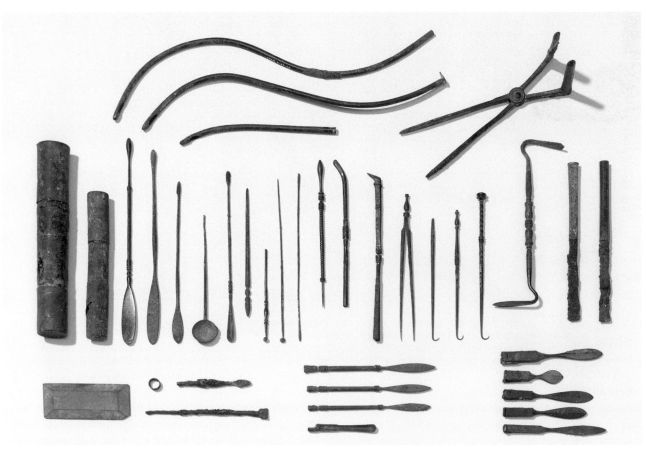

Figure 5 Set of Roman medical instruments from Italy, 1st/2nd century AD (Cat. nos 3.1–38)

found at named sites and in specific dated contexts (Cat. nos 3.153–7). Their acquisition formed an important part of the process of contextualising the Museum's medical collection, and enabling it to be displayed more effectively. Such copies are of great value for didactic purposes, and in 1999 the Museum commissioned reconstructions of the instruments in the then newly discovered surgical kit found in a grave at Stanway, near Colchester (British Museum reg. nos 1999,0701.1–13). The process of manufacture of those replicas, which involved detailed discussions between curator and craftsman, revealed fresh information about the form and function of the instruments.

A scalpel handle, a spring forceps and a possible surgical drill-bit (Cat. nos 3.71, 3.79, 3.88) were part of a slightly enigmatic group of 12 bronze and iron implements that was

Figure 6 Ointment pot from Corfu (Cat. no. 3.130) being analysed by XRF in the Department of Scientific Research, British Museum

donated to the Museum in 1932 following a sale of the collection of Dr Louis Sambon. All were said to have been found 'by Dr Sambon personally on the battle-field of Lake Trasimene'. Whatever the actuality of the find-spot the objects are a motley assortment with varied patinas and, although three have medical applications, the group is unlikely to represent a single closed medical find.

More securely provenanced, together with details of its find-place, is an instrument (Cat. no. 3.109) in the collection of Francis Greenway d'Aquila, a collection that was put on loan to the Museum in 1958 and purchased in 2005. Numbering over 100 objects, the collection was assembled in the City of London in the 1950s, when clearing of war damage and site development gave the opportunity to acquire finds of all periods. Greenway collected mainly finds of the Roman period, carefully recording details of their place and circumstances of discovery and of any dated and other associated finds. Most of his finds came from waterlogged deposits at Thames-side sites and locations in the valley of the River Walbrook where the anaerobic conditions of the deposits preserved wooden, bronze and iron objects in near-perfect condition. Already in the 19th century the Museum had acquired several more, similarly well-preserved, medical instruments from similar contexts in the City of London (Cat. nos 3.54, 3.77, 3.80, 3.90–3, 3.96, 3.108).

Significant instruments were added to the collection in 1990, 1992 and 2009 (Cat. nos 3.97–8, 3.105), and a bronze figurine of Asklepios, found near Chichester, Sussex, was purchased in 1995 (Cat. no. 6.32), but two acquisitions, in 1968 and in 1994, transformed the collection of Roman medical instruments. The first was a very large set of instruments from

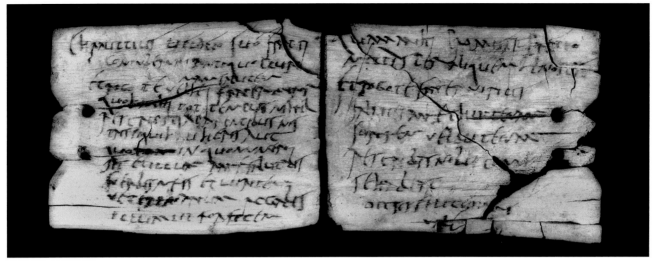

Figure 7 Wooden ink writing-tablet from Vindolanda comprising a letter in which a vet named Virilis is mentioned (Cat. no. 6.24)

Italy (**Fig. 5**) (Cat. nos 3.1–38), the second an example of a Greco-Roman doctor's small portable surgical kit of core tools (Cat. nos 3.40–8). The Italy set, one of the most extensive surviving Roman instrumentaria, consists of 37 pieces (see pp. 27–9 and 87–96). There are 32 instruments of copper alloy, two of iron, two of copper alloy and iron, and one object of stone. Eleven instruments were originally of copper alloy and iron but now lack their iron component, principally thin scalpel blades and slender needles which were casualties of corrosion. It is evident, too, from iron corrosion staining on several of the copper-alloy instruments that there were originally more objects of iron. Thin sheet-metal objects of copper alloy and iron are particularly susceptible to corrosion and objects made of organic materials are also likely to have been among the pieces lost to decay. Nevertheless, the set comprises an impressive array of instruments which equipped its user for a very wide variety of surgical interventions and medical treatments. Graded sets of scalpels, forceps, sharp hooks and probes are supplemented by utensils and implements for storing, preparing and applying medications and, most notably, by some rarely surviving specialised instruments – male and female catheters, a rectal speculum, a cataract needle and instruments of bone surgery – all of which were types of instrument hitherto unrepresented in the Museum collection.

The regrettable lack of information concerning the finding circumstances of the set from Italy was to some extent compensated for by the cornucopia of intrinsic evidence revealed by a comprehensive programme of scientific work on the set that its presence in the Museum collection enabled. Indeed, one of the advantages of curating the medical collection at the British Museum over many years is that throughout that time it has been possible to work with colleagues in the department formerly known as Conservation and Scientific Research (**Fig. 6**). Their scientific examinations and analyses have yielded a vast amount of new and important information on all the medical instruments in the collection as well as the Naples Foundry copies (Chapters 4 and 5). The scientific analyses included the establishment of alloy type and patina of the instruments, which shed light respectively on their manufacture and on their burial conditions. These proved crucial in assessing both the group of instruments in the Bristol Museum and Art Gallery (Appendix 1) and the British Museum's second set, the portable kit, which was acquired from Christies, London in 1994 (pp. 22–3 and 96–8). The acquisition of the kit materially expanded the British Museum collection, as it contained a number of new types of instrument and complemented the large set of instruments from Italy. A detailed macroscopic examination, combined with full scientific investigation, confirmed the integrity of the group of seven instruments as a belonging kit, while the unity of the instruments provided clues as to the process of assembly of the kit by the Roman practitioner. With 12 carefully selected operative components at his disposal – scalpel, blunt dissector, curette, smooth-jawed forceps, toothed forceps, sharp hook, needle, ear probe, pointed probe, hooked dissector, elevator and rasp – the practitioner had all that was required for a wide range of surgery on soft tissues and on bone.

Alongside the formation of the Museum's collection of surgical instruments, medical implements and objects related to divine healing, the acquisition, from the 1970s onwards, of a new and unexpected category of find has shone light onto an aspect of ancient medicine rarely revealed. The Vindolanda Tablets – wooden ink writing-tablets found at the Roman fort of Vindolanda, near Hadrian's Wall – provide a vivid glimpse of everyday life and the personal aspirations of officers and soldiers, including uniquely direct written evidence for patients as well as for the organisation and practice of medicine in a military context (**Fig. 7**). Miraculously preserved in waterlogged layers, these fragmentary military documents and letters – wafer-thin sheets of wood with Latin cursive script in carbon ink – include several concerned with health and healing which provide a sort of case study of medicine in action in a military setting in Roman Britain around AD 100. Included in the reports, lists and letters are a doctor, a pharmacist, two vets, a hospital, medical supplies, remedies and patients (see Chapter 6, Cat. nos 6.6–8, 6.12–13, 6.23–5). Between them the Vindolanda Tablets significantly extend and enliven the Greek and Roman medical collection of the British Museum and demonstrate the potential for other new and exciting future acquisitions.

Chapter 2
Greek and Roman Surgical and Medical Instruments

Note: In the following discussions, unless described otherwise, all objects are of copper and its alloys and are termed 'bronze' or 'copper alloy'. The more specific copper alloy formulation of analysed examples is given in the catalogue entries in Chapter 3.

Introduction

In the early Greek medical texts that bear the name of the great Hippocrates and date from the 5th century BC onwards a wide range of surgery is described and surgical tools named (see, e.g, Longrigg 1998, 178–90; Bliquez 2015, 23–50). Other written sources reveal the names and activities of some of the Greek medical practitioners. Yet very few of the ancient Greek instruments themselves have been identified. This may be because some instruments were made from non-metallic perishable materials and have simply not survived. But it is probably mainly because the basic instruments had not yet acquired distinctive recurrent forms and are therefore hard to differentiate from the contemporaneous domestic implements and craftsmen's tools – knives, needles, etc. Sometimes they probably did not differ at all and surgery might be performed with 'borrowed', adapted or individually created implements, as implied by the Hippocratic instruction 'you always have to use whatever is at hand' (*Joints* 4.7.43L; Bliquez 2015, 50). Only in a sealed archaeological context in conjunction with other recognisable medical objects like the cupping vessel is it possible to ascribe or suggest a medical or surgical function for individual instruments. That is the case with an exceptional burial group of the later 4th century BC found in a cist-grave (Tomb 66) in the southern cemetery at Pydna, Macedonia in 2000 (**Fig. 8**). For, in addition to two bronze vessels, an iron strigil and a small black-gloss phiale, the grave goods comprised a bronze cupping vessel, four small bronze medicine boxes (*pyxides*), a cylindrical ivory medicine bottle, a bronze double-ended probe, an iron spatula, an iron cross-legged forceps and four iron knives. The presence of the cupping vessel enables a secure identification of the other objects as a small group of medical, pharmaceutical and surgical instruments (Chrysostomou 2002, 105, 116, figs 4–6; Tsigarida 2011). As further discoveries from dated contexts are made we can anticipate the gradual recognition of recurrent forms and the emergence of a typology of early Greek instrumentation.

At any rate, by the late 1st century BC purpose-made surgical and medical instruments were being made and used throughout the Greco-Roman world. There was variety in the choice of materials and decoration, but the individual forms, once developed, remained surprisingly constant. Surgical and medical instruments became more numerous and widespread in the Roman Empire than in any other culture or at any other period up to the European Renaissance. It is surprising that so much survives, for the instruments had value, sometimes probably considerable value, and their loss, or intentional removal from circulation, requires explanation. Different processes are at work in the differing contexts of finds and these have to be taken into consideration when interpreting their meaning. Broadly, there are three categories of finds: site finds, grave finds and 'disaster' finds.

Figure 8 Pydna, Macedonia, burial group of medical instruments, including a cupping vessel, medicine boxes, a probe, iron knives and iron forceps, from Tomb 66, 4th century BC. Archaeological Museum, Thessaloniki, Py 7820-7826, 7830, 7840, 7842, 7845-7847. The rights to the depicted monuments belong to the Greek State and the Ministry of Culture (Law 4858/2021). The monuments are under the jurisdiction of the Archaeological Museum of Thessaloniki.
© Archaeological Museum of Thessaloniki. Image © AMTH. Photographer: Orestis Kourakis

Individual finds on occupation sites are unlikely to represent 'accidental' or 'casual' loss, but the actual circumstances of deposition can seldom be reconstructed with confidence. Nevertheless, whether from general layers or more specific contexts they can help to consolidate or broaden distribution patterns and sharpen the chronology of instrument types. Even in the absence of a secure context they can provide valuable new intrinsic information and they do, at least, attest medical activity, though not necessarily at the precise site of discovery (e.g. Jackson 1996b; Jackson 2011b). Particularly valuable are studies of site collections of medical implements, which often comprise both casual and surface finds and excavated assemblages, like that from Carnuntum, Austria, site of a legionary fortress, fleet base and town (Swoboda 1953; Hauff 1993/1994; Krug 1992b). The medical assemblage from the Roman town on the Magdalensberg, Austria is especially important because of the early and compact dating of the site – mid-1st century BC to mid-1st century AD – and it includes the earliest dated examples of a number of instrument types (see pp. 49, 59 and 63–5) (Gostenčnik 2004). Equally important are the assemblages from the *coloniae* at Augst (*Augusta Raurica*) and Avenches (*Aventicum*), Switzerland, which not only incorporate significant individual instruments but were also subjected to spatial analysis, which sheds light on medical foci and the zoning of medical activities within the domestic quarters of the towns (Riha 1986; Hirt 2000). Another town of major importance is Cologne, *Colonia Claudia Ara Agrippinensium*, capital of the Roman province of Lower Germany, in which a concentration of casual finds of medical instruments from the town has been importantly supplemented by excavations in the cemeteries. Nineteen graves with surgical instruments and pharmaceutical implements have been identified (including two of *medicae*, female practitioners), implying a high level of medical provision (Künzl 2002b, 66–7; Künzl 2005; Euskirchen 2018; Euskirchen 2022).

Grave finds provide a clear and often undisturbed context, an especially secure resting place for instruments.

Their burial was a controlled action, a deliberate, conscious decision to remove them from circulation and place them in the grave. In addition to their secure context the associated artefacts found with them have been an especially significant source of evidence for Roman medical instrumentation (Künzl 1983a; Jackson 2007a). However, the ritual aspect of ancient burial practice is seldom uncontentious, and generally it cannot be discerned or reconstructed with any great degree of certainty. There is, as yet, for example, no convincing explanation as to why valuable, functional medical tools were consigned to graves in this way. Furthermore, it is seldom clear whether, or how much, selection took place, and therefore it is rarely possible to determine whether or not the interred instruments represent a complete set, a part-set or merely a token instrument or instruments. Certainly, bulky items are seldom found. Critically, too, although the integrity and preservation of instruments are favoured in a burial context, those instruments had been removed from the setting in which they were used in life.

Thus, loose-finds and site finds provide intrinsic, chronological and statistical data, and the sepulchral finds add valuable information from securely associated medical and non-medical artefacts. To aim for the broader picture, however, to attempt to assess the reality of surgical treatment and to place medical practice in a social context, it is necessary to turn to the third category that may be termed 'disaster' or 'catastrophe' finds: volcanic eruptions, fires, floods and shipwrecks. These are unexpected, unpredictable or uncontrollable events that may isolate and preserve a whole assemblage of material remains in the place and form in which they were in use up to the moment of the disaster. Such finds are not numerous and they are seldom clear-cut. Ironically, too, their exceptional nature means that, while they are of immense importance and provide invaluable information, it is more necessary than ever to be cautious in attempting to generalise that information beyond the immediate setting. They may give a vivid glimpse of a particular circumstance in a particular place at a particular time, but it may be difficult to gauge how representative the set of circumstances are. Like the other categories of find, there is variation from one context to another.

Shipwrecks and other underwater finds rarely constitute a completely sealed context but, importantly, they can preserve wood and other organic materials (Künzl 2018, 28–31). Examples include 'Plemmirio B' (Syracuse), the wreck of a Roman merchantman of *c.* AD 200, which yielded two scalpel handles and a double-ended handle for a scalpel and needle (Gibbins 1988; 1989). Even more notable is the Pozzino wreck, a small vessel that foundered around the year 130 BC in the Gulf of Baratti, near the ancient Etruscan port of Populonia, off the west coast of Tuscany. As yet unpublished (but for interims see Spawforth 1990; Gibbins 1997, 457–8; Firmati and Romualdi 1998, 184–92), the Pozzino wreck preserved a variety of medical finds, most, seemingly, contained in a wooden chest. They include a bronze cupping vessel, a probe, a small mortar, a wooden right hand holding a libation dish, perhaps from a small statue of Asklepios, several rectangular wooden boxes with sliding lids, a stick of *collyrium* (desiccated eye-salve), its ingredients appropriately including zinc derivatives, a tin *pyxis* which contained six round tablets, and at least 136 small slender cylindrical lidded boxes (*pyxides*) of turned boxwood containing salves and powders. Scientific analysis of samples from some of the tablets in the tin *pyxis* has shown that they contain principally inorganic materials, mainly zinc oxide and haematite, as well as starch, beeswax, animal and plant fats, pine resin and other plant remains (Gourevitch 2011, 153–4; Touwaide 2011; Giachi *et al.* 2013). While their composition appears not to correspond exactly to any recipe in the ancient treatises on medication it is similar to some ancient eye remedies and treatment for wounds (Totelin 2013). Cinnamon, vanilla and cumin are among the ingredients of the medicaments so far identified in the boxwood *pyxides* and, together with the glass and ceramic items of the cargo assemblage, point to trading contacts with Chios, Rhodes, Syria-Palestine, Arabia, south-east Asia and southern China, and suggest that the ship's last voyage probably began in the Eastern Mediterranean. At present it is not possible to determine the exact status of the Pozzino medical assemblage: did it belong to a practitioner passenger; was it for use on board ship; or was it a medical consignment for onward trade?

Preservation of medical finds by flooding is much rarer, and unique at present is the catastrophic inundation event which overwhelmed the town of Allianoi, Turkey, including a medical site, in the 3rd century AD, and sealed it with a layer of silt (Baykan 2012) (see pp. 34–5). Conflagrations, that may simultaneously both destroy and preserve, are potentially more common disaster scenarios and the most important finds to date are the result of fires which destroyed medical sites at *Marcianopolis* and Rimini (see pp. 32–4). Although the violent fire that destroyed the Rimini *domus* del Chirurgo terminated the doctor's medical practice, and may also have resulted in his death, it preserved for posterity his professional equipment and other possessions in the places where he had last left them – it 'froze' a moment in time. Not only were the burnt contents

of the rooms sealed *in situ* beneath the rubble of the collapsed building, but also the subsequent abandonment of the site ensured that those contents remained almost completely undisturbed: they comprise the largest single find of ancient medical and surgical instrumentation yet discovered (Ortalli 2009; Jackson 2009b). The most celebrated disaster finds, and thus far the only example of preservation by volcanic eruption, are the medical finds at sites around the Bay of Naples, principally Pompeii and Herculaneum, sealed by volcanic debris from the eruption of Vesuvius in AD 79 (Bliquez 1994) (see pp. 35–6).

The recognition and identification of surviving Greco-Roman surgical instruments and medical implements relies in part on comparison with pre-modern instrumentation as well as on comparison with descriptions in the ancient medical texts. The texts range from the Hippocratic writings of the 5th century BC to those of Celsus (early 1st century AD) and Galen (second half of the 2nd century–early 3rd century AD) and to the Greek medical encyclopaedias – syntheses extracted from earlier writers – of Oribasius of Pergamum (4th century AD), Aëtius of Amida (6th century AD) and Paul of Aegina (7th century AD). Important, too, is the increasingly rich vein of written evidence found on papyri, especially the Oxyrhyncus Papyri (see, e.g. Marganne 1994; Marganne 1998; Marganne 2001; Marganne 2018; Andorlini ed. 2001). The 6th Book of Paul and Books 7 and 8 of Celsus' *On Medicine* are particularly invaluable sources of information on surgical instrumentation. Paul's text, which attests to the continuity and apparent success of the Alexandrian surgical tradition into the 7th century, covered a very wide range of surgery, 'everything from hernias and fistulae to sprained ankles and varicose veins, and from the removal of missiles from battlefield wounds to the surgical reduction of over-large breasts in a man' (Paul 6.65–6, 6.77–8, 6.120, 6.82, 6.88, 6.45; Nutton 2004, 295–6).

Celsus' work is especially appropriate because it was written early in the 1st century AD, coinciding with the time when, according to the archaeological record, diagnostic types of purpose-made surgical instruments and medical implements were beginning to emerge and to become more frequently found and widespread (Jackson 1994a). In Book 7 Celsus described numerous surgical interventions together with the instruments and implements required to perform them, and there are plentiful references, too, in the other books, especially Book 8, which details the tools of bone surgery. However, while his descriptions of some instruments and procedures are full and illuminating others are rather brief and imprecise. In the case of the commoner instruments Celsus probably felt it unnecessary to give a word-picture of an object that was generally well known. At the other extreme were less common instruments for which he knew no precise Latin name, so he then either used a Greek term or – of much more use to us in the elucidation of the instruments – he described their appearance. Thus, there is considerable scope for linking his more definitive descriptions to surviving instruments as, for example, catheters and lithotomy scoops (*On Medicine* 7.26.1, 7.26.2–4). The omission of several instruments from the *On Medicine* may be because at the time Celsus wrote some were still unknown to him. Most notable is the absence of any mention of bone levers, uvula forceps and bivalve and trivalve dilators (rectal and vaginal specula). The earliest archaeological find of a distinctive purpose-made surgical bone lever is one from Kalkriese, associated with the defeat of the Roman army under Varus in AD 9 (Künzl 1996, 2584–5, fig. 1.5); the earliest securely dated identifiable rectal and vaginal dilators are from Pompeii – buried half a century after the *On Medicine* was written (Bliquez 1994, 183–91, nos 291–5); and no uvula forceps has yet been found in a secure context as early as the 1st century AD (Jackson 1992, 175–6).

The specifically surgical texts of Celsus and Paul, together with selected passages from other ancient medical authors, have enabled and facilitated the recognition of some of the many named instruments amongst those in surviving instrumentation, especially those from sealed and dated contexts with closely associated finds (Jackson 1990a; Bliquez 2015). Inevitably, however, there are still many named instruments which have eluded discovery or identification in the archaeological record, just as there are instruments in the archaeological record which cannot yet be satisfactorily assigned to a specific usage in the ancient medical literature. We may anticipate new and important revelations as texts and finds continue to be examined together, and new discoveries of sets of instruments from secure contexts offer the greatest potential.

Design, manufacture and decoration of instruments

To judge from the Classical medical literature, healers in the Roman world potentially had access to an extensive range of medical equipment. Much of it would have been made from perishable organic materials, and Celsus mentioned instruments, implements and equipment of wood, leather, cloth, papyrus, reed and feather. Specialist craftsmen in those materials would have supplied medical practitioners with such things as splints, wedges, mallets, straps, slings, straws, quills, ligatures, sutures, dressings, plugs and bandages (Jackson 1994a, 198–200, tables 2–4; Bliquez 2015, appendix). Few of them have survived in recognisable form in medical contexts and even implements made from the more robust material, animal bone, and occasionally ivory, are relatively rarely found. It is important to keep in mind, therefore, that what does survive, principally the metal instrumentation, provides only part of the evidence for the extent of surgical and medical equipment.

By the time of Celsus, craftsmen in metals had a good understanding of, and control over, their materials. Those who made medical instruments generally employed copper and its alloys and wrought iron. Where an intricate form or surface treatment was required, whether for decorative effect or a specific function, or both, copper alloy was the normal medium. To judge by the results of scientific analysis, it would appear that medical instruments of copper alloy were made from a wide variety of alloy types, perhaps largely dictated by the metal that was to hand, whether in the form of ingots or recycled scrap. However, in his analysis of the instruments in the collections of the Römisch-Germanisches Zentralmuseum, Mainz (RGZM) (now Leibniz Zenter für Archäologie (LEIZA)), Riederer discerned a clear separation between the medical

instruments of bronze and those of brass (Riederer 2002, esp. 64–6, 73, 78). He suggested that this meant a purchaser could choose between metallic brown-coloured bronze and golden-coloured brass and that price/quality drove that choice rather than the selection of an alloy type with particular properties. He also concluded that the alloy formulation of the zinc-rich brass of some of the instruments from Asia Minor indicated a high-quality source of the metal located in the eastern Empire (Riederer 2002, 80).

Although in the RGZM (LEIZA) collections it was found that the spatula probes were mostly of bronze while the scoop probes and ear probes were mostly of brass, the scalpel handles were evenly divided between the two alloys and no close or coherent correlation could be seen between alloy type and instrument type. Indeed, it was notable that the three different types of instrument comprising the exquisitely made small kit of instruments said to be from the Rhineland – scalpel handle, two sharp hooks and two spring forceps – were all made from the same alloy type (Riederer 2002, 79, A61–A65). The same is true of the instruments in a portable kit in the British Museum collection (Cat. nos 3.40–8, see pp. 22 and 96) and those in a group of richly decorated instruments from Italy in the Bristol Museum and Art Gallery (Appendix 1). In larger sets of instruments, however, a more complex picture emerges. Thus, in an extensive set probably from Ephesus in the RGZM (LEIZA) (see p. 30), 17 analysed instruments were mostly brasses of different alloy formulations, indicating that the set had probably been gradually built up through the acquisition of individual instruments, while compositional analysis of the British Museum's large set of instruments from Italy (see pp. 156–8) demonstrated that it incorporates several distinct and discrete groups of instruments – scalpel handles (Cat. nos 3.7–9), bone chisels (Cat. nos 3.10–11) and catheters (Cat. nos 3.22–4), and that the formation of the set appears to have involved progressive acquisitions of both individual instruments and groups (see pp. 27–9 and 87–9).

Occasionally, however, a specific copper alloy type, or a combination of alloy types, was evidently chosen for their particular properties, in order to enhance the decoration, or to facilitate manufacture, or to improve function. A spectacular example of this sophisticated application of metallurgical knowledge is a unique plunger forceps in the Ashmolean Museum, an ostentatious instrument of innovative design and ingenious features (Appendix 2). Analysis by British Museum scientists revealed that the two main components were made from different alloy formulations, each specifically and appropriately selected for their metallurgical properties in order to maximise both the efficiency and appearance of the instrument. A rather different set of circumstances is likely to have applied to Cat. no. 3.101, a cross-legged uvula forceps formerly in the Meyrick Collection. Compositional analysis of the two components revealed that their alloys are slightly different, one a gunmetal, the other a leaded brass, a combination that would not have provided any obvious benefit. The forceps may have been made using two different sources of metal or perhaps one of the components was a replacement part.

Where robustness of an instrument or a component part was vital, as in the case of bone levers and dental forceps, iron was usually selected as the most appropriate material. It was also favoured, above all, for the manufacture of blades and needles, for which a hard, sharp and durable cutting edge or point was sought, because Roman smiths knew and exploited the advantages of steeling. A tough, durable, wrought iron blade could be given a sharp steeled edge by the process of carburisation. Alternatively, the naturally occurring steel ores of the Alpine province of Noricum might be used, as we know from Galen who specified Norican steel for the manufacture of the strong two-edged knife he used to dissect the spine: 'it should be made of the finest steel, like the Norican, that it be not blunted, bent or broken' (Galen, *Anatomical Procedures* 8.6 (2.682K), trans. Singer 1956, 214).

References in both lay and medical writers to gold or silver instruments – like the gold-handled scalpel, silver cupping vessel and ivory medicine box that Lucian of Samosata attributed to a medical charlatan (*Adversus Indoctum* 29) – should probably normally be taken to mean copper-alloy instruments with precious metal inlays, like the gold-banded handle in a small kit of instruments from the baths at Xanten (see **Fig. 53**) (Künzl 1986a, 491–5, fig. 2.3). Certainly, while there has not yet been a single discovery of an instrument of gold, and those of silver are restricted to rare examples of para-medical implements (e.g. Cat. nos 3.120–1), a growing number of instruments with decorative appliqués (e.g. Cat. no. 3.50) and, above all, inlays, of silver, niello, copper and Corinthian bronze is emerging (see scalpel grips, pp. 41–3). Corinthian bronze – *Corinthium aes* – is the name given to a copper alloy to which silver and gold were added to provide a distinctive black-patinated bronze (Craddock and Giumlia-Mair 1993; Giumlia-Mair and Craddock 1993). It was a byword for luxury and was incorporated into such high-status objects as couch-fittings (*fulcra*), boxes and inkwells, for which Roman connoisseurs were prepared to pay enormous prices (Giumlia-Mair and Craddock 1993, 3–7, 23–9, figs 11–19). Its use on surgical instruments would not have escaped the notice of discerning patients and was doubtless intended to impress them and gain their confidence.

The inlaid designs on surgical instruments are sometimes complex (e.g. Cat. no. 3.68) and sometimes minuscule masterpieces (e.g. Cat. no. 3.61), but most comprise relatively simple designs employing extremely thin wire strips, bands, rings and spirals (e.g. Cat. nos 3.43–4, 3.46–7, 3.62, 3.64–5, 3.85–6, 3.96, 3.100, 3.102, and, for example, the handles of the five cataract needles from Montbellet, France: Feugère *et al.* 1985, 443–5). All were designed to provide a colour contrast with the body metal of the instrument and would have been eye-catching when the instrument was clean and polished – silver and/or the reddish colour of copper and/or the black colour of niello and/or the black colour of Corinthian bronze, against the metallic brown colour of bronze or the golden colour of brass, or, as in the case of Cat. no. 3.68, silver against the black-patinated Corinthian bronze body metal. But the thin wire inlays are much more difficult to discern today on instruments with dark brown or green patinas and corrosion products, as is the case on the instruments in the British Museum's small kit (Cat. nos 3.40–8). Such inlay is easily overlooked and it is likely that

scientific examination of patinated and corroded instruments in other museum collections – like that undertaken on the British Museum instruments (see pp. 154–5) – would reveal more examples.

More common than inlay was cast and cut decoration with a wide variety of motifs, including handle ornament in the form of a stylised bunch of acanthus leaves and the club of Hercules (Bliquez 1992), shoulder decoration in the form of coils, scrolls and stylised dolphins, and handle finials in the form of snakes and lion-heads. The majority of instruments incorporated simpler decoration, combining series of crisply finished ring, disc-and-baluster mouldings with finely profiled linear-faceted stems. In addition to the decorative function there was a practical purpose: the practitioner was provided with a secure grip, most notably the finelytextured lattice-faceting of the upper stem of many sharp hooks, which was a vital benefit in the slippery context of surgery.

Tubes and probes of lead, and probes of tin, are specified in the medical literature. Perhaps because the metals do not survive well in the ground, they have hardly ever been encountered in secure medical contexts in the archaeological record, but they may always have been rare. However, lead and tin were put to a much more extensive use: alloyed together they formed a soft solder, which was commonly employed as a bonding medium for components of sheet metal objects. Most notable are the rectangular copper-alloy medicine boxes, the outer casing and internal compartments of which were assembled from many components, like the box from Yortan, Turkey (Cat. no. 3.124). Such boxes would not have been intended to be subjected to excessive heat so the relatively low melting point of the solder – 250 °C or less – would not have been problematic. For other instruments it would have been of particular benefit, because, as the work of British Museum scientists has shown (see p. 149), soft lead-tin solder was used above all to secure iron components to their copper-alloy handles and when those components – bone levers and occasionally the arms of composite forceps, but principally blades and needles – broke or wore out they could be removed from their socket by the combined use of heat and extraction tools. While most practitioners probably turned to specialist metalworkers or their local smith for such, and other, repairs, the soft solder would at least, in a case of necessity, have enabled them to remove and replace the part themselves.

Needles of iron were soldered into slender drilled cylindrical sockets in their copper-alloy handles (e.g. Cat. nos 3.106–7), while some iron scalpel blades were soldered into simple slotted sockets cut into the end of their copper-alloy grip (e.g. Cat. nos 3.66–7). Roman craftsmen employed both of these types of socket in the manufacture of non-medical implements and utensils, too, but one very distinctive form of socket, a carefully profiled keyhole-shaped slot, appears to have been used almost exclusively for surgical instruments. It occurs most frequently on scalpel handles (see p. 43) but also forms the means of attachment for other instruments which comprise iron operative parts fitted to copper-alloy handles, including a pointed-jawed forceps (Paris, Musée Nationale, St. Germain, inv. 35473), shears (Nijmegen: Leemans 1842, pl. I.3; Künzl 1983a, fig. 74; Braadbaart 1994, pl. I.2) and bone levers (e.g. Bingen: Künzl 1983a, fig. 56.10,11,13).

Duality of function is another characteristic feature of purpose-made Roman surgical instruments. Many, perhaps the majority, were designed as multi-purpose tools, for use in a wide variety of surgical interventions. Additionally, combination tools, consisting of a central handle or grip with an instrument at either end, are a common occurrence within sets of instruments. They are often composite instruments capitalising on the differing properties of bronze and iron, and the many different combinations include scalpel with blunt dissector, lithotomy knife with lithotomy scoop, knife with lever, forceps with sharp hook, forceps with needle-holder, forceps with probe, forceps with lever, sharp hook with needle-holder, sharp hook with blunt hook, double-ended blunt hook, double-ended needle, double-ended probe, double-ended bone lever. There were many advantages and sound practical reasons for the use of combination tools. Instrument costs could be reduced, the surgical kit could be kept relatively compact and portable, and an operation could be performed with the minimum number of instruments, saving valuable seconds at a time when speed was of the essence.

Roman surgical instruments are further distinguished by the high quality of their design and manufacture, which clearly demonstrates the attention paid to maximising the chance of success in medical and surgical interventions. Appropriately, it is the exact counterpart to the thoughtful and carefully composed descriptions of operations in the ancient medical texts. Some instruments are exquisitely decorated and some are essentially plain, but virtually without exception they are carefully designed precision tools finished to a very high standard. As with the tools of other craftsmen the optimum instrument design was developed in response to the required function, and that design remained unaltered until such time as the function changed or new manufacturing materials became available. In that the instruments were designed for interventions and operations on the human body their function, and therefore their form, did not change over the centuries, and such change as there was tended to be restricted to the style and techniques of decoration. Their basic design and quality of manufacture seem to have remained much the same from the 1st to the 5th century AD throughout the Roman world. Some, like catheters and rectal dilators (Cat. nos 3.22–5), are closely paralleled even by their modern counterparts.

Rather frustratingly, the identity of the craftsmen who made medical instruments is not known, neither their personal names nor any specific professional term, for they did not mark their name on their wares nor are they referred to in texts or inscriptions. Some were probably among those craftsmen called *artifex aerarius* or *faber aerarius*; others may have been known simply as *faber* (Künzl 1984a, 59). There are a few exceptions, though they appear to be atypical, one a bronzesmith named Agathangelus, the other a group of people termed *organikoi* – 'instrumentists'. The latter, mentioned in a number of fragmentary papyri from Greco-Roman Egypt, were technicians who made medical equipment, like the Hippocratic Bench, employing the latest technological innovations. However, their activities were the subject of criticism by medical writers at the time, since, on occasion, in their quest to perfect medical equipment they were seen to have lost sight of what should have been the overriding principle, the best overall interest of the patient (Marganne 1998, 35–66, 110–47, and esp. 157–8). The (not uncommon) name Agathangelus (perhaps a bronzesmith who gave his name to a workshop) is stamped on a small range of copper-alloy implements, dating from the early 1st century AD on, which are distinctive, quite numerous and widely distributed and were sometimes imitated by other manufacturers (Künzl 1984a, 63–4; Gostenčnik 2002). Just one, from the Magdalensberg, is a recognisable medical instrument, a spring forceps, though lacking the end of its jaws (Gostenčnik 2002, fig. 2.5; Gostenčnik 2004, 383, 426–7, pl. 16.7). None of the others are of types found in medical contexts, and, while evidently not for medical use, their function remains enigmatic – serrated and asymmetrical 'tweezers', double-ended 'moulding tools' and double-ended 'brush handles'.

Although there is very little written evidence to shed light on the personnel and processes of manufacture – on the designers and makers of the instruments – there are a few snippets in the texts and on inscriptions and papyrus fragments. They combine with the intrinsic evidence of the instruments themselves to indicate that, as might be anticipated, the high quality of instrumentation is attributable to a close collaboration between medical practitioners and the artisans who made their medical equipment. Most evocative are some inscriptions from the populous city of Ephesus which, by the 2nd century AD, had become a healing centre of considerable importance, the hub of medical activity in Asia Minor. It had a Museum – a community of scholars and intellectuals – like that of Hellenistic Alexandria, and its residents included the great physician and influential medical writer Rufus of Ephesus (*fl.* 98–117), a follower of Hippocratic tradition, and predecessor and important source for Galen, as has become clear with the discovery of Arabic translations of otherwise lost texts of Rufus (Nutton 2004, 6–7, 138, 202, 208–11; Sideras 1994; Ullmann 1994). A manifestation, perhaps, of this concentration of healing personnel was the organisation of annual medical contests, part of the Great Festival of Asklepios, the results of which were recorded on public inscriptions. A series of these inscriptions, of the 2nd–3rd centuries AD, has survived and records four categories of competition (*agon*) between doctors, including essays on surgery, public displays of surgical skill and one – *organa* – which seems to have entailed the design of new medical instruments (Engelmann *et al.* 1980, nos 1161–9, 4101b; Nutton 2004, 211; Bubb 2022a). Just as remarkable as the survival of these inscriptions is the occasional survival, too, of sophisticated, ingenious and finely crafted instruments which can be envisaged as entrants in the *organa* contest. A prime contender is the plunger forceps in the Ashmolean Museum (**Fig. 9**) (Appendix 2), which combines expertise in design with sophisticated manufacture, perhaps reflecting the respective complementary roles of surgical practitioner and craftsman.

Certainly the manufacture of Roman surgical instruments is just as impressive as their design, and, for

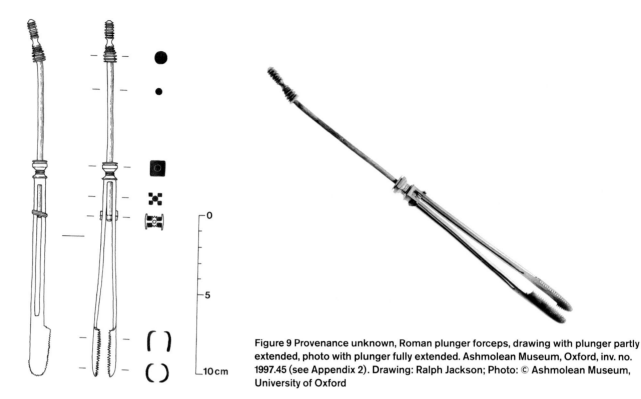

Figure 9 Provenance unknown, Roman plunger forceps, drawing with plunger partly extended, photo with plunger fully extended. Ashmolean Museum, Oxford, inv. no. 1997.45 (see Appendix 2). Drawing: Ralph Jackson; Photo: © Ashmolean Museum, University of Oxford

example, wherever burial conditions have preserved the original surface of the instruments they reveal, almost invariably, that whether cast or hand-forged all have been subject to a precise and thorough finishing process. This ranges from the immaculately smooth surface of those parts of instruments intended for insertion into the natural body orifices, wounds or incisions, to the finely incised, often decorative, texturing of the handle and stem of those instruments which required a secure, non-slip grip, or to the precise interlocking of finely cut teeth on the jaws of toothed fixation and uvula forceps. These and other requirements of medical and surgical instruments were very particular, and while some domestic implements and craft tools might be pressed into service *in extremis* and others lent themselves well to medical and surgical use, as is evident from their occasional inclusion in sets of instruments, most surgical instruments called for specialised production. Some were single-piece instruments of copper alloy or of iron, but many combined those two metals and some were fitted with handles of wood or bone, often incorporating a copper-alloy strengthening collar. Just as fine jewellery, which involved a variety of skills in working with several different materials, was made by specialists, so too would be medical instrumentation. Naturally, a local craftsman might be called upon, *faute de mieux*, but the evidence of the instruments points to specialist workshops, both for the manufacture of metal instruments and for the manufacture and fitting of the wooden and bone components that some required. As Künzl observed, citing the unity of design and manufacture of the nine instruments in a set from Milos, Greece, a specialist workshop would be able to provide a practitioner with a complete set of instruments, doubtless, too, together with the box or case in which they were to be contained (Künzl 1984a, 60). To be envisaged is a workshop with several craftsmen, who, between them, specialised in the casting and working of copper and its alloys and of tin and lead, the forging, and

sometimes steeling, of iron, and the working of bone and wood. In addition, some of those workshops had craftsmen with the skills to manufacture and work with precious metals, like silver and Corinthian bronze, and to apply them, or inlay them, in more or less ornate designs, onto or into the handles of some instruments. For bronze instrumentation there were probably master moulds and perhaps wax models, even perhaps pattern books, but, as already seen, a key component would undoubtedly have been the direct input from medical and surgical practitioners, a fruitful collaboration between *fabri* and *medici*.

Another remarkable discovery illuminates just such a collaborative process, at the top of the medical profession. It is a brief section in a formerly lost treatise of Galen, his *Avoiding Distress* (*De indolentia* /περì άλυπησίας), a 15th-century copy of which was found in the Vlatadon Monastery, Thessaloniki, in 2005 (**Fig. 10**) (Boudon-Millot 2008; Boudon-Millot and Jouanna 2010; Nutton 2013). The composition of *Avoiding Distress* was precipitated by, and written immediately after, Rome's disastrous fire of AD 192, which devastated the Temple of Peace region. Amongst the great swathes of public and private buildings destroyed by the fire was the stone warehouse in which, we discover, Galen, believing the building to be fireproof, had rented space to store many of his books and unpublished drafts, together with his most precious *materia medica* and instrumentation. Galen wrote *Avoiding Distress* in response to a friend's question as to how he had managed to avoid giving in to despair at the loss of his most prized possessions. Early on in the treatise he says:

> ... you were surprised, not that I had felt no sorrow when the fire destroyed part of the silver, gold ... and numerous IOUs that were kept there, but rather that I also hadn't when it burned the great quantity of books I had written there, as well as a wide selection of varied medicines, both simple and compound, and instruments of all kinds. (Galen, *Avoiding Distress* 4, trans. V. Boudon-Millot)

Continuing, he describes the instruments as:

> Instruments fit for medicine that obviously I had lost, but I could hope to buy again, and instruments that I had created which were part of those for which I myself made the wax models and gave them to the bronze-casters, so that it is not possible to obtain them again without a considerable amount of time and great pain. (Galen, *Avoiding Distress* 5, trans. P.L. Tucci)

Brief as it is, this vivid snippet clearly demonstrates the practitioner and craftsman collaboration in action. For, while Galen had purchased some of his specialised surgical instruments, others he had invented himself and had made wax prototypes to lend to metalsmiths for manufacture (Tucci 2008, 141). This new information is entirely in line with what was already known of Galen: that is, his attentiveness in securing the finest customised surgical instrumentation – he sourced Norican steel for the knife-blade he devised to dissect the spine – just as he ensured himself supplies of the most effective and sought-after *materia medica* (Nutton 2004, 245–6). Although Galen was rather exceptional he would not have been alone among medical practitioners in devising and specifying the exact form of his instrumentation. So the process alluded to in *Avoiding Distress* is likely to have been followed by other attentive practitioners, including the comprehensively equipped surgeon who was practising in Rimini just a few decades after the death of Galen (see pp. 32–4). Others may be represented by the inclusion of unique or adapted instruments in some sets of instruments, as, for example, the clyster/syringe in a set from Nea Paphos, Cyprus (see p. 29).

In the absence of specific written evidence for instrument manufacture, scientific analysis and examination of the instruments themselves provide the most fruitful avenue of research, as is revealed by the results of large-scale work on the British Museum and Mainz RGZM (now LEIZA) collections. It is to be hoped that similarly extensive investigation of excavated and securely contexted sets and collections of instruments will progressively take place to provide a fuller and more nuanced picture.

Sets of instruments

Sets of instruments in the British Museum collection: Cat. nos 3.1–48.
Large comprehensive sets of instruments are rare finds and only slightly less so are the kits of basic instruments, the portable sets that contained the instruments which were essential for the majority of surgical interventions (Künzl 1983a; Bliquez 1994; Jackson 1995a; 2009b). To the former category belongs the first of the sets in the British Museum collection, said to be from Italy (Cat. nos 3.1–38). To the latter category belongs the second British Museum set, of unknown provenance (Cat. nos 3.40–8). The word 'set' is used to indicate a range of instruments selected and used by a medical practitioner. As such, a set of instruments differs from a group of instruments which may be a random collection. Critical to bear in mind, as already flagged, is the partial nature of both types of set: it is usually only the metal instruments, and principally those of bronze, that survive, and the sets would undoubtedly originally have incorporated, too, instruments and equipment made of organic materials.

Figure 10 Vlatadon 14 codex, a 15th-century manuscript incorporating Galen's *Avoiding Distress* (*peri alypias*). Vlatadon Monastery, Thessaloniki. Photo: Ralph Jackson

Context is crucial in the identification of sets, and, as already seen, the sealed context of burial groups constitutes one of the best settings for the preservation of instruments and the recognition of sets. In addition, the securely dated context of associated artefacts in graves has greatly enhanced knowledge of Roman instrumentation in general and the composition of sets in particular. By combining the sepulchral evidence with that of the exceptional surgical finds from the Vesuvian sites and from Rimini, *Marcianopolis* and Allianoi, where sets of instruments were discovered in medically meaningful contexts, it has been possible to gain a much clearer understanding of the composition of medical kits. It has also revealed the essential uniformity of instrumentation throughout the Empire from the 1st to the 4th century AD.

Kits of basic instruments

In the Hippocratic writings a doctor was advised always to have ready to hand, in addition to the full equipment of the surgery, a portable carrying case (*parexodos*) containing a kit of instruments for use away from the surgery (*Decorum = De decente habitu* 9.8.8–9L; Bliquez 2015, 24). Such a kit is likely to have comprised one or more examples of each of the basic tools of surgery – scalpel, forceps, sharp hook, needle, probe and cautery, which are the instruments most frequently referred to several centuries later by Celsus in the surgical books of his *On Medicine* (*De medicina* 7–8). Iconography, whether on votive reliefs or tombstones, tends to support the written evidence, showing discrete ranges of instruments, often quite accurately depicted and sometimes shown in hinged rectangular boxes (see, e.g., Tabanelli 1958, pls 10–15; Matthäus 1989, figs 38–44; Hillert 1990, 187–97; Hillert 2005; Krug 2008, figs 7, 10, 14–22, 25; Verbanck-Piérard *et al.* 2018, 305–6) (**Figs 11–14**). However, a degree of caution is necessary, because the imagery probably had in part a symbolic or emblematic intent. Instruments and cupping vessels appear to have been seen as the epitome of healing, and they would thus be ready identifiers of 'doctoring' or 'medicine', as, for example, the cupping vessel shown on the early 2nd-century AD tombstone of Jason from Athens (Cat. no. 6.4), the opened box of instruments in the relief on the

Figure 11 (left) Provenance unknown, marble tomb relief, *c.* 300 BC, re-worked, probably in the 1st century AD, to show a doctor with papyrus scrolls and a box of instruments. Archäologische Sammlung, Universität Freiburg, inv. 535. Photo: J. Hartmann

Figure 12 (above) Provenance unknown, marble relief, showing a doctor and a hinged case of surgical instruments, 1st century BC/1st century AD. Staatliche Museen zu Berlin, Antikensammlung, Berlin, inv. no. Sk 804. Photo: Staatliche Museen zu Berlin, Antikensammlung/Johannes Laurentius CC BY-SA 4.0

Figure 13 Ostia, terracotta relief from the mid-2nd century AD tomb of Marcus Ulpius Amerimnus (Isola Sacra Tomb 100), showing instruments and treatment. Museo Archeologico, Ostia Antica, inv. 5204. Photo © Archivio Fotografico Parco archeologico di Ostia antica

Figure 14 Ostia, marble sarcophagus, detail of the central panel, showing a physician reading from a scroll with a hinged case of surgical instruments on top of the cupboard in front of him, 4th century AD. Metropolitan Museum of Art, New York, inv. 48.76.1. Gift of Mrs Joseph Brummer and Ernest Brummer, in memory of Joseph Brummer, 1948. Photo: Metropolitan Museum of Art, New York

later 2nd-century AD grave-altar of Publius Aelius Pius Curtianus from Palestrina (Krug 2008, fig. 18), and the opened box of instruments flanked by cupping vessels shown both on the 1st-century AD tombstone of Lykourgos, from Aedipsos, Euboea (Ritsonis 2014) and on an uninscribed 2nd/3rd-century AD tombstone of a female practitioner said to have been found in the environs of Kelli, Florina, Macedonia (Moschakis 2014) (**Fig. 15**). Therefore, the depictions cannot necessarily be regarded as evidence of the true appearance of a practitioner's normal complete instrumentarium. Nevertheless, they are likely to show some of the key instruments, the commonest, most recognisable essential tools. That this is probably the case is suggested by archaeological finds of sets of instruments, in virtually all of which the essential 'core' tools form an integral part or even the entire kit (Jackson 1995a, tables 1, 2); and because they have been found in the controlled conditions of archaeological excavations, which add contextual

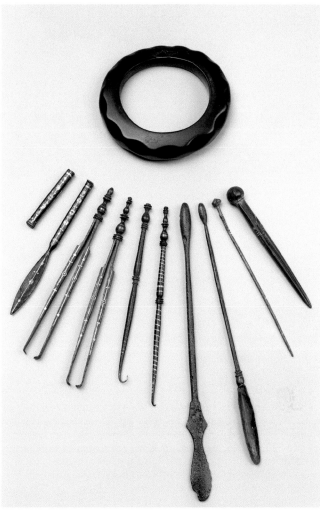

Figure 15 Kelli, Macedonia, marble grave stele, showing a female practitioner and a range of surgical instruments, some in a hinged case, mid-2nd/early 3rd century AD. Photo: Ephorate of antiquities of Kozani region/K. Moschakis

Figure 16 Cologne, set of Roman medical instruments, including scalpel handles, forceps and sharp hooks, with silver inlay, and probes and needles. Part of a burial group from the Luxemburgerstrasse Roman cemetery, 1st/2nd century AD. Römisch-Germanisches Museum, Köln, inv. nos 1072-1081. Photo: © Römisch-Germanisches Museum der Stadt Köln/Rheinisches Bildarchiv Köln, Anja Wegner

information to their intrinsic value, they are of especial importance. The surviving components of the sets are usually restricted to metal instruments, the great majority of bronze (copper alloy) and a smaller number of iron. Regrettably, the iron blades and needles originally secured to bronze scalpel handles and needle-holders have usually corroded and broken away.

Significant examples of small or moderate-sized kits include those from burials at Milos, south-west Cyclades, Greece; Cologne; and Aschersleben, Saxony-Anhalt, Germany. The 19th-century find from Milos comprises a set of nine instruments: four scalpels (lacking their iron blades), a toothed spring forceps, a pointed-jawed forceps combined with a needle-holder, a sharp hook, a needle and a curette (sharp spoon) (Deneffe 1893, 50, 52, pl. 5, fig. 1; Künzl 1983a, 40–1). Probably dating to the early Roman Empire, their distinctive mouldings and profile suggest they were made together, probably as a set, by the same craftsman or in the same workshop. The set from Cologne, also a 19th-century find, from the extensive Luxemburgerstrasse Roman cemetery, consists of an inlaid handle and bone fragments,

probably the remains of a box, and nine instruments: two scalpels (lacking their iron blades), two smooth-jawed spring forceps, two sharp hooks, a needle and two probes. The scalpels, forceps and hooks are almost certainly the product of a single workshop, for they are richly decorated with a very distinctive silver-inlaid design (**Fig. 16**) (see p. 43): on the flat faces of the scalpels and forceps, a series of tiny stars, discs, peltas, pellets and lozenges ranged along a line (as on scalpel handle Cat. no. 3.68); on the curved surface of the hooks, spirals and rings (Künzl 1983a, 33, 89–90; Büsing-Kolbe 2001, Type B). Evidently the product of a single workshop, too, is the small set from Aschersleben – beyond the Roman frontier in Free Germany – which was found with a bronze jug in an urn burial of probable 3rd-century AD date. The instruments, which may be earlier than the 3rd century, comprise a knife/scalpel which retains much of its long straight iron blade, a pointed-jawed forceps combined with an elevator, a sharp hook with snake-head handle finial, the broken handle, probably of a second sharp hook, and a composite bronze and iron bone lever. Excepting only the plain handle of the knife all the instruments are

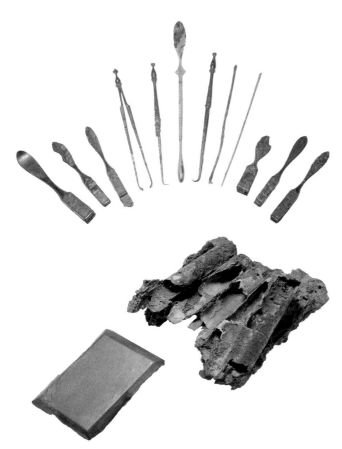

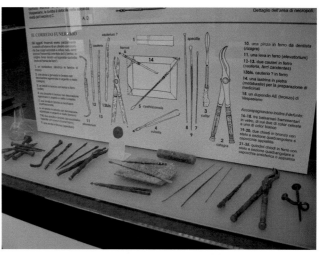

Figure 18 Luzzi, Cosenza, set of Roman medical instruments from a late 1st century AD inhumation burial, as displayed at the National Archaeological Museum of Sibaritide, Sibari. Photo: Ralph Jackson

Figure 17 Herculaneum, set of Roman medical instruments, tubular medicine boxes and mixing palette found in the north-east corner of waterfront Vault 12 (Fornice 12), 1st century AD. Archaeological Park of Herculaneum, Invv. 78999-79000. Photo: © Ministero della cultura – Parco Archeologico di Ercolano

decorated with finely worked stylised acanthus mouldings (Künzl 1983a, 100–1).

However, some of the best and most informative examples of the basic sets are those from sealed contexts, as at Pompeii, Herculaneum, Luzzi and Rimini in Italy, Dulgata Mogila, near Karanovo, in Bulgaria, Wehringen in Germany, Nijmegen in the Netherlands and Stanway in England.

The Pompeii find, discovered in 1936 in the region of the so-called 'Grande Palestra' adjacent to the amphitheatre, was dropped in transit by a luckless fugitive from the Vesuvian eruption of AD 79. He was one of a group of young and old, probably family members, fleeing from a nearby house. Beneath his skeleton was found the remains of a wooden box containing 16 instruments: four scalpels with partially preserved iron blades (three of them of common bellied form), two sharp hooks, two spring forceps (one with smooth jaws, the other toothed), a cataract needle, a double-ended needle-holder and a set of six probes in a tubular box along with four tubular drug boxes (Maiuri 1939, 218–21; Künzl 1983a, 12–15; Bliquez 1994, 87–8, 207–8 (A21–A27), pl. 23).

A very similar find was made at Herculaneum in 1992 during excavations in the waterfront vaults that supported the terrace overlooking the beach next to the Suburban Baths. The skeletons of hundreds of fugitives were found, some on the ancient beach but most in the vaults. Adjacent to one of the 32 huddled bodies in Vault 12 were the remains of a rectangular wooden box with hinged lid. Inside were six scalpels (their iron blades lacking), one with a lever-like

terminal in place of the normal blunt dissector, two sharp hooks, a toothed spring forceps, a needle, two probes and several unidentified corroded iron instruments. The box also contained seven tubular drug boxes and a stone palette for drug preparation (**Fig. 17**) (Pagano 2003, 135–6; Roberts 2013, 291).

These two finds, from Pompeii and Herculaneum, are particularly revealing. Each was a compact box of instruments and medications grabbed in haste in the devastating circumstances of the eruption. While they may represent the complete medical instrumentation of their owner, it is more likely that they comprised just the portable kit of instruments held in readiness for an emergency visit to a patient, the equivalent of the doctor's black bag of recent times, and that the large implements and more specialised instruments were left behind with other bulky medical equipment in their surgery.

A near-contemporary kit was found with a late 1st-century AD inhumation burial in excavations at Luzzi (Cosenza). It comprised a scalpel, complete with iron bellied blade, a sharp hook with silver-inlaid handle, a toothed spring forceps, four probes, two iron styli (probably used as cauteries), a bone forceps, an iron bone lever and an iron dental forceps, as well as a tubular drug box and a stone mixing palette (**Fig. 18**) (Guzzo 1974, 469–75 (grave 17); Künzl 1983a, 106–7).

At Rimini, amongst the astonishingly large assemblage of instruments in the *domus* del Chirurgo, which was burnt down in the mid-3rd century AD, are two clusters whose juxtaposition and composition indicate that they are core kits of essential tools, ready for use in or away from the surgery. One had been held in a hinged box and included five scalpels (four complete with their tiny straight and bellied iron blades), a toothed spring forceps, two sharp hooks, a composite bronze and iron bone lever and three composite bronze and iron instruments combining a knife and a lever (**Fig. 19**). The other kit appears to have been stored in a rolled cloth pouch and consisted of three scalpels complete with their tiny triangular and bellied iron blades, a spring forceps, a sharp hook, an iron file and an iron saw-knife (Jackson 2009b, 77, 83, pl. 1, 87).

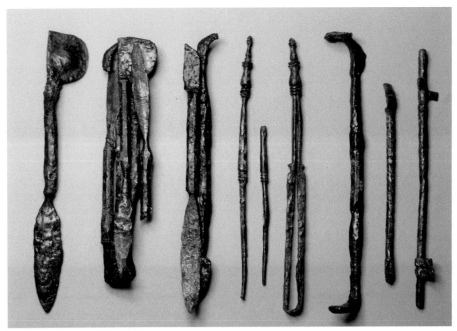

Figure 19 Rimini, *domus* del Chirurgo, portable kit of surgical instruments with, at right, the hinge of the wooden case in which they were contained, mid-3rd century AD. City Museum, Rimini. Photo: Ralph Jackson

Beneath the tumulus Dulgata Mogila, near Karanovo in the Nova Zagora region of Bulgaria, rescue excavations in 1976 revealed three vaulted brick burial chambers of late 1st/early 2nd-century AD date, two of which contained medical instruments. Grave 3 included a small kit of two scalpels, a spring forceps, a scoop probe and a tubular box alongside a broader range of personal grave goods for the afterlife comprising weaponry, a bronze lamp and inkwell, a silver *denarius* of Trajan, glass and ceramic *unguentaria* and other vessels, and a fine bronze patera and ewer, oil flask and pair of strigils. Grave 1 incorporated a similar but still richer range of grave goods together with a more extensive kit of instruments: three scalpels with inlaid handles, four spring forceps comprising smooth, toothed, pointed and coudée jaw types, a sharp hook, three scoop probes, two ligulae, a tubular box, a stone mixing palette, weighing scales, and a rectangular box containing stamped *collyria* and other medicaments (Kančeva-Ruseva *et al.* 1996, 17–70, pls 1–12 and 17–22, esp. 8–10 and 21).

Another kit, from a mid-3rd century AD inhumation (Grave 7) in a very rich necropolis at Wehringen, near Augsburg, excavated 1961–7, although only a modest-sized instrumentation, yielded a wealth of information (**Fig. 20a–c**). The grave contained an extended male skeleton, originally in a wooden coffin, with two pottery flagons and a glass vessel at his feet. Next to his head were a further two glass vessels and a rectangular bronze box with five compartments and a sliding lid. In the box's central compartment were three silver coins, the latest an almost unworn *antoninianus* of Gordian III, dated AD 238/9, indicating burial soon after that date. In the four side compartments were *materia medica*. The surviving plant remains included a laurel leaf, but the principal contents were medications for eye diseases – fragments of dried *collyrium* sticks. They had been stamped with the abbreviated details of two salves of Claudius Ingenuus and one of Quintus Simplicius Nedo. Chemical analysis indicated that the principal detectable substance was lead oxide, but the organic component was not detectable and can only be suggested from the stamped inscriptions, for example balsam, that is plant resins and essential oils. No stone collyrium-stamp was found in the grave so the stamped *collyria* had probably been purchased rather than blended by the deceased man. A spatula probe and a stone mixing palette next to his right elbow were for use in the preparation of the *collyria* and other medications. Immediately beneath them was a folding wooden case covered in gilded leather. Top-to-tail inside this fancy case were three scalpels intact with their tiny iron blades, a sharp hook, a toothed spring forceps, and a composite bronze and iron bone lever. The form of the handles and the decorative mouldings indicate that the instruments were made together as a set. The skeleton was that of an over-70-year-old man suffering from advanced osteoporosis. He may have been a retired military doctor from the fortress at Regensburg, or one of the nearby forts, who established a civilian practice in nearby Augsburg (*Augusta Vindelicum*), or a slave in a wealthy household, for his grave was positioned next to a substantial enclosed grave monument. Whatever his exact status he was an elderly man who died soon after AD 239, seemingly a 'general practitioner' using medications and surgical tools to treat the sick and injured, including those afflicted with eye diseases or with bone fractures and dislocations (Künzl 1983a, 120–1; Nuber 2004).

A more extensive instrumentation, also of the mid-3rd century AD, was found in 1840 in a stone sarcophagus burial on the Hunerberg at Nijmegen (**Fig. 21a–c**). Carefully placed within the sarcophagus were five medicine containers of glass, pottery and bronze; a stone palette for preparing medications; a chisel, with bronze handle and broad thin iron blade, of the type believed to have been used to remove wax from writing-tablets (though here perhaps adapted to use as a bone chisel); two bronze inkwells; an ingeniously constructed shears (ancient scissors), with a bronze spring handle and a pair of iron blades secured to the handle in the type of socket more normally used to fasten scalpel blades to their handle; and a rectangular drug box, with four lidded compartments, made of wood with decorative bone inlays.

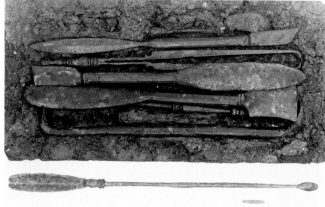

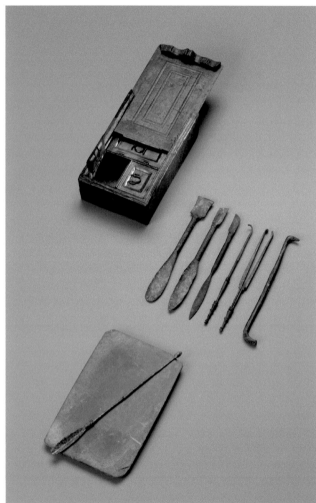

Figure 20a–c Wehringen, near Augsburg, small kit of Roman medical instruments and medicine box, from a mid-3rd century AD inhumation burial (Grab 7): a) (top left) the burial; b) (top right) the instruments, as excavated, in the remains of their leather-covered wooden case; c) (left) the medicine box, instruments and stone mixing palette. Prähistorische Staatssammlung, Munich. Photos Figs 20a–b © Bayerisches Landesamt fuer Denkmalpflege, Photo: Ruppaner; photo Fig. 20c © Archaologische Staatssammlung (Bavarian State Archaeological Collection). Photo: M. Eberlein

Associated with the wooden box, and probably originally contained within it, were 11 surgical tools comprising three scalpels (their iron blades lacking), a sharp hook, a combined double blunt and sharp hook, a toothed spring forceps, a double-ended needle-holder, two needles, a scoop probe and a composite bronze and iron bone lever. In addition there was a bundle of five iron needles, probably for use in the needle-holder. Like those in the Wehringen set, the instruments share common mouldings and profiles indicating that they were probably made together as a set (Leemans 1842; Künzl 1983a, 93–6; Braadbaart 1994, inv. nos NHa 1–27; Jackson 2018a, 142–4, figs 8A–C).

The earliest surviving firm evidence of instrumentation for surgical practice in Britain – and, indeed, one of the

earliest dated kits from the Roman Empire – was excavated in 1996 at Stanway, a sacred site close to the major Iron Age centre at Gosbecks, near Colchester. In one of the burial enclosures a set of 14 iron and bronze surgical instruments (as well as other objects that may have had healing applications) was found with cremated remains – presumably those of the healer who used them – in a grave dated c. AD 50–60 (**Fig. 22a–d**). The instruments comprise two single-piece iron scalpels with bellied blades, an iron knife with straight blade, two combined blunt and sharp hooks (one of bronze, one of iron), a smooth-jawed spring forceps, an iron pointed-jawed tweezers, three iron-handled needles, a scoop probe, a small iron saw, a possible retractor and a broken handle. Although the healer may have continued practising until his demise, it is likely that the manufacture and first use of his instruments ante-dated the conquest. If he were a native Briton or an incomer, perhaps a refugee from Gaul, that might help to explain the idiosyncratic nature of the instruments: the composition of types corresponds to that of other Roman sets, implying contact with Roman and Gallo-Roman medical practitioners, but the precise forms of the instruments and the predominant use of iron may reflect British Iron Age or Celtic influences (Crummy et al. 2007; Jackson 2007a; Crummy et al. 2008; Jackson 2011c).

A group of eight instruments, said to have been found at the Roman fort at Cramond, near Edinburgh, may constitute a small kit, but the finding circumstances are unknown and the provenance insecure (Gilson 1983). Unconfirmed, too, are the unpublished 'medical box' with instruments, reported to have been found in excavations at Corbridge in the 1930s but lost during the Second World War, and a possible kit from early excavations of the military site at Wilderspool (Gilson 1981, 5; Allason-Jones 1999, 141; Jackson 2011a, 252–3).

New finds continue to emerge, and a significant discovery was recently made some 35 miles east of Budapest, at

Figure 21a–c Nijmegen, set of Roman medical instruments from a mid-3rd century AD burial in a stone sarcophagus found on the Hunerberg: a) (top) the medical instruments and implements; b–c) (above left and right) illustrations of the grave group in Leemans' 1842 publication. Rijksmuseum von Oudheden, Leiden, inv. no. NHA 1-26. Photo © National Museum of Antiquities, Leiden

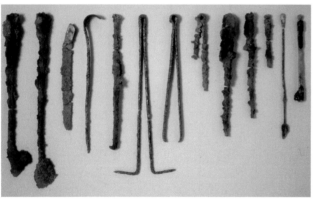
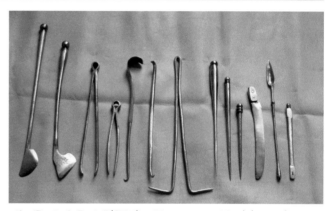

Figure 22a–d Stanway, near Colchester, set of medical instruments from the 'Doctor's Burial' (CF47), mid-1st century AD: a) (top left) the grave as excavated; b) (top right) the grave group as displayed at the British Museum in 1997; c) (above left) the medical instruments – scalpels, saw, sharp and blunt hooks, forceps, needles, probe, handle; d) (above right) reconstructions of the instruments. Colchester Museums, COLEM:1996.34.CF47.26-39. Photos: Fig. 22a) Philip Crummy; Fig. 22b–c) British Museum; Fig. 22d) Ralph Jackson

Jászberényi in the Jászság region of central Hungary. A grave, dating to the 1st or 2nd century AD, was revealed in archaeological excavations following a magnetometer survey. It contained the skeleton of a 50–60 year-old man with a kit of surgical instruments and the remains of medicaments in two wooden boxes at his feet. The find has not yet been published but has received press coverage (see e.g. www.heritagedaily.com/2023/04/medical-equipment-found-in-roman-burial/147093 Accessed 27/4/2023), from which it appears that the instruments include forceps, needles, a bone lever and three scalpels complete with their iron blades and with silver-inlaid handles. From the form of the instruments, and like the find from Aschersleben (p. 17), it would appear that the grave was that of a Roman doctor practising well beyond the Roman frontier, for this region only became part of the Roman Empire, as the province of Pannonia, after the Marcomannic Wars of AD 166–188.

To these important archaeological finds may be added a number of other kits which, though unfortunately lacking in contextual information or even their place and circumstances of discovery, provide considerable intrinsic interest. One of these is the small kit in the British Museum collection (**Fig. 23**) (Cat. nos 3.40–8), acquired from Christies, London in 1994. A detailed macroscopic

examination combined with full scientific investigation confirmed the integrity of the set (see pp. 22–3 and 96–8). It comprises a scalpel (its iron blade lacking), a smooth-jawed spring forceps and a curette (sharp spoon) – probably originally the two ends of a single combination instrument, a toothed spring forceps, a sharp hook, a sharp-pointed probe/needle, an ear scoop combined with a now broken terminal, a hooked dissector combined with a ridged lever, and a small broken finial. A high proportion of the instruments are double-ended, resulting in the provision of 12 different operative components. That carefully selected range of instrumentation would have enabled the practitioner who assembled and used the kit, probably in the 1st or 2nd century AD, to maximise the scope of medical provision while maintaining portability of the kit and ease of use (Jackson 1997a, 228, 239, fig. 1; Jackson 2007b, 21–4, fig. 7).

Another kit, acquired by the Berliner Museen in the early 20th century, was said to have come from Kyzikos, Mysia, in north-west Anatolia, Turkey, though without any further information. It consisted of a rectangular bronze box and nine instruments: three scalpels (their iron blades broken), a toothed spring forceps, a smooth-jawed spring forceps, two sharp hooks (one combined with a needle-holder), and two probes. All except the forceps and hooks were lost in the

Second World War, but photographs survive to enable an assessment. Unusually, the box appears to have had a two-tiered construction, like one from Pompeii (Beck 1977, 62, pl. VII,5; Sobel 1991, 134), one from an early 2nd-century AD cremation burial in the Traianoupolis tumulus at Loutra, Alexandropouli, Eastern Macedonia, and two from 2nd-century AD cremation burials in the grave tumulus of Mikri Doxipara-Zoni, Greek Thrace (Triantafyllos 2014). In one tier were four slender open compartments and two rectangular lidded compartments, for the storage and preparation of medications. The instruments had been stored in the other tier, as indicated by their silhouettes preserved in the corrosion products on the dividing panel (Heres 1992; Bliquez 2015, 274–5, fig. 83).

An important kit on the antiquities market in 2009/10, without any accompanying provenance or finding information, was acquired in 2015 by the RD Milns Museum at the University of Queensland, Brisbane. It comprises a rectangular bronze box, a tubular bronze box, a cylindrical bronze box, a stone mixing palette and 12 instruments, all in a fine state of preservation to judge from photographs (**Fig. 24**). The instruments consist of three scalpels complete with their iron blades (two with bellied cutting edges and one concave), a sharp hook, a smooth-jawed spring forceps, a toothed coudée-type spring forceps, two spatula probes, two scoop probes, a ligula and a composite bronze and iron bone lever. The rectangular box appears to be of unusual design, with the stone palette forming its sliding lid on one face, covering five hinged lidded compartments with omega-shaped wire handles, while the other face was also provided with a sliding lid, in the form of a silver- and copper-inlaid bronze panel showing a draped standing male figure on a plinth, framed by a laurel leaf and rosette border. The figure was surely intended as Asklepios – as seen on other rectangular box lids –

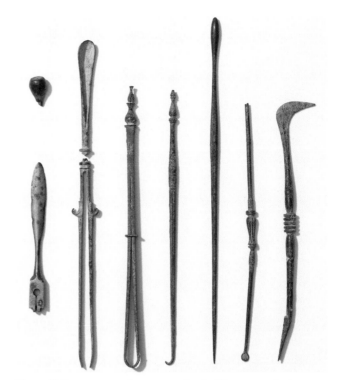

Figure 23 Provenance unknown, small set of Roman medical instruments, 1st/2nd century AD. British Museum, London (cat. nos 3.40–8)

though, unusually, he lacks both of his most distinctive attributes, the staff and snake. The long slender tubular box is a probe case of normal form. The hinged cylindrical box is less common and, with a number of internal compartments, appears to be a version of the hinged cylindrical cases found in several 4th-century BC tombs in Macedonia (Ignatiadou 2015, 91–7, 107–9). But, as an ensemble with the rectangular box and the tubular box, it is much more closely paralleled by the composite instrument and medicine case from the

Figure 24 Provenance unknown, set of Roman medical instruments, probably 1st/2nd century AD. RD Milns Antiquities Museum, The University of Queensland, inv. nos 15.001a-h. Purchased from Charles Ede Ltd with funds from Dr Glenda Powell AM in Memory of Dr Owen Powell OAM, 2015

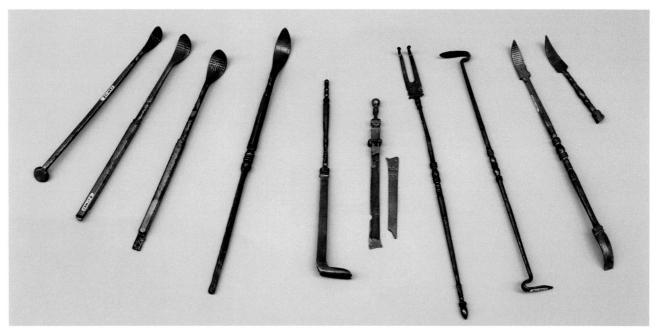

Figure 25 Near Rome, set of lithotomy instruments, probably from a tomb in the Roman Campagna, 2nd century AD. Cambridge, Museum of Classical Archaeology, CAM167–176. Photo © Museum of Classical Archaeology, Cambridge

early 2nd-century AD Cremation B in the Traianoupolis tumulus. That comprised a two-tier rectangular box, with a sliding bronze lid closing one face and a sliding stone palette the other, flanked on one side by a tubular bronze probe case and on the other by a hinged cylindrical case containing *materia medica* in three compartments (Triantafyllos 2014). The presence of close parallels from north-west Anatolia, eastern Macedonia and Thrace is suggestive of an eastern Empire origin for the unprovenanced set.

The broad similarity in the range of instrument types in all these sets is a repeating pattern which can also be identified as a component of more extensive sets of instruments (see pp. 26–34, and, e.g. Jackson 1986; Jackson 1995a, tables 1–2). We may cautiously accept that it reflects the composition of the metal tools in a typical set of basic medical instruments during the period of the Roman Empire and probably earlier, too. Indeed, the recurrence of this range of instruments has enabled the recognition of 17 instruments in the British Museum collection (formerly in the collection of the duc de Blacas d'Aulps) as a probable set (see p. 99 and **Fig. 105**). Notable, too, is the frequency with which combination instruments are found in the basic kits, for two-ended instruments could double the range of operative components while still maintaining portability of the kit. Design, craftsmanship, ingenuity, decoration and economy all combined to increase the practitioner's control over the operations that he (or she) undertook.

Thus, written, iconographic and archaeological sources converge to reveal that the basic metal instrumentation of Greek and Roman practitioners almost invariably comprised one or more examples of scalpel, forceps, sharp hook, needle and probe, most of which could also be heated to serve as cauteries, as required. With those instruments, in conjunction with fingers and the occasional non-medical implement, the great majority of surgical interventions could be accomplished, as Celsus' text demonstrates. Many

kits were also accompanied by drug boxes and implements for preparing medicaments, while a cupping vessel was sometimes included, as also, especially, a bone lever, reflecting respectively the integration of surgery with medical treatment and humoral therapy and the prevalence of fractures and dislocations.

Specialist kits

Some kits include instrument types indicative of specialist surgery. One such is the burial group found in 1988 in a mid-4th century AD grave during excavations at Gadara, Syria. It included utensils probably for the storage, preparation and application of medicaments – several small glass flasks and stone mixing palettes, a spoon, a scoop probe and a spatula probe – as well as a smooth-jawed spring forceps, an iron shears and an iron dental forceps. The dental forceps, a stout cross-legged instrument with in-turned close-gripping jaws, was specifically designed for the extraction of teeth and implies that the grave was that of a dentist (Künzl and Weber 1991).

Perhaps the clearest specialist set is the group of ten instruments believed to have been found in a tomb in the vicinity of Rome in the late 19th century and donated to the Cambridge Museum of Classical Archaeology in 1921/22 (inv. 167–176) (**Fig. 25**). It is the instrumentation of a Roman lithotomist, the λιθοτόμος in Galen's list of medical specialists (*On the Parts of Medicine* 2–3; Baader 1967, 233–4). The instruments comprise four roughened scoops – one single-ended, two double-ended and two combined with an iron blade (now lacking), a bifurcated blunt hook, two slender double-ended ridged levers/scoops, a slender double-ended blunt hook and two coudée-type toothed spring forceps. Probably dating to the 2nd century AD, the kit is clearly a belonging set and one that is probably complete and in which all of the instruments appear to have been intended exclusively for lithotomy – cutting for stone in the urinary bladder (vesical calculus) (Künzl 1983b; Jackson 1986, 142 fn.

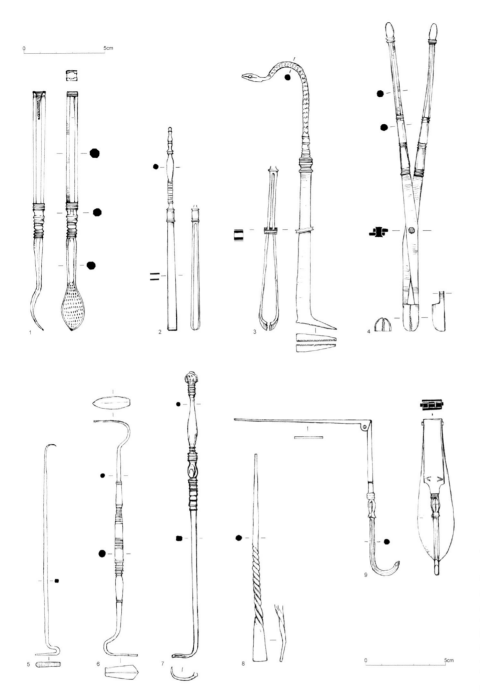

Figure 26 Cyrene, Libya, set of Roman medical instruments: 1) lithotomy knife and scoop (blade lacking); 2) smooth-jawed fixation forceps; 3) toothed fixation forceps; 4) uvula forceps; 5) double-ended sharp and blunt hook; 6) double-ended blunt hook; 7) suture needle; 8) styloid probe; 9) tongue-depressor. 1st/3rd century AD. Shahat Museum, Cyrene, inv. nos 1063-1071. Drawings: Craig Williams and Jim Thorn

80; Jackson 1995a, 194, 204, pl. 4; Jackson 2010; to the lithotomy instruments listed there may now be added another combined lithotomy scoop and knife in the Halûk Perk collection of instruments from Anatolia: Perk 2012, 39, 1.3.3).

Lithotomy was also among the specialist interventions enabled by another small kit of nine finely crafted instruments found at Cyrene, Libya before the Second World War (**Fig. 26**). There are examples of all the basic general-purpose metal tools of ancient surgery – knife, smooth-jawed and toothed forceps, sharp and blunt hooks, needle and probe. In addition there are instruments of more specialised use – a combined lithotomy knife and scoop, a toothed uvula forceps, a hinged tongue depressor and, exceptionally, a suture needle. The set is probably from a tomb and dates to the 1st/3rd century AD. It would appear that it had belonged to a practitioner experienced in Greco-Roman medicine who carried out both general and

specialised surgery, including lithotomy and operations in the throat (Jackson 2021).

Throat operations could also have been accomplished by a practitioner using a group of four instruments from Italy, probably part of a once larger set, in the Bristol Museum and Art Gallery (**Fig. 27**) (Appendix 1) (Jackson 1995a, 194, 205, pl. 5; Jackson 1997a, fig. 3). The smooth-jawed uvula forceps, double sharp hook, combined sharp and blunt hook and scalpel (blade lacking) were the instruments required for uvulectomy, tonsillectomy and other surgical interventions in the throat. The instruments are products of the same workshop: all are richly ornamented with distinctively worked lion-head finials and stylised acanthus mouldings, and scientific analysis revealed that three have virtually identical metal compositions.

Another unprovenanced kit on the antiquities market in 1991 comprised nine instruments, a bronze cupping vessel

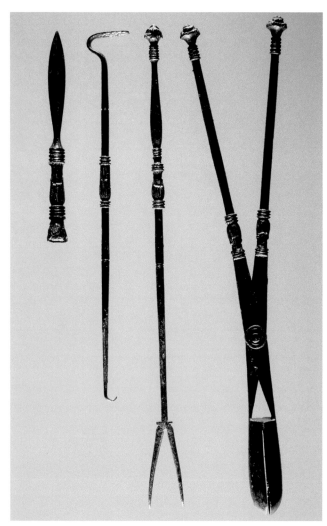

Figure 27 A group of four Roman surgical instruments from Italy, probably part of a once larger set, 1st/3rd century AD: scalpel handle, double-ended sharp and blunt hook; double sharp hook; uvula forceps (see Appendix 1). Bristol Museum and Art Gallery, inv. nos Ft.1449, Ft.1450, Ft.1452, Ft.1510. Photo: British Museum

and a glass pot or stand (Gods, Beasts and Men 1991). To judge from a colour photograph, the similarity in appearance of the patina on all the instruments strongly suggests that they are a belonging set, as does the range of instrument types: two scalpel handles, a combined pointed-jawed forceps and elevator, three probes, a double sharp hook, a toothed uvula forceps and a hinged tongue depressor. The last three instruments mirror those in the Cyrene set and those in the group from Italy in the Bristol Museum and Art Gallery and once again indicate that throat surgery was within the ambit of the practitioner who used the kit. However, like the Cyrene instrumentation the kit would also have enabled a much wider range of operative procedures, too.

Eye diseases, common and troublesome in antiquity, correspondingly loom large in medical texts and in surviving medical papyri (see, e.g., Marganne 1994 and Andorlini Marcone 1993, nos 40, 70, 94–5, 99, 104, 108–9, 117, 123, 129, 143, 152–3, 155, 159, 161, 174–5, 177, 196, 204), and they were high on the list of medical specialisms. The instruments in the Pompeii fugitive's kit (see p. 18), which included a cataract needle, indicate that he was both an eye doctor and a surgical practitioner, as too, probably, was the

Wehringen practitioner (see p. 19) whose kit included dried eye *collyria*. A tubular probe case, found in the River Maas at Maaseik, Belgium, also once belonged to an eye doctor, for it contained a cataract needle and four probes (Heymans 1979; Künzl 1996, 2610–11; Künzl 2018, 29–30, fig. 12), while an exceptional discovery in the River Saône at Montbellet, France, was the lost kit of an eye specialist who had the instruments – solid and hollow cataract needles – both to couch and to extract a cataractous lens (**Fig. 28**) (Feugère *et al.* 1985; Feugère *et al.* 1988; Künzl 1996, 2612–13).

Further evidence for an eye specialist is provided by a kit of nine instruments found in the late 1st- or early 2nd-century AD Tomb G1–1075 in the Više Grobalja necropolis at *Viminiacum*, the capital of the Roman province of Moesia superior, modern Kostolac, Serbia (Korać 1986; Heres 1992, 158–60; Kirova 2002, fig 12; Künzl 2018, 26–7, fig. 9; Pardon-Labonnelie *et al.* 2020). The instruments comprise four scalpels, two retaining broken iron blades, two sharp hooks, a spring forceps combined with a needle-holder, a cataract needle and a double-ended bronze and iron bone lever. In addition to a coin of the emperor Nerva (AD 96–8) and six gaming counters there are several medical utensils and the remains of medicaments – a stone mixing palette, a glass phial, the broken neck of a glass flask and a rectangular bronze box with sliding lid containing fragments of dried *collyrium* sticks stamped with the salve names *crocodes* and *stactum*. The grave was that of a man of about 40 years of age and his instruments had been stored in a wooden case placed on top of his rectangular bronze drug box. While the incorporation of the bone lever, together with the other instruments, suggests that the doctor who used the *Viminiacum* kit was a 'general practitioner', the presence of a cataract needle, as well as the combined forceps and needle-holder and the remains of dried eye medications, indicate that eye medicine and eye surgery also formed an important part of his practice.

Large sets of instruments

While a very large part of the surgical interventions described in Greek and Roman medical texts could have been accomplished using the restricted range of instruments in the basic kits, some surgery required additional instruments or instruments specifically designed for particular operations, as, for example, the lithotomy instruments, dental forceps and uvula forceps already noted. Corresponding quite closely to the range of medical and surgical specialists mentioned in lay and medical texts are the specialised instruments encountered in some of the surviving large sets of instruments (Jackson 1995a, table 3). Thus, the texts record, amongst others, specialists in eye diseases, ear disorders, dentistry, throat operations, hernia, lithotomy, rectal complaints and gynaecology, while the component instruments of the large sets include cataract needles, dental forceps, uvula forceps, lithotomy scoops, rectal and vaginal dilators and, above all, instruments of bone surgery, from dislocations and fractures to trepanation. The majority of the surviving large sets of instruments have been found in graves, thus removed from their places of first use and from circulation but, importantly, preserved as sealed groups of associated instruments. However, there are a number of other exceptional finds that come from settlement sites and shed even more valuable light, not only on the composition and extent of instrumentation but also on some of the settings in which medical treatment and surgery took place.

One of the largest grave finds is the set of about 50 surgical instruments found in 1924 with other medical implements and utensils in a cremation burial of the late 1st or early 2nd century AD at Bingen am Rhein, Germany (**Fig. 29a–c**). Some of the instruments are the basic tools of surgery, with which the Bingen practitioner was especially well provided, including 13 scalpels (nine complete with their iron blades), six sharp hooks, three spring forceps, a double-ended needle-holder and a spatula probe as well as three cupping vessels. But the majority of the other instruments were selected for – and some specifically designed for – bone surgery. They comprise five composite bronze and iron double-ended bone levers, a curette (sharp spoon), two double-ended spatulas, an iron knife, an iron gouge, at least three iron chisels, a possible iron drill-bit and, most spectacularly, two toothed cylindrical drills (crown trepans) and their folding handle. The crown trepans, the only certain surviving Roman examples to date, enabled the practitioner to remove a disc of bone from a patient's skull. This is cranial trepanation, an operation required especially for depressed skull fracture consequent on a serious wound or injury to the head. The other instruments permitted a full range of operative procedures on dislocated, fractured and injured bones, some of which would also have entailed the use of traction and other equipment at the practitioner's surgery. The grave group indicates, then, that at Bingen, around the year AD 100, there was a doctor who was well equipped for general practice but above all for specialist surgical treatment of bone and soft tissue injuries (Como 1925; Künzl 1983a, 80–5; Künzl 2002b, 36–8; Jackson 2005a, 104–9).

Another large set of similar date which also includes three cupping vessels is that said to have been found near Colophon, some 25 miles south of Smyrna, Turkey, in 1911/1912 (Caton 1914) (**Fig. 30**). Almost certainly a grave group, it comprises, in addition to the cupping vessels, which are graded in size, a large glass beaker and 32 surgical and medical instruments. The entire assemblage is in the Johns Hopkins Archaeological Museum, Baltimore (inv. Buckler 1–35), except for the glass beaker which is in the collection of the Ashmolean Museum, Oxford (acc. no. 1953.636). The instruments consist of six scalpels (lacking their iron blades), two knives, two sharp hooks, a double sharp hook, a blunt hook, four spring forceps, a double-ended needle-holder, three probes, a cautery/tongue depressor, a bone forceps, a folding drill handle, a double-ended bone lever, a double-ended curette, a double-ended spatula, two catheters, a pair of scales comprising a beam and two pans, a tubular drug box and a stone mixing palette. Although one of the forceps and the double sharp hook have very ornate handles, none of the instruments is closely dateable. However, the glass beaker supplies a date for the set: it is the largest known example of an East Mediterranean type and can be dated *c.* AD 75–100 (Jennifer Price, *pers. comm.*). Even lacking the iron objects and those made of organic materials, which

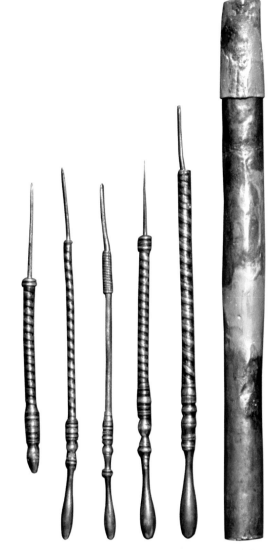

Figure 28 Montbellet, near Tournus, group of five Roman cataract needles found in a tubular box in the River Saône, 1st/2nd century AD. Musée Greuze, Tournus. Photo © Leibniz-Zentrum für Archäologie

would undoubtedly have formed part of the original instrumentation (see, e.g., Jackson 1994a, tables 2–4; Bliquez 2015, appendix), we can say that the practitioner who used the Colophon instrumentation had at his (or her) disposal the equipment to carry out a wide range of general surgery as well as, specifically, bone surgery, eye surgery, catheterisation of the urinary tract, humoral therapy (utilising the cupping vessels) and medication (as witnessed by the drug box, palette and scales).

That combination of medical and surgical practice is also indicated by the composition of the large set of instruments from Italy, probably from a grave of the 1st or 2nd century AD, acquired by the British Museum in 1968 (**Fig. 31**) (Cat. nos 3.1–38). The 37 objects comprise eight scalpels (lacking their iron blades), three sharp hooks, a double-ended spring forceps combining smooth and toothed jaws, a pointed-jawed forceps, a double-ended needle-holder, eight probes (a dipyrene, an ear probe, three spatula probes, two scoop probes and a ligula), an iron stylus, a spoon, two bone chisels (complete with their iron blades), a curette (sharp spoon), a double-ended blunt hook, an iron drill-bit (?), a cataract

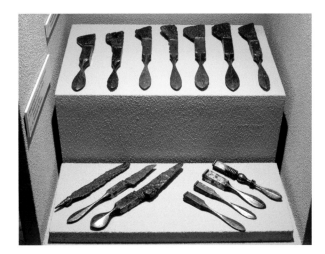

Figure 29a–c Bingen am Rhein, part of the extensive late 1st/early 2nd century AD set of Roman surgical instruments: a) (top left) scalpels, nine complete with blades; b) (above) three cupping vessels, with stand and hippopotamus figure; c) (left) folding trepan handle, two cylindrical drills (*modioli*) and bone lever. Historisches Museum am Strom, Bingen

needle, two male catheters, one female catheter, a bivalve dilator (rectal speculum), a tubular drug box, a cylindrical box system and a stone mixing palette. This carefully selected comprehensive instrumentation consists of three groups. First, a full range of the essential tools of surgery (the scalpels, hooks, forceps, needle and probes); secondly, a group for the storage, preparation and application of medications (the drug boxes, mixing palette, scoop probes, spatula probes and spoon); and thirdly, a number of specialist instruments (the bone chisels, curette, double blunt hook, drill-bit, cataract needle, catheters and rectal speculum). With the first two groups the practitioner could have operated on, and prescribed for, many of the more common injuries, afflictions and diseases, while the

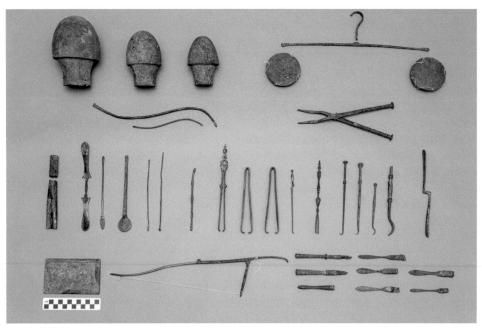

Figure 30 Colophon, near Smyrna, set of Roman medical instruments, probably from a burial, late 1st/early 2nd century AD. Johns Hopkins Archaeological Museum, Baltimore, Maryland, inv. no. Buckler 1–35. Image courtesy of the Johns Hopkins Archaeological Museum, photography by James T. VanRensselaer

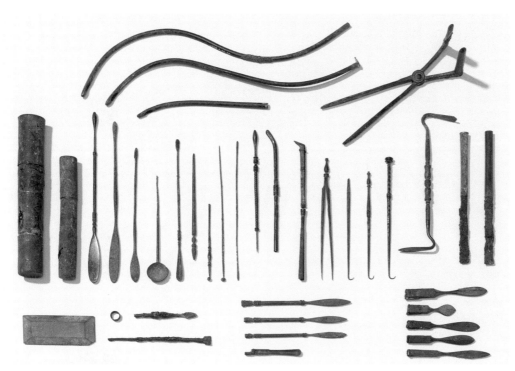

Figure 31 Italy, set of Roman medical instruments, probably from a burial, 1st/2nd century AD. British Museum, London (cat. nos 3.1–38)

instruments of the third group, in combination with those of the first, would have permitted a range of more specialised operations: the chisels, scalpels, curette, double blunt hook, pointed-jawed forceps and drill-bit were instruments of bone surgery; the needles, sharp hooks, fine scalpels and spring forceps would have enabled eye surgery, including the operation for couching cataract; the catheters, dipyrene and ear probe would have permitted treatment of patients with urinary disorders, especially strangury; while anal lesions, anal fistula and internal haemorrhoids could have been operated upon through use of the speculum (Jackson 1986; Jackson 1987).

A firm and specific sepulchral context exists for an assemblage of about 30 surgical and medical instruments found in 1983 during the archaeological excavation of a rock-cut tomb (Tomb 22/83) at Nea Paphos, Cyprus. Dated mid-2nd/early 3rd century AD, the instrumentation comprises a cupping vessel, three scalpels (one retaining the long stem of its iron blade), an iron shears, three double blunt hooks, an iron spring forceps, an ivory needle, an iron stylus and two long tubular boxes, one of which was used as a probe case containing a dipyrene, a spatula probe, a scoop probe, a ligula and a simple probe; also two iron bone levers, a composite bronze and iron instrument, possibly a bone chisel or file, a syringe or cyster, a tapered tube, five tubular drug boxes, four of which contained residues of medicaments, and a stone mixing palette (Michaelides 1984; Foster *et al.* 1988). Once again the instrumentation encompasses general surgery and pharmacy together with some more specialised treatments. The cupping vessel indicates venesection and humoral therapy, while the levers and double blunt hooks are instruments of bone surgery. The syringe, to date a unique find from the Roman world, comprises a slender pipe attached to a broader tube with what may be the remains of a close-fitting wooden plunger inside. Thus, it appears to have been a plunger-driven device, rather than a cyster. As such it would have been

capable both of withdrawing fluids and of injecting liquid medicaments with some force and it has been identified as probably an example of the pus extractor (*puoulkos*) that had been invented by Heron of Alexandria in the 1st century AD (Bliquez and Oleson 1994; Bliquez 2015, 217–19). The presence, too, of a fragmentary tapered tube, probably a cannula or a clyster nozzle, suggests that drainage and instilling were significant parts of the surgical interventions undertaken by the Nea Paphos practitioner.

At Rheims in 1854 a grave find, probably a cremation burial, yielded 35 surgical and medical instruments that had been contained in a wooden chest (Künzl 1983a, 61–7; Künzl 1985, 467–8, pls 61–6). In addition to the instruments the find included the lock and handle from the chest, a balance beam and its two pans, a small steelyard complete with hooks and weight, three bronze dishes, two iron flasks and two bronze coins of Antoninus Pius and Marcus Aurelius. The coins and one of the bronze dishes give a date of deposition of the grave group within the late 2nd or first half of the 3rd century AD. The instruments comprise large numbers of the basic tools of surgery: six scalpel handles (lacking their iron blades), three of which have inlaid decoration, two sharp hooks, two combined sharp and blunt hooks, three smooth-jawed spring forceps, three toothed spring forceps, a slotted-jawed forceps, a spatula probe and a scoop probe. In addition there are four slender round handles with a flattened head and a small circular socket (the iron component now lacking), one octagonal handle with an olivary terminal and a small circular socket (its iron component also lacking) and four double-ended octagonal handles combining a small circular socket at one end with a slotted socket at the other end (all iron components now lacking). The loss of every iron component from these handles is particularly unfortunate because without their operative part their precise function cannot be unequivocally determined. Although their small circular sockets very likely originally held iron needles (Künzl 2002b,

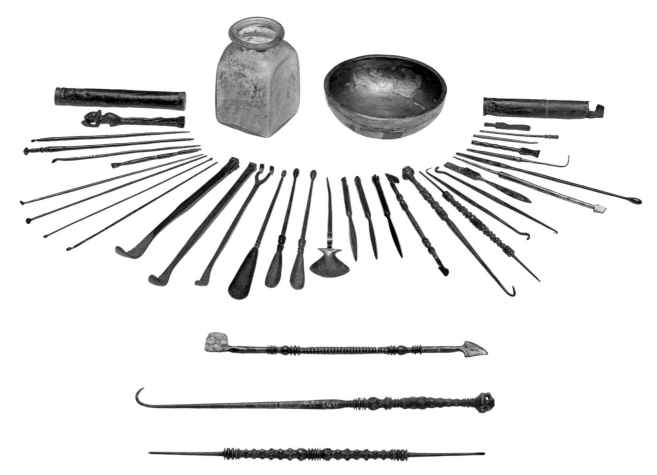

Figure 32 Ephesus (probably), set of Roman medical instruments, first half of the 3rd century AD, and detail showing, top to bottom, the probable *phlebotomon*, the sharp hook with lion-head finial and the cataract needle. Leibniz-Zentrum für Archäologie, Mainz, inv. no. 0.37829-0.37864. Photos © Leibniz-Zentrum für Archäologie / S. Steidl

81, fig. 106) there is another possibility, because examples of the same type of octagonal handle in the Rimini assemblage preserve not needles but iron blades (Jackson 2009b, 75, fig. 1, 7–9; Jackson 2014a, fig. 18.12, 5, fig 18.16, 1–2, 141). That at least the Rheims round handles with flat heads were probably needle handles, however, is implied by the inclusion in the grave group of a stone collyrium-stamp and 21 fragments (40g) of dried stamped *collyrium* sticks. The single die of the collyrium-stamp is inscribed retrograde with the name of Gaius Firmius Severus and his myrrh-salve – *diasmyrnes* (Voinot 1999, no. 104). None of the surviving *collyrium* stick fragments was stamped with that die. Instead several are stamped with the salve name *nardinum* and several others with a two-line die with the name Marcellinus and salves to be used for eye inflammation (*lippitudo*) and corneal scars (*cicatrices*). With those the Rheims practitioner treated eye diseases by medication but handled needles together with the sharp hooks and the various jaw types of the spring forceps would have enabled surgical interventions on the eye and its margins, including the operation to couch cataract. Together with the medical equipment, *collyria* and other medications and a full basic instrumentation for general surgery, this suggests that the Rheims practitioner was a general practitioner who also specialised in eye medicine.

Another large set of instruments that incorporates a needle for couching cataract is a burial group said to be from south-west Asia Minor acquired by the Römisch-

Germanisches Zentralmuseum, Mainz (LEIZA) in 1963 (Künzl 1983a, 45–8). Subsequently Künzl has shown that the burial group was very likely from Ephesus (Künzl 2002a, 12–20). The find comprises 31 surgical and medical instruments as well as a small silver bowl, a silver spoon, a silver stylus, a square glass bottle, and an inscribed bronze handle in the form of a mouse (**Fig. 32**). The silver bowl and glass bottle indicate a likely date for the burial in the first half of the 3rd century AD, while the inscribed handle connects the set and the practitioner who used it to Ephesus and, in particular, the sanctuary of Artemis (Künzl 2002a, 13–15; Künzl 2002b, 75–6). The instruments include four scalpel handles (lacking their iron blades), a slender double-ended handle mounted at one end with a tiny iron blade (probably a *phlebotomon* for blood-letting) and at the other with a tiny iron cautery, two sharp hooks, two combined sharp and blunt hooks, ten probes (a dipyrene, three ear probes, a spatula probe, a scoop probe and four ligulae), a broken needle, two tubular drug boxes, a double-ended cataract needle, two double-ended lithotomy knives combining a roughened scoop with an iron blade (now lacking), a lithotomy scoop combined with a double blunt hook and two lithotomy scoops combined with an olivary probe. Once again, only the less perishable, inorganic, parts of the instrumentation have survived. Nevertheless, they point to a potentiality not only for general surgery and medication but also specifically for eye surgery and, in particular, for urinary treatments, above all lithotomy. Such

Figure 33 Paris, avenue de Choisy, 13th arrondissement, set of Roman medical instruments, 3rd century AD. Musée Carnavalet, Paris. Photo CC0 Paris Musées / Musée Carnavalet – Histoire de Paris

specialisms were needed and enabled by population-dense cities like Ephesus.

As already seen, the cataclysmic events in the Bay of Naples in AD 79 caused a number of medical practitioners, unsuccessfully fleeing the Vesuvian eruption, to take part of their instrumentation away from their surgery. So, too, did different, but also probably dangerous, circumstances cause another practitioner in the Roman town of *Lutetia* (Paris) to take and conceal his medical instrumentation, together with a stash of 75 coins (*antoniniani* from Victorinus to Tetricus I and II, AD 269–74) (**Fig. 33**). In the event the hoard was never recovered by its owner. Often called the 'Paris Surgeon' set, it was discovered in 1880 at 180, avenue de Choisy in Paris's 13th arrondissement (Deneffe 1893, 23–65) and is now in the Musée Carnavalet, Paris. The coins point to a date of burial of the hoard around the year AD 275, a time of great instability in *Gallia* and *Germania* as the Franks and Alamanni crossed the frontier and plundered the provinces, and the Paris practitioner may have been a casualty. The coins and instruments were contained in a deep bronze bowl, itself almost certainly part of the medical equipment (Künzl 1983a, 74–8; Sorel 1984; Velay 1989 – but note that colour plate 38 has been reversed; Künzl 2002b, 43, fig. 56). The instruments and implements include a large cupping vessel and part of a second, three scalpel handles (lacking their iron blades), a smooth-jawed spring forceps, a toothed spring forceps, two coudée-type toothed spring forceps, two pointed-jawed forceps, a pointed-jawed forceps combined with an elevator, a toothed uvula forceps, a sharp hook, a spatula probe, a broken probe, a large pouring spoon, a tube with a disc terminal, probably an insufflator for blowing powdered medicaments into the nose or throat (Bliquez 2015, 231), a rectangular drug box, its sliding lid decorated with silver-inlaid animals, five (fragmentary) tubular drug boxes, a white marble mixing palette and a buckle and strap-end. Although the uvula forceps and insufflator indicate a degree of specialisation in throat operations, the set as a whole is that of a well-equipped

general practitioner who performed surgery, prepared and administered medications, let blood or dry-cupped the patient when necessary and doubtless advised on other therapies and regimens, too.

Another extensive instrumentation is an unprovenanced set in the Ashmolean Museum (acc. nos 1990.8-44). It is reputed to have come from Asia Minor or Syria, a provenance supported by the identification of surviving textile remains, a plain-weave linen fabric of Eastern Mediterranean type, adhering to some of the instruments – it would appear that each instrument had been individually wrapped (Jackson 1995a, 196–202, tables 1–2, pl. 2; Jackson forthcoming). Additional intrinsic evidence – surface indications and the preservation of vulnerable objects – suggests that the set probably came from a tomb. It is of exceptional interest in a number of ways, not least in the sheer number and variety of instruments: it comprises 37 pieces and incorporates many unique and specialised instruments as well as the essential instruments of surgery and pharmaceutical equipment (**Fig. 34a–b**). There are four slender scalpel handles (lacking their iron blades), two slender handles with a small socket for an iron needle or blade, four handles lacking their operative iron components, two toothed spring forceps, one combined with a blunt hook, two spatula probes, two styloid probes, one scoop probe, two uvula forceps, one of which is intact, while the jaws of the other were already broken at the time of burial, and a cross-legged toothed broad-jawed forceps, so far unique, but whose lion-head handle terminals and stylised acanthus mouldings are closely paralleled by those on instruments in the small sets from Italy and Cyrene (see pp. 22 and 25). Like one of the uvula forceps this forceps, too, was broken at the time of burial. There is an iron dental forceps, a double-ended bronze and iron bone lever, the handle of a bone chisel, a clyster nozzle (Jackson 1994a, 186, 207, fig. 4, 5), a broken bone tube, perhaps an ear syringe or clyster, two strainer spoons, a pouring spoon, two tubular drug boxes, a balance beam and pivot, four glass vessels (a jar, a small

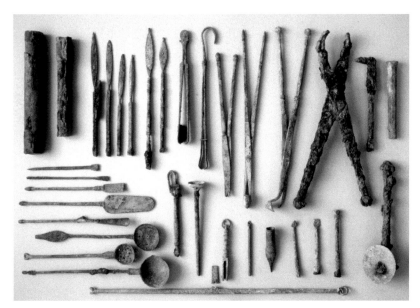

Figure 34a–b Asia Minor/Syria (reputedly), set of Roman medical instruments and glassware, probably from a burial, late 4th/early 5th century AD. Ashmolean Museum, Oxford, acc. nos 1990.8-44. Photos: Ralph Jackson

flask, a small bowl and a stand or stopper), and two unidentified implements. Equipped with these instruments and others made of organic materials the practitioner could have encompassed bone surgery, dentistry, rectal, gynaecological and throat interventions in addition to general surgery and medical treatments. Interestingly the set combines instruments of varying date: the form of the glass jar, the chip-carved mouldings on the bone lever and the stumpy olivary terminal of the probes belong to the 4th or early 5th century AD, indicating a likely deposition date for the set; but the complete uvula forceps is undifferentiated from examples of 3rd-century AD date, like that in the Paris instrumentation; while one of the toothed spring forceps is identical in form to one of 3rd-century AD date from Rimini and 1st-century AD examples from Pompeii and Bingen. Thus the set includes many functioning instruments suited to a wide range of surgical and medical treatments, together with others already broken or damaged at the time of burial, perhaps awaiting repair, and others of a form which may mean they were several hundred years old at the time of burial. This implies a very long usage of the set and is a reminder of the value of purpose-made medical instruments. It would also appear to show the strength of continuity of certain types, which continued to be made in traditional forms, either perhaps using handed down moulds or else moulded from existing instruments. Alternatively, it may represent the longevity of use of individual instruments, which might be maintained in good working order and passed on from healer to healer, generation after generation. Either way, the instruments are a tribute to Greek and Roman medical practitioners and craftsmen who developed carefully designed and finely crafted tools perfectly adapted to human anatomy and the demands of specific surgical interventions.

Key site assemblages of instruments: 'disaster finds'

A similarly large and varied set of instruments, deposited at about the same date as the Ashmolean set, is of especial importance for it not only has a known provenance but also a secure context, not from a burial but from a settlement site near the west coast of the Black Sea. It was found at Devnya,

eastern Bulgaria, during archaeological excavations following chance discoveries in the late 1970s in the town of *Marcianopolis*, the capital of the Roman province of Moesia inferior. On the floor of a large room of a very large late Roman *villa urbana*, destroyed by fire in the late 4th or first half of the 5th century AD, were about 30 surgical instruments and medical implements (Minchev 1983; Kirova 2002). Several of the instruments are broken, fragmentary or damaged by the fire which, in the absence of a full, illustrated publication, makes it difficult to ascertain their use. Nevertheless, it is possible to determine that the instrumentation includes at least one scalpel, a composite shears with bronze spring and iron blades (now lacking), a sharp hook, two handled needles (the iron needles lacking), several probes, including a dipyrene, several medical accessories, a bone lever, a folding drill handle, two uvula forceps (one with smooth jaws, the other toothed), a broken hinged tongue depressor, three double-ended lithotomy knives combining a roughened scoop with an iron blade (now lacking), a lithotomy scoop, a slender double-ended blunt hook (one end broken), a bivalve dilator (rectal speculum) and a trivalve dilator (vaginal speculum). The instrumentation gives the impression of a well-equipped healer, probably with a practice in his own home, who carried out routine surgery and medical treatments but who had in addition a very wide-ranging surgical expertise including bone surgery, throat operations, lithotomy, rectal and gynaecological treatments.

At *Marcianopolis* the instrumentation may have been used by a doctor based in his own home, but we can make a much firmer identification of a *taberna medica domestica* at the Roman town of *Ariminum*, modern Rimini, where a truly astonishing find was made in Piazza Ferrari. Archaeological excavations between 1989 and 1997, once again following a chance discovery, brought to light the so-called *domus* del Chirurgo which, since 2007, has been preserved under a cover building (**Fig. 35a–b**). The house, occupying a triangular plot in the north-east quarter of *Ariminum*, was burnt down in the mid-3rd century AD (Ortalli 2000; Ortalli 2008; Ortalli 2009; Ghiretti 2010; Ortalli 2011; Ortalli 2018). The burning down of the *domus*, together with contemporary

Figure 35a–b Rimini, *domus* del Chirurgo: a) the cover building; b) the principal room (top right) with mosaic of Orpheus, in which most of the medical instruments were found. Rimini, Piazza Ferrari. Photos: Ralph Jackson

conflagrations elsewhere in *Ariminum* and at other nearby coastal sites, has been linked to the Alamannic raids of AD 257/8 (Ortalli 2009, 26), a date that corresponds closely to that provided by the coin assemblage from the *domus*. The subsequent walling of the town resulted in the desertion of the site (which was in the lee of the rampart and the *intervallum* road) and its destruction deposits were sealed and re mained intact. They disclosed a two-storey residence, built in the second half of the 2nd century AD, with six main ground floor rooms with fine mosaics, a communicating corridor and a small courtyard garden. The rooms included a *triclinium* and *cubiculum*, but the medical equipment was found principally in one room, interpreted as the consulting room and surgery. In here was found a great profusion of surgical instruments and medical paraphernalia in positions suggesting storage on shelves and in cupboards. There are around 150 metal instruments and implements as well as ceramic medicine pots and a graded set of seven stone mortars and seven stone pestles. As well as introducing instrument types never before found, the Rimini assemblage provides the best evidence yet for what the complete metal instrumentation of a Roman medical practitioner may have looked like (Jackson 2002b; 2003; 2009b; 2011d; 2011e). It is important to emphasise the word 'metal', because what did *not* survive is the undoubtedly large quantity of instruments and implements made from organic materials – wood, bone, leather and textile – which all burnt away, as may be seen from several of the instruments that originally had wooden or bone handles. From Roman medical writers we know that medical equipment included bone and wooden probes, mallets, tubes, syringes, splints and medicine boxes, quills and reeds, and leather straps and bottles, as well as linen bandages, dressings, ligatures and sutures (Jackson 1994a, 198–200, tables 2–4). All of those the Rimini practitioner is likely to have possessed in some quantity together, probably, with wooden apparatus for the extension and reduction of fractures. In addition his *materia medica* – healing plants and drugs, prepared tablets, salves, ointments and potions – which was likely to have been as extensive and carefully chosen as his metal instrumentation, would all have perished. Even their glass containers were changed beyond

recognition, having been reduced to solidified 'puddles' of glass, which probably also included at least one cupping vessel, for none of bronze was found. Above all, as a literate healer conversant with Latin and Greek, we may be sure that the Rimini doctor would have equipped himself with an equally comprehensive collection of medical and other texts on papyrus scrolls (*rotuli*). So the destruction of the texts is perhaps the most regrettable loss of all, for it is likely that they would have included his marginal annotations, amendments and comments which would have given an even clearer picture of the nature of his practice.

Despite the loss of the organic materials destroyed by the fire, the intensity of which had also fused together many of the metal instruments (**Fig. 36a–e**), the Rimini *domus* find still sheds uniquely important light on the potential range of surgical and medical treatments available to the population of *Ariminum* in the mid-3rd century AD. The instruments include: 30 scalpels (most complete with their iron blades and unique in number and variety); 12 smooth-jawed and toothed spring forceps; two coudée-type toothed forceps; four hollow-jawed toothed forceps; five sharp hooks, one combined with a needle-holder; two double-ended blunt hooks; and several probes. In addition, there are three bone forceps, two drill handles, seven iron dental forceps, four bronze and iron double-ended bone levers, three iron double-ended bone levers, three iron gouges, 12 bone chisels (complete with their iron blades), four lenticulars, a small iron saw and a small iron file. There are three lithotomy scoops, two toothed uvula forceps, a smooth-jawed uvula forceps, a cautery, a tube, a tongue depressor, a double-ended spatula. There are two pouring spoons, a probable insufflator, several fragmentary rectangular boxes, including a lid engraved with the image of the goddess Diana (sister of the healing god Apollo), many fragmentary tubular drug boxes, two inscribed ceramic medicine pots, two balance beams, pans and weights, a large basin, a strigil and a ceramic foot used for thermal treatments. The instrumentation thus combines a very large number of basic surgical tools, some, as already noted (see p. 18 and **Fig. 19**) rolled in bundles to form the basic kits ready for use away from the surgery, with a wide range of medicine containers,

a

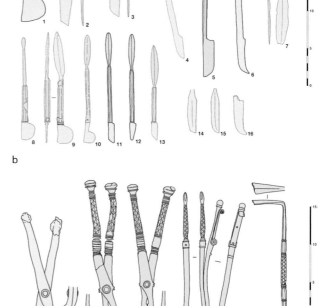

b

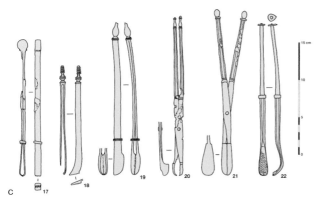

c

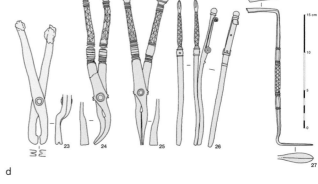

d

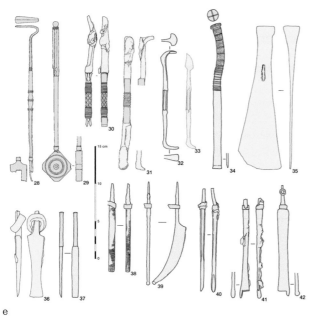

e

Figure 36a–e *Domus* del Chirurgo, Rimini, mid-3rd century AD: a) one of the fused clusters of instruments; b–e) drawings of a selection of instruments from the assemblage: b) scalpels; c) forceps and lithotomy scoop; d) dental and bone forceps, folding drill handle and double ended blunt hook; e) instruments of bone surgery. Rimini, City Museum. Photo: Ralph Jackson; drawings: Ralph Jackson and Stephen Crummy

(Ortalli 2000; Ortalli 2008; Jackson 2003). With his extensive instrumentation the Rimini practitioner, perhaps named *Eutyches* (Ortalli 2009, 37–8), and perhaps with one or more assistants or apprentices, could have faced a steady stream of sick and injured patients with some confidence, especially if, as seems likely, he had a correspondingly large library of medical texts and wide array of *materia medica*. Whether the patients were suffering from bad teeth, bone fractures, dislocations or soft tissue wounds, or from an occasional serious skull injury requiring trepanation, or from conditions like bladder stones (vesical calculus), haemorrhoids or chronic inflammation of the uvula, the practitioner had the instrumentation and doubtless, too, the medications, book learning, experience and practical skills to operate effectively.

At about the same time that the Rimini instruments were sealed beneath the debris of the *domus* a different kind of disaster helped to preserve medical instruments in their last-use context at Allianoi. This Roman-period spa town, 10 miles north-east of Pergamon in western Turkey, was embellished in the 2nd century AD in the reign of the emperor Hadrian. Archaeological excavations from 1998–2006, in advance of reservoir construction, uncovered

utensils and equipment and many specialised surgical instruments, most notably the 40 instruments designed for bone surgery. It would appear that the *domus* was the residence, surgery and possibly clinic of an extremely well-equipped healer, a generalist and specialist, of Greek extraction or, at least, Greek-speaking, probably originating in the East Mediterranean, and perhaps with experience of military medicine, who had become a fairly prosperous member of the community in which he lived and practised

Figure 37 Pompeii, the so-called House of the Surgeon (Casa del Chirurgo). Photo: Ralph Jackson

Figure 38 Pompeii, the *taberna medica* of Aulus Pumponius Magonianus. Photo: Ralph Jackson

over 30 distinctive and diagnostic medical instruments, together with many multi-purpose implements whose uses included medical applications (Baykan 2012: the catalogue also includes numerous socketed hooks (nos 120–80) which are not medical instruments but spindle hooks for textile production: see Gostenčnik 2001; Nutton 2014a). Most of the instruments were found *in situ* in several rooms of a large courtyard building (sadly incompletely excavated at the time of inundation behind the Yortanli Dam) adjacent to the hot spring and thermal baths complex. The instruments (Baykan 2012, especially nos 221–5, 252–8, 263, 291–306, 323, 335, 343–8) were found in later 1st- to mid-3rd century AD contexts (Baykan 2012, 165). They consist of basic surgical tools, including nine scalpels, one with its iron blade, three spring forceps, a double-ended needle-holder, several adapted hooks, two dipyrenes, six spatula probes and a double-ended spatula; pharmaceutical equipment, including five fragmentary tubular drug boxes and many scoop probes; and several more specialised instruments, including a composite double-ended bone lever, a probable skull saw, two toothed uvula forceps, two male catheters, a female catheter, a dilator and a clyster or cannula. Galen of Pergamon, close to the flourishing spa town of Allianoi, recommended baths for those suffering from urinary diseases, so it is interesting to note the presence among the instruments of male and female catheters. The Allianoi assemblage of instruments was preserved in the position of last use prior to a catastrophic flood that overwhelmed and eclipsed the town in the 3rd century AD. The archaeological evidence appears to demonstrate that several of the rooms, if not the entire courtyard building, were devoted to medical treatment, perhaps some sort of joint practice in a clinic (or even a hospital) catering to the needs of sick and injured visitors to the spa (Nutton 2014b, 382–9).

While the finds from Rimini and *Marcianopolis* provide particularly vivid glimpses of the medical and surgical activity of individual practitioners in a *taberna medica domestica*, and the assemblage from Allianoi hints, tantalisingly, at a larger-scale provision of treatment in a public building associated with spa facilities, the finds from Pompeii provide unparalleled evidence of the medical facilities available to a whole town (Bliquez 1994; Jackson 1994c; Künzl 1998; Künzl 2002b, 56–68; Künzl 2018, 16–19). Pompeii, unlike Herculaneum, was not totally sealed

by volcanic debris from the eruption of Vesuvius in AD 79. The upper parts of the highest buildings projected from the covering of lapilli and ash after the eruption had ended, providing landmarks orientating those survivors intent on the retrieval of their (or other people's) property. Subsequent removal of high-value goods, such as statuary and gold and silver possessions, undoubtedly occurred, and coins of Marcus Aurelius and Lucius Verus in the upper debris of the Casa del Medico Gladiatori may indicate that looters were still operating a century after the eruption. Nevertheless, the subsequent scavenging is most unlikely to have had as its primary aim the retrieval of medical kits. More significant is likely to have been the effect of the longer period of evacuation that appears to have been possible at Pompeii. This would have enabled an unknown number of people to escape (at least beyond the town walls) taking with them an unknown quantity of possessions. As already seen, the portable sets of instruments from Pompeii and Herculaneum carried by individuals – presumably healers – who had been fleeing the Vesuvian eruption are likely to represent part of, or even the whole of, their surgical and medical equipment. Their discovery in transit, away from the buildings in which they had been used, means that the former surgeries are impossible to identify. To those two 'invisible' surgeries, however, may be added about 20 to 25 houses which have yielded sufficient instruments to suggest the full- or part-time practice of medicine, many including surgery, by their occupants (Eschebach 1984; Bliquez 1994, 79–98; Dasen 2011b, 42–5). None was identified by the form of the building in which they were found, for ancient surgeries, like their modern counterparts, were located in houses that, though varied in size and type, were undifferentiated architecturally from other habitations or structures. The identifications have been made from *in situ* discoveries of identifiably medical and surgical instruments and paraphernalia. Unfortunately, accurate recording of objects and their find-places in the excavations at Pompeii was virtually absent

Figure 39 Pompeii, the Casa del Medico Nuovo II. Photo: Ralph Jackson

until the later 19th century, and even after that, somewhat erratic and incomplete. That makes it very difficult, often impossible, to retrospectively assign specific locations to all of the medical instruments preserved in the collections of the Pompeii and Naples museums. The provenance and finding circumstances of many are irretrievably lost, but some 240 instruments can be traced back to Pompeii and Herculaneum with confidence.

The most famous medical site at Pompeii, the so-called House of the Surgeon (Casa del Chirurgo) on the Via Consolare (**Fig. 37**), was the earliest excavated – in April 1771 – and only two surgical instruments can now be certainly associated with it, a probable *phlebotomon* (blood-letting knife) and a tube. A second tube, one or more cupping vessels, a toothed forceps and several scalpels and sharp hooks, appear to have been part of the find, but it is most unlikely ever to have numbered the 'over 40 instruments' often referred to from the early 19th century onwards (Bliquez 1994, 79–80). Less well known but much more significant is the medical assemblage from the *taberna medica* of Aulus Pumponius Magonianus, whose name survives painted on the lintel above the entrance to his house on the Via dell'Abbondanza (**Fig. 38**), just a step away from the south-east corner of Pompeii's forum. In 1818 and 1819 some 70 medical and pharmaceutical implements and surgical instruments were noted as having been found here, mostly in a large shop which opened onto the street. The surgical instruments included a trivalve dilator (uterine speculum), three embryo hooks and four cupping vessels (Bliquez 1994, 81; Jackson 2018b). Two more embryo hooks as well as a clyster and another uterine speculum, a unique quadrivalve dilator, were found between 1841 and 1882 in excavations at the Casa del Medico Nuovo (I), on the Via dell'Abbondanza close to the Stabian Baths (Bliquez 1994, 81–2). At both these houses the distinctive instrumentation indicates that the practices included gynaecology and the patients may well have stayed at the premises during and after treatment. The finds in these two houses also highlight the importance of Pompeii in preserving instrumentation seldom found elsewhere. For example, it has yielded a significant proportion of all the known rectal and uterine dilators, including the so far unique quadrivalve dilator (Bliquez 1994, 62–66, 183–91,

nos 291–5; Bliquez 1995). These large, undoubtedly expensive, metal instruments have only rarely been found in burials or on settlement sites and the Pompeii circumstance provides the opportunity to set them in the context of the broader surgical instrumentation and medical provision of the town. Equally interesting, if not always readily explicable, is the absence of certain types of instrument from the Pompeii assemblage: no dental forceps, no uvula forceps, no lithotomy instruments and no trepanation instruments have yet been found.

The most important medical site at Pompeii – because it has the best documented medical assemblage – is the Casa del Medico Nuovo (II), a small house on the Via di Nola (**Fig. 39**). It has the largest confirmed instrumentation, about 40 pieces, found in the atrium in 1887. In addition to basic surgical instruments – scalpels, spring forceps, sharp hooks, needle, probes and probe cases – and pharmaceutical implements – several tubular drug boxes, a medicine pot and a scale and weights – there were a number of specialised instruments: a cataract needle, a clyster, a bivalve dilator (rectal speculum), a trivalve dilator (uterine speculum) and an embryo hook (Bliquez 1994, 84–6). Here, then, was a medical and surgical practitioner equipped to treat a steady stream of patients presenting with a broad spectrum of wounds and afflictions as well as some more specific conditions, from cataract and other eye diseases to rectal and gynaecological disorders. While this modest house yielded a rich instrumentation, conversely a large and wealthy residence, the House of Marcus Lucretius, on the Via Stabiana, next to the Central Baths, yielded a more modest range of instruments. Found in several rooms, they comprised scalpels, sharp hooks, spring forceps, several tubular boxes, one containing instruments, and a cupping vessel (Bliquez 1994, 82–3). This assemblage mirrors that of the kits of basic instruments, found throughout the Roman world, and may perhaps be interpreted as the instrumentation of a private doctor, possibly a slave or freedman, tending to the medical needs not of all Pompeians but specifically the household of Marcus Lucretius (Künzl 2002b, 61). A similarly restricted range of instruments was found in several other houses, in two cases including a cataract needle, implying the surgical and medical treatment of those with eye diseases in addition to general medicine and surgery. Bearing in mind that some Pompeian medical practitioners may not have left any identifiably medical objects, and that about one-third of Pompeii remains unexcavated, it has been estimated that in AD 79 medical provision in Pompeii, a top-rank town (*colonia*) in a prosperous region, with a population of probably between 10,000 and 20,000, may have been as high as one practitioner for every 500 inhabitants (1:1000 if the population of the surrounding territory is included), a ratio that compares favourably with medical provision in recent times in some towns and cities in western Europe (Künzl 2002b, 68; Künzl 2018, 16–19). While the nature of the evidence means that such an estimate must be treated with caution, it nevertheless gives an impression of the potential scale of treatment available.

Types of instrument and their uses

Cupping vessels

Cupping vessel in the British Museum collection: Cat. no 3.49 (see also Cat. no. 6.4 and Cat. no. 6.27) (**Fig. 40**).

The letting of blood – venesection – has been a therapeutic measure employed at many different times in many different cultures. It was a very common expedient in Classical medicine designed primarily to restore the equilibrium of the body by bringing the bodily humours back into harmony (Jackson 1988, 70–3). Already hallowed by centuries of usage, venesection was enthusiastically endorsed and championed in the 1st century AD by Cornelius Celsus who frequently advocated the practice (*sanguinem mittere*), asserting that there was 'scarcely any malady in which blood may not be let' (Celsus, *On Medicine* 2.10.1; Jackson 1994a, 182–4). Blood was let by incising a vein, usually at the inner part of the elbow, though the lower leg is shown on the scene of venesection on the terracotta relief from the tomb of the surgeon Marcus Ulpius Amerimnus at Ostia (**Fig. 13**) (Hanson 2006, 503–4; Künzl 2013, 75–7, fig. 24; Olivanti 2014, 262–3; Verbanck-Piérard *et al.* 2018, 307–8), and many other sites were selected for specific conditions (see e.g. Paul of Aegina 6.40). This was a relatively straightforward procedure which could be accomplished without purpose-made instruments, since a domestic or craft knife would suffice. Thus it is archaeologically impossible to detect.

Although a specific blood-letting knife, a *phlebotomon*, was often named in Greco-Roman medical texts (e.g. Galen, *Anatomical Procedures* 2.387K; Pseudo-Galen, *Introduction or Physician* 14.787K; Paul of Aegina, 6. 22.1, 6.55.1, 6.62.2; Bliquez 2015, 87), few examples have yet been firmly identified. The most convincing is part of the large instrumentation from the probable Ephesus grave group, a tiny iron blade mounted at one end of a slender double-ended handle (**Fig. 32**) (Künzl 2002a, 17–18, A12, pl. 3). Another is an idiosyncratic instrument from the House of the Surgeon at Pompeii which may have been a variant of the *phlebotomon* (Bliquez 1994, 39, 122, no. 53; Bliquez and Munro 2007, 491–3). And if we restore three blades to the now empty sockets of a unique triple instrument of copper alloy from Rome (Jackson 2014a, fig. 18.16.6), we may have the triple-bladed scalpel which Paul of Aegina tells us was used by some practitioners to make three scarifications at one stroke before venesection (Paul of Aegina 6.41; Milne 1907, 28). Significantly, though, Celsus makes no mention of a *phlebotomon*, invariably naming the knife for use in venesection *scalpellus* – scalpel (Jackson 1994a, 182–3). So it is very likely that the *phlebotomon* was no more than a particular form of iron blade fixed into the socket of the general-purpose Roman copper-alloy scalpel handle. Any of the scalpel handles in the British Museum collection could have been mounted with blades suitable for venesection. More readily recognisable, however, and one of the earliest identifiable pieces of purpose-made medical equipment, is the cupping vessel, often termed 'bleeding cup'. (For the fullest discussion of cupping and cupping vessels, together with the literary testimonia, see Bliquez 2015, 56–72.)

The cupping vessel was developed to apply suction to the surface of the skin which, in cases of venesection, accelerated

Figure 40 Corfu, cupping vessel. British Museum, London (Cat. no. 3.49)

the flow of blood from an incised vein. Accordingly, Celsus' long and detailed chapter on blood-letting is followed by a comprehensive chapter on cupping and cupping vessels. It is the best source in Latin, while the later account of Oribasius, much of which was derived from Antyllus (Antyllus of Alexandria, an expert surgeon of the 2nd century AD), is the fullest in Greek and was also condensed by Paul (Celsus, *On Medicine* 2.10 and 2.11; Oribasius, *Medical Compilations* 7.16; Paul 6.40–1). The cupping vessel was the principal instrument of humoral pathology, employed as a suction cup to speed up the letting of blood from an incised vein or to extract 'vicious humour' through the pores. Thus, cupping did not invariably involve the incision of a vein, and Celsus' references to the *cucurbitula* are divided fairly evenly between cupping with incision (wet-cupping) and cupping without incision (dry-cupping). Wet-cupping, in addition to its primary role of extracting vitiated blood, was used amongst other things for diversionary bleeding, for draining corrupt matter from an abscess, and for the treatment of animal bites (Celsus, *On Medicine* 5.26.21C, 7.2.1–3, 5.27.1–3). Dry-cupping was often aimed at stimulating or attracting, and it had a special application in the relief of headache and of painful or paralysed joints and sinews (Celsus, *On Medicine* 4.2.8, 3.27.2B, 3.27.1D). It was a relatively mild intervention which Celsus also recommended for patients who were too weak to submit to venesection. He also considered it appropriate in some cases to try dry-cupping before resorting to wet-cupping as, for example, in the treatment of dropsy (Celsus, *On Medicine* 2.11.5–6, 3.21.9). In summarising the seemingly endless list of diseases and conditions in all parts of the body perceived to be relieved by cupping, Galen highlighted the drawing up of deep-seated humours, the staunching of haemorrhage, the reduction of fever, the relief of pain, menstrual problems, fainting and flatulence, the stimulation of appetite and the bracing of a weak stomach. Sometimes leeches were used in place of, or in addition to, cupping vessels, especially in areas where it was difficult to fasten a cup (Galen, *Leeches, Revulsion, Cupping* 11.320-321K; Bliquez 2015, 58).

So frequent was the use of the cupping vessel in Greco-Roman medicine, especially its role in humoral therapy, and so distinctive its shape, that already by the time of Hippocrates it had became the foremost indicator of medical practice and continued to be so into the Roman Imperial

Figure 41 Athens, tombstone of the physician Jason, with a larger-than-life depiction of a cupping vessel at right, symbol of his profession. British Museum, London (Cat. no. 6.4)

Figure 42 Atrax, Thessaly, coin reverse showing a cupping vessel, 4th century BC. British Museum, London (Cat. no. 6.27)

era. It was quintessentially the utensil of Greco-Roman healers and effectively their 'badge of office' as, for example, in the case of the scene on the early 2nd-century AD tombstone of the physician Jason from Athens (see pp. 174–5; Cat. no. 6.4) (**Fig. 41**), on the 1st-century AD tombstone of the physician Lykourgos from Aedipsos, Euboea (Ritsonis 2014) and on an uninscribed 2nd-/3rd-century AD tombstone of a female physician said to have been found in the environs of Kelli, Florina, Macedonia (see **Fig. 15**) (Moschakis 2014).

Celsus described two varieties of cupping vessel, one, of horn (*cornea*), worked by mouth suction, the other, of bronze (*aenea*), achieving suction by means of a vacuum, which was created by setting light to a scrap of lint inside the cup. The heated cup was applied to the appropriate part of the body, most often an arm, and as it cooled a vacuum was formed and caused the cup to adhere and suck. To avoid skin contact with the burning lint the cupping vessel was made with a distinctively shaped body. From its resemblance to a gourd it was named *sikua* in Greek medical literature, while its Latin name was *cucurbita* or the diminutive *cucurbitula* – little gourd. No cupping vessel of horn has yet been discovered, but about 40 copper-alloy cupping vessels are known, ranging in date from the 6th century BC to the 3rd century AD (Künzl 1982a). The earliest examples, of about 500 BC, are from Greek graves at Rhodes, Corinth and Thebes, while Hellenistic examples include those from a grave at Tanagra and from the 4th-century BC grave group at Pydna. They are matched in form and date by the images

of cupping vessels used to epitomise healing on the famous tombstone of a healer of *c.* 500 BC, possibly from Bodrum (Halicarnassus), Turkey, and on the reverse of a number of coins, including one of the 4th century BC issued at Atrax in Thessaly (Cat. no. 6.27 (**Fig. 42**). A cupping vessel is reported from the 2nd-century BC Pozzino wreck, and of those from the Roman Empire 14 were found at Pompeii, three in the Bingen grave group, and single examples from Masada, Colophon, Balčik, Nea Paphos, Paris and Corfu (Cat. no. 3.49; **Fig. 40**), as well as a possible variant in the Allianoi assemblage (refs in Bliquez 2015, 61–2). Two, of 1st-century BC/1st-century AD date, come from a tomb at Priene (Verbanck-Piérard *et al.* 2018, 285). No example has yet been found in Britain.

The cupping vessels, which were normally raised from a single piece of metal, comprise a thin-walled domed body, a carinated shoulder, a tapered neck and a lightly flared mouth which had a neatly thickened and smoothed rim to ensure an even, airtight contact with the patient's skin. A common feature, soldered to the apex of the dome, was a domed mount equipped with looped staple and ring, which probably aided removal of the cup when cupping was completed, and also enabled the cup to be suspended when not in use, like those on the stand in the Bingen instrumentation (**Fig. 29b**) (Künzl 2002b, 55, fig. 73; Jackson 2014a, fig. 18.3). The ring mount is visible, too, on the cupping vessel depicted on the tombstone of Jason (Cat. no. 6.4; **Fig. 41**) and those on the votive relief from the temple of Asklepios in Athens (Jackson 1988, 115, fig. 28). In the Roman period cupping vessels, like that from Corfu (Cat. no. 3.49; **Fig. 40**), there is a tendency towards a more pronounced division – a sharper carination – between the body and the neck, and there is some variation in the size, but the overall form remained remarkably constant over a period of at least eight centuries (Künzl 1982a, figs 1–2; Bliquez 2015, figs 4–7). In fact, the size variation may correspond to the directions of medical writers who recommended different forms and volumes of cup according

Figure 43a–b Scalpel handles, front and side views (left to right, Cat. nos 3.52, 3.53, 3.55, 3.56, 3.57, 3.58, 3.59). British Museum, London

to the required drawing power. Broader bodies, longer necks and narrower mouths gave greater drawing power, while the intensity of the vacuum could be varied according to the degree of heating (Bliquez 2015, 57–9).

If a purpose-made cupping vessel was not available, Celsus advised the use of a small drinking cup or narrow-mouthed porridge bowl. He made no mention of a glass cupping vessel, which may not have come into use until the 2nd century AD when it was recommended by Antyllus for close monitoring of the flow of blood (Oribasius, *Medical Compilations* 7.16.13). It may be that cupping vessels of glass were never as common as those of copper alloy, not least, as Paul noted, because the heating process made them susceptible to breakage (Paul 6.41.2). As yet no certain glass example has been identified, although, as already suggested, it might be anticipated that one or more form part of the melted glass 'puddles' in the extensive Rimini medical assemblage.

Scalpels, knives and shears

Scalpels in the British Museum collection: Cat. nos 3.50–77 (see also Sets of instruments, Cat. nos 3.1–9 and 3.40) (**Fig. 43a–b**).
Just as the cupping vessel was an instant visual identifier of healing in the Classical world, the surgical knife or scalpel was the foremost symbol of surgery. It was the surgical practitioner's principal tool and at least one knife is almost invariably included in surviving sets of Greek and Roman medical instruments. The scalpel was required for treatment of injuries and wounds, when soft tissue and structures needed cutting. It was also used to create an incision in elective surgery, and to puncture, excise, scrape, dissect and cauterise in a myriad of surgical interventions ranging from the simple cutting of a vein in blood-letting to such complex, hazardous and radical operations as hernia repair, lithotomy and mastectomy (for the numerous specified uses of the scalpel see Jackson 1994a,169–71 and 196–7, table 1; and Bliquez 2015, 81–4).

In the Hippocratic writings the preferred term for the surgical knife was *machaira* – simply 'knife' – and its diminutive *machairion*. But by the time of the Roman Empire the medical authors who wrote in Greek, while continuing to use *machaira/machairion*, tended to prefer the more specific technical name *smile* and its diminutive *smilion* (Bliquez 2015, 75–7). For those who wrote in Latin the surgeon's knife was *scalpellus*, and Celsus tended to restrict the less specific *ferrum* to those places where he was speaking more generally, as in

'the knife' or 'the surgeon's knife', as opposed to 'a knife'; and sometimes he substituted *ferrum* for *scalpellus* as a literary device as, for example, *ferro et medicamentis* – 'by the knife and by medicaments' (Jackson 1994a, 169; Bliquez 2015, 76).

The idiosyncratic single-piece iron knives with solid handles and curved blades in the small set of instruments in the late 4th-century BC grave group at Pydna (see pp. 8–9) may be examples of the *machaira/machairion*. But by the Roman Imperial period the surgical knife had acquired a form specific to surgery, a purpose-made scalpel designed to maximise function, economy and ease of use. Scalpels were still occasionally single-piece instruments, either made entirely of copper alloy, like an example in the Naples National Archaeological Museum (Bliquez 1994, 121, no. 52), or entirely of iron, like two scalpels of the 3rd century AD from Asia Minor (Künzl 2002a, 28, pl. 17, B1, B2; Jackson 2014a, fig. 18.12.6) and two of the early 1st century AD in the grave group from Stanway, near Colchester (Jackson 2007a, 236–8). However, most Roman scalpels were composite instruments comprising an iron blade fastened to a copper-alloy handle. That arrangement maximised utility and economy, enabling the most appropriate metal to be used for each of the two components. It also provided a double-ended instrument, a combination tool, because the handle comprised at one end the grip, which incorporated a socket to hold the blade, the principal component, and at the other end a terminal, which was usually in the form of a leaf-shaped spatula, the secondary component, used for blunt dissection.

Scalpel handles with a leaf-shaped blunt dissector and a rectangular block-like grip (**Fig. 43**) were the principal type of the 1st century AD. However, they continued long in use – for the more vulnerable iron blade could be replaced when necessary – and those from medical finds at Pompeii (AD 79) are undifferentiated from the examples in the Bingen surgeon's tomb (about AD 100) and those from the *domus* del Chirurgo at Rimini (about AD 250). It is probable that they continued still longer in use and they are likely to be the type of scalpel handle referred to as 'common' by Aëtius and 'simple' by Paul of Aegina (Bliquez 2015, 74).

The requirements of the handle were best accomplished in copper alloy, usually cast in a mould and finished with cold working, but sometimes worked up from a rod (see pp. 149–50). But although the need to provide the functional features largely dictated the form of the handle, there was

Figure 44 Scalpel handle and socketed needle-holders (left to right, Cat. nos 3.76, 3.106, 3.107). British Museum, London

comprising a blunt dissector, a grip and a socket, and its iron blade.

Blunt dissector

The most commonly depicted and surviving type of Roman scalpel handle, including virtually all of those in the British Museum collection, has a handle terminal in the form of a leaf-shaped spatula with blunt edges – a blunt dissector. The dissectors differ from, and cannot be confused with, the leaf-shaped spatula of spatula probes because they invariably have a median ridge on both faces, giving a diamond-shaped cross-section, unlike the spatula probes which generally have a median ridge on only one face, giving a plano-convex cross-section. Thus broken examples of both types may be distinguished. Their differing forms were developed to serve different medical applications. The majority of blunt dissectors are in the form of a slender myrtle leaf, with outliers ranging from extremely squat (Cat. nos 3.2, 3.50) to extremely slender examples (Cat. nos 3.60–1), but their median ridges ensured that all were robust. They vary in size and in proportion to the size of the grip and doubtless served a similarly varied range of secondary applications in addition to blunt dissection. The eight blunt dissectors of the scalpel handles in the set of instruments from Italy (Cat. nos 3.1–5 and 3.7–9) are all of slightly differing shape, length or thickness and may have been selected intentionally as a graded set. The grip and squat dissector of scalpel handle Cat. no. 3.5 are nearly identical to those on an example from Pompeii which retains its long triangular blade (Jackson 2014a, fig. 18.13.2). It is possible that Cat. no. 3.5 may once have had a similar blade.

Some blunt dissectors were evidently designed for (or adapted to) a very particular purpose, as implied by their idiosyncratic form. Of those in the British Museum collection, one is turned to one side (Cat. no. 3.64), another is lightly offset (Cat. no. 3.70), and another made with a distinctive slender crescent shape (Cat. no. 3.65). A rare form of the leaf-shaped terminal has a tiny spherical knob at its tip, like that of Cat. no. 3.76 (**Fig. 44**), an arrangement also found on some needle-holders (e.g. Cat. nos 3.106–7). While not well suited to blunt dissection, the knob may have been designed to serve some other medical application, perhaps to be heated as a button cautery, if it was not intended as a purely decorative feature. Other examples include one from Butrint, Albania (A15 Forum 2007, SF945 (859), details kindly supplied by Pippa Pearce and Dave Hernandez), two in the group of instruments found in the 'Maison de Bacchus', at Cuicul/Djémila, Algeria, two unprovenanced examples in the Musée de la Médecine, Brussels (Jackson 2018a, 139, fig. 3, 3rd and 4th from left), one in the Bibliothéque Nationale, Paris (illustrated but wrongly identified as a 'probe-pointed blade' by Milne 1907, 43, pl. 8.2), one in Solingen (Deutsches Klingenmuseum, inv. 65.42), and three in the Halûk Perk collection of instruments from Anatolia (Perk 2012, 36, 1.2.5.1–3).

It is important to reiterate that on surviving examples the edges of the copper-alloy scalpel handle's leaf-shaped terminal are almost invariably blunt, as they were made. Complementing the sharp iron blade mounted at the other end of the handle, the principal role of the leaf-shaped

also scope for the inclusion of decorative elements. As on other medical instruments, decoration of the scalpel handle was restricted to its non-operative parts – the central grip and its margins – and usually took the form of cut mouldings or, less often, inlay. The result was a robust, functional handle sometimes enhanced by exquisitely applied decoration. The blade, however, was purely functional and needed to be sharp and hard-edged, qualities which were best obtained through the use of wrought iron. This was forged to shape and could be provided with a steeled cutting edge by means of the carburisation process, while iron ores in the Alpine province of Noricum were famous in antiquity for yielding naturally a high-quality steel which Galen advocated for scalpel blades (Galen, *Anatomical Procedures* 8.6 (2.682K)). The blades were made in a wide variety of shapes and sizes, as vividly demonstrated by the Rimini find (Jackson 2009b, fig. 1), but were mostly very thin. In consequence, only in exceptional circumstances have they been preserved intact (Jackson 2014a, 137–44, figs 18.11–18.16), and the great majority of surviving scalpels are represented only by their copper-alloy handle, the vulnerable iron blade having corroded away. That is the case with the scalpels in the British Museum collection, which, with only one possible exception (Cat. no. 3.77), include no intact example, although several retain in their socket the corroded tang and stub of the blade. Thus, the components of the scalpel were its copper-alloy handle,

terminal was as a blunt dissector and not a blade, a point which still occasionally eludes those who do not have direct experience of examining large numbers of ancient scalpel handles (e.g. H.H. Dedo, 'Observations on a set of Greco-Roman eye, ear, nose, and throat surgical instruments', *Laryngoscope* 127, February 2017, 354–8). In fact, there is confirmation of the use of the scalpel handle's spatulate terminal as a blunt dissector in the Classical medical texts. It comes in the form of five references in Celsus' *On Medicine* (Jackson 1994a, 169–70; Bliquez 2015, 52, 77, 80, 83–4). Celsus specified the use of the scalpel handle – *scalpelli manubriolo* – as a blunt dissector in a number of surgical applications. They range from eye surgery to operations for hernia and they correspond to the variety in shape and size of surviving examples. In two eye operations Celsus described the use of the *manubriolum* in conjunction with its opposing blade, first to remove a cyst on the edge of the eyelid (chalazion), and secondly in the delicate surgery to detach and excise pterygium (*On Medicine* 7.7.3 and 7.7.4B). Similarly, in surgery of the scrotum he twice advised use of a finger or the *manubriolum*, first in repairing an inguinal hernia, and secondly in separating a varix before excision in varicocele (7.19.7 and 7.22.2). Once more, in the removal of a dermoid cyst (steatoma), he advocated use of the *manubriolum* (7.6.4): 'Then as soon as the white and tight coat is seen, it is to be separated from the skin and flesh by the handle of the scalpel (*scalpelli manubriolo*), and turned out together with its contents'. In each instance both ends of the scalpel were deployed, the role of the blunt dissector being to separate safely skin from flesh, cyst from tissue, pterygium from eyeball, tunic from scrotal wall, veins from scrotal tunic. In just one instance – lancing hydrocephaly – is there mention of a dissector sharp enough to lance or cut, and that probably involved adaptation of a standard blunt dissector (Aëtius 6.1.53; Bliquez 2015, 77).

Grip

Essential to the successful use of the scalpel was the provision made for the practitioner to hold it securely: the grip. Almost without exception, the grip takes one of two carefully profiled forms: Type I, a rectangular block (Cat. nos 3.1–5, 3.40, 3.50–67); and Type II, a slender rod of octagonal cross-section (Cat. nos 3.7–9, 3.69–74) or of square cross-section (Cat. nos 3.68, 3.75–6) – with a blunt dissector at one end and a blade socket at the other. Each type of grip, but especially the first, varies quite widely in length, width and thickness. Although some of the handles with Type I grips are quite slender, most are stout, and where examples have survived intact their iron blades tend to be large (Jackson 2014a, figs 18.11–18.13). Unsurprisingly it is the slender octagonal and slender square Type II grips which generally secured smaller blades, some of them very diminutive (Jackson 2014a, fig. 18.14.3–9). However, it is important to note that the form and size of the grip and socket do not necessarily reflect the potential size of the blade that might be attached, as is clear from several of the Rimini scalpels whose slender grips secure a variety of large long-stemmed blades (Jackson 2003, fig. 1.1–3; Jackson 2014a, fig. 18.15.1–3). A variant of the octagonal grip incorporated a socket at both ends which enabled the mounting of two blades (Jackson 2014a, fig. 18.12.5).

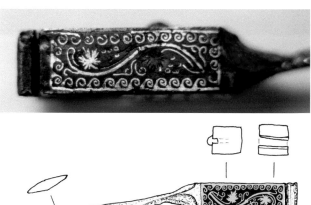

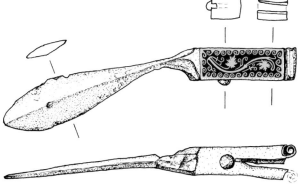

Figure 45 Scalpel handle, with silver-inlaid vine-spray and wave-crest ornament on the grip, from Cologne. Römisch-Germanisches Museum, Köln, inv. no. N3923a. Photo: Ralph Jackson; drawing: © Römisch-Germanisches Museum der Stadt Köln, Silke Haase

On most scalpel handles the junction of the leaf-shaped terminal and the grip usually comprises a simple constriction, but a variant with a tiny Type I block-like grip and a correspondingly small leaf-shaped terminal has in between a slender circular-sectioned baluster stem and a series of ring-and-disc mouldings. The mouldings are often extremely finely finished and served both to enhance the appearance of the scalpel handle and, in some cases, to facilitate the practitioner's grip, as for example those on Cat. no. 3.65. The stem was sometimes further elaborated as a stylised 'club of Hercules' (Bliquez 1992), as on Cat. no. 3.63, and other examples include an early 1st-century AD scalpel handle from the town on the Magdalensberg (Gostenčnik 2004, 371–2, figs 2–3, 396–7, pl. 1.3) and a richly ornamented idiosyncratic scalpel handle from the Roman town of *Aventicum* (Hirt 2000, 103, fig. 4, 116, pl. 2.5, 123, cat. no. 5). The stem also lent itself well to the addition of banded and spiral inlays of silver as, for example, on handles Cat. nos 3.62 and 3.65. The tiny rectangular grips themselves also occasionally provided sufficient space for exquisite polychrome inlays in miniature. Scalpel handle Cat. no. 3.61, for example, has two zones of inlay: the zone on the stem, just 3mm wide, comprises five silver strips interspersed with four ridges of the bronze body metal (see **Figs 109, 174**); the other principal zone, just 3.3mm wide, on the two main faces of the grip, comprises a mirror-image arrangement with a central inlaid copper strip flanked on both sides by five inlaid strips interspersed with six ridges of bronze body metal. The inlaid strips comprise copper, plain silver and twisted silver wire, the twist orientated to give a herring-bone effect (see **Fig. 187**). The baluster of the fine handle from Myndus (Cat. no. 3.64), flanked by crisply cut mouldings, was given further prominence by the contrasting colours of its inlays, a double spiral of silver and Corinthian bronze (see **Figs 109, 174**). The form of the handle is very

Figure 46 Scalpel handle, with vine-scroll and wave-crest ornament on the grip. British Museum, London (Cat. no 3.50)

Figure 47 Scalpel handle with silver-inlaid Corinthian bronze grip, with close-up detail of inlaid grip. British Museum, London (Cat. no. 3.68)

closely paralleled by other examples with spiral silver inlay, one from the necropolis at La Cañada Honda (Gandul) (Hibbs 1991, 116, 118, fig. 3.1), two unprovenanced examples in Solingen (Deutsches Klingenmuseum inv. 65.39–40), and one in the late 3rd-century AD cremation burial at Saint-Privat d'Allier (Künzl 1983a, 33, 57–8, fig. 26.1; Künzl 1996, 2594–5, fig. IX.3). The latter, according to Künzl, is almost identical to another from the Roman baths at Weissenburg, and it is possible that all are products of the same workshop.

A popular form of decoration on the two principal faces of large Type I grips, was an inset rectangular panel with a design in the form of a vine-spray enclosed by a wave-crest motif ('laufender Hund'). The design was inlaid – singly or in combination – with silver, niello and copper, as, for example, a silver-inlaid handle from *Aventicum* (Hirt 2000, 116, pl. 2.7, 123, no. 7) and another from the Luxemburgerstrasse cemetery, Cologne (**Fig. 45**) (Jackson 2014a, fig. 18.9). Cat. no. 3.50 is an example of this type, but its panels are now devoid of their inlay. Nina Crummy has reminded me (*pers. comm.*) that this type of decoration is also to be found on inlaid metal inkwells, especially Type Noll, but also Type Cologne (Eckardt 2018, 76–80). Less common variants of the design include bird and ivy-leaf motifs (Künzl 2002a, 28–9, pl. 17, B3, B4). Silver, niello and copper would have given the designs a vivid colour-range of silver, black and red within the dull gold backing of the bronze scalpel grip. This is a distinctive and widespread type (Büsing-Kolbe Type A) with over 30 examples ranging from Syria to Scotland and Spain to the Crimea but with a concentration in north-east Gaul and the Rhineland suggestive of manufacture in that region (Künzl 1986a, fig. 7; Künzl 1994a, fig. 133; Büsing-Kolbe 2001, map 1, Type A). An example from Xanten is virtually identical to the unprovenanced British Museum handle Cat. no. 3.50 (**Figs 46, 174**), both in the exact design of its inlaid panels and in the squat form of its blunt dissector, leading Künzl to suggest that they may be products of the same workshop (Künzl

1994a, 216). These showy, doubtless expensive, scalpel handles probably often had a very long life, but a manufacture date in the 1st century AD has been proposed in view of the fact that the Xanten handle was found in the area of the legionary fortress Vetera I, which was garrisoned from the time of Augustus until AD 70, and that dating evidence for the squat blunt dissectors also points to the 1st century (Künzl 1994a, 211–13). For the type more widely a production date range of mid-1st to late 2nd century AD is suggested (Büsing-Kolbe 2001, 107), while contextual dates imply continued usage well into the 3rd century and beyond. On the grip of Cat. no. 3.51 the panels evidently took the form of inset sheets, which are now lacking – accidentally or deliberately detached – leaving only remnants of the soft solder bonding medium on the surface of the rectangular recesses.

The same combination of motifs was also applied to Type II scalpel handles with slender octagonal grips, as on an example from Cologne, dated 2nd/3rd century AD (Bonn, Rheinisches Landesmuseum inv. 35.142; Künzl 1986a, 503–4, C1, fig. 9; Büsing-Kolbe Type C) and another from the fort at Gilău, Romania (Gui 2011, 119–20, 130, pl. 1.2), both of which have the running vine-spray motif engraved on the four broader faces of the grip interspersed with the running wave-crest motif on the four narrower faces. Only a few vestiges of the silver inlay remain on the Cologne handle, but the entire silver inlay survives on three more examples of this type of grip with the same decoration, part of a splendid set of ten richly ornamented instruments in the Halûk Perk collection said to be from the Antalya region of Asia Minor (Çulha 2009, 78–9; Perk 2012, cover illustration and pages 31, 52–3, 56, 64, 69, 79). In addition to the scalpel handles the set comprises a pointed-jawed forceps combined with an elevator, a double-ended blunt hook, a ligula probe, a coudée toothed spring forceps, a probable chisel handle and two further grips. Other examples of this type, which is similarly widespread but less numerous than Büsing-Kolbe

Type A, are known from Wiesbaden, Rheims and Dura Europos (Syria), and a date range for manufacture of second half of the 1st century to first half of the 2nd century AD has been proposed (Büsing-Kolbe 2001, 109, map 1, Type C).

Another form of decoration so distinctive that it even more clearly identifies products of a particular workshop, and helps to refine the dating of poorly contexted instruments, is that applied to a Type II slender rectangular grip from Rome, once in the Castellani Collection (Cat. no. 3.68). The four sides are inlaid with an elegant symmetrical linear design of rosettes, double peltas and pellets (**Figs 47, 174**). Analysis (see p. 155) has shown the inlay to be silver alloy while the body metal was made from the even more precious alloy Corinthian bronze. In use, in its uncorroded state, the silver-inlaid design of the Rome handle would have been set off by the induced black patina of its Corinthian bronze body metal. Other products of this workshop, active, perhaps, at least as early as the 1st century AD (since the design is reminiscent of the Third Style of wall-painting at Pompeii (Künzl 1984a, 60–1)), are known from the provinces of Gaul, Germany, Britain, Pannonia and Moesia inferior in 2nd- to 3rd-century AD contexts. The products include two spring forceps, two needle-holders, a sharp hook and an indeterminate long slender handle, but they are principally Type II scalpel handles, with examples from Saint-Privat d'Allier (2), Worms, Cologne (2), Constanța, Arles and Carnuntum, all of which, in contrast to the Rome grip, are octagonal-sectioned (chamfered square-sectioned) handles (Künzl 1983a, figs 26, 53, 68, 87; Krug 1992b, 155, no. 2; Büsing-Kolbe 2001, map 1, Type B; Künzl 2011, 127–8). There is a fragmentary grip, too, in the *Marcianopolis* instrumentation (Kirova 2002, 90, fig. 13.1). All bear variations on the silver-inlaid rosette/double pelta/pellet design, but none, other than the British Museum's Rome handle, appears to have had scientific analysis of the body metal undertaken, so it remains unknown whether the use of Corinthian bronze for the grip was normal or exceptional for the type.

In every case the inlaid design extends onto the leaf-shaped terminal, as it does, too, on the grip and leaf-shaped terminal of a needle-holder from Rochester, Kent (Roach Smith *c*.1855, 209, pl. XXXIV, 3; Jackson 2011a, 256–7, fig. 19d). It is evident, therefore, that the plain leaf-shaped terminal of the Rome handle Cat. no. 3.68, though ancient, does not belong with the grip, and the handle appears to be a 19th-century pastiche combining parts of two or three Roman scalpel handles. The closest parallels to the decoration of the Rome grip are the designs on the handles from Cologne, Worms and Rochester, the last of which also shares the rectangular form of the grip. The Saint-Privat d'Allier grave dates to the late 3rd century AD, at which time the inlaid scalpel handles in the grave group may have been 200 years old. But, as with the vine-spray inlaid handles, the implication of a very long working life for these instruments is not surprising. They remained eminently functional instruments and their finely crafted, costly, impressive-looking handles signified wealth, while their age probably invested their user with authority, and the operative parts – steel blades and needles – could be repeatedly replaced as necessary.

Socket

The great majority of scalpel handles had their socket cut into the side of the grip so that the blade and the blunt dissector were set in the same plane (**Figs 48–9**). That common orientation facilitated the practitioner's use of each operative end of the scalpel. It also enabled the scalpel more readily to be stored in a folding instrument box, as demonstrated by all of the depictions of the time as well as by the scalpels in the box of instruments found at Wehringen (see **Fig. 20**) (Krug 2008, figs 14–25). Occasionally, however, the socket was cut into the broader face of the grip, as on Cat. no. 3.40. The reason for this is not known, but unless the tang of the blade incorporated a 90° turn this arrangement would have affected the manner in which the instrument was used.

There are two principal forms of socket by means of which the tanged iron scalpel blade was secured to its copper-alloy handle, either a simple cut slot or a carefully profiled keyhole-shaped slot (keyhole socket) distinctive to Roman medical instruments. On both socket types the distal end of the grip, at the mouth of the socket, was frequently worked into rolled terminals or less elaborate grooved terminals. These had no practical purpose and were a purely decorative feature, like the mouldings on other non-functional parts of Roman surgical instruments. The suggestion that rolled terminals were intended to anchor a wire to secure the blade has long since been discounted (Milne 1907, 24; Jackson 1986, 133). The keyhole socket occurs most frequently on Type I scalpel handles, less often on Type II handles, and it is also occasionally the form of attachment of other composite copper-alloy and iron instruments. In both types of socket, where analysis has taken place, traces have usually been found of soft solder which fastened the iron scalpel blade to its handle. Such solder traces, indicated by high levels of lead and tin in and around the socket, have been detected on the majority of the scalpel handles in the British Museum collection (Cat. nos 3.1–5, 3.7–9, 3.52, 3.54–5, 3.57–9, 3.63–4, 3.66–8, 3.70, 3.73–5), demonstrating that blades fixed with lead-tin solder were the norm (see p. 149; Jackson 1986, 133–4; La Niece 1986, 161; Krug 1993). That form of bonding medium secured the blade but permitted a straightforward replacement for a broken or worn blade by the localised application of heat together with the use of appropriate tools. It is quite possible that in addition to re-sharpening their blades some medical practitioners were also equipped to repair or replace blades (soft lead-tin solder melts at 250 °C or less), but it is more likely that where practicable the practitioner went to a blacksmith, a specialist instrument-maker or a cutler. A terracotta relief on the 2nd-century AD tomb of Verrius Euhelpistus, a blacksmith from Ostia, suggests as much – it shows a display of his wares featuring a wide range of bladed tools including two scalpels in a box (Meiggs 1960, pl. 27a; Matthäus 1989, fig. 38; Krug 2008, 27–8, fig.14). So, too, does an intact Type I scalpel from London (Wheeler 1930, 81, pl. 38, 1; Jackson 2008, fig. 4.4.1.1), the handle of which appears to have been cast-on to the iron blade, which would have required a visit to a smith to detach it. Also instructive in this context is Galen's comment that he went to smiths with wax models of instruments he wanted made (Galen, *Avoiding Distress* 5; see

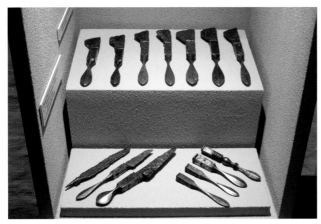

Figure 48 Scalpels, nine complete with blades, part of the extensive late 1st/early 2nd century AD set of Roman surgical instruments from Bingen am Rhein. Bingen, Historisches Museum am Strom

above, p. 15). At all events, while Roman scalpel blades were not as readily detachable as their modern counterparts they were replaceable, meaning that their handles might have a very long life indeed.

The additional benefit of the keyhole socket over the simple slotted form was the potential for a greater rigidity of the blade, an important factor where particular force was to be applied to the cutting edge. For, the tang of the iron blade could be made to terminate in a solid cylinder which fitted snugly in the distal end of the 'keyhole' when the blade was inserted from the side (see **Fig. 107**; Cat. nos 3.50–1). This arrangement, clearly revealed by X-radiography (Cat. no. 3.61; see **Fig. 177**), was evidently designed to prevent movement of the blade in either plane even if the solder failed. In two cases (Cat. nos 3.3–4), X-radiography of the British Museum scalpel handles revealed a variant of the keyhole socket. In place of the cylindrical fixing, the back of the socket was cut into a V shape with which a corresponding negative V shape cut into the back end of the blade tang could engage to provide a precise and rigid fit.

Solder was poured into the join by means of a small circular hollow drilled at the extremity of the slot from the top and bottom faces (Jackson 1986, 134; La Niece 1986, 161). Only scientific analysis enables the various forms of keyhole socket to be differentiated.

A much rarer slender tubular socket into which the blade tang was pegged occurs on a number of 3rd-century AD instruments, particularly in the Rimini assemblage (Jackson 2014a, 140–1, fig. 18.16.1). Its discovery signals the need for caution because the handle on its own would otherwise have been identified as that of a surgical needle: clearly there was sometimes a degree of interchange with handles, blades and needles.

While the keyhole socket provided a strong and secure seating, it appears sometimes to have proved difficult or impossible to remove an old blade, and several modifications have been found as, for example, on a Type II handle from Neuss (Rheinisches Landesmuseum, Bonn, inv. 11846; Künzl 1986a, 504, C2, fig. 10), and on a Type I handle of unknown provenance in Mainz (Künzl 2002a, 44, pl. 48, C2). In both cases the blade had defied removal and had to be cut off flush with the socket terminal and a fresh socket cut at right angles to accommodate the new blade. In some instances, as with the keyhole socket of scalpel handle Cat. no. 3.64, a replacement blade with a simpler tang was substituted leaving the terminal cylinder filled only with solder (Jackson 2014a, fig. 18.8). In other instances the socket was modified by the addition of a rivet, as on Cat. no. 3.65, perhaps to strengthen or to supersede the original soldered fastening (see **Figs 180–1**).

Blade
Like most ancient scalpels, all of the copper-alloy scalpel handles in the British Museum collection now lack their iron blade. Where Roman scalpel blades have survived they have tended to be large stout examples, the majority of deep bellied D-shape with a convex cutting edge, which are also

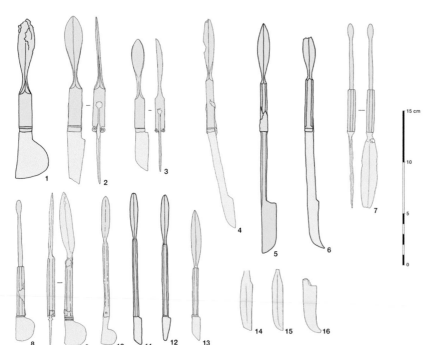

Figure 49 A selection of the scalpels from the *domus* del Chirurgo, Rimini, mid-3rd century AD. City Museum,Rimini. Drawing: Ralph Jackson and Stephen Crummy

the blades most commonly depicted in surviving imagery of the time (Jackson 1990a, fig. 1; Krug 2008, 23–41). Many other varieties of blades are named in Greek and Roman medical texts for specific surgical interventions. They include a suture knife, polyp knife, lithotomy knife, fistula knife, spatula knife, raven's bill knife, tonsillotome and knives to excise pterygium and uvula (Bliquez 2015, 87–105). Within the rather sparse sample of intact scalpels, examples of some of these knives have been tentatively proposed. Although few can be unequivocally identified, the surviving instruments demonstrate the many different types of knife and blade potentially available to Roman practitioners, while close study of the instruments and the ancient texts also advances our understanding of the *modus operandi* and surgical finesse of some of those practitioners.

The most famous complete scalpels (at least 15) are those from Pompeii, few of which, however, have survived unscathed the long and chequered history following their discovery. Fortunately some were drawn in the 1840s and a series of photos was taken at the end of the 19th century preserving important information on the now missing, broken or separated iron blades (Vulpes 1847, pl. VII; Bliquez 1994, pls 14–16). Another valuable source of intact blades (nine) is the late 1st- to mid-2nd-century AD cremation grave group from Bingen (**Fig. 48**) (Como 1925; Künzl 1983a, 80–5; Künzl 2002b, 36–8); while the small kit of basic surgical tools from the mid-3rd-century AD inhumation burial at Wehringen includes three scalpels complete with their tiny iron blades (Künzl 1983a, 120–1, 293–4. Nuber 2004). Most important of all are the scalpels in the remarkable assemblage of surgical instruments from the Rimini *domus* del Chirurgo – there are 30 complete scalpels together with a further 17 blades and 10 handles (Jackson 2003, figs 1–3; Jackson 2009b, fig. 1). The complete Rimini scalpels include some with the common bellied D-shaped blades in a range of sizes, including very small blades. But there is also an extremely diverse array of other blade shapes, at least 10 distinct forms (**Fig. 49**). The cutting edges are convex, straight, angled, concave, hooked, combined concave/convex, combined straight/convex, and combined convex/convex. The blades also vary greatly in size, from robust to diminutive examples, and in the length and alignment of the stem securing them to their handle; while the handles, equally varied, range from stout Type I block-like grips to very slender Type II octagonal grips.

Drawing together the information on intact scalpels from these and from other finds (Jackson 2014a, appendix) there is evidence for both continuity and change. Most immediately apparent is the unchanging nature and wide distribution of the robust Type I scalpel handle with D-shaped bellied blade that appears to have predominated in the 1st and 2nd centuries AD (**Fig. 50a**). Thus, early examples from Pompeii, Bingen, Cologne and London are indistinguishable from those in use in Rimini some 200 years later (Jackson 2014a, 137, 144, type 1, figs 18.11–18.12). Many of the stouter Type I scalpel handles in the British Museum collection (Cat. nos 3.1–5, 3.50–9) are likely often to have held blades of that type. Examples are also clearly depicted on stone and terracotta reliefs of the 1st to 2nd centuries AD from Athens, Ostia, Palestrina and Kom Ombo (Matthäus 1989, figs

38–44; Stettler 1982; Krug 2008, figs 11, 14, 15, 16, 18, 20). D-shaped blades were also mounted on Type II handles, as in the late 1st-century AD instrumentation from Luzzi (Guzzo 1974, 471–2, fig. 32, no. 91; Künzl 1983a, fig. 85, no. 3) and the mid-3rd-century AD Rimini instrumentation (Jackson 2003, fig. 3; Jackson 2014a, fig. 18.16.3). It seems reasonable to continue to regard that type of scalpel blade as the commonest general-purpose surgical knife designed to serve the majority of needs.

A similar longevity appears to apply to another robust scalpel type, which has a Type I handle and a long triangular blade with straight back and sloped cutting edge (**Fig. 50b**). Once more, examples from Pompeii, Bingen and Rimini are indistinguishable (Jackson 2014a, 137, 144, type 4, fig. 18.13.1–3), and this type of blade is likely sometimes to have been mounted on some of the stouter Type I handles in the British Museum collection, notably Cat. nos 3.5 and 3.50. Ubiquitous, too, is a smaller pointed blade type with convex back and straight cutting edge. It is represented in the 1st/2nd-century AD finds from Bingen and Cologne (Künzl 1983a, fig. 56. 7, fig. 67. 7), in a 2nd/3rd-century AD context at Sontheim an der Brenz (Künzl 2002b, 42–3, fig. 55; Künzl 2018, 27, fig. 8) and in the 3rd-century AD Rimini find (Jackson 2014a, 137, 144, type 7, fig. 18.14.1–4), and examples are included in the boxes of instruments depicted on the 2nd-century AD tomb reliefs of Publius Aelius Pius Curtianus at Palestrina and Marcus Ulpius Amerimnus at Ostia (Krug 2008, figs 18–21; Olivanti 2014, 262–3).

It is possible that some of the Rimini scalpel handles had been long in use, continuously or sporadically, and handed down over the centuries, but it is equally possible that they were freshly manufactured (**Fig. 50c**). Moulds were integral to bronze-working, either as existing moulds within the craftsman's stock, which might have been built up over many decades or longer, or new moulds made to replicate an existing object, which might equally have been of considerable age. And, as already assumed, but now with added emphasis for surgical tools on account of an enlightening passage in Galen's *Avoiding Distress*, the use of wax for moulding or modelling medical instruments was second nature. Thus, moulding with wax permitted continuity of form. But for Galen, and doubtless, too, many of his medical peers, modelling with wax also enabled innovation, the development of new and customised instruments.

Correspondingly, in the 3rd century AD alongside continuity of certain types of scalpel there also appears to be change, with an increased use of longer and more slender handles mounted with smaller blades (**Fig. 50d**). There is a close resemblance between the scalpel handles from the 3rd-century finds at Rimini, Wehringen and Nijmegen and those in other mid- to late 3rd-century groups, including the so-called Paris Surgeon set and those in the large sets from Rheims and Asia Minor/Ephesus (Künzl 1983a, 45–8, 61–67, 74–78, 93–6, 120–1; Sorel 1984; Braadbaart 1994; Künzl 2002a, 12–20, A19–A21; Nuber 2004; Jackson 2009b). The changing blade forms are seen most strikingly in the several rolled bundles of portable kits at Rimini, the kit from Wehringen, and a small kit in the Louvre, in all of which the tiny parallel-sided pointed blade type predominates

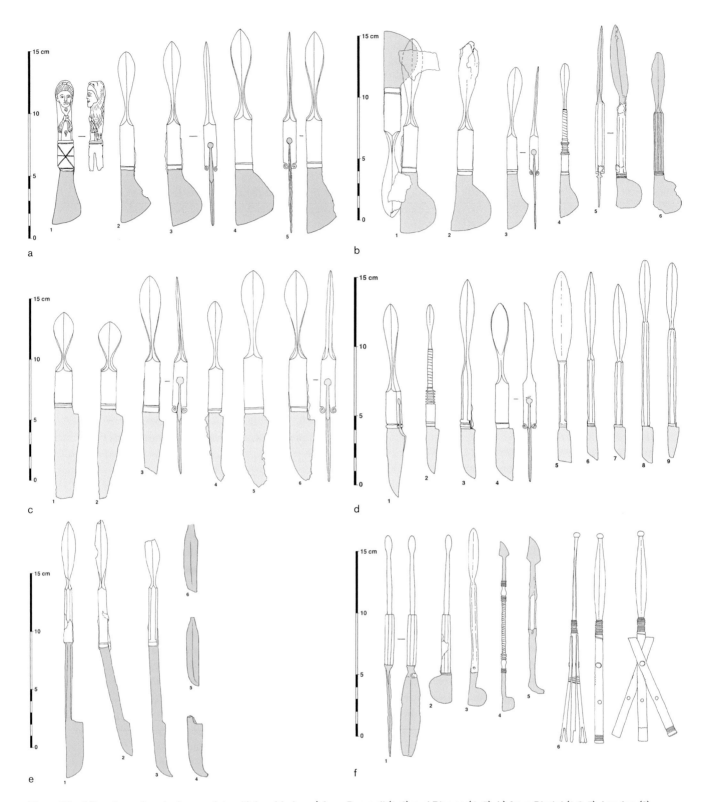

Figure 50a–f Drawings of scalpels complete with iron blades: a) from Pompeii (1–3) and Bingen (4–5); b) from Rimini (1, 2, 5), London (3), Cologne (4) and Asia Minor (6); c) from Pompeii (1, 4–6), Bingen (2) and Rimini (3); d) from Bingen (1), Cologne (2), Sontheim an der Brenz (3), Rimini (4, 7–9) and Wehringen (5–6); e) Rimini (1–6), f) Rimini (1–3, 5), Asia Minor (4) and Rome (6). Drawings: Ralph Jackson and Stephen Crummy

(Jackson 2014a, 140, 144, types 12 and 13, fig. 18.14. 5–9). It is likely that these slender scalpels were employed in a very wide variety of fine surgical interventions, including eye operations, and it is probable that such blades were once mounted on British Museum scalpel handles Cat. nos 3.7–9, 3.60–5 and 3.72–6. Several of the surviving tiny blades (Jackson 2014a, 140, 144, type 12, fig. 18.14.5–8) may be tentatively identified as the suture knife and/or pterygium

knife advocated by Aëtius (2.3.60) and Paul of Aegina (6.18) for dissecting away the pterygium and by Paul (6.8) in the operation to remedy trichiasis (entropion) (Jackson 1996a, 2245–6; Bliquez 2015, 90–2). This identification accords well with the other evidence for eye medicine (desiccated *collyria*) in the Wehringen assemblage. The blades also appear identical to that figured in the *Surgery* of Albucasis (al-Zahrawi *c.* AD 976–*c.* 1013) to accompany his Arabic rendering of Paul of Aegina's passage on pterygium (Milne 1907, pl. 9.2; Spink and Lewis 1973, 230–1, II, 16, fig. 55).

Even more striking is the change from stout handles with short-stemmed blades to slender handles with a very elongated blade stem that would have given the scalpels a longer reach (**Fig. 50e**). They are a notable feature of the Rimini assemblage (Jackson 2014a, 140–1, fig. 18.15.1–3) and are paralleled by a fragmentary example in the late 2nd/early 3rd-century Nea Paphos find (Michaelides 1984, fig. 1.19). The Rimini blades are of very varied form, few of which have been preserved elsewhere. One distinctive variety has a slender hooked blade with an angled heel, a concave cutting edge, a strongly curved tip, a convex back and a very long rectangular-sectioned stem in line with the slender handle (Jackson 2003, fig. 1.1 and fig. 3; Jackson 2009b, 75, 78, 88, fig. 1.6 and 1.16; Jackson 2014a, 141, 144, type 10, fig. 18.15.3). It may be the 'knife called from its shape "the raven"' which Celsus recommended for use in opening the scrotum for the radical cure of hernia, Oribasius used to lance an intercostal abscess, and Paul of Aegina advocated for the removal of corns (Celsus, *On Medicine* 7.19.7–8; Oribasius, *Medical Compilations* 44.7.5; Paul of Aegina 6.87.1; Bliquez 2015, 87–8). Alternatively or additionally it may have been a fistula knife (*suringotomon*), for its falciform blade conforms quite closely to Paul's description of that instrument used in the surgical treatment of anal fistula (Paul of Aegina 6.78.2; Bliquez 2015, 104–5). A short-stemmed version of this blade form is included in the folding box of instruments depicted on the stone votive relief from the Athens Asklepieion (Krug 2008, fig. 16).

Two more of the Rimini scalpels are especially notable because they are a complementary pair with their blade curved in two planes. Each comprises a parallel-sided blade with a profiled heel and a lightly convex cutting edge, strongly curved at the end as it slopes up to meet the straight back, which is in line with the very long slender octagonal-sectioned stem, itself in line with the handle. Viewed from above, one blade curves to the left and the other to the right (Jackson 2003, fig. 1.2; Jackson 2009b, 75, 78, 88, fig. 1.5; Jackson 2014a, 140–1, 144, type 6, fig. 18.15.1). They may be identified with some confidence as the tonsil knives in Paul of Aegina's account of tonsillectomy: 'we take a sharp hook and perforate the tonsil with it and drag it outwards as much as we can without dragging the capsule out along with it, and then we cut it off by the root with the tonsillotome suited to that hand, for there are two such instruments having opposite curvatures' (Paul of Aegina 6.30; Bliquez 2015, 102–3).

Two of the Rimini blades (Jackson 2014a, 141, 144, type 11, fig. 18.15.5–6) are slender and double-edged, with a midrib on both faces and a strongly curved tip (**Fig. 50f**). Combining a convex with a lightly concave cutting edge, their distinctive form corresponds closely to the type of scalpel advocated by Galen for dissection of the thorax: 'Use especially the convex part of the double-edged scalpel with both cutting edges curved, but concave on one side, convex on the other' (Galen, *Anatomical Procedures* 8.4 (2.673K), transl. Singer 1956, 210).

Another novel form of scalpel in the Rimini assemblage may be an example of the knife known as *spathion* – spatula knife. It is another double-edged blade, a myrtle-leaf-shaped

iron blade pegged into the circular socket of a handle with a narrow octagonal grip and a slender-stemmed olivary terminal (Jackson 2014a, 141, 144, type 2, fig. 18.16.1). This type of handle, also represented in the extensive Rheims instrumentation, but there lacking the iron operative component, was previously thought to have held a surgical needle or fine cautery (Künzl 1983a, fig. 36.31; Künzl and Feugère 2002, fig. 1, no.1e, fig. 6, no. C3). It is now apparent that handles with this type of socket could accommodate blades as well, probably, as a number of other alternative operative attachments. The Rimini blade, which is broken at the tip but otherwise complete, is sharp on both convex edges and, with a central midrib on both faces, it is quite robust. It is conceivably the type of scalpel Galen had in mind for the opening of the vertebral canal. Galen says:

> I perform this … with an instrument of my own devising, like the so-called sharp-pointed knife. It should be made of the finest steel, like the Norican, that it be not blunted, bent or broken. It must be thicker than a common scalpel, so that, as you press on the junction of the vertebrae, the operation is accomplished with ease. (Galen, *Anatomical Procedures* 8.6 (2.682K), trans. Singer 1956, 214)

However, there are other possible applications in descriptions given by Soranus, Aëtius and Paul, including puncturing of the foetal cranium in obstructed labour and lancing abscess of the womb (Soranus, *Gynaecology* 4.10.2; Aëtius 16.89.20; Paul of Aegina 6.73.2; Bliquez 2015, 96–7). Additionally, if we restore its broken tip, its appearance is close to that of the lancet used for venesection in Milne's day and, as already discussed, while it is probable that for much blood-letting in antiquity a wide variety of scalpels was used, this blade may correspond to the phlebotome specifically called for in some cases of venesection and for the opening of abscesses (Milne 1907, 34). Furthermore, Bliquez believes it likely that references to the *spathion* generally signified the polyp knife, which was used above all in the removal of nasal polyp (Bliquez 2015, 93–7).

New, too, amongst the Rimini scalpels is a composite instrument combining a small, strong, ivy-leaf-shaped blade at one end with a broken elevator at the other (Jackson 2014a, 141, 144, type 14, fig. 18.16.5). The blade shape is broadly paralleled by a smaller, thinner example on a double-ended instrument, also of 3rd-century AD date, from Asia Minor (Jackson 2014a, fig. 18.16.4; Künzl 2002a, A12, this instrument is closely paralleled by another from Asia Minor in the Halûk Perk collection: Perk 2012, 41, 1.4.1) and it resembles that of a scalpel in the box of instruments depicted on the well-known 4th-century AD sarcophagus of a physician from Ostia (McCann 1978, 138–40, figs 174–5; Jackson 1988, frontispiece; Krug 2008, fig. 25). The Rimini instrument is also similar to a 17th-century instrument (Scultetus 1655, pl. II, no. VII), which combines a blade with a ridged lever and was used at the start of cranial trepanation. As the Rimini instrumentation includes a very wide range of tools for bone surgery, including trepanation, it is possible to suggest that this is another new instrument of bone surgery and represents a further expansion of the known surgical arsenal of Roman orthopaedic practitioners.

As we have seen, the comparison of intact scalpels with descriptions in medical texts occasionally allows the

Figure 51 Cologne, Richard-Wagner-Strasse, Roman medical instruments and implements, including a surgical shears with bronze spring and iron blades, in a 3rd century AD grave group. Römisch-Germanisches Museum, Köln, inv. no. 91.204, 91.206, 91.161,1, 91.162,1-9, 91.162,12-31. Photo: © Rheinisches Bildarchiv Köln, Anja Wegner, rba_d037855

identification of a surgeon's knife intended for a specific operation, though over-identification should be avoided, since it is clear that in antiquity one instrument often served numerous roles. Even without their blade, however, two distinctive double-ended tools in the specialist set of 10 instruments found in the Rome region (see p. 24) have been recognised as lithotomy knives, used by a Roman specialist to cut for stone in the urinary bladder (Künzl 1983b; Jackson 2010). As Künzl pointed out, the combination of a roughened scoop with an iron-stained socket for the now missing blade allow the identification of two of these tools (Jackson 2014a, fig. 18.17, second and third from left) as the *lithotomon* (lithotomy knife) used in that most perilous of ancient operations and clearly described by Celsus and Rufus of Ephesus (Celsus, *On Medicine* 7.26.2H-L; Rufus, *On Diseases of the Kidneys and Bladder* 9.9–10; Sideras 1977). Celsus' account continued with a description of the procedure for a less straightforward operation in which the stone had a very irregular or spiny surface. While noting that 'many use a scalpel here also', by which we may take him to mean the bladed end of a lithotomy knife, Celsus warned that the blade might not be strong enough to completely divide the tissue above projections or spines. To avoid the potentially fatal consequences that might follow a failed operation a more robust instrument was developed for the removal of this type of stone, an invention that Celsus attributed to Meges (of Sidon), a Greek surgeon practising in Rome in the 1st century BC (Celsus, *On Medicine* 7.26.2M-O). In view of the perceived need for strength a single-piece knife of iron or steel is likely, but despite Celsus' quite detailed description, and several attempts to identify or picture Meges' knife (Milne 1907, 41–3, pl. 8.4–6), it has remained stubbornly elusive. However, an ingenious and closely argued case has been made for the idiosyncratic knife with curved blade and sinuous handle depicted on the Berlin relief (Krug 2008, 42–3, fig. 26), on the strength of which an example in a secure ancient medical context may one day be found.

Another bladed instrument available to Greek and Roman practitioners was the U-shaped spring shears (*forfex*).

This tool was common and widespread in the ancient world, and with its pair of opposed blades it fulfilled many functions, including those of the hinged scissors which only became current in medieval times. Shears were usually made of iron, but sometimes of copper-alloy. In a range of sizes they were variously a household item, an agricultural implement and a craftsman's tool. Shears also had medical and, albeit rarely, surgical applications, as in the removal of a type of wart from the penis (Paul of Aegina, 6.58.1). Celsus recorded a more radical application in the excision of mortified omentum in abdominal wounds and prolapse, though he pointed out that this was an exceptional use and he took issue with those surgeons who risked haemorrhage by using shears to cut away unmortified tissue in the treatment of scrotal hernia (Celsus, *On Medicine* 7.16.3; 7.21.1C). Mostly, though, shears would have been used, both in human and veterinary medicine, to cut dressings, bandages, sutures and ligatures, also even to cut the tails off leeches to facilitate their use in blood-letting (Galen, *Compound Drugs Arranged by Kind* 13.685K; Oribasius, *Medical Compilations* 7.21.6; *Mulomedicina Chironis* 64; further references in Bliquez 2015, 107–8).

As the shears used by medical practitioners did not differ significantly from household or craft tools it is not a diagnostic surgical type and can only be ascribed a probable medical use when found in association with other recognisable medical instruments. (Shears are included in images of instrumentation from Malta, Kom Ombo and Kelli (see **Fig. 15**) and the image of shears appears sometimes to have been used as an indicator of medical practice (Dasen 2008, 50–7; Moschakis 2014)). Iron-bladed shears have been found in sets of medical instruments dating from the 1st to the 5th century AD, including those from Verona (Künzl 1983a, 104), Merida (Künzl 1983a, 102), Nea Paphos (Michaelides 1984, 318, no. 18, 324, fig. 2.1, pl. 71.3), Cologne, Richard-Wagner-Strasse (**Fig. 51**) (Jackson 2018a, fig. 1; Euskirchen 2018, 313, 315, no. 28), Nijmegen (see **Fig. 21**) (Künzl 1983a, 93–6, fig. 74; Braadbaart 1994, 165, NHa 1, pl. 1.2; Jackson 2018a, 142–4, figs 8A–C), Gadara (Künzl and Weber 1991, 89–90, fig. 5, pl. 34c) and *Marcianopolis* (Minchev 1983, 144). The examples from Nea Paphos and Gadara are closely similar in form and size (197 and 194mm long); that from Nijmegen is slightly smaller (132mm long) and is of different and distinctive form, comprising a spring handle of bronze with a pair of iron blades fastened in the type of keyhole socket found on scalpel handles; that from Cologne, Richard-Wagner-Strasse (173mm long) also has iron blades held on a spring handle of bronze, as does an example from Dion.

Chisels, gouges and lenticulars

Chisels in the British Museum collection: see Sets of instruments, Cat. nos 3.10–11 (**Fig. 52**)

Just as the standard Roman scalpel comprised an iron blade with a bronze handle, so too, the other main bladed instrument in surgical kits, the purpose-made surgical chisel, also combined a bronze handle with an iron blade. The chisel (*scalper/scalprum*) was an instrument of bone surgery deployed in cutting, dividing, excising, scraping and smoothing diseased and fractured bone. Its many roles included the division of bone in complex fracture, the re-

Figure 52 A pair of bone chisels in the set of Roman medical instruments from Italy. British Museum (Cat. nos 3.10, 3.11)

Figure 53 A pair of bone chisels, two scalpel handles and a broken handle (probably a bone lever) with inlaid gold bands, from a room at the south-west corner of the town baths at Xanten, 2nd/3rd century AD. Archäologischer Park/Regionalmuseum, Xanten, C3718, CVT 1963

fracturing of bone in cases of distorted union, the removal of an embedded weapon, the division of a rib or clavicle, and the amputation of supernumerary digits (Bliquez 2015, 191–5). For the latter two applications Galen and Paul described the use of a pair of chisels in opposition (Galen, *Anatomical Procedures* 8.6 (2.686K); Paul 6.77.3 and 6.107.2, Bliquez 2015, 193). Above all, though, the chisel was an instrument of skull surgery. In addition to cutting and dividing cranial bone, the chisel was used to reveal fracture fissures, to smooth sharp projections, to excise fragments of fractured bone, to cut the small pit needed to locate the centre-pin of the crown trepan (*modiolus*) (see Drills, below, p. 53), and to smooth the margin of trepanations (Jackson 2005a, 110.). The *planus scalper*, used to level the elevated section of a depressed cranial fracture, probably had a flatter and wider cutting edge than the normal chisel.

Wide-bladed chisels are known in the instrumentaria from Bingen, Germany (1st/early 2nd century AD: Künzl 1983a, 84, fig. 58.13 and .15) and from Nijmegen (see **Fig. 21c**) (3rd century AD: Leemans 1842, pl II. 27; Künzl 1983a, 94, fig. 74.27). But the normal form of *scalper* is probably that of the two chisels in the set from Italy (1st/2nd century AD), Cat. nos 3.10–11. In form and size they are nearly identical, each with a narrow iron blade and a lightly waisted, octagonal-sectioned brass handle. Evidently they were made together as a pair, for scientific analysis, too, revealed that the handles have a virtually identical metal composition (see p. 151 and **Table 4**; and La Niece 1986, 162). X-radiography demonstrated that the tang of the iron blade of both chisels was embedded to a depth of about 15mm in the handle and as no trace of solder was detected it is inferred that the handles were cast-on to the blades, a joining technique that would have ensured a particularly strong bond. The heavy-duty usage that required such a bond is evidenced by the slight burring of the low-domed head of the handles, a consequence of repeated mallet blows.

Closely similar is another pair of chisels, part of a small group of surgical instruments found in a room at the south-west corner of the town baths at Xanten (**Fig. 53**) (*Colonia Ulpia Traiana*), Germany (Künzl 1986a, 492–5, figs 1–3; Künzl 2002b, 43–4, fig. 57; Künzl 2018, 20–1). Silver-coloured residues at the handle/blade junction of the Xanten chisels (2nd/3rd century AD) are probably remains of lead-tin solder, which helped to secure the tang of the blade within the socketed handle. Other complete examples of this type of chisel include those from Kallion, Greece (3rd century AD: Künzl 1983a, 40–2, fig. 11) and, in some numbers, from Pompeii (1st century AD: Bliquez 1994, 132–3, nos 94–8 and 102). All these chisels have a slender iron blade pegged into a waisted copper-alloy handle, of circular or octagonal cross-section, with a flat or low-domed head. One of these distinctive chisel handles was found in an Augustan context at the Magdalensberg, the earliest example yet known (Gostenčnik 2004, 373–4, fig. 5.2, 398–9, pl. 2.1). When the precise form of the cutting edge is still identifiable, their blade usually corresponds to a small example of the two commonest general-purpose chisels used by Roman woodworkers. Those are, in modern terminology, either a firmer chisel, which tapers evenly on both faces down to a lightly splayed cutting edge, or a mortise chisel, which is bevelled on one face of the cutting edge only (cf. Manning 1985, 21–4 and fig. 4). However, the requirements of the surgical chisel were hardly different to those of some of the chisels used by craftsmen who worked on wood, bone and stone. Thus, the chisels used by surgical practitioners were probably often the same as some of those used by carpenters and sculptors and probably acquired from the same toolmakers. Certainly, some of the chisels found in surgical kits comprise an iron blade with a tang to secure a wooden or bone handle and differ little from carpentry tools, as, for example, one in the Bingen set (Künzl 1983a, 84, fig. 58.6). Others are single-piece iron chisels, some of which are also virtually indistinguishable from the tools of other craftsmen.

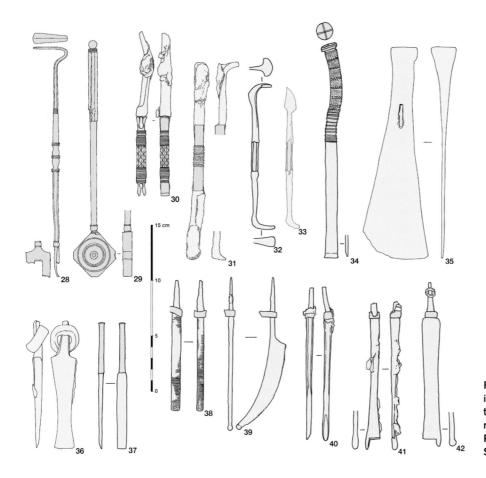

Figure 54 A selection of the instruments of bone surgery from the *domus* del Chirurgo, Rimini, mid-3rd century AD. City Museum, Rimini. Drawing: Ralph Jackson and Stephen Crummy

The potential extent of a surgeon's set of bone chisels has been vividly revealed in the extraordinary 3rd-century AD find from the Rimini *domus* del Chirurgo. Of over 150 surgical instruments more than 40 are tools of bone surgery, of which 13 are chisels (Jackson 2005a, 99, fig. 5.1; Jackson 2009b, 82–4, fig. 4.32–3). They range from tiny, bronze-handled, narrow-bladed instruments (**Fig. 54**, 37), to bronze-handled chisels with blades like those in the Italy set and Xanten find (**Fig. 54**, 34), to stout wooden-handled iron carpentry chisels (**Fig. 54**, 36), to fine flat-bladed examples with bronze handles (of wax spatula form) and to single-piece iron chisels with a long tapered blade, wide flat cutting edge and solid head (**Fig. 54**, 35). They include firmer and mortise type blades in a wide variety of sizes which enabled the practitioner to select the most appropriate instrument for the task in hand. There are two matching pairs which, like the finds from Italy and Xanten, recall Galen's description of the use of a pair of chisels as osteotomes.

The blade of one of the Rimini chisels is distinctive and unparalleled and may have been designed and commissioned by the Rimini practitioner. It is offset at its lower end and appears to have been sharp on one side as well as on the cutting edge. Its wooden or bone handle was strengthened by a bronze collar at the junction with the blade, an arrangement in common with four other specialised chisels, also thus far unique to the Rimini find (**Fig. 54**, 41–2). These 'guarded chisels' have a small lentil-shaped projection at one end of the cutting edge and they correspond exactly to Galen's description of the *phakotos ekkopeus* – lenticular – which was used exclusively in cranial

trepanation. Struck by a mallet, the lenticular divided the cranium while safely separating it from the underlying membrane (Galen, *Method of Healing* 10.445–9K; Oribasius, *Medical Compilations* 46.21.20–2; Paul of Aegina 6.90.6; Jackson 2005a, 99, fig. 5.1.5, 116–17; Jackson 2009b, 82, fig. 4.34–5, 84–5, 88–9; Bliquez 2015, 195–7).

The instrument Celsus most frequently named in skull surgery – *scalper* – was usually, but not always, a chisel. The *scalper excissorius* and its Greek equivalent were occasionally used to indicate a gouge, a 'hollow chisel' (Galen, *Method of Healing* 10.445K; Oribasius, *Medical Compilations* 46.21.17; Bliquez 2015, 194–5). The gouge was a tool of skull surgery and it is instructive to find an example in the Bingen instrumentation which included both carpentry tools and purpose-made tools of bone surgery and cranial trepanation (Künzl 1983a, 84, fig. 58.7). Three smaller surgical gouges in a range of sizes (as recommended by Paul 6.90.4) formed part of the Rimini instrumentation and the best preserved has the same form of handle construction as the lenticulars (**Fig. 54**, 40) (Jackson 2005a, 99, fig. 5.1.4, 116–17; Jackson 2009b, 82, fig. 4.36, 84–5, 88–9). It would have been used to cut a track for the lenticular in the operation for skull fracture so clearly described by Galen (Galen, *Method of Healing* 10.446K) and vividly revealed in use in the trepanned skull of a hydrocephalic child, now known to have been a girl (Valentina Gazzaniga, pers. comm., 1 August 2023), who was buried in the small cemetery of a *villa rustica* at Fidenae, near Rome in the late 1st/early 2nd century AD (**Fig. 55a–b**) (Mariani-Costantini *et al.* 2000; Jackson 2005a, 116–17; Gazzaniga and Marinozzi 2018).

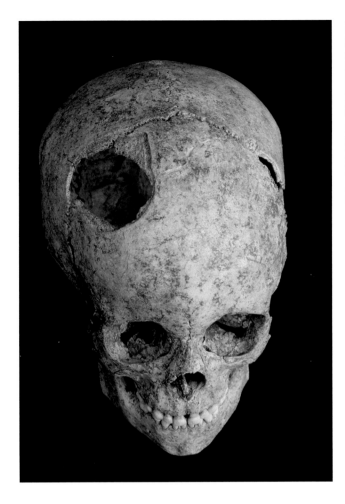

Figure 55a–b Fidenae, near Rome, trepanned skull from the skeleton of a hydrocephalic child buried in the small cemetery of a *villa rustica*, late 1st/early 2nd century AD. Soprintendenza Speciale per il Colosseo, il Museo Nazionale Romano e l'Area Archeologica di Roma. Photos courtesy of Luciana Rita Angeletti and Renato Mariani Costantini

Curettes

Curettes in the British Museum collection: see Sets of instruments, Cat. nos 3.6 and 3.42, and Levers, Cat. no. 3.80

The third instrument indicated (according to context) by the term *scalper/scalprum* by Celsus and other Latin medical writers was a curette, called *xuster*, a scraper, by Greek writers (Bliquez 2015, 39–40, 199–200). It was a key instrument of bone surgery in which it was used principally to remove necrotic tissue from chronically diseased bone that had become carious (Jackson 2005b, 102–4, fig. 5.2, 6). Scoops with a semi-sharp or fine-toothed rim have been found in a number of surviving medical kits and identified as curettes (sharp spoons). Most are robust instruments of bronze with a stout stem, a smoothly rounded or finely faceted convex exterior surface, a capacious interior and a carefully made rim, upright and semi-sharp at the mouth. Certainly, their form accords well with the described uses of the *scalper/xuster*. It is probably significant, too, that several have been found in sets which include other instruments of bone surgery, as in the case of the British Museum set from Italy (Cat. no. 3.6) and the sets from Colophon (Caton 1914, 117, pl. 11, 24) and Bingen (Künzl 1983a, 82, fig. 56.14). The Colophon instrument is double-ended, combining a semi-sharp with a fine-toothed curette; the Bingen instrument retains its scoop with finely toothed rim but is broken at the other end; and the example in the Italy set has a semi-sharp rim and was a combination instrument with a keyhole socket at the other end probably originally mounted with a scalpel blade. Other curettes include one in the large set of instruments from Ephesus (Künzl 1983a, 47, fig. 15.15), one in

the small set of instruments from Milos (Künzl 1983a, 41, fig. 10.5), a broken example in the British Museum's small kit (Cat. no. 3.42), and a fine example of iron, combined with a bone lever, from London (Cat. no. 3.80).

Saws

Saws in the British Museum collection: see Varia, Cat. no. 3.147

Saws appear to have had a restricted surgical use in antiquity and were only occasionally referred to in ancient medical texts, where they were termed *prion* in Greek and *serrula* in Latin (Bliquez 2015, 39, 183–4). They were an instrument of bone surgery and an obvious area of use was in limb amputation, which, although seemingly avoided wherever possible by Hippocratic practitioners, was described by Celsus in the 1st century AD, the earliest surviving account of the operation (*On Medicine* 7.33), and by Paul (6.84 – excerpting from Leonides of Alexandria). The reality of limb amputation by Roman practitioners has been confirmed in the form of skeletal remains of 2nd-century AD date from Ephesus (Kanz and Grossschmidt 2009; Kanz 2011) and from Rome's Isola Sacra necropolis, where the end of a thigh bone showed not only the serrated marks of a surgeon's saw but also bone remodelling and chronic osteomyelitis indicative of months or even years of survival after the operation (Weaver *et al.* 2000). However, very few saws have been identified in an ancient medical or surgical context and none, yet, as large as the frame saws that were used for limb amputation from the late 15th century on (Kirkup 2006, 379–90). As Kirkup observes (2006, 378), specifically designed surgical instruments are not essential for elective amputation, and when necessary a borrowed carpenter's bow saw or frame saw would have sufficed. Furthermore, it was not until the 18th and 19th centuries that operative indications widened and the surgical uses of saws proliferated (2006, 202).

For long, Cat. no. 3.147 was the only Roman saw blade regarded as a surgical tool (Milne 1907, 130, pl. 41.3), but with neither a context nor a provenance its surgical use could not, and still cannot, be proven. In recent decades, however, a number of more certain examples of surgical saws have been brought to light in dated medical contexts on archaeological excavations of Roman period sites. As Bliquez pointed out (2015, 184), Celsus' use of the diminutive *serrula* would appear to indicate that most surgical saws were relatively small, and that is indeed the case with those so far found. There is one in the set of instruments found in the cemetery at Stanway (see **Fig. 22c**) (1st century AD), one amongst the instrumentation from Allianoi (later 1st to 3rd century AD), and one in the extremely rich medical assemblage from the Rimini *domus* del Chirurgo (see **Fig. 54**, 39) (mid-3rd century AD). All are small saws and differ in their form and blade shape. The Stanway saw, which may have been of British Late Iron Age manufacture, comprises a slender, near parallel-sided, iron blade, 112mm long, with a blunt-nosed tip and a small block-like handle/grip made of iron, bronze and wood or bone. The finely toothed cutting edge is 86mm long and very lightly concave, with 14 teeth per cm. The teeth are neither set nor raked allowing the blade to cut in both directions (Jackson 2007a, 237–40, 250–1, fig. 121.CF47.28). The Allianoi saw comprises a double-edged flat rectangular blade of copper alloy, probably originally provided with a central handle. To judge from the published illustrations, the two straight, serrated cutting edges, 32mm long, appear to have had about 7–9 teeth per cm (Baykan 2012, 152, no. 323, 206, fig. 20). The Rimini saw, part of the very comprehensive range of instruments of bone surgery in the assemblage, comprises a crescent-shaped iron blade with a knobbed tip and a slender tang which, with a small copper-alloy collar, secured the now lacking wood or bone handle. The blade back is concave and the finely serrated convex cutting edge, 86mm long, has 16 unset and unraked teeth per cm (Jackson 2009b, 82, fig. 4.31, 85). Similar in appearance to the Rimini saw is one from the 2009–13 excavations of the *domus* dei Fondi Cossar at Aquileia (Dolenz *et al.* 2021, 681–8, figs 1, 3, 4, pl. 1.2). Although found in a 5th–6th century AD context and lacking any associated medical instruments, the distinctive form and decoration of its slender copper-alloy handle are closely paralleled by the handles of several surgical instruments of the early 1st century AD. It measures 191mm in overall length; its triangular iron blade, 84mm long, has a lightly convex cutting edge with five forward-raked teeth per cm.

Although the blade form of the Stanway and Rimini saws differs, their size and tooth count are closely similar. Both may correspond to the knife-shaped saw mentioned by Galen (*Commentary on Hippocrates' Fractures* 18b.331K; Milne 1907, 130–1; Bliquez 2015, 184). Such saws would have been well suited to the amputation of fingers or toes and it is interesting to note the close similarity in form and size between the narrow linear Stanway saw and the Larrey's early 19th-century 'Keyhole' finger saw for minor amputations and joint resection (Kirkup 2006, 203–4, fig. 258A), a type that was still included in the Thackray instrument catalogue of *c.* 1955 (Thackray *c.* 1955, 464, B2489). Strikingly similar to the curved Rimini saw are 16th-century hand saws designed for excision of compound fractures and ulcerated bone, while the Allianoi double-edged saw is closely paralleled by the small tenon saws, often incorporated in skull trepanation sets, which were used for bone excision in compound fractures of skull and limbs from the 16th to the 19th century (Kirkup 2006, 203, fig. 257). So

the Stanway, Rimini and Allianoi saws would also have been appropriate for the division of slender bones like ribs and the trimming of projecting splintered bone in complex fractures. Nor should their use in limb amputation or skull surgery be excluded, and it is instructive to note that Celsus specified a small saw in his detailed account of the amputation of a gangrenous limb:

> ... Therefore, between the sound and the diseased part, the flesh is to be cut through with a scalpel down to the bone, but this must not be done actually over a joint, and it is better that some of the sound part should be cut away than that any of the diseased part should be left behind. When the bone is reached, the sound flesh is drawn back from the bone and undercut from around it, so that in that part also some bone is bared; the bone is then to be cut through with a small saw (*serrula*) as near as possible to the sound flesh which still adheres to it ... (Celsus, *On Medicine* 7.33.1–2, trans. Spencer 1938b, 470–1)

To the Roman period saws may be added three further examples from much earlier contexts, the 3rd- to 2nd-century BC La Tène C burial groups from München-Obermenzing, Germany, Batina-Kisköszeg, Croatia and Galatii Bistriței, Romania. Each includes an iron skull saw, and the first two also an iron instrument closely resembling the form of the Roman *meningophylax* (see Levers, pp. 56–7). The saws have a long-stemmed tanged handle terminating in a small triangular blade with a finely serrated cutting edge of varying form. All three grave groups reflect the independent and innovative nature of medical and surgical equipment in the Celtic world (De Navarro 1955, fig. 2.3, fig. 3d; Künzl 1991a; Künzl 1995a, 223–4, 234–5, fig. 3.a, fig. 4.d).

Drills

Drills in the British Museum collection: Cat. nos 3.78–9 (see also Sets of instruments, Cat. no. 3.12)

Bow drills, whether for making fire or for drilling, have had a very long history. They were simple to make and easy to use, consisting of a drill-bit rotated by a length of cord or sinew held taut on a springy wooden bow handle. By Greek and Roman times they were an essential craft tool used by a wide range of artisans, including jewellers who adapted the bow drill to engrave gems (see, e.g., Kleibrink 1997, fig. 5). But they were most characteristically the tool of carpenters, such as Publius Licinius Demetrius, one of two freedmen commemorated on a late 1st-century BC marble relief from Frascati (**Fig. 56**). The tools of his trade were very clearly depicted – a chisel, an adze-head, a plane iron and, most graphically, a bow drill (Manning 1985, 25–7, pl. I; Jackson 2005a, 108–9, fig. 5.6). The drill and its bow handle are shown in great detail, and it is evident that the drill comprised an iron drill-bit secured at the end of a bi-partite wooden stock, the lower part of which was rotated by the corded bow handle while the upper static part formed the head on which it turned. The user held the bow handle in one hand and the stock head in the other. Where greater force was required the bow handle was replaced by a strap which was operated by an assistant. Essentially, these drills, especially the bow drill, were the type used by medical practitioners for, like other carpentry tools, they were either simply appropriated for, or adapted to, medical and surgical uses. Those uses included the release of suppuration from

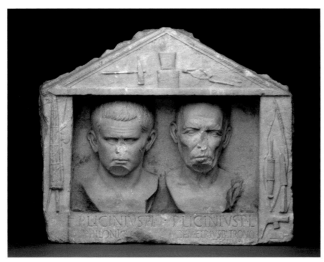

Figure 56 Villa Muti, Frascati, marble relief, commemorating the freedmen Philonicus and Demetrius and showing blacksmithing and carpentry tools. Prominent amongst the carpentry tools at right is a bow drill, late 1st century BC. British Museum, London, reg. no. 1954.1214,1

Figure 57 A folding trepan handle, two cylindrical drills (*modioli*) and a bone lever, part of the extensive late 1st/early 2nd century AD set of Roman surgical instruments from Bingen am Rhein. Bingen, Historisches Museum am Strom

behind ribs, the removal of sling shot embedded in a bone, the boring of holes in carious bone to enable cauterisation and, with a tiny version of the drill, perforation of the nasal bone in cases of fistula lachrymalis (Celsus, *On Medicine*, 8.4.14. 7.5.4B. 8.2.4; Galen, *Compound Drugs Arranged by Place* 12.821K, Paul 6.22.1). But the drill was employed principally as a trepan in skull surgery, to remove diseased or damaged bone resulting from trauma fractures or chronic ulceration (Arnott *et al.* 2003; Rocca 2003; Jackson 2005a, 101–4; Bliquez 2015, 185–9).

A surgical drill – *trupanon* – is mentioned in several Hippocratic treatises and to judge by the recommended applications took two forms, a solid-tipped trepan and a crown trepan (Bliquez 2015, 38–9). Although the Hippocratic drills were not described – and none has yet been identified in the archaeological record – the reference in *On Head Wounds* 21.6 to examining 'the circular track of the trepan' indicates that the drill employed there was a crown trepan. Subsequently surgical drills were referred to, and sometimes described, by many medical writers, including Celsus, Heliodorus, Pseudo-Galen, Galen, Oribasius and Paul (Bliquez 2015, 185–6). Celsus' descriptions are particularly detailed and full (*On Medicine* 8.2–4; Jackson 1994a, 191–4). He recommended three types of drill. One, which he called *terebra*, was a trepan with a solid drill-bit, which corresponds to the carpenter's bow drill. A second was a variant of the *terebra* with a longer, guarded, drill-bit. The third was a crown trepan, a *modiolus*, with a hollow cylindrical drill-bit which, he noted, 'the Greeks call *choinikis*'. If the diseased or damaged bone was confined to the skull's outer table then the use of either a *modiolus* or a *terebra* was appropriate. The *modiolus* was to be used if the area involved was small enough to be encompassed by its cylindrical drill-bit, but if the area was more extensive the *terebra* was required.

Celsus' description of the appearance and operation of the *modiolus* is one of the clearest such passages from antiquity:

The modiolus is a hollow cylindrical iron instrument with its lower edges serrated; in the middle of which is fixed a pin which is itself surrounded by an inner disc. ... When the disease is so limited that the modiolus can include it, this is more serviceable; and if the bone is carious, the central pin is inserted into the hole; if there is black bone, a small pit is made with the angle of a chisel for the reception of the pin, so that, the pin being fixed, the modiolus when rotated cannot slip; it is then rotated like a trepan ... The pressure must be such that it both bores and rotates; for if pressed lightly it makes little advance, if heavily it does not rotate. It is a good plan to drop in a little rose oil or milk, so that it may rotate more smoothly; but if too much is used the keenness of the instrument is blunted. When a way has been cut by the modiolus, the central pin is taken out, and the modiolus worked by itself; then, when the bone dust shows that underlying bone is sound, the modiolus is laid aside. (Celsus, *On Medicine* 8.3.1–3, trans. Spencer 1938b, 497–9)

No Greek or Hellenistic crown trepan has yet been identified and only one Roman crown-trepanning kit is so far known, that in the Bingen instrumentation (late 1st/early 2nd century AD) (Como 1925; Künzl 1983a, 80–5; Jackson 2005a, 104–6, fig. 5.3,1, fig. 5.4). The Bingen trepanning kit (**Fig. 57**) consists of a folding handle and two cylindrical drills (*modioli*), all of copper alloy. The handle has perforations to secure the cord that rotated the drills. The drills, which now lack their wooden stock and head, are tubular, with a toothed cutting edge. They differ slightly in length and diameter, and the teeth vary in number and thickness. Since the backwards and forwards movement of the handle provided a clockwise/anti-clockwise rotation of the drill, the teeth are symmetrical so that they could cut in both directions. Corresponding to Celsus' description the drills are provided with a centre-point mounted on a retractable cross-plate.

Although Celsus' use of the phrase *modiolus ferramentum* suggests that the drill-bit of the crown trepan was made of iron, the two *modioli* from Bingen are of copper alloy, and no other certain examples – of copper alloy or of iron – have yet been identified. It is probable that the great majority of

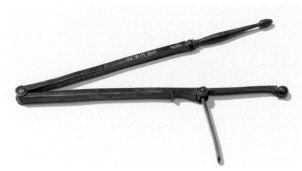

Figure 58 Folding drill-handle, with the handle near fully folded. British Museum, London (Cat no. 3.78)

modioli were indeed of iron and have corroded beyond recognition. However, a further seven folding copper-alloy handles are known, one each, of unknown provenance, in the British Museum (Cat. no. 3.78) and the Berlin Antikenmuseum (Jackson 2005a, 105–6, fig. 5.3, 2–3), two from the Rimini *domus* del Chirurgo (3rd century AD) (Jackson 2009b, 76–7, fig. 3.26, 84, pl. 2), one each from the instrument finds at Colophon (1st/2nd century AD) (Caton 1914, 116–17, fig. 2) and *Marcianopolis* (late 4th/early 5th century AD) (Minchev 1983, 146, no. 18; Kirova 2002, 81, 86, fig. 5.4) and one from the House of Poseidon (House 1) at Zeugma, south-east Turkey (mid-3rd century AD destruction deposit) (M. Feugère in Dieudonné-Glad *et al.* 2013, 210–11, no. 1186, 407, pl. 63, 1186a–d). It was the discovery of the folding handle in the Colophon set and its comparison with the unprovenanced example in the British Museum (Cat. no. 3.78) that led to the recognition of the handles as a specifically medical type (p. 108).

In each instance the folding handle comprises a bi-partite crossbar, of rectangular cross-section, hinged near the centre and with a short projecting hinged strip set near one end (**Fig. 58**). The tip of the strip and a moulding set a short distance in from the terminal of the opposing bar were provided with a small drilled perforation, by means of which each end of the cord was secured. When unfolded and strung with a cord the handle was operated in a to-and-fro action, like that of an artisan's bow drill, to rotate a solid or tubular drill-bit secured in a wooden stock (see **Fig. 114c**). The terminals of most of the handles are in the form of a decorative moulded knob, but the two unprovenanced examples and one of those from Rimini have a stylised snake-head finial, like those found also on a sharp hook in the set of instruments from Aschersleben and on a coudée-type forceps in the set of instruments from Cyrene (Künzl 1983a, 100–1; Jackson 2021, 546–9, fig. 3.3). The Aesculapian snake was a powerful symbol of healing and was probably incorporated in all these instruments to imbue them and their user with the divine powers of Aesculapius. Thus the form of the folding handles is distinctive, and those from Bingen, Colophon, Rimini and *Marcianopolis* are all components of medical instrumentaria, so even though, in theory, the handles could have been used for non-surgical purposes, or by other artisans, the handle type was clearly designed for surgical use – a drill handle, principally for cranial trepanation. Thus, the handle from Zeugma, although lacking associated surgical or medical instruments, may be regarded as formerly part of a surgical instrumentation as, too, the unprovenanced British

Museum handle, Cat. no. 3.78, and the unprovenanced handle in the Berlin Antikenmuseum.

The Bingen handle and *modioli* were employed as crown trepans in the manner so clearly described by Celsus, but the Bingen handle and all of the other folding handles could also, or alternatively, have been used to drive a solid drill-bit, a *terebra*. Celsus also described clearly when and how the *terebra* type of drill should be used:

> But if disease is too extensive for the modiolus to cover, the operation must be carried out by the trepan (*terebra*). With this a hole is made exactly at the margin of the diseased and sound bone, then not very far off a second, and a third, until the whole area to be excised is ringed round by these holes; ... Next the excising chisel is driven through from one hole to the other by striking it with a mallet, and cuts out the intervening bone, and so a ring is made like the smaller one cut by the modiolus. (Celsus, *On Medicine* 8.3.3–5, trans. Spencer 1938b, 499)

Thus, where carious cranial bone was too extensive to be encompassed by the *modiolus* Celsus advised use of the *terebra*, with which the diseased area was encircled by a series of drilled holes. A mallet and chisel (like Cat. nos 3.10–11) were then used to cut through the intervening 'bridges' and detach the diseased bone. The chisel was also used to smooth down the edges of the trepanation and the surface of the inner table, if that was not to be removed.

Celsus reserved his second type of *terebra* drill-bit for the removal of deeper carious bone, in the case of the skull for those occasions on which the disease had penetrated both the outer and inner tables. Further descriptions of the instrument are given by Galen (*Method of Healing* 10.446–447K) and Paul of Aegina (6.90.5) (Bliquez 2015, 185–6). It, too, was a solid-tipped drill, but longer, and with an expansion above the tip in order to provide a more precise control over the depth of penetration, which was of critical importance in skull surgery where the cerebral membranes lay immediately beneath the inner table.

No definite example of either type of *terebra* has yet been found and the reason is not hard to understand. For both varieties of drill-bit would have comprised a small, slender iron object in a wooden stock, easily destroyed or altered by corrosion, while the handle was probably often the simple wooden artisan type rather than the more durable (and costly) purpose-made folding copper alloy handle. It is possible, however, that one of the iron implements in the Bingen instrumentarium is a pointed drill-bit for surgical use (Künzl 1983a, fig. 58.9; Manning 1985, fig. 5.1). Certainly, the Bingen find includes a number of other generic woodworking tools – an iron gouge and three iron chisels – in addition to the more distinctive tools of bone surgery: the trepanning kit, a curette, four bone levers and a rasp. But even with their secure medical association these iron tools can be interpreted in various ways. They might actually be purpose-made tools of bone surgery, or perhaps carpentry tools acquired by the healer for use in bone surgery, or even carpentry tools used as such to make splints, traction equipment, walking aids and the like (Jackson 2002a, 89).

A similar uncertainty attaches to Cat. no. 3.12 in the set of instruments from Italy, a small iron implement with spear-shaped tip (once tentatively identified as a cautery: Jackson

1994a, 179, 206, fig. 3.5), and the near-identical Cat. no. 3.79, part of a small group of implements, including a scalpel handle and a forceps (Cat. nos 3.71 and 3.88), from Lake Trasimene (**Fig. 59**). There is a third example, of closely similar form and size, but of bronze, from the Dacian site of *Porolissum*, Romania (Cociş 1993, 242–3, fig. 1.6). Each of these implements comprises a short tang, a neatly cut moulding and a carefully profiled robust stem which expands and then tapers towards the operative spear-shaped tip, which corresponds to that of the carpenter's diamond bit (cf. Manning 1985, fig. 5.2). A wooden stock (or handle) would have been secured to the tang and braced by the moulding and, in the case of Cat. no. 3.12, its end further reinforced by a small brass binding-ring (Cat. no. 3.13). Corrosion has removed the surface and obscured the original form of the tip of Cat. no. 3.12, which now has a flat spear shape, but Cat. no. 3.79 is well preserved and its tip has a flattened triangular cross-section. In both cases slight damage at the point appears consistent with the rotary use of a drill; and they are closely paralleled by perforators in 18th-century trepanning sets (Bennion 1979, 30, 35, fig. 19). The Italy set includes a number of instruments of bone surgery but no folding trepan handle; nor was there a folding handle with the Lake Trasimene group. So if the identification of these implements as drill-bits is correct it is likely that they were used with the artisan-type wooden bow handle.

Similarly rare are surviving identifiable examples of trepanned skulls, partly, no doubt, because of burial practice: cremation was the Roman norm from the 4th century BC to the 2nd century AD, thus erasing most evidence of pathology and therapy for much of the periods of the Republic and Empire (Toynbee 1971, 40; Germanà and Fornaciari 1992; Cruse 2004, 187, 189–91; Tullo 2010, 166–7). In fact, some of the best evidence for the use of the crown trepan comes not from the Roman Republic or Empire but from beyond the frontier, from the Celtic sites of Katzelsdorf, Guntramsdorf and Dürrnberg/Hallein, Austria (Urban *et al.* 1985; Breitwieser 2003). The skulls of three 3rd- to 2nd-century BC inhumations at Guntramsdorf (Graves 5, 6 and 29) and one at Katzelsdorf (Grave 1) yielded a total of nine circular drilled trepanations measuring between 17mm and 20mm in diameter (compare the Bingen *modioli* with diameters of *c.* 24mm and *c.* 25mm). In one case (Katzelsdorf) an incomplete triple trepanation also preserved the impression of a centre-point. The earliest evidence for the use of a crown trepan comes from the Dürrnberg, where the skull of a male inhumation of the first half of the 4th century BC revealed a six-fold trepanation (Breitwieser 2003, 149–50, fig. 2). The majority of Celtic trepanations were performed by cutting or scraping, and it is generally assumed (though unproven) that the crown trepan was a Greek or Hellenistic introduction. Of the seven patients with drilled trepanations at Guntramsdorf and Katzelsdorf, two appear to have undergone surgery following cranial injury. Four seem to have survived their operations, but, as the survival rate for cutting and scraping trepanations was significantly higher, it may be that Celtic practitioners rejected the crown trepan in favour of safer traditional techniques (Künzl 1995a, 222–3).

Figure 59 Probable drill-bits. British Museum, London (left to right, Cat. nos 3.12 and 3.79)

Levers (elevators)

Levers in the British Museum collection: Cat. no. 3.80 (see also Sets of instruments, Cat. no. 3.19 and Hooks, Cat. no. 3.105)
The treatment of dislocated and fractured bones must have loomed large in the practice of ancient medical and surgical practitioners, and the bone lever is one of the commonest specialist components of surviving sets of surgical instruments. Tellingly, too, a bone lever was often included as one of the essential instruments in basic kits (see p. 24). For, in addition to straps and bandages and other parasurgical equipment made of organic materials, the reduction of compound fractures and the manipulation of dislocated bones required powerful robust levers (elevators) (see, e.g. Paul of Aegina 6.107.2; 6.107.1.23). The function and form of surgical levers corresponded to those used by stonemasons, so it is unsurprising to find a shared vocabulary – in the Hippocratic treatises *Fractures* and *Joints* the lever is often called *siderion* but alongside it, too, *mochlos*, the stonemason's lever, together with its diminutive *mochliskos* (Bliquez 2015, 202–4). In Roman times the term *anaboleus* was added, but it is likely that all three names were interchangeable. Galen noted that a small version of the mason's *mochliskos* was adapted for surgery. He also emphasised the need for the practitioner to have several levers to hand, varying in size and in the form of their operative ends (*Commentary on Hippocrates' Fractures* 18b.592K; Bliquez 2015, 203).

Perhaps because many early Greek and Hellenistic bone levers were made of iron, and were often borrowed or reused mason's tools (or were levers that hardly differed from those), the earliest surgical levers thus far identified are of Roman date: two examples of copper alloy from Haltern and from Kalkriese, Germany, both dated to the early years of the 1st century AD (Künzl 1996, 2451, 2584–5, fig. 1.5; Künzl 2002b, 30, figs 31–2). Other Roman bone levers include double-ended copper-alloy examples from Pompeii (1st century AD; Bliquez 1994, 131, nos 91–2), Colophon (1st/2nd century AD; Caton 1914, 115, pl. 10, 15), Wehringen (3rd century AD;

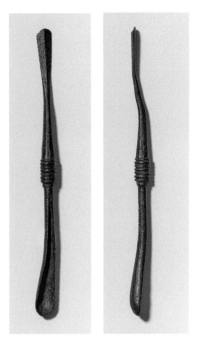

Figure 60 Iron combined bone lever and curette, front and side view. British Museum, London (Cat. no. 3.80)

Künzl 1983a, 120–1, fig. 96, 1; Nuber 2004) and ?Rome (Musei Vaticani inv. 6075); and double-ended iron examples from Luzzi (1st century AD; Guzzo 1974, 472–3, fig. 32, no. 99), Nea Paphos (2nd/3rd century AD; Michaelides 1984, 317, 320–1, fig. 1.15–16) and Rimini (3rd century AD; Jackson 2009b, 83, 88). All of these are identifiable because they were found in association with other more readily recognisable surgical instruments. But often Roman bone levers were distinctive purpose-made composite tools consisting of a copper-alloy centre grip with an iron lever mounted at each end in a socket of keyhole type, as used above all to secure scalpel blades to their handles (Jackson 2005a, 110–11, fig. 5.2.3). This type of bone lever is widespread and examples include those found at Pompeii (Bliquez 1994, 131, no. 93, 206, no. A19), Bingen (1st/early 2nd century AD; Künzl 1983a, 80, 82, fig. 56, 10–13 and 18), Allianoi (later 1st to 3rd century AD; Baykan 2012, 154, no. 335), Nea Paphos (Michaelides 1984, 317–20, 326–7, fig. 1.21–2), Aschersleben (2nd/3rd century AD; Künzl 1983a, 100–1, fig. 80, 4–5), Nijmegen (3rd century AD; Leemans 1842, pl. 2.19; Künzl 1983a, 93, no.19) and Rimini (Jackson 2009b, 82–4, 88, fig. 4.28–29, pls 1–2).

Whether of copper alloy, iron or a combination of the two, Roman bone levers are almost invariably double-ended, usually combining two levers. However, a fine iron example from London (1st/2nd century AD) (**Fig. 60**) (Cat. no. 3.80) combines a lever with a curette; one of the Rimini examples combines a lever with a blade (Jackson 2009b, 82, fig. 4.29); and several small slender levers, probably cranial elevators, are combined with a pointed-jawed spring forceps, as in the Aschersleben and Paris instrumentations and an example from the 2nd century AD fort at Lancaster (Künzl 1983a, 100–1, fig. 80, 2; Sorel 1984, 231, fig. 133c, top right; Jackson 2005a, 110–11, fig. 5.2.4; Jackson 2011a, 254–5, fig. 18c). All of these combinations are specifically appropriate to bone surgery.

Frequently, the inner concave face of the lever has, like its modern counterpart, a ridged surface to ensure a more

secure hold. Some of these were intended for the elevation of cranial bone, others used in place of forceps to extract teeth, but the larger examples were primarily for use in the reduction of fractured long bones. The Bingen instrumentation, so fully provided with instruments of bone surgery, included five levers, in accord with Galen's advice. Likewise, the Rimini practitioner, as in so many other realms of his surgery, and most notably in orthopaedics, was equipped with an even wider range of levers (**Fig. 54**, 30–2): there are four single-piece iron levers and five of the composite type with copper alloy grip and iron levers; all are double-ended, some are diminutive, others stout, two are included in a boxed kit of basic instruments, and the surviving lever ends include curved, angular, broad, narrow, tapered, splayed, crescentic and kite-shaped forms (Jackson 2009b, 82–4, 88, fig. 4.28–29, pls 1–2).

Curiously, Celsus did not name a bone lever. On one of the rare occasions when he made specific reference to the levering of bone he advised that a blacksmith's tongs would serve to provide the necessary leverage (*On Medicine* 8.10.7G). On two other occasions, the excision of diseased cranial bone and the elevation of depressed skull fragments, he advised use of an instrument he called *membranae custos* (*On Medicine* 8.3.8, 8.4.17). Precision was critical when the cerebral membranes were to be exposed during the removal of diseased or fractured cranial bone, so it is hardly surprising that a specialised instrument was recommended. Celsus called it 'a guard of the membrane (*membranae custos*) which the Greeks call *meningophylax*'. He continued:

> This consists of a plate of bronze, its end slightly concave, smooth on the outer side; this is so inserted that the smooth side is next the brain, and is gradually pushed in under the parts where the bone is being cut through by the chisel; and if it is knocked by the corner of the chisel it stops the chisel going further in; and so the surgeon goes on striking the chisel with the mallet more boldly and more safely, until the bone, having been divided all round, is lifted by the same plate, and can be removed without any injury to the brain. (Celsus, *On Medicine* 8.3.8–9, trans. Spencer 1938b, 500–3)

For treating depressed skull fracture he advocated the same approach:

> ... the plate which I suggested as a guard of this membrane is to be passed underneath in order that all pointed fragments which project inwards may be cut away over the plate, and any depressed bone is to be raised by means of the same plate. (Celsus, *On Medicine* 8.4.17, trans. Spencer 1938b, 515)

The use of three instruments, simultaneously, demonstrates that at least two medical personnel were involved in these operations, one manoeuvring the *meningophylax*, while the other divided the bone with mallet and chisel.

Evidently, the *meningophylax* was primarily a protector and treatment platform, not only in skull operations but wherever vital parts lay beneath the bone to be excised. Paul of Aegina, for example, described its use in conjunction with a chisel when dividing a fractured clavicle, and also to assist with the cutting out of a rib when operating to remove a weapon embedded in the chest (Paul 6.77, 6.93, 6.88). It would appear to have been a copper-alloy instrument with a plate-like terminal, which was sufficiently narrow, flat and smooth to insert easily and safely between the cranium and the dura mater as soon as a large enough opening had been made. The plate needed a very lightly convex outer face, so as not to injure the membrane, a flat inner face, upon which the cranial bone could be resected, and a handle, in order to raise the bone. A type of instrument with distinctive terminals which fits this description has been found with other tools of bone surgery in several Roman instrumentaria and may be the tool Celsus had in mind (Jackson 1986, 140–3; Bliquez 2015, 190–1). There is a fine example in the British Museum set from Italy, Cat. no. 3.19 (**Fig. 61**) (1st/2nd century AD; Jackson 1986, 124–5, fig. 2.16), one each in the grave groups from Bingen (1st/early 2nd century AD; Künzl 1983a, 82, fig. 56, 17) and Nea Paphos (2nd/3rd century AD; Michaelides 1984, 317–18, 327, fig. 1.20), and two in the assemblage from Rimini (3rd century AD; Jackson 2009b, 82, fig. 4.27). The unprovenanced Cat. no. 3.105, though broken at one end, is of the same type. Each is a copper-alloy Z-shaped double-ended blunt hook (*tuphlankistron/hamulus retusus*) with a very robust central grip. The terminals almost invariably comprise one kite-shaped and one leaf-shaped hooked plate to allow the practitioner to select that best suited to the specific circumstance.

A more slender version of this instrument combines a kite-shaped and leaf-shaped hook, or a blunt hook and a two-pronged blunt retractor, or a blunt hook and a sharp hook, and some have been found in association with lithotomy instruments (Jackson 2010, 396, fig. 2.6, 410–11). Thus, like so many Roman surgical instruments, these double hooks probably served several different roles, in orthopaedics, in lithotomy and in other surgical interventions, too. As Bliquez has observed, the instrument was the same but what it was called would have varied according to the specific use to which it was put – *meningophylax* or *tuphlankistron* (Bliquez 2015, 191). The link with cranial surgery of the stouter version is also supported by instruments found in a number of Celtic (La Tène C) grave groups of 3rd–2nd century BC date, in particular the finds from München-Obermenzing and Batina-Kisköszeg, both of which include an iron skull saw and an iron instrument closely resembling the form of the Roman double hooks identified as the *meningophylax* (De Navarro 1955, fig. 2.1, fig. 3e; Künzl 1991a; Künzl 1995a, 234–5, fig. 3.a–b, fig. 4.d–e).

Forceps
Forceps in the British Museum collection: Cat. nos 3.81–101 (see also Sets of instruments, Cat. nos 3.14–15, 3.41 and 3.43)

Spring forceps
Forceps, like scalpels, were one of the principal instruments of Greek and Roman surgery. The simplest, most widespread type, almost invariably included in even the most basic sets of instruments, was the spring forceps (*labis/volsella/myzon*). It was essentially a mechanical extension of an opposed thumb and index finger and, appropriately, was operated by those two digits. In his discussion of the many applications of the hand and fingers in surgery, Kirkup drew attention to the effective and continuing use of thumb and fingers as forceps and pincers (Kirkup 2006, 42–51). That

Figure 61 Double-ended blunt hook, probably used variously as a *meningophylax* and *tuphlankistron*, part of the set of Roman medical instruments from Italy. British Museum (Cat. no. 3.19)

use was longstanding, and is specifically attested in Roman surgery, for example by Celsus who advised use of the fingers and thumb as an alternative to forceps in the removal of a tooth or of an embedded arrowhead or slingshot, and by Paul for the removal of skull fragments (Celsus, *On Medicine* 7.12.1B, 7.5.2B-C, 7.5.4B; Paul 6.90.5; Jackson 1994a, 174–6; Bliquez 2015, 233). Inflammation and infection were constant hazards, which made any surgery a risky venture, and it may have proved advantageous to use fingers and thumb whenever possible to avoid even the slight tissue damage caused by forceps.

The development of the spring forceps arose from the need for a more accurate and rigid grip than could be achieved by finger and thumb or nail to nail contact. To provide the required combination of springy arms and strong, accurately opposed jaws a metal forceps was needed and, though iron was sometimes used, copper alloy was generally the metal of choice, as is the case with all of the British Museum examples (**Fig. 62**). The spring forceps, similar in form to modern dissecting forceps, was usually a single-ended instrument but was occasionally combined with a second spring forceps (Cat. no. 3.14) or another instrument (Cat. nos 3.41, 3.90–2). Two principal techniques were used in their manufacture (see p. 151), cutting a bar (Cat. nos 3.15, 3.41, 3.43, 3.84–7, 3.96–8) or bending a strip (Cat. nos 3.81–3, 3.88–9, 3.94–5). Finishing striations are sometimes visible on the inner face of the arms of the cut bar type (Cat. nos 3.84–5). The folded strip type is usually plain but the cut bar type sometimes has ornately moulded shoulders (Cat. nos 3.41 and 3.96) and generally has a decorative disc-and-baluster finial, some of which were enhanced with fine rings or spirals of silver inlay (Cat. nos 3.86 and 3.96). A sliding lock-ring was often provided on

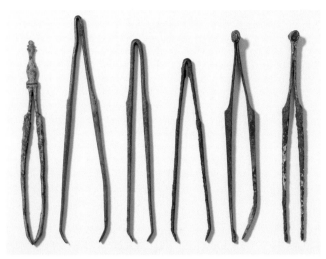

Figure 62 Smooth-jawed spring forceps. British Museum, London (left to right, Cat. nos 3.87, 3.81, 3.82, 3.83, 3.88, 3.89)

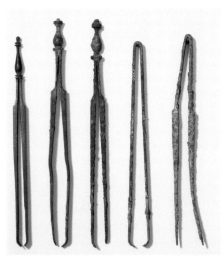

Figure 63 Smooth-jawed, toothed, and pointed-jawed spring forceps. British Museum, London (left to right, Cat. nos 3.84, 3.85, 3.86, 3.94, 3.95)

smooth-jawed and toothed fixation forceps so that the jaws could be clamped when a firm and prolonged grip was required (Cat. nos 3.14, 3.43, 3.86, 3.94, 3.99). As one of the basic instruments of surgery, spring forceps formed a part of a practitioner's portable kit and the presence of mineral-preserved wood and patches of iron corrosion on spring forceps Cat. no. 3.94 are suggestive of storage in a wooden box alongside iron-bladed scalpels.

Spring forceps were occasionally specified for particular surgical interventions, but the great majority of surviving examples were made with one of three principal jaw types – pointed-jawed, smooth-jawed and toothed – which, together, were expected to cover most eventualities (**Fig. 63**). Pointed-jawed forceps, like Cat. no. 3.15 and Cat. nos 3.95–6, have long slender arms tapered evenly in width and thickness to accurately aligned, thin, pointed jaws. The outer surface of the arms was carefully rounded and smoothed in order to avoid damage to adjacent skin and tissue when in use. Often, too, as on Cat. no. 3.95, there is fine ridging on the contact face of the jaws, like the serrated jaws of modern anatomical forceps, to maximise grip and minimise tissue damage. In addition to use as a splinter forceps this type must have had many other applications in delicate surgery, including skull surgery. It was probably the small forceps Celsus advised for removal of bone splinters in tooth extraction and nasal fracture (Celsus, *On Medicine* 7.12.1D, 8.5.5) and the narrow-bladed forceps specified by Paul, too, for removing bone splinters in fracture of the nose (Paul 6.91), and again in the extraction of foreign bodies from the ear (Paul 6.24).

Sometimes pointed-jawed forceps were combined with a second instrument as, for example, a pointed-jawed forceps with a needle-holder in the small kit from Milos (Künzl 1983a, 40–1, fig. 10.1). A distinctive double-ended type has a pointed-jawed forceps at one end and a small elevator at the other, both with ridged contact faces. That combination was particularly well suited to the elevation and retrieval of detached cranial fragments and splinters in skull surgery (Jackson 2005a, 114–15 and fig. 5.2,4) and, significantly, examples have been found in the 2nd/3rd-century AD surgical kit from Aschersleben, Germany and the extensive

3rd-century AD instrumentation from Paris, both of which included other instruments of bone surgery (Künzl 1983a, 100–1, fig. 80.2; Sorel 1984, 231, fig. 133c, top right). There is an example in one of the unprovenanced kits (Gods, Beasts and Men 1991) and further examples from the 2nd-century AD fort at Lancaster, England (Jackson 2011a, 254–5, fig. 18c), from Gauting, near Münich, Germany (Prähistorische Staatssammlung, München, inv. 1951.440) and from Asia Minor, two (Künzl 1985, pl. 60.2b; Perk 2012, 53, 4.1). A rarity is a composite instrument comprising a copper-alloy spring with pointed-jawed arms of iron secured in sockets of the keyhole type (Paris, Musée Nationale, St. Germain, inv. 35473).

The commonest spring forceps was smooth-jawed, usually with in-turned jaws, a type that was closely related to the tweezers that had for long been widely and commonly used in cosmetics and toiletry. Tweezers were small, usually about 5cm in length, and many of them, like other toiletry implements, had a looped terminal for suspension which was almost never present on medical instruments. Therefore, it is seldom hard to differentiate tweezers from forceps, which rarely measure less than 10cm (Jackson 2002a, 87–8, figs 1.1, 1.4 and 2.2; Eckardt and Crummy 2008). Nevertheless, as in other cases where craft tools or domestic implements were borrowed for medical or surgical use, if a spring forceps was not available and fingers would not suffice tweezers might be pressed into service. However, since they were not primarily designed for surgical use, and are not found in the surviving sets of medical instruments, tweezers have not been included in this catalogue.

Smooth-jawed spring forceps were variously named *volsella/labis/tricholabis* (Bliquez 2015, 234–5). With their long smooth flat arms, often provided with a sliding lock-ring, and in-turned, smooth, square-ended jaws, they were the general-purpose forceps for seizing and fixing, or drawing out, growths and foreign bodies. Specific uses included dissection and surgical epilation for in-growing eyelashes (trichiasis), a painful condition consequent on granular ophthalmia, and which, to judge from Greek and Roman medical writers, was particularly prevalent at that time (Celsus, *On Medicine* 7.7.8; Paul 6.13; Jackson 1996a, 2245–6).

Interestingly, and perhaps significantly, some of the earliest dated spring forceps, those from the Magdalensberg, are predominantly of folded strip type, all with smooth in-turned jaws, and dated *c.* AD 15–50 (Gostenčnik 2004, 426–7, pl. 16).

The British Museum smooth-jawed spring forceps (Cat. nos 3.14, 3.41, 3.81–93) comprise both cut bar and folded strip types. Of the examples from London two are combined with a ligula (Cat. nos 3.90–1) and one with an olivary probe (**Fig. 64**) (Cat. no. 3.92), like examples from Trier (Künzl 1984b, 163, pl. 10, D12–D14) and from *Aventicum* (Hirt 2000, 117, 123, pl. 3.21), while the example in the British Museum unprovenanced small set of instruments appears to have been combined with a curette (Cat. nos 3.41–2). All of these are logical and practical combinations which would have facilitated and speeded up a variety of operative procedures. That is also certainly the case with the double-ended spring forceps in the set of instruments from Italy, Cat. no. 3.14 (see **Figs 94, 170**). This had, within a central moulding, a joining iron component, now corroded and broken, that united a smooth-jawed forceps at one end with a toothed forceps with jaws angled to one side (coudée type) at the other. There is a near-identical smooth-jawed end from a double spring forceps of this type from Asia Minor (Künzl 2002a, 32, pl. 29, B33). The combination of toothed and smooth-jawed forceps was evidently considered useful, for exactly the same variety of double-ended forceps is encountered again in a small group of instruments from a burial found near Ohrid, North Macedonia (Künzl 1983a, 108–9, fig. 86.4); and in two examples in a group of instruments from Asia Minor, one of which twins a smooth-jawed and a pointed-jawed forceps, the other a toothed and a coudée-type toothed forceps, the ultimate provision – four varieties of forceps in two instruments (University History of Medicine Museum, Istanbul; Uzel 1995, 135–6, fig. 3; Künzl 2002b, 51, fig. 66). Almost as fully equipped was the user of the British Museum Italy set who, with two instruments (Cat. nos 3.14–15), could select one of three different spring forceps – pointed-jawed, smooth-jawed or toothed. Similarly well provisioned was the Rheims practitioner who had four smooth-jawed fixation forceps, including a rare form with blunt crescent-shaped jaws, and three toothed fixation forceps (Künzl 1996, 2622–3, fig. 26).

Toothed spring forceps, where named in the Classical medical literature, were often referred to as *myzon* (Greek *mudion*). However, the terms *labis/vulsella/myzon* were probably often interchangeable, with the specific surgical context indicating which type of forceps was to be selected (Jackson 1994a, 174–5; Bliquez 2015, 235–6). Widespread, though less numerous than the smooth-jawed variety, the toothed fixation forceps was a similarly versatile instrument with applications in general surgery and in particular operations and it is part of many of the surviving basic surgical kits. The long smooth flat arms, frequently provided with a sliding lock-ring, are often lightly flared at the operative end; and the jaws, similar to those of modern tissue forceps, have between three and six very finely cut and closely interlocking tiny triangular teeth per jaw. The British Museum examples comprise one of cut bar type (Cat. no. 3.43) and one of folded strip type (Cat. no. 3.94), each with

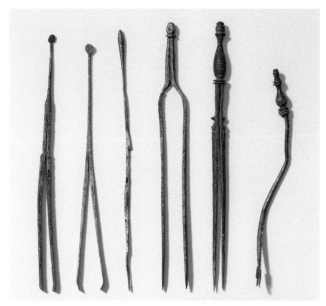

Figure 64 Smooth-jawed, pointed-jawed, and re-worked spring forceps. British Museum, London (left to right, Cat. nos 3.90, 3.91, 3.92, 3.93, 3.96, 3.97)

three into four teeth on their square-ended, in-turned jaws, and each provided with a sliding lock-ring. The fine interlocking teeth enabled an even firmer and more secure grip than the smooth-jawed fixation forceps. Consequently, in addition to dissection it was used, above all, to seize, fix and raise skin or tissue and wherever else traction was required (Bliquez 2015, 236–7). The double-ended spring forceps combining toothed and smooth-jawed varieties has already been discussed. Other combinations include a toothed forceps with a sharp hook from Cologne (Römisch-Germanisches Museum, Köln, inv. Lü 194) and a toothed forceps with a blunt hook from Asia Minor/Syria (Jackson 1995a, pl. 2, centre right).

The less common coudée-type variant of the toothed forceps has broader jaws turned to one side and tapered to a blunt point, with tiny, finely cut, triangular teeth along the jaw rims (Cat. nos 3.14 and 3.98). When fully interlocked the jaws enclosed an elongated hollow space which could be securely clamped by the sliding lock-ring that was frequently provided, as on Cat. no. 3.14. The hollow, finely toothed jaws were especially well adapted to seizing and making traction on small growths and tumours prior to excision as, for example, in the raising and excision of the surplus skin of the eyelid in trichiasis and the seizing for excision of anal condylomata (warty excrescences) (Paul 6.8; Celsus, *On Medicine* 7.30.2). But the forceps was probably used, too, for clamping blood vessels. In addition, the firm grip of its capacious jaws would have enabled the extraction of foreign bodies from organs or tissue as, for example, slingshot and bladder stones and, significantly, a coudée forceps from the Rome region is part of a lithotomy kit (Jackson and Leahy 1990, 272–3; Bliquez 2015, 236, fn. 665).

Coudée forceps have been found widely throughout the Roman Empire, with examples from Silchester (Jackson 2011a, 254–5, fig. 18d), Littleborough (Jackson and Leahy 1990), Paris (Sorel 1984, 231, fig. 133c, top row, centre), Trier (Künzl 1984b, 162, 212, pl. 8, D2), the Rhineland (Künzl 2002a, 24–5, pl. 15, A61), Vindonissa (Wiedemer 1962, 42–3,

Figure 65 Uvula forceps. British Museum, London (left to right, Cat. nos 3.101, 3.100)

fig. 19), Carnuntum (Swoboda 1953, pl. 19.2), Rimini (Jackson 2009b, 76, fig. 2.18), the Rome region (Jackson 1995a, pl. 4, centre; Künzl 1996, 2602–3, fig. XIV.5; Jackson 2010, 396, fig. 2.9), Herculaneum (Bliquez 1994, 172, no. 245), Italy (Cat. no. 3.14), Ohrid (Künzl 1983a, 108–9, fig. 86.4), Milos (Künzl 1983a, 40–1, fig. 10.2), Asia Minor (1) (Künzl 2002a, 32, pl. 29, B29), Asia Minor (2) (Uzel 1995, 135–6, fig. 3; Künzl 2002b, 51, fig. 66), Asia Minor (3) (Künzl 1985, pl. 60.2d), Asia Minor (4) (Perk 2012, 56, 4.3.1.1–3) and Cyrene (Jackson 2021, 546–9, fig. 3.3). Of those from dated contexts the chronological range is 1st to 3rd century AD. Many retain their sliding lock-ring. The forceps from the Rhineland is very long – 231mm – but the majority measure between 125 and 160mm in length, have a jaw length within the range 14 to 25mm and have between 10 and 23 teeth per jaw. Apart from the double-ended forceps from Ohrid and Italy all have a decorative baluster-moulded finial except for the forceps from Cyrene, Trier and Littleborough, which have an ornate hooked finial in the form of a stylised Aesculapian snake's head: in addition to a decorative/symbolic purpose (see p. 54) this may have functioned as a fingergrip or even as a blunt hook.

The example in the extensive instrumentation from Paris is part of a very full provision of spring forceps in the set – three pointed-jawed, one smooth-jawed, one toothed and two coudée forceps. The Rimini practitioner was even more fully equipped, with 19 spring forceps all carefully selected to form a graded series of jaw type and size (see **Fig. 36c**). In addition to smooth-jawed, toothed and coudée-type forceps they include four examples of a distinctive type of hollow-jawed toothed forceps, a fifth example of which, from Colchester, is in the British Museum collection (Cat. no.

3.99) (Jackson 2009b, 76, fig. 2.19; Jackson 1992, 179, pl. 2, 185, no. 20). This type has a decorative disc-and-baluster finial, very long flat arms, and large, capacious, hollow jaws, with a straight un-toothed side opposite a long, curved, in-turned, finely toothed rim. It extended still further the range of forceps from which the Rimini practitioner could select the instrument best suited to the task in hand. While the normal toothed forceps had a relatively narrow end grip, with 3–6 teeth per jaw, and the coudée-type forceps extended that to a broader end grip, with 10–23 teeth per jaw, the hollow-jawed type provided a long side grip as well as an end grip, with 22–29 teeth per jaw. The Rimini hollow-jawed toothed spring forceps measure between 175 and 215mm long, with a graded range of jaw size and shape, and all four have a sliding lock-ring for firm and/or prolonged clamping of the jaws, as does, too, the example from Colchester. The jaw form of the hollow-jawed spring forceps is similar to that of a unique and sophisticated plunger forceps, now in the Ashmolean Museum (**Fig. 9**; and see Appendix 2) (Jackson 1997b; Jackson 2007b, 17–19, figs 4–5; Jackson 2014a, 133–4, fig. 18.6).

The surgical applications of these hollow-jawed forceps likely overlapped those of the toothed and coudée forceps but, with the long arms and side gripping jaws, they might have enabled interventions beyond the reach and capabilities of other forceps, while the plunger forceps would have been able to operate in still deeper and more confined spaces. In addition, the size and form of the jaws correspond quite closely to those of the cross-legged uvula forceps and it seems probable that the hollow-jawed spring forceps was sometimes substituted for that instrument, even though the Rimini practitioner also had two uvula forceps at his disposal (Jackson 2009b, 76, fig. 2.20).

Cross-legged forceps

The British Museum collection includes two examples (Cat. nos 3.100–1) of the distinctive type of copper-alloy cross-legged forceps with hollow toothed jaws which has been identified as the uvula forceps (*staphylagra*) (**Fig. 65**) (Milne 1907, 97–100; Jackson 1992; Bliquez 2015, 243–5). The uvula (Latin *uva*, Greek *staphule*) is the small fleshy appendage which hangs from the free edge of the soft palate at the back of the mouth. Today it rarely requires surgery, but passages in Greek and Roman medical writers reveal that elongation of the uvula, following chronic or acute inflammation arising from a variety of causes, was quite prevalent and troublesome – choking was one of the consequences (Caelius Aurelianus, *On Acute Diseases* 3.1.6, 3.4.32; Galen 14.785K; Oribasius, *Medical Compilations* 24.10). If the uvula did not respond to treatment by cupping, purging or medication, a practitioner might need to resort to surgery. In the Hippocratic *Diseases* 2.29 and in Celsus' *On Medicine* 7.12.3 partial amputation of the uvula is described, but only recommended if the uvula was not in a severely inflamed state. Using a simple spring forceps, probably a pointed-jawed forceps, the uvula was to be seized and stretched before trimming away with a scalpel 'what is in excess of the natural length of the uvula'. But Aëtius (8.44.7–14) and Paul (6.31) described a purpose-made forceps, the uvula crusher (*staphylagra*), which was to be used in an intermediate step, to avoid the danger of haemorrhage, by clamping and strangling the neck of the uvula while its tip was twisted with the other forceps to render it completely lifeless prior to excision.

For those patients who would not tolerate the toothed jaws of the *staphylagra* a smooth-jawed version, the *staphylocaustes*, was to be used. The hollow jaws were filled with a caustic paste and clamped over the end of the uvula to remove it by cauterisation. Paul noted that the *staphylagra* was further employed in an operation on anal fistula, and that both types of uvula forceps were also used in the operation to remove haemorrhoids (Paul 6.78.2 and 6.79; Bliquez 2015, 243–7). In common with most other Roman medical instruments, uvula forceps doubtless had additional medical and surgical applications for which the combination of a powerful grip and capacious jaws was required, notably the extraction of missiles and other foreign bodies. The worn and damaged teeth of some examples of the uvula forceps and hollow-jawed forceps certainly accord better with such use than with uvulectomy.

Each of the British Museum uvula forceps has stylised pine-cone finials on their long, slender handles, flat elongated lozengiform arms, and a simple pivot. Their capacious hollow jaws enclose a sub-rectangular space, with tiny, precisely interlocking, triangular teeth set around the outer two edges, Cat. no. 3.100 with 24 teeth per jaw and Cat. no. 3.101 with 19. Their form corresponds closely to the requirements of the *staphylagra*, as does that of the other 27 known examples. Nineteen have a provenance demonstrating that the type was in use throughout the Roman Empire, from Britannia to Syria and Moesia to Numidia: examples have been found at Ancaster, Caerwent, Dorchester, Leicester, Trier, Sauchy-Lestrée, Augst, Avenches, Ostia, Rome, Tartûs, Cuicul/Djémila and Anatolia; and in the sets and assemblages of instruments from Cyrene, Paris, *Marcianopolis*, Rimini (2) and Allianoi (a single broken jaw made, exceptionally, of iron), in contexts which provide a date range of 1st–5th century AD (references and illustrations in Jackson 1992; also Jackson 2009b, 73–91, fig. 2.20; Baykan 2012, 145, no. 295, 205, fig. 16; Perk 2012, 54, 4.2; Vanwalscappel *et al.* 2015; and Jackson 2021, 547–9, fig. 3.4). The *staphylocaustes* is a much rarer instrument, and just four are so far known, one each in the dated medical contexts of the Rimini and *Marcianopolis* finds, one in the small group of instruments from Italy in the Bristol Museum and Art Gallery (Appendix 1) and an unprovenanced example in the Kunsthistorisches Museum, Vienna (Jackson 1992, fig. 5.24–5; Jackson 2009b, fig. 2.21).

The *staphylagra* type forceps is very constant, with the majority measuring 185–210mm long and, like other Greco-Roman instrumentation, mostly very finely crafted, with precisely interlocking teeth and a very smooth outer jaw surface. Decoration was restricted to the handles and their finials and comprises principally fine faceting and cut mouldings, but Cat. no. 3.100 has thin bands of inlay on its handles and finials (**Fig. 66**). Scientific analysis (see p. 155) revealed that the inlay consists of a copper base with minor amounts of gold, silver and arsenic and with an artificially induced black patina. This has been identified as the highly prized inlay Corinthian bronze (Craddock and Giumlia-

Figure 66 Detail of the handles of uvula forceps showing the six inlaid bands of Corinthian bronze. British Museum, London (Cat. no. 3.100)

Mair 1993; Giumlia-Mair and Craddock 1993, esp. 15, table 2, 27–9, 34–5, figs 16–17). Against the golden-coloured background of the gunmetal handles the black bands of inlay would have been both striking and recognisable. Indeed, the cost of the inlay may have repaid the practitioner who used the forceps by the confidence it perhaps gave the patient, who may have been impressed by a practitioner with expensive instrumentation. Just one other uvula forceps with black inlaid bands on its handles is known (**Fig. 67a–b**), another unprovenanced example, 'formerly in a German private collection' and now in the R.D. Milns Museum at the University of Queensland, Brisbane (Charles Ede Limited: Catalogue 186, July 2013, no. 40).

A much stouter cross-legged forceps, with ornate robust handles and powerful jaws, usually of copper alloy but occasionally of iron, has been recognised as the *ostagra*, a sequestrum forceps, which was recommended for the removal of detached or partially detached cranial fragments. It was evidently capable of many other functions too, including the clamping of blood vessels and the removal of embedded projectiles. Two principal varieties have been identified, one with straight, the other with curved jaws, in both cases with elongated close-fitting gripping faces, usually with accurately cut ridging to ensure the firmest possible grip. Examples of the copper-alloy curved-jawed type include those found at Pompeii (1st century AD), Luzzi (1st century AD) and Rimini (3rd century AD), while the straight-jawed variety is known in copper alloy from Colophon (1st/2nd century AD), Rimini, and Potaissa/ Turda, Romania, and, in iron, from Luzzi and from Carnuntum (Künzl and Weber 1991, 107, figs 20–2, pls 36, 38b; Bliquez 1994, 171, no. 242, pls 5, 13, 20; Jackson 2009b, fig. 3.24–25, pl. 2). A particularly ingenious copper alloy example from Rome combines both jaw types in one instrument by means of a loose-hinge assembly (Jackson 2005b, 114, fig. 5.8.3; Jackson 2007b, 18–23, figs 8–9). There is no ancient *ostagra* in the British Museum collection, but the

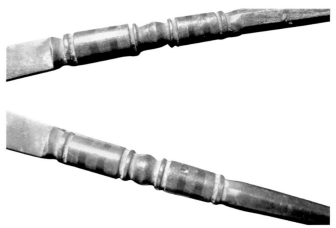

Figure 67a–b Provenance unknown, uvula forceps with bands of black inlay on the handles. Brisbane, University of Queensland, RD Milns Antiquities Museum, inv. no. 13.021. Photos: Ralph Jackson

type is represented by a Naples Foundry copy (Cat. no. 3.153) of the famous example from Pompeii.

Another stout, cross-legged forceps, invariably of iron, has been identified as the *odontagra*, sometimes referred to as *rhizagra*, a forceps designed specifically for dental use (Künzl and Weber 1991, 107–9; Jackson 1994a, 175–6, 209, fig. 6.1; Dude 2005; Bliquez 2015, 239–41). The powerful bowed jaws, usually offset, and with in-turned, often notched, tips, were precisely adapted to the extraction of teeth (e.g. Celsus, *On Medicine* 7.12.1; Paul 6.28); but they were equally well applied to the grasping and repositioning of fractured bones and the removal of arrowheads or slingshot. Examples are widespread, and include those in medical contexts from Kallion (late 3rd century AD), St. Privat d'Allier (late 3rd century AD), Wederath (late 1st/2nd century AD), Merida (late 2nd/early 3rd century AD), Luzzi (late 1st century AD), Rimini (see **Fig. 36d**, 23) (mid-3rd century AD), Gadara (mid-4th

Figure 68 Pompeii, Casa di Sirico, fresco panel showing Iapyx treating the wounded Aeneas, a scene from the *Aeneid*. Naples, Museo Archeologico Nazionale, inv. no. 9009. Photo © Adam Eastland/Alamy Stock Photo

century AD), and Asia Minor/Syria (late 4th/early 5th century AD) (Künzl 1983a, 40–2, fig. 11.1, 57–8, fig. 26.4–5, 71–3, fig. 45, fig. 46.1, 102, 106–7, fig. 85.10; Künzl and Weber 1991, 87–9, fig. 4; Jackson 1995a, pl. 2, bottom right); and as site finds from Autun, Vindonissa and Saalburg-Kastell (Künzl and Weber 1991, 107–9, pl. 37a-c, pl. 38a) and from the fort site of Porto Quintela, Ourense in north-west Spain (Vega Avelaira 2017, 226, no. 3, figs 8–9). The occurrence of some in small basic kits has led to the suggestion that those were used by practitioners who specialised in dentistry. Dentistry was evidently one of the medical realms in which the Rimini practitioner operated, for, as in other areas of surgical instrumentation, he was especially fully equipped, with seven *odontagrae* of graded size and jaw form (Jackson 2003, 319–20, fig. 4; Jackson 2009b, 77, fig. 3.23, and 80–1).

The chronology of surviving dental forceps from dated contexts is wide, ranging from the 1st to the 5th century AD. However, a reference to the *odontagra* in a Hippocratic treatise (*Physician* 9P), together with the survival of an iron cross-legged forceps (though sadly lacking its jaws) in the 4th-century BC Pydna grave group (see **Fig. 8**) (Chrysostomou 2002, fig. 4; Tsigarida 2011, 14), and the probable depiction of one on the reverse of a 4th-century BC bronze coin from Atrax in Thessaly (Cat. no. 6.27) indicate that the type originated in the Hippocratic era, if not earlier. Another depiction, the famous 'wounded Aeneas' fresco panel from the Casa di Sirico, Pompeii (VII, 1,25 and 47), illustrating an episode from Vergil's *Aeneid* (12.391–422), almost certainly shows the use of an *odontagra* (or an iron *ostagra*) (**Fig. 68**). For the instrument involved is clearly a cross-legged forceps with bowed and in-turned jaws and the fact that it is silver-coloured and not gold-coloured indicates that it was intended to show an iron, not a bronze, forceps. Here, then, is the accompaniment to the surviving texts and instruments, a rare scene of surgery in action showing the doctor/patient experience as Iapyx, mythical surgeon, favourite of Apollo, endeavours to extract the arrowhead embedded in Aeneas' thigh, while the hero stands stoically, under the protection of Venus (Künzl 2002b, 62, fig. 84; Bliquez 2015, 241).

With their shared plier-like construction, robust handles and powerful jaws, the *ostagra* and the *odontagra/rhizagra* were similar in their overall form (Jackson 1994a, fig 6.1–3), and for some applications they were probably interchangeable (Bliquez 2015, 241). That is certainly indicated by references in Paul, on the removal of an arrowhead from the chest and on the extraction of fractured cranial bone (6.88 and 6.90), and in Paul and Soranus, on the removal of cranial fragments in embryotomy (6.74; *Gynaecology* 4.63), where both types of forceps are specified on an either/or basis. Such an overlap was probably very necessary, for they were substantial and probably quite costly instruments and, excepting the Rimini practitioner, even a well-equipped surgeon may not have possessed both types. Thus, like the great majority of Greek and Roman surgical instruments, the bone and tooth forceps were adapted to several different uses – very few instruments were restricted to a single function.

Hooks (retractors)

Hooks in the British Museum collection: Cat. nos 3.102–5 (see also Sets of instruments, Cat. nos 3.16–19 and 3.44; and forceps adapted as triple hook?, Cat. no. 3.97)

By the time of Celsus the sharp hook – Latin *hamus/hamulus/hamulus acutus*, Greek *ankistron* – had become indispensable in ancient surgery and, as an essential component of basic surgical kits, it has been found widely throughout the Roman Empire, from Spain to Asia Minor and from Britain to Cyrenaica (**Fig. 69**) (Künzl 1983a, 19; Jackson 1994a, 172–4; 1995a, 198–9, table 2; Bliquez 2015, 173–7). One of the earliest examples is a broken sharp hook from the Magdalensberg found in a context pre-dating 20 BC (Gostenčnik 2004, 374–5, fig. 5.4, 398–9, pl. 2.3). The sharp hook's principal function was to retract and fix the margins of wounds and incisions or underlying tissue and structure, as, for example, in the exposure of varicose veins (Celsus, *On Medicine* 7.31.2; Oribasius, *Medical Compilations* 45.18.13; Paul of Aegina 6.82.1) and in the treatment of inguinal hernia:

> … in a case which is suitable for treatment by the knife, as soon as the incision made in the groin reaches the middle tunic, this must be seized near the margins by a couple of hooks (*duobus hamulis*), when, after drawing down all the fine membranes the surgeon sets it free. (Celsus, *On Medicine* 7.20.4, trans. Spencer 1938b, 410–11)

Often several sharp hooks were required, as in the operation for varicose veins and the retraction and opening of the prepuce in the operation for phimosis (Paul of Aegina 6.55.1), a requirement reflected in the numbers of sharp hooks found in some sets of instruments, for example three in the British Museum set from Italy (Cat. nos 3.16–18), three in the set from Colophon (Caton 1914, 117, pl. 10.16–18) and six in the Bingen instrumentation (Künzl 1983a, 83, fig. 57.15–18). Sharp hooks additionally served to seize and raise for excision small structures or tissue, as, for example, in the operations for tonsillectomy, pterygium (surgery in the angle of the eye) and contraction of the vulva (Celsus, *On Medicine* 7.12.2, 7.7.4B, 7.28.2; Paul of Aegina 6.30, 6.72.1), as well as in another delicate eye operation:

> Sometimes, when the pterygium has not been quite cut away or from some other cause, a small tumour, called by the Greeks encanthis, forms at the angle and this does not allow the eyelids to be completely drawn down. It should be caught up with a hook (*hamulo*) and cut round, but with so delicate a touch that nothing is cut away from the angle itself. (Celsus, *On Medicine* 7.7.5, trans. Spencer 1938b, 332–3)

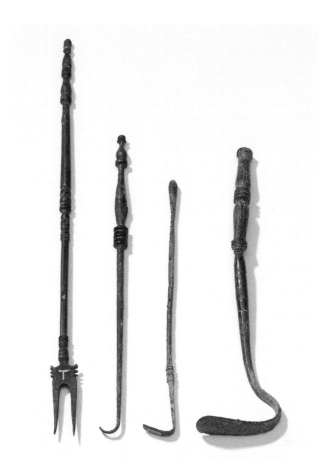

Figure 69 Sharp and blunt hooks. British Museum, London (left to right, Cat. nos 3.103, 3.102, 3.104, 3.105)

Sharp hooks were also used as haemostats, to arrest bleeding by seizing and twisting a severed blood vessel (e.g. Oribasius, *Medical Compilations* 50.47.4; Majno 1975, 403–5, fig. 10.6.2. For further applications of the sharp hook, see Bliquez 2015, 174–6).

A combined sharp and blunt hook in the idiosyncratic Stanway instrumentation is of iron (Jackson 2007a, 239–40, fig. 122, CF47.30), but other surviving sharp hooks are invariably of copper alloy. They occur in a range of sizes corresponding to the different degrees of delicacy of treatment, but all are slender-stemmed and most have a length within the range 110–170mm. To avoid tissue damage and inflammation the tapered tip was worked to a smooth and very fine, evenly curved point. At the other end the slender stem was usually decorated with finely cut facets and mouldings which terminated in a knobbed finial, as on Cat. nos 3.16–17, 3.44 and 3.102–3. These enhanced the appearance of the instrument but also provided the operator with a secure grip. The cut mouldings were often supplemented with inlaid bands, as on Cat. no. 3.44 (silver flanked by copper) and Cat. no. 3.102 (Corinthian bronze flanked by silver). The handle of an unprovenanced example in Solingen is inlaid with a spiral of silver (Deutsches Klingenmuseum inv. 74.B25), while, exceptionally, even the tips of the pair of ornate silver-inlaid sharp hooks in the set of instruments from Cologne, Luxemburgerstrasse cemetery, were made of silver (Künzl 1983a, 89–90, fig. 68.5; and Römisch-Germanisches Museum, Köln, inv. 1076: Jackson 1986, 140).

For a wider more secure retraction, sharp hooks sometimes terminated in a pair of tips, like Cat. no. 3.103, which is closely paralleled by an example in the lithotomy kit from the Rome region (Jackson 2010, fig. 2.5); and one in the group of instruments from the 'Maison de Bacchus' at Cuicul/Djémila, Algeria; and there are further, ornate, bifurcated sharp hooks in the Colophon instrumentation (Caton 1914, 115, pl. 10.16), in the group of instruments from Italy in the Bristol Museum and Art Gallery (Appendix 1) and in one of the unprovenanced kits (Gods, Beasts and Men 1991). Occasionally, too, sharp hooks were double-ended instruments, like an example from Cologne paired with a toothed spring forceps (Römisch-Germanisches Museum, Köln, inv. Lü 194), one from London paired with a socketed needle (Jackson 2008, fig. 4.4.1.4), one in the Nijmegen kit paired with a bifurcated blunt hook (Künzl 1983a, 93–4, fig. 75.12; Braadbaart 1994, inv. no. NHa 12) and one from the River Tiber at Rome with a sharp hook at each end (Museo Nazionale Romano inv. 7551). There is logic to all of these combinations, but the most common pairing was a sharp hook with a blunt hook.

The less commonly found blunt hook – Latin *hamulus retusus*, Greek *tuphlankistron* – was used for operations in which sensitive retraction was involved and puncturing was to be avoided, above all in the raising of blood vessels, either to isolate them or as a preliminary to excision. For such interventions slender-stemmed double-ended instruments combining sharp and blunt hooks were an obviously useful combination. They were especially well suited, for example, to the operation to excise varicose veins, in which several of both types of hook were required:

> The skin is ... incised over the vein, and the margins held apart by hooks (*hamulo*); with a scalpel the vein is separated from surrounding tissue, avoiding a cut into the vein itself; underneath the vein is passed a blunt hook (*retusus hamulus*); the same procedure is repeated ... throughout the course of the vein which is easily traced by pulling on the hook. When the same thing has been done wherever there are swellings, at one place the vein is drawn forward by the hook and cut away; then where the next hook is, the vein is drawn forward and again cut away. (Celsus, *On Medicine* 7.31.2–3, trans. Spencer 1938b, 467–9)

The size and form of the blunt hook of two near-identical combined sharp and blunt hooks in the large instrumentation from Ephesus (Künzl 2002a, 17, pl. 2.A7, . A8) appear particularly well suited to this type of surgery. So, too, does the slender swan's-neck blunt hook on the combined sharp and blunt hook in the group of instruments from Italy in the Bristol Museum and Art Gallery (Appendix 1), an instrument that is closely paralleled by one in the Cyrene kit (see **Fig. 26**, 6) (Jackson 2021, 547–8, fig. 4.5) and two from Rome (Museo Nazionale Romano inv. 65830–1). The Rome instruments also include four slender, double-ended, swan's-neck blunt hooks (Museo Nazionale Romano inv. 65832–5) as well as a much more robust double-ended blunt hook of distinctive elongated Z-shape with stout central grip (Museo Nazionale Romano inv. 65836), of the same type as Cat. nos 3.19 and 3.105. Cat. no. 3.105 preserves only one end, with a kite-shaped hook but, as we have seen, Cat. no. 3.19 and the other robust Z-shaped double-ended blunt hooks (*tuphlankistron/hamulus retusus*), which may be examples of Celsus' *meningophylax* (see Levers,

p. 56), almost invariably combine a kite-shaped and a leaf-shaped hooked terminal. Some are more gracile than others and usually combine a leaf- or kite-shaped hook with a sharp hook. Between them the two varieties of Z-shaped double-ended hooks probably fulfilled many roles in addition to those in bone surgery and lithotomy, being variously used as a lever, a guard and a blunt retractor. Again, one of the earliest examples, a broken grip with a kite-shaped terminal, comes from the Magdalensberg and pre-dates AD 50 (Gostenčnik 2004, 370, 374–5, fig. 5.5, 398–9, pl. 2.4).

Hooks were essentially simple instruments and if a purpose-made sharp or blunt hook was not available a practitioner could fairly easily adapt another instrument. That appears to have happened in the case of Cat. no. 3.104, formerly a scoop probe, converted to use as a blunt hook by truncating, flattening and bending the scoop. Similarly, a sharp hook in the large set from Ephesus comprises a reworked stylus (Künzl 2002a, 17, pl. 2.A9), while Cat. no. 3.97, formerly a spring forceps of sawn bar type, appears to have been reworked as a triple hook.

Needles
Needles in the British Museum collection: Cat. nos 3.106–7 (see also Sets of instruments, Cat. nos 3.20–1 and 3.45)
Needles – Latin *acus*, Greek *belone* – were an integral part of the surgical instrumentation of antiquity, as is clear from their frequent mention in medical texts (for a full treatment of the literary testimonia see Bliquez 2015, 149–52). Most would have been tiny, very slender instruments and, like their domestic counterparts, the majority would have been made of iron. Thus, very few survivors have been identified partly because most have corroded away and partly because they were named, in the texts but rarely described. Celsus, for example, used the unadorned word *acus*, with no further description, to denote needles of at least five different varieties, so their form has to be visualised from their given usage (Jackson 1994a, 176–7, 200, table 4).

Eyed needles included a domestic type for stitching the end of a bandage (Celsus, *On Medicine* 5.26.24B) as well as surgical needles for suturing (5.26.23D, 7.7.8, 7.9.4, 7.16.4–5), for carrying a ligature (7.7.11, 7.14.5, 7.17.1B, 7.21.1B, 7.30.3B–C) and for passing a thread (7.7.4B, 7.25.3). Correspondingly, eyed copper-alloy needles, undifferentiated from the domestic type, have been found in several surgical contexts, including those in the 1st-century AD set from Morlungo, and the 3rd-century AD sets from Nijmegen and Kallion (Künzl 1983a, 105, fig. 84, 94, fig. 75.9, 42, fig. 11.10; Bonomi 1984; Pardon-Labonnelie 2014, 107–11). Until recently, however, no example of a suture or ligature needle was known, but now a unique survival in the set of instruments from Cyrene has been identified. What had appeared from a photograph to be a damaged copper-alloy sharp hook turned out on examination to be a complete instrument with an intact operative end comprising a double curved and eyed sharp hook terminal (see **Fig. 26**, 7) (Jackson 2021, 547–9, fig. 4.7). It is a close analogue to a pre-modern ligature needle and another for stitching the palate (Windler 1912, 165, no. 2896e and 164, no. 2890d-e) and may also be compared to needles for hernia, bladder, perineum and tonsil (Thackray *c.* 1955, G869, U1251, M1685, T2058). It is evidently a suture or ligature needle, perhaps the instrument Galen specified – an eyed hook or a curved needle – to position a thread under an intercostal nerve (*Anatomical Procedures* 2.668K; Bliquez 2015, 177). The Cyrene instrument may always have been a rare and specialised needle, for much of the stitching of wounds and incisions must have been done with small purpose-made surgical needles of iron or, *in extremis*, with the thinnest of household needles. However, it is also a reminder to be cautious when interpreting broken instruments: if the operative tip of the Cyrene needle had been missing it would have been impossible to differentiate it from a pointed probe or a sharp hook.

Un-eyed needles with a fine point were used for dissection and cauterisation (Celsus, *On Medicine* 7.7.8B, 7.7.10, 7.8.3) as well as for perforating pustules (5.28.4D), puncturing skin and haemorrhoids (5.28.19C, 6.18.9C), raising the skin of the eyelid (7.7.8F) and transfixing small tumours on the eyeball (7.7.12). Needle cauteries were used for delicate surgery on the eyes and ears (7.7.8B, 7.7.10, 7.8.3), and that used in the treatment of trichiasis was specified as of iron (7.7.8B). These un-eyed needles probably equate with the handled and socketed-holder varieties identified in archaeological contexts. For, although most needles have not survived, a number of distinctive varieties have been identified (Jackson 1994a, 176–7, 206, fig. 3.1–4). As we have seen (pp. 29–30) an iron needle point may well have been the missing component once fixed into the socket of a distinctive type of cylindrical or hexagonal copper-alloy handle, as in the large set of instruments from Rheims (Künzl 1985, 467–8, pl. 62.1–2; Künzl 1996, 2614–15, fig. 20).

An even more distinctive type of handled needle, often found in surgical kits, comprises a slender copper-alloy grip with a thin tubular socket at one or both ends (Künzl and Feugère 2002, 120–3, type D), into which, to judge by the corroded residues often found in the sockets, an iron component was soldered, almost certainly a needle in view of the diminutive size of the sockets. In fact, an example from Pompeii provides more certain evidence, for the corroded iron needle is preserved, bent back against the exterior of the socket (Bliquez 1994, 53–4, 165–6, no. 227). The British Museum set from Italy includes a double-ended example, Cat. no. 3.20. With one straight and one angled socket it would have enabled many of the interventions listed above and its central multiple ring moulding provided a secure grip for whichever end was in use. The effectiveness of this type of needle is indicated by its chronological span (early 1st to late 3rd century AD, at least), its wide distribution, and its prevalence: there are additional examples with one straight and one angled socket in the sets from Colophon (Caton 1914, 117, pl. 11.28) and Bingen (Künzl 1983a, 83, fig. 57.20), from Pompeii – nine examples (Bliquez 1994, 164–6, nos 222–4 and 226–9; Jackson 1994c, 202, no. A2 and 206, no. A18) and from Allianoi (Baykan 2012, 137, no. 263, 204, pl. 14); examples with two straight sockets from Pompeii (Bliquez 1994, 164–5, no. 221), from the Magdalensberg (Gostenčnik 2004, 373–4, fig. 5.3, 398–9, pl. 2.2), in the Savaria grave group (Künzl 1983a, 117–18, fig. 92.5) and in the set from Nijmegen (Künzl 1983a, 93–4, fig. 75.13); with a straight socket and a sharp hook from Pompeii (Bliquez 1994, 166, no. 230) and from Rome (Museo Nazionale

Figure 70 Socketed needle-holders. British Museum, London (left to right, Cat. nos 3.106, 3.107)

Romano); with an angled socket and a sharp hook from London (Jackson 2008, fig. 4.4.1.4), from Rimini (inv. 184537), and in the set from Kyzikos (Heres 1992; Bliquez 2015, 274–5, fig. 83, bottom left); with an angled socket and a pointed probe from Pompeii (Bliquez 1994, 165, no. 225); with a straight socket and a pointed probe from Pompeii (Jackson 1994c, 203–4, no. A9 and 213–14, no. A51), and with an angled socket and a pointed-jawed forceps in the Milos set (Künzl 1983a, 40–1, fig. 10.1) and in the set from *Viminiacum* (Kirova 2002, fig 12.6; Künzl 2018, 26–7, fig. 9.6; Pardon-Labonnelie *et al.* 2020, fig. 1).

Cat. nos 3.106 and 3.107 (**Fig. 70**) are a rare single-ended variant of this type of handled needle, with a straight socket at one end and at the other a leaf-shaped terminal with a tiny spherical knob at its tip like that on scalpel handle Cat. no. 3.76 (see p. 40). They are closely paralleled by two socketed handles in the large unprovenanced set in the Ashmolean Museum (acc. nos 1990.23–24; Jackson 1995a, pl. 2, top right; Jackson forthcoming). Another example of this variant, from Rochester, Kent (Jackson 2011a, 256–7, fig. 19d) is a product of the workshop making instruments with the distinctive richly ornamented silver-inlaid symmetrical linear design of rosettes, double peltas and pellets (Büsing-Kolbe 2001, Type B) already discussed in relation to scalpel handles (see p. 43).

The user of the Nijmegen instrumentation was particularly well provisioned with needles. In addition to the double straight-socketed needle-holder the set included, almost uniquely preserved, a bundle of five slender iron needles (their precise form sadly no longer recognisable), a domestic eyed copper-alloy needle, and a very slender simple

Figure 71 Cataract needle and double-ended needle-holder, part of the set of Roman medical instruments from Italy. British Museum, London (left to right, Cat. nos 3.21, 3.20)

double-ended copper-alloy needle or double-pointed probe (Leemans 1842, pl. 2.9–10, 2.13, 2.18; Künzl 1983a, 93–4, fig. 75.13, 75.9–10; Jackson 2018a, 142–4, fig. 8A-C). Cat. no. 3.45 in the British Museum small kit of instruments is a similarly simple, though finely wrought, slender needle or pointed probe, with an olivary terminal at the other end. Excepting the applications requiring a needle with an eye it could have been used for many different interventions even including, since it has an olivary terminal, the operation to couch cataract.

The couching of cataracts is not mentioned in the Hippocratic Corpus, but by the 3rd century BC Greek practitioners were performing the operation, and by the time of Galen, and probably before, there were practitioners who specialised in cataract alone (Longrigg 1988, 464–6; Marganne 2001). There are two very full descriptions of the operation, together with its preliminaries and post-operative care, one an extensive account by Paul of Aegina, who drew on Galen, and the other, equally extensive, and the earliest surviving account, by Celsus (Paul 6.21; Celsus, *On Medicine* 7.7.14; Bliquez 2015, 152–3; Leffler *et al.* 2016.). Extracting the passages relating to the instrumentation, Celsus says:

> Thereupon a needle (*acus*) is to be taken pointed enough to penetrate, yet not too fine; and this is to be inserted straight through the two outer tunics at a spot intermediate between the pupil of the eye and the angle adjacent to the temple, away from the middle of the cataract, in such a way that no vein is wounded. The needle should not be, however, entered timidly ... When the spot is reached, the needle is to be sloped against

the suffusion itself and should gently rotate there and little by little guide it below the region of the pupil. (Celsus, *On Medicine* 7.7.14D–E, trans. Spencer 1938b, 350–1)

Paul says:

> ... then mark with the olivary end of the couching needle (*parakenterion*) the place to be perforated ... Bringing round the pointed end of the perforator which is round at the tip we push it firmly through ... Then raising the needle to the apex of the cataract (the bronze of it is plainly visible through the transparent part of the cornea) we depress the cataract to the underlying parts. (Paul 6.21.2, trans. Milne 1907, 70)

Pooling the information from both writers it would appear that the cataract needle was a double-ended bronze instrument with an olivary terminal at one end and a slender, round-pointed needle at the other. While Cat. no. 3.45 answers that description quite well, another distinctive type of needle, a single-piece copper-alloy instrument with a round-pointed tip, a slender, often decorated, stem and an olivary terminal, has been convincingly identified as the needle principally designed for couching cataract (Künzl 1983a, 26–7; Feugère *et al.* 1985, 436–68; Künzl and Feugère 2002, 119–23, type B). Cat. no. 3.21 (**Fig. 71**), a single-piece needle of brass in the British Museum set from Italy, is now one of around 20 known examples of this type, which is widely distributed around the Roman Empire and has a minimum date range, like the needle-holders, of 1st–3rd century AD. There are four from Pompeii, including one in the 'Grande Palestra' kit and one in the Casa del Medico Nuovo (II) instrumentation (Künzl 1983a, 12–15, fig. 4; Bliquez 1994, 164–5, no. 220; Jackson 1994c, 203–4, no. A10 and 209, no. A35), three in the extraordinary find from the bed of the River Saône at Montbellet (see **Fig. 28**) (Feugère *et al.* 1985, 439–47, pl. 53.1–2 and 4), one from the find in the River Maas at Maaseik (Heymans 1979, 97, fig. 2.5; Künzl 1985, 448, 451, fig. 8A.5), one in the set from *Viminiacum* (Korać 1986, pl. 4.9; Pardon-Labonnelie *et al.* 2020, fig. 2), one in the set from Milos (Künzl 1983a, 40–1, fig. 10.4), one in the set from Kallion (Künzl 1983a, 42, fig. 11.9), one in the Ephesus set (Künzl 1983a, 45–7, fig. 15.10), one from the villa site at Piddington, England (Jackson 2011a, 256–7, fig. 19e), one from Termes, Spain (Künzl 1985, 453–4, pl. 59.3), one from Rome (Museo Nazionale Romano, inv. 65806) and one from Asia Minor (Künzl 1985, pl. 60.2a). Broken examples are difficult to distinguish from broken scoop probes and a fragmentary implement identified as a cataract needle from the Brading Roman villa, Isle of Wight, is, in fact, a broken scoop probe (Summerton 2007, 39–40, fig. 27).

The couching – breaking up – of the lens with the tip of the cataract needle was a delicate, audacious operation, the only ancient surgery within the eyeball, but one with a reasonable chance of success and it remained popular up to recent times (Jackson 1988, 121–3; Jackson 1996a, 2248–50). However, as already seen, it should not be assumed that cataract couching was done exclusively with this type of needle or that the instrument identified as the cataract needle was restricted to that one operation – it would have been suitable for many other surgical applications, like most of the instruments practitioners included in their surgical kits.

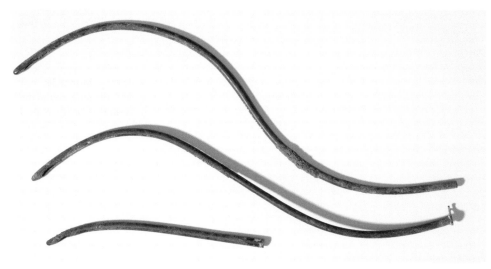

Figure 72 Catheters, two male and one female, part of the set of Roman medical instruments from Italy. British Museum, London (top to bottom Cat. nos 3.23, 3.22, 3.24)

Catheters

Catheters in the British Museum collection: see Sets of instruments, Cat. nos 3.22–4 and Varia, Cat. no. 3.154

One instrument that had a very specific and quite restricted use was the catheter (Greek, *auliskos/katheter*, Latin, *fistula aenea*), a slender curved tube developed for catheterisation of the urinary tract (**Fig. 72**). Catheters are among the most readily identifiable of ancient surgical instruments because their form is closely similar to their pre-modern and modern counterparts. They were designed to reach the bladder via the urethra in order to treat a number of urinary disorders and diseases, principally the retention of urine, a painful condition which Celsus attributed to stricture, blockage and inflammation of the urethra (*On Medicine* 7.26.1A). Appropriately, his description of catheters and their usage is included in the brief account of urinary complaints which precedes his long discussion of lithotomy, the operation to remove a bladder stone (*On Medicine* 7.26.1A–B, 7.26.2–7.27). For stricture often occurred as a result of vesical calculus (stone in the urinary bladder), which was particularly prevalent in boys and young men (Künzl 1983b; Jackson 2010). But female patients were also treated for urinary dysfunctions, as in Soranus' instructions for the easing of one of the causes of a difficult labour:

> If the excreta have been kept back, one should get rid of the faeces by introducing an enema of water mixed with oil or hydromel [honey-water], while the urine should be removed by means of the catheter if the bladder is full of urine. If a wedged-in stone is the cause, one must push the stone with the catheter out of the neck of the bladder and drive it back into the cavity. (Soranus, *Gynaecology* 4.7.8, trans. Temkin 1956, 186)

Rufus of Ephesus, too, advised use of the catheter as a bladder sound to dislodge a calculus impacted in the urethra or at the neck of the bladder: 'Those that are stuck fast push back with the catheter if you prefer not to do lithotomy' (Rufus, *On Diseases of the Kidneys and Bladder* 12.3.1–2; Milne 1907, 145). Lithotomy was always a hazardous operation, to be avoided wherever possible, and many other medical writers recommended the same procedure (Bliquez 2015, 222, fn. 600).

In another role – to irrigate the bladder in cases of ulceration, abscess and inflammation – the catheter was used as a clyster by attaching to the proximal end a pouch filled with water or medication, which could be squeezed to instil the liquid when the tip of the catheter had reached the neck of the bladder: 'But since we have often occasion to wash an ulcerated bladder ... we may fix a skin or the bladder of an ox to the catheter, and throw in the injection through its opening' (Paul of Aegina 6.59, trans. Adams 1846, 351).

But the primary role of the catheter seems to have been in the treatment for retention of urine, as succinctly described by the early 2nd-century AD author known as Pseudo-Galen:

> When urine is not passed on account of excessive dilation of the bladder so that it cannot contract, we draw off the urine with a catheter. Therefore an instrument like the Roman letter S is let down into the bladder by the urethra. (Ps. Galen, *Introduction or Physician* 14.787K, trans. Milne 1907, 143)

The differing position and configuration of the male and female urinary tract and bladder was known and accordingly two different instruments were made. Thus Aëtius (11.5.83) and Paul of Aegina (6.59.1) specified catheters suited to the sex of a patient, but also to their age (Bliquez 2015, 221), while Celsus gave a more detailed instruction:

> For this purpose bronze tubes (*aeneae fistulae*) are made, and the surgeon must have three ready for males and two for females, in order that they may be suitable for every body, large and small: those for males should be the longest, 15 finger-breadths (*digiti*) in length, the medium 12, the shortest nine; for females, the longer nine, the shorter six. They ought to be a little curved, but more so for men, and they should be very smooth and neither too large nor too small'. (Celsus, *On Medicine* 7.26.1A–B, trans. Spencer 1938b, 424–5)

The earliest discovery of a Greco-Roman catheter, probably at Herculaneum, was made in the mid-18th century, the male catheter now in Naples Museum (Bliquez 1994, 14–24, 168–9, no. 235, pls 4 and 7), a copy of which is in the British Museum collection (Cat. no. 3.154). Celsus' specification of bronze tubes finds confirmation in the Herculaneum catheter and in the other surviving examples, all of which were made from copper-alloy sheet, and specifically bronze sheet in the case of Cat. nos 3.22–4, the three catheters in the British Museum set from Italy (see pp. 152–3 and **Figs 171**, **183**). The seam where the sheet edges were butted together is remarkably close-fitting, hardly visible to the naked eye, and represents a very high order of craftsmanship. The slightly spiral line of the seam observed on some male catheters may have been a deliberate feature, perhaps intended to increase the tensile strength of the instrument. In all other respects the catheter changed hardly at all from the 1st to the 20th century (see e.g. Windler 1912, 488). The surviving Greco-Roman instruments conform to the differing anatomy, and are in accord with the written descriptions, the male catheter long and S-shaped, the female catheter shorter and J-shaped. Like other instruments which were required to be inserted into natural body cavities, considerable care was taken in their manufacture to ensure the smoothest possible contact surface. Both male and female instruments were provided with an elongated oval eye a short distance back from the lower end to ensure a completely smooth tip, and to prevent any blockage of the eye occurring before the neck of the bladder was reached. The solid tip itself was tapered, round-ended and immaculately smooth, like the rest of the instrument, and, in common with many sounds, in particular the most slender ones used for especially sensitive probing, the handle region was also completely smooth, enabling great delicacy of touch. A variety of lubricants may have been pressed into service, but the most usual would have been olive oil, and Paul (6.59.1) noted that the catheter was to be immersed in oil before insertion into the urethra.

Of particular interest in the context of the catheters in the British Museum is the need for a surgeon to have a graded set of catheters, a stipulation, as we have seen, that is implicit in Aëtius and Paul but explicit in Celsus. It would appear that the single female and two male catheters (Cat. nos 3.22–4) in the instrumentarium from Italy formed such a set, although less comprehensive than the set of five recommended by Celsus. There is certainly a difference, both in degree of curvature and overall length, as well as a slight difference in gauge, between the two male catheters, so that they complement rather than duplicate each other; and, as Celsus reveals, there was seen to be less of a need for variation in the size of female catheters. Indeed, as recently as the 18th century a single size was regarded as sufficient for all female patients (Bennion 1979, 78). These finely designed, versatile instruments are very standard and tend to confirm the ancient descriptions. They have survived in only small numbers partly, no doubt, because they were specialised and probably quite costly instruments, but also because when broken if the operative end with its distinctive eyed tip is lacking they cannot easily be differentiated from other thin tubular copper-alloy implements, like the broken barrel of split-nib pens (e.g. a fragment from Allianoi: Baykan 2012, 134, no. 251).

Of the 12 catheters listed in 1986 (Jackson 1986, 150, table 3) one may now be discounted, the 'female catheter' from Pompeii/Herculaneum cited by Milne, which is a simple un-diagnostic tube (Milne 1907, 145, pl. 45.2; Bliquez 2015, 223, fn. 606). Additionally, it has not been possible to locate the instruments themselves, or images, of the two fragmentary examples from Baden and the fragment from Rome, all of which, therefore, remain uncertain (Milne 1907, 144–5; Tabanelli 1958, 143; Jackson 1986, table 3.10–12). To the remaining eight catheters a further six may now be added to bring the total of certain survivors to 14 – 11

male and three female. It is still the case that the one female (L. 144mm) and two male catheters (L. 303mm; 280mm) in the 1st/2nd-century AD Italy instrumentarium, Cat. nos 3.22–4, comprise the most complete surviving set, followed by the smaller set of two male catheters (L. 322mm; 165mm) in the 1st/2nd-century AD Colophon instrumentation (Caton 1914, 116, pl. 11.20–1). The important later 1st–3rd-century AD medical assemblage from Allianoi includes three catheters – two male (L. 181mm; 149mm – broken), one female (L. 106mm) – though not in direct association (Baykan 2012, 134, nos 252–4, 202, pls 10–11), while the site collection from Carnuntum includes a male (L. 223mm) and a female catheter (L. 144mm) (Krug 1992b, 155–6, nos 7–8), and a broken male catheter of uncertain provenance may be part of the assemblage from the Magdalensberg (Gostenčnik 2004, 374–6, fig. 5.6, 398–9, pl. 2.6). Although there is a published photo of the male catheter (L. 153mm), part of a supposed grave group said to be from Ephesus (Meyer-Steineg 1912, 43, pl. 7.1), it has been established that the instrument is no longer extant and now exists only in the form of a copy (Künzl 1991b, 533, no. 32, pl. 46.32). The fine male catheter (L. 272mm) in Naples Museum, not from Pompeii's House of the Surgeon, as once thought, but probably from Herculaneum (Bliquez 1994, 55–7, 168–9, no. 235), is still one of the earliest dated examples (pre-AD 79), the others being a fragmentary male catheter found in a Flavian context at Silchester (Insula IX, SF 3404 – Crummy in Fulford, in prep. I am most grateful to Nina Crummy for supplying details in advance of publication), and the male catheter (L. 290mm) found in a Tiberian context (AD 14–37) in the excavations at Neuss (Simpson 1977, fig. 1.11), and therefore coeval with the text of Celsus' *On Medicine*. However, an example in an earlier context may yet be discovered, for catheters were evidently in use in the Hellenistic era, when Erasistratus of Iulis was credited with the development (or more probably a refinement) of the male catheter, and they are attested still earlier in the *Hippocratic Corpus* (*Diseases* 1.6P; Bliquez 2015, 221). At the other end of the chronological spectrum, Late Antiquity, the time of Aëtius and Paul, their use is recorded by John of Ephesus, writing in the late 560s AD, who related the story of a patient reliant upon a metal catheter for many years (*Lives of the Eastern Saints* 38 – I thank Vivian Nutton for this reference).

The male catheters vary in length from 153mm to 322mm, but most lie within the range 272mm–303mm; one of the female catheters measures 106mm, the other two 144mm. All of these measurements are broadly in accord with Celsus' recommended scale of sizes – 15 *digiti* = 278mm; 12 *digiti* = 222mm; 9 *digiti* = 167mm; 6 *digiti* = 111mm. Corrosion inhibits an accurate measurement of the diameter of several of the catheters, but where measurable there is a range of 3–6mm, though most have a diameter of about 5mm, equivalent to Nos 8 and 9 on the pre-modern English Catheter Gauge (Windler 1912, 482; Thackray c. 1955, U194). Only two of the male catheters are substantially different: the smaller of the two catheters from Colophon is both short and slender and may have been intended for boy patients, while the instrument from Ephesus, though similar in gauge to the other male catheters, is extremely short, an idiosyncrasy harder to explain. A small bracket is soldered to the upper end of male catheter Cat. no. 3.22 and similar brackets were probably once fastened to the male and female catheters Cat. nos 3.23 and 3.24, to judge from the remains of solder at their upper end. There is a simpler flange at the upper end of one of the male catheters from Colophon and one from Allianoi. The purpose of the brackets and flanges was probably to facilitate manipulation of the catheter and to more readily enable a pouch to be attached when it was to be used as a clyster.

Other tubes

Other tubes in the British Museum collection: see Varia, Cat. nos 3.156–7

Catheters were one type of tubular instrument but a number of other types were widely used in ancient medicine and surgery. A slender copper-alloy tube with a flanged disc at its mouth in the Paris instrumentation (Sorel 1984, 229, fig. 133b, far right) and a similar, but broken, example in the Rimini assemblage (inv. 184419) were probably insufflators for blowing powdered medication into the nose or throat. But most tubes, like catheters, were used to extract fluids from, or introduce them into, the body (Jackson 1994a, 184–7, 207, fig. 4; Bliquez 2015, 207–33). Simple tubes of lead, copper alloy or bone would serve many of the procedures described in medical texts from the *Hippocratic Corpus* onwards (Bliquez 2015, 45–8), as for example the small tube used in the Hippocratic treatment of empyema to drain pus from the pleural cavity (*Diseases* 2.47P; Majno 1975, 156–8, fig. 4.14) or the lead tube which Celsus advocated both in the treatment of a fistula consequent on lithotomy, and in the treatment of an occluded vagina (*On Medicine* 7.27.8, 7.28.2). In the former case the function of the tube was to ease closure of the fistula; in the latter it was to promote healing of the incision and prevent adhesion. Tubes were also used as guards to protect surrounding organs and tissue when applying a heated cautery, as in the treatment of haemorrhoids and nasal polyp (Bliquez 2015, 167). Such tubes would be hard to identify as medical instruments unless found in a sealed context with other distinctive medical instruments. Even then the specific use, or more probably uses, would be difficult to determine, as is the case with two simple tapered copper-alloy tubes from the House of the Surgeon at Pompeii (Bliquez 1994, 55–7, 80, 167–8, nos 233–4).

Much more secure is the identity of the tube described by Celsus in his account of the procedure to drain water from patients with dropsy. After piercing the abdomen and peritoneum with a scalpel:

> ... a lead or bronze tube should be inserted, either with lips curved back at its outer end, or with a collar round the middle so that the whole of it cannot slip inside. The part of the tube within the abdominal cavity should be a little longer than the part outside, in order that it may project inwards beyond the deeper membrane. Through this tube the humour is let out .... (Celsus, *On Medicine* 7.15.2, trans. Spencer 1938b, 382–5)

The presence of a flanged mouth, and a collar on the shaft, together with the instruction that rather more than half of the tube should be inserted into the abdomen, has allowed the identification of the instrument as a cannula. With the additional comment from Paul of Aegina (6.50), in his account of dropsy, that the operative end of the tube

should have an opening like that of split-nib pens, it has also permitted the recognition of the instrument itself. Two copper-alloy examples, probably from Herculaneum – one of which is represented by a Naples Foundry copy in the British Museum collection, Cat. no. 3.156 (see **Fig. 168**) – correspond closely to the ancient descriptions (Milne 1907, 112–13, pl. 39.2–3; Bliquez 1994, 169, nos 236–7; Bliquez and Oleson 1994, 98–100, 115, fig. 12; Jackson 1994a, 184, fig. 4.1–2; Bliquez 2015, 224–6, fig. 60); and a slightly simpler version has been identified in the Allianoi assemblage (Baykan 2012, 135, no. 256, 203, pl. 12). A slender pipe with a hollow reservoir tube, part of the Nea Paphos instrumentation, has been identified as probably a syringe, originally provided with a wooden plunger, for instilling or withdrawing fluids, perhaps the *puoulkos* – pus extractor – described by Heron of Alexandria in the 1st century AD (Michaelides 1984, 318, no. 20, 327–8, fig. 2.7, pl. 74.1; Bliquez and Oleson 1994, 95–6, 114, fig. 11; Bliquez 2015, 217–19).

Drainage was a principal function of many tubes but just as frequent was the administration of enemas – the doctor whose first and constant recourse was to bleed and purge his patients was a stock character of Greek and Roman satirists. Whether an anal or a vaginal/uterine injection was involved, both the procedure and the apparatus were termed *kluster* (Bliquez 2015, 208). Since the clyster comprised simply a short slender tube fastened to a bladder or pouch containing the liquid to be instilled it has proved an elusive instrument to identify. However, two finely made examples of bronze, with carefully rounded tip and funnel-like mouth, were found with a cupping vessel and medicine box in a 5th-century BC grave (Tomb 457) at Ialysos, Rhodes (Verbanck-Piérard 1998, 205–6, I. 10–12; Stampolidis and Tassoulas 2014, 308–9, no. 186). A small, slender, tapered, copper-alloy tube with an expanded dished mouth in the large set said to be from Asia Minor or Syria in the Ashmolean Museum may well have been a clyster, as also, perhaps, in the same set, a still finer, but broken, example of bone (acc. no. 1990.11 and 1990.9; Jackson 1995a, 196–202, tables 1–2, pl. 2, centre left; Jackson 1994a, 186, 207, fig. 4.5; Jackson forthcoming). It is likely, too, that the Allianoi cannula also served as a clyster (Baykan 2012, 203, pl. 13.2).

More certainty attaches to the identification of two instruments from Pompeii as uterine clysters. One can be securely associated with other gynaecological instruments in one of the most notable medical sites at Pompeii, the Casa del Medico Nuovo (II), while the other was probably part of the medical assemblage in the Casa del Medico Nuovo (I) (Bliquez 1994, 54–7, 82, 84–5, 167, nos 231–2; Majno 1975, fig. 4.16, centre). The second example is represented in the British Museum collection by another of the Naples Foundry copies, Cat. no. 3.157 (see **Fig. 169**). Their form corresponds closely to that of the clyster described in medical texts from the *Hippocratic Corpus* up to the time of Paul of Aegina – a tube with tapered tip and multiple perforations along the sides. From the time of Soranus (mid-2nd century AD) it was named *metrenchutes* and used to instil medications for the treatment of a wide range of female conditions, including uterine haemorrhage swelling and prolapse, irregular and excessive menstruation, and hysterical suffocation (Bliquez 2015, 211–12).

Figure 73 Trivalve vaginal dilator (*dioptra*), from Asia Minor, probably 1st/2nd century AD. Leibniz-Zentrum für Archäologie, Mainz, inv. no. 0.38171. Photo © Leibniz-Zentrum für Archäologie/S. Steidl

Dilators (specula)

Dilators in the British Museum collection: see Sets of instruments, Cat. no. 3.25.

By the Roman Imperial period, if not before, some medical practitioners – but probably not many – had at their disposal expanding specula: bivalve and trivalve copper-alloy dilators, designed to give access to treat disorders of the anus, rectum and vagina. The trivalve dilators, used to dilate the vagina for internal examination and for treatment of gynaecological disorders, are among the most striking of all ancient medical instruments, not least because they are one of the earliest tools to incorporate a screw mechanism (**Fig. 73**) (Krause 1995, 41–5). They are complex, composite, technically advanced instruments. By turning a handled worm, which passes through a screw-bearing, the three valves of the projecting *lotos/priapiscus* – smooth on the outside, prismatic on the inside – could be parted for dilation, at the same time as the side handles folded out to allow the operator to hold the instrument steady. Soranus was one of the first medical writers to mention the uterine speculum (*dioptra*), recommending it as a safe means of determining the affected part in cases of uterine haemorrhage (*Gynaecology* 3.40). There are particularly instructive accounts, too, of its use in the operation for abscess of the womb (Aëtius 16.89.1–18; Paul of Aegina 6.73; for other gynaecological treatments involving the *dioptra* see Bliquez 2015, 255).

Surviving uterine specula have been found in contexts dated from the 1st to the 5th century AD. There are three fragments – from Augst, *Marcianopolis* and Varna (Riha 1986, 89, 176, pl. 61, no. 679; Kirova 2002, 80–4, 87, fig. 8.1; Künzl 1983a, 112) – and nine complete examples, three of which are from Pompeii – from the Casa del Medico A. Pumponius Magonianus, from the Casa del Medico Nuovo

(II) and, the so far unique quadrivalve dilator, from the Casa del Medico Nuovo (I) (Bliquez 1994, 62–6, 183–9, nos 291–3; Deppert-Lippitz *et al.* 1995, 43, fig. 25, 183–5, G3,1–3; Bliquez 2015, 253–4). There are single trivalve dilators from Rome (probably) (Reggiani 1988, 460–1, fig. 11), from Dion (Pantermalis 1997; Bouzakis *et al.* 2008), from Merida (Künzl 1983a, 102–3, fig. 81; Deppert-Lippitz *et al.* 1995, 42, fig. 23, 181–2, G2; Krug 2011, 554, fig. 10), from Asia Minor (Deppert-Lippitz *et al.* 1995, 41, fig. 22, 180, G1; Künzl 2002a, 31–2, pls 22–28, B 28) and from Lebanon (Longfield-Jones 1986, which on pages 84–8 includes a discussion of the results of scientific analysis by the British Museum (Scientific Research File 4264)), and one in the Lambros Collection in Athens, of unknown provenance (but possibly a copy) (Milne 1907, 152, pl. 48; Meyer-Steineg and Sudhoff 1921, 75, fig. 48; Deppert-Lippitz *et al.* 1995, 185, G4; Stampolidis and Tassoulas 2014, 307, no. 184).

The smaller and simpler bivalve dilator may have originated as early as the 5th century BC, for in the Hippocratic treatises on fistulas and haemorrhoids there are references to an 'instrument for viewing', a *katopter* (*Fistulas* 3.331; *Haemorrhoids* 5). However, no information on the appearance of the instrument was given, and no surviving speculum of the Hippocratic era has yet been identified. All other references to a rectal speculum belong to the Roman Imperial period, as do all the surviving identifiable bivalve dilators, so it is uncertain whether, or how closely, the Greek instrument resembled the Roman one. Though incapable of proof one way or the other, the instrument depicted on the 4th-century BC bronze coin from Atrax, Thessaly, Cat. no. 6.27, may in fact have been intended to show a bivalve dilator rather than a dental forceps.

Like the trivalve speculum, the bivalve dilator was a diagnostic rather than an operative instrument, designed to hold apart the walls of a cavity. For its principal use in the operations for fistula and haemorrhoids it required a smooth projecting expandable prong (*priapiscus*) and handles with the strength and leverage necessary to dilate the strong sphincter muscles of the anus and rectum. Accordingly, most of the surviving bivalve dilators are sturdy instruments, with a length in the range 139–184mm, and a *priapiscus* length in the range 62–95mm, like the cast bronze example in the British Museum set from Italy, Cat. no. 3.25 (**Figs 74, 172**). Its two long plain handles pivot on a strong hinge beyond which they are angled outwards to terminate in powerful jaws. Each jaw has a projecting blunt blade, with flat inner face and convex exterior, which dilate when the handles are compressed. In the closed position the blades form a smooth, tapered prong, the *priapiscus*. Some examples have a slight swelling at the distal end of the *priapiscus*, a feature which may have been intended to discourage the instrument from slipping out when in use. The hinge pivots on a stout central rivet, braced by a pair of disc washers and positioned close to the blades. Both the *priapiscus* and the handles have a very carefully finished smooth surface, in common with that of catheters and clysters and other instruments designed for use in the natural body cavities.

Galen (19.110K) called the *katopter* an 'instrument for widening the passage of the anus' (*hedrodiastoleus*), and it was recommended primarily to enable the treatment of anal and rectal disorders. Thus, in the 1st–2nd century AD, the celebrated surgeons Heliodorus, Antyllus and Leonides of Alexandria were all credited with using it in the operation for anal fistula (Oribasius, *Medical Compilations* 44.20.66; Paul of Aegina 6.78; Bliquez 2015, 249–50). Also known as *mikron dioptrion* (small speculum), on occasion it was probably also used in place of the larger trivalve speculum, as was the equivalent instrument in post-Renaissance Europe (Jackson 1991, 105). It may have been considered more appropriate for some women or girls, at least for examination if not for more lengthy treatment. It is interesting to note, therefore, that a bivalve dilator from the Casa del Medico Nuovo (II), Pompeii, is part of an instrumentarium that also includes a trivalve uterine speculum and other gynaecological instruments (Bliquez 1994, 190–1, no. 294; Bliquez 2015, 250–1). A further ten Roman bivalve dilators are known: two unprovenanced examples (Bliquez 1982, 216–17, no. 41, fig. 8; Deutsches Klingenmuseum, Solingen, inv. 74.B24), and single examples from Herculaneum (probably) (Bliquez 1994, 190–1, no. 295), from the River Tiber at Rome (Reggiani 1988, 460–1, fig. 10), from Italy (Cat. no. 3.25), from Italy (probably) (Künzl 1979/81, 52–4, pl. 3.5), from Vechten, The Netherlands (Braadbaart 1994, 164, 170, pl. 1.1), from Sarmizegetusa (Micia), Romania (Deva, Muzeul Judetean Hunedoara, inv. 2762), from Valeria, Spain (Fuentes Dominguez 1987, 255, fig. 4, 1 and 5), and from *Marcianopolis* (Kirova 2002, 78–81, fig. 5.3). Like the uterine specula, the surviving rectal specula have a date range of 1st–5th century AD.

As with so many ancient medical and surgical instruments, bivalve dilators could be adapted to a number of different interventions. It is possible that the very small example from *Marcianopolis*, which is only 102mm long, with a *priapiscus* length of just 17mm, was intended for use as a nasal dilator instead of, or in addition to, rectal dilation. Probably, too, some of the bivalve dilators were also used to dilate wound cavities. In particular, it would appear to be the instrument Celsus recommended for the extraction of an embedded arrowhead. His detailed description includes the sentence 'When a passage out has been laid open the flesh ought to be stretched apart by an instrument like a Greek letter …' (*On Medicine* 7.5.2). Unfortunately the figure of the Greek letter is not preserved in the manuscripts, but the restoration of an upper case *upsilon* would provide a letter-image – Y – virtually identical to the Roman bivalve dilator in its fully open position (**Fig. 74**) (Jackson 1991, 105–8). The advantages of using a hinged dilator for certain types of wound are clear: by dilating the entry wound, dissection and exploratory probing could be minimised, the situation could be assessed, the method of removal decided upon, and the extraction effected, all in a comparatively controlled manner. An added benefit would be that the practitioner could dilate the wound with one hand while extracting the weapon with a forceps held in the other hand. As a military surgeon could not always rely on the presence of medically skilled assistants, an instrument that enabled self-sufficiency would be highly desirable. In fact, the bivalve dilator from Vechten may well have been used in this way. Vechten lies close to the mouth of the River Rhine, and was the site of an early Roman fort, *Fectio*, which was used in 12 BC by Drusus in his waterborne attack on the Chauci and, a few years

Figure 74 Bivalve rectal dilator, in fully dilated position. British Museum, London (Cat. no. 3.25)

later, by Germanicus prior to his defeat by Arminius (Wells 1972, 101–16). In that context it seems reasonable to suppose that the Vechten dilator was used in the treatment of weapon wounds as well as for rectal and anal disorders.

Copies
Uterine and rectal specula were part of the range of Naples Foundry copies. There are none in the British Museum, but in the London Science Museum's Wellcome Collection there is a copy (A75897) of the trivalve dilator from the Casa del Medico A. Pumponius Magonianus, Pompeii; six copies (A67433, A75899, A129733, A646073, A646075, A646755) of the quadrivalve dilator from the Casa del Medico Nuovo (II), Pompeii; and two copies (A624705, A645719) of a bivalve dilator, almost certainly the example, probably from Italy, in Worms Museum, of which there is also a copy in the Römisch-Germanischen Zentralmuseum, Mainz (LEIZA) (inv. 12270). (Other museums with copies are noted in Longfield-Jones 1986, 81–2, fn. 5).

Probes
Selected probes in the British Museum collection:
Dipyrenes: Cat. nos 3.108–9 (see also Sets of instruments, Cat. no. 3.26)
Selected ear probes: Cat. no. 3.110 (see also Sets of instruments, Cat. nos 3.28 and 3.46)
Selected scoop probes: Cat. nos 3.111–13 (see also Sets of instruments, Cat. nos 3.29–30)
Selected spatula probes: Cat. nos 3.114–21 (see also Sets of instruments, Cat. nos 3.31–3)
Selected ligulae (see also Sets of instruments, Cat. no. 3.27) (**Fig. 75**)
As a supplement to the use of fingers, probes would have formed part of the instrumentation used in surgery and medicine from earliest times. Most were probably made of perishable organic materials, especially wood or bone. The few examples identified in Egyptian, Mesopotamian, Mycenaean and Celtic contexts are generally simple slender rods of copper alloy which differ little from those later in use in the Classical world (Kirkup 2006, 163–73; Sternitzke 2012; Arnott 1997; Künzl 1995a).

At a time when much internal anatomy was ill-understood, surgical probes (Greek *mele*, Latin *specillum*) had

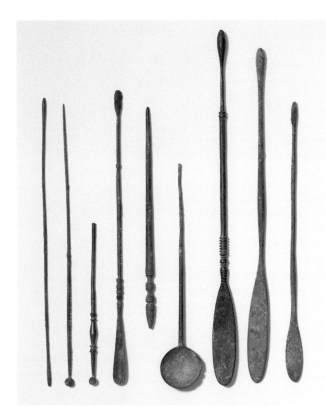

Figure 75 Probes in the set of Roman medical instruments from Italy. British Museum, London (left to right, dipyrene, ligula, ear probe, scoop probes, spoon, spatula probes – Cat. nos 3.26, 3.27, 3.28, 3.29, 3.30, 3.35, 3.31, 3.32, 3.33)

an enduring and important role for Greek and Roman practitioners, as underlined by the fact that they are more frequently mentioned in medical texts and more frequently found in medical sets than any other instrument. They were widely used multi-purpose implements which usually combined two functional ends. However, few types of probe were restricted to surgery or medicine and, as most varieties were also to be found in common domestic use in the extraction and application of unguents and cosmetics, individual examples cannot be regarded as surgical instruments unless found in a secure context with other distinctive surgical equipment.

The principal surgical use of probes was in the exploratory sounding, in advance of surgery, of wounds, injuries, incisions, fistulae and diseased or fractured bone. These were manipulations in which the surgeon's tactile sense needed to be highly developed, as is evident, for example, from Celsus' account of the probing of fistulae, in which subtle gradations were to be detected in order to indicate what stage the disease had reached:

> ... pass a probe (*specillum*) into the fistula, that we may learn both its direction and depth, and at the same time whether it is moist or rather dry.... we can also learn whether the fistula has reached and penetrated the bone or not, and how far the damage has gone. For if what is touched by the end of the probe is soft, the disease is still limited to the flesh; if it meets with more resistance, the fistula has reached the bone. But when the probe slides smoothly, there is not yet decay; if it does not so slide, but meets with an even surface, there is some decay although still slight; if what underlies is uneven also and rough, the bone has become more seriously eaten away. (Celsus, *On Medicine* 5.28.12C–E, trans. Spencer 1938a, 151–3)

Probes also had many other surgical and medical uses, from the elevation of cartilage in a broken nose, to use as a bougie for the urethra in an operation on the glans penis, and from use as a director for a scalpel in treating a fistula, to the application of medication to the eyeball and to many other parts of the body (Celsus, *On Medicine* 8.5.1, 6.18.4, 5.28.12L, 6.6.11; Jackson 1994a, 180–2; Bliquez 2015, 108–39). In consequence, sets of instruments almost invariably include one or more bronze examples of a range of probes (and originally may well have included other non-metallic probes). Often they were contained in tubular bronze boxes, as in the small kit in a late 1st-century AD cremation burial at Morlungo, Italy (Künzl 1983a, 105, fig. 84; Bonomi 1984; Pardon-Labonnelie 2014, 107–11), sometimes together with needles and other slender instruments, as in some of the Pompeii finds (Bliquez 1994, 194–5, nos 304 and 306, 202–4, figs 211–12, pl. 18). The inclusion of probes in the following sets provides them with an assured surgical, medical or pharmaceutical use.

The mid-1st-century AD kit from Stanway includes a scoop probe (Jackson 2007a, 243–4, fig. 124, CF47.37). The 1st-century AD kit found near the amphitheatre at Pompeii includes a spatula probe, a scoop probe, two ear probes and two broken probes (Künzl 1983a, 12–15, fig.3). The 1st-century AD kit from Luzzi includes a *dipyrene*, a scoop probe and two ligulae (Guzzo 1974, 469–75; Künzl 1983a, 106–7, fig. 85.5, 7, 8, 9). The late 1st/early 2nd-century AD set from Colophon includes a *dipyrene*, a spatula probe and a ligula (Caton 1914, 117, pl. 11.25, 29, 26). The British Museum 1st/2nd-century set from Italy includes a *dipyrene*, an ear probe, two scoop probes, three spatula probes and a ligula (Jackson 1986, 128–9, fig. 4.27–31, 33–5; Cat. nos 3.26–33). The late 2nd/early 3rd-century AD grave group from La Favorite, Lyon includes an ear probe, a scoop probe and a spatula probe contained in a tubular probe case (Boyer *et al.* 1990, 229–33, fig. 25) The mid-2nd/early 3rd-century AD Nea Paphos set includes a *dipyrene*, a scoop probe, a spatula probe, a ligula and a simple probe (Michaelides 1984, 324–6, fig. 1.7–13). The mid-3rd-century AD tomb group from Cologne, Richard-Wagner-Strasse includes an ear probe, a scoop probe and a spatula probe contained in a tubular probe case (Euskirchen 2018, 313–14, nos 13–15). The 3rd-century AD set probably from Ephesus includes a *dipyrene*, a spatula probe, three ear probes and three ligulae (Künzl 2002a, 12–20, pl. 2, A11, pls. 6–7, A30–A36). The 4th/early 5th-century AD set in the Ashmolean Museum said to be from Asia Minor or Syria includes a scoop probe, two spatula probes and two styloid probes (Jackson 1995a, pl. 2; Jackson forthcoming). Particularly significant are the sets from Pompeii and Nea Paphos, each of which incorporated a tubular probe case containing a selection of six probes (Bliquez 1994, 87–8, pl. 23b; Stampolidis and Tassoulas 2014, 316–7, no. 195) – examples of spatula probe, scoop probe, ear probe, ligula and *dipyrene*. Like the probes in the Italy set (Cat. nos 3.26–33), they were evidently carefully selected to cover all eventualities.

The *dipyrene* (*dipurenon*, 'double olive') is one of the slenderest exploratory probes. Like the British Museum examples in the Italy set and from London (Cat. nos 3.26 and 3.108–9) it is a double-ended instrument with an extremely thin flexible stem and a tiny olivary expansion (*puren*) at each terminal. It was probably the type Celsus intended for probing fistulae and it appears also to have been the instrument Paul advocated for the same purpose : 'We first examine them ..... with a double-headed *specillum* of a very flexible nature, such as those made of tin, and the smallest of those made of copper' (Paul 6.77.2, trans. Adams 1846, 396). Its diminutive size also made it an appropriate instrument to cauterise the root of eyelashes removed to treat trichiasis (Paul 6.13). In addition to the *dipyrenes* in the sets listed above there are examples from Allianoi (Baykan 2012, 135, nos 257–8), from Asia Minor (Künzl 2002a, 36, pl. 35, B92–4), from London (Cat. nos 3.108–9), Colchester and various other sites in Britain (Jackson 2011a, 256–8, fig. 19f). As is the case with one of the British Museum examples from London (Cat. no. 3.109), one of the olivary terminals was sometimes provided with a tiny eye (fenestration). That enabled it to be used to insert a thread in such delicate operations as the treatment of anal fistula and the removal of a nasal polyp (Celsus, *On Medicine* 7.4.4A-D; Paul of Aegina 6.25.3 and 6.78.3). Other eyed *dipyrenes* include one in the small kit of instruments in the tubular probe case found in the River Maas at Maaseik (Heymans 1979, 98–9, fig. 2.4; Künzl 1996, 2610–11, fig. 18.4).

Ear probes and ligulae are common components of sets of instruments. The ear probe, like Cat. nos 3.28, 3.46 and 3.110, combines a tiny round-bowled spoon with a simple pointed probe, while the ligula, like Cat. no. 3.27, comprises a tiny angled disc at the end of a slender pointed probe. Both types had medical and pharmaceutical uses, especially removing medicaments from containers and instilling liquids into the ear and eye by squeezing them from a twist of wool wrapped round the stem so that it ran down and fell in droplets from the pointed end. But they also had surgical applications, the ligula, for example, as a dental scaler, a fine cautery and a blunt hook. They probably equate to the *oricularium specillum* which Celsus recommended for removing wax and foreign bodies from the ears, and for removing linen threads in an operation on haemorrhoids, and which Aëtius advised for curetting the inside of a small cyst on the eyelid (Celsus, *On Medicine* 6.7.7A–B, 6.7.5, 6.7.9A, 7.30.3D; Aëtius 2.3.81). The *oricularium specillum* advocated for the extraction of a bladder stone (Celsus, *On Medicine* 7.26.1C) is likely to have required a larger scoop, and in order to perform the range of Celsus' recommended operations the scoop of the *oricularium specillum* must have varied in size and shape. Some interventions would have been appropriate to the tiny round spoon of the ear probe or the disc of the ligula, but others would have been better accomplished with the longer scoop of a scoop probe. Thus, to the practitioners of Greco-Roman medicine *oricularium specillum*, rather than meaning 'ear probe' in the strictest sense, was probably intended to signify a plain, slender, pointed probe with a scoop of variable size (on the complexity of the terminology of probes see Bliquez 2003 and Bliquez 2015, 125–38).

Scoop probes and spatula probes – olivary-ended probes combined with a slender scoop or a flat spatula – are numerous in the domestic context, but are also regularly found in sets of instruments, as in the set from Italy (Cat. nos

3.29–33). They vary considerably in size and shape according to the specific usage or range of functions intended, as exemplified by those in the British Museum collection, which also include two made of silver (Cat. nos 3.29–33 and 3.111–21). The scoop, of varied depth and capacity, is sometimes broad at the tip, sometimes narrow (see **Fig. 127**). The spatula is even more varied, ranging from very broad to extremely narrow, its sides sometimes straight, sometimes convex and sometimes concave, usually with one flat and one low-ridged face, and with a rounded, straight or blunt-pointed tip (see **Fig. 128**). The principal medical role of both scoop probes and spatula probes was in the preparation of medicaments – extracting, crushing, stirring and mixing – and in their application – dabbing, pouring and spreading. The olivary terminal of both varieties was recommended as a small cautery, as a probe for exploring large cavities, and, wrapped in wool, as a plug for occluding the nostrils. The use of some scoop probes in lithotomy has already been mentioned, and the form of the scoop of some others would have enabled them to function as curettes. Further surgical applications of the scoop probe include its use to support, force or elevate tissue and vessels for incision or excision and to cause or regulate blood flow (Bliquez 2003, 330). The instrument employed in the separation of adhered eyelids and the re-opening of a prematurely adhered bladder incision following lithotomy could have been either a scoop probe or a spatula probe (Celsus, *On Medicine* 7.7.6B, 7.27.8). Other surgical applications of the spatula probe included use as a blunt dissector, as a tongue depressor in throat operations, and as a substitute for the *meningophylax* in skull surgery. It was also used to apply plasters, to prevent prolapse of the bowel and to replace veins in the treatment of a scrotal varix (Celsus, *On Medicine* 7.25.1C, 7.21.1A, 7.22.4).

Writing-styli, of bronze or of iron, are quite often found in sets of instruments, including those from Nea Paphos (Michaelides 1984, 318–19, no. 14, fig. 2.4, pl. 74.2) and the British Museum set from Italy (Cat. no. 3.34). Like other implements, notably spoons, they are generally undifferentiated from their domestic counterparts and were probably incorporated into sets of instruments to fulfil medical or surgical roles, but perhaps also to be used for non-medical purposes. Thus the stylus might be used simply as a writing-implement or as a medical instrument – a styloid probe or a dental lever (Aëtius 8.36.17) – or both. In addition, like many other surgical instruments, styli and all the other types of probe, with their wide variety of terminal shape and size, were also sometimes used as cauteries – vehicles for transferring and applying heat. Though considered extreme and often a last measure, cauterisation was frequently referred to in the medical texts, especially in delicate or small-scale interventions. It is likely that the beneficial effect of a heated instrument had registered even though there was no knowledge of the need for sterilisation. The main applications were in staunching haemorrhage, destroying unhealthy or mortified tissue (especially ulcerations or carious bone) and removing healthy tissue to gain access to underlying organs or structure. The requirement for a correspondingly wide variety of size and shape of cautery was mostly met within the existing instrumentation, whether

Figure 76 Spouted spoons. British Museum, London (upper to lower, Cat. nos 3.122, 3.123)

probes, blades or needles, and few purpose-made cauteries have been identified (Jackson 1986, 154–6; Jackson 1994a, 177–9; Bliquez 2015, 157–72).

Spoons

Spouted spoons in the British Museum collection: Cat. nos 3.122–3 (see also Sets of instruments, Cat. no. 3.35)

Spoons are occasionally found in sets of medical instruments (Künzl 1983a, *passim*), in which they would have supplemented the much smaller spoons at the end of ear probes and scoop probes, as indicated by a Galenic reference 'Let the application be made by a spoon (*kochliarion*) or by a spoon of a probe' (Aëtius 8.43.31; Bliquez 2015, 144). Often, like the round-bowled spoon in the Italy set (Cat. no. 3.35) or a fiddle-shaped spoon in the set probably from Ephesus (Künzl 2002a, 16, pl. 1, A4) they are undifferentiated from domestic spoons. In fact, they probably are just that – domestic utensils pressed into service for medical use, for dispensing, measuring, heating and pouring liquid medicaments (for other everyday objects adapted to medical usage see e.g. Jackson 1994a, 199, table 3). However, in some cases they were probably used for other medical applications too, and the slender pointed handle of Cat. no. 3.35 may well have served as an additional instrument, a probe or perforator.

Spouted spoons had clear advantages in medicine where precise pouring was critical, and Cat. nos 3.122–3 (**Fig. 76**) are examples of a distinctive type with a spout on a capacious round bowl. This type has been found in three of the most comprehensive Roman sets of medical instruments: one in the 3rd-century AD 'Paris Surgeon' set (see **Fig. 33**) (Sorel 1984, fig 133b, centre, pl. 17, front); two in the 3rd-century AD Rimini *domus* del Chirurgo find (inv. 184417, 184482; Jackson 2009b, 80–1); and one in the 4th/early 5th-century AD set in the Ashmolean Museum said to be from Asia Minor or Syria (**Fig. 34a**) (Jackson 1995a, pl. 2, top left; Jackson forthcoming); and there is another in the small set of instruments in the mid-3rd-century AD cremation burial from Cologne, Richard-Wagner-Strasse (**Fig. 51**) (Euskirchen 2018, 314, no. 16). All five spoons, together with the two British Museum spoons, have their spout in a position that favours right-handed use. Cat. no. 3.123 has engraved concentric rings on the inner face of the bowl, like several of the other lipped spoons. Although it is tempting to think of these as dosage lines their occasional presence also on the exterior surface of the bowl rather suggests

decoration, and the same simple decorative motif is commonly found on tubular medicine boxes, as on Cat. nos 3.36 and 3.126–7. One of the Rimini spoons was part of a fused group comprising also a knife and two dental forceps and the Ashmolean set also includes a dental forceps, while the mid-4th-century AD Gadara grave group, probably the instrumentation of a practitioner specialising in dentistry, also combines a dental forceps with a large round-bowled spoon (Künzl and Weber 1991, 87–9, 94, figs 4 and 10, pl. 34c). These associations are suggestive of a specific role for the spoons in dental treatment, perhaps for administering gargles and pain-alleviating liquid medications. However, they would doubtless have been used more generally in medicine, too.

Drug containers

Drug containers in the British Museum collection: Cat. nos 3.124–30 (see also Sets of instruments, Cat. nos 3.36–7)

The proper storage of medicines was essential if their efficacy was to be ensured and the care taken to select the most appropriate type of container was succinctly described by the 1st-century AD pharmacologist Pedanius Dioscorides:

> Flowers and such parts that have a sweet-smelling fragrance should be laid down in small dry boxes of limewood, but occasionally they can be serviceably wrapped in papyrus or leaves to preserve their seeds. As for moist drugs, any container made from silver, glass or horn will be suitable. An earthenware vessel is well adapted provided that it is not too thin, and, among wooden containers, those of boxwood. Copper vessels will be suitable for moist eye-drugs and for drugs prepared with vinegar, raw pitch or juniper-oil. But stow animal fats and marrows in tin containers. (Dioscorides, *Materials used in Medicine* Preface, 9.7–15, trans. Scarborough and Nutton 1982, 197)

In addition to leaves, sheets of papyrus and containers of horn, glass, earthenware and silver, boxes of wood, copper and tin were variously chosen according to the medicine to be stored (for the wide variety of containers from graves with associated medical instruments see, e.g., Künzl 1983a, *passim* and Bliquez 2015, figs 86–91). The written descriptions are closely matched by the drug boxes found in the archaeological record as, for example, the round box, of which only the lead lid survived, from Haltern, Germany, inscribed *ex radice britanica* (Fitzpatrick 1991), and the lidded round tin canister (*pyxis*) from a 2nd-century AD context in a temple precinct at Tabard Square, Southwark, London, the uniquely preserved contents of which – a white, creamy substance still retaining finger impressions of the last user – were interpreted after analysis as a form of moisturising cream (Evershed *et al.* 2004; Gourevitch 2011, 152–3). Round lidded drug boxes – *pyxides* – of tin or bronze were widespread and of very long standing, but that many had also long since been made from wood is implied by the assemblage from the 2nd-century BC Pozzino wreck in the Gulf of Baratti which, in addition to a tin *pyxis* containing six tablets, preserved several rectangular wooden boxes and at least 136 small *pyxides* of turned boxwood containing salves and powders (Gourevitch 2011, 153–4; Touwaide 2011; Giachi *et al.* 2013).

By the time of the Roman Empire, however, purpose-made drug boxes, as opposed to glass and ceramic drug

Figure 77 Rectangular medicine box from Yortan, with upper sliding lid removed. British Museum, London (Cat. no. 3.124)

Figure 78 Lyon, La Favorite, Roman rectangular and tubular medicine boxes and stone mixing palette, lying on ground after excavation. Desiccated *collyria* are visible in the rectangular box compartments. Musée de la civilisation gallo-romaine, Lyon. Photo © Jean-Michel Degueule, Christian Thioc/Lugdunum

containers, took two principal forms, rectangular and tubular, and most surviving examples of each are made of copper alloy (Beck 1977; Künzl 1983a, *passim*; Boyer *et al.* 1990, 224–31; Sobel 1991; Heres 1992; Bliquez 1994, 66–9, 192–7, 202–3, pls 18 and 24–6; Künzl 1996, figs 12, 17–19, 32–4; Künzl 2002a, B119, B120). The rectangular boxes appear to have been known by the name *deltos* or *deltarion*, the tubular boxes *narthex* or *narthekion* (Fischer 1997; Marganne 2003; Bliquez 2015, 276–8). Remains of medicaments have been found in both types of box, confirming their primary use in medicine, though of course they could also be used for the storage of other materials. Indeed, some of the rectangular boxes not from medical contexts have been found to contain jewellery and powdered pigments – perhaps cosmetics or artists' colours (e.g. Beck 1977, 61, 64) and, even if that represents a reuse of the box, unassociated boxes and those not found in a medical context cannot be automatically assumed to have had a medical use.

The rectangular drug boxes have a sliding lid, often with a fastening catch on the end-plate, and between three and six rectangular internal compartments, all or some of which have a hinged lid with a round or, more often, omega-shaped wire handle (**Fig. 77**) (Jackson 1988, 74–5; Bliquez 1994, 191–2, pls 24–5). Those found as part of a set of medical instruments – often also with a stone mixing palette, tubular drug boxes and other medicine containers – include one in the 3rd-century AD grave group from Vermand, Aisne, France (Künzl 1983, 68–9, fig. 43), one in the mid-3rd-century AD Wehringen grave group (Künzl 1983a, 120–1; Nuber 2004), and one in the 3rd-century AD 'Paris Surgeon' instrumentation (Sorel 1984; Künzl 2002b, 43, fig. 56). Both of the British Museum rectangular bronze boxes (Cat. nos 3.124–5) lack a specifically medical context and associated finds and neither is recorded as having contained any object or substance. Each has a sliding outer lid and five internal compartments, though differently arranged. That from Yortan (Cat. no. 3.124) is an intricate and carefully constructed example with a catch to secure its sliding lid. The provision of an outer sliding lid and inner

hinged compartment lids permitted the safe storage together of different medical substances, free from contamination, as, for example, at least three of the rectangular bronze boxes from Pompeii, which preserved pills and other medicaments in their compartments (Milne 1907, 172, pl. 54; Bliquez 1994, 2F, 191–2, no. 196, and pl. 24; Bliquez 2015, figs 79–81); the rectangular bronze box in the late 2nd/early 3rd-century AD grave at La Favorite, Lyon (**Fig. 78**), where desiccated sticks of eye-salve (*collyria*) were stored in four of the five compartments (Boyer *et al.* 1990, esp. 224–35; Künzl 2002b, 85, fig. 114); the rectangular bronze box in the late 1st/early 2nd-century AD grave group from *Viminacium*, which also contained fragments of dried *collyrium* sticks (Korać 1986; Heres 1992, 158–60; Künzl 2018, 26–7, fig. 9; Pardon-Labonnelie *et al.* 2020); and the rectangular bronze box in the mid-3rd-century AD Wehringen grave (see **Fig. 20**), which contained *materia medica*, including dried *collyria*, in four compartments and coins in the fifth (Künzl 1983a, 120–1; Nuber 2004).

Sometimes a rectangular box was adapted in order to combine a number of functions. Thus, the base plate of the Lyon box was replaced by a bronze sheet with circular bowl-like depression for the preparation of medications (Boyer *et al.* 1990, 224–7, figs 11–14 and 17). A much simpler, more compact version from Andernach, Germany, combined a small square lidded salve container with a bowl-like depression for mixing, an adjacent tubular container for instruments or medicaments and a stone mixing palette which formed the lower sliding lid (Künzl 1984b, 169–70, 220–1, pls 16–17, I1). Even more multi-functional is a rectangular bronze box from Tomb 427 at Marquion-Sauchy-Lestrée, Pas-de-Calais, France, which was contrived to accommodate a three-compartment rectangular box with an adjacent slender rectangular box, each with a sliding lid fastened by a catch, the juxtaposition of which provided a space which allowed the inclusion of a bowl-like depression in the base plate which was accessed from the lower face and was sealed when not in use by a stone mixing palette which formed the lower sliding lid (Verbanck-Piérard *et al.* 2018, 325).

Another variation of the rectangular bronze box comprised a two-tier construction which neatly provided

Figure 79 Wooden rectangular
medicine box from Eenum, near
Groningen. Groninger Museum,
inv. no. 1949/IV 1. Photo
© Collection Groninger Museum:
Photo Marten de Leeuw

storage for a practitioner's instruments as well as
medicaments, as in the case of that from Kyzikos, which was
provided with drug storage in six compartments at the lower
level and storage for medical instruments in the upper tier
(Heres 1992). Other two-tiered examples have been found at
Pompeii (Milne 1907, 173; Beck 1977, 62, pl. VII, 5; Sobel
1991, 134); at Loutra, Alexandropouli, eastern Macedonia,
in an early 2nd-century AD cremation burial in the
Traianoupolis tumulus; and at the grave tumulus of Mikri
Doxipara-Zoni, Greek Thrace, in two 2nd-century AD
cremation burials (Triantafyllos 2014). The Traianoupolis
and Mikri Doxipara-Zoni boxes were further elaborated by
incorporating a stone mixing palette as well as a tubular
probe case on one side and a hinged cylindrical box with
three compartments on the other side. The hinged
cylindrical box, which comprised two half cylinders with a
longitudinal hinge, may have had its origins in northern
Greece, where examples have been found in two 4th-century
BC burials in Thessaloniki – Derveni Grave B and
Stavroupolis – the former, like the Traianoupolis box, still
containing desiccated *materia medica* in its three
compartments (Ignatiadou 2015).

Although most surviving rectangular boxes are made
from copper-alloy sheet, the same design was applied to
boxes of wood or bone, which were probably much
commoner than their metal counterparts, and occasionally
boxes of ivory (Milne 1907, 173; Matthäus 1989, fig. 35; Sobel
1991, 138–44; Künzl 2002b, 103, fig. 152), including one in
the mid-3rd-century AD instrumentation in the burial group
from Cologne, Richard-Wagner-Strasse (Künzl 2002b, 67,
fig. 88; Jackson 2018a, 134, fig. 1; Euskirchen 2018, 314, no.
16). In addition to the rectangular wooden boxes in the
Pozzino wreck assemblage, a very finely preserved
rectangular box of yew-wood with sliding lid and four lidded
compartments was found at Eenum, Loppersum, near
Groningen in 1917 'during digging in the Eenum terp'
(Groninger Museum) (**Fig. 79**), while the four-compartment
rectangular wooden box with decorative bone inlays which
survived in the mid-3rd-century AD sarcophagus burial at
Nijmegen (see **Fig. 21a**) was part of a grave group that
included surgical instruments and other medicine containers

of bronze and glass (Künzl 1983a, 93–6; Verbanck-Piérard *et
al.* 2018, 141–4, 285–6).

The outer and inner lids of the rectangular boxes were
usually decorated with a simple incised linear design, like
that on both of the British Museum boxes, but sometimes the
outer lid was ornately ornamented with incised and inlaid
figural designs (e.g. Diana on a lid in the assemblage from
the Rimini *domus* del Chirurgo: Ortalli 2000, 523–4, no. 191;
Ortalli 2009, 38, fig. 25), some of which had a direct medical
association, above all the attributes or images of the great
healer deities Asklepios and Hygieia – Roman Aesculapius
and Salus (Beck 1977, 56–7, pls 5–6; Künzl 1996, figs 32–3;
Künzl 2002b, 102–4, figs 150–3; De Carolis 2009, 53–8, fig.
6). As with other medical instruments, the combination of
ingenious design and fine craftsmanship with the addition of
Asklepian imagery was doubtless intended to impress and
reassure the patient.

The tubular bronze drug boxes, rather like modern cigar
tubes, comprise a slender cylinder with a precisely rebated,
close-fitting lid, and are a shorter version of the boxes used to
contain probes and other slender instruments (**Fig. 80**) (see
also **Fig. 28**). The simple incised linear design of the
rectangular boxes is also found on both the tubular drug
boxes and the probe boxes in the form of a series of incised
girth rings together, usually, with incised concentric rings on
the end face of the lid. Like the probe boxes the body and lid
of the tubular bronze drug boxes were usually each raised in
a single piece, as scientific investigation proved to be the case
with all four British Museum examples (Cat. nos 3.36 and
3.126–8). The late 1st/early 2nd-century AD set of
instruments from Colophon included just one tubular drug
box, together with a stone mixing palette and a pair of scales
(Caton 1914, 116, pls 11.22, 11.31, 12.32), but often several
tubular drug boxes are found together, for they would
normally have held only a single medicament – a powder, a
moist ointment, pills or sticks of desiccated *collyria*. The mid-
2nd/early 3rd-century AD Nea Paphos instrumentation, for
example, included four tubular drug boxes, two of which
contained pills and the other two powders (Michaelides
1984, fig. 1.1–3 and 5, 331; Foster *et al.* 1988, 229–30), while
the wooden box in the Vault 12 find on the Herculaneum

Figure 80 Tubular medicine boxes. British Museum, London (left to right, Cat. nos 3.126, 3.127, 3.128)

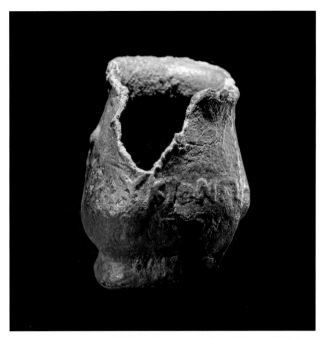

Figure 81 Miniature lead *lykion* ointment pot from Athens. British Museum, London (Cat. no. 3.129)

beach-front included seven tubular drug boxes and a stone palette for drug preparation (Pagano 2003, 135–6; Roberts 2013, 291). Scientific analysis of the British Museum's tubular drug boxes Cat. nos 3.126–8 found evidence indicative of the former presence of medicaments, but the tubular drug box in the Italy set, Cat. no. 3.37, proved to be empty (see pp. 162–3). The practitioner who used the Italy set was also equipped with drugs in a novel storage system: Cat. no. 3.36 comprises a stack of cylindrical boxes – a lid section and three close-fitting boxes. As with the tubular boxes, scientific investigation demonstrated that each of the stacking boxes was raised from a single sheet of metal (see pp. 152–3 and **Figs 100, 173**). The compartments provided good conditions for preservation of their contents and residues of medicaments have been detected in all four sections (see pp. 162–3, **Tables 5–6**, **Figs 190–2**). Like the tubular and rectangular bronze boxes the stacking cylindrical boxes are simply decorated with bands of incised girth rings and incised concentric rings on the end face of the base. At present no other example of this ingenious form of drug storage has been found.

The British Museum collection includes two examples of another form of purpose-made drug container, miniature lead pots, with a pedestal base, globular body and everted rim, one from Athens (**Fig. 81**) and the other from Corfu, Cat. nos 3.129–30. These pots were quite simply cast in two-piece moulds without any subsequent surface finishing – the casting flashes are still visible. Their rudimentary manufacture is in stark contrast to their contents: they were micro-containers designed to transport a very precious medication – λύκιον/*lykion* – and their minuscule size reflects the costliness of the product. As its name suggests one variety of *lykion* was sourced in the region of Lycia, where it was obtained from the branches and roots of a shrub of the Boxthorn family. It was a tannin-rich astringent, and Celsus rated it highly, advocating its use in staunching haemorrhage, inducing wounds to heal,

relieving ulcerations, checking discharges from ear and nose and, above all, as an ingredient in eye-salves (*collyria*) (Spencer 1938a, xl–xli).

Even better was Indian *lykion* extracted from shrubs of the Berberis family and acclaimed by most medical writers of the time (Jackson 1996a, 2238; Maddoli 1998). As an eye medicine it was singled out for praise by Dioscorides (*Materials used in Medicine* 1.132), Galen (*Mixtures and Properties of Simples* (7.64K)) and Marcellus Empiricus (*On Drugs* 8), while Scribonius Largus (*Drug Recipes* 19) claimed it was more effective as a simple than any of the compounded *collyria*. As it was one of the most highly prized drugs of antiquity, Galen rejoiced in obtaining some from a caravan on the Indian trade route (12.216K). The success of Indian *lykion* – still in use in India in the 19th century – can be attributed to the fact that its constituent, berberine, has an antibiotic action (Boon 1983, 9–10; Riddle 1985, 50). Galen subsequently used his *lykion* very sparingly, employing a secret technique to make a little go a long way (Nutton 1985, 143). In doing so he was following a long tradition, for *lykion* had been imported, packaged and marketed around the Mediterranean in minuscule quantities in the probably mass-produced (see p. 154) lead micro-containers (like Cat. nos 3.129–30) from the 3rd century BC until the 1st century AD. One was part of a 'home pharmacy' kit found in an early 3rd-century BC context with other ceramic juglets and unguentaria in House 4, West Quarter, Eretria (Stampolidis and Tassoulas 2014, 279–81); while on Sicily, the many lead and ceramic *lykion* micro-containers found at Agrigento, Syracuse and Morgantina have led to the suggestion that these were *lykion* production centres (Taborelli and Marengo 1998; Taborelli and Marengo 2010; Taborelli 2012; Marengo and Taborelli 2013). The inclusion of imagery and personal names on some of these pots, like Apollo's tripod and the name Mousaios on Cat. no. 3.129, were probably intended as symbols guaranteeing an unadulterated, high-quality drug.

Figure 82 Collyrium-stamps. British Museum (Cat. nos 3.131–44)

Other small and miniature ceramic pots were also used to transport medicines. Early 1st-century BC examples of a distinctive biconical form from Delos have painted inscriptions naming their contents which include *lykion* and *kentaurion* (Stampolidis and Tassoulas 2014, 278–85, nos 143, 149, 151–2). Two pots of the same biconical form were part of the 3rd-century AD Rimini *domus* del Chirurgo assemblage and their scratched inscriptions, in Greek, and partly in Latin, name their contents as ΧΑΜΑΙΔΡΥΣ (*camedrio*, possibly *Teucrium chamaedrys*, wall germander, a medicinal herb used for the treatment of gout, rheumatism and limb pains) and ΑΒΡΟΤΟΝΟΥ (*abrotono*, perhaps *Artemisia abrotanum*, southernwood, used as a vermifuge to expel intestinal worms) (Ortalli 2009, 33, 37, fig. 24).

Collyrium-stamps (Tables 1–3)

Collyrium-stamps in the British Museum collection: Cat. nos 3.131–45
These small stone tablets, often called 'oculist's stamps' (or 'cachets d'oculistes' or 'Okulistenstempel'), are more correctly termed collyrium-stamps (or 'cachets à collyres' or 'Augensalbstempel'), since their function was to stamp *collyria* – eye-salves – and their users were probably not exclusively oculists (Nielsen 1974, 58–62 'collyrium seals'; Boon 1983, 2 'collyrium-stamps'; Voinot 1999 'cachets à collyres'. But note a more recent suggestion that 'cachets oculistiques' may, in fact, be a better term: Pardon-Labonnelie 2013b, 49). Over 350 collyrium-stamps have been recorded, the great majority from the north-west provinces of the Roman Empire, principally Gallia, Germania and Britannia (*CIL* XIII, 3.1, 10021, 1–229; Künzl 1985, 468–81; Voinot 1999, maps 1–3; Pardon-Labonnelie *et al.* 2020, 56). Most are rectangular, but circular, triangular and hexagonal forms are occasionally found. Thirty-three

collyrium-stamps have a secure British provenance (*CIL* VII; Jackson 1990b, 279–81; *RIB* II, 4: 2446; Jackson 1996b, 178–80; plus subsequent finds from Ashton Keynes (*Wiltshire Archaeological & Natural History Magazine* 101, 2008, 40, fig. 8.1, 45–6), Hockwold and Colchester).

From the earliest recorded finds in the 17th century the stamps fascinated collectors and antiquaries alike, both for their attractive appearance – small tablets of stone in various colours (**Fig. 82**) – and for the intrinsic interest of their dies – abbreviated, finely engraved, reversed Latin inscriptions, recording an extensive range of *collyria*, credited to numerous salve-blenders, for the treatment of an assortment of eye diseases. The stamps are now widely distributed across the collections of almost 100 museums in Europe, mostly as singletons. The 14 stamps in the British Museum, Cat. nos 3.131–44 (**Fig. 83**) – four from France, seven from Britain, three probably from Britain – comprise a very significant collection, exceeded only by the 41 examples in the Cabinet des Médailles, Paris (Voinot 1999, 30–8). The British Museum collyrium-stamps were found between 1739 and 1927 and few have well-recorded details of their place and circumstance of finding. The two stamps from Naix-en-Barrois (Cat. nos 3.131–2) were part of the largest single find of collyrium-stamps – seven – so far made, but apart from having been found with a quantity of pottery vessels no other details of the context are known (for the archaeological context of collyrium-stamps see e.g. Baker 2011). Of the British finds, three are from Roman towns (Cat. nos 3.135, 3.139, 3.140) and three probably from burials (Cat. nos 3.136, 3.138, 3.141).

The fundamental importance of vision, the vulnerability of eyes to injury and disease and the relative ease of access to them resulted in the early development of eye medicine as a speciality (Jackson 1996a, 2231–5). However, in areas of low population density specialisation may not have been feasible and eye treatments were probably administered by *medici* and other 'general practitioners'. Such is suggested by the distribution of the British collyrium-stamps which, with few exceptions, come from sites located on the main Roman road network, often from towns or their hinterland, places where a resident 'general practitioner' might access a viable 'market' (Jackson 1996b, 178–9, fig. 21.1).

Collyria, some of which were liquid or semi-liquid lotions probably contained in labelled glass phials, became specifically associated with the treatment of eye complaints (on the meaning of *collyrium* see Pardon-Labonnelie 2013b). In the north-western provinces of the Roman Empire they were used in a dried form often bearing an inscription marked with a collyrium-stamp. Over 120 *collyria* are named on the collyrium-stamps (Voinot 1999, 41–9) reflecting Celsus' observation that 'there are many salves (*collyria*) devised by many inventors, and these can be blended even now in novel mixtures, for mild medicaments and moderate repressants may be readily and variously mingled' (*On Medicine* 6.6.2). Likewise, the 'many inventors' mentioned by Celsus are also reflected in the evidence from the collyrium-stamps – over 300 named salve originators or blenders, very few of whom are recorded more than once (Voinot 1999, 23–8). While some of the individuals named on collyrium-stamps may have been exclusively salve-blenders, many may also have been medical practitioners. Certainly, Euelpides, the most celebrated eye doctor of his day, whose *collyria* were listed by Celsus, Scribonius Largus and Galen, both compounded and administered eye-salves (Celsus, *On Medicine* 6.6.8, 17, 20, 25C, 31A-B; Scribonius Largus, *Drug Recipes* 19–22; Galen, *Mixtures and Properties of Simples* (12.767K)). As the *collyria* named on collyrium-stamps often correspond specifically to those listed by medical writers their recommended composition is known. *Collyrium* ingredients generally comprised active and aromatic

Name on collyrium-stamp	Cat. no.
Amandus, C. Valerius	Cat. no. 3.141
Ariovistus, T. Vindacius	Cat. no. 3.139
Clodi(anus(?)), P(...)	Cat. no. 3.143
Crescens, M. Vitellius	Cat. no. 3.144
Deciminus, L. Ulpius	Cat. no. 3.137
Iuvenis, L. Iulius	Cat. no. 3.140
Minervalis	Cat. no. 3.136
Polytimus, Hirpidius	Cat. no. 3.133
Satyrus, M. Iulius	Cat. no. 3.142
Secundus, Flavius	Cat. no. 3.140
Sedatus, P. Anicius	Cat. no. 3.135
Sedatus, Sex. Iulius	Cat. no. 3.134
Senex, L. Iulius*	Cat. no. 3.145
Taurus, Q. Iunius	Cat. no. 3.132
Taurus, Iunius	Cat. no. 3.131
Tutianus, M. Iuventius	Cat. no. 3.138
Valentinus, C. Valerius	Cat. no. 3.141

Table 1 Names on the British Museum collyrium-stamps (and samian vessel*)

substances blended with an agglutinant, usually gum, the latter being especially advantageous in the manufacture of the dried *collyria* as, according to Celsus, it prevented them from crumbling (Celsus, *On Medicine* 6.6.3). Thus, one of Celsus' featured famous *collyria*, the salve of Dionysius, consisted of poppy-tears, frankincense, zinc oxide and gum (Celsus, *On Medicine* 6.6.4). It was not just the composition of *collyria* that was seen as therapeutic, but their colour, too. Active ingredients could be supplemented by active colours, and green especially, but also white and orange-yellow were regarded as particularly beneficial for the eyes. Thus, at least

Figure 83 Collyrium-stamps. British Museum, London (upper row, left to right, Cat. nos 3.131, 3.132, 3.133, 3.134; middle row, left to right, Cat. nos 3.135, 3.136, 3.137, 3.138, 3.139; lower row, left to right, Cat. nos 3.140, 3.141, 3.142, 3.143, 3.144)

Salve name	Salve type	Cat. no.
acharistum	rapid-working salve	Cat. no. 3.133b
anicetum	infallible salve	Cat. no. 3.139a
anodynum	pain-relieving salve	Cat. no. 3.132b
chloron	green salve	Cat. no. 3.139b
collyrium	eye-salve	Cat. no. 3.143
crocodes	saffron salve	Cat. nos 3.134c, 3.145*
crocodes dialepidos	saffron salve with copper oxide	Cat. nos 3.131b, 3.134a, 3.137b
crocodes diamisus	saffron salve with misy (copper pyrites)	Cat. no. 3.131c
crocodes paccianum	saffron salve of Paccius	Cat. nos 3.131d, 3.134b
crocodes sarcofagum	saffron salve with sarcophagus stone	Cat. no. 3.131a
diaglaucium	salve made from juice of herb *glaucium*	Cat. nos 3.133c, 3.141c
dialepidos	salve made from scales of copper oxide	Cat. no. 3.142b
dialibanum	salve made from frankincense	Cat. nos 3.132a, 3.136a, 3.142c
diamysus	salve made from misy (copper pyrites)	Cat. no. 3.138
diapsoricum opobalsamatum	itch-salve made from balsam tree sap	Cat. no. 3.140a
diasmyrnes	salve made from myrrh	Cat. nos 3.140b, 3.142d
dicentetum	doubly-biting salve	Cat. no. 3.133d
dioxum	vinegar salve	Cat. no. 3.141a
melinum	quince-coloured salve	Cat. no. 3.136b
mixtum	mixture	Cat. no. 3.141d
nardinum	salve made with nard oil	Cat. no. 3.139c
penicillum	salve applied with a brush	Cat. no. 3.137a
penicillum lene	mild salve	Cat. no. 3.142a
stactum	drops	Cat. no. 3.141b, 3.144
turinum	salve made from frankincense	Cat. nos 3.139d

Table 2 Eye-salves on the British Museum collyrium-stamps (and samian vessel*)

a part of the perceived healing powers of *collyria* like *chloron* (Cat. no. 3.139), *melinum* (Cat. no. 3.136) and *crocodes* (Cat. nos 3.131, 3.134, 3.137, 3.145) lay in their colour, and also, probably, in the colour of the collyrium-stamps that were used to mark them (Krug 1987; Baker 2011; Pardon-Labonnelie 2021. On the power of colour see also, e.g. Mastrocinque 2011).

Soft, fine-grained types of stone were usually selected for the manufacture of collyrium-stamps in order to facilitate the cutting of dies on their edges. The majority of rectangular collyrium-stamps have dies on all four edges, though examples with three, two and one inscribed edge(s) also occur. Most of the dies consist of two-line inscriptions, but many have a single line and a few are three-line dies. On two- and three-line dies, lightly incised guidelines were often provided in order to regularise the inscriptions. The inscriptions, usually finely cut in Latin capitals (very occasionally in Greek characters: Voinot 1999, nos 154, 207, 221, 260), were engraved in reverse so that they gave a positive impression. Abbreviations, sometimes extreme, and ligatured lettering, sometimes complex (e.g. Cat. no. 3.136, die a; Cat. no. 3.141, die a), are common; stops, and spaces between words, are only occasionally used. Sometimes a letter is given a flourish (e.g. Cat. no. 3.132, dies a and b; Cat. no. 3.136, die a; Cat. no. 3.140, die b), and a decorative leaf is used in place of a stop (e.g. Cat. no. 3.131, dies a and d), while other leaves and simple decorative motifs are occasionally

inserted to fill a space (e.g. Cat. no. 3.134, die b; Cat. no. 3.138). The resulting complicated medical jargon, as well as the occasional user's name incised on the planar faces (e.g. Cat. no. 3.139), implies that the healers who used the collyrium-stamps were often literate. It is a reminder that the most important missing part of the material evidence is the medical literature – treatises, manuals and herbals – that some practitioners would have possessed. Functional features of the stamps include the bevelling of faces adjacent to the dies (e.g. Cat. nos 3.131–2, 3.135, 3.141) probably to improve impression of the die into the *collyrium* and, as in the case of Cat. no. 3.141, the cutting of abbreviated un-reversed versions of its four named *collyria* on the relevant edges of the planar faces in order to facilitate the selection and use of the correct die. Many collyrium-stamps bear evidence of long or secondary use: Cat. nos 3.135 and 3.140 were originally larger but were re-cut in antiquity and, in the case of Cat. no. 3.140, provided with a secondary die; while traces of whetting and probable drug preparation are quite often found, as on Cat. nos 3.134, 3.136, 3.138, 3.139.

The dies usually incorporate the name of a *collyrium*, the name of its originator or blender and, often, the name of an eye ailment or indication for use (**Tables 1–3**). Sometimes the *collyrium* or the ailment was omitted, more rarely the personal name, and, very occasionally, both the personal name and ailment are absent. The dies were engraved retrograde because they were intended for impressing into

Eye condition	Indication for use	Cat. no.
aspritudo	roughness of the eyelids, trachoma	Cat. nos 3.131a, 3.142b, 3.145*
caligo	dim sight, poor or blurred vision	Cat. no. 3.141b
cicatrices	scars, corneal scarring	Cat. nos 3.131b, 3.131d, 3.138, 3.140c
claritas	clear vision	Cat. nos 3.140a, 3.141d, 3.144
diathesis	affections	Cat. nos 3.131c, 3.134c
lippitudo	inflammation, ophthalmia	Cat. nos 3.132b, 3.136a, 3.137a, 3.140b, 3.141c, 3.142a, 3.142d
omnes dolores	all afflictions	Cat. no. 3.136b
omnia vitia	all defects	Cat. no. 3.137b
reumatica	running eyes	Cat. nos 3.131c, 3.131d, 3.141a
scabrities	roughness and itching of the eyes	Cat. no. 3.131b
suppurationes	suppurations, purulent inflammation	Cat. nos 3.132a, 3.142c

Table 3 Eye conditions/indications for use on the British Museum collyrium-stamps (and samian vessel*)

sticks of *collyria*, the ingredients of which were mixed to a dough-like consistency, rolled into strips, impressed with the appropriate die of the collyrium-stamp and allowed to dry. The marked and dried sticks of *collyria* could then be stored together in a box or bag and, after noting the inscription, the user crumbled off the requisite amount, ground it to a powder, and mixed it with water, wine, vinegar, honey-water, milk or egg albumen and then instilled it into the patient's eye. This was perhaps accomplished using the same technique as that for the administration of ear-drops, by squeezing the liquid from a twist of wool wrapped around the stem of a probe so that it ran down the stem and fell, in carefully guided droplets, from the tip of the probe (Milne 1907, 67; Jackson 1986, 158). This system enabled ready-made desiccated eye-salves to be carried, ready for use as the occasion arose, by medical practitioners, whether they were in the surgery or away from home as itinerant healers or 'circuit doctors' (Nutton 1972; Jackson 1996b, 177–8).

On rare occasions fragments of the dried *collyrium* sticks themselves have been preserved, some of them with stamped inscriptions (Nielsen 1974, 62–7; Gourevitch 1998). They include stamped fragments from Rheims, Cologne and Morlungo, the latter stored in a small round bronze box (Pardon-Labonnelie 2014, 111–16). The 40g of dried stamped *collyria* from the large Rheims instrumentation comprised 21 fragments, some stamped with the *collyrium* name *nardinum*, others with the name of the salve-blender Marcellinus together with abbreviated details of ailments, including *cicatrices*, *lippitudo* and *aspritudines*. Although a collyrium-stamp was part of the Rheims grave group, its single die, with the name of Gaius Firmius Severus and his myrrh-salve – *diasmyrnes* – had not been used to mark any of the surviving dried *collyria* (Künzl 1985, 473–4, pl. 66; Jackson 1996b, 178; Voinot 1999, no. 104). It is likely that stamped *collyria* often, and the stamps themselves presumably less often, passed quite freely between healers, none of whom was necessarily the person named in the prescriptions.

Sometimes, as already noted (above, p. 75), dried *collyria* were one of the medications stored in rectangular bronze drug boxes like those in the late 1st/early 2nd-century AD grave group from *Viminiacum*, those in the late 2nd/early 3rd-century AD grave group from Lyon, La Favorite (**Fig. 84**), and those in the mid-3rd-century AD grave group from Wehringen, and those secure contexts provide the valuable

opportunity for scientific analysis (Korać 1986; Boyer *et al.* 1990; Jackson 1996a, 2234–5, 2240–3; Künzl 2002b, 87–8; Pardon-Labonnelie *et al.* 2020). However, volatile ingredients are elusive, and even organic components have proved difficult to detect and characterise in the usually fragmentary and degraded surviving *collyria*. This was graphically demonstrated when the 11 stamped and nine other fragments of dried *collyria*, from the Lyon cremation grave, were analysed (Boyer *et al.* 1990, 235–43). That grave group provided the clearest and best-recorded archaeological evidence for a healer specialising in eye medicine, yet no close correspondence could be demonstrated between the *collyria* of Zmaragdus named in the stamped impressions (*stratioticum*, *dialibanum*, *crocodes*, *dielaeum*), the ingredients of those *collyria* as given in the contemporary pharmacopoeias and the substances detected in the scientific analyses (pollen analysis, chemical analysis and Raman spectrometry). The discordance appears not to have been attributable solely to the limitations of analysis: it was concluded that pharmaceutical terminology may have been subject to change both in time and in region (Boyer and Guineau in Boyer *et al.* 1990, 235–46; Jackson 1996a, 2235, 2242–3; Jackson 2012a, 226; Pardon-Labonnelie *et al.* 2020, 63).

So, *collyria* stamped with the *acharistum* die of Hirpidius Polytimus on the British Museum collyrium-stamp Cat. no. 3.133, die b, also from Lyon, may or may not have comprised the ingredients that Celsus attributed to 'the *collyrium* of

Figure 84 Lyon, La Favorite, detail of dried *collyria* stored in a rectangular bronze drug box. Musée de la civilisation gallo-romaine, Lyon. Photo © Jean-Michel Degueule, Christian Thioc/Lugdunum

Figure 85 Detail of regimental strength report recording those soldiers unfit for service, comprising three categories – *aegri* (the sick), *volnerati* (the wounded) and *lippientes* (those suffering from inflammation of the eyes). Ink writing-tablet, Vindolanda. British Museum, London (Cat. no. 6.12)

Theodotus himself, which by some is called achariston', which contained castorium, Indian nard, lycium, poppy-tears, myrrh, saffron, white lead, lign aloes, zinc oxide, copper scales, gum, acacia juice, antimony sulphide and rain-water (Celsus, *On Medicine* 6.6.6). Such a costly cocktail of antibiotic, antiseptic, anodyne, astringent, desiccant and caustic substances may well have proved beneficial in the prescribed treatment of ophthalmia (*lippitudo*) and in other eye diseases, too, even if the combination of some ingredients may have caused unforeseen and unwelcome side-effects.

Study of the inscriptions on collyrium-stamps has shed light on the relative frequency of different eye diseases: some 30 ailments are referred to on the dies of over 350 stamps (Jackson 1990b; 1996b, 182–4; Voinot 1999, 39–49). Many of the ailments or conditions referred to have only a single occurrence, and some others are rather generic, for example *diathesis* (affection), *omnes dolores* (all afflictions) and *omnia vitia* (all defects) (**Table 3**). Some are more specific and more frequently mentioned, for example *ad claritatem* ('for clearing the vision') which accounts for some 16% of references on the dies of collyrium-stamps, *cicatrices* (corneal scars) 12.5%, *caligo* (dim sight) 7.5% and *suppurationes* (suppurations) 2.5%. But almost half of the treatments were focused on just two, clearly very troublesome and widespread, conditions – *lippitudo* (25%) and *aspritudo* (20%) (Jackson 1996a, 2229). Celsus used *aspritudo* for the Greek *trachoma* and *ophthalmia*, but he also included *ophthalmia* under *lippitudo*, a condition with the symptoms of inflamed and running eyes with sticky secretions, sometimes chronic, and sometimes consequent on, or contributing to, *trachoma*. Between them, *aspritudo* and *lippitudo* also correspond to our conjunctivitis and to other eye diseases displaying the symptoms of inflamed and running, sticky eyes (Celsus, *On Medicine* prooemium 30, 1.5.1, 6.6.1, 6.6.27; Spencer 1938a, 184–5; Nielsen 1974, 90–1; Jackson 1990b, 276–7; Voinot 1999, 39–40; Pardon-Labonnelie 2004).

Patients with the milder versions of *lippitudo* and other minor eye ailments might treat themselves rather than seeking treatment by medical practitioners (Jackson 2013, 55–6). Such self-medication, as for other diseases, is likely to have been so routinely practised that it was generally not worthy of comment. However, it is evidenced both by a reference of Pliny the Elder to ready-made eye-salves (*collyria*) freely available on the open market – 'iam pridem facta emplastra et collyria mercantur' (Pliny, *Natural History* 34.108) – and, more specifically, by a Greek text on an early 2nd-century AD *ostrakon* from Mons Claudianus, a letter from one Isidorus to his two sons in which he requests, amongst other things, two sticks of eye-salve (*O.Claud.* 174; Cuvigny 1992, 161–3. See also Youtie 1976 and Sofroniew 2014. But eye medicaments were not always available in Egyptian desert locations: *O.Claud.* 1171; *O.Did.* 323, 2–6; Hanson 2019, 126). We do not know the exact nature of Isidorus' eye complaint, nor that of Pliny the Younger who, writing at about the same time as Isidorus, has left an interesting patient's account of his eye troubles ('infirmitati oculorum') in a letter to a friend (Pliny, *Letters* 7.21). However, from his description we can deduce that he may well have been suffering from *lippitudo*. For Pliny submitted himself to bed-rest in a darkened room, abstinence, baths and a sparing diet, a regime which corresponds closely to that which Celsus prescribed for *lippitudo* (*On Medicine* 6.6.1F–G). This was presumably in addition to medication since Pliny completes his account with the words 'and now I am under medical supervision'.

Lippitudo was foremost in Celsus' chapter on eye diseases (*On Medicine* 6.6.1) and it was clearly one of the most prevalent eye-infections of antiquity, not least, presumably, because of the highly contagious nature of one of its manifestations, conjunctivitis. Although a minor complaint today conjunctivitis can still be difficult to cure, even with effective medication and high standards of hygiene. It would have been a much more daunting prospect for ancient healers who, lacking a proper understanding of the cause and spread of disease, were unable to deploy effective preventive measures. In the close-packed barracks of a fort it might spread rapidly to pose a threat to the effectiveness of the garrison, and a document on one of the ink writing-tablets from the fort of Vindolanda, near Hadrian's Wall, indicates the seriousness with which *lippitudo* was viewed by military leaders. A regimental strength report of about AD 100 (Cat. no. 6.12) recorded 31 soldiers absent from duty because they were unfit, a figure divided into three groups, the sick (*aegri*), the wounded (*volnerati*) and those suffering from inflammation of the eyes (*lippientes*) (*Tab. Vindol.* II,154; Bowman and Thomas 1994, 90–8) (**Fig. 85**). The three-way division implies not only that the *lippientes* were separated from the healthy but that they were also segregated from the other sick and wounded. It might also be taken to suggest the presence of an eye specialist amongst the medical personnel of the fort, although until now the writing-tablets attest only a doctor (*medicus*) and a pharmacist (*seplasiarius*).

Just as *lippitudo* clearly encompassed a range of eye diseases so, too, did *aspritudo*, and both were inter-connnected, as is evident from Celsus' description of *aspritudo*:

> Now this condition generally follows inflammation of the eyes; sometimes it is more serious, sometimes less so. Often, too, as the result of trachoma (*aspritudo*), inflammation (*lippitudo*) is set up, which in its turn increases the trachoma, and sometimes lasts a short time, sometimes long, and then it is scarcely ever terminated. (Celsus, *On Medicine* 6.6.27A; trans. Spencer 1938a, 215–17).

Trachoma, one of the eye diseases indicated by the term *aspritudo*, is a contagious inflammation of the conjunctiva, cornea and eyelids. It was a scourge of the past, often endemic, and has continued to be so in some countries up to the present, though it can be cured with antibiotics (Boon 1983, 10–11). The resulting roughness and granulation of the eyelids and corners of the eyes (granular ophthalmia) caused unpleasant irritation and soreness that if not treated in a timely and effective way might easily trigger further diseases, including trichiasis (abnormal in-turned eyelashes which irritate the cornea and conjunctiva causing secondary infection), and ultimately could lead to blindness. As a bacterial infection, trachoma would have responded well to those *collyria* containing copper as, for example, the *collyrium* of Hierax containing myrrh and copper filings which Celsus recommended '*ad aspritudinem*' (*On Medicine* 6.6.28). For *aspritudo* he also recommended *pyxinum* and *sphaerion*, both of which are *collyrium* names found on some collyrium-stamps (e.g. Voinot 1999, nos 19, 81, 260, 149 and 204). But the *collyrium* by far the most frequently encountered on collyrium-stamps as a treatment for *aspritudo* was *crocodes*, saffron salve.

Of the more than 120 different *collyria* recorded on collyrium-stamps just seven – *diasmyrnes, crocodes, diamisus, dialepidos, stactum, diapsoricum* and *opobalsamatum* – account for almost half of the occurrences, and of those saffron salve (*crocodes*) is second only to myrrh-salve (*diasmyrnes*). Saffron, like myrrh, was a highly esteemed and very costly substance. It was obtained from the styles and stigmas of the autumn flowering *crocus sativus* and from it an orange-coloured oil was expressed, leaving a residue known as crocomagma, saffron dregs (Spencer 1938a, xxviii–xxix). Both saffron and saffron dregs are regularly included in the ingredients for eye-salves recorded in the medical literature (e.g. Celsus, *On Medicine* 6.6.5–8, 20, 22, 24–5, 31, 33; Jackson 2012a, 229), and saffron salve was frequently advocated on collyrium-stamp dies (**Table 2**; Voinot 1999, 44). Usually it was simply named *crocodes* (e.g. Cat. no. 3.134, die c), but often it was combined with another substance, and occasionally it bore the name of a particular salve-blender, as in the case of Cat. no. 3.134, dies a–b and 3.137, die b. Especially significant is Cat. no. 3.131 from Naix-aux-Forges which, for the treatment of several of the commonest eye afflictions, has four alternative saffron salves of (Quintus) Iunius Taurus – *crocodes sarcofagum* (saffron salve with sarcophagus stone), *crocodes dialepidos* (saffron salve with copper oxide), *crocodes diamisus* (saffron salve with misy) and *crocodes Paccianum* (saffron salve of Paccius) (see **Figs 138–9**). The seven collyrium-stamps in the Naix-aux-Forges find (Voinot 1999, nos 35–41), six of them with the prescriptions of Quintus Iunius Taurus and the seventh with those of Lucius Iunius Philinus, represent what must have been a flourishing family business manufacturing eye-salves and probably other medicines, too. For, in addition to Iunius Taurus' stamp with four saffron salves another of his stamps has four salves for the treatment of the various stages of *lippitudo* and the dies of the other five stamps bring the total of named *collyria* to 20 for the treatment of all ten of the most common eye conditions recorded on collyrium-stamps.

Figure 86 Impression of the collyrium-stamp of Lucius Iulius Senex on the inside of the broken base of a samian cup, Cat. no. 3.145. Photo: Ralph Jackson

Just one of Iunius Taurus' saffron salves was specifically for the treatment of *aspritudo*, but, where a use was given, *crocodes ad aspritudines* was the application stipulated for the salve on the great majority of other collyrium-stamps. Clearly, *crocodes*, one of the most popular *collyria* marked on collyrium-stamps, was the principal salve to be deployed in the treatment of *aspritudo*, one of the most troublesome of Roman eye diseases. That exact combination of eye disease and *collyrium* is found again in a rather unexpected place, on the inner base of a number of samian vessels – six cups and four dishes (Jackson 2012a). Instead of the normal potter's stamp there is the stamped impression of a diminutive collyrium-stamp, a two-line die inscribed *L(uci) Iul(i) Senis crocod(es) ad aspr(itudines)*, 'Lucius Iulius Senex's saffron salve for granulation (of the eyelids)'. Cat. no. 3.145 (**Fig. 86**), the base of a Drag. 33 cup found in the City of London in 1854, was the first to be recognised, since when further examples have been found at the La Graufesenque samian kiln site, another in London, and several at a number of military sites (Jackson 2012a, table 22.1, fig. 22.5). Although the evidence is inconclusive, it is possible that Lucius Iulius Senex was a salve-blender who lived and practised in the region of La Graufesenque in the late 1st–early 2nd century AD; who received a contract to supply medication to units of the Roman army in the north-western provinces; and who commissioned samian vessels as containers for the quite large quantities of his semi-solid saffron salve for the treatment of trachoma that would have been required by those densely populated military garrisons (Jackson 2012a, 232).

Varia

Mouse handles
Mouse handle in the British Museum collection: Cat. no. 3.146
In 1982/3 Ernst Künzl published a large set of instruments from a burial group of the 3rd century AD said to be from south-west Asia Minor and now thought to be probably from Ephesus (Künzl 1983a, 45–8; Künzl 2002a, 12–16) (see pp. 30–1 and **Fig. 32**). The set included a bronze mouse handle inscribed in Greek lettering with a name – Hygeinos Kanpylios – which Künzl believed to be that of the surgeon/physician who had owned and used the set of instruments

Figure 87a–b Inscribed mouse handle, said to have been found in the Artemision at Ephesus. British Museum, London (Cat. no. 3.146)

Figure 88 Saw blade. British Museum, London (Cat. no. 3.147)

(Künzl 1982b). A reassessment of this distinctive handle type was triggered in the light of the recognition of two more examples with the same inscription, one on the antiquity market, the other in the British Museum (Cat. no. 3.146) (**Fig. 87a–b**), as well as a bronze clasp-knife handle, also on

Figure 89 Two-pronged forks. British Museum, London (left to right, Cat. nos 3.149, 3.148, 3.150)

the antiquity market, in the form of a leonine pedestal bearing the same Greek inscription as the mouse handles – Hygeinos Kanpylios *neopoiós* (Jackson 1994b). Subsequently, a further two inscribed mouse handles appeared on the antiquity market, one with the same name and one with a new name – Elpidephoros *neopoiós* (Künzl 2001, fig. 5; Biers 2004, 71–2, no. 6.81).

Of the five mouse handles (Jackson 2014b, 228, nos 61–5) three lack a provenance, but the handle in the set of medical instruments and that in the British Museum (Cat. no. 3.146) are both said to be from Ephesus, the latter specifically from the sanctuary of Artemis whence, it is conceivable, all five mouse handles and the clasp-knife handle derive. The word *neopoiós* signified a temple official, and while Hygeinos Kanpylios, *neopoiós* is otherwise unattested the name Elpidephoros is found again, and at Ephesus, on a late 2nd-century AD inscription, an *archon* of the Ephesian Mouseion, the body that organised annual medical contests as part of the Great Festival of Asklepios (see p. 13) (Künzl 2002a, 15; Nutton 2004, 211). Though none of the mouse handles preserves the iron 'business end', Künzl has suggested they were the handles of writing implements, probably the spatula used for spreading and clearing the wax surface on stylus tablets (Künzl 2002a, 15, pl. 1.A5). The clasp-knife might also have been part of the paraphernalia of writing, used to cut the nibs of quill-pens. So, the mouse-handled spatula and leonine clasp-knife may be proposed as examples of Martial's *xenia* (like the fancy pen- and stylus-cases and writing-tablets of citrus wood and ivory: Martial *Epigrams* 14.3–7, 19 and 21), that were distributed as gifts by Elpidephoros and Hygeinos Kanpylios during or on completion of their term of office (Künzl 2001; Künzl 2002a, 16; Künzl 2002b, 75–6). One found its way into the possessions of a medical practitioner, but the mouse-handled implements were almost certainly not medical instruments.

Saw blade
Saw blade in the British Museum collection: Cat. no. 3.147
This small copper-alloy saw blade (**Fig. 88**) was included in the 'Surgical and Other Instruments' section of Walters Bronzes catalogue in 1899 and was termed a surgical saw both by Milne (1907, 130, pl. 41.3) and in the *Guide to Greek and Roman Life* 1908 (179–80, fig. 189h). That identification was accepted by several subsequent medical historians including the present author (e.g. Scarborough 1969, pl. 41; Marganne-Mélard 1987, 410, fig. 8; Jackson 1990a, fig. 5.7). However, the saw blade lacks a context or even a provenance and its form is unparalleled (see pp. 51–2) so its postulated surgical use, while feasible, remains unproven.

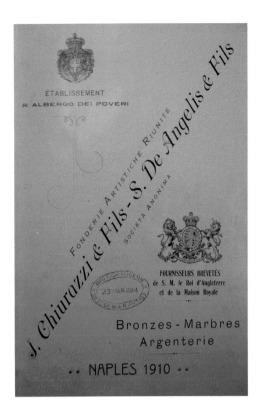

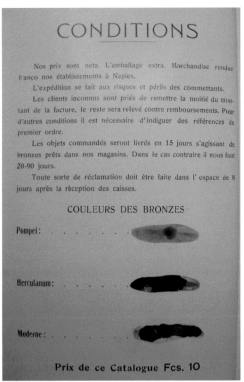

Figure 90 (far left) Title page of the Chiurazzi/De Angelis 1911 catalogue: *Fonderie Artistiche Riunite, J. Chiurazzi & Fils – S. De Angelis & Fils, Catalogo 1911: Bronzes – Marbres – Argenterie*, Naples 1910. Photo: Ralph Jackson

Figure 91 (left) Chiurazzi/De Angelis 1911 catalogue: the three available induced patinas for the bronze copies – 'Pompei', 'Herculanum', 'Moderne'. Photo: Ralph Jackson

Two-pronged forks

Two-pronged forks in the British Museum collection: Cat. nos 3.148–52

Milne identified a number of implements as bifurcated probes (Milne 1907, 83–4, pls 21–22), but they include only one example of what we would now regard as a Roman surgical instrument (Milne 1907, pl. 22.3), a double sharp hook with one broken and one straightened hook tip (Cat. no. 3.103). The remaining implements he illustrated are either certainly not surgical tools (Milne 1907, pl. 21.3 – a netting needle), or cannot be proven to be so (Milne 1907, pl. 21.1 and .6), or are neither Roman period nor surgical tools. Into the latter category fall two examples of a distinctive type of implement (Milne 1907, pl. 22.1–2). They are two of three similar copper-alloy implements in the British Museum collection (Cat. nos 3.148–50) (**Fig. 89**) and may be characterised by their slender decorated handle, omega-shaped loop and pair of long diamond-sectioned prongs which taper to a blunt-pointed tip. Ever since Milne appended them to the end of his discussion of bifurcated probes they have been regarded as Roman surgical or medical instruments. However, they do not correspond to any ancient description of bifurcated probes, their form does not clearly lend itself to any obvious surgical application, none has been found in a secure medical context, and their decoration points to a Late Antique or post-Roman date. Some are closely paralleled by Sasanian silver forks of 5th–7th-century AD date and also by Byzantine bronze examples, several from Corinth in 9th–12th-century AD contexts, and one from Constantinople in an early 11th-century AD context (Davidson 1952, nos 1377–83; Bliquez 1984, 187–8; Parani 2010, 147–50, 155–62, figs 9, 10, 13. See also Sherlock 2007, 250–5 and 259–64). Therefore, this type of two-pronged fork should be regarded not as a Roman surgical instrument but as a Byzantine, Late Antique, or

later utensil, probably a table-fork, a type that continued in use in the medieval and later period (for 16th-century examples see Brown 2001, 73, fig. 26.a–f). Of the two other two-pronged implements in the British Museum illustrated by Milne (1907, pl. 22.4–5), one is probably another post-Roman dining utensil (Cat. no. 3.152), while the other is possibly a surgical instrument of medieval date (Cat. no. 3.151).

Copies

Copies in the British Museum collection: Cat. nos 3.153–7

By the late 19th century, photography of the surgical and medical instruments from Pompeii and Herculaneum, especially by Allinari, Brogi and Anderson (see, for example, Bliquez 1994, pls 13–20), diffused knowledge of their extraordinary range and number worldwide. The instruments were evocative of an advanced medical provision and enabled the visualisation of medical and surgical practice in the Roman era in a way that had not before been possible. Many individuals, including the staff of museums and institutes, were keen not just to go to southern Italy to see the instruments or to have photographs of them but to acquire something more tangible for their collections. This desire for copies of bronze antiquities from the Vesuvian cities, of which the medical instruments were just a small part, had quickly been anticipated, and from the 1860s the Museo Archeologico Nazionale di Napoli started to grant permits for the production of copies. That resulted in the establishment in Naples of a number of foundries, including the 'Fonderie Artistique G. Sommer & Figlio' in Piazza Vittoria. But the 'Fonderie Artistiche Riunite' of Gennaro Chiurazzi, established in 1870, was one of the earliest, most enduring and most successful. By the early 20th century, as G. Chiurazzi & Figli /S. De Angelis & Figli (Chiurazzi/De Angelis), the Fonderia Chiurazzi employed hundreds of craftsmen and supplied museums and individuals all over the world. Their reproductions fulfilled a number of different purposes but in museums their intended role was principally didactic. In London, in addition to the copies of surgical instruments acquired by the British Museum in 1920, many more entered the Wellcome Collection around the same time, while in Italy, for example, copies of 17 instruments were accessed into the collection of the Museo dell'Istituto di Archeologia dell'Università di Pavia in 1940 (Tomaselli 1983, 58, 97–106, 190–5, nos M44–M60), and there are copies, too, in the Museo di Storia della Medicina dell'Università di Roma "La Sapienza".

Often called replicas (or 'modello', 'fac-simile' or 'imitazione moderna' – Tomaselli 1983, 58, 97), the Naples Foundry products are better termed simply copies because they are neither electrotypes nor *exact* copies, as is evident in the case of all five of the British Museum copies. Prospective purchasers selecting from the retail catalogues (e.g. J. Chiurazzi & Fils – S. De Angelis & Fils 1911; G. Sommer & Figlio 1914) (**Fig. 90**) made their choices based not on photos of the copies but on photos of the originals in the Naples National Museum captioned with their museum inventory number. The copies were available with a finish in three different induced patinas – 'Pompei' ('green and blue copper-oxidised, imitation of the excavation Pompeii'), 'Herculanum' ('dark green, half polished, imitation of the excavation of Herculaneum'), 'Moderne' ('brown polished') (**Fig. 91**). The dark grey to black patina of all five instrument copies in the British Museum collection appears to correspond to the Herculaneum finish. However, despite the favourable display and storage conditions of the British Museum collection, small patches of blue-green and green corrosion products are present in some places on Cat. nos 3.154–7, all of which are changes to the patina that have occurred since 1920. This was observed to be the case, too, on some of the copies in the Rome Museo di Storia della Medicina, which the author had the opportunity to examine in 2000. If, in other cases, the acquisition details of Naples Foundry products are lacking or insufficient, and unfavourable storage results in the development of more active corrosion, that is a combination that may lead to uncertainty as to whether an object is a copy or a genuine ancient instrument. Bearing in mind the large output, worldwide distribution, and age of the Naples Foundry products – most, now, over a century old – and because no scientific analysis of them was known to have been undertaken, it was decided to examine the British Museum instrument copies to establish their techniques of manufacture and composition. As was hoped, and may be seen below (see pp. 158–60 and **Fig. 189**), the scientific work revealed differences and distinctive indicators that characterise the British Museum's copies and will facilitate the differentiation of copies from originals in cases of uncertainty. The scientific work extended the results of visual examination of form, dimensions and manufacturing methods (Cat. nos 3.153–7) in comparison to those of the original instruments examined by the author in the Naples National Museum.

Chapter 3
Catalogue of Greek and Roman Surgical and Medical Instruments in the British Museum

Note: the copper alloy formulation of all analysed instruments is incorporated in the description in their catalogue entry, e.g. 'bronze', 'leaded bronze', 'brass', 'gunmetal'. For the alloy nomenclature see pp. 155–6.

BMRL numbers refer to files held historically in the British Museum Research Laboratory (now known as the Department of Scientific Research).

Sets of instruments

Set 1 (Cat. nos 3.1–38) (1968,0626.1–39) (Figs 92, 170–3)
From Italy.
1st/2nd century AD.

This extensive instrumentation was purchased by the British Museum from a London antiquity dealer in 1968. With almost 40 objects it is one of the largest and richest surviving sets of Roman medical instruments. The comprehensiveness of the instrumentation, however, is not matched by information on its place and circumstances of discovery: no more than the bare provenance 'Italy' was supplied by the dealer. Such a provenance is perfectly compatible with the instruments and their patinas. Furthermore, the survival together of such a large number of instruments, including some fragile pieces, the similarity of the corrosion products, and the presence of soil particles within the mouldings combine to suggest that the instrumentation probably came from a tomb or grave; though from what region of Italy, if indeed the set truly was found in Italy, it is not possible to say.

Scientific investigation (see pp. 156–8 and **Table 4**) tends to support the results of optical examination, namely that the instruments do indeed comprise a belonging set. However, the fact that the set was not discovered in controlled archaeological excavations means that we cannot be sure that it includes every piece found. There are no indeterminate fragments nor any specifically non-medical objects of the kind often encountered in Roman medical grave groups, so if any had existed they must have become separated. Additionally, there is neither a cupping vessel nor any other metal vessel, and while these are by no means invariably found with sets of medical instruments they might have been anticipated in a set as large and comprehensive as the present one. However, objects of thin sheet metal are particularly vulnerable to corrosion and if they survive at all they require considerable care during and after excavation, conditions that may not have prevailed in the present case. In fact, there is some evidence indicating that the set did originally incorporate at least one sheet metal object no longer in existence: iron corrosion staining on the long sides of the stone palette (Cat. no. 3.38) is probably the remains of a sheet metal slide in which it was contained.

Even more vulnerable are implements and containers made of wood, but evidence survived to show that at least one wooden box was included in the set: wood traces and iron corrosion products on the Type I scalpel handles (Cat. nos 3.1–5) and the scalpel/curette (Cat. no. 3.6), combined with their distinctive patina, as revealed by X-ray diffraction analysis (see Chapter 4, p. 158), demonstrate that all six had been contained top-to-tail in a hinged wooden scalpel box.

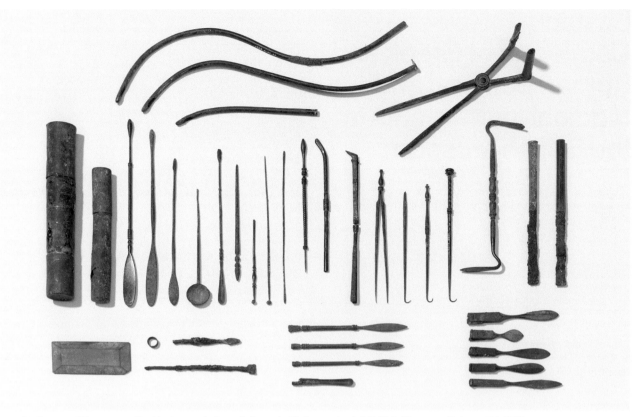

Figure 92 The set of Roman medical instruments from Italy, probably from a burial. British Museum, Cat. nos 3.1–3.38

Similarly, shared corrosion products on the Type II scalpel handles and the spring forceps (Cat. nos 3.7–9 and 3.14–15) indicate that these slender instruments may have been contained in a second box or case, perhaps together with the sharp hooks (Cat. nos 3.16–18). The set almost certainly would have included additional boxes, instruments and utensils made of wood, bone and other organic materials. Thus, it is evident that the set, like many others, lacks some of the objects that were part of the group as deposited. Evident, too, is the intrusive nature of a folding knife with suspension ring (Cat. no. 3.39) which must have been added to the set at some point following its discovery, as also, probably, was one of the spatula probes (Cat. no. 3.31). The folding knife is not a Roman medical instrument and its rather rudimentary manufacture is also in complete contrast to that of the uniformly finely crafted medical instrumentation. The spatula probe, like its counterparts in the set, is a paramedical implement, but its surface appearance and corrosion products, like those of the folding knife, are significantly different to those of the rest of the set and indicate different burial conditions (see p. 156 and **Table 4**).

Since publication of the set in 1986 new finds from elsewhere, which have enriched the database of ancient surgical instruments, together with a fresh investigation of the instruments themselves, have led to a reinterpretation of some pieces. In particular it is now evident that the smooth-jawed and toothed spring forceps were probably not each combined with a second missing iron component, as originally thought, but were, instead, united by means of an iron fixing as a double-ended forceps (Cat. no. 3.14), a type now represented by two further examples from Asia Minor (see p. 59). In addition, the small tanged iron instrument

(Cat. no. 3.12), originally identified as probably a cautery, is now considered to be more likely the solid-tipped drill-bit (*terebra*) from a surgical drill – trepan (see pp. 54–5 and **Fig. 59**). Additional scientific investigation (see Chapters 4 and 5) has also revealed important new information as, for example, the much fuller results obtained from analysis of the drug residues in the medicine boxes (Cat. nos 3.36–7) than was possible in 1986, and which has shed fascinating light on the variety and potential sophistication of the original medicaments (see pp. 162–3).

Despite the lack of contextual information for the find, the intrinsic evidence of the instruments themselves provides pointers towards their date, towards the likely processes of formation of the set and towards the medical provision and surgical interventions it enabled. The scalpel handles are all of forms characteristic of the 1st and 2nd century AD, a chronology supported by the absence of 3rd-century AD types and also by the lack of inlaid decoration in any of the instruments, a fashion that became popular in the 3rd century AD, while the stylised acanthus decoration of the double-ended blunt hook is paralleled on instruments of 1st–3rd century AD date. Thus, the form and decoration of the instruments indicates a date of manufacture in the 1st or 2nd century AD. The set as it now exists combines basic surgical instrumentation – scalpels, forceps, sharp hooks, needle and probes – with an array of medical implements linked to pharmacy – medicine boxes, mixing palette, spatulae, scoops and spoon – and an important component of specialised surgical instruments – catheters, rectal speculum, cataract needle and orthopaedic tools. It is likely that the set was never static, that it fluctuated with the fortunes of the practitioner, and that its present state was determined by his or her death, if it is correct to assume that

Figure 93a–b Scalpel handles, front and side views. British Museum, left to right, Cat. nos 3.1, 3.2, 3.3, 3.4, 3.5, 3.6

the set probably derived from a burial. The existence of discrete groups of instruments within the set – most notably the three delicate scalpels and double-ended spring forceps, and the three catheters – which on the basis of stylistic and scientific analysis were almost certainly each made together in the same workshop, indicates that each of those groups was a separate acquisition. Likewise, the rectal speculum, the cataract needle and the stacking medicine box were all probably individually acquired. The practitioner who owned and used the set, therefore, whether a man or a woman, may have started in medicine, like many of his or her peers, as the son, daughter or apprentice of an established physician. In time he/she may have taken over the practice and inherited a set of instruments which was progressively expanded as the practice flourished and the young practitioner increased the range of surgical and medical expertise. Taking into account only what has survived – the metal instrumentation – the set nevertheless gave the potential for an impressive range of surgery and medication for both male and female patients, from eye surgery, including the couching of cataract, to rectal disorders, including anal fistula and haemorrhoids, to urinary complaints, especially the relief of strangury caused by stone in the bladder, and to orthopaedic surgery, including the treatment of complex fractures, skull surgery, and even cranial trepanation. All that was in addition to the treatment of soft tissue wounds and injuries and a steady flow of patients with disorders and infections requiring medication.

Jackson 1986; La Niece 1986; Jackson 1987.
BMRL 5305-24395-Pi–iv.

3.1. Scalpel handle, Type I (1968,0626.2) (Figs 93a–b, 170)
Length 88.9mm (including blade stub 92.5mm); grip width 10mm; weight 28.29g

A standard Type I scalpel handle of bronze. The blunt dissector has a pronounced median ridge on both faces, a blunt tip and a faceted stem. The plain rectangular grip has rolled terminals and a keyhole socket (revealed by X-radiography). The iron blade tang, still in position in the socket, projects a few millimetres beyond the rolled terminals, and XRF analysis suggests that it was originally

secured by a soft solder of lead and tin. Adhering to the tang, and to both narrow sides of the grip, are fragments of mineral-preserved wood, the grain running along the main axis of the grip. There is a small patch of iron corrosion on one face of the dissector.

Jackson 1986, no. 1.

3.2. Scalpel handle, Type I (1968,0626.5) (Figs 93a–b, 170)
Length 55mm (including mineral-preserved wood fragment 57mm); grip width 9mm; weight 16.64g

A stout example of bronze. The short, broad dissector has a strong median ridge on both faces, a blunt tip and a faceted stem. The plain rectangular grip has rolled terminals and a keyhole socket which retains the end of the iron blade tang. XRF analysis suggests that the blade was originally secured by a soft solder of lead and tin. Mineral-preserved wood adheres to both sides of the grip and there is a patch of iron corrosion on one face.

Jackson 1986, no. 2.

3.3. Scalpel handle, Type I (1968,0626.3) (Figs 93a–b, 170)
Length 82.8mm (including blade stub 83.8mm); grip width 8mm; weight 17.45g

Similar to Cat. no. 3.1, though of gunmetal, and smaller, with a proportionately large blunt dissector. The dissector has a blunt tip, faceted stem and a median ridge higher on one face than the other. The plain rectangular grip has rolled terminals and a variant of the keyhole blade attachment: X-radiography revealed that in place of the cylindrical fixing of Cat. nos 3.1–2 and 3.5–6, the back of the socket slot was cut into a V shape with which a corresponding negative V shape cut into the back end of the blade tang engaged. To enable solder to be poured into the join a small circular hollow was drilled at the extremity of the slot from the top and bottom faces. The iron blade tang is still in position, and XRF analysis suggests that it was originally secured by a soft solder of lead and tin. Fragments of mineral-preserved wood adhere to one side of the grip and there are small patches of iron corrosion on one face of the grip and dissector.

Jackson 1986, no. 3.

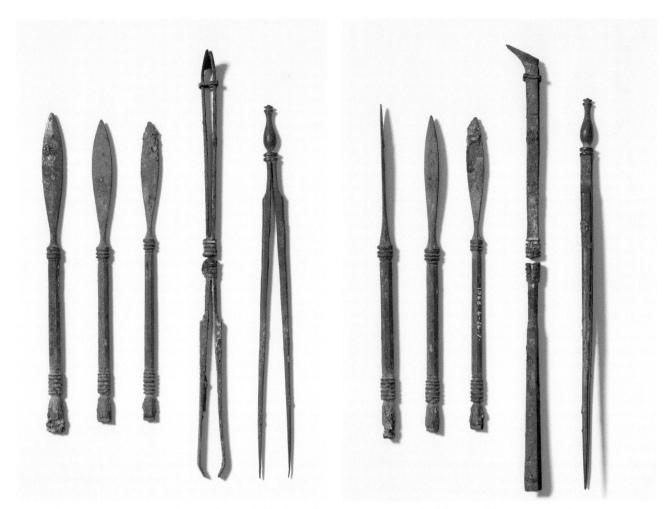

Figure 94a–b Scalpel handles and forceps, front and side views. British Museum, left to right, Cat. nos 3.7, 3.8, 3.9, 3.14, 3.15

3.4. Scalpel handle, Type I (1968,0626.4) **(Figs 93a–b, 170)**
Length 76mm; grip width 7.7mm; weight 16.01g

A small example, of bronze. The dissector has a blunt tip, a faceted stem and a median ridge on both faces, on one of which is a patch of iron corrosion. The plain rectangular grip has rolled terminals and the same variant of the keyhole socket as Cat. no. 3.3. Like Cat. no. 3.3, too, the end of the iron blade tang is still *in situ*, and XRF analysis suggests that it was originally secured by a soft solder of lead and tin. There are fragments of mineral-preserved wood on one side of the grip and clearly visible manufacturing file striations on one face.

Jackson 1986, no. 4.

3.5. Scalpel handle, Type I (1968,0626.1) **(Figs 93a–b, 170)**
Length 94.3mm; grip width 7mm; weight 19.01g

A slender example, of leaded bronze. The long, narrow dissector, with blunt-pointed tip, faceted neck and median ridge on both faces, is very slightly bent. There is a patch of iron corrosion on one face. The long, slender, plain rectangular grip has rolled terminals and a narrow keyhole socket with the end of the iron blade tang corroded in position. XRF analysis suggests that the blade was originally secured by a soft solder of lead and tin. Fragments of mineral-preserved wood adhere to the sides of the grip and there is a patch of iron corrosion on one face.

Jackson 1986, no. 5.

3.6. Scalpel?/sharp spoon (1968,0626.9) **(Figs 93a–b, 170)**
Length 63.3mm; grip width 5mm; weight 6.16g

A finely crafted double-ended instrument, of bronze, probably combining a scalpel blade with a sharp spoon (curette) instead of the more normal blunt dissector. The long, slender, capacious, thin-walled scoop has a rounded V-shaped cross-section and a broad upturned tip with semi-sharp rim. The grip, at the base of the scoop, is a tiny rectangular block with finely finished mouldings. Its terminals are broken but were probably of rolled type. Its broken keyhole socket retains fragments of an iron tang while fragments of mineral-preserved wood adhere to one face. XRF analysis suggests that the blade was originally secured by a soft solder of lead and tin.

Jackson 1986, no. 6.

3.7. Scalpel handle, Type II (1968,0626.8) **(Figs 94a–b, 170)**
Length 116.1mm (including blade stub 121.2mm); grip width 4.5mm; weight 12.2g

A long, slender, finely finished example, of brass. The slender, thin dissector, with blunt-pointed tip and faceted neck, has one flat face, the other with a very low median ridge. The long, very slender, octagonal-sectioned grip is flanked by crisply cut multiple ring-and-disc mouldings. The tang of the iron blade is corroded in position in the simple tiny slot socket, which has a neatly chamfered end. XRF analysis suggests that the blade was originally secured by a soft solder of lead and tin. There is a patch of iron corrosion on one face of the dissector.

Jackson 1986, no. 7.

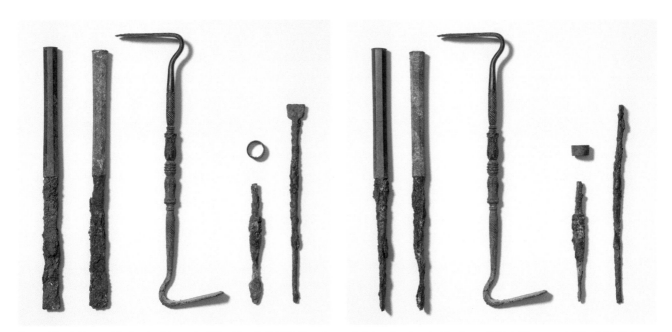

Figure 95a–b Bone chisels, double-ended blunt hook, ?drill-bit, collar and stylus, front and side views. British Museum, left to right, Cat. nos 3.10, 3.11, 3.19, 3.12, 3.13, 3.34

3.8. Scalpel handle, Type II (1968,0626.6) (Figs 94a–b, 170)

Length 114.5mm; grip width 4.2mm; weight 10.48g

The slender dissector has a very low median ridge on both faces. Otherwise this example, also of brass, is almost identical to, though slightly smaller than, Cat. no. 3.7. XRF analysis suggests that the blade was originally secured by a soft solder of lead and tin.

Jackson 1986, no. 8.

3.9. Scalpel handle, Type II (1968,0626.7) (Figs 94a–b, 170)

Length 113mm; grip width 3.9mm; weight 8.48g

This example, also of brass, is almost identical to Cat. nos 3.7 and 3.8, but smaller than both. XRF analysis suggests that the blade was originally secured by a soft solder of lead and tin. A small iron blade fragment adheres to the end of one face of the dissector.

Jackson 1986, no. 9.

3.10. Bone chisel (1968,0626.19) (Figs 95a–b, 170)

Length 152.5mm; cutting edge width 10.7mm; weight 54.71g

The neatly faceted octagonal-sectioned handle, of gunmetal, is lightly waisted. Its low-domed head bears slight traces of burring. The narrow iron blade, of rectangular cross-section, has a slightly splayed cutting edge sufficiently well preserved to show that it is lightly bevelled on one face.

Jackson 1986, no. 17.

3.11. Bone chisel (1968,0626.20) (Figs 95a–b, 170)

Length 150mm; cutting edge width 10.7mm; weight 46.53g

Almost identical to Cat. no. 3.10. Although slightly shorter in overall length the width of the cutting edge appears to have been the same. The octagonal-sectioned handle, of gunmetal, has a more pronounced waist and the head is more heavily burred.

Jackson 1986, no. 18.

3.12. Drill-bit (?) or cautery (?) (1968,0626.34) (Figs 95a–b, 24a–b, 170)

Length 69.5mm; weight 7.69g

A tanged iron instrument with lanceolate tip. The elongated baluster stem, of circular cross-section, has a plump ring-and-double-disc moulding. The functional spatulate end appears to be substantially complete but corrosion at the edges has obscured its precise original shape and dimensions. Critically, too, it is difficult to determine whether the edges were sharp or blunt. The slender tang, of square cross-section, is broken short. It bears mineralised remains of its wooden stock or handle, the end of which was probably bound with collar Cat. no. 3.13. Perhaps a wooden-handled cautery, but more likely a drill-bit which would have been mounted in a wooden stock.

Jackson 1986, no. 25.

3.13. Collar (1968,0626.12) (Figs 95a–b, 170)

Width 6.5mm; diameter 10.5mm; weight 0.86g

This small circular band of brass was registered with forceps Cat. no. 3.15, but it does not belong to it – its form and size are incompatible with use as a lock-ring. It is almost certainly a binding-collar from the end of the wooden handle or stock into which the tang of Cat. no. 3.12 was once fitted. A white fibrous substance adhering to the inner face is probably degraded wood.

Jackson 1986, no. 12.

3.14. Double-ended spring forceps (1968,0626.10–11) (Figs 94a–b, 170)

Smooth-jawed forceps: length 82.5mm; jaw width 5.3mm; weight 7.62g
Toothed forceps: length 77.5mm; weight 6.54g

A double-ended forceps of brass, combining smooth-jawed and toothed spring forceps, with a central multiple-ring moulding.

The short arms of the smooth-jawed forceps are divided by their stepped shoulder into a slender, neatly faceted upper part and a lower part which tapers in thickness and gently splays in width to the in-turned, smooth, straight-edged jaws. There is a patch of iron corrosion on the inner face of one of the arms.

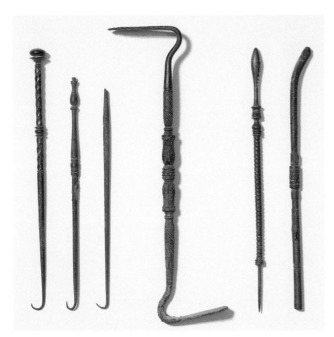

Figure 96 Sharp hooks, double-ended blunt hook and needles. British Museum, left to right, Cat. nos 3.16, 3.17, 3.18, 3.19, 3.21, 3.20

The toothed forceps is of coudée type. Its short, slender arms are near parallel-sided and of even thickness. They terminate in broad, angled, in-turned jaws, turned to one side, with finely cut tiny interlocking teeth (10 per jaw). Most of the teeth tips are now damaged. A thin band of corrosion on the lower outer face of one arm registers the 'as found' position of the (now moved) small rectangular sliding lock-ring. At this point the lock-ring holds the jaws in the fully compressed closed position.

The central iron component that once held the two forceps together is broken. Scientific analysis demonstrated that it comprised a small bar secured by lead-tin solder in a slot within the central mouldings and that the two forceps are of very similar composition (Chapter 4, **Table 4**).

Jackson 1986, nos 10–11.

3.15. Pointed-jawed forceps (1968,0626.12) **(Figs 94a–b, 170)**
Length 141.5mm; weight 16.95g

A leaded bronze example, of cut bar type, with a neat double-ring-and-baluster finial above plain shoulders. The long slender arms, carefully chamfered on their outer face, taper in width and thickness to the thin, pointed, accurately opposing, blunt-tipped jaws.

Jackson 1986, no. 12.

3.16. Sharp hook (1968,0626.21) **(Figs 96, 170)**
Length 140.5mm; weight 11.80g

A very fine and intricately finished example, of bronze. Beneath the large cup-and-button finial the upper stem is divided into two unequal zones by a ring-and-squat-baluster moulding. Both zones have a finely cut, multi-faceted 'latticework' surface. A simple disc moulding, near the centre of the instrument, separates the upper grip from the lower stem, of finely striated octagonal cross-section, which tapers evenly to a gently curved, fine, sharp-pointed hook.

Jackson 1986, no. 13.

3.17. Sharp hook (1968,0626.22) **(Figs 96, 170)**
Length 124.5mm; weight 7.29g

A slender example, of bronze, shorter than Cat. no. 3.16 and with a more tightly curved hook. The upper part of the instrument comprises a disc-and-baluster finial and a plain, waisted, circular-sectioned stem. Beneath a multiple-ring-and-disc moulding the lower stem, of finely striated, octagonal cross-section, tapers evenly to a fine sharp-pointed hook.

Jackson 1986, no. 14.

3.18. Sharp hook (1968,0626.23) **(Figs 96, 170)**
Length 117.6mm (broken); weight 5.53g

A simple example, of brass, lacking part of the upper stem and finial. The finely striated, octagonal-sectioned stem tapers in both directions from its point of maximum girth. The lower stem terminates in an open-angled, fine, sharp-pointed hook.

Jackson 1986, no. 15.

3.19. Double-ended blunt hook (1968,0626.13) **(Figs 95a–b, 96, 171)**
Length 158.5mm; weight 33.96g

A finely made, robust instrument, of bronze, with elaborately decorated grip and hooked, blunt, spatulate terminals turned back in opposing directions. The symmetrical decoration of the circular-sectioned grip comprises a central double-ring moulding flanked by a pair of stylised acanthus mouldings and an outer zone of fine candy-twist engraving. Beyond a simple ring moulding the stem tapers to form a swan's-neck loop at the back of each hook. Both hooks are of plano-convex cross-section with a marked median ridge on the outer (convex) face. One is of rounded laurel leaf shape; the other, of angular kite shape, is bent to a more acute angle with the stem. There is a patch of iron corrosion on the loop behind the kite-shaped terminal. Amongst other uses this instrument may be the *meningophylax* (or a variant of it) that Celsus recommended as a guard of the membrane in cranial trepanation (see pp. 56 and 64).

Jackson 1986, no. 16.

3.20. Socketed needle-holder (1968,0626.36) **(Figs 96, 171)**
Length 139.7mm; internal socket diameters *c.* 2.5mm; weight 13.52g

The slender grip, of bronze, of a double-ended instrument. Either side of the central moulding – multiple rings flanked by simple cylinders – the stem is of plain circular cross-section. A simple ring-and-cushion moulding separates each end of the stem from its terminal socket. One terminal is straight with an ovoid socket, the other is angled with flattened sides and a sub-triangular socket.

Jackson 1986, no. 24.

3.21. Cataract needle (1968,0626.31) **(Figs 96, 171)**
Length 141.5mm; weight 11.04g

A finely crafted instrument, of gunmetal, with circular-sectioned, spirally cut stem. At one end a large olivary terminal surmounts a neatly formed multiple-disc-and-baluster moulding. At the other end a straight, slender, round-pointed needle projects from a disc-moulded shoulder.

Jackson 1986, no. 23.

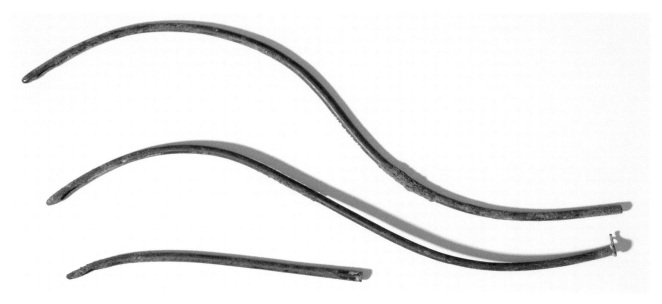

Figure 97 Catheters, two male and one female. British Museum, top to bottom, Cat. nos 3.23, 3.22, 3.24

3.22. Catheter, male (1968,0626.24) (Figs 97, 171)

Length 280mm; outer diameter 4.9–5.1mm (equivalent to English Catheter Gauge No. 8); weight 24.93g

A long S-shaped tube, of bronze, of uniform diameter, with an elongated oval eye on the inner curve just above the neatly tapered and carefully rounded solid tip. The instrument is made from a rolled strip and the lightly spiralled butt-join is just discernible along its whole length, except at the distal end in the region of the eye where considerable care was taken in the closing and smoothing of the seam. Wherever the original metal surface survives it can be seen to be both even and very smooth. At the proximal end a small, lobate plate-like bracket soldered to, and encircling, the mouth of the tube, was probably intended to facilitate manipulation of the instrument.

Jackson 1986, no. 20.

3.23. Catheter, male (1968,0626.25) (Figs 97, 171)

Length 302.5mm; outer diameter 5.1–5.2mm (equivalent to English Catheter Gauge No. 9); weight 32.58g

Another example, of bronze, almost identical to Cat. no. 3.22, but a little longer, more strongly curved and of slightly larger gauge. The ovoid eye is slightly smaller and the butt seam is visible only at the neck and within the patch of corrosion. A tiny patch of white metal at the neck is a remnant of lead-tin solder, probably used to attach a small bracket of the kind seen on Cat. no. 3.22.

Jackson 1986, no. 21.

3.24. Catheter, female (1968,0626.26) (Figs 97, 171)

Length 143.8mm; outer diameter 5.1–5.9mm; weight 10.26g

A short, J-shaped tube, of bronze, very gently tapered, with a lentoid eye on the inner curve, just above the neatly rounded solid tip. Like the two male catheters this instrument was made from a rolled strip, and the carefully smoothed butt-join can be discerned over the entire length, particularly below the eye where corrosion has forced the edges slightly apart. Traces of lead-tin solder detected near the mouth imply the former presence of a small bracket like that on Cat. no. 3.22.

Jackson 1986, no. 22.

3.25. Bivalve dilator (rectal speculum) (1968,0626.27) (Figs 98a–c, 172)

Length 156mm. Length *priapiscus*: tip to shoulder 65mm; tip to arm angle 76mm. Maximum outer width between fully open blades: at tips 44mm; at shoulder 54mm. Diameter of closed blades: at tips 8mm; at shoulder *c.* 10mm. Weight 104.11g

A precisely designed and finely crafted bivalve dilator (*speculum ani*), of bronze. When compressed the handles, of plano-convex cross-section, form a slender, elongated tear shape, their tips carefully tapered and rounded. A neatly moulded shoulder marks the junction with the arms, which do not cross but pivot on a simple strong hinge secured by a central rivet and braced by a pair of ribbed disc washers. Beyond the pivot the arms, of softened rectangular cross-

Figure 98a–c Bivalve dilator, in closed, part open and fully dilated position. British Museum, Cat. no. 3.25

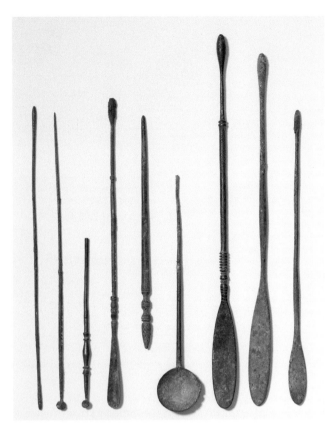

Figure 99 Probes and spoon. British Museum, left to right, Cat. nos 3.26, 3.27, 3.28, 3.29, 3.30, 3.35, 3.31, 3.32, 3.33

section, terminate in a carefully rounded end. To one side, above a slight shoulder, the two slender, lightly tapered blades (valves) project perpendicularly to the arms. They are of solid semi-circular cross-section with carefully tapered, smoothly rounded blunt tips. When closed the tips meet, but a slight gap between the blades, increasing towards the arms, gives a tapered *priapiscus* of round or sub-oval cross-section. There is a band of iron corrosion around one of the blades, perhaps the remains of a dislodged collar or slide.

Jackson 1986, no. 19; Jackson 1991.

3.26. Dipyrene, solid (1968,0626.17) (Figs 99, 172)
Length 161.5mm; weight 2.69g

An extremely slender double-ended olivary probe, of gunmetal. The tiny olivary tips are very narrow and elongated, while the flexible circular-sectioned stem is a mere 1.3mm in diameter.

Jackson 1986, no. 27.

3.27. Ligula (1968,0626.28) (Figs 99, 172)
Length 158mm; weight 2.92g

A very slender-stemmed example, of bronze, one end terminating in a simple point, the other in a tiny angled disc. Just below the point of maximum girth of the plain circular-sectioned stem is a simple paired double-ring moulding. There are traces of iron corrosion on the lower stem.

Jackson 1986, no. 28.

3.28. Ear probe (1968,0626.29) (Figs 99, 172)
Length 90mm (broken); weight 3.45g

An example of brass, its plain, circular-sectioned stem broken at one end. At the other end, beyond a reel-and-

baluster moulding, the spirally engraved stem tapers towards a tiny circular spoon. After discovery, but before its acquisition by the British Museum, this piece was cleaned. Probably at the same time an unsuccessful attempt seems to have been made to repair the stem: there is a trace of solder on the broken end and a marked blackening of the adjacent stem. It has not proved possible to find a prospective join with any of the other broken instruments in the set.

Jackson 1986, no. 29.

3.29. Scoop probe (1968,0626.18) (Figs 99, 172)
Length 165mm; weight 6.51g

A finely worked example, of bronze, divided by its mouldings into three zones – grip, scoop and olivary probe. The slender grip is of square cross-section with finely swaged corner mouldings; the scoop is separated from the grip by a multiple-ring-and-squat-baluster moulding; and the slender-stemmed olivary terminal (lightly coated with iron corrosion) projects from a small double-ring moulding.

Jackson 1986, no. 30.

3.30. (Scoop) probe (1968,0626.32) (Figs 99, 172)
Length 123.5mm (broken); weight 10.61g

A broken example, of brass, with plain tapered stem of circular cross-section. The tapered end terminates in a blunt point, possibly reworked in antiquity. The other end terminates in a multiple-disc-and-hourglass moulding with a lattice-engraved baluster broken (in antiquity) at the neck. The missing part was probably a scoop, while the opposing end may have comprised a plain pointed probe or an olivary terminal.

Jackson 1986, no. 31.

3.31. Spatula probe (probably intrusive) (1968,0626.14) (Figs 99, 172)
Length 198mm; weight 18.16g

A large ornate example, of bronze. A double-ring moulding separates the olivary tip and its long slender stem from the grip. At the other end a multiple-ring-and-squat-baluster moulding precedes the spatula with its spirally engraved neck. The ovoid spatula is plano-convex in cross-section with a marked median ridge on one face. In profile it has a clear concavo-convex curve. Unusually, the grip has been adorned with a carefully applied tubular sheet, of copper – the butted vertical seam is clearly visible – covered with fine linear engraving. The underlying stem is unbroken and this appears to be an original feature, not a repair. Scientific examination of the composition and patina of this instrument suggests that, like Cat. no. 3.39, it had different burial conditions and is intrusive to the set.

Jackson 1986, no. 33.

3.32. Spatula probe (1968,0626.15) (Figs 99, 172)
Length 186mm; weight 17.17g

A plain example, of bronze, with slender laurel leaf-shaped spatula and large blunt-ended olivary probe. There is a patch of iron corrosion on the octagonal-sectioned grip, off-centre towards the olivary tip. The spatula, turned slightly to one side, has a plano-convex cross-section and, like Cat. no. 3.31, a concavo-convex curve.

Jackson 1986, no. 34.

Figure 100a–b Mixing palette, tubular box and cylindrical box system, closed and open. British Museum, left to right, Cat. nos 3.38, 3.37, 3.36

3.33. Spatula probe (1968,0626.16) (Figs 99, 172)

Length 155.5mm; weight 8.28g

A small plain example, of bronze, with slender olivary probe, octagonal-sectioned stem and short oval spatula of plano-convex cross-section. In profile the spatula is turned slightly to one side. There is a small patch of iron corrosion on the olivary tip.

Jackson 1986, no. 35.

3.34. Stylus (1968,0626.33) (Fig. 95a–b, 173)

Length 115mm; weight 6.86g

A simple example, of iron, with a plain circular-sectioned stem, corroded and bent, and a broad tulip-shaped eraser. The other end of the stem is broken short of the writing point. The breakage and distortion probably occurred after deposition.

Jackson 1986, no. 26.

3.35. Spoon (1968,0626.30) (Figs 99, 173)

Length 125mm (broken); bowl diameter 24.3mm; weight 5.56g

A standard round-bowled spoon, of bronze, with slender tapered handle, its tip now broken. Both faces of the thin-walled circular bowl are tinned, as also the lower part of the handle. On one side the rim of the bowl is chipped and slightly distorted.

Jackson 1986, no. 32.

3.36. Cylindrical box system (1968,0626.37) (Figs 100a–b, 173)

Length: segment I: 57.5mm; segment II: 60mm; segment III: 58mm; segment IV: 45.5mm. Diameter 29–30mm; weight 73.46g

An unusual drug storage system of stacking cylindrical boxes comprising three upper segments, of bronze, and a base segment, of brass. The four segments are: I) lid, with plain, 'dimpled' end face; II) box, open at the top and

rebated at both ends; III) box, open at the top and rebated at the lower end; IV) base unit, with recessed, concentric ring decoration on the end face. The sides of all segments are decorated with paired bands of incised girth rings, three pairs on lid segment I and two pairs each on box segments II–IV. The contrast in patina, decoration and metal composition between segments I, III and IV implies that IV, the base segment, is of different origin, perhaps a replacement (see pp. 152–3 and **Table 4**). Medicinal residues were detected in all four segments. Variation in their constituents – organic and inorganic ingredients – is indicative of four different ointments, one of which may even have been Pliny's 'Punic wax'. For the results of analysis of the residues see pp. 162–3, **Tables 5–6** and **Figs 190–2**.

Jackson 1986, no. 36; Stacey 2011.

3.37. Tubular box (1968,0626.38) (Figs 100a–b, 173)

Maximum length *c.* 145mm; minimum length 105mm; length of lid 47.5mm; length of base 95.5mm; diameter 19–20mm; weight 21.20g

A short, slender cylindrical, two-part box, of bronze. The end face of the base segment is plain, while that of the lid bears engraved concentric ring decoration. There are pairs of simple incised girth rings on the sides at top and bottom and at the mouth of the lid segment. A long rebate – almost half the length of the base segment – provides a secure seating for the lid. The interior is empty, and scientific investigation detected no remains of former contents. However, differential corrosion shows that on burial the lid was extended to its greatest length, as though the box had then contained something since gone.

Jackson 1986, no. 37; Stacey 2011.

3.38. Mixing palette (1968,0626.39) (Figs 100a–b, 173)

Length 82mm; width 36mm; thickness 5mm; weight 29.96g

A small, thin, narrow rectangular example, of dull green fine-grained stone, with a flat working face and neatly

Figure 101 Clasp-knife. British Museum, Cat. no. 3.39

faceted underside. Although the facet angles on the underside are rounded off, and three of the corners were chipped in antiquity, there is little sign of wear on the working face, and manufacturing saw/file marks are visible on the squared-off edges. The long sides and part of the working face are stained with iron corrosion, while a small stripe of copper corrosion is present on the underside.

In 1985 the stone was examined by Dr Ian Freestone and Mavis Bimson who kindly provided the following note: 'Non-destructive X-ray diffraction analysis indicated that the mineralogy is predominantly chlorite with some quartz. Thus it is a low-grade metamorphic rock of a type which is fairly widespread, and may even occur as erratic pebbles.'

Jackson 1986, no. 38.

3.39. Clasp-knife [*aliena*] (1968,0626.35) (Figs 101, 173)
Length, blade extended 174mm; length, blade folded 119mm; weight 24.50g

A rather rudimentarily made folding knife, of gunmetal. The handle comprises a sawn bar with central slot and splayed and bevelled sides. At one end is a worn and rather coarsely cut multiple-ring-and-baluster moulding terminating in a circular eyed plate, in which is held a simple butted suspension ring of thick circular cross-section. At the other end a knife blade is hinged on a small rivet, which also braces the end of the handle plates. The blade, which now hangs loosely, is small and very thin, apparently heavily whetted, with a burred tip. Scientific examination of the composition and patina of this instrument suggests that, like Cat. no. 3.31, it had different burial conditions and is intrusive to the set.

Jackson 1986, no. 39.

SET 2 (Cat. nos 3.40–8) (1994,0726.1–9) (Figs 102, 174)
Provenance unknown.
Probably 1st/2nd century AD.

This small set of instruments was seen and recorded by the author at Christies, London, on 24 June and 1 July 1994. Although the instruments were without provenance and listed only as 'a group of Roman bronze medical instruments', the author's preliminary examination indicated that they were almost certainly a belonging set, and they were purchased by the British Museum at auction on 6 July 1994 (Christies 'Fine Antiquities' catalogue for 6 July 1994, p. 136, Lot no. 417). Subsequently, a more detailed macroscopic examination yielded strong intrinsic evidence

for the integrity of the group of instruments as a belonging set. This evidence was supported by that of a full scientific investigation of the instruments. The combined results may be summarised under five heads:

1) The consistency of the patina: this is uniformly mid-brown-green in appearance on all except the finial fragment and (for obvious reasons) the cleaned scalpel handle.

2) The consistency of the corrosion products: excepting the cleaned scalpel handle, this is copper carbonate (malachite or azurite) in every case.

3) The consistency of the metal composition: within the limitations of non-destructive qualitative analysis it is significant that all the instruments are of bronze with low to moderate lead contents. In addition, the shared low trace element content further unites the instruments and suggests the use of a high quality or well-refined metal.

4) Shared stylistic traits, features of manufacture and decorative inlays: Cat. nos 3.41 and 3.42 are linked by fine faceting; Cat. nos 3.44–7 are linked by fine longitudinal tapered faceting; Cat. nos 3.43 and 3.44 are linked by the form of their finials; and Cat. nos 3.44, 3.46 and 3.47 are linked by their distinctive inlay design (revealed by energy dispersive X-ray analysis – see p. 154), comprising a thin triple-ring 'sandwich' of Corinthian bronze and silver.

5) The range of instruments: whether counted as seven or eight instruments (depending on whether Cat. nos 3.41 and 3.42 are regarded as formerly a single, double-ended, instrument, or not) the set includes examples of all those most commonly found in the basic kits of Roman instruments. The inclusion of the tiny broken fig-shaped finial is also of significance, for it suggests that nothing was discarded from the group, and that this was the complete surviving metal instrumentation as found.

In terms of number, the instruments comprise one of the smaller basic sets of metal instruments. However, most of the instruments are double-ended, which broadened the scope of the set by providing at least 12 operative instruments – scalpel, blunt dissector, curette (which could also be used as a scoop), smooth-jawed forceps, toothed forceps, sharp hook, needle, ear probe, pointed probe, hooked dissector, elevator and rasp. These certainly have the appearance of instruments carefully selected by a practitioner to correspond to the wide range of medical and surgical interventions anticipated. As well as the range, the idiosyncratic alignment of the scalpel blade hints at an individual and purposeful acquisition, as does the incorporation of the distinctive inlaid decoration on three of the instruments, which suggests the practitioner appreciated the positive benefit that costly instrumentation could provide.

Together the instruments would have enabled surgery on both soft tissues and on bone, including ear, nose, throat and eye operations, the removal of small growths and foreign bodies and the treatment of fractured and diseased bone. In addition, the copper-alloy instruments would have been supplemented by others made of more perishable materials. Iron instruments or components of instruments (usually made from thin rods or sheet) rarely survive intact or in recognisable form, even those retrieved in the controlled

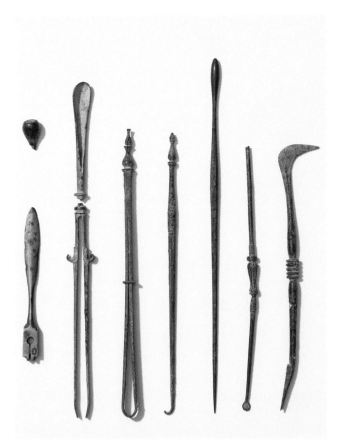

Figure 102 The small set of Roman medical instruments. British Museum, Cat. nos 3.40–3.48

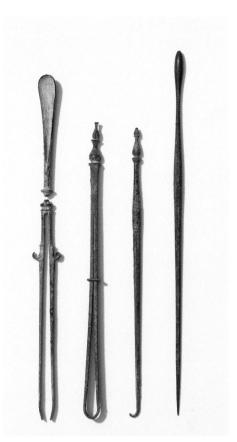

Figure 103 Part of the small set of Roman medical instruments – sharp spoon, smooth-jawed forceps, toothed forceps, sharp hook, needle. British Museum, left to right, Cat. nos 3.42, 3.41, 3.43, 3.44, 3.45

conditions of an archaeological excavation, and, as with many other instrument finds, there is none in this set. Only the last vestige of the iron blade remains in the socket of the scalpel handle, and it is possible that there were originally other instruments of iron, notably fine suturing needles, just as the practitioner would also have possessed instruments and implements made from organic materials.

Jackson 1997a, 228, 239, fig. 1; Jackson 2007b, 21–4, fig. 7. BMRL File 7071.

3.40. Scalpel handle, Type I, variant (1994,0726.1) (Figs 102, 104, 174)
Length 76.5mm; grip width 8.05mm; weight 9.2g

A small example, of bronze, which had been ruthlessly cleaned prior to acquisition by the British Museum, a process that has exposed the dull golden colour of the substrate metal. The bases of occasional corrosion pits have survived, preserving remnants of the original mid-brown-green patina. In consequence of this attrition, especially at the edges, the precise shape and dimensions of the blunt dissector are indeterminate. However, it appears to have been of slender form with a low median ridge on both faces. The grip, a tiny rectangular block, has plain faces. Its terminals are simply stepped, lacking the distinctive 'rolls' of most Type I scalpel handles, but it is conceivable that they were removed during cleaning. An idiosyncratic feature of this scalpel handle is that the keyhole socket was cut through the broader faces of the grip. Unless the iron blade tang incorporated a 90° turn this would have positioned the blade in a different plane to the dissector and would have affected

the manner in which the instrument was used and stored. Heavy cleaning has emptied the socket – just one tiny fragment of the iron blade tang has survived.

3.41. Smooth-jawed spring forceps (1994,0726.3) (Figs 102–3, 174)
Length 106.9mm; jaw width 4.5mm; weight 9.8g

A finely made example, of leaded bronze, of cut bar type. The upper end of the instrument is broken across the neck of a ring-and-disc moulding. The arms are unequally divided by their decorative shoulders: the short upper arms have a neatly faceted external face; the shoulders are of crisply cut step-and-scroll form; the lower arms taper in thickness and gently and evenly expand in width towards the in-turned smooth straight-edged jaws.

The fine faceting of the upper arms is exactly mirrored by that on the neck of the sharp spoon Cat. no. 3.42, which very probably was originally part of this instrument.

3.42. Sharp spoon (1994,0726.4) (Figs 102–3, 174)
Length 58.5mm; scoop width 9.5mm; weight 4.8g

A finely made elongated deep scoop, of bronze, with fine faceting on the underside and a semi-sharp rim at the broad upturned end. The object, a curette or scoop (or both), is broken across the neck of a ring moulding of the same type and dimension as that of forceps Cat. no. 3.41 and is very likely its missing component.

3.43. Toothed spring forceps (1994,0726.5) (Figs 102–3, 174)
Length 143.2mm; jaw width 4.4mm; weight 18.3g

**Figure 104 Part of the small set of Roman medical instruments –
finial, scalpel handle, ear probe, hooked dissector and lever. British
Museum, left to right, Cat. nos 3.48, 3.40, 3.46, 3.47**

A well-crafted leaded bronze example of cut bar type,
complete with sliding lock-ring. The finial is in the form of
two superimposed balusters, the tiny upper one fractured,
the lower plump one with a single slender girth ring inlaid
with a band of silver. The elegant arms are un-shouldered,
plain, well-finished, crisp rectangular-sectioned bars which
maintain a constant width but taper in thickness towards the
smoothly curved in-turned jaws. The teeth – three opposing
four, complete except for one tip – interlock precisely. A
square sliding lock-ring (7.8 × 6.5mm), still in place at the
mid-point of the arms, holds the jaws in their fully
compressed closed position.

3.44. Sharp hook (1994,0726.2) (Figs 102–3, 174)
Length 140.3mm; weight 8.6g
    A finely made and carefully finished slender leaded
bronze example of normal type. The elegant disc-and-
baluster finial, closely similar to that on Cat. no. 3.43,
though it lacks its tip, has a single slender girth ring inlaid
with a band of silver. As usual, the stem, itself of elongated
baluster form, is divided into two unequal parts by a
circular-sectioned zone at the point of maximum girth: a
series of three slender bands of inlay – silver flanked by
copper (but probably actually Corinthian bronze – its gold
component masked by copper corrosion products) – is
framed top and bottom by a pair of double-disc mouldings.
Above is a zone of fine 'scaly lattice'; below, the finely faceted
octagonal-sectioned stem tapers evenly to the smoothly
curved sharp hook, its tip now lacking.

3.45. Pointed probe or needle (1994,0726.6) (Figs 102–3, 174)
Length 177.5mm; weight 10.1g
    A very precisely made and carefully finished instrument,
of leaded bronze. Beneath the round-tipped olivary terminal
the long slender stem, of finely faceted octagonal cross-
section, first tapers and then expands to form a swollen grip,
beyond which it tapers evenly to the point, which is circular-
sectioned and sharp.

3.46. Ear probe and ? (1994,0726.7) (Figs 102, 104, 174)
Length 131.8mm; spoon diameter 4.3mm; weight 5.6g
    A finely made double-ended instrument of leaded bronze,
one end broken. The very slender, precisely faceted,
octagonal-sectioned stem is divided into two parts flanking a
central grip in the form of a neat stylised acanthus moulding,
its pedestal foot inlaid with a narrow band of Corinthian
bronze. The complete surviving part, slightly bent at the
junction with the grip, comprises a slender vase-shaped
moulding inlaid with three thin bands – Corinthian bronze
flanked by silver – beyond which the stem tapers evenly to
the neck of the tiny circular spoon. The other part comprises
a slender cylindrical moulding, also inlaid with three thin
bands – and again Corinthian bronze flanked by silver –
beyond which the straight, parallel-sided stem extends to the
point of breakage. Assuming symmetry around the central
grip little is lacking and breakage may have occurred near
the end of the missing component – probably a pointed
probe or (less likely) an olivary terminal.

3.47. Hooked dissector and lever (1994.0726.8) (Figs 102, 104, 174)
Length 132.9mm; weight 13.0g
    A very precise and carefully wrought symmetrical
double-ended instrument, of bronze, combining a hooked
dissector with a ridged lever. The central grip, comprising a
crisply cut series of double-disc and cushion mouldings, is
flanked by slender vase-shaped mouldings, each
ornamented, like those on Cat. no. 3.46, with three thin
bands of inlay – Corinthian bronze flanked by silver – and a
disc moulding. These are followed by an evenly tapered,
finely faceted, octagonal-sectioned stem. One end
terminates in a curved, bill-like blade or dissector (like that
on scalpel handle Cat. no. 3.65), with a low median ridge on
both faces, semi-sharp convex and concave edges and a
pointed tip. The other end comprises an angled, lightly
splayed wedge, with a bifurcated tip and a series of 14 raked
ridges on the inner, very lightly concave, face.
    Cf. an example in the late 2nd/early 3rd-century AD
Verona 'Tomba del Medico' instrumentation (its hooked
dissector part-broken) (Künzl 1983a, 104; Bonomi 1984;
Bolla 2004); one in Solingen (Deutsches Klingenmuseum)
inv. 74.B26 (L. 120mm); and one in the Halûk Perk collection
of instruments from Anatolia (Perk 2012, 37, 1.3.1 – wrongly
identified as a decapitator, L. 137mm).

3.48. Finial? (1994,0726.9) (Figs 102, 104, 174)
Length 15.2mm; diameter 9.2 mm; weight 4.1g
    A fig-shaped finial, of heavily leaded bronze, with flat end
and circular cross-section, broken at the narrow neck.
Function uncertain, but possibly a handle finial.

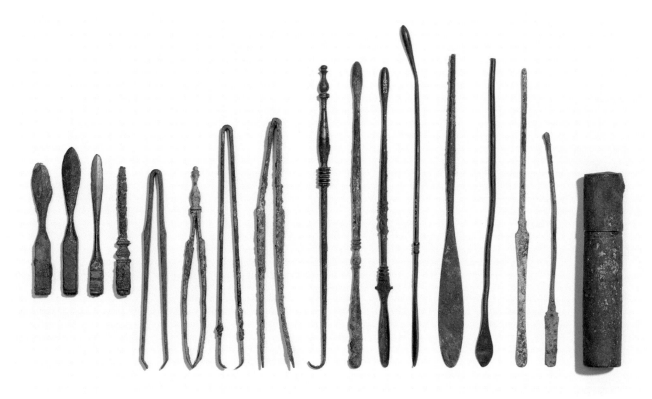

Figure 105 The possible set of Roman medical instruments formerly in the Blacas collection – scalpel handles, forceps, sharp hook, probes, tubular box. British Museum, left to right, Cat. nos 3.58–9, 3.61–2, 3.82, 3.87, 3.94–5, 3.102, 3.112–13, 3.128

?SET (Cat. nos 3.58–9, 3.61–2, 3.82, 3.87, 3.94–5, 3.102, 3.112–13, 3.128) (1867,0508.118*–119*, 120–32, 140, 168 Blacas Collection) (Fig. 105)

Provenance unknown.

Probably 1st/2nd century AD.

Seventeen medical instruments were included in the large acquisition of antiquities purchased by the British Museum in Paris in 1866 at the sale of the Collection of Louis Charles Pierre Casimir de Blacas d'Aulps, 2nd Duke of Blacas (1815–1866). Much of the extensive collection had been formed by his father, Pierre-Louis Jean Casimir, duc de Blacas d'Aulps, the 1st Duke (1771–1839), on whose death he had inherited it, but the 2nd Duke increased the collection in size and scope. It is not known which of the Dukes acquired the instruments. The 1st Duke had been French Ambassador at Naples and at Rome for many years and, as noted in 1867, 'his official position, ample fortune and high reputation as a connoisseur, gave him advantages as a collector of antiquities such as few foreigners resident in Italy have possessed' (Newton 1867, 3). It is unfortunate, though not unusual for the time, that no information was supplied with the instruments. Their place and circumstances of discovery are thus irretrievable, but a find-spot in the region of Naples or of Rome would not be unexpected.

No record survives to show even that the instruments were found or acquired together, but there are reasons to believe not only that they were acquired, but also that they were found, together and comprise a belonging set. For they comprise the number and varieties of metal instruments recurrently found in the basic sets in the Greco-Roman world – there are two plain (Cat. nos 3.58–9) and two inlaid (Cat. nos 3.61–2) scalpel handles graded in size, two smooth-jawed spring forceps (Cat. nos 3.82 and 3.87), a toothed spring forceps (Cat. no. 3.94) and a pointed-jawed spring forceps (Cat. no. 3.95), a sharp hook (Cat. no. 3.102), three scoop probes (Cat. nos 3.112–13) and four spatula probes in a range of forms and sizes, along with a tubular medicine box (Cat. no. 3.128). In addition, all 10 instruments which were analysed (all except the probes) are made from bronze or leaded bronze; and the appearance of the surface of the instruments – a brown patina, in places lightly encrusted with pale green corrosion products – is very similar (in some cases near-identical, e.g. Cat. nos 3.94–5), especially when taking into consideration their long period out of the ground, during which time some selective cleaning probably took place. There is a further linkage between scalpel handle Cat. no. 3.62 and toothed forceps Cat. no. 3.94: both preserve mineral-preserved wood in their surface corrosion products, suggestive of storage with others of the instruments in a wooden case.

Thus, several features unite the instruments and make a compelling case for regarding them as a belonging set when acquired, rather than adventitiously acquired individual instruments. We may probably discount the possibility that either of the Dukes of Blacas would have acquired individual instruments in order to put together a set. Even if they had thought it worthy of their time to do so they would probably not have known which were the appropriate instruments to seek. For it was only with the discovery of sets of instruments in secure contexts on archaeological excavations, mostly in the 20th and 21st centuries, that the composition of the ancient sets was established. Proof is lacking, therefore, but the likelihood is that the Blacas instruments are a set, assembled by a knowledgeable and discerning medical practitioner, probably within the period 2nd–3rd century AD.

Figure 106a–b The cupping vessel from Corfu. British Museum, Cat. no. 3.49

Cupping vessels

3.49. Cupping vessel (1868,0110.230 Woodhouse Collection) (Figs 106a–b, 174)

From Corfu, Greece. No known finding details, but probably from a grave.

Height 98.7mm; maximum girth 65.8mm; diameter at mouth 38.8mm; weight 74.3g

A finely crafted bronze cupping vessel (*cucurbitula*) of normal form, raised in one piece, with a narrow domed body, crisply carinated shoulder, tapered neck, lightly flared mouth and neatly thickened and smoothed rim. The metal varies in thickness: 1.3mm at the dome's apex; 0.3mm at the shoulder; 1mm above the rim and 0.9–1.3mm at the rim. There is localised breakage in three places on the shoulder. At the apex of the dome the dimpled centre-point (a remnant of manufacture) occupies a circle of differentially preserved patina, itself encircled by a grey-coloured halo, which analysis indicates to be degraded solder. These traces disclose the former presence of a domed mount with looped staple and ring, a common feature of Greek and Roman cupping vessels which enabled them to be suspended when not in use. There is no mention of a domed mount in Walters' Bronzes catalogue of 1899 and it is likely that the mount was a post-discovery loss prior to the accessioning of the cupping vessel into the British Museum collection.

1st/2nd century AD

Bronzes catalogue, 2313; Lambros 1895, 10, fig. 18; Milne 1907, 103, pl. 34; *Guide to Greek and Roman Life* 1908, 180, no. 440; Scarborough 1969, pl. 38; Berger 1970, 74, fig. 74; Künzl 1983a, 42–3, fig. 12.

BMRL 7191-57-R.

Scalpels

3.50. Scalpel handle, Type I (1975,1106.7) (Figs 107a–b, 174)

Provenance unknown.

Length 56.5mm (including blade stub 58.5mm); grip width 10.5mm; weight 23.8g

A small, heavy, seemingly worn example of leaded bronze. The blunt dissector is short and stubby, with a strong median ridge on both faces, a blunt tip and a short faceted stem. The rectangular grip has rolled terminals and a keyhole socket, with the end of the iron blade tang *in situ* in

the slot and its circular terminal. The two main faces of the grip incorporate a rectangular panel ornamented with a relief design comprising a vine scroll motif within a wave-crest border. The recessed areas of the design probably originally held inlays of silver and niello.

1st century AD.

Bronzes catalogue, 2338; Künzl 1994a, fig. 130; Büsing-Kolbe 2001, Type A.

Cf. Künzl 1994a, 216, a near-identical example from Xanten.

BMRL 7191-6-R.

3.51. Scalpel handle, Type I (1975,1106.6) (Fig. 107a–b)

Provenance unknown.

Length 88.1mm; grip width 9.9mm; grip thickness 7.6mm; weight 27.7g

A medium-sized example of leaded bronze. The dissector has a blunt tip, a rounded median ridge on both faces and a short neatly faceted stem. The rectangular grip has rolled terminals (one damaged) and a keyhole socket. The mouth of the socket has been forced slightly apart and is now empty, but the end of the iron blade tang occupies the back of the slot and the round terminal. A recessed rectangular area occupies most of the two main faces of the grip. It is bordered by a straight rim with a narrow channel on the inner side and evidently once held an inlay, presumably a silver foil sheet held in place with solder – there are slight traces of what looks like white metal in a few places.

1st/2nd century AD.

Bronzes catalogue, 2336.

BMRL 7191-73-R.

3.52. Scalpel handle, Type I (1856,1226.1033 Temple Collection) (Fig. 108a–b)

Provenance unknown.

Length 78.5mm; grip width 9.8mm; grip thickness 7.0mm; weight 23.7g

An example, of leaded bronze, of the 'standard' Roman scalpel handle. The leaf-shaped blunt dissector has a marked median ridge on both faces and a slender, neatly faceted, hexagonal-sectioned stem. The grip is a seemingly plain rectangular block with rolled terminals. Iron corrosion products on the sides prevent identification of the socket, which contains the corroded remains of the iron blade tang.

XRF analysis suggests that the blade was originally secured by a soft solder of lead and tin.

1st/2nd century AD.

BMRL 7191-28-T.

3.53. Scalpel handle, Type I (1878,1019.105 Meyrick Collection) (Fig. 108a–b)

Provenance unknown.

Length 87.5mm (including blade stub 90.9mm); grip width *c.* 10mm; grip thickness *c.* 7.8–8.9mm; weight 26g

An example, of leaded bronze, of the 'standard' Roman scalpel handle. The blunt dissector, damaged at its blunt tip, has a low median ridge on both faces and a faceted stem. The rectangular grip, apparently plain, expands in width and thickness towards the rolled terminals (one now damaged). The socket, of keyhole type, is still occupied by the end of the iron blade tang, which projects a few millimetres beyond the moulded terminals.

1st/2nd century AD.

BMRL 7191-34-N.

3.54. Scalpel handle, Type I (1865,1220.20 Given by Augustus Wollaston Franks) (Fig. 110a–b)

From City of London.

Length 92.1mm (including blade stub 93.1mm); grip width 8.8mm; grip thickness 7.9mm; weight 25.9g

A medium-sized, well-made example of leaded bronze. The blunt dissector is proportionately large, with a strong median ridge on both faces, blunt edges and a blunt tip. It is lightly offset by a kink in the neatly faceted stem, probably a deliberate adaptation by its user. The relatively long slender rectangular grip has rolled terminals and a deep keyhole socket. The corroded end of the iron blade tang remains in the round terminal and slot and projects slightly from the mouth of the socket. XRF analysis suggests that the blade was originally secured by a soft solder of lead and tin.

The distinctive finely preserved metallic surface with partial brown coating is characteristic of London finds from the bed of the River Walbrook and its tributaries. As such it may be dated 1st/2nd century AD.

BMRL 7191-62-K

3.55. Scalpel handle, Type I (1878,1019.106 Meyrick Collection) (Fig. 108a–b)

Provenance unknown.

Length 78.8mm; grip width 9.5mm; grip thickness maximum 10mm; weight 27.8g

A standard Type I scalpel handle, of leaded bronze. The leaf-shaped blunt dissector has a median ridge on both faces, and a neatly faceted stem. The small, rectangular block grip, with crisp angles, has neatly rolled terminals and a keyhole socket, still partially blocked with the corroded remains of the iron blade tang. XRF analysis suggests that the blade was originally secured by a soft solder of lead and tin.

1st/2nd century AD.

BMRL 7191-35-Q.

3.56. Scalpel handle, Type I (1975,1106.5) (Fig. 108a–b)

Provenance unknown.

Figure 107a–b Scalpel handles, front and side views. British Museum, left to right, Cat. nos 3.50, 3.51

Length 70.0mm (including blade stub 71.1mm); grip width 9.9mm; grip thickness 8.9mm; weight 26.6g

A small stout example of leaded bronze. The dissector is short and plump, with a strong median ridge on both faces, a blunt tip and semi-sharp edges. The strong stem is very neatly faceted. The plain rectangular grip has crisp angles, finely crafted rolled terminals (one damaged) and a keyhole socket which retains the corroded remains of the iron blade tang both in the slot and in the round terminal. The handle appears to preserve a wear polish.

1st/2nd century AD.

Bronzes catalogue, 2333.

BMRL 7191-74-W.

3.57. Scalpel handle, Type I (1814,0704.948 Townley Collection) (Fig. 108a–b)

Provenance unknown, but probably found in Rome or its environs (see pp. 2–3).

Length 82.1mm (including blade stub 84.8mm); grip width 9.2mm; grip thickness 7.8mm; weight 18.8g

A relatively light and slender example, of bronze. The small leaf-shaped blunt dissector, rounded and blunt at the tip, has a clear median ridge on both faces. It is angled very slightly to one side. Its tapered junction with the grip is a neatly faceted hexagonal-sectioned stem. The simple plain grip is a small rectangular block with rolled terminals and a keyhole socket, the latter still filled with the corroded remains of the iron blade, the stub of which protrudes slightly beyond the terminals. XRF analysis suggests that the blade was originally secured by a soft solder of lead and tin.

1st/2nd century AD.

Bronzes catalogue, 2334.

BMRL 7191-27-Q.

Figure 108a–b Scalpel handles, front and side views. British Museum, left to right, Cat. nos 3.52, 3.53, 3.55, 3.56, 3.57, 3.58, 3.59

Figure 109a–b Scalpel handles, front and side views. British Museum, left to right, Cat. nos 3.60, 3.61, 3.62, 3.64, 3.65

3.58. Scalpel handle, Type I (1867,0508.129 Blacas Collection) (Fig. 108a–b)

Provenance unknown.

Part of probable set, see p. 99.

Length 66.2mm; grip width 7.5mm; grip thickness 7.0mm; weight 15.4g

A small example, of leaded bronze, with short leaf-shaped dissector and slender grip. The blunt dissector has a low median ridge on both faces and a neatly faceted hexagonal-sectioned stem. The crisply cut grip, apparently plain, lacks one of its rolled terminals. The end of the tang of the iron blade is clearly visible in the keyhole socket. XRF analysis detected higher levels of lead in the vicinity of the socket suggestive of the use of soft solder to secure the blade.

ıst/2nd century AD.

BMRL 7191-29-X.

3.59. Scalpel handle, Type I (1867,0508.130 Blacas Collection) (Fig. 108a–b)

Provenance unknown.

Part of probable set, see p. 99.

Length 74.5mm (including blade stub 74.6mm); grip width 7.1mm; grip thickness 6.2mm; weight 12.5g

A small slender example, of leaded bronze. The blunt

dissector has a very low median ridge on both faces and a hexagonal-sectioned faceted stem. The slender grip is a plain rectangular block with grooved terminals. The socket, which appears to be a simple thin slot, is filled with the end of the iron blade tang. XRF analysis suggests that the blade was originally secured by a soft solder of lead and tin.

ıst/2nd century AD.

BMRL 7191-30-R.

3.60. Scalpel handle, Type I (1878,1019.108 Meyrick Collection) (Fig. 108a–b)

Provenance unknown.

Length c. 77mm (including blade stub 83.4mm); grip width c. 6.8mm; grip thickness c. 5mm; weight 7.9g

An extremely slender and light example, of leaded bronze. The thin leaf-shaped blunt dissector has a low median ridge on both faces and a very long thin faceted stem. The tiny grip is a flat rectangular block, its terminals and socket obscured by the corrosion products of the iron blade tang, which projects c. 6.4 mm. from the socket end, at which point it is 7mm wide.

ıst/2nd century AD.

BMRL 7191-37-X.

3.61. Scalpel handle, Type I (1867,0508.131 Blacas Collection) (Figs 109a–b, 174)

Provenance unknown.

Part of probable set, see p. 99.

Length 70.1mm (including blade stub 71.3mm); grip width 6.3mm; grip thickness 5.8mm; weight 6.9g

A small slender example, of leaded bronze, with fine minuscule inlay. The very slender blunt dissector has a blunt tip and a marked median ridge on both faces. The tiny rectangular grip has neatly stepped terminals and a keyhole socket filled with the end of the tang of the iron blade. Towards the grip end of the long, narrow, neatly faceted stem is a zone of inlay, *c.* 3mm wide, comprising five silver bands interspersed with four bands of the bronze body metal. The principal zone of inlay is on the two main faces of the grip. The design is the same on both faces and comprises a symmetrical mirror-image arrangement based on a central horizontal inlaid copper strip flanked on both sides by five inlaid strips interspersed with six ridges of bronze body metal. The inlaid strips comprise copper, anticlockwise twisted silver, copper, clockwise twisted silver, plain silver, copper, plain silver, anticlockwise twisted silver, copper, clockwise twisted silver, copper. The twisted strips were orientated to give a herring-bone or chevron effect. The width of each of the four 'layer-cakes' of five inlays and six interspersed ridges is *c.* 3.3mm. Each inlaid wire is just *c.* 0.3–0.4mm in diameter. See pp. 41 and 155 and **Figs 174, 187**.

   1st/2nd century AD.
   Bronzes catalogue, 2332.
   BMRL 7191-31-W.

3.62. Scalpel handle, Type I variant (1867,0508.132 Blacas Collection) (Fig. 109a–b)

Provenance unknown.

Part of probable set, see p. 99.

Length 64.6mm; grip width 5.9mm; grip thickness *c.* 6.5mm; weight 9.8g

A finely made, ornate, leaded bronze handle of unusual form, lacking its terminal. The simple grip is a tiny rectangular block with rolled terminals. Its socket is partially obscured by the corrosion products of the end of the iron blade tang which is still in position. Above the grip is a double-disc-and-baluster moulding (the baluster with two inlaid silver rings) surmounted by an elongated, slender, circular-sectioned stem (with inlaid silver spiral), a small ring-and-disc moulding and a further circular-sectioned stem, its end broken. Traces of mineral-preserved wood (*Prunus* sp.) in several areas are indicative of storage in a wooden instrument case.

   1st/2nd century AD.
   BMRL 7191-32-Y.

3.63. Scalpel handle, Type I variant (1856,1226.1034 Temple Collection) (Figs 112a–b, 174)

Provenance unknown.

Length 81.9mm (including blade stub 84mm); grip width 9mm; grip thickness 7mm; weight 18.3g

A well-made ornate example, of leaded bronze, with an elongated stem in the form of a stylised 'Club of Hercules'.

The blunt dissector is small and short, with a blunt tip and a median ridge on both faces. The small plain rectangular grip has moulded terminals. A series of finely cut rectangular mouldings divides the grip from the 'Club of Hercules' stem, itself probably used as a grip, especially when manipulating the blunt dissector. The corroded stub of the iron blade tang occupies and obscures the socket. XRF analysis suggests that the blade was originally secured by a soft solder of lead and tin.

   1st/2nd century AD.
   Bronzes catalogue, 2340.
   BMRL 7191-2-X.

3.64. Scalpel handle, Type I variant (1902,1212.2) (Figs 109a–b, 174)

Found at, or near, Myndus (modern Gümüslük), near Bodrum, Turkey.

Length 81mm; grip/socket width 5.3mm; weight 10.3g

A small, slender, finely made ornate example, of leaded bronze. The grip, a tiny rectangular block with rolled terminals, is little more than a seating for the keyhole socket. The end of the iron blade tang, *in situ* in the socket, occupies only the slot and not the circular terminal. A whitish deposit in the socket, concentrated in the circular terminal, is probably degraded lead-tin solder, as indicated by XRF analysis. The grip proper, above the socket block, is an elegant circular-sectioned baluster flanked by groups of crisply cut ring-and-disc mouldings. The baluster is inlaid with a double spiral of silver and Corinthian bronze, while the central ring of the mouldings is inlaid with a band of silver. The small leaf-shaped blunt dissector has a low median ridge on both faces and is angled to one side, seemingly a feature of manufacture rather than a later adaptation.

   1st/2nd century AD.
   Guide to Greek and Roman Life 1908, 179–80, fig.189g.
   BMRL 7191-4-M.
   Cf. Künzl 1983a, 33, 57–8, fig. 26.1; Künzl 1996, 2594–5, fig. IX.3, a near-identical example from Saint-Privat d'Allier, Haute-Loire, France; and Hibbs 1991, fig. 3.1, another, from a necropolis of cremation burials at La Cañada Honda (Gandul), near Seville, Spain.

3.65. Scalpel handle, Type I variant (1907,0523.1) (Figs 109a–b, 174)

Provenance unknown.

Length 80.6mm; weight 8.3g

A small, light instrument, of leaded bronze, with crisply cut mouldings and few visible manufacture marks. The grip has a central zone of ring-and-disc mouldings flanked by tiny plain blocks. Radiography (see p. 151 and **Figs 180–1**) revealed: 1) that the socket is of keyhole type with rolled terminals; 2) that a tiny perforation pierces the terminals at 90° to the slot and contains the remains of a pin or rivet, presumably fixing the iron blade tang (the stub of which is still *in situ*); and 3) that the central ring mouldings are inlaid with silver bands (confirmed by XRF). Projecting from the grip is a long very slender stem which terminates in a hooked crescent-shaped dissector (like that on Cat. no. 3.47) with median ridge on both faces, the concave and convex edges semi-sharp, the tip blunt.

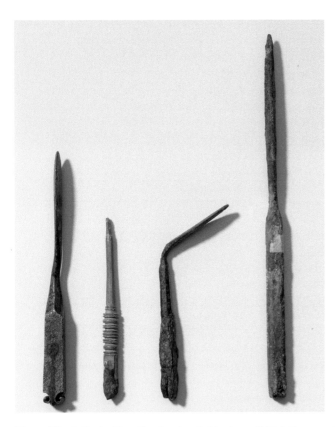

Figure 110a–b Scalpel handles, front and side views. British Museum, left to right, Cat. nos 3.54, 3.66, 3.67, 3.72

1st/2nd century AD.
BMRL 7191-5-P.
Cf. Cat. no. 3.47 and comparanda.

3.66. Scalpel handle, Type I variant (1949,0601.35) (Fig. 110a–b)

From Hammill Shaft, Eastry, Kent.
Length 64.0mm (including blade stub 66.8mm); grip width 5.1mm; grip thickness 4.6mm; weight 6.95g

This is a finely made slender leaded bronze handle of unusual form. The simple grip is a tiny rectangular block with rolled terminals. Within its slender slot socket is the corroded tang of the broken iron blade. Scientific investigation revealed that the socket is 11mm deep; and XRF analysis identified remains of a soft solder of lead and tin in association with the corroded iron blade tang.

Above the grip is a series of very finely cut ring-and-disc mouldings surmounted by an elongated, slender, octagonal-sectioned stem broken at the foot of its terminal, probably a blunt dissector.
1st/2nd century AD.
BMRL 7191-64-P

3.67. Scalpel handle, Type I variant (1985,1003.14) (Fig. 110a–b)

From Stonea Grange, Cambridgeshire, part of a metal-detected surface collection made prior to archaeological excavations.
Length 70.2mm (originally – unbent – 86.5mm); grip width 8.9 mm; grip thickness 5.8mm; weight 13.35g

This is a slender and idiosyncratic example, of leaded gunmetal, of the most common form of Roman scalpel handle. The small dissector has a low median ridge on both faces and has been bent at the neck. Scientific examination revealed a strip of metal wound around the bent neck of the dissector, an alteration which had occurred before burial as the patina developed over the added strip. There is no clear junction with the grip, for the flat octagonal-sectioned neck simply splays out to form a narrow, seemingly plain, rectangular block with grooved terminals. Within the simple slot socket are the corroded remains of the tang of the iron blade. XRF analysis suggests that the blade was originally secured by lead-rich solder.
1st/2nd century AD.
Jackson and Potter 1996, 354–6, fig. 114, no. 114.
BMRL 7191-63-M

3.68. Scalpel handle(s?), three fragments (1872,0604.879 Castellani Collection) (Figs 111a–b, 174)

From Rome.
Length 133.1mm; grip width and thickness: 1) 7.1 × 6.2mm 2) 7.3 × 6.6mm 3) 6.9 × 6.5mm; weight 32.6g

A rather enigmatic object in three pieces currently joined with adhesive.

1) The large dissector has a strong median ridge on both faces, a blunt-pointed tip and a neatly faceted stem. The surviving stub of the grip is a slender, plain, rectangular-sectioned block with crisp angles. A half dovetail mortise has been cut into its end permitting it to be joined to the decorated grip (3) by means of a corresponding (but full) mortise tenon of the same dimensions.

2) The socket end of an apparently plain, slender, rectangular-sectioned grip with crisp angles and rolled terminals. XRF analysis indicates the presence of decayed solder in the keyhole socket. A half dovetail mortise has been cut into the end enabling it to be joined to a

corresponding half dovetail tenon in the end of the decorated grip (3).

3) A fine, slender, regular, rectangular-sectioned block with crisp angles, inlaid with a design in white metal on all four faces: scientific analysis indicates that the body metal is Corinthian bronze and the inlay silver alloy. The two principal (broader) faces have a symmetrical design comprising a four-pointed star in a disc flanked by double-pelta discs and a double-pellet-and-lozenge motif, all ranged on a central line. The two narrower sides share a simpler arrangement of centre line, double-pelta disc and double-pellet-and-lozenge motif. It is a Büsing-Kolbe 2001, Type B grip. The design on all faces has been truncated by the working of a dovetail tenon onto both ends of the grip.

It is possible that pieces (1) and (2) are parts of the same scalpel handle, the central grip portion of which was at some point cut out in order to insert the highly ornate, though incomplete, component (3). The patina and corrosion products of (1) and (2) are similar and their surviving grip dimensions almost precisely the same, bearing in mind that (1) has been cleaned more than (2). However, scientific analysis, using surface XRF, perhaps suggests otherwise, for the composition of (1) corresponds to a leaded brass while that of (2) is gunmetal, although both analyses are actually fairly similar. Whatever the case, we may be fairly confident that component (3) is from a different instrument altogether – on all other scalpels with this very distinctive type of decoration the inlaid design continues onto the blunt dissector, and it is not present on (1). The present object may therefore be characterised as a pastiche, comprising pieces of two or three different scalpel handles. Such a confection is more likely to have been a product of the recent past than of antiquity. The second part of the short description of the instrument in Castellani's catalogue of 1872 as 'di bronzo intarsiato di argento' confirms the presence of the ornate component (3), while the first part, 'Instrumento (chirurgico?)', implies the presence of the other two pieces (1 and 2), since it would have been difficult in the 19th century to have characterised the instrument as 'chirurgico?' in the absence of the distinctive blunt dissector (1) and, to a lesser degree, of the distinctive socket type. Certainly, the annotated pen-and-ink thumb-nail sketch (showing the object in three joined pieces) and length measurement ('L 5¼in.') added in, or after, 1872 demonstrate the presence of all three pieces. In all probability, therefore, the pastiche had been contrived before Castellani acquired the object. The entry in Walters 1899 characterises the object as a 'bistoury' (i.e. a scalpel), 'complete', though 'broken in three pieces'. Misled by the black appearance of the Corinthian bronze Walters described the central component as an 'iron haft, inlaid with patterns in silver'. Nevertheless, he astutely added a reference to Roach Smith's 1850s publication of the (now missing) parallel piece from Rochester, Kent (Roach Smith c. 1855, 209, pl. XXXIV, 3).

1st/2nd century AD.

Castellani catalogue, 879; Bronzes catalogue, 2341.

BMRL 7191-7-W.

3.69. Scalpel handle, Type II (1883,0725.6) (Fig. 112a–b)
Provenance unknown.

Figure 111a–b Scalpel handle with silver-inlaid Corinthian bronze grip, front and side views. British Museum, Cat. no. 3.68

Length 97.5mm (incl. blade stub 98.1mm); grip width 7.1mm; grip thickness 7.1mm; weight 19.5g

The handle, of leaded bronze, has a slightly asymmetric dissector with a low median ridge on both faces, a blunt tip and a faceted stem. The octagonal-sectioned grip has a moulded and grooved terminal. The socket, which retains the corroded tang of the iron blade, is partially obscured by corrosion products but appears to be a simple slot. Traces of mineral-preserved wood (*Fraxinus* sp.) on the grip near the socket may suggest storage in a wooden instrument case.

2nd/3rd century AD.

BMRL 7191-39-M.

3.70. Scalpel handle, Type II (1878,1019.107 Meyrick Collection) (Figs 112a–b, 174)
Provenance unknown.

Length 77.5mm; grip width c. 6.9mm; grip thickness c. 6.8mm; weight 16.3g

A small example, of leaded bronze. The leaf-shaped blunt dissector, with median ridge on both faces, is lightly cranked at the faceted hexagonal-sectioned stem – apparently an original feature suggestive of an additional role as a bone elevator. The slender grip, of octagonal cross-section, has simple chamfered terminals. The socket, apparently of keyhole type, is blocked with the corroded remains of the iron blade tang. XRF analysis suggests that the blade was originally secured by a soft solder of lead and tin.

2nd/3rd century AD.

Bronzes catalogue, 2335.

BMRL 7191-36-T.

Figure 112a–b Scalpel handles, front and side views. British Museum, left to right, Cat. nos 3.69, 3.70, 3.71, 3.63

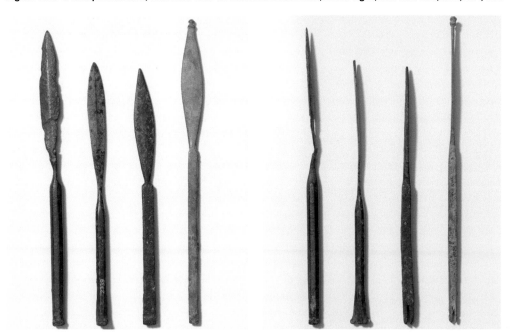

Figure 113a–b Scalpel handles, front and side views. British Museunm left to right, Cat. nos 3.73, 3.74, 3.75, 3.76

3.71. Scalpel handle, Type II variant (1932,1112.2 Ex-Sambon Collection) **(Fig. 112a–b)**

Lake Trasimene, Umbria, Italy.
Given by Dr Davies Sherborn, Natural History Museum, South Kensington; ex-Louis Sambon Collection (Glendenning's sale 25 July 1932, Lot 62); all said to have been found by Dr Sambon personally on the battlefield of Lake Trasimene – see also drill-bit? and forceps, Cat. nos 3.79, 3.88.
Length 94.2mm; grip width *c.* 7.8mm; grip thickness *c.* 4.4mm; weight 16.8g

A rather idiosyncratic and rudimentarily finished example, of brass, with an unusually thin flat grip. The blunt dissector has a low median ridge on both faces, a damaged tip and a short faceted stem. The plain grip is a flat rectangular block with lightly chamfered angles and simple grooved terminals (one broken). The socket, a simple slot, retains no trace of the iron blade.

2nd/3rd century AD.
BMRL 7191-40-Y.

3.72. Scalpel handle, Type II (EA67451 (WG.627))
(Figs 110a–b, 174)

Gebel Sheikh Embarak, Upper Egypt
Length 133mm; grip width 9.7mm; grip thickness 6.9mm; weight 26.19g

A long example, of brass, with plain, octagonal-sectioned grip and a slot socket with grooved mouth. The long slender leaf-shaped blunt dissector has a marked median ridge on both faces. Corroded remains of the iron blade tang are present in the socket. Analysis by inductively coupled plasma-atomic emission spectrometry (ICP-AES) yielded the following results: Cu 85.1, Sn 2.33, Zn 11.3, Pb 0.35, Ag 0.05 Fe 0.36, Sb 0.08, Ni 0.032, As 0.08, S 0.09 (Au, Co, Mn, Cd, Bi, not detected).

2nd/3rd century AD.
BMRL 6097-38888-X.

3.73. Scalpel handle, Type II (1877,0820.3) **(Fig. 113a–b)**

Provenance unknown.

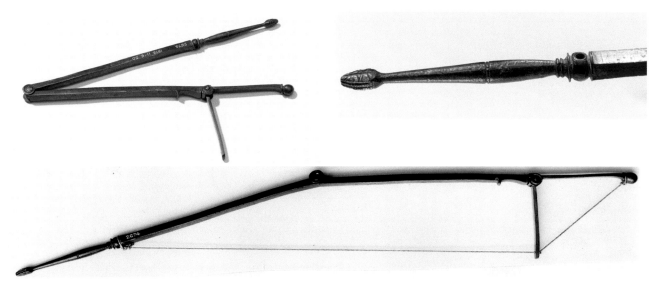

Figure 114a–c Folding drill-handle: a) (top left) the handle near fully folded; b) (top right) detail showing the stylised snake's head finial and the perforation for securing the distal end of the cord; c) (above) the drill-handle fully opened and strung with a cord. British Museum, Cat no. 3.78

Length 121.7mm; maximum grip width 5.2mm; maximum grip thickness 4.9mm; weight 14.8g

A long slender example, of low-zinc brass. The slender blunt dissector has a pointed tip and a median ridge on both faces. It is damaged and distorted at the hexagonal-sectioned faceted stem. The long, very slender grip, plain and octagonal-sectioned, has neatly moulded and grooved terminals and a very thin slot socket (depth 11.4mm), which still contains the end of the iron blade tang. XRF analysis suggests that the blade was originally secured by a soft solder of lead and tin.

2nd/3rd century AD.
Bronzes catalogue, 2364.
BMRL 7191-33-L.

3.74. Scalpel handle, Type II (1814,0704.955 Townley Collection) (Fig. 113a–b)

Provenance unknown, but probably found in Rome or its environs (see pp. 2–3).

Length 108.5mm; grip thickness 4mm; socket width 4.2mm; weight 8.7g

A small, light, neatly made example, of bronze, with a long, very slender, octagonal-sectioned grip. The long slender, laurel leaf-shaped blunt dissector has a low median ridge on both faces and a blunt tip. Its light curvature is more probably a result of distortion at the very thin neck than a deliberate adjustment by the user. The slotted socket, with neatly rolled terminals, is blocked by the iron tang of the now missing blade. XRF analysis suggests that the blade was originally secured by a soft solder of lead and tin.

2nd/3rd century AD.
Bronzes catalogue, 2339.
BMRL 7191-1-T.

3.75. Scalpel handle, Type II (1878,1019.109 Meyrick Collection) (Fig. 113a–b)

Provenance unknown.

Length 105.8mm; grip width 4.8mm; grip thickness 4.4mm; weight 13.9g

A long slender example, of leaded gunmetal. The leaf-shaped blunt dissector, with a very low median ridge on both faces and a pointed tip, is bent to one side. Likewise, the long slender rectangular-sectioned grip, with simple grooved terminal and thin slot socket, is lightly bent (in a different plane to the dissector). In both cases the distortion appears deliberate either as an original feature or an ancient adaptation of the instrument. A whitish substance filling the back of the socket is evidently the degraded remains of a bonding medium for the iron blade as XRF analysis identified it as a soft solder of lead and tin.

2nd/3rd century AD.
Bronzes catalogue, 2337.
BMRL 7191-38-K.

3.76. Scalpel handle, Type II (1899,0218.61) (Fig. 113a–b)

Provenance unknown.

Length 125.3mm; grip width and thickness 3.5–3.8mm; weight 10.9g

A light, simply made and quite rudimentarily finished scalpel handle, of leaded gunmetal, with manufacturing/finishing marks still visible in the well-preserved patina. The grip is long and extremely slender, of crisp rectangular cross-section. It terminates in a tiny slot socket with plain grooved moulding. No iron corrosion is visible but the back of the socket is blocked with soil or decayed solder. The elongated laurel leaf terminal has a very low median ridge on both faces, blunt sides and a moulded knob finial.

2nd/3rd century AD.
BMRL 7191-3-K.

Cf. Milne 1907, 43, pl. 8.2, a near-identical example, but wrongly identified as a probe-pointed blade; two unprovenanced examples in the Musée de la Médecine, Brussels (Jackson 2018a, 139, fig. 3, 3rd and 4th from left); and an unpublished example from excavations at Butrint, Albania (A15 Forum 2007, SF 945 (859).

3.77. Scalpel? (1934,1210.46) (Figs 116a–b, 174)

From City of London, bed of the River Walbrook.

Length 141mm; weight 33.7g

Figure 115a–b Probable drill-bits, front and side views. British Museum, left to right, Cat. nos 3.12 and 3.79

A single-piece iron implement, with a long slender circular-sectioned stem, terminating at one end in a small diamond-shaped spatula with blunt edges and a median ridge on both faces. At the other end is a broad flat triangular-sectioned blade with an oblique, lightly convex, cutting edge. Waterlogging in the bed of the River Walbrook has resulted in good preservation of the surface of the metal.

In the light of the single-piece iron scalpels found in the kit of medical implements in the mid-1st-century AD 'Doctor's Burial' at Stanway, near Colchester (Jackson 2007a, 236–8, fig 121, CF47.26 and CF47.27), and a single-piece copper-alloy example in Naples (Bliquez 1994, 121, no. 52), identification of the present implement as a Romano-British scalpel seems more probable than its former identification as a modelling tool (Manning 1985, 31–2, pl. 13, C10). Certainly its blade is close in appearance to the common 'bellied' form of Roman scalpels, while the opposing terminal is a small version of the blunt dissector which so frequently forms the terminal of Roman scalpel handles. It is, perhaps, instructive that the curette/elevator Cat. no. 3.80, another find from the River Walbrook deposits, is also a single-piece iron instrument, unlike most other Roman examples which are of copper-alloy or combined copper-alloy and iron.

1st/2nd century AD.

Jackson 2008, 196–9, fig. 4.4.2.3.

Drills

3.78. Folding drill-handle (1975,1106.30) (Figs 114a–c, 175)
Provenance unknown.
Length extended 405mm; length folded 207mm; weight 109.4g

This folding handle for a surgical drill is complete, except for the short hinged lower projection and its fastening rivet, which are recent (probably early 20th-century) replacements for the missing original parts. The handle comprises two equal-sized rectangular-sectioned brass bars hinged together, the hinge still operative but loosened through stress. Both pieces have a very lightly sinuous profile. The proximal (handle) piece has a knobbed finial and a rebated

section to accommodate the hinged projection when it was folded away out of use. An assortment of ancient scratched marks on the rebated surface appears fortuitous. The hinge (a one-and-two-plate strap-hinge) turns on a simple rivet (replacement, see below), the ends of which are burred over to brace the two flanking disc washers. The washers have a flat inner face and decorative outer face comprising a low dome with a moulded rim. Beyond the hinge the bar is decorated on its inner face with a neatly cut stylised dolphin moulding. The central hinge (an offset one-and-one-plate strap-hinge), designed to brace the handle in its extended (180+°) – operative – position, has a pair of washers matching those on the other hinge and secured by a central rivet with burred heads. The distal piece of the bar has a projecting, slender, baluster-like finial, at the tip of which is a stylised snake's head with incised decoration. In the mouldings at the base of the finial is a tiny cylindrical perforation, lightly countersunk on each face, by means of which the distal end of the cord was secured.

In 1899 H.B. Walters, with no known parallels to cite, included the handle in the 'Miscellaneous implements' section of his *Catalogue of the Bronzes … in the British Museum*, describing it as 'compasses, working on a hinge'. The work was revised by the then Keeper of the Department of Greek and Roman Antiquities, A.S. Murray and by Cecil H. Smith and Arthur H. Smith. Just over a decade later Arthur Smith, by then himself Keeper (1909–25), was to see another, more complete, handle, in the group of medical and surgical instruments found near the site of Colophon around 1911 and published by Richard Caton in 1914. Smith noted the identity of the two examples (Caton 1914, 117), while Caton, interpreting his instrument within the demonstrably medical/surgical context of the associated objects in the Colophon find, recognised its functional similarity to the drill-bow used by carpenters, ancient and modern, and related it to the trepan described by Celsus, Galen and the Hippocratic authors (Caton 1914, 116–17). His identification was fully endorsed in 1924 by the celebrated Bingen grave find, which included a folding drill-handle complete with two crown trepans (Como 1925). It is very likely, therefore, that it was in or around 1914, with Caton's and Smith's recognition of the type, that the hinged projection, imitating that on the Colophon instrument, was added to the British Museum handle, presumably for display purposes. To secure it to the hinge the rivet had to be removed (and scientific analysis indicates that the present rivet is a modern replacement) and the washers released and repositioned.

1st/3rd century AD.

Bronzes catalogue, 2674; *Guide to Greek and Roman Life* 3rd edition, 1929, 181, no. 586; Jackson 2005a, 105–6, fig. 5.3.2.

Department of Scientific Research File 7134.

3.79. Drill-bit? (1932,1112.7) (Fig. 115a–b)
Lake Trasimene, Umbria, Italy.
For acquisition and finding details see Scalpels, Cat. no. 3.71.
Length 73.1mm; weight 9.1g

A tanged iron instrument with lanceolate tip closely similar to Cat. no. 3.12. A plump ring-and-squat-baluster moulding separates the slender tang from the elongated baluster stem, of circular cross-section. The lanceolate end is of flattened triangular cross-section. Its tip and one adjacent edge are very slightly damaged consistent with use as a drill-bit.

1st/3rd century AD.

Levers (elevators)

3.80. Bone lever/curette (1928,0713.30) (Figs 116a–b, 175)

From City of London, 'Found during excavations for the rebuilding of the Bank of England'.

Length 159mm; maximum width of curette 11.4 mm; maximum depth of curette 6.4mm; weight 21.95g

A double-ended instrument wrought from a single bar of iron. The excellent preservation of the original surface reveals the fine and careful workmanship involved in its manufacture. It is a dual-purpose tool with two different terminals utilising a central neatly cut moulded grip. The mouldings comprise a sequence of seven circular discs – three plain ones alternating with four grooved ones. One terminal consists of a long capacious scoop with a broad sharp-rimmed end and a carefully smoothed rounded back. The other terminal, with stout stem of neatly profiled octagonal cross-section, consists of a cranked spatulate lever (its tip chipped) with a strengthening median ridge on both faces.

The very fine preservation of this iron instrument is a result of waterlogging in the bed of the River Walbrook and its tributaries.

1st/2nd century AD.

Jackson 2005a, 102–4, fig. 5.2.6; Jackson 2008, 196–9, fig. 4.4.2.1; Jackson 2011a, 258–60, fig. 20, c.

BMRL 7191-71-M.

Forceps

3.81. Smooth-jawed spring forceps (1926,0216.117) (Fig. 117a–b)

Provenance unknown.

Length 112.5mm; jaw width 4.5mm; weight 16.0g

An example, of bronze, of the type made from a folded rectangular-sectioned strip. The arms have a simple carinated shoulder and taper gently to the in-turned jaws which have a straight, smooth edge, one chipped.

1st/2nd century AD.

Bronzes catalogue, 2406.

BMRL 7191-50-N.

3.82. Smooth-jawed spring forceps (1867,0508.119* Blacas Collection) (Figs 117a–b, 175)

Provenance unknown.

Part of probable set, see p. 99.

Length 100.1mm; jaw width 4.7mm; width 15.3g

An example, of leaded bronze, of folded strip type, with simple carinated shoulders. The sharply angled in-turned jaws, with straight, smooth edges, are only slightly narrower than the arms.

1st/2nd century AD.

Bronzes catalogue, 2405.

BMRL 7191-48-P.

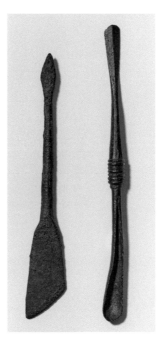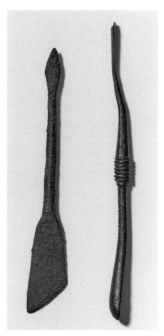

Figure 116a–b The probable scalpel and the combined bone lever and curette. British Museum, left to right, Cat. nos 3.77 and 3.80

3.83. Smooth-jawed spring forceps (1814,0704.960 Townley Collection) (Fig. 117a–b)

Provenance unknown, but probably found in Rome or its environs (see pp. 2–3).

Length 90.5mm; jaw width 4.0mm; weight 9.4g

A small simple example, of leaded bronze, of folded strip type, with lightly ridged shoulders. The rectangular-sectioned arms taper very slightly to the in-turned jaws, which have smooth straight edges.

1st/2nd century AD.

BMRL 7191-49-R.

3.84. Smooth-jawed spring forceps (1926,0216.118) (Fig. 118a–b)

Provenance unknown.

Length 125.1mm; jaw width 7.1mm; weight 18.6g

A well-crafted example, of leaded bronze, of cut bar type, with a slender disc-and-baluster finial. The rectangular-sectioned arms, with crisp shoulder mouldings, taper in thickness but expand in width towards the jaws. The neatly carinated in-turned jaws are broad, straight, smooth and accurately opposed. The careful finish of the outer surfaces contrasts with that of the inner surface of the arms where extensive cutting/filing striations are visible.

1st/3rd century AD.

Bronzes catalogue, 2411.2.

BMRL 7191-46-K.

3.85. Smooth-jawed spring forceps (1975,1102.1) (Fig. 118a–b)

Provenance unknown.

Length 136.1mm; jaw width 5.9mm; weight 21.8g

An example, of leaded bronze, of cut bar type, with a disc-and-baluster finial inlaid with a silver band at the point of maximum girth of the plump baluster. The arms, with neatly cut shoulders, are both a little distorted near their mid-point. They taper in thickness and gently expand in

Figure 117a–b Smooth-jawed spring forceps, front and side views. British Museum, left to right, Cat. nos 3.87, 3.81, 3.82, 3.83, 3.88, 3.89

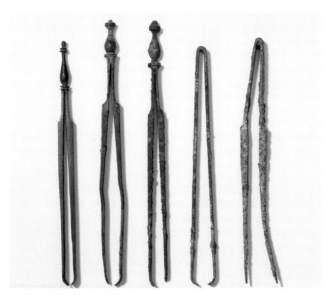

Figure 118a–b Smooth-jawed, toothed, and pointed-jawed spring forceps, front and side views. British Museum, left to right, Cat. nos 3.84, 3.85, 3.86, 3.94, 3.95

width towards the in-turned smooth-edged jaws, each chipped at one angle. Manufacturing filing striations are visible on the inner face of both arms.

1st/3rd century AD.
Bronzes catalogue, 2409.
BMRL 7191-14-R.

3.86. Smooth-jawed spring forceps (1856,1226.1025 Temple Collection) **(Fig. 118a–b)**

From Ruvo, Puglia, Italy.
Length 136mm; jaw width 4.7mm; weight 20.6g

An example, of leaded bronze, of cut bar type, with a fine disc-and-baluster finial. The baluster, as revealed by radiography and XRF analysis, is inlaid with four bands of silver. The three interspersed grooves may once have held an inlay of contrasting colour that has corroded away or fallen out. The arms, divided by a slightly asymmetric cut at the top, have simply formed shoulders and taper both in width and thickness towards the in-turned jaws. One smooth, straight jaw tip survives. A narrow band of corrosion products on both arms 24mm above the jaws probably indicates the former presence there of a sliding lock-ring.

1st/3rd century AD.

Bronzes catalogue, 2321.
BMRL 7191-11-K.

3.87. Smooth-jawed spring forceps (1867,0508.121 Blacas Collection) **(Fig. 117a–b)**

Provenance unknown.
Part of probable set, see p. 99.
Length 101.2mm; jaw width 4.7mm; weight 12.3g

An unusually small example, of leaded bronze, of the cut bar type, with a fine disc-and-baluster finial. The short arms, with simple pronounced shoulders, taper in thickness but gently expand in width towards the in-turned jaws, which have smooth, straight edges.

1st/3rd century AD.
Bronzes catalogue, 2410.
BMRL 7191-47-M.

3.88. Smooth-jawed spring forceps (1932,1112.3 Ex-Sambon Collection) **(Fig. 117a–b)**

From Lake Trasimene, Umbria, Italy.
For acquisition and finding details see Scalpels, Cat. no. 3.71.
Length 104.4mm; jaw width 3.9mm; weight 17.8g

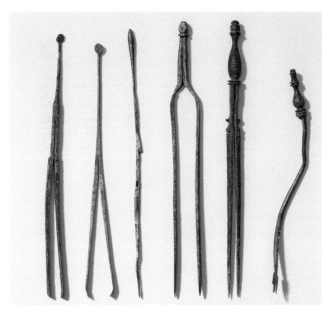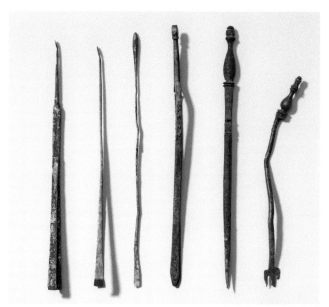

Figure 119a–b Smooth-jawed, pointed-jawed, and re-worked spring forceps, front and side views. British Museum, left to right, Cat. nos 3.90, 3.91, 3.92, 3.93, 3.96, 3.97

A simple bronze forceps of folded strip type. The broad looped head with flanged ends is blocked with soil and corrosion products. The rectangular-sectioned arms, with angular shoulders, taper in width and thickness towards the jaws. The surviving complete jaw has a straight, smooth edge. The jaws were not demonstrably in-turned.

1st/2nd century AD.
BMRL 7191-51-Q.

3.89. Smooth-jawed spring forceps (1814,0704.961 Townley Collection) (Fig. 117a–b)

Provenance unknown, but probably found in Rome or its environs (see pp. 2–3).
Length 104.3mm; jaw width *c.* 4.2mm; weight 12.4g

A simple, leaded bronze, forceps of folded strip type, with expanded looped head. The arms are markedly thickened below the pronounced shoulder and taper gently in width and thickness towards the broken jaws. It is not possible to determine whether the jaws were of simple smooth-jawed or in-turned smooth or toothed type.

1st/2nd century AD.
Bronzes catalogue, 2413.
BMRL 7191-52–T.

3.90. Smooth-jawed spring forceps/ligula (1896,0501.18) (Figs 119a–b, 175)

From Tower Street, City of London, 1868.
Length 125.1mm; ligula 4.4 × 3.6mm; weight 8.32g

A light slender instrument, of gunmetal, combining a ligula with a smooth-jawed spring forceps. The forceps has broad, smooth-edged, in-turned jaws. The arms taper upwards to simple stepped shoulders beyond which the rectangular bar of the top of the forceps meets the neck of the fine octagonal-sectioned stem of the ligula, an angled tiny flat ovoid disc.

The distinctive finely preserved golden-coloured body metal lightly coated with a dusty brown layer is characteristic of London finds from the bed of the River Walbrook and its tributaries.

1st/2nd century AD.
BMRL 7191-65-R.

3.91. Smooth-jawed spring forceps/ligula (1883,0509.7) (Fig. 119a–b)

From City of London.
Length 120.0mm; ligula 4.4 × 5.1mm; weight 3.61g

A light and slender instrument, of brass, combining a ligula with a smooth-jawed spring forceps. As Cat. no. 3.90 though even more slender and with more widely splayed arms and a longer, more slender, ligula stem. The angled ligula disc is extremely thin.

The distinctive finely preserved golden-coloured body metal lightly coated with a dusty brown layer is characteristic of London finds from the bed of the River Walbrook and its tributaries.

1st/2nd century AD.
BMRL 7191-66-W.

3.92. Smooth-jawed spring forceps/probe (1883,0502.9) (Fig. 119a–b)

From London Wall, City of London, June 1880.
Length 128mm; weight 2.21g

A very light, slender, smooth-jawed spring forceps combined with a probe in the form of an olivary finial. One arm of the forceps is lacking. The surviving arm is dented in two places and the in-turned tip of the jaw has become flattened.

The distinctive finely preserved golden-coloured body metal lightly coated with a dusty brown layer is characteristic of London finds from the bed of the River Walbrook and its tributaries.

1st/2nd century AD.

3.93. Smooth-jawed spring forceps (1883,0502.7) (Fig. 119a–b)

From London Wall, City of London, June 1880.
Length 131mm; weight 12.06g

A smooth-jawed forceps with plain rounded shoulders,

Figure 120a–b Coudée type and hollow-jawed toothed spring forceps, front and angled views. British Museum, left to right, Cat. nos 3.98, 3.99

blunt-pointed jaws and a simple moulded finial in the form of a flattened pine cone.

The distinctive finely preserved golden-coloured body metal lightly coated with a dusty brown layer is characteristic of London finds from the bed of the River Walbrook and its tributaries.

1st/2nd century AD.

3.94. Toothed spring forceps (1867,0508.118* Blacas Collection) (Fig. 118a–b)

Provenance unknown.
Part of probable set, see p. 99.
Length 122.2mm; jaw width 4.2mm; weight 15.2g

A simple, well-crafted, unadorned bronze example of folded strip type. The long thin rectangular-sectioned arms taper very slightly in width and thickness towards the smoothly curved, in-turned, toothed jaws. The teeth – three opposing four – are long, pointed and extremely finely cut and would have interlocked very precisely. The former presence of a sliding lock-ring is indicated by a line of encrusted corrosion products on the arms 29.5mm above each jaw. Traces of mineral-preserved wood on the outer and inner faces of the arms, together with concretions of iron corrosion, might be taken to imply storage in a wooden instrument case alongside iron-bladed scalpels.

1st/2nd century AD.
Bronzes catalogue, 2320.
BMRL 7191-12-M.

3.95. Pointed-jawed spring forceps (1867,0508.120 Blacas Collection) (Figs 118a–b, 175)

Provenance unknown.
Part of probable set, see p. 99.
Length 124.9mm; weight 20.1g

A well-crafted, leaded bronze, example of folded strip type, with simple stepped shoulders. The arms taper evenly in width (from the loop) and thickness (from the shoulders) towards the blunt-pointed jaw tips. Their cross-section changes from rectangular to plano-convex as the jaws are approached in order to present a smooth outer face to skin, tissue etc. The flat inner face has rifled faceting (to enhance grip) extending 21.5mm above the jaw tips. The size, form, manufacture, patina and corrosion products of this forceps are so similar to those of Cat. no. 3.94 as to indicate that they were formerly part of the same set of instruments.

1st/2nd century AD.
Bronzes catalogue, 2407.
BMRL 7191-13-P.

3.96. Pointed-jawed spring forceps (1869,0715.1) (Fig. 119a–b)

From Lothbury, City of London ('found 19 feet from the surface, in Charlotte Row, Lothbury, 5th July 1869')
Length 131.6mm; weight 14.25g

A finely made ornate brass example, of sawn bar type. The long slender arms, with flat inner face and hexagonal-faceted outer face, taper evenly to the finely pointed jaws, the tip of one now slightly bent. A fine dolphin moulding marks the shoulders. The finial, which stands on a pair of disc mouldings, is an elongated baluster with very fine silver spiral inlay. There is fine inlay, too, on the moulded terminal.

Scientific investigation of the finial revealed that it had been partially replaced: its top c. 23mm, made of copper, was secured to the forceps by means of a dovetail joint and held in place with soft solder. This is likely to be a 19th-century repair.

The distinctive finely preserved golden-coloured body metal lightly coated with a dusty brown layer is characteristic of London finds from the bed of the River Walbrook and its tributaries, a context that corresponds to the stated find-spot and depth of the forceps.

1st/2nd century AD.
BMRL 7191-67-Y.

3.97. Reworked spring forceps (1992,0503.1) (Fig. 119a–b)

From Little Burstead, Billericay, Essex.
Length 106.1mm; width fork plate 9.6mm; weight 5.40g

An adapted and reworked spring forceps, of gunmetal, of sawn bar type. The neatly moulded multiple-disc-and-baluster finial remains intact and reveals on the underside of the lower disc mouldings the stub of one broken forceps arm. The other arm, bent in two places (probably post-depositional damage), comprises a slender parallel-sided rod with neatly chamfered angles (evidently a wholesale reworking of the original form of the arm) which terminates in a flat plate with three prongs, all damaged at the tip. If, as seems likely, the tips were originally turned the instrument had probably been converted into a triple hook retractor.

1st/3rd century AD.
BMRL 7191-72-P

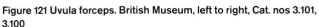

Figure 121 Uvula forceps. British Museum, left to right, Cat. nos 3.101, 3.100

Figure 122 Detail of the handles of uvula forceps Cat. no. 3.100 showing the six inlaid bands of Corinthian bronze

3.98. Coudée-type toothed spring forceps (1990,0623.1) (Figs 120a–b, 175)

Provenance unknown.

Length 131.3mm; jaw width 11mm; weight 24.4g

A bronze example of 'standard' form, made from a cut bar surmounted by a finely worked disc-and-baluster finial. The rectangular-sectioned arms retain a uniform width and thickness until the point where they start to curve to one side, where they expand in width and taper in thickness to the broad jaws, which now lack their in-turned toothed edges. Also lacking is the sliding lock-ring.

1st/3rd century AD.
BMRL 7191-59-Y.

3.99. Hollow-jawed toothed spring forceps (staphylagra variant) (1870,0402.220 Pollexfen Collection) (Fig. 120a–b)

From Colchester, Essex.

Length 198mm; jaw length 24.2mm (tip broken); jaw width 11.9mm; weight 27.46g

A long spring forceps, of bronze, with a fine multiple-disc-and-baluster finial. The jaw and lower half of one arm is lacking. The more intact arm is long and carefully profiled, of crisp rectangular cross-section. It is near parallel-sided but gently expands towards the jaw which is sub-rectangular and hollow at the back. The in-turned rim of the jaw had a curved row of extremely finely cut tiny triangular teeth set at about 11 teeth per cm; 24 are preserved on the lateral edge, seven of which are complete, but most lack their tip and the end of the jaw is damaged. There is a fragment of the neatly moulded sliding lock-ring corroded in position towards the upper end of the outer face

of the complete arm. Only the upper part of the symmetrical second arm survives.

1st/3rd century AD.
Jackson 1992, 185, no. 20, 179, pl. 2.
BMRL 7191-68-L

3.100. Uvula forceps (staphylagra) (1814,0704.969 Townley Collection) (Figs 121, 175)

Provenance unknown, but probably found in Rome or its environs (see pp. 2–3).

Length 202mm; length handle 99.5mm; length arm 85mm; length jaw 17.5mm; width jaw 10mm; 24 teeth per jaw; length handle to pivot 139mm; length pivot to jaw 63mm; ratio of handle/pivot:pivot/jaw 2.2:1; weight 51.6g

A finely crafted ornate example, of gunmetal, with straight arms, virtually intact and in good condition: the pivot operative, the handles slightly bent, and only the tips of a few teeth missing from the jaws. The slender handles comprise three distinct parts linked by disc mouldings: a stylised pine cone finial inlaid with a band of Corinthian bronze; an elegant, slender, tapered rod of neatly faceted octagonal cross-section; and a smooth, tapered, circular-sectioned rod inlaid with six evenly spaced bands of Corinthian bronze. The elongated lozengiform arms, of flat rectangular cross-section, pivot on a simple, plain, flat-headed rivet. The carefully offset capacious hollow jaws, which enclose a sub-rectangular space, have each 24 finely cut interlocking teeth along their outer elliptical edge. Corrosion products on the arms indicate that as discovered the instrument was in a closed position.

1st/3rd century AD.
Bronzes catalogue, 2317; Deneffe 1893, 54, pl. 6, fig. 6;

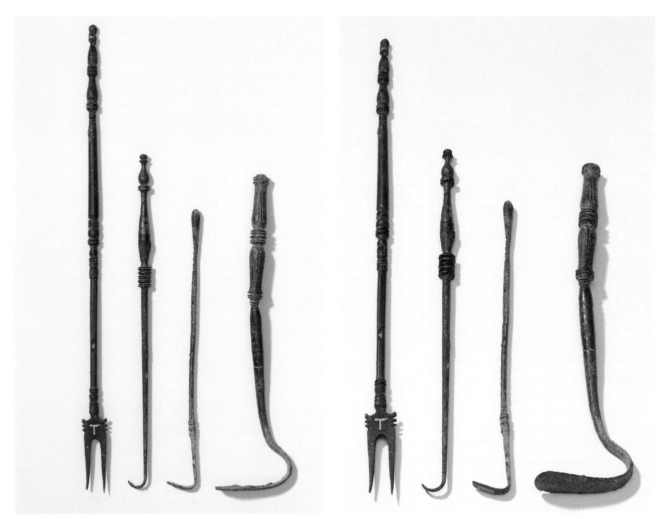

Figure 123a–b Sharp and blunt hooks, front and angled views. British Museum, left to right, Cat. nos 3.103, 3.102, 3.104, 3.105

Milne 1907, 97, pl. 30.1; *Guide to Greek and Roman Life* 1908, 179–80, no. 435, fig. 189k; Meyer-Steineg and Sudhoff 1921, 117, fig. 69; Tabanelli 1958, pl. 52; Jackson 1992, 171 ff., esp.176, fig. 4.11, 183, no. 11.

BMRL5969-34570-T.

3.101. Uvula forceps (staphylagra) (1878,1019.145 Meyrick Collection) (Figs 121, 175)

Provenance unknown.
Length 187mm; length handle 93.5mm; length arm 77mm; length jaw 16.5mm; width jaw 12mm; 19 teeth per jaw; length handle to pivot 137mm; length pivot to jaw 50mm; ratio of handle/pivot:pivot/jaw 2.7:1; weight 28.3g

A straight-armed example, virtually intact and in good condition: the pivot operative, one handle slightly bent, and only the tips of a few teeth missing from the jaws. The handles, one of leaded brass and the other of gunmetal, have stylised pine cone finials and are quite rudimentarily finished. They comprise a slender, tapered, rectangular-sectioned rod, with simple disc mouldings at either end. The elongated lozengiform arms, of flat rectangular cross-section, are lightly bevelled on their inner distal edge to avoid the necessity of an offset of the jaws. The pivot assembly, positioned a little beyond the point of maximum expansion of the arms, comprises a lightly domed rivet, with a disc washer on one face. The capacious hollow jaws, which enclose a sub-rectangular space, have each 19 imperfectly interlocking

teeth along their outer L-shaped edge. On the inner profiled edge of each jaw is a neat, countersunk, circular perforation. Excepting only the inner concave face of the jaws, the surface of the instrument bears extensive traces of file marks and wear, which, although seemingly ancient, may alternatively be a result of 'cleaning' after discovery.

The patina and surface treatment are very similar to those of socketed needle-holder Cat. no. 3.107 and suggest they may have been found together.

1st/3rd century AD.

Bronzes catalogue, 2316; Deneffe 1893, 54, pl. 6, fig. 3; Milne 1907, 97, pl. 30.2; Sudhoff 1926, 109–110, pl. 66; Tabanelli 1958, pl. 52; Jackson 1992, 175, fig. 3.12, 183–4, no. 12.

BMRL7191-60-T.

Hooks (retractors)

3.102. Sharp hook (1867,0508.140 Blacas Collection) (Figs 123a–b, 176)

Provenance unknown.
Part of probable set, see p. 99.
Length 152mm; weight 12.6g

An exquisitely crafted example, of bronze, complete and in fine condition. The ornate, circular-sectioned handle is in the form of an elongated baluster with five inlaid bands at its maximum girth. Even in their present state they show as three black interspersed with two grey bands, contrasting with the golden-coloured body metal. As Corinthian bronze, silver and bronze (identified by XRF analysis) the original colour tones are likely to have been black and silver on gold. At the upper end a disc-and-baluster finial is preceded by a ring moulding and a short zone of fine lattice faceting. At the lower end the baluster is divided from the stem by a symmetrical series of finely cut ring-and-disc mouldings. Beyond these is another short zone of fine lattice faceting followed by the very finely drawn striated surface of the gently tapered stem, which terminates in a large, evenly curved hook, its intact tip still sharp.

1st/2nd century AD.

Bronzes catalogue, 2318.

BMRL 7191-15-W.

3.103. Double sharp hook (1814,0704.947 Townley Collection) (Fig. 123a–b)

Provenance unknown, but probably found in Rome or its environs (see pp. 2–3).

Length 213.5mm; width between hook tips 8.8mm; weight 21.0g

A long, ornate, bifurcated sharp hook, of brass. The elongated, circular-sectioned handle tapers upwards to a double disc-and-baluster finial. At the lower end it meets the octagonal-sectioned stem at a series of bead, ring, disc-and-baluster mouldings. Another, shorter, series of disc-and-squat-baluster mouldings separates the stem from the flat, rectangular-sectioned hook plate, which has moulded shoulders and a pair of slender tapered hooks, now bent straight, with sharp-pointed tips – one lacking.

1st/2nd century AD.

Bronzes catalogue, 2323; Milne 1907, pl. 22.3; Meyer-Steineg and Sudhoff 1921, 117, fig. 69.

BMRL 7191-16-Y.

3.104. Blunt hook, adapted (1851,0813.117 Comarmond Collection) (Fig. 123a–b)

From Vaison, Vaucluse, France

Length 127.4mm; width hook 5.2mm; weight 5.2g

A scoop probe, of leaded bronze, adapted to use as a blunt hook by truncating, flattening and bending the scoop. The olivary terminal is well formed with a broad end, the stem has a very finely drawn, longitudinally striated surface and the hook (ex-scoop) is preceded by a neat small double-disc-and-baluster moulding. The hook has a broad, rounded-square end, now chipped at one corner.

1st/3rd century AD.

Bronzes catalogue, 2319; Milne 1907, pl. 23.3; *Guide to Greek and Roman Life* 1908, 179–80, no. 438, fig. 189d – where it is erroneously described as a sharp hook; Meyer-Steineg and Sudhoff 1921, 18, fig. 70.

BMRL 7191-17-L.

3.105. Double-ended blunt hook (2009,5017.1) (Figs 123a–b, 176)

Provenance unknown.

Length 143.5mm; original length (by projection) *c.* 230mm; width hook 14.4mm; weight 30.2g

Rather over half of an ornate, stout, Z-shaped double-ended blunt hook of fine workmanship, its surviving blunt,

Figure 124 Socketed needle-holders. British Museum, left to right, Cat. nos 3.106, 3.107

spatulate, hook terminal mounted at right angles to the stem. The instrument, of gunmetal, was originally symmetrical around its grip, which comprises a central ring-and-double-disc moulding flanked by a pair of balusters, finely incised with stylised acanthus leaves, and a further series of disc mouldings. These latter were clearly a point of weakness – they are the point of breakage of the missing hook and the point at which the stem of the surviving hook has been bent out of true. The surviving stem is a neatly formed, plain, circular-sectioned, tapered rod, with a single incised ring midway towards the (slightly distorted) swan's neck loop behind the hook. The hook, of rounded kite shape, has a flat inner face, a convex outer face, with low median ridge, and a smooth, rounded, blunt leading edge, one corner slightly chipped. By analogy with other examples the missing hook, likely of blunt leaf shape, would have been turned in the opposing direction.

1st/2nd century AD.

Charles Ede Ltd, *Antiquities* catalogue, 174, December 2003, no. 56.

BMRL 7191-58-W.

Needles

3.106. Socketed needle-holder (1814,0704.954 Townley Collection) (Fig. 124)

Provenance unknown, but probably found in Rome or its environs (see pp. 2–3).

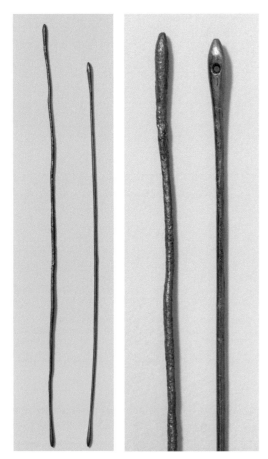

Figures 125–6 Solid and fenestrated dipyrenes. British Museum, left to right, Cat. nos 3.108, 3.109 and detail of the olivary tips of the solid and fenestrated dipyrenes

Length 125.2mm; length socket 21mm; internal diameter of socket mouth 3mm; weight 15.2g

A finely made slender handle, of gunmetal, with leaf-shaped finial, which has a low median ridge on both faces and a tiny terminal knob. The elongated baluster-type grip, of circular cross-section, is flanked at each end by a well-formed double-disc-and-ring moulding, while the slender flared socket, of hollow, circular cross-section, is decorated with a zone of interlocked triangular faceting flanked by a triple disc moulding. Iron corrosion products are present on the outer rim and interior of the part-broken socket, which retains the remnants of decayed solder – tin-lead soft solder, as determined by XRF analysis.

2nd/3rd century AD.
Bronzes catalogue, 2689.
BMRL 7191-18-N.

3.107. Socketed needle-holder (1878,1019.126 Meyrick Collection) (Figs 124, 176)

Provenance unknown.
Length 154mm; length socket 20mm; internal diameter of socket mouth 2.7mm; weight 20.1g

An exuberantly decorated example, of brass. The leaf-shaped finial has a very low median ridge on both faces (which retain file-finishing marks) and a small double-disc-and-knob terminal. The handle, of circular cross-section, comprises a wide variety of decorative mouldings – disc, ring, baluster, interlocked triangular faceting – centred on a zone of candy-twist. A square shoulder moulding separates

the handle from the slender flared socket, which is similarly decorated with a zone of candy-twist flanked by a baluster and discs. The socket, at least 6mm deep, is of hollow circular cross-section and, as revealed by XRF analysis (see p. 152 and **Fig. 182**), retains traces of tin-lead soft solder.

The patina and surface treatment are very similar to those of uvula forceps Cat. no. 3.101 and suggest they may have been found together.

2nd/3rd century AD.
Bronzes catalogue, 2688.
BMRL 7191-19-Q.

Selected probes

Dipyrenes (see also Sets of instruments, Cat. no. 3.26)

3.108. Dipyrene, solid (1896,0501.15) (Figs 125–6)

From Tokenhouse Yard, City of London.
Length 177mm; maximum width of tips 1.9mm, 2.0mm; weight 2.37g

An extremely thin, flexible, smooth, circular-sectioned probe, of brass, which terminates at each end in a tiny, elongated, solid, olivary tip.

The distinctive finely preserved golden-coloured body metal lightly coated with a dusty brown layer is characteristic of London finds from the bed of the River Walbrook and its tributaries. As such, and in conjunction with its find-spot, the probe may be dated 1st/2nd century AD.

BMRL 7191-69-N

3.109. Dipyrene, fenestrated (2005,0402.63 Greenway Collection DR1,63) (Figs 125–6)

From City of London, 'Thames-side, between London Bridge and Union Cold Storage Co.'.
Length 160.5mm; maximum width of solid tip 1.9mm; maximum width of eyed tip 2.4mm; eye 0.5mm; weight 1.80g

An extremely thin, flexible, smooth, circular-sectioned probe, of bronze, which terminates at each end in an elongated, slender, olivary tip, one solid, the other, slightly larger, with a tiny circular eye.

The distinctive finely preserved golden-coloured body metal is characteristic of London finds from the bed of the River Walbrook and its tributaries. The context date for the probe, based on associated finds, is mid-2nd century AD.

BMRL 7191-70-K

Selected ear probes (see also Sets of instruments, Cat. nos 3.28 and 3.46)

3.110. Ear probe (1851,0813.108 Comarmond Collection) (Fig. 127)

Provenance unknown, but probably from the neighbourhood of Lyon, France.
Length 147.4mm; spoon diameter 4.3mm; weight 5.0g

A well-made example, of gunmetal, of standard form, with a simple pointed tip, a slender circular-sectioned stem, a neatly cut double-ring-and-squat baluster moulding and a tiny angled circular spoon. The stem changes to an octagonal cross-section near the mouldings perhaps to give greater purchase in the area of grip.

    1st/2nd century AD.

    Bronzes catalogue, 2683.

    BMRL 7191-20-M.

Also:

Ear probe (1865,0720.63)
Provenance unknown.
Length 88.9mm

Ear probe (1900,1214.2)
Provenance unknown.
Length 141mm; spoon diameter 4.4mm
    A very slender example with circular-sectioned stem, blunt tip, prominent globe-and-ring moulding and narrow tapered rod terminating in a tiny circular spoon.

Ear probe (1900,1214.3)
Provenance unknown.
Length 153mm; spoon diameter 4.5mm
    In form, finish, patina and corrosion products the same as 1900,1214.2, but with an elongated baluster-and-ring moulding.

Selected scoop probes (see also Sets of instruments, Cat. nos 3.29–30)

3.111. Scoop probe (1838,1231.2) (Fig. 127)

Provenance unknown.
Length 142.7mm; weight 6.6g
    A finely made example, of gunmetal, with a large olivary terminal, a slender octagonal-sectioned stem, lightly swollen near the central grip area, and a crisply cut moulding comprising five discs between a pair of rings. The slender scoop has an elliptical cross-section and a rounded tip.

    1st/2nd century AD.

    Bronzes catalogue, 2356.i.

    BMRL 7191-25-L.

3.112. Scoop probe (1867,0508.123 Blacas Collection) (Fig. 127)

Provenance unknown.
Part of probable set, see p. 99.
Length 154mm
Octagonal-sectioned stem.
1st/2nd century AD.

3.113. Scoop probe (1867,0508.124 Blacas Collection) (Fig. 127)

Provenance unknown.
Part of probable set, see p. 99.
Length 151mm
Fine fluted stem.
1st/2nd century AD.

Also:

Scoop probe (1814,0704.951 Townley Collection)
Provenance unknown, but probably found in Rome or its environs (see pp. 2–3).
Length 161mm

Figure 127 Ear probe and scoop probes. British Museum, left to right, Cat. nos 3.110, 3.111, 3.112, 3.113

Scoop probe (1814,0704.953 Townley Collection)
Provenance unknown, but probably found in Rome or its environs (see pp. 2–3).
Length 172mm

Scoop probe (1814,0704.956 Townley Collection)
Provenance unknown, but probably found in Rome or its environs (see pp. 2–3).
Length 74mm (broken)
The scoop and part of the stem only remain.

Scoop probe (1824,0483.5)
Provenance unknown.
Length 185mm
The back of the stem has a series of incised graded lines.

Scoop probe (1824,0483.6)
Provenance unknown.
Length 67mm (broken)
The probe and much of the stem broken. Moulded, engraved and inlaid decoration on surviving part.

Scoop probe (1859,1226.646)
Provenance unknown.
Length 67mm (broken)
The tip of the scoop, most of the stem and the probe are broken.

Figure 128 Spatula probes. British Museum, left to right, Cat. nos
3.114, 3.115, 3.116, 3.117, 3.118, 3.119)

Scoop probe (1865,0720.58)
Provenance unknown.
Length 152.4mm

Scoop probe (1867,0508.122 Blacas Collection)
Provenance unknown.
Part of probable set, see p. 99.
Length 173mm ('unbent')
Octagonal-sectioned stem, bent.

Scoop probe (1868,0110.305 Woodhouse Collection)
From Corfu, Greece.
Length 193mm
Bronzes catalogue, 2349.

Scoop probe (1882,1009.20)
From Galaxidi, Phokis, Greece
Length 174mm
Scoop flattened.
Bronzes catalogue, 2354.

Scoop probe (1891,0624.12)
Provenance unknown.
Length 173mm
Octagonal-sectioned stem.

Scoop probe (1904,0204.219 Morel Collection)
Provenance unknown.

Length 161mm
Repaired at centre of stem.

Scoop probe (1904,0204.221 Morel Collection)
Provenance unknown.
Length 106mm ('unbent')
Probe end broken. Bent.

Scoop probe (1904,0204.372 Morel Collection)
Provenance unknown.
Length 160mm

Scoop probe (1904,0204.1062 Morel Collection)
Provenance unknown.
Length 107mm

Scoop probe? (1932,1112.4 Ex-Sambon Collection)
Lake Trasimene, Umbria, Italy.
For acquisition and finding details see Scalpels, Cat. no. 3.71.
Length 135mm

Scoop probe (1975,1106.40)
Provenance unknown.
Length 130mm

Selected spatula probes (see also Sets of instruments, Cat. nos 3.31–3)

3.114. Spatula probe (1868,0110.302 Woodhouse Collection) (Fig. 128)
From Corfu, Greece.
Length 192mm; weight 13.0g
    A finely finished ornate example, of leaded bronze, with a well-formed large olivary terminal, an octagonal-sectioned stem and a very neatly cut double-disc-and-baluster moulding. The extremely slender spatula has a finely cut moulded shoulder, concave sides and a rounded tip. The slight curvature of the stem may have been an intentional adaptation.
1st century AD.
BMRL 7191-24-Y.

3.115. Spatula probe (1814,0704.950 Townley Collection) (Fig. 128)
Provenance unknown, but probably found in Rome or its environs (see pp. 2–3).
Length 182.5mm; weight 17.1g
    A carefully made example, of leaded bronze, with a pronounced blunt-tipped olivary terminal and an octagonal-sectioned stem which swells in the area of grip towards the spatula. The profiled spatula has (unusually) a low median ridge on both faces. A slight curvature of the stem and spatula may be an intentional adaptation rather than damage.
    1st century AD.
    Bronzes catalogue, 2359.
    BMRL 7191-23-W.

3.116. Spatula probe (1878,1019.125 Meyrick Collection) (Fig. 128)
Provenance unknown.

Length 183mm
Octagonal-sectioned stem. Double convex spatula.
1st century AD.

3.117. Spatula probe (1814,0704.949 Townley Collection) (Fig. 128)

Provenance unknown, but probably found in Rome or its environs (see pp. 2–3).
Length 172.5mm; weight 16.3g

A well-crafted example, of brass, with a short plump olivary terminal, a softened square-sectioned stem and a triple ring-and-squat baluster moulding. The broad parallel-sided spatula has a moulded shoulder, one median-ridged and one flat face and a rounded tip.

2nd/3rd century AD.
Bronzes catalogue, 2343.
BMRL 7191-22-R.

3.118. Spatula probe (1878,1019.122 Meyrick Collection) (Fig. 128)

Provenance unknown.
Length 149mm
Plano-convex spatula.
2nd/3rd century AD.

3.119. Spatula probe (1772,0312.131 H. 131 – Hamilton collection?) (Fig. 128)

Provenance unknown.
Length 170.5mm; weight 6.6g

A very rudimentarily made idiosyncratic example, of brass, with a tiny olivary terminal formed mainly by a basal grooving. The slender stem is of chamfered square cross-section which modifies to a flat chamfered rectangular cross-section towards the spatula, which it meets at a simple flat moulding. The slender, near parallel-sided spatula has a rounded tip and flat faces.

1st/2nd century AD.
BMRL 7191-21-P.

3.120. Spatula probe (1868,0110.379 Woodhouse Collection) (Fig. 129)

From Corfu, Greece.
Length 152.4mm

A simple example of silver, with a large, elongated olivary terminal, a plain circular-sectioned stem and a simple shouldered spatula which tapers to a smoothly rounded tip. Bevelling of the spatula sides may have been a product of use or a consequence of adaptation rather than an original feature.

1st century AD.

3.121. Spatula probe (1881,0709.13) (Fig. 129)

Provenance unknown.
Length 165.1mm

A finely made example of silver, with a plump olivary terminal, a smooth circular-sectioned stem, a ring-and-baluster moulding and an oar-shaped spatula.

1st century AD.

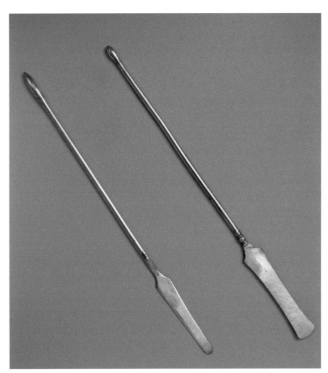

Figure 129 Spatula probes. British Museum, left to right, Cat. nos 3.120, 3.121

Also:
Spatula probe (1814,0704.970 Townley Collection)
Provenance unknown, but probably found in Rome or its environs (see pp. 2–3).
Length 185mm
Bronzes catalogue, 2342.

Spatula probe (1842,0728.691)
Provenance unknown.
Length 161mm
A large, crude, simple example with flat spatula.

Spatula probe (1856,1223.666)
Provenance unknown.
Length 136mm (broken)
Tip of flat spatula broken.

Spatula probe (1857,1226.210)
Provenance unknown.
Length 123mm
Flat spatula.

Spatula probe (1865,0720.57)
Provenance unknown.
Length 203.2mm
Bronzes catalogue, 2344.

Spatula probe (1867,0508.125 Blacas Collection)
Provenance unknown.
Part of probable set, see p. 99.
Length 158mm (broken)
Plano-convex spatula. Probe end broken.

Spatula probe (1867,0508.126 Blacas Collection)
Provenance unknown.

Part of probable set, see p. 99.
Length 156mm (broken)
A crude example, broken at the probe end, with flat spatula.

Spatula probe (1867,0508.127 Blacas Collection)
Provenance unknown.
Part of probable set, see p. 99.
Length 151mm (broken)
Probe end broken. Double convex spatula.

Spatula probe (1867,0508.128 Blacas Collection)
Provenance unknown.
Part of probable set, see p. 99.
Length 119mm (broken)
Probe end broken. Flat spatula.

Spatula probe (1868,0110.299 Woodhouse Collection)
From Corfu, Greece.
Length 186mm
Flat spatula.
Bronzes catalogue, 2353.

Spatula probe (1868,0110.300 Woodhouse Collection)
From Corfu, Greece.
Length 170mm
Flat spatula.
Bronzes catalogue, 2345.

Spatula probe (1868,0110.301 Woodhouse Collection)
From Corfu, Greece.
Length 191mm
Double convex spatula.
Bronzes catalogue, 2350.

Spatula probe (1868,0110.303 Woodhouse Collection)
From Corfu, Greece.
Length 151mm
A crude example, with flat spatula.

Spatula probe (1868,0110.304 Woodhouse Collection)
From Corfu, Greece.
Length 155mm
Double convex spatula.

Spatula probe (1878,1019.110 Meyrick Collection)
Provenance unknown.
Length 120mm
A very crude example.

Spatula probe (1878,1019.124 Meyrick Collection)
Provenance unknown.
Length 109mm (broken)
Probe end broken. Flat spatula.

Spatula probe (1891,0624.6)
Provenance unknown.
Length 185mm
A large example with a simple pointed probe and a plano-convex spatula.

Spatula probe (1891,0624.14)
Provenance unknown.
Length 167mm
A slender example with a double convex spatula.

Spatula probe (1891,0624.15)
Provenance unknown.
Length 126mm
Spatula recently cut and ground.

Spatula probe (1904,0204.217 Morel Collection)
Provenance unknown.
Length 164mm
Double convex spatula.

Spatula probe (1975,1106.31)
Provenance unknown.
Length 155mm
Plano-convex spatula.

Spatula probe (1975,1106.32)
Provenance unknown.
Length 171mm ('unbent')
Plano-convex spatula. Bent.

Spatula probe (1975,1106.33)
Provenance unknown.
Length 168mm
Double convex spatula.

Spatula probe (1975,1106.34)
Provenance unknown.
Length 154mm
A very thin flat spatula.

Spatula probe (1975,1106.35)
Provenance unknown.
Length 181mm
Plano-convex spatula.

Spatula probe (1975,1106.36)
Provenance unknown.
Length 227mm
A large example with double convex spatula.

Spatula probe (1975,1106.37)
Provenance unknown.
Length 150mm
Plano-convex spatula.

Spatula probe (1975,1106.38)
Provenance unknown.
Length 76mm (broken)
Probe and stem broken, spatula flat.

Spatula probe (1975,1106.39)
Provenance unknown.
Length 90mm (broken)
Probe end broken.

Spatula probe (1871,0619.60 (EA36742))
Egypt
Length 46.9mm
Fragment. The lightly waisted spatula and adjacent
mouldings survive but the remainder of the stem is lacking.

Selected ligulae (see also Sets of instruments, Cat. no. 3.27)
Selected examples of normal plain simple form, with a small
angled flat ovoid disc at one end of a slender circular-
sectioned stem, tapered to a pointed tip at the other end.

Ligula (1904,0204.228 Morel Collection)
Provenance unknown.
Length 144.5mm; disc 6 × 8mm
Normal form, the disc quite large, with lightly convex back
and smoothed edge.

Ligula (1904,0204.229 Morel Collection)
Provenance unknown.
Length 140mm
Normal form, distal half of disc broken.

Ligula (1904,0204.230 Morel Collection)
Provenance unknown.
Length 128mm; disc 5.3 × 6.5mm

Ligula (1904,0204.231 Morel Collection)
Provenance unknown.
Length 134.5mm; disc 4.5 × 5.5mm
Bent and roughly straightened.

Ligula (1904,0204.232 Morel Collection)
Provenance unknown.
Length 106.7mm; disc 4.8 × 4.0mm
Normal form, with finely cut ring-and-disc moulding, the
pointed end broken.

Ligula (1904,0204.233 Morel Collection)
Provenance unknown.
Length 97mm; disc 4.8 × 5.0mm
Short, simple, rudimentarily made example.

Ligula (1904,0204.373 Morel Collection)
Provenance unknown.
Length 181mm; disc 4.2 × 3.8mm
Normal form, with a tiny plano-convex disc and a very long,
slightly distorted, blunt-pointed stem.

Ligula (1904,0204.1039 Morel Collection)
Provenance unknown.
Length 171 mm; disc 4.5 × 5.2mm
A long example, with a slightly distorted pointed terminal.
At the other end simple cut mouldings flank a large
prominent cuboid moulding with chamfered angles, its four
faces decorated with a similar arrangement of an incised
four-ring motif.

Ligula (1904,0204.1057 Morel Collection)
Provenance unknown.

**Figure 130 Spouted spoons. British Museum, upper to lower,
Cat. nos 3.122, 3.123)**

Length 138mm; disc 5.2 × 7.5mm
Normal form, with a tapered octagonal-sectioned stem.

Ligula (1904,0204.1058 Morel Collection)
Provenance unknown.
Length 154.5mm; disc 4.8mm diameter
Normal form, with a very slender finely made stem and
pointed tip. At the other end, beyond fine disc-and-cup
mouldings, a tiny circular, angled disc.

Ligula (1904,0204.1059 Morel Collection)
Provenance unknown.
Length 137mm; disc 5.1 × 5.7mm
Normal form, with a well-made slender, rounded
rectangular-sectioned stem and pointed tip. At the other
end, beyond disc-and-baluster mouldings and a tapered
circular-sectioned stem, a plano-convex angled ovoid disc.

Spoons

3.122. Spouted spoon (1814,0704.968 Townley Collection) (Figs 130, 176)
Provenance unknown, but probably found in Rome or its
environs (see pp. 2–3).
Length 173.6mm; length handle 132.3mm; bowl diameter *c.*
41.2mm; weight 16.2g
    A light large-bowled spoon, of leaded bronze, with a very
thin rectangular-sectioned handle (slightly bent), which
tapers to a tiny baluster-moulded finial. The junction plate
between handle and bowl is decorated with notch-and-
groove mouldings on its upper face. The large thin-walled
circular bowl, with a broad spout on the left (optimal for a
right-handed user), is slightly raised at its centre – probably
accidental damage.
    3rd/4th century AD.
    Bronzes catalogue, 2314.
    BMRL 7191-26-N.

3.123. Spouted spoon (1891,0624.4) (Fig. 130)
From Orvieto, Italy, purchased from the Rev. Greville John
Chester in 1891.
Length 188.0mm; length handle 155.0mm; bowl diameter
c. 32.5mm; weight 12.8g
    A light round-bowled spoon, of brass, with long slender
handle, of chamfered rectangular cross-section, which ends
in a neatly cut double-disc-and-pine-cone finial. The

Figure 131a–b The rectangular box from Yortan. British Museum, Cat. no. 3.124

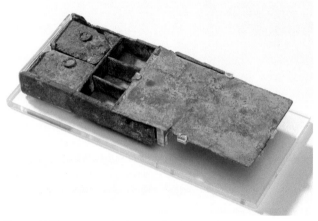

Figure 132 The rectangular box, probably from Cyrenaica. British Museum, Cat. no. 3.125

junction plate is ornamented on its upper face with notch-and-groove mouldings. The bowl is extremely thin-walled, resulting in (presumed) post-depositional damage/deterioration – denting, distortion, chipping, a small fissure and break-through at the centre (the thinnest point). The spout positioned at left favours right-handed use. A pair of incised rings on the inner surface midway down the wall is more probably a decorative motif than a dosage measure.

  3rd/4th century AD.
  Bronzes catalogue, 2315.
  BMRL 7191-45-X.

Drug containers

3.124. Rectangular box (1921,1220.122) (Fig. 131a–b)
Yortan, Turkey, from excavations of a cemetery by Paul Gaudin in the early 1900s.
Box: 129.4 × 74.4 × 24.4mm; sliding lid 126.8 × 70.1mm; compartment lids 1) 58.5 ×31.2mm 2–5) 38.5 × 28.5mm; weight 343.6g (box 243.8g; lid 99.8g)

A rectangular box, of bronze, with sliding lid, secured by a catch, and five rectangular compartments, each with a hinged lid. The box, an intricate construction, is made of a combination of cast components and sheet metal. It has an outer side-casing of sheet metal *c.* 0.7mm thick, joined at three of the four angles with lead-tin soft solder. Four flanges on the underside comprise the seating for the base plate, also

secured with solder. On the upper side flanging is restricted to the two long sides and one short side. Together with a similarly flanged inner casing this provides a slotted seating for the sliding lid, which has a neatly moulded bar-like grip soldered to its leading edge. The box's inner casing also comprises the outer wall for the five compartments, which are symmetrically disposed as two matching pairs flanking a large central unit. All the compartment walls are soldered in position and have flanged rims to enable hinging and seating for their lids, each of which is provided with an omega-shaped wire handle passed through a slit and engaged in the eye of two tiny staples. All of the lids and handles are mobile but part of one small compartment lid is broken and most of the compartment lid hinges are damaged. At the front, un-flanged, side of the box a lock mechanism is contrived in the gap between the inner and outer casing, its simple moulded catch corroded in position on the outer edge. There is a tiny rectangular bolt-hole in the inner flanged surface and a corresponding cavity in the underside of the leading edge of the lid. A simple decorative motif, comprising a pair of incised lines framing a lightly cambered moulding, is present in various adaptations to the available space on the lid, base and outer flanges of the box and on the compartment lids. All the compartments are empty.

  1st/3rd century AD.
  BMRL 7191-54-K.

3.125. Rectangular box (1866,0415.235 donated by George Dennis) (Fig. 132)
Probably from Cyrenaica, Libya.
Box 114.3 × 72.4mm; sliding lid 112.1 × 70.3mm

A copper-alloy rectangular box, corroded and sand-encrusted, with five compartments and a sliding lid. The box construction is relatively simple, with single-thickness walls flanged inwards at the top to provide the seating for the sliding lid. The flanges bear simple incised paired-line decoration (the only decoration now visible on the box) and are neatly angled at the corners. The base and long side walls appear to have been made from a single sheet. The two end walls – both now lacking – were separately made and secured in position with solder. There are three long open rectangular compartments at one end of the box and two broader, shorter, lidded rectangular compartments at the other. The two dividing walls of the open compartments and the transverse wall dividing the open from the lidded compartments have rolled-over tops and their edges and bases were evidently fixed in position with solder. The two compartment lids are provided with a simple wire ring-handle held in the eye of a tiny staple. The sliding rectangular lid, apparently unornamented, has broken sections of the wall-flanges corroded to its edges in a number of places.

1st/3rd century AD.
Guide to Greek and Roman Life 1908, 181, no. 441.

3.126. Tubular box (1851,0813.93 Comarmond Collection) (Fig. 133)

From Vaison, Vaucluse, France.
Length 91.2mm; box length 75.0mm; box diameter 14.0mm; lid length 24.8mm; lid diameter 14.3mm; weight 12.3g (box 8.4g; lid 3.9g)

A small cylindrical two-part box, of bronze. Box and lid were each raised from a single sheet. Decorative incised rings are present on the box base and lid top as well as on the wall near top and bottom of the lid and near the mid-point and base of the box. The very lightly tapered offset of the box top for the seating of the lid permitted an overlap of *c.* 9mm. The lid is detachable.

For the results of analysis of sampled residues from the box see pp. 167–8, **Tables 5–6** and **Fig. 191**.

The register entry records that the box contained three bodkins – two bronze, one bone – but these were not found in 1981. A small paper label stuck to the side of the box near the base is marked with the number 167 in sepia ink.

1st/3rd century AD.
Guide to Greek and Roman Life 3rd edition, 1929, 138, fig. 156; Stacey 2011.
BMRL 7191-8-Y.

3.127. Tubular box (1904,0204.264 Morel Collection) (Fig. 133)

From Vaison, Vaucluse, France.
Length 88.3mm; box length *c.* 81.5mm; box diameter 14.0mm; lid length 14.9mm (broken); lid diameter 13.5mm; weight 13.0g

A small cylindrical two-part box, of bronze, complete except for the top of the lid. Each component is raised from a single sheet. Very finely incised rings are visible on the base of the box, on the wall at its junction with the base and on the wall 28.5mm above the base. At the upper end of the box a marked angular offset to seat the lid extends for *c.* 20mm. The lid is corroded in a partially removed position.

For the results of analysis of sampled residues from the box see pp. 166–7, **Tables 5–6** and **Figs 191–2**.

1st/3rd century AD.
Stacey 2011.
BMRL 7191-10-X.

3.128. Tubular box (1867,0508.168 Blacas Collection) (Fig. 133)

Provenance unknown.
Part of probable set, see p. 99.
Length 96.5mm; box length 73.7mm; box diameter 19.7mm;

Figure 133 Tubular boxes. British Museum, left to right, Cat. nos 3.126, 3.127, 3.128

lid length 29.8mm; lid diameter 20.0mm; weight 23.1g (box 17.8g; lid 5.3g)

A short two-part cylindrical box, of bronze, each component raised from a single sheet. Decoration appears to be restricted to a dimpled centre-point on the base of the box and top of the lid and a single incised ring around the rim of the lid. The very lightly offset close-fitting seating for the lid extends 9.6mm back from the mouth of the box. The lid is detachable.

For the results of analysis of sampled residues from the box see p. 167, **Tables 5–6** and **Fig. 191**.

1st/3rd century AD.
Stacey 2011.
BMRL 7191-9-L.

3.129. Ointment pot (1842,0728.569) (Figs 134a–c, 176)

From Athens, Thomas Burgon Collection, acquired by the British Museum in 1842.
Height 27.5mm; maximum girth 24.1mm; weight 21.1g

A miniature lead pot (micro-container) with solid pedestal base, globular body and simple flared rim, classified as an Athenian or central Mediterranean form (Taborelli and Marengo 1998, 222, 226, Group C). The pot, which lacks much of the rim and part of the upper body, is of somewhat irregular form. It was cast in a two-piece mould and retains the casting flashes on the exterior surface. Integral to the casting are an image of a tripod, adjacent to one of the casting seams, and a line of relief lettering in Greek (the characters 3–3.5mm high) which follows and encircles the body just above its maximum girth, straddling the second casting seam. It reads:

ΛΥΚΙΟΝΠ/ΑΡΑΜΟΥΣΑΙΟΥ,

that is: ΛΥΚΙΟΝ ΠΑΡΑ ΜΟΥΣΑΙΟΥ,

which translates: 'Mousaios' lykion ointment'.

For the results of analysis of sampled residues from the pot see p. 168, **Tables 5–6** and **Fig. 193**.
Probably 3rd century BC.

Figure 134a–c
Miniature ointment
pot. British Museum,
Cat. no. 3.129

Simpson 1855, 48–9, pl. 2, no. 1; *Guide to Greek and Roman Life* 1908, 182, no. 444; Taborelli and Marengo 1998, 226, 228, fig. 4.13, 231, fig. 6.4, 234, 259.

BMRL 7191-56-P.

3.130. Ointment pot (1868,0110.219 Woodhouse Collection) (Fig. 135)

From Corfu, Greece.

Height 23.7mm; maximum girth 19.4mm; weight 10.8g

A miniature lead pot with solid pedestal base, globular body and neck-moulded flared rim. About half of the rim and one-third of the body is broken away. The pot was cast in a two-piece mould and the casting flashes on the exterior surface are still clearly visible as a prominent rib. Immediately above the maximum girth are two relief letters (5 and 6mm high), an integral part of the casting. They are:

AJ

For the results of analysis of sampled residues from the pot see p. 168, **Tables 5–6** and **Fig. 193**.

Guide to Greek and Roman Life 1908, 182 – where the letters are read as AT.

BMRL 7191-53-X.

Figure 135 Miniature ointment pot. British Museum, Cat. no. 3.130

Collyrium-stamps (Figs 136–7)

3.131. Collyrium-stamp (1879,0916.1 Franks Collection) (Figs 138–9)

Naix-aux-Forges (formerly known as Naix-en-Barrois), Meuse, France. One of seven collyrium-stamps found on 19 September 1807 'dans une fouille' together with a quite large number of complete and broken pottery vessels (Voinot 1999, nos 35–41). At the present day three stamps are in the Musée du Louvre, Paris, two at the British Museum (Cat. nos 3.131–2), one in the Cabinet des Médailles, Paris and one in the Kunsthistorisches Museum, Vienna. Cat. no. 3.131 was first acquired by the Chevalier de Barthélemy à Celles, was then sold to Froehner in 1867, subsequently passed to Auguste Parent in Paris, after which it entered the collection of Augustus Wollaston Franks, who donated it to the British Museum in 1879.

53.8 × 52.9 ×14.5mm; dies 52 × 8mm; weight 100.54g

A large, thick, nearly perfect square tablet of pale green fine-grained stone with a creamy band and small cream inclusions ('green steatite'). The planar faces have a raised flat central square and regularly formed broad bevels towards the die faces. The surface is regular and smooth with no markings or wear. Finishing file striations are visible in areas of the planar faces and bevels. The die faces are perfectly flat regular rectangles with lightly chamfered corner angles. One corner is slightly damaged. The two lines of reversed lettering on all four die faces are each set between a pair of lightly incised guide lines. The letters (Latin capitals) are finely cut, well formed and regularly spaced. Only die (a) has dot stops, but there are decorative gap-filling leaf-stops at the end of dies (a) and (d). There is much abbreviation and several instances of simple (two-letter) ligaturing on dies (b), (c) and (d).

Collyria of Iunius Taurus.

A. Two-line dies engraved retrograde on four edges:
(a) IVNI.TAVRI.CROCOD.SAR/
COFAGUMADASPRIT leaf-stop
Iuni Tauri crocod(es) sar/cofagum ad asprit(udines)
'Iunius Taurus's saffron salve with sarcophagus stone for trachoma'

Figure 136 Collyrium-stamps. British Museum, Cat. nos 3.131–44

Figure 137 Collyrium-stamps. British Museum, upper row, left to right, Cat. nos 3.131, 3.132, 3.133, 3.134; middle row, left to right, Cat. nos 3.135, 3.136, 3.137, 3.138, 3.139; lower row, left to right, Cat. nos 3.140, 3.141, 3.142, 3.143, 3.144

Figure 138 Collyrium-stamp. British Museum, Cat. no. 3.131, with impressions of the four dies

(b) [I]VNITAVRICRODIALEP /
ADCICATRICEISCABRIT

[I]uni Tauri cro(codes) dialep(idos) / ad cicatric(es) et scabrit(ies)
'Iunius Taurus's saffron salve with copper oxide for scars and roughness/itching (of the eyes)'

(c) IVNITAVRICROCODDIA /
MISVSADDIATHESISEIRE

Iuni Tauri crocod(es) dia/misus ad diathesis et re(umatica)
'Iunius Taurus's saffron salve with misy for eye affections and running eyes'

(d) IVNITAVRICROCODPAC /
CIANADCICAIEIREVM leaf-stop

Iuni Tauri crocod(es) pac/cian(um) ad cicat(rices) et reum(atica)
'Iunius Taurus's saffron salve of Paccius for scars and running eyes'

CIL XIII 10021.111; *Guide to Greek and Roman Life* 1908, 181–2, no. 442, fig. 191; Franks List, no. 25; Voinot 1999, no. 37; Jackson 2014c, 289–90, no. 157.

3.132. Collyrium-stamp (1879,0916.2 Franks Collection) (Fig. 140)

Naix-aux-Forges (formerly known as Naix-en-Barrois), Meuse, France. Details as Cat. no. 3.131.
48.8 × 27.7 × 13mm; dies 46 × 9.5mm; weight 45.48g

A regular rectangular block of pale green fine-grained stone ('green steatite'). There is slight scratching on one planar face and a finely incised letter G on the other. Finishing file striations are present on both of the plain end faces. Both long sides of the planar faces have a narrow bevel above the two die faces. Each line of the dies is set between a pair of lightly incised guide lines. The reversed lettering is deeply cut, well formed and mostly regularly spaced; the punctuation is rather irregular; and there is just one simple (two-letter) ligature at the end of the second line of die (b).

Figure 139 The four inscribed die faces of collyrium-stamp, British Museum, Cat. no. 3.131, with their retrograde Latin inscriptions together with reversed images to show their impressions. Top to bottom, dies a, b, c, d

The tail of the letter Q (for Quintus) at the start of both dies is given a flourish.

Collyria of Quintus Iunius Taurus.

A. Two-line dies engraved retrograde on two edges:

(a) Q.IVNITAVRIDIALIBAN / ADSVPPVRAT. EXOVO

Q(uinti) Iuni Tauri dialiban(um) / ad suppurat(iones) ex ovo
'Quintus Iunius Taurus's frankincense salve for suppuration (of the eyes) (to be used) mixed with egg'

(b) Q.IVN.TAVRIANODY / NVMADOMN.LIPPIT

Q(uinti) Iuni Tauri anody/num ad omn(em) lippit(udinem)
'Quintus Iunius Taurus's pain-relieving salve for all kinds of eye inflammation'

CIL XIII 10021.113; Franks List, no. 24; Voinot 1999, no. 39.

Figure 140 The two inscribed die faces of collyrium-stamp, British Museum, Cat. no. 3.132, with their retrograde Latin inscriptions together with reversed images to show their impressions. Top to bottom, dies a, b

3.133. Collyrium-stamp (1879,0916.3 Franks Collection) (Figs 141–2)

Lyon, Rhône, France. Found before 1845 in the River Saône, upstream from the Pont du Change, the earliest bridge in central Lyon.

38.5 × 36.5 × 8mm; dies (a) and (c) 35 × 4mm; dies (b) and (d) 34 × 4mm; weight 26.28g

A nearly square thin tablet of olive-green fine-grained stone ('green steatite'). There are irregularities on both planar faces and one has a rudimentarily incised torc-like motif. The die faces are narrow with neatly tapered ends. The reversed lettering of the dies is deeply cut, quite well formed and regularly spaced. There is just one simple (two-letter) ligature at the middle of face (d).

Collyria of Hirpidius Polytimus.

A. One-line dies engraved retrograde on four edges:
(a) HIRPIDI.POLYTIM
Hirpidi Polytim(i)
'Hirpidius Polytimus's (salves)'

(b) ACHARISTVM
acharistum
'acharistum'

(c) DIAGLAVCEV
Diaglaucium
'glaucium salve'

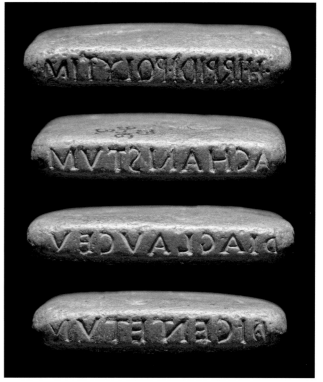

Figure 141 The four inscribed die faces of collyrium-stamp, British Museum, Cat. no. 3.133, with their retrograde Latin inscriptions together with reversed images to show their impressions. Top to bottom, dies a, b, c, d

(d) DICENIETVM
Dicentetum
'dicentetum'

CIL XIII 10021.81; Franks List, no. 49; Voinot 1999, no. 73.

3.134. Collyrium-stamp (1984,0328.1) (Fig. 143)

Provenance unknown, but probably from the Auvergne, France. This stamp was once believed to have been in the collection of Sir Hans Sloane and probably found in Britain. However, current opinion is that it was more probably found in 1773 at an unrecorded site in the Auvergne (references in *RIB* II, 4, 2446.32 and Voinot 1999, no. 29: 'Trouvé en 1773 chez les Arvernes' (?) Beraud). It is possible that its acquisition by the British Museum corresponds to an entry for the year 1819 in the Donations Register of the

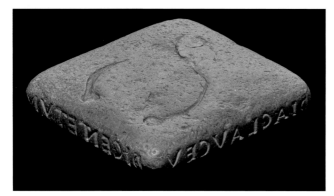

Figure 142 Collyrium-stamp, British Museum, Cat. no. 3.133, showing the torc-like motif incised on one of the planar faces

Figure 143 The three inscribed die faces of collyrium-stamp, British Museum, Cat. no. 3.134, with their retrograde Latin inscriptions together with reversed images to show their impressions. Top to bottom, dies a, b, c

Department of Antiquities and Coins. The entry reads: '1819 June 12. A Roman stamp supposed to be one of those used by the Roman oculists for stamping their medicines: from Taylor Combe Esq.' Taylor Combe was Keeper of Antiquities from 1807 to 1826.

54.5 × 51.5 × 9.1mm; die (a) 54 × 8mm; die (b) 49 × 8 mm; die (c) one end damaged; weight 59.79g

A nearly square tablet of pale olive-brown fine-grained stone ('green schist') damaged at one corner. On one planar face there is wear polish, slight bevelling and a number of natural irregularities. Scratching and light hollowing of the other planar face are suggestive of drug preparation. The plain die face bears no sign of ever having been inscribed. The reversed lettering of the three dies, set between two pairs of lightly incised guide lines, is quite clear, deeply cut and well formed, consistent with fitting in to a relatively confined space. The 'A's are blind. Die (b) has a space-filling stylised palm-frond at both ends.

Collyria of Sextus Iulius Sedatus.

A. Two-line dies engraved retrograde on three edges:
(a) SEXIVLSEDATICRO / CODESDIALEPIDOS
Sex(ti) Iul(i) Sedati cro/codes dialepidos
'Sextus Iulius Sedatus's saffron salve with copper oxide'

(b) SEXIVL SEDATI / CROCODPACCIAN
Sex(ti) Iul(i) Sedati / crocod(es) paccian(um)
'Sextus Iulius Sedatus's saffron salve of Paccius'
(c) [...]IVLSEDATICRO / [..]DESADDIATHES
[Sex(ti)] Iul(i) Sedati cro/[co]des ad diathes(es)
'Sextus Iulius Sedatus's saffron salve for affections (of the eyes)'

CIL VII 1313; *CIL* XIII 10021.107; Franks List, no. 61; *RIB* II, 4, 2446.32; Voinot 1999, no. 29.

3.135. Collyrium-stamp (1928,0714.3) **(Fig. 144)**
Caistor St. Edmund, Norfolk, England. Found in the Roman town of *Venta Icenorum* in 1927.
24 × 24 × 5.5mm; weight 8.28g

A tiny square thin tablet of pale grey-green fine-grained stone. In its present form the stamp bears only one inscribed die face, with a single line of neatly cut reversed lettering. However, a slight bevel on the planar margin of the inscribed edge and on that of the adjacent edge and the absence of this feature from the other two edges suggests that the latter pair was truncated and that the stamp was originally larger. In addition, illegible traces of incised lettering survive on the adjacent edge and indicate that its die had been deliberately erased. If the surviving die had indeed been truncated then the point of truncation – at the end of the name of the salve-blender – would most probably originally have been followed by the name of a salve.

Collyria of Publius Anicius Sedatus.

A. One-line die engraved retrograde on one edge:
P.ANIC.SEDATI [
P(ublii) Anic(ii) Sedati[
'Publius Anicius Sedatus's (salve)'

Jackson 1990b, esp. 277–8 and fig. 3B; *RIB* II, 4, 2446.24; Voinot 1999, no. 244.

3.136. Collyrium-stamp (1872,0520.1) **(Figs 145, 146a–b)**
Cirencester, Wiltshire, England. From the Roman town of *Corinium Dobunnorum*, found near the Leauses Garden, in an urn, in 1818.
50 × 19 × 12mm; weight 29.32g

A slender rectangular block of dark grey-green fine-grained stone ('green schist'). The engraved reversed lettering and spacing are rather irregular although this is partly a product of heavy wear and slight damage on the die

Figure 144 The inscribed die face of collyrium-stamp, British Museum, Cat. no. 3.135, with its retrograde Latin inscription together with reversed image to show the impression

faces. The planar faces also show signs of wear, perhaps from whetting. Separating the two lines of lettering on die (a) there is a lightly incised central line, with five-pellet finial, which stops short of the exuberant long descender of the letter 'x' of *ex o(vo)*. Heavy ligaturing compresses the letters NPETLIPPIT into just four letter blocks.

Collyria of Minervalis.

A. Two-line dies engraved retrograde on two edges:
(a) MINERVALISDEALEB /
ANUMADINPETLIPPITEXO
Minervalis dealeb/anum ad inpet(um) lippit(udinis) ex o(vo)
'Minervalis's frankincense salve, to be mixed in egg white, for the onset of eye inflammation'
(b) MINERVALISMELIN[V] / [A]
DOMNEMDOLOREM
Minervalis melinu(m) / ad omnem dolorem
'Minervalis's quince ointment for the treatment of all ailments'
   B. Incised on both of the end faces is a six-point star, probably nothing more than a simple decorative motif – it is closely paralleled on the two end faces of a collyrium-stamp from Sainte-Colombe, France (Voinot 1999, 191). Probably not a Chi-Rho symbol as suggested in the 1922 edition of the British Museum *Guide to the Antiquities of Roman Britain*, 34.
   CIL VII 1316; *CIL* XIII 10021.138; Franks List, no. 57; Jackson 1990b, table 1, no. 7; *RIB* II, 4, 2446.19; Voinot 1999, no. 49.

3.137. Collyrium-stamp (1892,0801.1 Franks Collection) (Fig. 147)
Probably from Colchester (*Camulodunum*), Essex, England, where the stamp was acquired in or before 1892.
41 × 41 × 13mm; weight 54.71g
   A thick square tablet of olive-grey stone with mottled cream and brown inclusions, probably Purbeck marble (and thus likely British made). In this relatively hard stone the reversed lettering appears to have been cut with some difficulty, though the rudimentary appearance of the lettering may in part be a product of subsequent wear (which hinders the reading of die a). No guide lines are visible on the three inscribed faces, and one face is uninscribed. The planar faces are blank. The stamp is idiosyncratic both in the choice of stone and in the layout of the die inscriptions –

Figure 145 The two inscribed die faces of collyrium-stamp, British Museum, Cat. no. 3.136, with their retrograde Latin inscriptions together with reversed images to show their impressions. Top to bottom, dies a, b

Figure 146a–b The six-point stars incised into the two end faces of collyrium-stamp, British Museum, Cat. no. 3.136

two lines on die (a), three lines on die (b), one incomplete line on die (c).

Collyria of Lucius Ulpius Deciminus.

A. Two-line, three-line and one-line dies engraved retrograde on three edges:
(a) LVLPDECIMIN / PENICADLIP *or* PENICILLE
L(ucii) Vlp(ii) Decimini / penic(illum) ad lip(pitudinem) or
penicil(lum) le(ne)
'Lucius Ulpius Deciminus's salve, to be applied with a fine brush, for inflammation of the eyes' *or* 'Lucius Ulpius Deciminus's mild ointment (to be used at the onset of eye inflammation)'

(b) LULPDECIMINIDIA / [L]EPIDOSCROCOD / [A]
DOMNIAVITIA
L(uci) Ulp(i) Decimini dia/lepidos crocod(es) / [a]d omnia vitia
'Lucius Ulpius Deciminus's saffron salve (made with) copper oxide for all defects (of the eyes)'

(c) LVLP.DEC
L(uci) Ulp(i) Dec(imini)
'Lucius Ulpius Deciminus's.... '

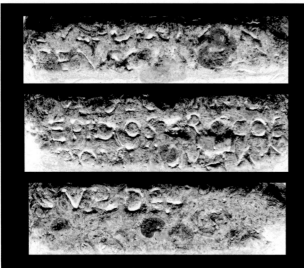

Figure 147 The three inscribed die faces of collyrium-stamp, British Museum, Cat. no. 3.137, with their retrograde Latin inscriptions together with reversed images to show their impressions. Top to bottom, dies a, b, c

CIL XIII 10021.198; Jackson 1990b, 276, fn. 50, table 1, no. 10; *RIB* II, 4, 2446.8; Voinot 1999, no. 205.

3.138. Collyrium-stamp (1864,0602.1) **(Fig. 148)**

Golden Bridge, near Clonmel, County Tipperary, Ireland. Found near the village of Golden Bridge on the River Swire, in a dike in the Spittefields, together with human bones, in about 1842.

37 × 28 × 8.5mm; weight 24.29g

A small rectangular tablet of dark grey/black fine-grained stone, engraved on one face only – there is no sign of any former lettering on the other three faces. The die's reversed lettering, set between lightly incised guide lines, is neat and regularly cut, with a decorative leaf-stop at the end of the upper line. The planar faces are plain, while hollowing and grooving on the long edge opposite the die are suggestive of whetting.

Figure 148 The inscribed die face of collyrium-stamp, British Museum, Cat. no. 3.138, with its retrograde Latin inscription together with reversed image to show the impression

Collyria of Marcus Iuventius Tutianus.

A. Two-line die engraved retrograde on one edge:
MIVVENTTVTIANI leaf-stop/ DIAMYSVSADVETCIC
M(arci) Iuvent(i) Tutiani / diamysus ad vet(eres) cic(atrices)
'Marcus Iuventius Tutianus's salve made from misy for corneal scars'
 CIL VII 1315; *CIL* XIII 10021.117; Franks List, no. 60; Jackson 1990b, table 1, no. 14; *RIB* II, 4, 2446.28; Voinot 1999, no. 68.

3.139. Collyrium-stamp (1931,0211.1) **(Figs 149–51)**

Kenchester, Hereford and Worcester, England. Found in 1848 at the Roman small town of *Magnis*.

39 × 39 × 9.5mm; weight 37.59g

A square tablet of pale green fine-grained stone. The deeply engraved reversed lettering is regular and well spaced, with no visible guide lines. The lower line of die (d) is partly erased by what appears to have been heavy whetting, damage which extends onto one adjacent planar face. On each of the two planar faces a name has been cut retrograde – Senior on face (a), Seni on face (b). It may be more than fortuitous that each name is positioned so that when upright they face the top of two dies – Senior facing dies (a) and (b), Seni facing dies (c) and (d) – thus perhaps aiding selection of the appropriate die the correct way up when marking the *collyria*.

Collyria of Titus Vindacius Ariovistus.

A. Two-line dies engraved retrograde on four edges:
(a) T.VINDAC.ARIO / VISTIANICET
T(iti) Vindac(ii) Ario/visti anicet(um)
'Titus Vindacius Ariovistus's infallible salve'

(b) [T.] VINDAC.ARI / OVISTICHLORON
[T(iti)] Vindac(ii) Ari/ovisti chloron
'Titus Vindacius Ariovistus's green salve'

(c) T.VINDACIAR / [I]OVISTINARD
T(iti) Vindaci(i) Ar/[i]ovisti nard(inum)
'Titus Vindacius Ariovistus's nard-oil salve'

(d) T.VINDAC.ARIO / VISTIT[V]RINVM

T(iti) Vindac(ii) Ario/visti t[u]rinum
'Titus Vindacius Ariovistus's salve made from frankincense'

B. Roughly incised retrograde lettering on the two planar faces:
(a) SENIOR

(b) SENI
  CIL VII 1320; *CIL* XIII 10021.195; Franks List, no. 58; *Guide to the Antiquities of Roman Britain* 1964, 73, fig. 38; Jackson 1990b, table 1, no. 17; *RIB* II, 4, 2446.3; Jackson 1996b, 183–4; Voinot 1999, no. 94.

3.140. Collyrium-stamp (SL Antiq. 1130 Sloane Collection) (Fig. 152)

St Albans, Hertfordshire, England. Found in 1739 at the Roman town of *Verulamium*.
31 × 31 × 16mm; weight 36.20g

A small, thick square block of pale green fine-grained stone ('green steatite'). This is part of a larger stone tablet that was broken in antiquity. What survives, extrapolating from the remnants of the original inscriptions on the two adjacent die faces (a) and (b), is probably about a quarter of the size of the original of *c.* 60 × 60 × 16mm. The broken edge of face (c) was then smoothed to receive a secondary die text. The reversed lettering of dies (a) and (b) is set between lightly incised guide lines and is neatly cut, regular and evenly spaced, with a flourish given to the upper branches of the 'Y' of *di]asmyrnes* on die (b). The secondary die (c) has no guide lines and the reversed lettering is larger and less regular. The original margins of the planar faces are lightly bevelled, while an incised line on one planar face adjacent to die (c) may have been intended to prioritise that die.

Collyria of Lucius Iulius Iuvenis and Flavius Secundus.

A. Two-line dies engraved retrograde on three edges:
(a) LIVLIVENISD[. . .] / OBALSAMATV[...]
L(uci) Iul(i) Iu(v)enis d[iapsor(icum) op]/obalsmatu[m ad clar(itatem)]
'Lucius Iulius Iuvenis's anti-irritant balsam [for clear sight]'

(b) [. . .]ASMYRNESBIS / [. . .]MPETVEXOVO
[L(uci) Iul(i) Iuvenis di]asmyrnes bis / [post lippitu(dinis) i]mpetu(m) ex ovo
'Lucius Iulius Iuvenis's myrrh salve (to be used) twice (a day) with egg [after] the onset of [eye inflammation]'

(c) FLSECVNDI / ATALBAS
Fl(avi) Secundi / at albas (cicatrices)
'Flavius Secundus's salve for white (scars)'

  CIL VII 1310; *CIL* XIII 10021.70; Jackson 1990b, table 1, no. 23; *RIB* II, 4, 2446.11; Voinot 1999, no. 16.

3.141. Collyrium-stamp (1882,0819.1) (Figs 153–4)

Sandy/Biggleswade, Bedfordshire, England. Found in 1873 at Tower Hill, Sandy (near Biggleswade railway station),

Figures 149–50 Planar faces of collyrium-stamp, British Museum Cat. no. 3.139, showing the incised names SENIOR and SENI

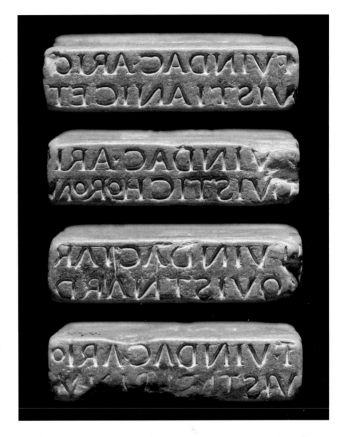

Figure 151 The four inscribed die faces of collyrium-stamp, British Museum, Cat. no. 3.139, with their retrograde Latin inscriptions together with reversed images to show their impressions. Top to bottom, dies a, b, c, d

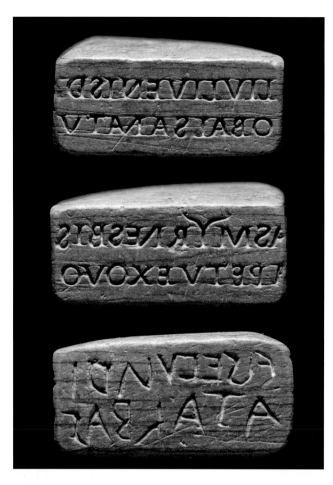

Figure 153 The three inscribed die faces of collyrium-stamp, British Museum, Cat. no. 3.140, with their retrograde Latin inscriptions together with reversed images to show their impressions. Top to bottom, dies a, b, c

where quarrying for ballast between 1866 and 1902 revealed a cemetery with cremations and inhumations. The stamp is therefore likely to have come from a burial. A coin of Antoninus Pius issued between AD 155–61 was reported to have been found with it (D.E. Johnston 'Sandy', in *The 'small towns' of Roman Britain* (ed. W. Rodwell and T. Rowley), British Archaeological Reports 15, Oxford, 225–31, esp. 228, figs 1 and 3).

54 × 41 × 12mm; weight 64.75g

A rectangular tablet of mid-grey-green fine-grained stone ('green schist') with bevelled margins on the planar faces. The reversed lettering of the dies was confidently engraved, with large lettering set between incised guide lines, though the curved letters S and C were evidently the hardest to achieve. The spacing is rather irregular – large lettering at the start of the lines reduced to smaller lettering and spaces towards the ends where there are multiple complex ligatures, especially VMATI of *reumatic(a)* on die (a) and IMP LIP of *imp(etum) lip(pitudinis)* on die (c). It is possible, however, that the differing letter sizes and layout were intentional in order to give prominence to the name of the salve-blender and the salve.

Collyria of Gaius Valerius Amandus and Gaius Valerius Valentinus. Roger Tomlin has suggested that these two salve-blenders, who shared the same praenomen and nomen, might have been father and son, or brothers, or freedmen of the same owner (*RIB* II, 4, 2446.2).

A. Two-line dies engraved retrograde on four edges:
(a) C.VAL.AMANDI / DIOXVMADREVMATIC
G(ai) Val(erii) Amandi / dioxum ad reumatic(a)
'Gaius Valerius Amandus's vinegar salve for running eyes'

(b) CVALAMANDI / STACTVMADCAL
G(ai) Val(erii) Amandi / stactum ad cal(iginem)
'Gaius Valerius Amandus's drops for dim sight'

(c) C.VAL.VALENTINI / DIAGLAVCPOSTIMPLIP
G(ai) Val(erii) Valentini / diaglauc(ium) post imp(etum) lip(pitudinis)'
'Gaius Valerius Valentinus's celandine (*or* poppy) salve (to be used) after the onset of eye inflammation'

(d) CVALVALENTINI/ MIXTVMADCL
G(ai) Val(erii) Valentini / mixtum ad cl(aritatem)
'Gaius Valerius Valentinus's mixture for clear sight'

B. Roughly incised lettering on the two planar faces:
On each of the two planar faces are two graffiti, not retrograde, which are abbreviated versions of the four named *collyria*. Each of the four graffiti is juxtaposed adjacent to the relevant die face to aid selection of the appropriate stamp when marking the *collyria*. This system is paralleled on a hexagonal collyrium-stamp from Caceres, Spain (Voinot 1999, 251), which has on one planar face the initial letter of each of the six *collyria* adjacent to the relevant die face.
(e) near (a) DIOX – dioxum
(f) near (b) STAC – stactum
(g) near (c) DIAGLAVC – diaglaucium
(h) near (d) MIXT – mixtum

Figure 153 Planar face a) of collyrium-stamp, British Museum Cat. no. 3.141, showing the un-reversed, abbreviated *collyrium* names DIOX and STAC adjacent to the relevant die-faces

Figure 154 Planar face b) of British Museum collyrium-stamp, Cat. no. 3.141, showing the un-reversed, abbreviated *collyrium* names DIAGLAVC and MIXT adjacent to the relevant die-faces

Figure 155 The four inscribed die faces of collyrium-stamp, British Museum, Cat. no. 3.141, with their retrograde Latin inscriptions together with reversed images to show their impressions. Top to bottom, dies a, b, c, d

CIL XIII 10021.186; Jackson 1990b, table 1, no. 3; *RIB* II, 4, 2446.2; Voinot 1999, no. 143.

3.142. Collyrium-stamp (1878,1019,1 Meyrick Collection) (Figs 156–8)

Provenance unknown, but probably from Britain. Found before 1775, lost in 1778 'out of a pocket that had a hole in it' (*Gentleman's Magazine* 48, 1778, 472,) but evidently re-found since it was (still) 'in the possession of Francis Dowse, Esq. of Grays Inn' (*Archaeologia* 9, 1789, 239); in Sir Samuel Rush Meyrick's collection at Goodrich Court in 1869; and donated to the British Museum by his cousin General Augustus Meyrick in 1878.

48.8 × 47 × 11mm; dies (a) and (c) 48 × 9mm; dies (b) and (d) 45.5 × 7mm; weight 65.82g

A nearly square tablet of pale green-grey fine-grained stone ('green steatite'). The planar faces, which bear some damage and a number of smoothed off natural irregularities, are covered with an assortment of simple linear 'doodles' and other unintelligible markings. The reversed lettering of the dies, set between incised guide lines, is deeply cut, competent and mostly well spaced. There is a single simple (two-letter) ligature at the middle of the second line of die (d).

Collyria of Marcus Iulius Satyrus.

A. Two-line dies engraved retrograde on four edges:
(a) MIVLSATYRIPENI / CILLENEEXOVO
M(arci) Iul(i) Satyri peni/cil(lum) lene (ad impetum lippitudinis) ex ovo
'Marcus Iulius Satyrus's mild ointment (to be used) mixed with egg (at the onset of eye inflammation)'

(b) MIVLSATYRIDIA / LEPIDOSADASPR
M(arci) Iul(i) Satyri dia/lepidos ad aspr(itudines)

'Marcus Iulius Satyrus's copper oxide salve for granulation (of the eyelids)'

(c) MIVLSATYRIDIALI / BANVADSVPPVRAT
M(arci) Iul(i) Satyri diali/banu(m) ad suppurat(ionem)
'Marcus Iulius Satyrus's frankincense salve for suppuration (of the eyes)'

(d) MIVLSATYRIDIASMY[.] / [.]ESPOSTIMPETLIPPIT[...]
M(arci) Iul(i) Satyri diasmy[r/n]es post impet(um) lippit[u](dinis)
'Marcus Iulius Satyrus's myrrh salve (to be used) after the onset of eye inflammation'

CIL VII 1312; *CIL* XIII 10021.106; Franks List, no. 32; Jackson 1990b, 275, fn. 48; *RIB* II, 4, 2446.23 (where it was

Figure 156 Planar face a) of collyrium-stamp, British Museum, Cat. no. 3.142

Figure 157 Planar face b) of collyrium-stamp, British Museum, Cat. no. 3.142

Figure 158 The four inscribed die faces of collyrium-stamp, British Museum, Cat. no. 3.142, with their retrograde Latin inscriptions together with reversed images to show their impressions. Top to bottom, dies a, b, c, d

recorded as lost, the author seemingly unaware that it had been in the British Museum collection since 1878); Voinot 1999, no. 31.

3.143. Collyrium-stamp (1976,0109.1 Sloane Bequest) (Fig. 159)

Provenance unknown, but probably from Britain, which has yielded the only other example of a stamp with a die of P. Clod (from the Roman fort of Watercrook, Cumbria: *RIB* II, 4, 2446.5). Known to have been found before 1850 and thought to have been in the collection of Sir Hans Sloane, which was acquired by the British Museum in 1753.
25.4 × 22.3 (broken) × 5mm; die 25 × 4mm; weight 5.95g

A tiny thin broken tablet of pale green fine-grained stone ('green steatite'), probably originally square. The planar faces are flat, smooth and plain. The lettering of the die, reversed except for the D, is well formed and regularly spaced. The two part-broken edges bear no trace of lettering.

Collyria of Publius Clodius or P... Clodianus.

A. One-line die engraved retrograde (except D) on one edge:
COLLYR.P.CLOD
collyr(ium) P(ubli) Clod(i) or *P(...) Clod(iani)*
'The salve of Publius Clodius [*or* P... Clodianus]'
   CIL VII 1317; *CIL* XIII 10021.143; Franks List, no. 62; Jackson 1990b, 275, fn. 48; *RIB* II, 4, 2446.6; Voinot 1999, no. 95.

3.144. Collyrium-stamp (1851,0605.16) (Figs 160–1)
Provenance unknown, but possibly from Britain. Found before 1851 when the Trafford Leigh Collection was acquired by the British Museum.
28.5 × 12 (broken) × 10.5mm; die 28.5 × 9.5mm; weight 7.33g

A small broken block of black fine-grained stone ('schist') – the broken edge of a once larger tablet. There is rudimentarily incised lettering at the surviving end of one planar face – SOLI – and at the surviving end of one edge – VI. The reversed lettering of the die, set between very lightly incised guide lines, is deeply cut, regular and regularly spaced.

Collyria of Marcus Vitellius Crescens.

Figure 159 The inscribed die face of collyrium-stamp, British Museum, Cat. no. 3.143, with its retrograde Latin inscription together with reversed image to show the impression

Figure 160 The inscribed die face of collyrium-stamp, British Museum, Cat. no. 3.144, with its retrograde Latin inscription together with reversed image to show the impression

Figure 161 Planar face of collyrium-stamp, British Museum, Cat. no. 3.144, showing the un-reversed incised word SOLI

A. Two-line die engraved retrograde on one edge:
M.VITELCRES / STACTADCLAR
M(arci) Vitel(li) Cres(centis) / stact(um) ad clar(itatem)
'Marcus Vitellius Crescens's drops for clear sight'.

B. Roughly incised lettering, not retrograde, on one planar face and one edge:
(b) SOLI
(c) [...]VI
    CIL VII 1321; *CIL* XIII 10021.197; Jackson 1990b, 275, fn. 48; *RIB* II, 4, 2446.7; Voinot 1999, no. 97.

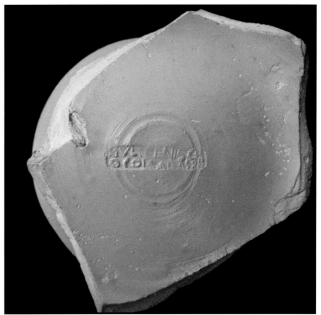

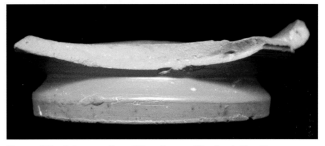

Figure 162a–b Impression of the stamp of Lucius Iulius Senex on the inside of the broken base of a samian cup, Cat. no. 3.145. Photos: Ralph Jackson

3.145. Collyrium-stamp impression on samian cup (1856,0701.595 Roach Smith Collection) **(Fig. 162a–b)**

Found in 1854 at an unrecorded site in the City of London.

The broken base of a Dragendorff 33 samian cup, an early version of the form, dating to around the end of the 1st century AD. At the centre of the inner face, in place of a potter's stamp, there is a rectangular cartouche with the impression of a diminutive two-line die from a collyrium-stamp.

L.IVL.SENISCR / OCOD.ADASPR
L(uci) Iul(i) Senis cr/ocod(es) ad aspr(itudines)
'Lucius Iulius Senex's saffron salve for granulation (of the eyelids)'

Charles Roach Smith, *Catalogue of the Museum of London Antiquities* (London 1854), 47, no. 208; *CIL* VII 1314; *CIL* XIII 10021.231; *RIB* II, 4, 2446.25(i) (where the form of the cup is wrongly given as Dr. 27); Jackson 2012a, no. 8.

(See also Cat. no. 6.3, the seal of a medical practitioner engraved retrograde HEROPHILI OPOBALSAMVM)

Varia

3.146. Mouse handle (1909,0620.3) **(Fig. 163a–c)**

Said to have been found in the Artemision, Ephesus.
Length 78.6mm; socket width 10.7mm; weight 24.6g

A rectangular-sectioned bar handle of leaded bronze, its finial in the form of a crouching mouse nibbling a nut or fruit held between its fore-paws. The creature's coat is simply

Figure 164 Saw blade. British Museum, Cat. no. 3.147

rendered with incised lines. The circular pitted eyes may have been set with an inlay of contrasting colour – one is still part-filled with corroded metal. The tail extends in a straight line onto and along the 'upper' broad face of the handle. The other three faces of the handle bear an incuse inscription in Greek letters. The rather rudimentarily moulded handle terminal has a very short and thin slot-type socket, filled with a lead-rich light grey material, probably a bonding medium for the missing iron component. The handle feels 'right' when held in a position in which the socket is horizontal. This suggests that the missing functional part of the implement was more likely to be an iron spatula than an iron knife blade.

To read the inscription the correct way up and in the correct sequence it is necessary to hold the handle by its mouse finial in the left hand. Starting with the mouse upside down the first side is viewed, then the handle is turned anticlockwise twice to view the 'lower' broad face and the second side. This gives:

(a) ΥΓΕΙΝΟΥ

(b) ΚΑΝΠΥΛΙΟΥ

(c) ΝΕΟΠΟΙΟΥ

that is 'of Hygeinos Kanpylios, *neopoiós*'.

The careful, if simplified, modelling of the sleek-bodied mouse contrasts with the quite indifferent workmanship of the handle and socket and with the rather cavalier treatment of the inscription. Prior to casting it would appear that the wax model was pared away on the upper and lower faces of the handle to give prominence to the mouse's tail and to reduce the thickness of the handle. This was at the expense of the inscription on the two sides which have lost the base of their letters, especially the tail of upsilon and gamma at the start of ΥΓΕΙΝΟΥ. Clearly the paring must have occurred before the word ΚΑΝΠΥΛΙΟΥ was cut into the lower face of the model. The reason for it is not completely clear but is more likely to have had an economic than an ergonomic explanation, a saving of metal rather than a design feature. At all events it implies that the figure of the mouse and the *cognomen* Kanpylios

took precedence over the side components of the inscription.

Jackson 1994b, 326–8 and fig. 6a; Künzl 2002a, 13–14, fig. 7; Jackson 2014b, 221 and 228, no. 61.

BMRL 7191-41-L.

3.147. Saw blade (1851,0813.101 Comarmond Collection) (Fig. 164)
Provenance unknown, but probably from the neighbourhood of Lyon, France.
Length 113.6mm; thickness 0.95–1.05mm; length of toothed edge 100.0mm; weight 20.5g

A small sub-trapezoid saw blade made from a flat sheet of leaded bronze about 1mm thick. The straight 100-mm-long cutting edge has 66 tiny un-raked teeth, closely set at *c.* 7 per cm, the tip of many now damaged. The back is straight and sloping; the sides are neatly cut crescentic hollows, the upper tip at the broader end damaged. During scientific examination (see p. 154 and **Fig. 185**) radiography revealed a row of three small diamond-shaped holes close to the broader side and at right angles to the line of the blade back. They contain the remains of tiny round pins or rivets, probably the remnants of a handle fixing.

Bronzes catalogue, 2328; *Guide to Greek and Roman Life* 1908, 179–80, fig.189h; Jackson 1990a, fig. 5.7.

BMRL 7191-55-M.

3.148. Two-pronged fork (1847,0806.141 Millingen Collection) (Fig. 165)
Provenance unknown.
Length 150.7mm; length of prongs 77.6mm; width between tips 6.1mm; weight 18.7g

A two-pronged fork, of gunmetal, with long prongs and an ornate handle. The handle, symmetrically arranged with a moulded finial and intricate fenestrated units flanking a central moulding, surmounts an omega-shaped loop from which the prongs, of diamond-shaped cross-section, extend in an even taper to sharp-pointed tips.

Bronzes catalogue, 2324; Milne 1907, pl. 22.1.

BMRL 7191-42-N.

3.149. Two-pronged fork (1923,0117.1) (Fig. 165)
Provenance unknown.
Length 128.9mm; length of prongs 73.4mm; width between tips 6.5mm; weight 14.0g

A two-pronged fork, of brass, with long (distorted) prongs and an ornate handle. As the previous example, though a little smaller and with a simpler finial.

BMRL 7191-43-Q.

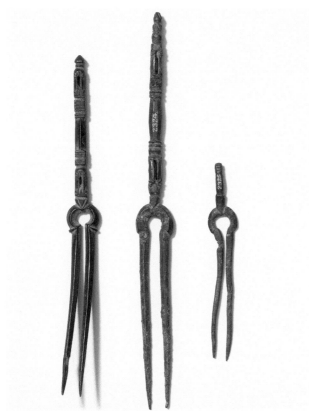

Figure 165 The two-pronged forks. British Museum, left to right, Cat. nos 3.149, 3.148, 3.150

Figure 166 Bone forceps, Naples Foundry copy. British Museum, Cat. no. 3.153

3.150. Two-pronged fork (1975,1106.2) (Fig. 165)
Provenance unknown.
Length 75.4mm; length of prongs 59.0mm; weight 4.2g

A two-pronged fork, of brass, lacking much of the handle, with slender distorted prongs of irregular ovoid cross-section. Similar to the two previous examples, though smaller, more damaged and of much inferior workmanship.

Bronzes catalogue, 2325; Milne 1907, pl. 22.2.
BMRL 7191-44-T.

3.151. Two-pronged fork (1866,0101.328)
From Cyprus.
Length 140 mm

A slender tapered stem, with decorative moulded finial, which terminates at the other end in a pair of everted slender pointed prongs.

Closely resembles the drawing of a bifurcated instrument in *folio* 86 of the 13th–14th-century *Chirurgia* of Bruno da Longobucco (reproduced in *La scuola medica Salernitana: storia, immagini, manoscritti dall' XI al XIII secolo* ed. Maria Pasca, Soprintendenza per I beni ambientali architettonici, artistici e storici di Salerno e Avellino (Naples 1988)).

Bronzes catalogue, 2326; Milne 1907, pl. 22.4.

3.152. Two-pronged fork (1824,0498.7)
Provenance unknown.
Length 102mm; length of prongs 22mm; width between tips 9mm.

A bifurcated implement, of rather indifferent workmanship. The rectangular-sectioned handle is decorated with a series of ring-and-baluster mouldings and terminates in a pair of short, thick, blunt prongs. Probably not a surgical instrument.

Milne 1907, pl. 22.5.

Copies (see also Chapter 4, pp. 158–60)

3.153. Bone forceps, copy (1920,0717.4) (Fig. 166)
Pompeii.
Modern copy, of Museo Archeologico Nazionale di Napoli Inv. No. 78029, purchased from Chiurazzi-De Angelis, Naples, 1920.
Length 197mm; length of handle 83.5mm; length of leg from handle to hinge 39mm; length of leg from hinge to jaw 74.5mm; weight 211.5g

The instrument is effectively as made, a fully functioning copy, with no apparent post-1920 corrosion. The patina appears to correspond to the dark grey 'Herculanum' patina, one of the three finishes offered in the Chiurazzi/De Angelis 1911 retail catalogue. Small casting blemishes (blow-holes) are visible a) at one handle finial and b) on the plain bar section just beyond the handle mouldings of one leg. File-finishing striations are visible on the surface of all undecorated zones.

The object is well made and looks close in appearance to the original. However, there are some very clear differences:
1) Most notably, the object has been made in reverse – the two legs have been transposed.
2) It is substantially smaller than the original – 90% of the length (197mm as opposed to 220mm).
3) The zones of disc-and-baluster mouldings are quite crude in comparison to the crisply cut originals.
4) Although the jaws and the decorated handles are close in size to the original there is a marked disparity in the size of the plain cross-legged section, in particular the section between the handle moulding and the hinge, which is less than two-thirds the length of the original – 39mm as opposed to 57mm. This changes the leverage and the general feel quite considerably.
5) The form and degree of curvature and offset of the plain cross-legged section between hinge and jaw is substantially different – it is more highly curved than the original.

On the 'plus side', although the 'candy-twist' zone of the handles is rather shorter than it should be the twisting itself is quite accurately rendered.

Figure 167 Male catheter and tube, Naples Foundry copies. British Museum, Cat. nos 3.154, 3.155

Figure 168 Cannula, Naples Foundry copy, British Museum, Cat. no. 3.156

The great advantage of this functioning copy is that it permits experimental use. Thus, it became apparent that the span of the user's hand in a position to give a controlled grip of the forceps handles (themselves transmitting control of the jaws) dictates the degree of opening of the jaws and thus a maximum diameter/width for objects or structure that can be successfully gripped. In the average-size male right hand this measurement is *c*. 25mm (30mm at the outside) and the preferred size is *c*. 15mm. Objects of that order of size could be readily grasped and manipulated at various positions in the beaked jaws and could be held with very considerable pressure. Tiny objects can also usually be grasped firmly in the jaw tips. It seems clear that the forceps would function very effectively when dealing with cranial fragments or with other fractured bones of similar size and with digits, ribs and long bones up to a diameter of 20–25mm. Obviously, because of the inexactitude of this copy, its jaw capacity differs from that of the original, which was probably a little less. With its much longer handles the original would also have exerted a greater leverage on the jaws, resulting in a still firmer grip.

Chiurazzi – De Angelis Catalogo 1911, 407, no. 78029 (with photo of museum original, not copy). For the original instrument see Bliquez 1994, 171, no 242.

BMRL File 7070.

3.154. Male catheter, copy (1920,0717.5) (Fig. 167)
Pompeii.
Modern copy, of Museo Archeologico Nazionale di Napoli inv. no. 78026, purchased from Chiurazzi-De Angelis, Naples, 1920.
Length 262mm; external diameter 5.5mm; weight 35.0g

The object is virtually as made, but a) the apparently 'Herculanum' applied patina has flaked or been chafed away in small areas in one or two places, and b) there is a bright green corrosion patch, of limited extent, in two places along the manufacture seam on the upper part of the instrument, and bright blue-green corrosion products within the eye at the tip of the catheter, all presumably post-1920.

The copy is close in appearance to the original but by no means an exact replica.
1) Its length, at 262mm, is 10mm short of the original.
2) The degree of curvature of both parts of the S-shape is a little more acute than that of the original.
3) The incuse girth ring near the top of the copy is not a feature of the original.
4) The form of the eye and tip varies slightly from the original and is slightly less well finished.
   On the positive side, the copy was made, like the original,

with a close-fitting butt-join which runs the full length of the instrument. Like the original, too, the butt-join of the copy is not straight but spirals very slightly over its length (to give greater tensile strength?). Being a copy it is possible to test the flexibility: there is none at all.

Chiurazzi-De Angelis Catalogo 1911, 423, no. 78026 (with photo of museum original, not copy). For the original instrument see Bliquez 1994, 168–9, no. 235.

BMRL File 7070.

3.155. Tube, copy (1920,0717.6) (Fig. 167)
Pompeii.
Modern copy, of Museo Archeologico Nazionale di Napoli Inv. No. 78027, purchased from Chiurazzi-De Angelis, 1920.
Length 103.8mm; external diameter at mouth 7.1mm, at tip 4.5mm; weight 15.2g

The copy is almost as made, but a) the 'Herculanum' patina has flaked away in a small area near the mouth revealing liver-red metal, and b) bright blue-green crystals and powdery corrosion products within the tube mouth and tip and a light dusting of greenish corrosion powder on the exterior surface at the mouth are all presumably post-1920. File-finishing marks are visible over most of the exterior surface and a fine casting seam, partly filed away, is discernible from top to bottom of the tube.

A close copy of the original but not an exact replica:
1) The length, at 103.8mm, is a little greater than the original at 102mm.
2) The diameter is a little engrossed at all points.
3) The curvature at the tip is less acute than the original.
4) A roughly worked incuse girth ring, not present on the original, has been applied near the mouth.
   For the original instrument see Bliquez 1994, 170, no. 241.
   BMRL File 7070.

3.156. Cannula, copy (1920,0717.7) (Fig. 168)
Probably Herculaneum.
Modern copy, of Museo Archeologico Nazionale di Napoli inv. No. 78008, purchased from Chiurazzi-De Angelis, 1920.
Length 139.5mm; width of handle 30.4mm; diameter of disc 27mm; diameter of tube 5.9mm; weight 50.5mm

The copy is just about as made, but a) a tiny flake of the 'Herculanum' patina is missing near the tip of the tube and b) there are pale blue powdery corrosion products on the rod and within the tube, both presumably post-1920.

A rather inaccurate copy of the original:
1) The length (even allowing for the now missing broken T-bar from the handle of the original) is too great, probably by about 10mm.

2) The rod and tube are too thin, while the disc diameter is too great.
3) The seam-like girth expansion midway along the tube of the original is lacking on the copy, as is also the side eye above the tip of the original.
4) It appears that some licence has been used in re-creating a functioning instrument, namely that the 'thick ring' or disc-like expansion at the top of the tube of the original has been interpreted, and reconstructed, as a box-like component with the rebated 'lid' part attached to the T-handled rod. Bliquez (1994, 169) makes no reference to such a possible configuration of the original. The 'box' was machined and pegged and ?soldered onto the tube. The tube was cast – its seam, running top to bottom, is still clearly visible despite file-finishing of the tube. The T-handled rod was made in three pieces – T-bar, rod and rebated lid – the components being soldered together.

Chiurazzi-De Angelis Catalogo 1911, 421, no. 78008 (with photo of museum original, not copy). For the original instrument see Bliquez 1994, 169, no. 236.

BMRL File 7070.

3.157. Uterine clyster, copy (1920,0717.8) (Fig. 169)

Pompeii, probably from Casa del medico nuovo I.
Modern copy, of Museo Archeologico Nazionale di Napoli inv. No. 78235, purchased from Chiurazzi-De Angelis, 1920.
Length 152.7mm; length of tube 118.3mm; diameter of tube 7–7.5mm; height of 'cup' 34.4mm; diameter of 'cup' 31.5–32.5mm; weight 26.9g

The object is virtually as made, but a) several flakes of the 'Herculanum' patina are lacking around the outer surface of the rim of the 'cup' revealing copper-coloured metal, b) there are tiny specks of green corrosion along the seam of the tube, and c) there is a whitish crystalline and powdery

Figure 169 Uterine clyster, Naples Foundry copy. British Museum, Cat. no. 3.157

corrosion product on the inner face of the 'cup', all presumably post-1920.

This is a quite close copy of the original, but:
1) The tube is 4mm too long.
2) The tube is markedly more slender than the original.
3) The 'cup' is not slightly crushed, like the original, and its wall is vertical, unlike that of the original, which is wider at the rim than the base.
4) Unlike the original, the tip of the tube is too pointed and has no end perforation, while the side perforations of the tube are too close together and too close to the tip. The copy was made in three pieces: the tube was cast – the partially file-finished seam is visible; while the base and the wall of the 'cup' were separately made from sheet metal – the lap join of the wall is visible as also is the butt-join of the wall to the base and the pegged join of the base to the tube. All joins are soldered.

Chiurazzi-De Angelis Catalogo 1911, 414, no. 78235 (with photo of museum original, not copy). For the original instrument see Bliquez 1994, 167, no. 231.

BMRL File 7070.

Drawings of sets and selected instruments

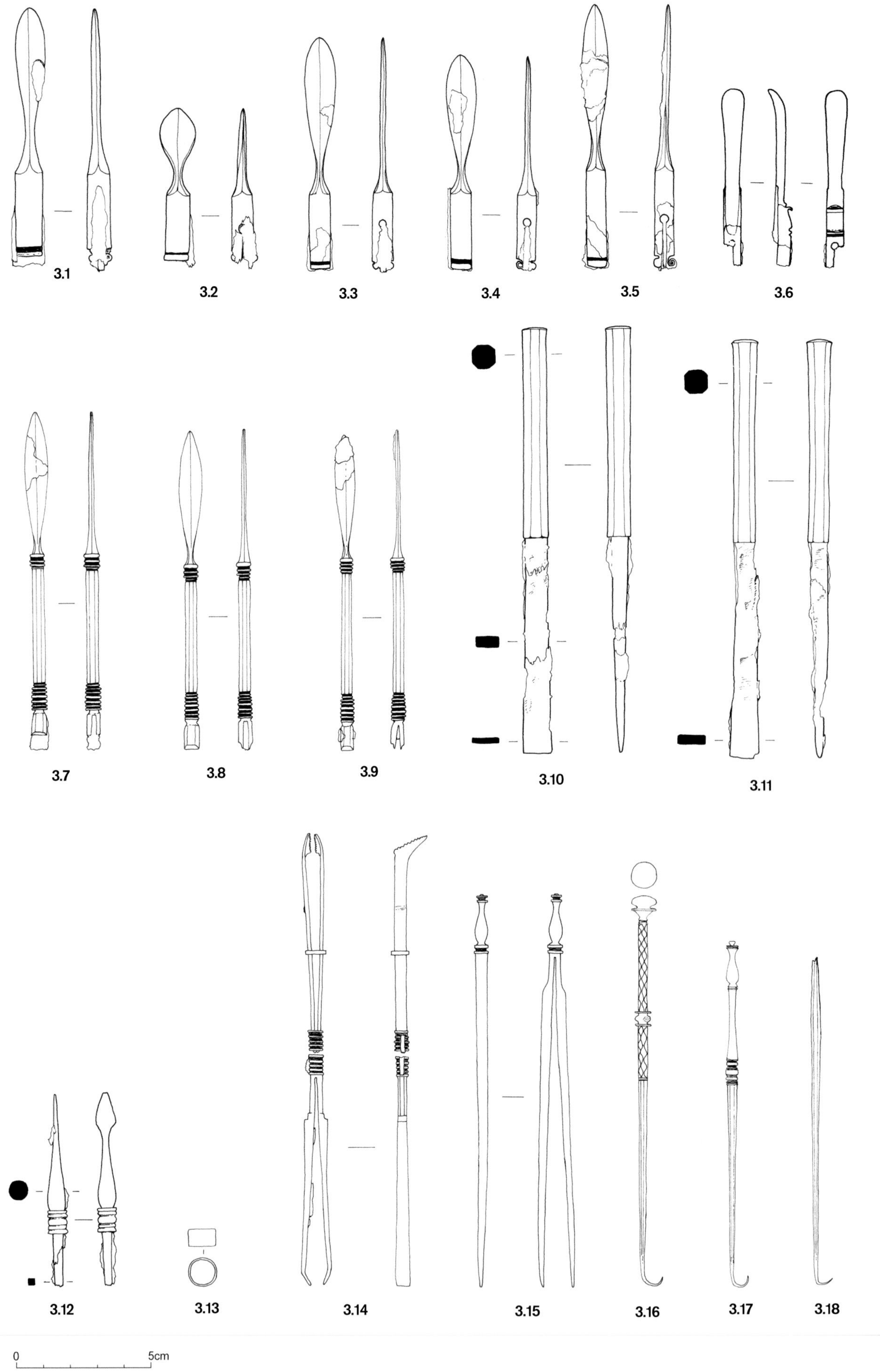

3.1 3.2 3.3 3.4 3.5 3.6

3.7 3.8 3.9 3.10 3.11

3.12 3.13 3.14 3.15 3.16 3.17 3.18

0   5cm

Figure 170 Drawings of cat. nos 3.1, 3.2, 3.3, 3.4, 3.5, 3.6, 3.7, 3.8, 3.9, 3.10, 3.11, 3.12, 3.13, 3.14, 3.15, 3.16, 3.17 and 3.18

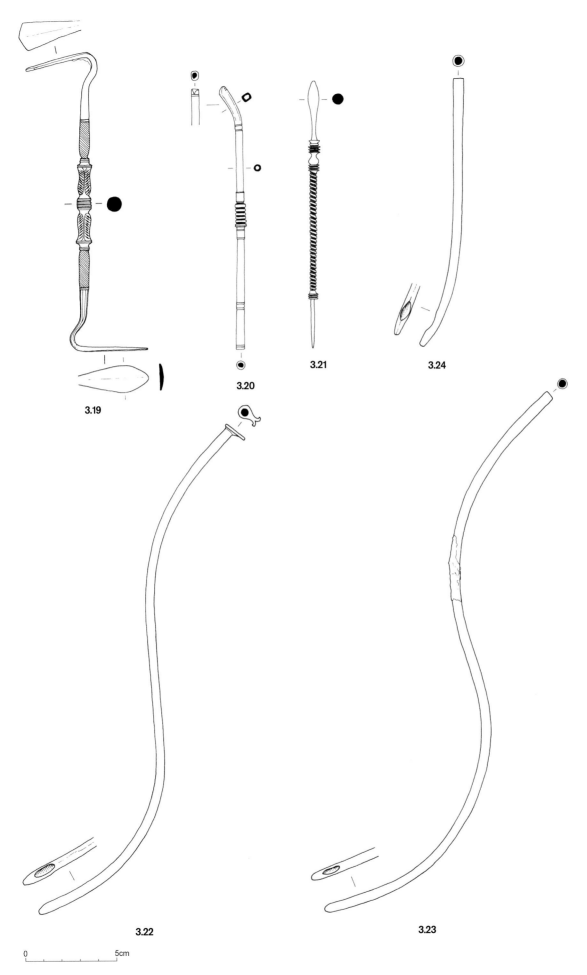

3.19

3.20

3.21

3.24

3.22

3.23

0   5cm

Figure 171 Drawings of cat. nos 3.19, 3.20, 3.21, 3.22, 3.23 and 3.24

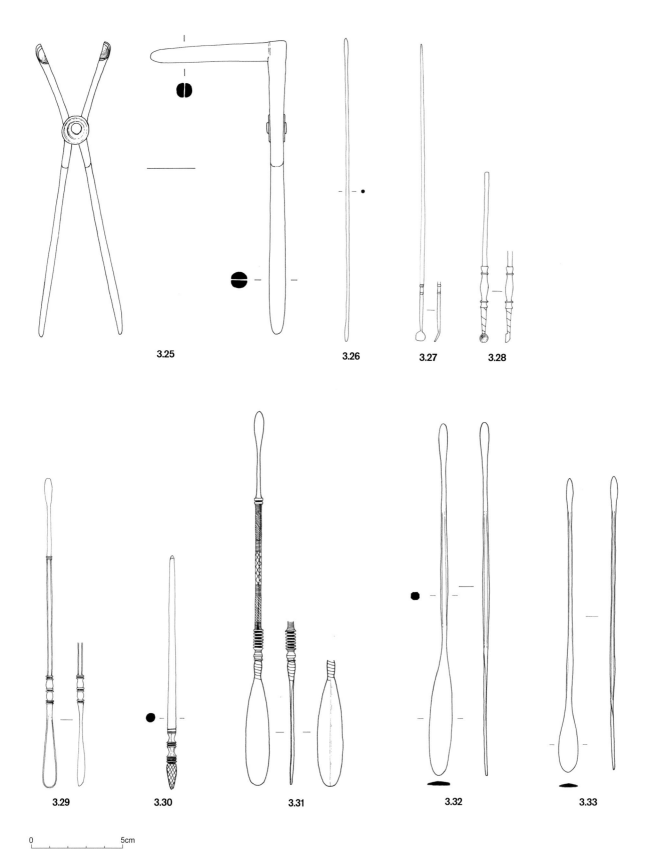

3.25

3.26

3.27

3.28

3.29

3.30

3.31

3.32

3.33

0   5cm

Figure 172 Drawings of cat. nos 3.25, 3.26, 3.27, 3.28, 3.29, 3.30, 3.31, 3.32 and 3.33

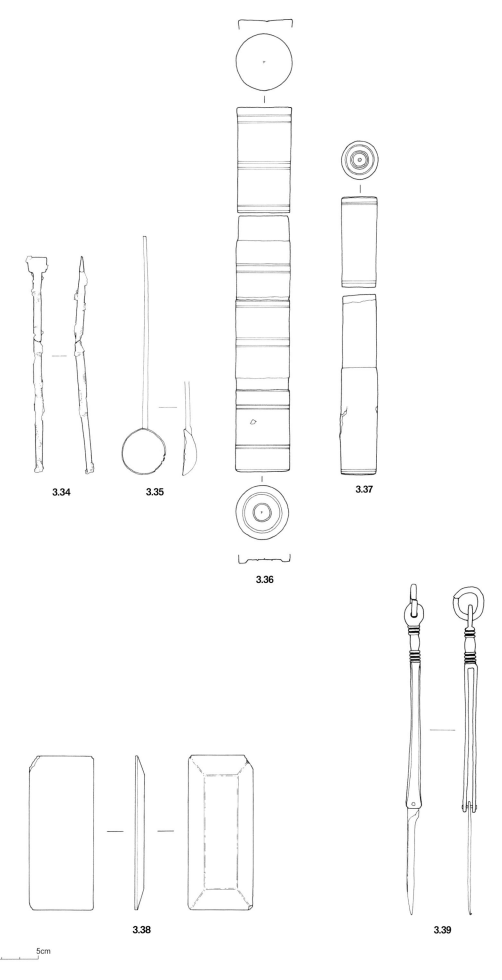

3.34

3.35

3.36

3.37

3.38

3.39

0   5cm

Figure 173 Drawings of cat. nos 3.34, 3.35, 3.36, 3.37, 3.38 and 3.39

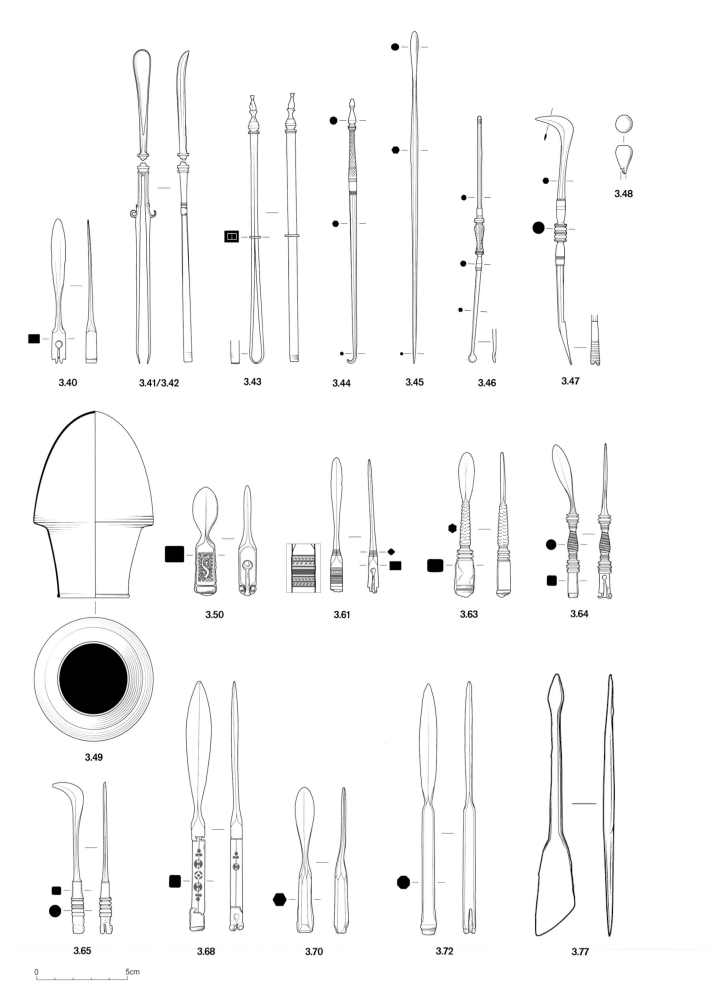

3.40   3.41/3.42   3.43   3.44   3.45   3.46   3.47   3.48

3.50   3.61   3.63   3.64

3.49

3.65   3.68   3.70   3.72   3.77

0   5cm

Figure 174 Drawings of cat. nos 3.40, 3.41, 3.42, 3.43, 3.44, 3.45, 3.46, 3.47, 3.48, 3.49, 3.50, 3.61, 3.63, 3.64, 3.65, 3.68, 3.70, 3.72 and 3.77

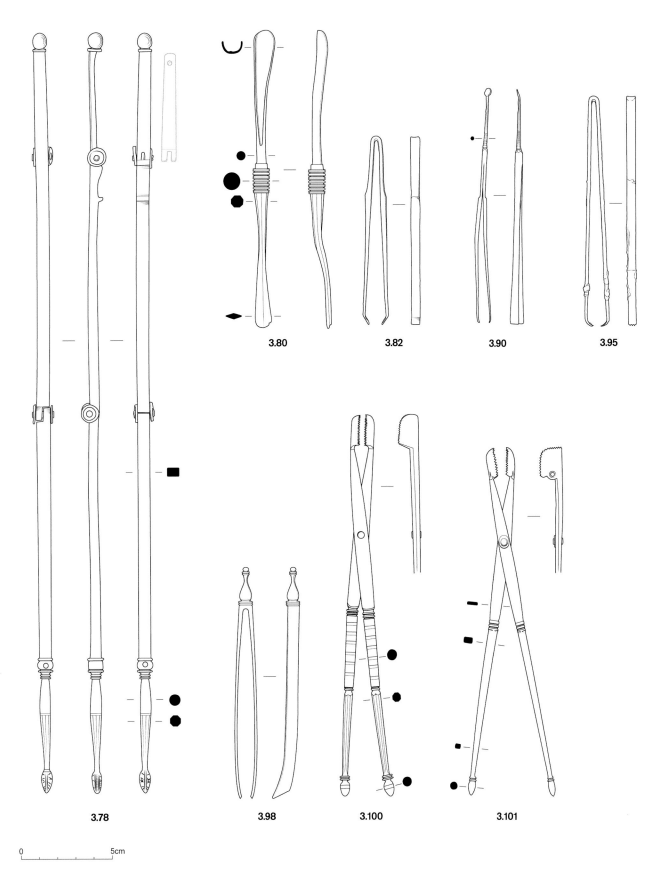

3.80

3.82

3.90

3.95

3.78

3.98

3.100

3.101

0   5cm

Figure 175 Drawings of cat. nos 3.78, 3.80, 3.82, 3.90, 3.95, 3.98, 3.100, 3.101

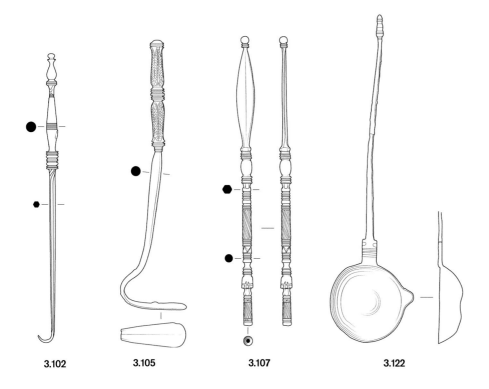

3.102   3.105   3.107   3.122

ΛΥΚΙΟΝΠ ΑΡΑΜΟΥΣΑΙΟΥ

3.129

0   5cm

Figure 176 Drawings of cat. nos 3.102, 3.105, 3.107, 3.122 and 3.129

Chapter 4
Scientific Examination of the Metal Medical Instruments

Susan La Niece and Duncan Hook

Introduction

The aim of this scientific study of medical instruments was to provide data on a broad range of types, building on the 1986 study of a set of 39 Roman medical instruments from Italy in the collection of the British Museum (La Niece 1986). Our results have been integrated into the full description of each instrument as set out in the catalogue section of the volume (Chapter 3), with this chapter drawing together the overall conclusions from the scientific data. The full armoury of a medical practitioner would of course have comprised items of glass, stone and a range of organic materials as well as of metal, but it is the copper-alloy instruments that have survived best and it is these that are reported here, with some comments on lead ointment pots and iron/steel blades and instruments.

There are a considerable number of recognisable and purpose-made medical instruments known from the Greek and Roman world and the types of instruments and the composition of sets owned by individual physicians can provide invaluable insights into the actual practice of medicine in that period (see Chapter 2). It is clear that the instruments are highly specialised and specific to medical use but there are surprisingly few published technical studies of their materials and methods of manufacture. By far the most extensive analytical study is by Riederer (2002) in Künzl's major publication of the collections of Roman medical instruments, mostly found in the eastern Empire and now in the Römisch-Germanisches Zentralmuseum (LEIZA), which provides a valuable data set. Healy (1978) included a general discussion of metals and alloys used in Roman medicine, reporting a metallurgical study of seven copper-alloy instruments from the Wellcome Collection by Dr Rees C. Rawlings of Imperial College, London but no analyses of the alloys were carried out (Healy 1978, 290 n. 172). A few small-scale metallurgical studies have been published, for example Jakielski and Notis (2000) examined an ear scoop and a spatula of unknown provenance, purportedly of Roman date, and Giumlia-Mair and Lucchini (2005) analysed the decorative patina of an instrument from a Roman physician's grave in Cologne. This study of the British Museum collection will provide a substantial addition to the understanding of this class of metalwork.

Methodology of the study

The first stage of the study was to make a detailed examination of the surfaces of the instruments under a stereo microscope, using magnifications from ×6 to ×80, with the aim of recognising decorative features, and assessing the number of components present and how they were made and fitted together. Stereo microscopy was also used to look for evidence of how the instruments were packed during burial, for example traces of a wooden box or textile bag, or evidence of contact with other items or now missing components such as organic handles. Examination in a Hitachi S-3700N Variable Pressure Scanning Electron Microscope (SEM) with a large chamber and Energy Dispersive X-ray analysis (EDX) was carried out on some pieces to allow study at higher magnification, particularly of fine inlays or decorative patination.

To facilitate the understanding of construction of the instruments and to detect any damage or repairs, X-radiographic images were taken of all the instruments. This was carried out using a Siefert DS1 X-ray tube with 0.6 and 1.1mm copper filters. The images were collected at a distance of 1 metre from the tube on Agfa Structurix D4 and D7 films held in rigid cartridges with 0.125mm lead sheets on either side of the film. These films were scanned using an Agfa RadView digitiser with a 50mm pixel size and 12-bit resolution.

Examination of metal microstructures is the ideal method of determining manufacturing methods such as casting, working and annealing but the necessity to limit the impact of the investigation on these generally small and sometimes delicate instruments meant that metallographic examination could only rarely be carried out. Where it was possible, a small area was polished directly on the surface of the instrument while it was held steady in a purpose-built clamp. The area was examined using a Zeiss inverted stage metallographic microscope with magnifications up to ×200, first in the polished state and then etched with an alcoholic ferric chloride solution to reveal the metallographic structure. In most cases, however, the manufacturing methods, as given in the description of the instruments, was deduced from microscopic examination of the surfaces combined with the X-radiographic information.

In most cases, compositional analysis of the instruments was carried out using X-ray fluorescence analysis (XRF) (e.g. Cowell 1977; Cowell 1998). The technique is widely used in museums as it is rapid and non-destructive – it does not harm an object and it can be used without having to prepare an area for analysis or remove a sample. However, it should be noted that XRF measures the composition of only the surface layers of an object, which may have undergone alteration as a result of corrosion or contamination during burial, or from cleaning or conservation processes. The depth of analysis varies depending on the analytical conditions used, but also by element and on the density of the matrix. When XRF is used in this manner any quantitative results obtained are not reliable. Thus here XRF was used to determine the presence/absence of the major and minor elements only, but at least allowing the alloys to be more suitably described rather than just using the term 'copper alloy'.

XRF was also used in this way to identify areas of inlay such as silver and Corinthian bronze, for which the small beam size of the equipment (c. 0.5–1.5mm in diameter) was especially useful. It was also adopted to identify materials used in fabrication, such as the presence of lead-tin solder used to hold scalpel blades in place, and for the identification of some of the inorganic components of the medicine residues analysed for organic components (see Chapter 5).

However, XRF can be used to produce reliable, quantitative results if any unrepresentative surface material is removed prior to analysis – this was the case for most of the instruments in the 'Italy set' (**Table 4** below). Used in this way, XRF can detect most elements likely to be present in ancient copper alloys above levels of c. 0.05–0.2%, with an approximate precision (a measure of reproducibility) of c. ±1–2% relative for copper, and c. 5–20% for tin, zinc and lead, deteriorating as the levels present approach the detection limits.

In a few cases, it was possible to carry out fully quantitative analysis of the major, minor and trace elements using different analytical methods, although this involved the removal of samples (weighing approximately 10mg, taken using a 1mm diameter drill). One instrument (scalpel handle Cat. no. 3.72) was analysed using inductively coupled plasma-atomic emission spectrometry (ICP-AES) (e.g. Hook 1998). A further four instruments from the Bristol Museum and Art Gallery (see Appendix 1) were analysed using atomic absorption spectrophotometry (AAS) following the procedures of Hughes et al. (1976). These two techniques are significantly more sensitive than XRF and also more reliable given that any unrepresentative surface material is discarded prior to analysis. The analyses thus obtained should have a precision (a measure of reproducibility) of c. ±1–2% relative for copper, c. ±5–10% for tin, zinc and lead, and c. 10–30% for the minor and trace elements, deteriorating to ±50% at their respective detection limits (ranging from c. 0.2% for tin to between 0.02–0.002% for the remaining elements).

Mineral analysis of some patinas was carried out on small samples by Debye-Scherrer powder X-ray diffraction analysis (XRD) (Azaroff and Buerger 1958). As well as identifying fake patinas on instruments that had been made or repaired in modern times, this method was useful for confirming, for example, that one instrument (Cat. no. 3.39) purporting to belong to a set was in fact intrusive as it had been buried in a different environment with consequential different corrosion products on its surface.

Manufacture of Roman copper-alloy instruments

The conclusions of the study of manufacturing methods of the following general classes of metal instruments are discussed below based on the examples from the British Museum collection, in the order presented in the catalogue. This chapter should be read in conjunction with the detailed information and illustrations in the catalogue entries in Chapter 3.

Metal cupping vessel

The only example of a metal cupping vessel examined for this project (Cat. no. 3.49) is made of bronze with very low lead levels. The manufacturing method, as determined by optical microscopy and X-radiography, is the same as that for small Roman copper-alloy vessels for domestic use: it was worked from a single disc of virtually lead-free bronze held firmly against a stake while hammering in concentric circles, with cycles of annealing, to raise the sides and shape the seamless cup. The rim was thickened and smoothed to ensure close contact with the skin of the patient. An area on the apex of the vessel differs in colour from that of the general body patina. XRF analysis of this area detected the presence of lead and higher levels of tin than in the body metal, indicating the presence of soft solder. This is interpreted as the attachment point for a now missing suspension ring (see catalogue entry).

Scalpel handles

Copper-alloy scalpel handles make up a very large proportion of the instruments. The typical form is one-piece,

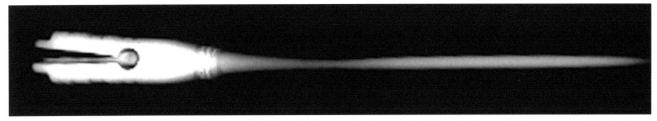

Figure 177 X-radiograph showing the remains of an iron blade inside a key-hole socket (on the left) of a leaded bronze scalpel handle Cat. no. 3.61 (see Fig. 187 for detail of inlay). Length 70.1mm

double-ended with a central grip (see e.g. **Figs 50, 93**). Commonly, at one end is a blunt dissector (see pp. 40–1) and at the other, a slot or socket for the iron/steel scalpel blade (**Fig. 177**). Some instruments other than blunt dissectors are also paired with scalpels, for example Cat. no. 3.6 is paired with a curette. Sets of scalpel handles generally vary in dimensions but are similar in form. A number of the handles are elaborately decorated, some with inlays of other metals (see below pp. 154–5). Others are very simple but almost all are single piece castings with working after casting. The most visible evidence of finishing is filing, particularly to create or sharpen decorative details.

In most cases the blade socket and the blunt dissector are at the same orientation, allowing the instruments to lie flat in a box or on a table; indeed Cat. nos 3.1–6 from the so-called Italy set have fragments of wood embedded in their corrosion, interpreted as evidence they were buried together in a wooden case (see discussion of sets, pp. 156–8 below, and Jackson 1986, 135 n. 33). Cat. no. 3.40, a delicate bronze example, is an exception to the rule that the blade socket and dissector were at the same orientation: its blade is set in at 90° to the usual position. X-radiography showed no evidence of post-manufacture alteration so this would seem to be a deliberate feature. Cat. no. 3.70, a leaded bronze, has a slightly offset blunt dissector and the smoothness of the patina at the bend in the neck suggests it was not damaged post-burial, so this was likely an intentional variation to allow its use as a bone elevator. Cat. no. 3.64, a finely made and decorated scalpel handle from Asia Minor, has a small dissector turned slightly to one side, which could be a later adaptation but probably was a feature of manufacture. The slender scalpel handle Cat. no. 3.73, on the other hand, is cracked and bent at the narrow neck with the blunt dissector. This area is deeply pitted with corrosion and the concentration of the corrosion attack at this point suggests that the deformation may well have occurred during use.

Iron corrosion products are often visible in and around the sockets of the scalpel handles and occasionally remains of the blade survive (see **Fig. 177**). Analyses of residues in the sockets by XRF and XRD were able to detect corrosion

products of tin or lead or a combination of both, indicating the use of a low melting temperature soft solder to secure the scalpel blades in place. Soft solder would allow the iron blades to be changed when worn or damaged but this task could not be done rapidly, hence the need for several scalpels, perhaps with different blade types, to be readily to hand during a procedure, and this is confirmed by the relatively large number of scalpel handles found together in instrument sets (Jackson 1986, 133). There is insufficient metal remaining in the sockets to determine either the quality of the ferrous blade or the original shape, though in the scalpel handle seen in the X-radiograph of Cat. no. 3.61 (see **Fig. 177**) may be the remains of the type of blade with a thickened tang, providing stability within the keyhole socket (Jackson 2014a, 135). There is evidence from surviving examples, depictions on tombstones and in Classical medical literature that a variety of blade shapes were used (Jackson 2014a, 137–42 and 144). Galen, a Greek physician practising in the Roman Empire, regarded the iron ores in the Alpine province of Noricum as best for scalpel blades (Galen, *Anatomical Procedures* 8.6 (2.682K); see pp. 15, 47).

A common feature of Roman scalpel handles is that the metal on both sides of the socket opening is rolled outwards, giving more flexible support to the blade during use than a simple groove or slot cut into the handle. Metallographic examination of a taper section polished directly across the side of the rolled terminal of a typical bronze scalpel handle with keyhole socket (Cat. no. 3.56, unknown provenance; **Fig. 178**) confirmed that its rolled terminals had been heavily worked and annealed, evident from the recrystallization of the metal and presence of annealing twins (**Fig. 179**), and that further down the side of the socket the bronze had been worked to a lesser extent, evident from the larger grain size.

Lost-wax casting would have been the most practical method for making ornate handles for scalpels and other instruments. A case in point is Cat. no. 3.146, a mouse-shaped handle (not for a scalpel) that is cast in leaded bronze. Ornaments to scalpel handle grips, for example multiple ring-and-disc mouldings, would have been more easily cut

Figure 178 Cat. no. 3.56 bronze scalpel handle (length 70mm), polished area on rolled terminal, upper left. Note the iron corrosion around the keyhole socket from the corroded iron blade tang

Figure 179 Detail of Cat. no. 3.56 (Fig. 178).
Polished and etched tip of the rolled
terminal showing the corroded outer
surface and the recrystallized bronze with
annealing twins, indicative of heavy
working and annealing in its formation.
Field of view 1.5mm

into a wax model than into metal, though additional work to sharpen the details is likely to have taken place. Evidence for lost-wax casting of at least some cast medical instruments comes from the writings of Galen (AD 129–216), which recorded that he had personally designed and made wax models for specialised medical tools to be cast for him (Tucci 2008, 141).

Another possible method could have been to cast in two-part clay moulds which had been impressed with a model made in a durable material like wood or metal. This method allows several instruments to be cast simultaneously in the same mould assemblage to facilitate rapid production from one crucible of metal. Archaeological evidence for moulds for scalpel handles or other medical instruments is lacking. Large numbers of fragments of clay moulds for casting multiple copper-alloy spoons together in one mould have been excavated from Roman Castleford, Yorkshire (Bayley and Budd 1998) and scalpel handles are not so dissimilar in size and form. If, like the Castleford spoons, a set of instruments had been cast together in one mould, they would be of identical composition and evidence for this seems to be rare. An example of virtually identical alloy composition is the pair of handles for bone chisels Cat. nos 3.10–11 (see below).

Whatever the casting method, extensive finishing of the as-cast surface would have been necessary, and many of the handles show evidence of this. Furthermore, not all scalpel handles seem to have been cast to a final form, but instead were shaped from a rod. This may be the case for scalpel handles Cat. nos 3.7–9 which, like many other sets, are graded in increasing size of dissector and thickness of grip, and are stylistically and analytically similar to each other, made of brass containing tin and a little lead (c. 12% zinc, 2.5% tin and 1% lead). The longitudinal striations along the eight-sided grips are evidence of scraping to sharpen the faceting. These three scalpel handles, together with the double forceps Cat. no. 3.14, constitute a group which visually appear to have been manufactured together, within the larger set of instruments known as the Italy set (Jackson 1986).

Figure 180 Detail of the scalpel socket of Cat. no. 3.65 in Figure 181
showing the remains of the iron pin (left) which secured the blade.
Note the fine detail of the mouldings seen in the X radiograph is
obscured by iron corrosion

Figure 181 X-radiograph of scalpel handle Cat. no. 3.65 with hooked dissector. Note the sharpness of the mouldings and the hole in the
scalpel socket for the iron pin securing the blade. Length 80.6mm

One unusual scalpel handle (Cat. no. 3.65) has an iron pin or rivet fixing for the blade (**Figs 180–1**). No evidence was found amongst all the scalpel handles examined to support the now discounted suggestion that a wire was threaded through the rolled terminals to fix the blades in place (Jackson 1986, 133). The majority of those examined for this study still retain traces of soft solder, which would have held the ferrous blade in position. Some of the sockets for the blades are simple slots (e.g. Cat. no. 3.67), but the majority are shaped like an inverted keyhole (see **Fig. 177**). Interestingly the keyhole type of socket seems to be an adaptation exclusive to medical instruments, especially scalpels. The advantages of the keyhole form would be to provide a generous space into which to apply the soft solder to ensure the blade was held securely, and to make it easier to melt out the solder when a replacement insert was needed. If blades with thickened tangs were used, it would provide greater stability.

Bone chisels

The two bone chisels (Cat. nos 3.10–11) from the set of instruments from Italy are bi-metallic in construction, with iron chisel blades set into octagonal-sectioned copper-alloy handles. These two handles are of virtually identical metal composition, with 9% zinc, 1% lead and 11% and 12% tin respectively, thus they would appear to have been made as a pair. X-radiography indicates that the iron chisel is embedded in the handle to a depth of *c.* 1.5cm and no soft solder was detected visually or analytically so it is suggested that the copper-alloy handle was cast onto the iron chisel. This would provide a strong bond, better able to withstand the impact of a mallet during bone surgery: as evidenced by the splayed metal at the top of the handle, the force used was considerable.

Surgical drills

Surgical drills are multi-component tools utilising different materials including copper alloy, iron, wood and cord, though the organic materials are rarely preserved. Cat. no. 3.78 is a folding drill-handle constructed of hinged rectangular bars of brass (see p. 108). The two (unrelated) probable drill-bits Cat. nos 3.12 and 3.79 are tanged iron points, the former having traces of wood and an associated brass collar. The drill-handle has undergone some restoration (see Cat. no. 3.78), so evidence of its original form is now lost. The main folding sections are slightly twisted, which suggests some change in alignment has occurred in what was probably a precision tool used for cranial trepanation, and could support the suggestion that it once had the curving profile of other known folding drill-handles operating as bow-drills. The instrument is certainly not in its original condition: XRF has shown that the components believed to be original are medium zinc brasses, whereas the replacement components are modern high zinc brass and much of the patina is artificial.

Levers

Bone lever/curette (Cat. no. 3.80) is a rare example of a well-preserved iron instrument, the result of deposition in waterlogged ground in the City of London. The double-ended instrument, 159mm long, was wrought from a single bar of iron with a sharp-rimmed scoop beaten out at one end and a lever at the other.

Forceps

Forceps, like scalpels, were a standard piece of equipment in a Roman doctor's kit. The class of instrument defined as forceps comprises several different forms designed for specific tasks (see pp. 57–63). There were two main methods of manufacture of the arms of the forceps in this study. The first was to cast or forge a single bar and saw down the centre, most of the way down its length, to create the two arms, for example Cat. nos 3.15, 3.84–7, 3.96–99. The second was to cut a strip of copper-alloy, fold it in half and bend it inwards at the tips, for example Cat. nos 3.81–3, 3.88, 3.89, 3.94 and 3.95. A few of the more slender forceps show evidence that the arms were at least partly worked to shape rather than cut to separate the arms, for example Cat. nos 3.90–1, both of which are from Britain and are double-ended instruments.

The jaws of some forceps are smooth, for example Cat. nos 3.87–8. Others have cut/filed grooves on the inner surfaces of the jaws to aid grip, for example Cat. no. 3.95. The toothed fixation forceps Cat. no. 3.94 have interlocking teeth cut with precision into the opposing folded-strip arms. Cat. no. 3.14 is an unusual double-ended forceps, comprising smooth-jawed forceps at one end and toothed forceps at the other, joined by a small iron bar and soft solder. The alloy composition and decorative details link this double forceps to three scalpel handles (Cat. nos 3.7–9; **Table 4**).

In some cases a copper-alloy sliding ring which served to hold the forceps in the closed position is still preserved (Cat. nos 3.14, 3.43 and 3.99).

Forceps Cat. no. 3.88 is made from a single rectangular-sectioned strip of bronze, folded in half to form the two arms. Just below the top it is pinched together forming a tubular cavity that is now filled with soil and iron corrosion, perhaps indicating there was once an iron suspension ring. Forceps Cat. no. 3.89 has the same type of tubular cavity. In this case no iron was detected; perhaps it was lost or removed, or possibly a cord of organic material was threaded through the tube.

Hooks

Sharp and blunt hooks were both made from a single rod of metal. The sharp hooks are delicate instruments with a thin hook worked at the end of a bronze or brass rod which, like a number of other instruments, is finely decorated. Sharp hooks often have a decorative finial and a grip cut into the metal rod (Cat. nos 3.16–18). Cat. no. 3.102 has five narrow bands of alternating Corinthian bronze and silver inlay around the bronze grip (see below for discussion of inlays).

The blunt hooks, on the other hand, are more heavy duty instruments, though Cat. no. 3.105 is now broken at what may have been a weak point created by cutting the decoration into the gunmetal rod. Cat. no. 3.19 is complete and is a *c.* 9% tin bronze double-ended instrument with the blunt hook terminals worked flat and bent back in opposing directions at each end of an ornately decorated rod. This highly textured decoration may have been partly cast but exhibits extensive post-casting work.

Figure 182 X-radiograph of brass socketed needle-holder with multiple decorative mouldings Cat. no. 3.107. The socket, which retains traces of soft solder, is on the right of the image. The leaf-shaped finial (left) appears darker in the image because it is thinner than the central grip. Length 154mm

Socketed needle holders

Cat. no. 3.20, from the Italy set, is double-ended with a hollow tube or socket added at both ends of a decorated rod. No needles are now preserved in its tubular sockets, which, like the catheters from the same set (see below) were made of sheet bronze with a single, butted seam running lengthwise. There appears to be no overlap and the join is very precise. The central decorated grip appears from the X-radiograph to be solid. It is not known how a needle would have been secured in this example, but in the case of Cat. no. 3.106, where iron corrosion products are present on the outer rim and interior of the damaged socket, presumably from the needle, traces of tin-lead solder remain inside the socket. This socket was cast in one with the grip and was at least 7mm deep, thus providing a good holder for the needle. Cat. no. 3.107 was also made from a single rod, with its leaf-shaped finial worked and filed. The socket was *c.* 10mm deep, with tin-lead soft solder residues detected (**Fig. 182**).

Cataract needle

Cat. no. 3.21, a handled needle from the Italy set, is very finely made. It appears to have been manufactured from a single, circular-sectioned rod, and the working end has a rounded tip. The instrument (analysed semi-quantitatively) is made of a copper alloy with zinc in the range 10–15% and between 2% and 5% of lead and tin. The decoration is very crisp, probably cut rather than cast, and there is no evidence that the spiral grooves ever held any inlay.

Catheters

The three catheters (Cat. nos 3.22–4) in the Italy set (Jackson 1986) are finely made tubes of sheet bronze of very regular thickness with 9–15% tin and little or no lead and zinc. They have a single, butted seam with no overlap of the edges, running lengthwise, twisted slightly off-centre (**Fig. 183**). No evidence for solder at the join was detected: they were clearly fabricated to the highest standard, to present the smoothest possible surface. Tin-lead solder was found around the open necks of Cat. nos 3.23–4, probably for attaching a collar like that preserved on Cat. no. 3.22 to enable manipulation of the catheter.

Draw-plates are not generally thought to have existed in the Roman period for the manufacture of fine wire, but a similar tool, with large aperture, could have been used to make tubes for catheters with the aid of a removable mandrel to retain the diameter of the internal cavity (Untracht 1975, 45). The workmanship of these examples is indicative of the high level of skill of the maker and, no doubt, the ability of the doctor who bought them to pay a high price.

Dilator

The bivalve dilator (Cat. no. 3.25) is sturdy and well engineered. The instrument operates by pivoting on a hinge rather than with a scissor action. Each arm, with its smooth tip of solid semi-circular section projecting at right angles, was cast in bronze (with 11.7% tin, 0.8% lead and no detectable zinc) and is joined to the other arm by a rivet with a washer on each side (the washer and rivet are of almost identical alloy composition to the arms so undoubtedly are original).

Probe, scoops and spoons

Slender instruments such as probes, scoops, spoons, dipyrene and ligulae were worked from a single rod of metal, for example Cat. no. 3.110, a gunmetal ear probe terminating in a tiny angled spoon. X-radiography revealed internal folding at several points along its length, consistent with extensive working to shape before the mouldings were filed (**Fig. 184**). X-radiography of a brass pouring spoon (Cat. no. 3.123) also reveals longitudinal internal creasing in the metal of its long handle, confirming it was extensively hammered to shape it. Its decorative details were probably filed. The bowl of spoon Cat. no. 3.35 was tinned, presumably to protect the bronze from corrosive materials. The tin plating continues a little way up the stem, likely an unintentional result of the tinning process.

Containers

Four narrow tubular boxes with lids (Cat. nos 3.37, 3.126–8) were examined optically and by X-radiography. Neither the boxes nor their lids had soldered or mechanical joins and the metal exhibited the impressions of repeated hammering. The lid is of similar form to the lower part of the container but slightly wider to enable it to be pushed down tightly outside the lip of the box. These tubular boxes and their lids were made from discs of metal worked by hammering around a stake to raise the sides, forming seamless containers. This is the metalsmithing technique used to make cupping vessel Cat. no. 3.49 and is the same as that employed more generally to make small metal cups for non-medical use.

Cat. no. 3.36 is somewhat larger than the tubular boxes discussed above and has more components, all of which were initially corroded together (see **Figs 100, 173**). It was only when an X-radiograph was taken that it became clear that it was in fact made up of four separate containers which fit tightly together. As is the case for the tubular boxes discussed above, each was made from a single disc of metal worked by hammering around a stake to raise the sides and form seamless containers, three of which still contain residues. These residues have been the subject of intensive analyses which has led to the conclusion that there was a different ointment in each compartment (see Chapter 5). The X-radiograph showed the hammer impressions left by the shaping and that each individual container was made without any mechanical or soldered joins. Three of the

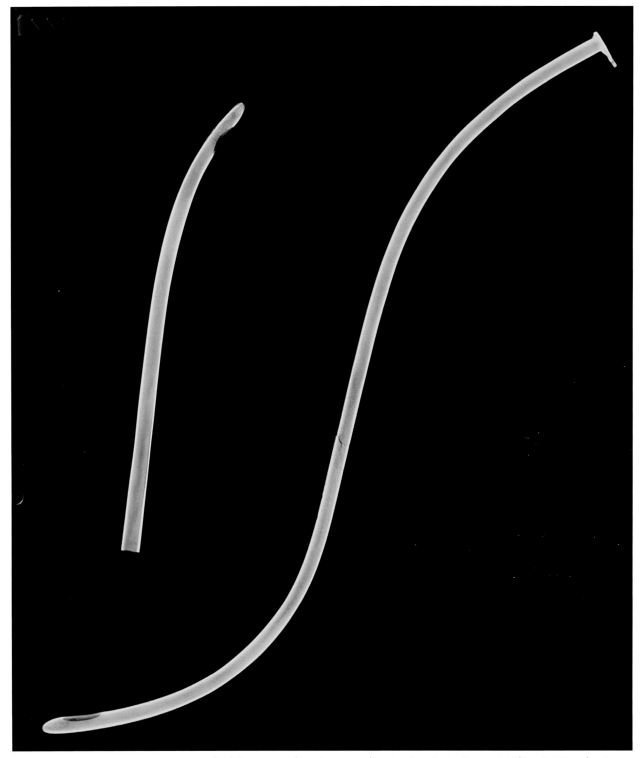

Figure 183 X-radiograph of female catheter (left) Cat. no. 3.24 (length 143.8mm) and male catheter Cat. no. 3.22 (length 280mm) with separately made collar (top right). Note the regularity of the metal tubes, made from sheet bronze with a single butted seam running lengthwise

containers are of bronze with *c.* 7.5% tin but the fourth is brass with *c.* 15% zinc and only a trace of tin detectable. This component would have looked very much more golden than the other containers and is suggested to be a later addition. XRF indicates that the lead content of the alloys of every box is only at trace levels, a deliberate choice by the maker for a copper alloy which was to be extensively hammered.

All the tubular boxes examined are without seams, which requires much more skill than constructing a cylinder from a roll of sheet metal joined down the side and sealed at one end with a soldered disc, particularly as these boxes needed to fit tightly together. It suggests that there was a practical requirement for this extra work; perhaps it was a deliberate ploy to avoid the possibility that the lead-tin solder might contaminate the medicines or ointments, and/or that the contents might actively corrode the solder, weakening the container.

Cat. no. 3.124 is a rectangular box made of a combination of cast components and sheet metal. All the cast components have higher lead contents in the bronze

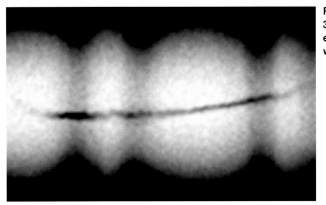

Figure 184 (a, above) X-radiograph of gunmetal earprobe Cat. no. 3.110, formed by extensive working (length 147.4mm) and (b, left) enlarged detail showing a crease in the metal (dark line) created by working the rod

than the sheet metal components (some lead improves the casting properties of copper alloys but its presence is deleterious during working). The sheet metal lids of the compartments are hinged by means of a strip of sheet metal threaded through a slit in the lid. Their handles are of bent wire loops fixed with wire staples. The lids and their handles all have similar compositions. The decoration on the lids and the base of the box is engraved. The walls of the compartments and the bottom of the box are soldered in place with lead-tin soft solder. The catch for the sliding lid is operated by rotating a knob in the end wall of the box, which pushes a metal catch up into a hole in the underside of the thick metal edge of the lid. The hole next to the knob may be part of a locking mechanism.

Ointment pots

Ointment pots (Cat. nos 3.129–30) are made of lead and exhibit a casting flash running under the base and up both sides on the exterior surface only. These features indicate that they were cast in two-part moulds with a core. These pots are very small, 27.5mm and 23.7mm high respectively, and no attempt has been made to remove the casting flash from the exterior surface. Cat. no. 3.130 has the letters AJ in relief on its side, and Cat. no. 3.129 has relief Greek lettering around its girth, abutting the casting flash and continuing into the other half. The lettering is likely to have been

impressed into the inner surface of both of the mould parts, suggesting an element of mass production with a reusable model.

Saw blade

Cat. no. 3.147 is a tiny saw blade of unknown provenance and its use in a medical context is unproven. The length of the toothed edge is only 100mm but 66 teeth have been cut into the sheet of leaded bronze. X-radiography revealed three tiny round pins or rivets set into diamond-shaped holes, indicating where a handle, likely of organic material, was once fixed to the blade (**Fig. 185**).

Inlaid decoration

Metal inlay, especially silver, is not uncommon on medical instruments and drug boxes, especially from the 2nd and 3rd centuries (Jackson 2014a, 135–7; Künzl 1983a, 106–7). No niello, gold or enamel was found surviving on any of the items examined for this study, though this may be a result of the poor condition of some of the surfaces. The inlays identified on the British Museum instruments are silver, copper and the black patinated copper alloy known as Corinthian bronze (see below) (Craddock and Giumlia-Mair 1993), applied in sheet form and/or as wire. The spiral silver wire decorating scalpel handle Cat. no. 3.62 was hammered into a groove (**Fig. 186**). An extremely delicate example is

Figure 185 Enlarged X-radiograph of tiny leaded bronze saw blade Cat. no. 3.147 (length 100mm). Corrosion pitting appears mid-grey in the image. Note the three diamond-shaped holes, top left (dark outline in image) each filled with a round pin (white)

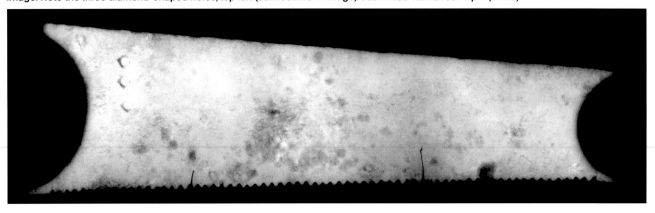

Figure 186 X-radiograph (inverted image) of leaded bronze scalpel handle Cat. no. 3.62 inlaid with silver wire (dark spiral). The metal of the handle is cracked. Length 64.6mm

Figure 187 Backscatter electron image taken in a scanning electron microscope of leaded bronze scalpel handle Cat. no. 3.61 (see Fig. 177 for X-radiograph). Detail of some of the very fine inlay bands. The darkest areas in the image are recesses filled with iron and copper corrosion products. The bands from left to right in this image: (1) bronze body of handle; (2) copper strip; (3) anticlockwise twisted silver strip (white); (4) copper strip; (5) clockwise twisted silver strip; (6) plain silver strip. After the broad inlaid copper strip (7) the same sequence is repeated in the reverse order. Each inlaid strip is only c. 0.5mm wide. White scale bar = 2mm

the leaded bronze scalpel handle Cat. no. 3.61, with narrow strips of copper and silver inlay only c. 0.3–0.4mm in width (**Fig. 187**). The decoration is so fine it is difficult to see with the naked eye.

Corinthian bronze is recognisable analytically by the minor amounts of gold, silver and arsenic in a copper matrix, and visually by its even matt black patina. Corinthian bronze inlays were found to be present on six instruments, three of them from Set 2 (Cat. nos 3.44, 3.46–7), the rest apparently unrelated to each other: a scalpel handle (Cat. no. 3.64), uvula forceps (Cat. no. 3.100; **Fig. 188**) and a sharp hook (Cat. no. 3.102). A rectangular-sectioned block of Corinthian bronze alloy inlaid with silver now forms part of Cat. no. 3.68, a pastiche acquired from the Castellani collection. The use of Corinthian bronze together with silver and copper inlays is found on luxury items such as fine furniture fittings (e.g. BM GR 1784,0131.3 and 4) and ink pots (e.g. 1853,0218.6).

The extent of decoration of medical instruments might seem surprising, and not in keeping with modern surgical hygiene, but a medical practitioner with fine instruments would perhaps inspire greater confidence in his patients than one with a basic set of knives.

Compositions of the copper-alloy instruments

The requirement to minimise the impact of analysis on these mostly small and often delicate instruments necessitated the use of non-invasive analysis, largely carried

out using X-ray fluorescence (XRF) without the removal of any unrepresentative patina or corroded surface metal. The qualitative results obtained and visual assessments of each individual XRF spectrum were used to produce descriptive alloy types, which have been reported in the catalogue entries. Only for the Italy set (Cat. nos 3.1–37) was there the opportunity to remove any surface material to leave a flat area of clean metal suitable for quantitative analysis using XRF. The alloy concentrations and alloy types of the majority of the Italy set are reported in **Table 4**. The results of quantitative analysis on drilled samples by ICP-AES on scalpel handle Cat. no. 3.72 are reported in the catalogue entry, and those by atomic absorption spectrophotometry (AAS) on four instruments from the Bristol Museum and Art Gallery are reported in Appendix 1.

Assigning a meaningful descriptive alloy term based on composition for ancient copper alloys is, perhaps surprisingly, not straightforward, and a definitive 'system' has not been widely accepted, Discussions about the lack of consistency of nomenclature goes back at least to Rickard (1932). Some authors have given definitions of common copper alloy types (e.g. Bayley 1991) with others using slightly different definitions where opinions differed or to suit a particular data set (e.g. Hook 1988). Perhaps it is best not to be too prescriptive here, especially for those analyses which were carried out using surface XRF. The body metal of the instruments have been assigned one of the following descriptive alloy types: bronze (here defined as copper with

Figure 188 Detail of the arms of uvula forceps Cat. no. 3.100. Six bands of the black patinated alloy known as Corinthian bronze are inlaid into the polished gunmetal, now corroded green but would originally have had a soft yellow colour, contrasting with the black inlay

more than *c.* 5% tin with little or no zinc); brass (copper with more than *c.* 5% zinc with little or no tin); and gunmetal (a modern term for an alloy of copper with significant amounts of both tin and zinc, here defined as containing more than 2% of both tin and zinc, and with tin (Sn) and zinc (Zn) being at relatively similar levels. It would seem likely that gunmetal first became widespread as a result of the mixing and recycling of bronze and brass, although its useful properties and the golden colour of gunmetal have led to its use continuing to the present day. Most of the instruments contain at least some lead, either as a trace impurity in the original copper (perhaps 1% or less), or in larger quantities, from mixing with lead-containing scrap or as a deliberate addition to the alloy. The prefix 'leaded' has been added to all these alloys when more than of *c.* 5% lead was detected.

The range of compositions of the surgical instruments analysed here compares well with many of those of instruments undertaken by Riederer (2002) and with Roman copper alloys more generally (e.g. Craddock 1978; Craddock 1985; Bayley and Butcher 1981).

Bronze, brass and gunmetal are all suited to casting, or being worked to shape. Unsurprisingly the cast instruments and cast components of instruments analysed for this study were generally found to have higher lead contents than those which had been heavily worked: lead can facilitate casting (adding even a small amount makes the molten metal more fluid) but it is detrimental to metal shaping by hammering.

Brass is the alloy most golden in colour and can be worked to very thin sheets if no lead is added. Bronze and gunmetal were widely used in the Roman world for small robust implements, but interestingly, from our study there does not appear to be a correlation between instrument type/degree of robustness required and alloy type, which is in agreement with the findings of Riederer (2002) in his analysis of the instruments in the Römisch-Germanisches Zentralmuseum (LEIZA). He argues that the colour of the alloys was more important to the purchaser than the properties of the metal, with zinc-rich brass, i.e. a golden appearance, being more prestigious than the browner-coloured bronze (Riederer 2002, 73 and 78).

Instrument 'sets'

In this volume 'set' is used to indicate a group of instruments which appear to have been selected and used by an individual medical practitioner in his or her day-to-day practice. The understanding of what might constitute a set has been developed from study of groups of instruments from well-recorded find-spots, for example from excavation of graves and of contexts sealed by disasters such as the eruption of Vesuvius in AD 79 (see pp. 15ff). Many of the extant collections of instruments, however, do not have either a general or even any find context. An example of this lack of a specific provenance is Set 1, the so-called Italy set (Cat. no. 3.1–38; Jackson 1986). It encompasses a selection of instruments which could be considered a useful tool kit, with no obvious duplication, and the overall appearance was of consistent, high-quality workmanship. It was hoped that scientific examination could establish the extent to which copper-alloy instruments in this collection might truly be considered a set. The results of the scientific examination are as follows.

The patinas of most of the instruments in the Italy set are similar in colour. X-ray diffraction analysis (XRD) (Azaroff and Buerger, 1958) identified the main corrosion product as basic copper carbonate ($Cu_2CO_3(OH)_2$). The only exceptions were the clasp-knife Cat. no. 3.39 and spatula probe Cat. no. 3.31. In the case of the clasp-knife, this confirmed an earlier suspicion, based on the poorer quality of workmanship and the colour of the patina, that it was not part of this group when it was buried. The second exception, spatula probe Cat. no. 3.31, has a smooth, dark patina which stands out from the rest of the instruments and analysis of the corrosion product on both these instruments by XRD identified it as a basic copper chloride ($Cu_2Cl(OH)_3$), not a carbonate, indicating different burial conditions to the other instruments.

Another feature of many, but not all, of the objects in the Italy set is visible staining with iron corrosion, probably from now lost iron components such as blades, and a calcareous deposit, identified by XRD as a mixture of calcite ($CaCO_3$) and dolomite ($CaMg(CO_3)_2$), suggesting burial in a region of limestone, rich in magnesium. This burial environment would be consistent with the formation of a carbonate patina. That they have the same patina is good supporting evidence that they belong together, but does not prove they are a set: basic copper carbonate ($Cu_2CO_3(OH)_2$) is commonly found on copper-alloy objects from many geographical areas.

Cat. no.	Description	Copper wt %	Tin wt %	Zinc wt %	Lead wt %	Other	Alloy
3.1	Scalpel handle	83.7	14.8	<0.2	1.5		Bronze
3.2	Scalpel handle	81.9	13.3	2.1	2.9		Bronze
3.3	Scalpel handle	85.3	3.8	9.2	1.7		Gunmetal
3.4	Scalpel handle	90.2	7.9	<0.2	1.9		Bronze
3.5	Scalpel handle	82.5	10.4	<0.2	7.1		Leaded bronze
3.6	Scalpel?/sharp spoon	84.0	10.9	1.4	3.7		Bronze
3.7	Scalpel handle	83.2	2.9	12.7	1.1		Brass
3.8	Scalpel handle	85.1	2.2	12	0.8		Brass
3.9	Scalpel handle	85.9	2.3	11	0.7		Brass
3.10	Bone chisel (handle)	78.6	10.9	9.2	1.3		Gunmetal
3.11	Bone chisel (handle)	77.7	11.9	9.3	1.1		Gunmetal
3.13	Collar	82.0	0.2	17	0.4		Brass
3.14	Double-ended forceps (smooth-jawed)	85.1	2	12.3	0.6		Brass
3.14	Double-ended forceps (toothed)	86.0	2.2	11	0.9		Brass
3.15	Pointed-jawed forceps	79.5	10	<0.2	10		Leaded bronze
3.16	Sharp hook	85.9	9.7	1.5	3		Bronze
3.17	*Sharp hook*	XX	8-13	nd	tr.		Bronze
3.18	Sharp hook	86.5	1.5	11.4	0.6		Brass
3.19	Double-ended blunt hook	89.5	9.4	<0.2	1		Bronze
3.20	Socketed needle-holder	87.6	11.5	<0.2	1		Bronze
3.21	*Cataract needle*	XX	2-5	10-15	2-5		Gunmetal
3.22	Catheter, male	90.6	9.1	0.2	0.4		Bronze
3.23	Catheter, male	87.6	12.1	<0.2	0.2		Bronze
3.24	Catheter, female	84.2	14.8	<0.2	1.1		Bronze
3.25	Bivalve dilator	87.5	11.7	<0.2	0.8		Bronze
3.26	*Dipyrene*	XX	5-10	1-5	tr.		Gunmetal
3.27	*Ligula*	XX	X	nd	tr.		Bronze
3.28	*Ear probe*	XX	nd	X	tr.	tr. As	Brass
3.29	Scoop probe	91.1	6.4	<0.2	2.4		Bronze
3.30	*(Scoop) probe*	XX	2-5	15-20	tr.		Brass
3.32	Spatula probe	87.3	9	1.1	2.5		Bronze
3.33	Spatula probe	86.6	11.3	<0.2	2.1		Bronze
3.35	*Spoon*	XX	X	nd	tr.	Tinning	Bronze
	Stacking cylindrical boxes:						
3.36	Components I to III	92.5	7.5	<0.2	<0.1		Bronze
	Component IV	*c.* 85	tr.	*c.* 15	tr.		Brass
3.37	Tubular box	90.9	9	<0.2	0.2		Bronze
	Intrusive to the set:						
3.31	Spatula probe	86.8	12.7	<0.2	0.4		Bronze
3.39	Clasp-knife	85.5	2.4	8.8	3.3		Gunmetal

Table 4 X-ray fluorescence analyses of the copper alloy instruments in the Italy set

KEY: *Italics* = semi-quantitative/qualitative analysis; XX = major component; X = alloying component; < = less than; nd = not detected; tr. = trace

Scalpel handles Cat. nos 3.7–9 from the Italy set are graded in increasing size of dissector and thickness of grip and are stylistically similar to each other. These three instruments are also analytically similar, made of brass containing tin and a little lead (c. 12% zinc, 2.5% tin and 1% lead). This is good evidence that they belong together.

Scalpel handles Cat. no. 3.1-5 and scalpel/curette Cat. no. 3.6 have the same patina as the rest of the Italy set, together with patches of iron corrosion, but the calcite and dolomite deposit was not detected on them. Instead, traces of mineral-preserved wood were noted on the surface of these six instruments. The traces of mineral-preserved wood were very small but Caroline Cartwright (Department of Scientific Research) was able to take samples from scalpel handles Cat. no. 3.1 and 3.2 for examination by Paula Rudall, at the Jodrell Laboratory, Royal Botanic Gardens, Kew. Dr Rudall reported:

> The wood is in too poor a condition to permit an exact identification. However, it is certainly a hardwood (not a softwood i.e. a conifer) and the vessels are clearly visible with marked spiral thickenings on their walls, although very little other structure remains. The most likely candidates are Lime (*Tilia* sp.), Sycamore or Maples (*Acer* sp.), Cherry (*Prunus* sp.) or Spindle (*Euonymus* sp.), but several other woods have spiral thickenings and cannot be ruled out e.g. Pear (*Pyrus* sp.), and other Rosaceae and Elm (*Ulmus* sp.)

In spite of their very poor condition it was possible to determine that the samples from both instruments had similar characteristics, consistent with identification as a hardwood. It might therefore be concluded that the five scalpel handles had been buried in a wooden box, perhaps with Cat. no. 3.6. Furthermore, the position of the wood traces and the patches of iron staining on each of the instruments could be explained by the positioning of them, top to tail, next to each other inside the same box. This of course would account for the lack of calcareous deposits on their surfaces as they were not in direct contact with the soil during burial, but they would still have been corroded by the groundwater. Thus they could be considered to be a set within a set. However, the metal compositions of the instruments from this putative lost box are not the same, or even particularly similar (**Table 4**): Cat. nos 3.1–2, 3.4 and 3.6 are of bronze, but with variable tin contents ranging from 7.9% to 14.8%, and differing zinc and lead contents; Cat. no. 3.3 is a gunmetal; and Cat. no. 3.5 is a leaded bronze. Clearly these six instruments, although of similar style, were not cast together.

The conclusion that must be drawn from the study of the Italy set is that, although it might initially be supposed that all the instruments in a set owned by a Roman medical practitioner would show similarities in metal composition, when this assumption is tested against the scientific evidence it is sometimes, but not necessarily, found to be the case. This point is reinforced by Riederer's analysis of a set of 17 instruments from a single excavated context, a grave at Ephesus: he found little similarity in alloy composition amongst them and proposed that the set was formed from individually acquired pieces (Riederer 2002, 78–9). This suggestion seems eminently likely if it is considered that the career of a medical practitioner could span many years,

starting with a basic set of instruments and building the collection as and when needed for particular treatments and with replacements for breakages. It also might be the case that some instruments during their lifetimes were owned by more than one practitioner. It must be concluded that it is difficult to be certain that a group of instruments was a set, acquired and used by a single medical practitioner, without well-documented evidence of the find-spot, but scientific study can of course add evidence for or against the identification.

Conclusions

The alloys, manufacturing and decorative techniques noted in the British Museum collection of Roman medical instruments are all to be found in the wider repertoire of metalwork from the Roman world. Certainly, from the evidence seen here, catheter manufacture was highly skilled, and the design of keyhole sockets for blades was interestingly specific to scalpel handles, but from a practical economic point of view it seems unlikely that there were makers who only manufactured items for medical use. Makers of cosmetic instruments and containers, razors, toothpicks, knives, carpentry tools etc. would have had the skills to make precision medical equipment (Gostenčnik 2002; Giumlia- Mair 2000). A medical practitioner, like any other customer, would have been able to commission the making of specific items, as is illustrated by Galen's comments that he had personally designed and made wax models for specialised medical tools to be cast for him (Tucci 2008, 141).

The ideal study would be of well-excavated material: a museum collection is not ideal. That said, microscopic examination combined with X-radiography has assisted in identifying manufacturing techniques, repairs and more recent restoration. Furthermore, scientific analysis of patinas and organic traces in or on the instruments, as well as compositional analysis of the metal itself, can provide valuable insights into less obvious aspects including decayed storage containers and other ephemeral contents of the medical practitioner's tool kit as well as identifying modern copies and fakes.

Modern copies of Roman instruments made by the Fonderia Chiurazzi, Naples

The group of five instruments, Cat. nos 3.153–7, were made by the Fonderia Chiurazzi, Naples. These instruments are closely similar in appearance to, but not exact copies of, individual Roman surgical instruments in the National Archaeological Museum in Naples. In the early decades of the 20th century copies of antiquities from Pompeii and Herculaneum were being made by Naples foundries. These are now to be found in collections worldwide and although they were originally sold as copies, some are now mistakenly labelled as genuine Roman items. The British Museum bought these five copies of surgical instruments directly from the Naples Foundry in 1920 and they have now been examined to determine how they were made and what scientific criteria might be used to distinguish these copies from genuine antiquities in cases where their original provenance has been lost.

The methods used to study these copies, like those used on the Roman instruments in the collections discussed above, were of necessity non-invasive, relying on microscopy and X-radiography for an understanding of the manufacture (metallography to confirm the method of manufacture was not permitted) and X-ray fluorescence analysis (XRF) for the alloy type. Most of the components of these five instruments were analysed using XRF at uncleaned areas, without the deliberate removal of the patina/corrosion products or potentially unrepresentative surface metal, and thus the results should therefore be regarded as qualitative only. However, in three cases small areas of patina had become detached, facilitating analysis of the underlying metal, and in one case (bone forceps Cat. no. 3.153) a worn area on one of the handles was cleaned using gentle abrasion allowing a more reliable, semi-quantitative result to be obtained.

The bone forceps (Cat. no. 3.153) is physically very similar to the bone forceps Naples Museum inv. no. 78029 from Pompeii, but smaller and the two legs are transposed. Cat. no. 3.153 has every appearance of being cast, with typical casting defects and some finishing by filing, but electroforming is a real possibility for copies at this period so had to be considered.

The observed mis-assembly of the Naples Foundry bone forceps in relation to the original suggests that separate moulds for the two legs were taken from the Roman original and perhaps the assembling craftsman did not have access to the Roman instrument, resulting in the legs being transposed. Taking a mould from anything can be the first step in making a copy by electroforming or by casting but an electroform copy will be identical in dimensions (and surface texture) to the original whereas a casting will be smaller than the original, as in this case, because cast metal shrinks within the mould when it solidifies. This observation adds weight to the conclusion that copies of cast Roman instruments were also cast, as might be expected of the products of a foundry.

XRF analysis on the surface metal and on the abraded area of the forceps gave consistent results for the major and some of the minor/trace elements: c. 70% copper, c. 27% zinc, c. 1% tin, c. 2% lead, with a trace of iron, but arsenic and antimony were not detected. Slight traces of silver and nickel were detected in the surface only, but as the amounts were at the detection limit of the technique, these results are uncertain and their significance is difficult to assess.

The examination and analysis of the bone forceps indicate that it was cast, using brass with a high zinc content (c. 27%), with the small amount of lead (c. 2%) being sufficient to give a greater fluidity to the melt, improving the casting characteristics of the alloy. Although it was technically possible to produce brasses with such high zinc contents by the cementation process used in the Roman period to produce brass (e.g. Craddock and Eckstein 2003), the level is higher than is observed in Roman period medical instruments for which analyses are available (Riederer 2002) and from the results of this study. The overall trace element content of the metal is very low compared to that of much ancient metalwork.

The tubular components of the other instruments in this group also differ in dimensions and other details from the originals, but most are larger. The butting seams are similar in appearance to the Roman originals and X-radiography showed distinct density differences at these seams, confirming that they are real features of construction rather than the surface appearance of seams that an electroform might display. Thus, like their Roman originals, they were formed from sheet metal and are not electrotypes.

Analysis of the uncleaned surfaces of Cat. nos 3.154 (male catheter), 3.155 (tube) and 3.157 (uterine clyster) showed them to be almost pure copper containing about 0.3% of lead, but no detectable tin or zinc. Trace elements were barely detectable. Analysis of areas of underlying metal of the tube and clyster, where the patina had flaked away, gave similar results. This composition is typical of 20th-century sheet copper, which of course would be the material readily available to craftsmen of the Naples Foundry. It is rare for genuine Roman metalwork.

The outer casing of the cannula (Cat. no. 3.156) is of a composite construction, consisting of a copper tube attached to a brass disc. Analysis of an area of underlying metal of the copper tube gave a similar result to analyses of the catheter, tube and clyster above. Analysis of the surface metal of the brass disc showed it to be a high zinc brass containing a trace of tin, c. 1% lead and a trace of iron, but arsenic and antimony were not detected. Analysis of the surface metal of the inner plunger of the cannula showed it to be a high zinc brass rod with more than 27% zinc and no detectable tin, c. 0.4%, a trace of iron, and again arsenic and antimony were not detected.

The 1911 retail catalogue of the *Fonderie Artistiche Riunite J. Chiurazzi & Fils – S. De Angelis & Fils* offered its bronzes in three colours: Pompeii (green), Herculanum (dark grey) and Moderne (brown). The instruments discussed here appear to have the 'Herculanum' finish. The patina is very dark grey with a greenish tinge and with some fine, earthy deposits, particularly in the ribbing of the forceps handles. The patina is thin, smooth and even, with occasional rough patches of bright blue-green, especially in recesses and inside the tubes. The patinas of the five instruments examined are similar in appearance and the patina has flaked off small areas on several of the instruments revealing bare metal underneath (**Fig. 189**).

Energy dispersive X-ray analysis (EDX) of patina samples in a scanning electron microscope detected both copper with zinc in all the patina samples, surprisingly even on those from copper objects with no zinc in their metal. Other elements detected in the patinas were chlorine, sulphur, silicon and oxygen, with iron, phosphorous, potassium, calcium and aluminium also present in several samples.

X-ray diffraction analysis (XRD) of patina samples produced diffraction patterns which are difficult to characterise precisely, as is often the case with artificial patinas, i.e. rapidly formed patinas. No clear identification of the dark grey patina was produced by XRD analysis, but the green component on all the objects is a basic copper chloride. This does occur naturally on antiquities but is also relatively easy to promote artificially. The bright blue-green

Figure 189 Magnified detail of flaking patina on the edge of a 20th-century Naples Foundry copy of a Roman instrument from Pompeii, revealing the fresh metal beneath. This is typical of an artificial patina

corrosion appears to be a mixture of zinc and copper hydroxide hydrates, with some sulphates and nitrates also present. These corrosion products are not normally found on genuine antiquities. A red layer of cuprite (Cu_2O) is normally found under the green patina on genuine antiquities (e.g. Giumlia-Mair and Lucchini 2005) but was not consistently found on these copies (see **Fig. 189**).

Summary of findings for Naples Foundry copies

The copies were not made by electroforming; indeed, they appear to have been made by similar techniques to those of the Roman originals, either by casting or being constructed from sheet, though presumably using machine-rolled copper sheet rather than hand-made sheet metal. The finish of these copies is comparatively crude, with distinct file marks on their surfaces. Two kinds of alloy appear to have been used for the production of these five instruments: high purity copper containing little lead for the sheet metal components, and secondly, high zinc brass, containing lead (and in two instances tin) for the cast pieces. The alloy composition of the original instruments in Naples Museum is not known but we can assess these copies within the parameters of the alloys of the Roman instruments analysed for this research. The metal of the brass copies is characterised by high zinc levels, *c.* 27%, higher than was found for genuine Roman instruments in this study. Riederer's analytical survey identified a group of 14 'high zinc brass' Roman instruments, but these all had zinc contents lower than 26% and the four brass instruments he analysed with zinc in the range 29–37% were not identified as of Roman manufacture (Riederer 2002, 63–4).

The patination of the copies differs from that formed naturally over time. The zinc in the patinas on the copper objects may not be a deliberate component of the artificial patina, instead resulting from treating both copper and brass objects in the same patinating bath with zinc dissolved from the surface of the brasses being redeposited onto other items immersed in the patinating solution. The presence of more than trace levels of zinc in the patina of copper objects containing no zinc in the metal is a useful indicator of artificial chemical treatment, though it can also occur as the result of some chemical conservation treatments (and of course traces of zinc and iron may be picked up from a burial context). The bright blue-green corrosion seen inside the tubular components, probably caused by chemicals trapped inside the tubes, the even colour and smooth appearance of the thin patina, together with the lack of cuprite formation, are typical of 'antiqued' modern productions rather than genuine antiquities.

Chapter 5
Chemical Analysis of Medicinal Residues: Ingredients, Properties and Purpose

Rebecca Stacey

Introduction

Aims

Chemical analysis of residual material preserved inside medicine boxes was undertaken with the aim of learning more about the original medicinal contents. Such information can make an important contribution to the interpretation of the containers and their use in the past. For example, the unique form of the multi-compartment container (Cat. no. 3.36) presents particular questions about the comparative composition of the residues in the different compartments while identification of medicinal residues in the single tube containers would clarify their range of use.

Medicinal remains such as these are rare archaeological finds and thus there are few published data with which they can be compared. The accumulating data from increasing research of such material offer scope to investigate ingredients used in different kinds of treatment or different container types and to consider their properties and efficacy in tandem with evidence from the documentary sources and other texts such as collyrium-stamps. Comparative research is also vital for advancing our understanding of the preservation of medicinal materials in archaeological environments.

Background

The corpus of surviving Greek and Roman medicine containers is relatively small, for items which must have been commonplace in their time. The majority of containers made of organic materials are lost to us unless preserved by exceptional burial environments; surviving examples include a small rectangular 3rd-century wooden box with four compartments and sliding lid found at Nijmegen (Künzl 1983a, 94–5, figs 74, 76) and traces of a leather pouch (with medical instruments inside) found in a 3rd-century tomb at Wehringen (Künzl 1983a, 120, fig. 96).

Containers that survive are typically made of metal. A common form is the cylindrical lidded tube; these tube containers are sometimes interpreted as instrument cases and some of the longer examples of the form have been found to contain surgical instruments (Milne 1907; Tabanelli 1958; Künzl 1983a, 105, fig. 84; Jackson 1990a; Hibbs 1991; Bliquez 1994, pl. 26, fig. 1). Shorter forms, however, are ill-sized for this purpose (Milne 1907) and examples with *materia medica* preserved within are known: a silver tube containing a red powder was discovered in a 3rd-century noblewoman's grave in Judea (Ilani *et al.* 1999); fragments, possibly of pills, survive inside bronze tubes from the 2nd/3rd-century Roman surgeon's tomb at Nea Paphos (Michaelides 1984); medicine traces have also been reported from cylinder boxes at Pompeii (Bliquez 1994, 68, 196, nos 311, 312, 314).

Containers with multiple compartments can hold different types of medicine and this is attested in examples where the contents survive. The most usual form of multi-compartment box to survive is the metal rectangular form (see Cat. nos 3.124–5, alas with no contents). A rectangular box with six compartments containing different medicines is depicted by Milne (Milne 1907, pl. LIV) and attributed to the collection of Naples Museum, although it was not seen by Bliquez or Jackson in more recent examination of the material there (Bliquez 1994). Another, with four compartments, each still containing pills and fragments of pills, described as 'greyish in colour and shaped like the eraser on a pencil', was seen and recorded by Bliquez (1994, 66–9, 191–2, no. 296). A further four-compartment rectangular box from the 2nd/3rd-century Lyon eye kit contains 20 collyrium sticks, 11 of which bear stamps indicating different types of medicine (Boyer *et al.* 1990; Gourevitch 1998; Lioux 2016). A much earlier example dating to the 4th century BC from Thessaloniki (Katsifas *et al.* 2018) is a semi-cylindrical metal container with three compartments, each containing a mass of medicinal residue.

Single-compartment boxes of various forms have also been discovered with contents *in situ*. Examples from the Balkans include a rectangular box containing a block of medicines from Tomb 1 of the 1st–2nd century Dulgata Mogila tumulus physician's tombs at Nova Zagora, Bulgaria and a rectangular box with medicinal residues from the physician's kit at Kostolac, Serbia (Baykan 2017). A bronze box and boot from the 2nd/3rd century physician's tomb at Bankso, Bulgaria, both contained medicines (Michaelides 1988; Baykan 2017). A tin *pyxis* containing five grey discs of solid medicine was recovered from the 2nd-century BC Etruscan Pozzino shipwreck, part of the contents of a physician's chest (Giachi *et al.* 2013). Earlier still, the 4th-century BC Derveni tomb group at Thessaloniki included a lidded pyxis containing red powder (Katsifas *et al.* 2018). *Materia medica* can also survive as residues on instruments (Michaelides 1985), and the *collyria* that survive dissociated from containers (Gourevitch 1998).

The two Greek lead ointment pots in this catalogue (Cat. nos 3.129–30) are a type of miniature vessel widely known in the Mediterranean; they are commonly made of ceramic although other lead examples are known (Sjöqvist 1960; Işin 2002; Łajtar and Południkiewicz 2017; Taborelli and Marengo 2017;). The inscription on Cat. no 3.129 links this vessel to *lykion*, a medicine highly favoured in antiquity especially for the treatment of eye disorders. The active ingredient of *lykion* was extracted from the branches and roots of the 'lykion' plant, so-called because of its prevalence in Lycia and Cappadocia (Łajtar and Południkiewicz 2017), although it was widespread elsewhere in the Mediterranean. This plant is interpreted as buckthorn (either *Rhamnus cathartica* or *Rhamnus infectoria* L.) but the name was also applied to a plant and medicine from India (inferred to be *Berberis lyceum royale*) which was more highly regarded according to Galen (Simpson 1855; Jackson 1996a, 2238). Some 14 examples of vessels with stamped *lykion* inscriptions survive (Işin 2002) but none are described as containing residues of their original contents. Analysis of the residues in pots Cat. nos 3.129–30 provides a unique opportunity to investigate the composition of this anciently renowned salve.

The importance of the chemical and biological evidence embodied by surviving *materia medica* has long been recognised, although detailed published scientific studies of the materials are few. Chemical analysis of the *collyria* from Rheims was undertaken on their rediscovery in the mid-19th century and in successive analytical campaigns in the following years (Gourevitch 1998 and refs therein). The contents of the multi-compartment medicine box from

Lyon, with its 20 *collyrium* sticks, have been the subject of detailed analytical investigation combining elemental, mineralogical and pollen analysis (Guineau 1989; Boyer *et al.* 1990). More recently, the medicine discs inside the *pyxis* from the Pozzino shipwreck have been subject to similarly thorough study (Giachi *et al.* 2013). More often the scientific investigations are limited to elemental and mineralogical investigation of inorganic components of the material, as, for example, in the study of the pills and powders from Nea Paphos (Foster and Kanada 1988), the medicines from Bankso (Michaelides 1988), and the red powder from Judea (Ilani *et al.* 1999); Michaelides (1988) documents further examples. Greater attention to organic composition has been given to residues of ointments and unguents where the original consistency of the material demanded a higher proportion of organic ingredients (see for example Ribechini *et al.* 2008; Colombini *et al.* 2009; Zachariou-Kaila 2009).

Increased analytical study of ancient medicines follows increasing sophistication of analytical methods which permit detection of a greater range of materials from ever smaller samples. New analytical tools, however, cannot overcome the limitation of preservation which dictates the material that survives to be studied. Preservation of *materia medica* favours dry material or semi-solids, explaining the predominance of *collyria*, pills and powders in the physical record. It also accounts for the emphasis until recently on inorganic ingredients in analysis. The more organic-rich ointments survive where protected by containers, often metal containers (as in, for example, the Roman cosmetic pot from London, Evershed *et al.* 2004). Association with metal has significance for preservation of the residues, leading, for example, to soap formation in the fats (Stacey 2011). This process can also be attributed to the mineral ingredients of the medicine, and the presence of metals from either source may inhibit microbial action leading to further enhanced preservation. Even so, chemical changes such as hydrolysis and oxidation will reduce diagnostic information such that precise identification of organic materials is impossible unless specific stable diagnostic compounds (biomarkers) are present (Evershed 2008; Craig *et al.* 2020). Moreover, in any formulation carrier ingredients are likely to be proportionally more abundant than active ingredients, although many carrier substances such as fats and waxes have therapeutic properties which were recognised in antiquity, as discussed below. These materials are more likely to be identified in analysis. Therapeutic components are more likely to be biologically active and thus more vulnerable to alteration and loss over time, as has been demonstrated for opiates (Chovanec *et al.* 2012; Smith *et al.* 2018).

Objects and residues

The British Museum collection includes nine medicine containers: two multi-compartment rectangular boxes with sliding lids (Cat. nos 3.124–5); a cylindrical box system in bronze, comprising four separate containers that stack together to form a single tube (Cat. no. 3.36; **Fig. 190**); four simple lidded bronze tubes (Cat. nos 3.37, 3.126–8) and two lead pots (Cat. nos 3.129–30).

The rectangular multi-compartment boxes contain no trace of original contents. However, with the exception of

Figure 190 Cylindrical box system (Cat. no. 3.36) open at section IV and interior view of section IV with mass of medicinal residue. Images previously published in Stacey 2011

tube Cat. no. 3.37, all the other containers exhibit residues ranging from well-preserved masses of original contents to scant surface deposits, see **Table 5**. In the cylindrical box system (Cat. no. 3.36) each section of the tube contains extensive well-preserved deposits of the original contents: all are buff-coloured powdery solids, tinged with green from corrosion products of the container. The single tubes exhibit more ambiguous interior surface deposits (more powdery and variable in colour) that may be residues of medicinal contents. Of the two Greek lead pots, one contains a well-preserved waxy solid that bears impressions made by needle-like tools, the other has a residual waxy coating on the interior surface.

Methods

Prior to sampling, the deposits were visually examined using optical microscopy. The multi-compartment container was sampled in two campaigns: in the first (see Stacey and Hook, unpublished 2005) only sections I–III were sampled because the fourth section could not easily be opened. After analysis of the first batch a case could be made for intervention to release section IV so that the residue inside could be investigated; further samples from sections I–III were taken at the same time. Details of the samples taken from each container are given in **Table 5**.

Inorganic components in the samples were analysed non-destructively by X-ray fluorescence (XRF), and in some cases Raman spectroscopy. Separate sub-samples of 0.5mg were then prepared for analysis by gas chromatography – mass spectrometry (GC-MS) using two different preparation methods: method (1) extracting wax, lipid and resin components; and method (2) extracting saccharide (sugar) components. In both cases laboratory blanks (no sample)

Table 5 Summary of materials analysed
*= The compartment numbers are as given in Jackson (1986, 130). See also BM/SR (British Museum Department of Scientific Research) reports 5305; 6001; 7070; 7071; 7134; 7191)

Cat. no. and BM Reg. no.	Object details	Residue description	BMRL no.	Analyses
Cat. no. 3.36 (1968,0626.37)	Cylindrical box system (composed of four stacking sections, I–IV* in bronze and brass). From a set of surgical instruments and accessories. Roman (from Italy)	Contents of section I: Grey/green solid, residue slightly powdery surface	5305-24395-P I	XRF, XRD, GC-MS (1) & (2); starch test
		Contents of section II: Grey/green solid, residue slightly powdery surface	5305-24395-P II	XRF, XRD, GC-MS (1) & (2); starch test
		Contents of section III: Grey/green solid, residue slightly powdery surface	5305-24395-P III	XRF, XRD, GC-MS (1) & (2); starch test
		Contents of section IV: Grey/green solid, residue slightly powdery surface	5305-24395-P IV	XRF, XRD, GC-MS (1) & (2); starch test
Cat. no. 3.127 (1904,0204.264)	Lidded bronze tubular box. Roman (from France). L. 88.3mm; dia. 14mm	Black powdery deposit	7191-10-X	XRF, XRD, GC-MS (1) & (2)
Cat. no. 3.126 (1851,0813.93)	Lidded bronze tubular box, which once contained two bronze and two bone needles (now missing). Roman (from France). L. 91.2mm; dia. 14mm	Black powdery residue. Minute sample	7191-8-Y	XRF, GC-MS (1)
Cat. no. 3.128 (1867,0508.168)	Lidded bronze tubular box. Roman (unknown provenance). L. 96.5mm; dia. 19.7mm	Thin surface deposit	7191-9-L	XRF
Cat. no. 3.130 (1868,0110.219)	Lead ointment pot inscribed around body. Greek (from Corfu)	Waxy solid with impressions from needle-like tools	7191-53-X	XRF, GC/MS (1)
Cat. no. 3.129 (1842,0728.569)	Lead ointment pot inscribed '*Lykion from Mousaios*'. Greek (from Athens)	Wax-like surface film	7191-56-P	GC-MS (1)

Cat. no. and BM reg. no.	Ingredients		
	Sample details	Organic	Inorganic
Cat. no. 3.36 (1968,0626.37) Section I*	Grey/green solid. 24395P I	Beeswax, conifer resin, fat or oil, plant gum, cellulosic material	Lead, zinc
Cat. no. 3.36 (1968,0626.37) Section II*	Grey/green solid. 24395P II	Beeswax, conifer resin, fat or oil, plant gum, cellulosic material	Trace lead
Cat. no. 3.36 (1968,0626.37) Section III*	Grey/green solid. 24395P III	Beeswax or Punic wax, conifer resin, fat or oil, plant gum, cellulosic material	Lead, zinc
Cat. no. 3.36 (1968,0626.37) Section IV*	Grey/green solid. 24395P IV	Beeswax, conifer resin, fat or oil, plant gum, cellulosic material	Trace lead
Cat. no. 3.127 (1904,0204.264)	Black powdery deposit 7191-10-X	Trace fat, plant gum, cellulosic material	Lead, calcium, carbon
Cat. no. 3.126 (1851,0813.93)	Black powdery residue. 7191-8-Y	Conifer resin, fat or oil	Zinc, lead, carbon
Cat. no. 3.128 (1867,0508.168)	Thin surface deposit. 7191-9-L	Trace fat	Zinc, lead
Cat. no. 3.130 (1868,0110.219)	Waxy solid 7191-53-X	Beeswax, fat or oil	
Cat. no. 3.129 (1842,0728.569)	Wax-like surface film 7191-56-P	Fat or oil	

Table 6 Summary of ingredients identified (contaminants excluded)
* = The compartment numbers are as given in Jackson (1986, 130)

were prepared alongside to monitor for background contamination. Small sub-samples of residues from the multi-compartment tube (Cat. no. 3.36) were tested for starch with a solution of iodine and potassium iodide. The analytical techniques applied to each sample are detailed in **Table 5**. For full details of sample preparation and analytical methods, see Appendix to this chapter, p. 171.

Results and discussion

The results of analysis for each sample are summarised in **Table 6**. Some of these results have already been published and discussed elsewhere: see Stacey 2011. Example chromatographic data for residues from the bronze tube containers are presented in **Figs 191–2**; see Stacey (2011) for full results. Data obtained from the lead pots are presented in **Figure 193**. Compound identifiers in brackets throughout this discussion refer to the peak labels in the figures.

Object-by-object: detection and interpretation of ingredients

Cylindrical box system (Cat. no. 3.36)
The materials inside the four compartments of this box are very alike in appearance and similar in composition (**Fig. 190**).

Residues from compartments I and II were previously analysed by X-ray fluorescence (XRF) and X-ray diffraction (XRD), with results indicating the presence of lead and wax respectively (La Niece 1986, 163–4). Further XRF analysis on samples indicated that the residues in compartments I, III and IV display levels of both zinc and lead that are higher relative to the metal of the box (see pp. 152–3) while in the compartment II residue only the lead content is

enhanced. All four residues contain an abundance of copper likely to be from the corrosion of the box.

Analysis by GC-MS confirmed the presence of wax in all four residues, specifically beeswax, indicated by the range of wax esters (W40–W52), odd-carbon-number n-alkanes (C_{27}–C_{33}) and even-carbon-number long-chain fatty acids (F_{22}–F_{34}) (Heron et al. 1994). In the residue from section III the beeswax exhibited a slightly different composition, lacking the characteristic long-chain fatty acids (F_{22}–F_{34}). In other archaeological specimens this phenomenon has been attributed to preferential loss of these compounds due to salt formation in saline or alkaline burial environments (Evershed et al. 1997). The original burial environment for this container is unknown, but the residues have been well protected and should in any case have all been subject to similar conditions; moreover, the shorter chain fatty acids in the residues have not been lost. The composition in this case may therefore point to modification of the wax in antiquity. Pliny describes the processing of beeswax to produce Punic wax, a method involving boiling the wax in salt water with the addition of soda (Pliny, *Natural History* IV, trans. Rackham 1961, 221–3). This treatment should lead to the loss of the long-chain fatty acids as salts and experiments have been undertaken to demonstrate the similarity of the resultant wax product to the composition seen here (Stacey 2011).

Hydrolytic degradation of the wax esters in beeswax leads to formation of even-carbon-number n-alkanols, present only at low levels in these samples (and so not labelled in **Fig. 191**), and palmitic acid. Palmitic acid is present in large quantities in all the residues and accompanied by stearic and oleic acids. This suggests that not all of it derives from beeswax degradation. Although oleic acid could derive from degradation of unsaturated

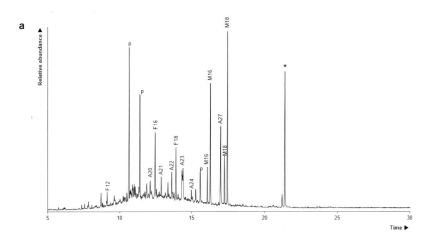

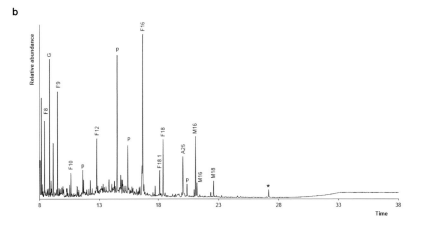

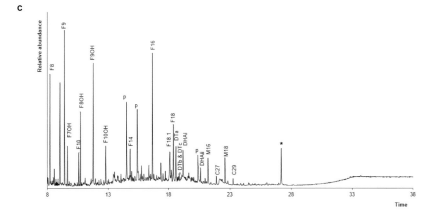

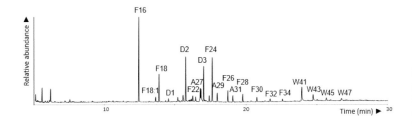

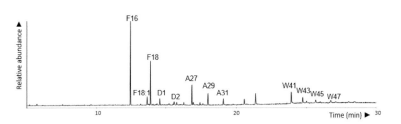

Figure 191 Partial (5–30 min) total ion chromato-grams obtained by analysis of the solvent extracts (TMS derivatives) of samples from:
a) Bronze tubular box Cat. no. 3.127;
b) Bronze tubular box Cat. no. 3.126;
c) Bronze tubular box Cat. no. 3.128;
d) Cylindrical box system, section I (Cat. 3.36);
e) Cylindrical box system, section III (Cat. no. 3.36).
Peak identities: F*n* fatty acids, A*n* *n*-alkanes, W*n* wax esters, D1 dehydroabietic acid, D2 7-oxode-hydroabietic acid, D3 7-oxo-15-hydroxydehydro-abietic acid, DTa pimaric acid, DTb sandaracopi-maric acid, DTc isopimaric acid. * internal standard (tetratriacontane). The data are presented as originally published in Stacey 2011

a

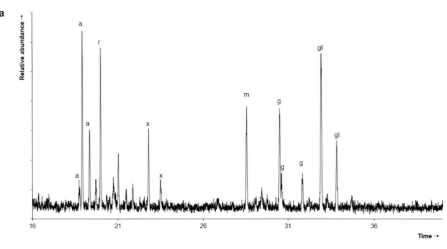

b

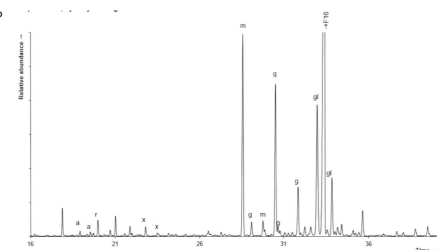

Figure 192 Partial (16–40 min) total ion chromatograms obtained by analysis of hydrolysed sample extracts from:
a) Cylindrical box system, section I (Cat. no. 3.36);
b) Bronze tubular box (Cat. no. 3.127).
Peak identities: F*n* fatty acids, a arabinose, r rhamnose, m mannose, g galactose, gl glucose, x xylose. Data presented as originally published in Stacey 2011

monoesters in beeswax (Garnier *et al.* 2002) it has seldom, if ever, been observed. Instead, these shorter chain fatty acids (F16–F22, F18.1), and their relative abundances, are typical of a highly degraded fat or oil. The presence of diacids in the residue from section II supports this further; diacids are degradation products of unsaturated fats and thus may suggest an oil rather than a fat. The material is too degraded to infer the source further, although no evidence was observed for the presence of the distinctive biomarkers of brassica or castor oils (Copley *et al.* 2005; Romanus *et al.* 2008).

Diterpenoids observed in all four residues indicate a softwood resin. The three diterpenoids detected (dehydroabietic, 7-oxodehydroabietic and 7-oxo-15-hydroxydehydroabietic acids) are oxidation products of the original resin constituents (Pastorova *et al.* 1997) so they cannot be linked to a specific botanical origin. Nevertheless, a Pinaceae origin might be tentatively inferred because the abietane and pimarane diterpenoid precursors of these oxidation products are particularly characteristic of this family (Mills and White 1994, 101).

Sugars observed in all four residues (although most abundantly in section I, see **Fig. 192**) might suggest the presence of a plant-derived gum. The typical gum sugar constituents (arabinose, rhamnose, xylose, mannose and galactose) are accompanied in the residues by glucose. The most obvious sources of glucose – honey, juice or nectar – can be excluded as no free glucose or sucrose could be

identified in unhydrolysed extracts. Starch can also be discounted as iodine starch tests were negative. Glucose is not considered a typical constituent of plant gums (see for example Ha and Thomas 1988, 576; Mills and White 1994; Vallance *et al.* 1998, 299) but it has been reported by Al-Hazmi and Stauffer (1986) as a major ingredient of gum tragacanth (from *Astragalus* sp.), along with mannose. Mannose is also present in some abundance in the residues, but the absence of fucose which is always present in gum tragacanth steers away from interpreting a tragacanth source. Mannose also occurs in locust bean gum (also known as carob gum, from *Ceratonia siliqua*) and, in lower levels, in *Prunus* spp. (i.e. cherry, plum, almond etc.) gums; it is possible that sugars from a mixture of gums are present. An important alternative source for the glucose could be cellulose, perhaps derived from pulverised herbs, and the presence of xylose, a constituent of hemicellulose, might support this explanation.

Bronze tubular box (Cat. no. 3.127)
This box contains a very small amount of black powdery residue. Preparation of samples for GC-MS left the black material undissolved and analysis of the samples revealed little evidence from which to interpret original organic ingredients.

Some of the most abundant components detected are plasticisers (p) of modern origin and the range of *n*-alkanes

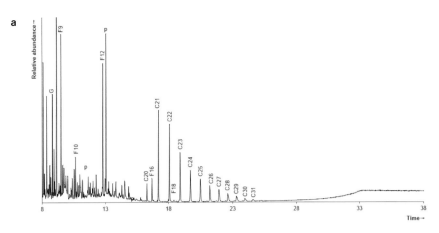

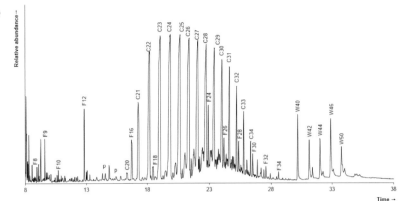

Figure 193a–b Partial (8–38min) total ion chromatograms obtained by analysis of the solvent extracts of residue samples from two lead pots: a) Cat. no. 3.129 and b) Cat. no. 3.130.
Peak identities: F*n* fatty acids; A*n* n-alkanes; W*n* wax esters; p plasticiser (modern)

(C_{20}–C_{24}) most likely to derive from a modern petroleum wax. The presence of modern materials means that other components must be interpreted with caution.

Traces of fat are indicated by the fatty acids (F12, F16, F18) and monoacylglycerides (M16, M18) but these are not distinctive to any particular fat source and such compounds can be seen as modern contaminants in archaeological residues.

A range of sugars (arabinose, rhamnose, xylose, mannose, galactose and glucose) was detected, similar in distribution to those seen in residues from Cat. no. 3.36 (see **Fig. 193**), and probably indicates the presence of a plant gum, although the alternative interpretations for the presence of glucose that have already been discussed are also possible.

The insoluble black powder gave no XRD result, but Raman analysis confirmed that it was elemental carbon (soot). XRF analysis indicated the presence of lead, and possibly calcium, as well as copper from the box itself. Despite the similarities in described appearance, the composition of this powder is very different to the black powder medicament from Nea Paphos which, using XRD, was identified as the mineral carphosiderite (Foster and Kanada 1988, 229).

Bronze tubular box (Cat. no. 3.128)

The sample from this box comprised a surface scraping from the interior. The organic composition of the extracted sample offers little information diagnostic of original ingredients.

A range of fatty acids was detected, including the unsaturated oleic acid and shorter chain fatty acids which are common degradation products of unsaturated fats. None

of the diacids that are typical constituents of degraded oils could be detected, although as these are more polar and they could be subject to differential loss in leaching burial environments. This limited range of compounds could tentatively be interpreted as a fat or oil, but the possibility they derive from an introduced contaminant cannot be ruled out. Phthalate peaks indicate that the interior of the box has been exposed to some contamination from plasticisers.

Inorganic components in the residue include lead and zinc which appear enhanced relative to the metal of the cylindrical container and are likely to be original ingredients.

Bronze tubular box (Cat. no. 3.126)

The black powdery residue in this box, like that in box Cat. no. 3.127, left an undissolved black residue after extraction of samples for GC-MS. However, on analysis the sample extracts yielded much more evidence for organic ingredients. Diterpenoid compounds indicative of conifer resin were seen; these are better preserved than those observed in the residues from the cylindrical box system (Cat. no. 3.36): the oxidised diterpenoid products are accompanied by some of the original diterpenoid resin acids, including pimaric, sandaracopimaric and isopimaric acids. Together these point to the Pinaceae family as the likely source of the resin, probably a pine (*Pinus* sp.) (Mills and White 1994, 101).

Fatty acids in the residue point to a fat or oil component. As in the sample from Cat. no. 3.127, short-chain fatty acid fat/oil degradation products are seen, but no diacids. However, an abundant range of short-chain hydroxy fatty acids (F7OH-F10OH) have chain lengths which imply their origin as degradation products of similar unsaturated components. Such compounds are not commonly reported but have been observed in ancient fat residues preserved in pottery (Regert *et al.* 1998a).

As in other residues analysed here, phthalate compounds are indicative of recent contamination from plastics.

Inorganic components in the residue detected by XRF include lead and zinc, which are enhanced relative to the metal of the cylindrical container and so are likely to be original ingredients. The insoluble black powder can be attributed to be elemental carbon (soot) identified from the two diffuse peaks at *c.* 1360 and 1590 cm^{1} observed in the Raman spectrum. No phosphate peak (*c.* 960 cm^{-1}), indicative of carbon derived from burnt bone or ivory, was observed (Coccato *et al.* 2015).

Lead ointment pots (Cat. nos 3.129–30)

In both of these pots large amounts of petroleum wax (C20–C34) dominate the residue composition (see **Fig. 193**), presumably introduced as a conservation treatment at some time; the phthalate plasticisers (p) are also modern contaminants.

Some fatty acids are present in both samples which indicate the presence of an oil or fat, but the range and distribution of these compounds is not diagnostic to source. The short-chain acids suggest that the fat is degraded, and therefore perhaps a component of the original vessel contents, but the possibility that the fat may have been introduced with the conservation treatment cannot be ruled out.

The sample from Cat. no. 3.130 contains beeswax, and although, again, this may have been introduced with the petroleum wax, *n*-alkanols formed by hydrolysis of the wax esters are just discernible in among the smaller peaks eluting between 23 and 28 minutes so it may be an original component of the material – this would certainly be consistent with its ointment-like appearance.

XRF indicated the presence of lead, although this is most likely to have originated from the container itself. In addition, very slight traces of iron, nickel, copper and zinc were detected in the sample from Cat. no. 3.130, but are, again, thought likely to be contaminants.

Ingredients in context

The ingredients identified present only a partial picture of the formulations represented by these residues. Many constituents will have been lost: volatile compounds typical of fragrance extracts seldom survive in archaeological residues (Serpico and White 2000) and many biologically active compounds are likely to be more vulnerable to alteration or loss, as has been demonstrated for opiate compounds (Chovanec *et al.* 2012; Smith *et al.* 2018). Important medicinal ingredients may be included in only small quantities meaning that more abundant carrier or bulking materials may be more likely to be detected, especially for those that are more stable. Others will not have been captured by the analytical methods used; particular methodologies are required for detection of, for example, opiates and bitumen (Smith *et al.* 2018; Fulcher *et*

al. 2020). It is possible that the application of alternative analytical approaches (such as liquid chromatography – mass spectrometry) could uncover further medicinal biomarkers that would be less amenable to the techniques employed in this study.

The inorganic analysis conducted here is largely confined to elemental analysis so the mineral forms of inorganic ingredients have not been determined. No micro-organic analysis was conducted to look for evidence from pollen or other cellular material, evidence which has provided valuable insights into herbal ingredients in other studies (see for example Giachi *et al.* 2013 and the Lyon *collyria* too (Gourevitch 1998; Boyer *et al.* 1990)).

This partial picture of ingredients precludes interpretation of specific applications for these materials or identification of the conditions they were intended to treat. Nevertheless, all the substances identified here had therapeutic value according to the Classical sources and many have been demonstrated also to have therapeutic value according to modern science. They are consistent with evidence from other finds, which further enforces their importance in the ancient pharmacopoeias.

Wax: beeswax and Punic wax

Among the material analysed here, wax seems to be confined to ointment type residues. Beeswax is present in one of the Greek miniature ointment pots (Cat. no. 130) in combination with fat or oil and inorganic components. In the multi-compartment box system, wax is seen in all four of the residues, combined with fat/oil, conifer resin, gums, inorganic compounds and possibly herbs. Comparisons can be drawn with other unguents, for example beeswax reported in mixtures with conifer resin and fat (Ribechini *et al.* 2008) and in unguent from a Hellenistic *pyxis* (Zachariou-Kaila 2009). Wax has also been reported in the solid tablet medicines from the Pozzino shipwreck (Giachi *et al.* 2013)

This physical evidence accords with the applications described in the Classical sources. Celsus, for example, defines wax as discutient and emollient, effective in promotion of tissue growth and filling in ulcerations (Celsus, *On Medicine* 5.14, 5.15). Dioscorides describes a plaster made of asphalt, barley meal, beeswax and natron for treatment of gout, arthritis and lethargy (Dioscorides, *Materials used in Medicine* 1.101). Non-topical uses are also noted such as mixing beeswax into broths for dysentery (Dioscorides, *Materials used in Medicine* 2.105).

Preparation of Punic wax from beeswax would lead to a modification of the properties of the material. Much has been written about the use of this modified product as a painting medium (White 1978; Botticelli *et al.* 2012; Stacey *et al.* 2018) but Pliny also observes that Punic wax is good for use in medicines (*Natural History* 21.49). Its appearance in just one section of the box points to different applications for the materials in this container.

In the modern world beeswax is widely used in cosmetics, on account of its very low irritant and comedogenic effects and in pharmaceutical applications it is widely used as a thickener, binder, drug carrier and release retardant (Cornara *et al.* 2017). It also has significant therapeutic properties and the bioactive compounds responsible for these have recently been reviewed (see Cornara *et al.* 2017). The antimicrobial properties of beeswax have been tested in formulations against skin infections and it has been found effective against a variety of skin disorders, specifically mixed with oil and honey (Fratini *et al.* 2016), which is interesting in view of the fat/wax/sugar ointment mixtures identified here.

Conifer resins

Conifer resins were detected in all four ointments preserved inside the different sections of the cylindrical box system and in the black powdery residue from one of the simple cylindrical boxes (Cat. no. 3.126). Conifer resins have been reported as ingredients in other Roman unguents (Ribechini *et al.* 2008) and in Etruscan cosmetics (Colombini *et al.* 2009) as well as in the solid tablets recovered from the Pozzino physician's chest (Giachi *et al.* 2013).

A broader range of resins was valued for medicinal purposes; myrrh was tentatively suggested as an ingredient in some of the *collyrium* sticks from the Lyon medicine box (Boyer *et al.* 1990) while frankincense is indicated in inscription(s) on stick(s) from the oculist's tomb at Rheims (Gourevitch 1998). Ancient trade routes bringing resins to the Mediterranean attest to the importance of these products (Lardos *et al.* 2011) and Pliny describes the harvesting of frankincense and myrrh in southern Arabia and their overland transport by camel to the Mediterranean (Pliny, *Natural History* 12.30, 12.35). Other resins such as mastic (from *Pistacia* sp.) and resins from Pinaceae conifers such as *Pinus* sp. and *Cedrus* sp. would have been available more locally as the source plants are widely distributed in the Mediterranean (Langenheim 2003).

Resins were used in a range of preparations; Dioscorides describes their use in cough treatments, diuretics, plasters, poultices and salves (*Materials used in Medicine* 1.91–5). Resins were considered to have a warming effect (Lardos *et al.* 2011, citing *Materials used in Medicine* 1.91) and to promote tissue growth and fill in ulcers (Antwi 2000, citing Celsus 5.14). Cedar oil was added to analgesic compresses and used in treatment of toothache (Jocks 2020; Pliny, *Natural History* 24.11). Dioscorides (*Materials used in Medicine* 1.96) recommends the use of soot made from pine resin (and frankincense, 1.81 and 1.84) for eye remedies, which is particularly interesting given the black powder form of the residue in box Cat. no. 3.126.

In reviewing the Greek Byzantine *iatrosphia* ('medical wisdom') texts of Cyprus, Lardos *et al.* (2011) note some 30 recipes containing pine products, directed especially towards dermatological treatments, and topical applications of conifer resins persist in modern folk medicine in the Eastern Mediterranean (Lardos *et al.* 2011). Modern studies have shown that poultices of pine resin increase blood flow and have analgesic and anti-inflammatory effects (Lardos *et al.* 2011) and recent research has demonstrated the efficacy of Pinaceae resins in the treatment of chronic wounds (Jokinen and Sipponen 2016). Experiments have shown that compounds are bioavailable when topically applied (Lardos *et al.* 2011) and microbiological testing has proved the antibacterial properties of various resin acids (Leandro *et al.* 2014; Vainio-Kaila *et al.* 2015).

Lipid/fat

Fats and oils (lipids) are commonly reported from ancient cosmetics (e.g. Cotte *et al.* 2005; Evershed *et al.* 2004; Colombini *et al.* 2009) and are important ingredients in modern cosmetic formulations where their purpose is to form a protective barrier and to hydrate and emolliate the skin (Bonnet 2018; Berdick 1972). These properties are also important for the use of lipids in pharmaceutical applications, as is the role they play in cell membrane structure, fitting them for use as trans dermal carriers (Hernandez and Kamal-Eldin 2013). The same properties were valued for therapeutic purposes in the past; fats were considered to be cleansing and emollient (Celsus, *On Medicine* 5.5) and Dioscorides lists the fats of bears, goats, lions, sheep, duck, geese and more for use in treatments, as well as milk and the blood of reptiles, birds and mammals (Scarborough 1996). Olive oil was used a carrier for other medicines and uses of specific oils are described by Pliny, for example the well-known purgative properties of castor oil but also its beneficial action on joint problems and for skin and hair treatments (Pliny, *Natural History* 23.41). Pliny praised the emollient properties of almond oil and describes its use with wax as a cure for boils (*Natural History* 23.42).

An abundance of fats was reported in the residues within the 4th-century BC multi-compartment box from Thessaloniki, which have the appearance of similar ointment-based topical treatments to most of those analysed here (Katsifas *et al.* 2018). Interestingly, lipids were also detected in one of the Cologne *collyrium* sticks (Gourevitch 1998), where the presence of a pork bristle was inferred as supporting evidence to suggest a very specific animal fat source (although the possibility that this was deposited by a brush cannot be excluded); the case provides a precedent for the lipids seen in the more powdery residues analysed here.

Gums

Plant-derived polysaccharide gums were observed in all the cylinder tube residues. They cannot be linked to a specific botanical source, but the range of gums that were available were all used medicinally according to the Classical sources. Some plant gums (acacia, tragacanth) are specifically mentioned in relation to eye medicines (Celsus, *On Medicine* 6.6.7 and 6.6.25) and Pliny (*Natural History* 13.20) states that 'the Egyptian thorn (acacia) supplies the best kind of gum'. Paulus Aegineta mixed gum arabic with herbs for dysentery (Lardos *et al.* 2011, 20) and gums were also used to arrest bleeding and agglutinate wounds and to relieve irritation (Celsus, *On Medicine* 5.13).

In modern folk medicine plum gum is used as a tonic, laxative and vermifuge and gum arabic is used today as a traditional medicine for dysentery in Senegal (Lardos *et al.* 2011). The positive effects of gum arabic in the gastrointestinal tract have been demonstrated and other medical benefits are proven, including its efficacy as a topical treatment for skin disorders (Lardos *et al.* 2011; Salih 2018; Ali 2018). In modern pharmaceuticals a wide range of gums are used as binders and thickeners (Karmakar 2016) and Celsus explains the benefits of gums as binding agents for salves (Celsus, *On Medicine* 6.6.3). It is impossible to know if the gum in the residues examined here was included as a therapeutic ingredient or carrier substance: it is possible they acted as both, the morphology of the residues being consistent both with topical treatments (in the box system) and powders perhaps derived from a more solid form. The *collyria* from Lyon were found to contain gum (identified by Fourier-transform infrared spectroscopy, Gourevitch 1998) but in the absence of more organic analysis on solid medicine remains it is not possible to judge how typical the occurrence of gums is in this type of material.

Carbon

The presence of carbon in the two black powders is perhaps unsurprising given their form, although the black powder medicine Foster and Kanada describe from the Roman surgeon's tomb at Nea Paphos is very different, being mineral in character (Foster and Kanada 1988, 299). Charcoal has also been reported as a component of the tablets from the Pozzino shipwreck (Giachi *et al.* 2013) and carbon black has been identified in the medicines from Lyon (Gourevitch 1998). The written sources supply lots of examples of the use of soots in medicines, particularly valued as antiseptic ingredients (Dioscorides, *Materials used in Medicine* 5.183). Cherry, plum and conifer resin soots were used in remedies for eye complaints, as were burned date kernels (Dioscorides, *Materials used in Medicine* 5. 89, 86, 93, 149; Pliny, *Natural History* 28.47). Pliny describes soot in treatments for epilepsy, chlorosis and anthrax (*Natural History* 36.69). In modern medicine the adsorbent properties of carbon mean it is still widely used in the treatment of ingested poisons and other toxins (Roy 1994).

Inorganic materials

In the absence of mineralogical analysis interpretation of the elemental evidence for inorganic ingredients is limited to generalities. Nevertheless, as discussed below, the presence of lead and zinc is consistent with evidence from other sources. It is interesting that these residues lack the broader range of inorganic ingredients that have been reported for other some other medicines, especially haematite (Giachi *et al.* 2013; Katsifas *et al.* 2018), and these absences may also have significance for interpretation of the intended application.

Lead was detected in all the residues analysed here, in common with reports from a number of other medicinal residues that have been analysed. For example, lead (or lead minerals) have been reported from analysis of *collyrium* sticks from Pompeii (Milne 1907), Cologne, Rheims and Lyon (Gourevitch 1998) as well as in the medicines from Bankso (Baykan 2017) and the powder medicine from Judea (Ilani *et al.* 1999). As these are mostly solid or powder medicine formulas it is notable that lead is identified here in ointments as well as in powder residues, particularly as no lead was detected in the Hellenistic ointments analysed by Katsifas *et al.* (2018). Celsus recommends the use of lead in various forms of external treatments which could be consistent with the ointment form: galena (lead sulphide) was used to arrest bleeding and lead slag as an emollient and in dressings for burns and ulcers (Celsus, *On Medicine 5.1)*; litharge and other oxides of lead were used to clean wounds and skin lesions (Celsus, *On Medicine* 5.19.23−8).

Zinc oxide was used for similar therapeutic applications; Celsus describes it as exedent, desiccant and extractive and recommends it for relief of irritation and as an ingredient in eye salves (Celsus, *On Medicine* 5.13, 6.6). Zinc was detected here in residues from two compartments of the box system and in residues from two of the simple bronze tubes. Elsewhere it has been reported (as hydrozincite) in the tablets from the shipwreck (Giachi *et al.* 2013), *collyrium* sticks from Pompeii (Milne 1907) and Lyon (Gourevitch 1998) and in the medicine from the Bankso tomb (Michaelides 1985). Of the residues in the Greek multi-compartment box (Katsifas *et al.* 2018) just one contained hydrozincite, implying, as here, that the separate ointments were different formulations.

One of the residues, from Cat. no. 3.127, contained calcium. Calcium carbonate has previously been reported in pills and powders from the Nea Paphos tomb (Foster and Kanada 1988), in *collyrium* sticks from Pompeii (Milne 1907) and in the Bankso medicines (Baykan 2017). The therapeutic applications of calcium were various according to the sources: Celsus describes calcined hard tissues from various animal sources as ingredients for treatments in wound cleaning and dentistry (Celsus, *On Medicine* 5.8; 6.9.6) and Galen notes the astringent qualities of calcium compounds recommending their use in haemorrhage treatments (Tegethoff *et al.* 2001).

Interpretation of residues and objects

The multi-compartment form of the cylinder box system (Cat. no. 3.36) implies a storage system for four different medicines intended for different therapeutic applications. Although the different sections contain broadly the same ingredients (beeswax, fat or oil, a conifer resin, plant gum(s) and possibly pulverised herbs as well as low levels of lead and zinc), there are differences: possible Punic wax in section III, more evidence for oil rather than fat and an absence of zinc in section II. These variations support the notion that the residues were different preparations. It seems likely that original 'active' ingredients, now lost or undetectable by the methods used here, could have been much more varied.

The ointment-like appearance of these residues (see **Fig. 190**), and those in the lead pots, is consistent with their lipid-rich waxy composition and points to their use as topical remedies for external application. The incorporation of fat or oil into the wax would soften it to create a creamy consistency and this is supported by tool marks visible in some of the residues. The absence of starch in the ointments is interesting. Starch was identified as a major ingredient in the well-preserved Roman cosmetic remains from London (Evershed *et al.* 2004); the starch would deliver a smooth powdery texture to skin after application so its absence in these ointments perhaps emphasises the different applications of the two 'creams': the cosmetic to beautify and the ointment to heal.

It is more difficult to interpret the type of medicinal preparations represented by the residues from the simple cylinder tubes, both because of their scant powdery form and the limited range of organic constituents detected. The formulations are certainly different to the ointments described above in terms of the absence of wax and presence of carbon, but the fat/oil components could still point to alternative forms of topical treatment. The solubility of gum (as in residue from Cat. no. 3.127) would have a cohesive effect after wetting of the powder for external application. It would also make a good binder for remedies intended for ingestion, for example in the form of pills. It is possible that the powders are a residue from larger medicinal blocks stored in the tubes; this would be consistent with the types of medicines that have been found in other tubes (Michaelides 1984) although there are precedents for powders as well (Ilani et al. 1999). Although the form of the medicines is unclear, their presence in these simple tube boxes is significant, lending support to the theory that these shorter tubes were widely used as drug boxes rather than as surgical instrument cases.

Conclusions

The contents of six containers have been investigated in this study, comprising nine discrete medicinal residues. A diversity of residue types is presented, including different coloured powders and ointment-like solids. The results represent a significant contribution to the corpus of scientific data on Roman materia medica in general and specifically to that relating to residues associated with medicine containers. A variety of ingredients have been identified, including beeswax, conifer resin, fat, oil and plant gum, as well as lead and zinc. The therapeutic potential of these substances can be assessed from modern understanding of their pharmacological properties, while the Classical literature grants insights into how they were valued and prescribed in the past. The nature of the formulations allows speculation on their mode of delivery and sheds light on the use of the containers with which they are associated. Advances in scientific technology make possible the analysis of ever smaller samples, so there is good reason to anticipate that more data will emerge, both from known and yet to be discovered material, thus further expanding the potential for interpretation and understanding of Roman medicinal practice.

Appendix: methods of analysis

Sampling and sample preparation
Samples of 1-2mg were removed using a clean scalpel blade and tweezers and stored in glass micro vials. After analysis of inorganic components by XRF and Raman spectroscopy, sub-samples of 0.5mg were prepared for analysis by gas chromatography – mass spectrometry (GC-MS) using two preparation methods:

1) For analysis of lipid (wax/fat/resin). Samples were placed in clean glass vials and extracted with 500μl of dichloromethane, assisted by gentle heating (45 °C) and ultrasonication. The solvent extract was decanted and divided into two aliquots from which solvent was evaporated under a stream of nitrogen. One aliquot was derivatised with 50 μl bis(trimethylsilyl)trifluoroacetamide (BSTFA) + 1% trimethylchlorosilane (TMCS) to form trimethylsilyl (TMS) derivatives, the other with diazomethane to form methyl ester derivatives.

2) For analysis of lipid sugars. Samples were placed in clean glass vials and hydrolysed by the addition of 500μl of

0.5M methanolic HCl followed by heating at 80 °C for 18 hours. Samples were then dried under a stream of nitrogen and derivatised by addition of 500μl of Sigma-Sil A (1:3:9 ratio of TMCS, hexamethyldisilazane and pyridine) followed by heating at 80 °C for one hour (procedure is based on the method described by Bleton et al. 1996).

In both cases laboratory blanks (no sample) were prepared alongside to monitor for background contamination.

Small sub-samples of residues from the multi-compartment tube (Cat. no. 3.36) were tested for starch with a solution of iodine and potassium iodide.

Gas chromatography – mass spectrometry (GC-MS)
Samples were analysed using an Agilent 6890N gas chromatograph coupled to an Agilent 5973N mass spectrometer (MS). An Agilent AS7683 autosampler was used to inject 1μl samples in splitless mode at 250 °C and 10 psi, purge time 0.8 min. An Agilent HP5-MS, 30m × 0.25mm, 0.25μm film thickness, column with 1m × 0.32mm pre-column was used. For the wax/lipid/resin analysis the carrier gas was helium in constant flow mode at 1.5ml/min. After a one minute isothermal hold at 35 °C the oven was temperature programmed to 300 °C at 10 °C/min. with the final temperature held for 12 min. The final temperature was raised to 340 °C with a 20 min. hold for the waxes. The gums were analysed with the carrier gas in constant flow mode at 1ml/min. The oven temperature was programmed from 40 °C to 130 °C at 9 °C/min, and to 290 °C at 2 °C/min with the final temperature held for 10 minutes. In all cases the MS interface temperature was 280 °C and the MS source temperature 230 °C. Acquisition was in scan mode (29-650 amu/sec) after a solvent delay of 5 minutes. Mass spectral data were interpreted manually with the aid of the NIST/EPA/NIH Mass Spectral Library version 2.0 and by comparison with published data (3,4,5,6). Identification of sugar components was further verified by comparing with retention data from reference standards.

Raman spectroscopy
Raman spectroscopy was carried out using a Jobin Yvon LabRam Infinity spectrometer using a green (531nm) laser with a maximum power of 2.4mW at the sample, a liquid nitrogen cooled CCD detector and an Olympus microscope system. A few grains of sample were placed on a clean glass slide and analysed with no further preparation. Spectra were identified by comparison the British Museum in-house database.

X-ray fluorescence (XRF)
Non-destructive analysis of samples by energy dispersive XRF was carried out using a spectrometer as described by Cowell (1998). The X-ray tube was operated at 45kV and 0.4mA; a large collimator was used to irradiate an area c. 1.5mm² and measurements were taken for 300 s. Light elements (e.g. sodium, magnesium and aluminium) could not be detected due to the air-path between the X-ray tube, sample and detector.

Chapter 6
Selected Greek and Roman Objects in the British Museum Related to Medicine and Health

In antiquity health was often fragile, the cure for many diseases elusive, and an outcome for the sick rarely predictable. It was critical not to fall ill. As is seen in contemporary lay and medical writings, the importance of a positive regimen for the maintenance of health was clearly understood. Lifestyle, dietetics and body care all had a role, but so too did religious ritual. The positive benefit of religious belief was of considerable significance in medicine, both for those suffering disease and for those who sought to heal them – the powers of Asklepios were as real to such eminent physicians as Galen and Rufus of Ephesus as they were to the long-suffering orator Aelius Aristides. Nor was there any great difference between the practical measures taken to restore health in either secular or religious settings (Nutton 2004, 110–14, 276–81; Nissen 2007; Israelowich 2015, 52–67). In the Greek and Roman world, therefore, patients afflicted with illness or injury might exercise a choice between various healing strategies, or a combination of them. Some of those strategies – all of them for those with limited means – will have involved self-help and the assistance of family and friends, but many depended on a wide spectrum of healing personnel, and many others relied on the healing powers of an equally wide spectrum of deities.

The reality of those various strategies for maintaining health, warding off disease, securing well-being and treating those suffering illness or injury is vividly, sometimes painfully, illuminated by a wide range of surviving objects in the British Museum collection: the material remains of medicine, so to speak. In that health and well-being are integral to life, of course, a large proportion of all surviving artefacts can be taken to have some bearing on our subject, but some are more directly relevant than others; so, for this chapter, those pieces have been chosen which have the greatest significance and impact. Between them, the artefacts catalogued here introduce us to Greek and Roman practitioners, patients and their afflictions, fertility and childbirth, *materia medica*, veterinary medicine and the paramount healing cult of Asklepios and Hygieia.

Greek and Roman practitioners

6.1. Decree honouring a doctor (1864,1007.54) **(Fig. 194)**
From Karpathos, Dodecanese, Greece.
Height 61cm; width 41cm; depth 12 cm

A blue marble stele inscribed in Greek with an honorific decree commissioned by the citizens of Brykountos. Breakage at top and bottom of the stele has destroyed the beginning and end of the inscription, including the date of the decree. It records that the *demos* of Brykountos granted a golden crown to Menokritos, son of Metrodoros, a Samian, for his experience and long service – an exceptionally long period, more than 20 years – as public physician of the town of Brykountos (one of the cities of the Tetrapolis of Karpathos (Strabo, *Geography* 10.5.17)).

Menokritos was honoured for his zeal and enthusiasm in curing all people and for his knowledge and his virtue – being both skilled in his practice and beyond reproach in his conduct. Special mention is made of his dedication at the time of an epidemic when he treated alike both the citizens and the visiting strangers resident in the town. 'Menokritos,

Figure 194 Marble stele with decree honouring a doctor, from Karpathos, Greece, 2nd/1st century BC. British Museum, Cat. no. 6.1

Figure 195 Marble stele with decree honouring a doctor, from Gytheion, Greece, 73/72 BC. British Museum, Cat. no. 6.2

by the power of his care and his patience, treated the majority of them and restored the public health ... he saved many infected citizens from dangerous diseases without accepting money, in accordance with law and justice.' Furthermore, he did not restrict himself to receiving patients in the town but went out to visit those in the suburban areas, too.

Appropriately, a proclamation was to be made during a festival of Asklepios, and to ensure the widest possible publicity for this honoured physician the consecration and erection of the decree was scheduled to take place in the town's sanctuary of Poseidon Porthmios.

2nd/1st century BC.

Newton 1883, 138–40, no. CCCLXIV; *IG* XII,1 1032; Massar 1998, 87–9, no. 3; Samama 2003; Nutton 2004, 153–4.

6.2. Decree honouring a doctor (1839,0806.12) (Fig. 195)
From Gytheion, Lakonia, Greece.
Height 49.5cm (top broken); width 29.2cm

A red marble stele, the top broken and sides damaged, inscribed in Greek with an honorific decree of the city of Gytheion. It confers the *proxenia* ('public guest') on Damiadas, a Lacedemonian, honouring him for his public service as a physician to the people of the city of Gytheion for two years. Only the end of a few lines of a second decree to Damiadas survive at the broken top of the stele. He receives fulsome praise for his expertise, wisdom, nobility and justice as well as for the fact that for part of the time, at a

period of military and financial instability in Gytheion, he provided his services free of charge.

73/72 BC.

Newton 1883, 5–7, no. CXLIII; Massar 1998, 89–94, no. 4; Samama 2003.

6.3. Engraved gem, seal of a medical practitioner (1859,0301.118) (Fig. 196)
Provenance unknown.
Width *c.* 17mm; height *c.* 20mm

Carnelian. A broad oval, plano-convex, translucent orange-red gem set in a modern gold ring. The convex front surface of the gem is rather eroded and pitted, but the engraved surface is mainly shiny and retains some working marks.

The gem was identified by Raman spectroscopy and optical microscopy as microcrystalline quartz, and, with its deep orange colour, is therefore best described as carnelian (Janet Ambers, CSR Report no. AR2009/17. See also Sax 1996, esp. 66).

The gem is engraved with an image of Athena, facing right (reversed in impression), seated on a throne with lion's legs, her shield leaning to one side. She wears a crested helmet, *chiton* and *peplos*, her gaze fixed on a tragic mask which she holds in front of her in her left hand. The goddess is framed by a two-word inscription engraved along the elliptical borders behind and in front of her. That behind (at left), rising upwards, reads, retrograde, OPOBALSAMVM; that in front (at right), descending downwards, reads,

Figure 196 Engraved and inscribed carnelian gem, probably the seal of a medical practitioner, 1st/3rd century AD. British Museum, Cat. no. 6.3

Figure 197 Marble tombstone of the doctor Jason, from Athens, early 2nd century AD. British Museum, Cat. no. 6.4

retrograde, HEROPHILI. When used as a seal the impression would thus have read from left to right HEROPHILI OPOBALSAMVM.

The words *Herophili opobalsamum* relate directly to the treatment of eye ailments. The second word of the inscription, *opobalsamum*, was a *collyrium* made from the valuable and celebrated resin of the balsam tree ('balsam of Mecca'). It was widely and enduringly recommended as an eye-salve in medical texts and on collyrium-stamps, where its uses included the treatment of poor vision and cataract (e.g. Celsus, *On Medicine* 6.6.34; Galen, *Compound Drugs Arranged by Place* 4.8 (12.781K); Voinot 1999, nos 64 and 192; Pardon-Labonnelie 2006, 45).

The blenders (*auctores*) of *collyria*, like other medical personnel, sometimes adopted a name which might give them added authority as a medical practitioner. Such names were selected from the most prestigious medical men of the past, like one Herasistratus recorded on a collyrium-stamp (Voinot 1999, no. 85), and this is likely to apply to this sealstone. For the first word of the inscription, the name Herophilus, was, most famously, that of the great anatomist, Herophilus of Chalcedon, who, in the first half of the 3rd century BC made astonishing medical advances in Hellenistic Alexandria. These included a new understanding and sophisticated description of the anatomy of the eye, amongst other things revealing the optic nerves and tracing their route from the brain to the eyes. He also wrote a specific treatise 'On Eyes', unfortunately no longer extant. His ground-breaking anatomical discoveries and ophthalmological work were of considerable influence on and through subsequent Greek and Roman medical writers up to and beyond the Byzantine era, and *opobalsamum* was frequently cited in the Herophilean ophthalmological tradition (von Staden 1989, 583–4; Jackson 1996a, 2235–7; Nutton 2004, 128–33).

In addition to the specific link between the famous medical authority Herophilus and the celebrated *collyrium opobalsamum* another feature of the sealstone evokes eye medicine, namely the intense eye contact between Athena and the mask: eyes are the focus of the engraved scene (Dasen 2011a, 72). Taken in combination these three aspects make a convincing case for regarding the gem as the seal of a medical practitioner, perhaps a specialist in eye medicine, who may have used it to mark sticks of *collyria*, whether or not he himself had assumed the name of the great Herophilus.

1st/3rd century AD.

C.W. King, *Antique Gems and Rings* II (London, 1872), 20; A.H. Smith, *A Catalogue of Engraved Gems in the British Museum (Department of Greek and Roman Antiquities)* (London, 1888),100, no. 670; Gems catalogue, 1366.

6.4. Tombstone of the doctor Jason (1865,0103.3 Pourtalès Collection) (Fig. 197)

From Athens.

Height 85cm; width 57cm; thickness 8.9cm

The tombstone was discovered in Athens by the French Consul Louis François Sébastien Fauvel (1753–1838) and obtained by him for the collection of Marie-Gabriel Florent Auguste de Choiseul-Gouffier (1752–1817), French ambassador to the Ottoman Empire from 1784 to 1792. After his death and the sale of his collection the tombstone (Dubois 1818, no. 156) passed into the collection of Comte James Alexandre de Pourtalès-Gorgier (1776–1855) (Panofka 1834, 78, pl. 26). Following Pourtalès' death his collection was sold at auction in Paris in 1865, when the Jason tombstone was one of the pieces purchased by the British Museum.

The marble tombstone commemorates an Athenian doctor called Jason. It has a five-line Greek inscription on the base and a series of mock architectural antefixes on the top. The well-known – and near-unique – relief scene in the centre shows a seated doctor examining a standing male patient. The doctor, either in accordance with his status or perhaps simply adapted to the available space on the tombstone, is rendered disproportionately large in comparison to the patient. He is bearded and draped in the manner of a philosopher and sits on a cushioned stool, while the patient stands naked before him. Because of his relatively diminutive size the patient has often been referred to as a boy or child (e.g. Phillips 1973, pl. 9). However, close examination reveals that he, also, is bearded and should be regarded as an adult. On the ground to the left of the patient is a prominent object immediately recognisable as an inverted cupping vessel, though of unrealistically large size.

The inscription begins: Ἰάσων ὁ καί Δέκμος Ἀχαρνεύς ιατρός, 'Jason, also known as Decimus, of the Acharnian deme, a physician' and continues, on lines 4–5, with a detailed genealogy of Jason's family (*IG* III, 1445; *CIG* 606; Hicks 1874, 141–2, no. 81).

The scene (the principal part of which is closely similar to that on engraved gem Cat. no. 6.5) was carefully chosen and skilfully composed to show, with great clarity, the archetypal image of a doctor at work, examining his patient. He does so in a calm and unhurried manner, in accordance with the contemporary medical writings on ethics and etiquette (e.g. Hippocrates, *In the Surgery* 3, 17–21; Celsus, *On Medicine* 3, 6,6; Rufus of Ephesus, *Medical Questions*; Krug 1985, 212; Jackson 1988, 68–9; Hillert 1990, 125–8; Nutton 2004, 209–10). The sculptor has very successfully captured the tension in the eye contact between the two individuals (**Fig. 198**): it is an anxious time for the patient, who seeks reassurance in the face of the doctor, while the doctor looks intently into the eyes of the patient. For this is a two-way process, and the doctor, who used all his senses in gathering tell-tale signs and symptoms from which to make a diagnosis and prognosis of the patient's condition, anticipated and sought meaningful signs above all in the face and especially the eyes, at that time regarded as the mirror of the soul and most sensitive indicator of physical and mental health (e.g. Hippocrates, *Prognosis*; Celsus, *On Medicine* 2, 6, 1–4; Galen, *On Affected Parts* 4, 2 (8.223K); *On the Method of Healing for Glaucon* 1, 2 (11.12K); Garcia-Ballester 1981; 1994).

Some have thought to discern in the patient signs of his condition or symptoms of a particular disease and various theories have been put forward (e.g. Grmek and Gourevitch 1998, 185–6, 355). Two things in particular have caused speculation: the perception that his ribs are protruding, and also that he has an abnormally swollen belly, leading to suggestions of malnutrition (e.g. Scarborough 1969, pl. 37) and malaria. However, retrospective diagnosis is a risky business and photographs can be misleading: while his swollen abdomen is evident enough, close inspection of the relief reveals that the perceived 'protruding ribs', visible only on the patient's left side, were almost certainly intended as the fingers of the doctor's left hand stabilising the side of the patient as he

Figure 198 Detail of doctor and patient on the tombstone of Jason (Cat. no. 6.4). Photo: Ralph Jackson

palpates the abdomen with his right hand (**Fig. 198**). What is clear is that the patient has been shown with a disproportionate and mal-formed physiology (Hillert 1990, 126).

The distinctive form of the cupping vessel – domed body, suspension loop, carinated shoulder, flared mouth and rolled rim – corresponds precisely to surviving examples of copper alloy, as, for example, Cat. no. 3.49 from Corfu, three in a contemporary surgeon's grave at Bingen, Germany (Künzl 1983a, 80–5) and one in the mid-2nd to early 3rd-century AD Nea Paphos assemblage (Michaelides 1984, fig. 2, no. 3). Whether for extracting 'vicious humours' through the pores of the skin or for speeding up the letting of blood, the suction cup, of bronze or glass, was both the epitomy of humoral pathology and quintessentially the utensil of Greco-Roman healers. Thus, it was effectively their 'badge of office', as was surely intended by the sculptor who carved this eye-catching example – if any ancient viewer failed to recognise the medical nature of the main scene and did not, or was unable to, read the epitaph then the cupping vessel alone was sufficient to show the profession of the dead man.

It seems probable, therefore, that the intention of those who commissioned the sculptor was simply to depict the attentive doctor Jason in that most characteristic of poses, examining an obviously unwell patient, while the inclusion of the image of the cupping vessel, which underlined Jason's role as a healer, was likely also intended as a clear indication of the humoral therapy that awaited the patient.

Early 2nd century AD.

Sculpture catalogue, 629, Hicks 1874, 81, Mould 671; *Guide to Greek and Roman Life* 1908, 180–1, fig. 190; Hillert 1990, no. 18; von Moock 1998, no. 445; Samama 2003, 19; Jackson 2014c, 345–6, no. 219.

6.5. Engraved gem showing a medical examination (1912,0311.1) (Fig. 199a–b)

Provenance unknown. The gem was auctioned in 1911 and purchased by the British Museum in 1912.
Width 21mm; height 13 mm
Carnelian. A long oval translucent orange gem, its edges chipped, especially at top left, set in a modern gold ring.

Figure 199a–b a) (left) Engraved carnelian gem, showing a doctor examining a patient observed by Asklepios, 1st/2nd century AD; b) (above) impression of the gem, British Museum, Cat. no. 6.5

Figure 200 Wooden ink writing-tablet recording a hospital (*valetudinarium*), from Vindolanda Roman fort. *c.* AD 92–115. British Museum, Cat. no. 6.6

The gem is engraved with a scene of medical examination closely similar to that on the tombstone of Jason (Cat. no. 6.4). At right (reversed in impression) is a seated physician of mature years, perhaps intended to represent Hippocrates, or a healer in the guise of Hippocrates. He has full hair, a beard and a moustache and sits on an elegant and well-cushioned chair. He extends both arms to examine the central figure, a standing male patient. The patient, probably intended to represent a young man, is un-bearded and naked and meets the gaze of the physician. A space separates them from the third figure, the god Asklepios, who stands at left, observing the proceedings. He, too, is shown as a bearded, mature figure. He leans on his most distinctive attribute and symbol of his miraculous powers, the snake-entwined staff. Both healer and god wear shoulder-slung drapery, which reveals the powerful physique and musculature of their naked torsos – as befits those who would bring others back to health – and contrasts with that of the patient, who is ill-proportioned with a swollen abdomen.

The miniature scene on this gem is likely to have evoked many visual messages. Above all, and at the forefront, is the close and critical relationship between healer and patient, like that shown also on the Jason tombstone, which chimes both with the advice of Celsus (*On Medicine* 3.6.6) and with the Hippocratic writings on medical etiquette (*The Physician*; *The Oath*). But the gem has an added dimension in the presence of Asklepios, who was needed in equal measure both by the patient and the physician. While the physician might use all his experience and senses as he palpates the patient's abdomen, and the patient himself might do all he could to combat his disease, the divine powers of Asklepios could be considered critical to a successful outcome. Just as the scene on the tombstone illustrated Jason's role as a doctor, the scene on this gem, too, shows a doctor at work. It seems probable, therefore, that the gem belonged to, and was the seal of, a medical practitioner.

1st/2nd century AD.

Gems catalogue, 2176; Richter 1971, 76, no. 362; Krug 1982; Wickkiser 2008, 53–8, fig. 3.4; Jackson 2014c, 263–4, no. 128.

6.6. Wooden ink writing-tablet recording a hospital (1980,0303.1) (Fig. 200)

From excavations at the Roman fort site of Vindolanda, Chesterholm, Northumberland. From location II, layer 10. Inv. no. 195 and 198.

93 × 77mm and 33 × 22mm.

This tablet was an official document, probably part of a list of military fatigues (duties). Unfortunately, it is extremely fragmentary, so that the reading is no more than a string of fractured phrases and words: '*vii Kalendas Maias fabricis hominess cccxxxxiii ex eis sutores xii structores ad balneum xviii ad plumbum ... ad ... ar...a... valetudinar... ad furnaces ... ad lutum ... tectores ...* ' etc. which translates '25 April, in the workshops, 343 men: of these: shoemakers, 12; builders to the bath-house 18; for lead ...; for ... wagons (?) ...; ... hospital (*valetudinarium*); to the kilns ...; for clay ...; plasterers ...' etc.

All that can really be deduced from this is that there was a hospital building at Vindolanda, and its appearance in this list implies that a number of soldiers were sent there to carry out a duty. This could have been construction work,

Figure 201 Wooden ink writing-tablet recording a doctor named Marcus, from Vindolanda Roman fort, *c.* AD 92–115. British Museum, Cat. no. 6.7

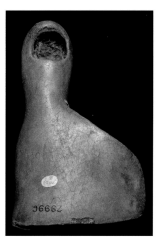 

Figure 202a–b A prosthetic toe made from cartonnage: a) (left) top b) (right) underside, said to be from Thebes, Egypt, before 600 BC. British Museum, Cat. no. 6.9

maintenance tasks or, slightly less likely in the context of the list, assistance for the medical personnel of the hospital. Interestingly, subsequent to the discovery of this tablet a bath-house was found at Vindolanda, so a hospital building might yet be identified at the fort.

Excavation context Period 3: *c.* AD 92–115.

Tab. Vindol. II, 155; Bowman and Thomas 1994, 98–100.

6.7. Wooden ink writing-tablet recording Marcus the doctor (1986,1001,223) (Fig. 201)

From excavations at the Roman fort site of Vindolanda, Chesterholm, Northumberland. From VIA (*praetorium* yard). Inv. no. 85.248.

96 × 30 mm

This tablet, another list of military fatigues (duties), includes the lines '*missi ad hospitium cum Marco medico faciendum structores numero xxx*', which translates 'sent with Marcus, the doctor (*medicus*), 30 builders to build the residence'.

Marcus, who would have had officer status, was evidently in charge of a detachment rather than, on that occasion, fulfilling a medical role. Unfortunately, the precise function of the residence is not given. It may have been an officer's house or a residence for guests.

Excavation context Period 3: *c.* AD 92–115.

Tab. Vindol. II, 156; Bowman and Thomas 1994, 100–1.

6.8. Wooden ink writing-tablet recording Vitalis the pharmacist (1995,0701.306)

From excavations at the Roman fort site of Vindolanda, Chesterholm, Northumberland. From SG (bonfire site). Inv. no. 93.1495.

88 × 63mm

This account of commodities, both dispensed and received, includes the entry '…. *Vitali seplasiario halicae modios v siliginis modium i …*', translating 'To Vitalis, pharmacist (*seplasiarius*), 5 modii of gruel and one modius of soft wheat'. Whether the gruel and wheat were for his own consumption or to be used as components of a remedy is unknown.

Excavation context Period 3: *c.* AD 92–115.

Tab. Vindol. III, 586; Bowman and Thomas 2003, 37–9, pl. 5.

Patients and their afflictions

6.9. A prosthetic toe (1881,0614.77 EA29996) (Fig. 202a–b)

From Egypt, said to be from Thebes.

Length 118mm; width 69mm; weight 44g

This ancient Egyptian artificial toe is made from cartonnage – linen impregnated with animal glue and gesso.

With its relatively light weight and smooth, tan-coloured, painted outer surface its appearance is comparable to pre-modern artificial limbs. It was designed to compensate for the loss of the big toe on a male right foot, and was said to have been found with a mummy. It is of sophisticated manufacture and was evidently originally intended for both utility and appearance – there is wear on the end of the toe, while the toe nail, now lacking, was an inlay, perhaps faience, glued in place. When the prosthesis was in use, in life, it was secured in position on a sandal and given the necessary flexibility by means of laces in eight holes along the long free edge and four holes in the shorter free edge. After death, and as part of the mummification process, the lacing requirement changed and the holes in the shorter edge were filled. Although the artefact is without context and only poorly provenanced, the specific manner of manufacture of the linen cloth, which preceded the introduction of 'draft-spun' yarns, indicates that the prosthesis was made before 600 BC (Reeves 1999).

This toe is one of the earliest surviving working prostheses from the ancient world. Another toe prosthesis, a female right big toe, from a tomb in the Thebes-West necropolis, has been dated to the 21st–22nd dynasty (*c.* 1065–740 BC). The Thebes-West prosthesis was still attached to the mummified corpse, which allowed extensive palaeopathalogical examination demonstrating that the prosthesis had been made subsequent to the amputation of the toe (Nerlich *et al.* 2000). As the big toe usually bears about 40% of walking weight, the need for replacement is clear enough. Also clear is the ability at this period for finely crafted functioning replacements to be made.

New Kingdom, before 600 BC.

Reeves 1999; Falder *et al.* 2003; Strudwick 2006, 268.

6.10. Figurine showing the impact of disease (1814,0704.277 Townley Collection) (Fig. 203)

Provenance unknown.

Height 101.6mm

An ivory figure of a huddled, hunch-backed man, naked and with close-cropped hair, seated on a circular plinth. The figure depicts with great clarity a gross spinal deformity, perhaps tuberculous osteomyelitis of the spine (Pott's

Figure 203 Ivory figurine depicting a man with a gross spinal deformity, 1st century BC. British Museum, Cat. no. 6.10

Figure 204a–b Pottery lamp with an enigmatic scene on the discus, perhaps intended as a satirical representation of surgery, c. AD 40/75. British Museum, Cat. no. 6.11

disease). The upper part of the vertebral column is the commonest site for tuberculous bone infection and the angular distortion and asymmetric 'pigeon-chest' are characteristic changes of the disease. As skilfully captured as the pathology is the careworn, melancholy expression of the man. It is an intensely moving sculpture and was intended to be so, an example of the move away from idealisation towards realism in Hellenistic art, and the attempt to communicate both the physical and emotional state of individuals.

Hellenistic, perhaps made in Alexandria in the 1st century BC.

Grmek and Gourevitch 1998, 211–12.

6.11. Lamp showing surgery satirised? (1814,0704.34 Townley Collection) (Fig. 204a–b)

Provenance unknown.

Length 106mm

A mould-made pottery lamp (Loeschke Type IV, with IIIa shoulder form) with finger-marked brown slip, voluted nozzle (tip missing) and an air-hole on the discus between the nozzle volutes. Parts of the left and lower right sides are missing.

The unusual and distinctive scene on the discus may have been intended as a satirical representation of surgery and medical practitioners in general, or of circumcision in particular, as depicted in a stage comedy. In Bailey's description (Lamps catalogue II, 163–4):

> a bearded man, seated … with his clothing drawn to one side, exposing his lower body, looks with well-founded apprehension as his penis, resting on an anvil, is gripped by a pair of forceps. The forceps are wielded by a bald-headed, bearded man, who … is draped about the lower limbs … The burlesque character of the scene is emphasized by a large hammer awaiting use below the block.

There are a number of possible witty conflations, not least the ambivalence in the appearance of the operator, who may be both the great healer Hippocrates and the lame smith-god Hephaestus/Vulcan, while the forceps (or shears) could be identified just as well as blacksmith's tongs and the operation easily (and perhaps deliberately) confused with castration. The conflation, confusion or at least association of castration and circumcision was not purely popular: Antoninus Pius' edict restricting circumcision was essentially an extension of the ban on castration, and in the legal texts the penalties were often the same for both (Modestinus, *Digest* 48.8.11; Robinson 1995, 51–3).

In view of the date of manufacture of the lamp it is further possible that it was in some way linked to a near-contemporary event, the vicious conflict between the Jewish and Greek communities in Alexandria in AD 38 (Josephus, *Antiquities of the Jews* 18.257; Philo of Alexandria, *Flaccus* and *On the Embassy to Gaius*; Schäfer 1997, 136–60). Tension between the two groups and the native Egyptians was longstanding, but in AD 38, as a result of inept political manoeuvring by the Roman prefect A. Avilius Flaccus, hostility turned to violent persecution in which many Jews were massacred. Subsequently, in AD 40, a delegation of Alexandrian Greeks was sent to Rome.

Figure 205a–b Wooden ink writing-tablet – a regimental strength report, from Vindolanda Roman fort: a) (top) the whole strength report; b) (bottom) detail of the entry for those unfit for service – *aegri*, *volnerati* and *lippientes*, *c*. AD 85–92. British Museum, Cat. no. 6.12

Figure 206 Wooden ink writing-tablet recording remedies, from Vindolanda Roman fort, *c*. AD 92–115. British Museum, Cat. no. 6.13

Made in Italy, *c*. AD 40–75.

Lamps catalogue II, 163–4, figs 66, 112, pl. 12, Q875; Scarborough 1969, pl. 11; Jackson 2005c, 25.

Broken examples can be hard to interpret, and a discus fragment of this type from Nin, Croatia has been erroneously identified as a scene of childbirth (Grmek and Gourevitch 1998, 314–15, fig. 249).

6.12. Wooden ink writing-tablet recording patients (1989,0602.21) (Fig. 205a–b)

From excavations at the Roman fort site of Vindolanda, Chesterholm, Northumberland. From ditch of first fort. Inv. no. 88.841.

86 × 394mm

This tablet, one of the most important military documents from Vindolanda, is a strength report of one of the units that garrisoned the fort, the First Cohort of Tungrians. The text is in three parts, starting with the date, the name of the unit, the name of its commanding officer and the total strength of the unit. Next, those absent on detached duties are listed and totals of those *absentes* and the remaining *praesentes* given. Finally the number of *praesentes* unfit for active service is recorded, followed by the total of the *praesentes* available for active service.

It is instructive to see that the patients – those soldiers unfit for active service – are divided into three categories: 15 were sick (*aegri*), 6 were wounded (*uolnerati*), and 10 were suffering from eye disease (*lippientes*). The division between the sick and those with eye disease may have been more than a paper exercise, for the eye disease was *lippitudinis* – ophthalmia – which included the highly contagious infection conjunctivitis (see p. 82). To avoid a mass outbreak of bleary-eyed soldiers in the garrison the fort commander and his medical staff may well have taken the decision physically to segregate the *lippientes* both from the healthy and from the other sick soldiers in different parts of whatever building was fulfilling the function of a hospital (*valetudinarium*).

Excavation context Period I: *c*. AD 85–92.

Tab. Vindol. II, 154; Bowman and Thomas 1994, 90–8, pl. 5; Jackson 1990a, 13.

Figure 207 Marble thank-offering to Asklepios and Hygieia, from Melos, Greece, 2nd century AD. British Museum, Cat. no. 6.14

6.13. Wooden ink writing-tablet recording remedies (1986,1001.63) (Fig. 206)

From excavations at the Roman fort site of Vindolanda, Chesterholm, Northumberland. From VIA (*praetorium* yard). Inv. no. 85.056a.

65 × 65mm

This tablet is a personal letter from a woman, probably called Paterna, to Sulpicia Lepidina, wife of Flavius Cerealis, a commander of the fort at Vindolanda. Its content, like that of Lepidina's other correspondence (including the famous 'birthday invitation') with Claudia Severa, the wife of another fort commander, Aelius Brocchus, is social and intimate and sheds a little light on the family life of literate women of the equestrian officer class. The letter includes a reference to remedies, including one probably for fever. The relevant section reads: '*ut ego duas an(tidotos) ... feram tibi alteram ... alteram febric ...*', translating 'I shall bring (?) you two remedies (?), the one for ..., the other for fever (?) ...'.

Excavation context Period 3: *c.* AD 92–115.

Tab. Vindol. II, 294; Bowman and Thomas 1994, 263–5, pl. 19.

6.14. Marble thank-offering for a divinely healed leg (1867,0508.117 Blacas Collection) (Fig. 207)

From Melos, Cyclades, Greece, formerly in the Collection of Louis Charles Pierre Casimir de Blacas d'Aulps, 2nd Duke of Blacas (1815–1866). Found in 1828 buried in a cave together with a colossal marble head of Asklepios (Cat. no. 6.38) and a number of other votive offerings relating to the cult of Asklepios and Hygieia.

Height 30.4cm; width 20.3cm; thickness 3cm.

A rectangular slab of medium-grained white marble with grey streaks, showing the lower part of a left leg carefully modelled in relief with an adjacent seven-line inscription in Greek. There is damage to the upper right and lower left corners, to the toes and to the upper edge of the leg, but the relief is otherwise in good condition and its front surface retains the original polish. As observed (Higgs 2014, 230), the lack of weathering indicates that the relief was originally displayed in an interior or sheltered setting. With its soft flesh and understated musculature the leg, which terminates just above the knee, was perhaps intended as female rather than male. No pathology is visible. Although it may originally have been painted on, it is more likely that it was not depicted. For the all-seeing deities would have known the nature of the disorder when a cure was sought, and, in any case, as a thank-offering, the leg, logically, would have been shown restored to its normal form.

The inscription, which has been re-coloured at some point since discovery of the relief, is incised in Greek capitals on seven short lines neatly accommodated to the space provided to the left of the leg. It reads: ΑΣΚΛΗ/ΠΙΩ/ΚΑΙ/ ΫΓΕΙΑ/ΤΥΧΗ/ΕΥΧΑΡΙΣ/ΤΗΡΙΟΝ, that is Ἀσκλη-/πιώ/ καί/Ὑγεία/Τύχη/εὐχαρισ-/τήριου, which is susceptible to two alternate translations, either '*Tyche (*dedicated this*) to Asklepios and Hygieia as a thank-offering*' (Cook 1987, 21; Forsén 1996, 103), or '*To Asklepios and Hygieia Tyche* (luck or good fortune) *as a thank-offering*' (Higgs 2014, 231).

2nd century AD.

Sculpture catalogue, 809, Inscription 365; Higgs 2014.

6.15a–f. Terracotta anatomical votives – body parts in need of a cure (Fig. 208a–c)

(a) ear, 1865,1118.135, length 50.8mm

(b) eye, 1865,1118.129, length 63.5mm

(c) breast, 1839,0214.54, diameter 101.6mm

(d) womb, 1865,1118.119, length 177.8mm

(e) male genitals, 1865,1118.104, length 129.5mm

(f) internal organs, 1839,0214.52, width 179mm

4th–1st century BC.

This selection of unprovenanced terracotta model body parts is, together with heads, hands, feet and limbs, typical of the range found in votive deposits at temples and sanctuaries in Magna Graecia and Republican Italy, especially Etruria and Latium, from the 4th–1st century BC. Clay was inexpensive so these often mass-produced objects, probably available at stalls adjacent to religious sanctuaries, were within the reach of most suppliants. As such, they offer a fascinating glimpse of individual and personal reactions to disease, albeit the pathology is rarely depicted. Sadly, too, the terracotta anatomical votives, unlike some of those of metal and marble, lack accompanying inscriptions with the names of suppliants and their afflictions, and even the deity to whom they were dedicated is seldom known. Like the marble leg, Cat. no. 6.14, some were doubtless dedicated to a deity as thank-offerings in fulfilment of a vow for the restoration of health to an affected part. Others, though, were probably dedicated as part of the initial approach, when the attention of the deity was drawn to the body part in need of divine powers. Additionally, it is possible that the purpose of many ear and eye models was to get the deity to hear the suppliant's prayer or see the part or parts of the body in need of attention rather than to represent specific

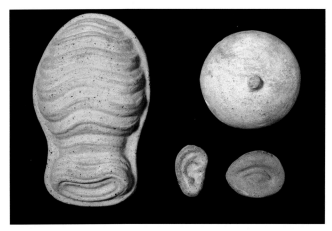

Figure 208 Terracotta model body parts dedicated at temples in the hope of, or in thanks for, divine attention, 4th/1st century BC. British Museum, Cat. no. 6.15a–f

Figure 209 Gold coin of the emperor Caracalla, commemorating his attendance at the Asklepian healing sanctuary in Pergamon, minted in Rome, AD 215. British Museum, Cat. no. 6.16

ear and eye complaints. Similarly, the dedication of reproductive organs might have been intended to focus attention on diseased parts but could equally well have been to seek aid with fertility or to give thanks for childbirth. So, the anatomical votives are an intriguing class of evidence for health and disease, but one that is open to many interpretations. At the very least, though, they provide vivid testimony of the importance and popularity of religious belief in the maintenance and restoration of health alongside the measures and treatments of mortal medical practitioners (see, e.g., Krug 1985, 31–6; Jackson 1988, 157–64; Deyts 1983; Deyts 1994; Draycott and Graham 2016; Hughes 2021).

6.16. Coin of an ailing emperor (1844,1015.239) (Fig. 209)
Minted in Rome.
Diameter 21mm; weight 7.31g

A gold *aureus* with, on the obverse, the laureate and bearded bust of the emperor Caracalla, to right, inscribed ANTONINVS PIVS AVG GERM. At the centre of the scene on the reverse Asklepios stands before his temple, his head facing right, his right hand on his serpent-entwined staff, a young servant depicted behind him with a staff over his right shoulder. On the right a toga-clad figure accompanies the emperor, who is in military dress and pours a libation over a garlanded and lighted altar. The inscription reads P M TR P XVIII COS IIII P P.

In the hope of divine relief, the emperor Caracalla (AD 198–217), suffering from chronic ill-health – both physical and mental disorders – embarked on an extended, Empire-wide tour of healing shrines in AD 213–15. His pilgrimage included the sanctuaries of Apollo Grannus in southern Germany and Sarapis in Alexandria. This coin illustrates his visit to the pre-eminent Asklepian healing sanctuary at Pergamon and was issued in commemoration the following year. Despite his personal attendance at the shrines, his lavish benefactions, and the earlier prayers and sacrifices made on his behalf, a cure proved elusive, according to Cassius Dio (Cassius Dio, *History* 77.15.3–7; Herodian, *History* 4.8.3; Engelmann *et al.* 1980, no. 802; Nutton 2004, 275).

AD 215.

Mattingly 1975, 458, no. 148; Carson 1980, no. 723; Penn 1994, 113, fig. 81; Stampolidis and Tassoulas 2014, 171, no. 53.

Fertility and childbirth

6.17. Figure showing a scene of childbirth? (1855,1101.26) (Fig. 210a–b)
Said to be from Idalion, Larnaka, Cyprus.
Height 150mm; length 220mm

A carved limestone figure showing a thickly upholstered bed on which a woman lies outstretched on her back with her legs akimbo. The head of a second woman is visible between her feet.

It is just possible that this rather enigmatic scene depicts childbirth. However, it is rather different in its arrangement both to the earlier (6th century BC) terracotta childbirth groups from a cave assemblage near Lapithos and from other sites in Cyprus (Alphos 2014, 267–9, nos 132–3) and to the much later celebrated childbirth scene from Tomb 100 in the Porto necropolis on the Isola Sacra at Ostia (**Fig. 211**) (Krug 1985, 195–7, fig 88; Jackson 1988, 97–9, fig. 24; Künzl 2002b, 98–9, figs 142–4; Hanson 2006, 503–4, fig. 25; Künzl

Figure 210a–b Limestone figurine, possibly showing a scene of childbirth, said to be from Idalion, Cyprus, 3rd century BC. British Museum, Cat. no. 6.17

2013, 75–7, figs 23–5; Olivanti 2014, 269–70; Verbanck-Pierard *et al.* 2018, 307–8). That 2nd-century AD terracotta relief, on the tomb of the midwife Scribonia Attice, shows her in the midst of delivering a woman seated on a birthing chair with a female assistant or relative standing behind and restraining her. Scribonia herself, wearing a simple tunic with bare arms, sits on a low stool in front of the labouring woman. The scene corresponds closely to near-contemporary passages in Soranus (who wrote the most substantial surviving treatise on obstetrics and gynaecology) and Galen, in which it was regarded as normal practice for a woman to be delivered in her home, to start her labour lying down in bed and, towards the end, to get up and sit on the birthing chair, which was part of the midwife's equipment

Figure 212 Black-gloss pottery vessel, perhaps a baby-feeder, from southern Italy, 4th century BC. British Museum, Cat. no. 6.18

Figure 211 Terracotta tomb relief, showing the midwife Scribonia Attice delivering a woman on a birthing chair, from Isola Sacra, Ostia, Tomb 100, mid-2nd century AD. Museo Archeologico, Ostia Antica, inv. 5203. Photo © Archivio Fotografico Parco archeologico di Ostia antica

and could be adapted to women of different sizes (Soranus, *Gynaecology* 2.2–3, 2.5–6; Galen, *On the Natural Faculties* 3.3). Only in difficult labour was the foetus to be extracted with the woman lying down.

The medically recommended manner of delivery described and depicted in some detail in the 2nd century AD was most unlikely to have been followed universally even at that time, and simpler childbirth processes naturally would have occurred quite frequently, especially where midwives and medical personnel were lacking. Thus, although the Idalion scene differs from that of the Ostia relief, it is several hundred years older, and a stylised scene of childbirth, perhaps at an early stage of labour, is probably the best explanation of the imagery.

3rd century BC.

Sculpture C412; V. Karageorghis, *Aspects of Everyday Life in Ancient Cyprus. Iconographic Representations* (Nicosia, 2006), 219, no. 218, fig. 234; A. Dierichs, *Von der Götter Geburt und der Frauen Niederkunft* (Mainz, 2002), 86–7, fig. 48.

6.18. Baby-feeder? (1836,0224.262) **(Fig. 212)**
From southern Italy (Magna Graecia).
Height 88.9mm; length 190.5mm

A boat-shaped black-gloss pottery vessel, with a plinth-like stand on the base, a circular mouth with flared rim at top centre, an upturned circular drinking spout at one end, and a looped handle on one side. On the other side is an inscription in Greek, incised, after firing, with a fine-pointed implement. It reads ΓΡΟΠΙΝΕΜΗΚΑΤΘΗΙΣ – 'Drink, don't drop'.

Maternal breast-feeding must have been the norm for most mothers in antiquity. It was favoured by Soranus, though he believed it should not begin until three weeks after the birth when the mother's bodily health would be restored and she could produce wholesome milk. Meanwhile a wet-nurse (*nutrix*) was to be employed and, in some cases, retained for the whole period of breast-feeding, normally between 18 months and 2 years (Soranus, *Gynaecology* 2.18, 38, 40). Contracts, some of them quite exacting, for the hiring of wet-nurses have survived from Roman Egypt, while reliefs on the side of a tombstone show the *nutrix*

Severina suckling and swaddling an infant in her care (Bradley 1986; Jackson 1988, 100–3, fig. 25; Künzl 2002b, 95–6, figs 135–6).

A number of similar types of glass and pottery vessels, provided with a small opening at the top and a fine spout at the side, have been postulated as baby-feeders, and they have been found quite frequently in infant burials. Suggested alternative uses include oil-fillers for lamps or feeding-vessels for the sick. Although none has provided firm evidence that they once contained milk, experimentation with a replica vessel has shown that they can be used effectively by a lactating woman who presses the top opening over her nipple and expresses and collects her breast milk by sucking the spout (Gourevitch 1991; Rouquet 2003).

4th century BC.

Vases catalogue, F596.

6.19. Uterine amulet (1986,0501.32) (Fig. 213a–b)

Provenance unknown.

Height 16mm; width 13.5mm; thickness 3mm

An oval magical gem made of haematite, with a bevelled edge on the reverse face.

The engraved scene on the obverse shows a naked pregnant woman squatting over a birthing chair with arm rests which end in an animal head, possibly a ram's head. The woman's hands are clasped above her head and her long hair falls on her shoulders. Below the woman is a womb symbol with a seven-bitted key with an adjacent Greek inscription, and the scene is encircled by an *ouroboros*. The inscription reads IAW/IAW = Iaô Iaô and OPOPIOYΘ ... ΘIPΔI (?) = Orôriouth.

The reverse face is engraved with the image of an octopus-like womb with a surrounding Greek inscription which reads, from top right, OPWPIOYΘAEHIOYW = Orôriouth.

From the time of the earliest Greek medical writers the womb was likened to an upside down pot or to the gourd shape of a cupping vessel, with a broad bulbous body, narrow neck and flared mouth, its size determining the size of the child. It was believed that it opened and closed periodically – opening for menstruation and for the reception of seed, closing for the retention of seed and nurturing of the growing foetus, and opening again at birth. The key on this and many other uterine amulets symbolised control over that process, which was to be vouchsafed through the divine power of the amulet, ensuring that the mouth of the womb opened and closed at the proper time. Magical power also resided in the gemstone itself, for the majority of uterine gemstones were made of the mineral form of iron oxide, haematite – a Greek word meaning bloodstone – which was believed to control blood flows. Further protection was provided against any malevolent force threatening the womb, in the form of the encircling *ouroboros*, an Egyptian image of a snake consuming its own tail. The word Orôriouth is commonly found on the reverse of the uterine amulets, in the present instance on the obverse, too. It is not a Greek word and there is no consensus as to its exact meaning, but it is regarded most probably as the name of a demon who controlled the womb or as a word or epithet of the womb itself.

Figure 213a–b A haematite uterine amulet, engraved on both faces with magical words and images, Eastern Mediterranean, 3rd century AD. British Museum, Cat. no. 6.19

Like the childbirth amulet (Cat. no. 6.20) the haematite uterine amulets were probably quite costly, and therefore most likely to be the possessions of relatively wealthy women. They demonstrate that belief in the power of magic permeated all levels of society: not unreasonably, in an uncertain world amulets may often have been perceived to be as effective as what might otherwise be thought of as more rational health-maintaining methods. For haematite uterine amulets see e.g. Kotansky 1991; Hanson 1995; Faraone 2011a; Faraone 2011b, 56–7; Dasen 2018. See also Hanson 2006, 517–19; Dasen 2015; Faraone 2018.

3rd century AD. Eastern Mediterranean.

Michel 2001, no.387.

6.20. Childbirth amulet (2009,8042.1) (Fig. 214)

From Cholsey, Oxfordshire. A metal-detector find from a possible Roman villa site.

Height 63mm; width 28mm; weight 1.49g

A tall rectangular sheet (*lamella*) cut from gold foil and inscribed with 16 lines of text across the short axis. The *lamella* is complete, though with extensive creasing and post-depositional crumpling. Originally it was probably rolled, and contained in a cylindrical amulet case worn close to the body, probably suspended on a cord or chain round the neck. The text is an invocation to deities, a protective magical amulet (phylactery), a charm to ensure safe childbirth for Fabia, daughter of Terentia. Twelve magical characters, perceived as investing the amulet with extra power, occupy the first three lines and are followed by the main text in Greek cursive writing, which translates: 'Make with your holy names that Fabia whom Terentia her mother bore, being in full fitness and health, shall master the unborn child and bring it forth; the name of the Lord and Great God being everlasting' (trans. R.S.O. Tomlin, *Britannia* 40, 2009, 353–4.)

Amulets were widespread and popular, and medical practitioners would have encountered them frequently. Soranus did not reject the use of amulets, for he understood and accepted the psychological benefit they brought to those who believed in them (*Gynaecology* 3.42; Jackson 1988, 88–9).

2nd–3rd century AD.

Tomlin 2008; 2018, 315–16. For other examples of gold *lamellae* see Kotansky 1994.

Figure 214 A charm to ensure safe childbirth, inscribed on a thin sheet of gold foil, from Cholsey, Oxfordshire, 2nd/3rd century AD. British Museum, Cat. no. 6.20

Materia medica

6.21. Silver coin showing a silphium plant (1891,1003.11) (Fig. 215)

Minted in Cyrene, Libya.

Weight 12.8g

A silver *tetradrachm* with, on the obverse, the head of Apollo Carneius, to left, on the reverse, a silphium plant.

Cyrene, founded by settlers from the Greek island of Thera in the 7th century BC (Herodotus, *Histories* 4.150–8), became the pre-eminent Greek colony in Africa under the Battiad kings reaching its zenith in the 5th and 4th centuries BC. Its wealth was based on cereals, vines and olives, but it was especially famous for silphium, a wild plant which grew in the pre-desert margin. Its leaves were a fattening food for cattle and sheep and a rich food-seasoning, but more importantly, its resin was renowned as a cure-all and a contraceptive (Theophrastus, *Enquiry into Plants* 6.3; Dioscorides, *Materials used in Medicine* 3.94; Riddle 1985; Riddle 1992; Riddle *et al.* 1994). In consequence silphium was extremely valuable and much sought after, and the image of the plant was an emblem for Cyrene, appearing on its coinage from the 6th to the 1st century BC. Silphium was governed by a Royal Monopoly, restricting its use, until 96 BC when Ptolemy Apion died and the colony was ceded to Rome. Perhaps because of over-harvesting in the Roman

Figure 215 Silver coin of Cyrene, with the head of Apollo and a silphium plant, minted in Cyrene, Libya, 435–375 BC. British Museum, Cat. no. 6.21

period the plant became extinct, the emperor Nero being presented with the only stick 'found within our memory', according to Pliny (*Natural History* 19.15). Silphium cannot now be identified unequivocally, but it was probably one of the *Ferula* species of giant fennel, similar to *asafoetida*. The twinning of the silphium plant and the head of Apollo Carneius on this coin accords with the legend that silphium was a gift of the paramount healer-deity, Apollo.

435–375 BC.

Robinson 1927, 37, no. 164.

6.22. Papyrus letter regarding drugs (British Library, formerly transferred on loan to the British Museum (GR1907,3–1,3)) (Fig. 216)

Height 193mm; width 103mm

An ink-written letter on a sheet of papyrus, with 18 lines of elegantly formed Greek text. It translates:

> Prokleios to Pekysis, his dear friend, greetings. You will please me, if, at your own risk, you can sell a good-quality drug from your stock, if you have it, so that my friend Sotas can take it to Alexandria. If you do otherwise, giving him a rotten product, it will not pass muster in Alexandria. You will hear from me about the costs. Greetings to all your family. Farewell. (trans. Lucilla Burn)

The letter highlights both the importance of drugs and the problem of drug fraud, together with Alexandria's enduring pre-eminence in medicine (Nutton 1985; Nutton 2004, 41, 172–7; Scarborough 1996). Another Greek text concerning medication has already been mentioned (p. 82), an early 2nd-century AD letter written on a pot-sherd (*ostrakon*) found at Mons Claudianus in the Egyptian desert, from a man named Isidorus to his two sons requesting two sticks of desiccated eye-salve (*O.Claud.* 174; Cuvigny 1992, 161–3). Another *ostrakon*, of the 4th century AD from Thebes, preserved a partial Greek text on both faces, listing the ingredients of two eye-salves, one of which was *dialibanum* – frankincense eye-salve (see Cat. nos 3.132, 3.136, 3.142), the other specified as a *collyrium* for children (Sofroniew 2014). In a fragmentary papyrus letter of the 5th century AD from Hermopolis Magna a patient reproaches his doctor for neglecting him (Verbanck-Pierard 1998, 216–17). Whether on papyrus or *ostraka* these letters, and others like them, preserve the voices of individual people and attest the reality of the ancient medical texts in daily life.

1st century AD.

F.G. Kenyon (ed.) *Greek Papyri in the British Museum Vol. II* (London, 1898; repr. Milan, 1973), Cat. no. 365

6.23. Wooden ink writing-tablet recording medical supplies (1995,0701.152)

From excavations at the Roman fort site of Vindolanda, Chesterholm, Northumberland. From location SG/N. Inv. no. 93.1350.

45 × 80mm and 45 × 80mm.

This tablet is a long, but fragmentary, account, which lists an extensive range of commodities that are almost certainly medical supplies for the fort hospital:

> *anesi ...; nucule ...; uvae ...; siliginis ...; fabae ...; aluminis ...; cerae pondo ...; bitumen pondo ...; glutem taurinam ...; picis pondo ...; atramenti pondo ...; ancusae pondo ...; senapidis pondo ...; aeruginis c...; lini mellari ...; resinae ...; cummini ...;gallae ...*

which translates:

> anise ...; nuts ...; berries ...; soft wheat flour (?) ...; beans ...; alum ...; wax, by weight ...; bitumen, by weight ...; bull's glue ...; pitch, by weight ...; blacking, by weight ...; anchusa, by weight ...; verdigris ...; linen soaked in honey ...; resin ...; cumin ...; oak-gall ...

These commodities, which can be found in various forms in Greek and Roman medical texts, especially in Celsus' *On Medicine*, are very much geared to the treatment of wounds, ulcers and sores (old and chronic wounds, perhaps) and eye diseases. As such, as highlighted by the patients listed in the strength report (Cat. no. 6.12), they would clearly be very appropriate to the needs of the garrison at Vindolanda. Furthermore, some of the commodities correspond to the ingredients for a specific wound treatment recorded by Celsus (*On Medicine* 5.19.9 and 5.26.9) raising the fascinating possibility that his *On Medicine*, or something similar, was among the texts being used by medical personnel at Vindolanda.

Excavation context Period 3: *c.* AD 92–115.

Tab. Vindol. III, 591; Bowman and Thomas 2003, 44–6, pl. 5.

Veterinary medicine

6.24. Wooden ink writing-tablet recording Virilis the vet (1988,1005.66) **(Fig. 217)**

From excavations at the Roman fort site of Vindolanda, Chesterholm, Northumberland. From VIA (*praetorium* yard). Inv. no. 86.470.

189 × 70mm

This complete and well-preserved diptych comprises a letter sent from Chrauttius to Veldedeius while the latter was in London serving as a groom of the governor (*equisio consularis*), perhaps involved in the supply and provision of horses for the army. Veldedeius was probably on detached duty and brought the letter with him on his return to Vindolanda. Amongst Chrauttius' greetings and his enquiries after relatives and friends is mention of a veterinary instrument that one Virilis was supposed to be supplying him with: ' ... greet ... Virilis the veterinary doctor (*veterinarius*). Ask him whether you may send through one of our friends the pair of shears (*forfex*) which he promised me in exchange for money.'

Evidence relating to *veterinarii* is quite scarce so this snippet is significant in revealing something of the reality of their day-to-day practice (Adams 1990; Jackson 2008, 199).

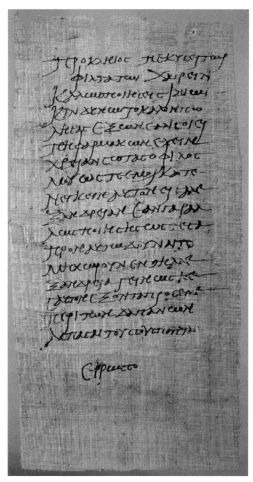

Figure 216 Papyrus letter concerning the supply of drugs, 1st century AD. British Library, Cat. no. 6.22. Photo: British Museum

Excavation context Period 3: *c.* AD 92–115.

Tab. Vindol. II, 310; Bowman and Thomas 1994, 289–94, pls 28 and 29.

6.25. Wooden ink writing-tablet recording Alio the vet (1989,0602.71) **(Fig. 218)**

From excavations at the Roman fort site of Vindolanda, Chesterholm, Northumberland. From room XIV (centurions' rooms). Inv. no. 88.944.

70 × 137mm

This diptych contains a cash account recording sums received and debts outstanding. Amongst those soldiers depositing money were 'Vitalis the bathman (*balniatore*)' and Alio the vet: '*ab Alione ueterinario (denarios) x*' – 'from Alio the veterinary doctor, 10+ *denarii*'.

Whether infantry or part-mounted regiments were in garrison at Vindolanda there would always have been a need for veterinary doctors to care for the horses of cavalry or scouts as well as for transport animals. The mention of a *balniatore* is also a reminder of the importance of baths in maintaining the health of the garrison.

Excavation context Period 4: *c.* AD 92–115.

Tab. Vindol. II, 181; Bowman and Thomas 1994, 129–31, pl. 10.

6.26. Graffito of a Greek vet (1899,1017.1) **(Fig. 219)**

From the River Thames at Amerden, Buckinghamshire. Width 105mm; height 82mm

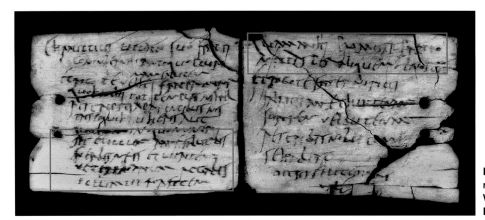

Figure 217 Wooden ink writing-tablet recording a vet named Virilis, from Vindolanda Roman fort, c. AD 92–115. British Museum, Cat. no. 6.24

Figure 218 Wooden ink writing-tablet recording a cash deposit by a vet named Alio, from Vindolanda Roman fort, c. AD 92–115. British Museum, Cat. no. 6.25

Figure 219 Sherd from a Romano-British pot incised with the graffito of a Greek-speaking vet, from the River Thames at Amerden, Buckinghamshire, 1st/4th century AD. British Museum, Cat. no. 6.26

A sherd from the body of a Romano-British dark grey coarse-ware pot, preserving part of a neatly scratched Greek text. Originally comprising at least three lines of writing, the rather enigmatic surviving legible remnant (on the central line) consists only of the latter part of a man's name and a description of his trade:

[...]...[...]

[...]ΜΑΝΤΙΟCΜΥΛΟΦΙCΙ[...]

EP   PΨ

[...]μαντιος μυλοφισι[χος]

EP   PΨ

[...]mantios mulophysi[kos]

'[...]mantius the mule-physician'

Identification of the sherd as of a normal Romano-British coarse-ware (Wright 1977, 280, fn.1) indicates that the pot was not an import and allows us to regard the pot, its contents (perhaps a healing substance) and the *mulophysicus* as part of the evidence for healing in Roman Britain. The word *mulophysicus* is hitherto unattested, but it is likely to equate with *mulomedicus*, the term normally applied to those who ministered to sick animals in the Roman world. Their principal role was the care of transport animals and beasts of burden. As with the healers who treated humans, many 'Roman vets' were Greek, of Greek extraction or Greek speakers. Their surgical instruments and medical equipment have rarely been identified, probably because they differed little (if at all) from the tools of other craftsmen and medical personnel. For veterinary medicine in the Greco-Roman world see, e.g., Walker 1973; Fischer 1981; Fischer 1988; Hyland 1990; Bliquez and Munro 2007; Gitton-Ripoll 2016.

1st/4th century AD.

Roman pottery catalogue, M 2838; Wright 1977; *RIB* II.8, 2503.537.

The healing cult of Asklepios and Hygieia

6.27. Coin from the land of Asklepios and Hippocrates (1866,1201.4268 Given by James Woodhouse, 1866)
(Fig. 220)
Minted in Atrax, Thessaly.
Diameter 13.5mm; weight 2.58g

Bronze coin, with, on the obverse, the laureate head of Apollo to left and, on the reverse, a cupping vessel flanked by a cross-legged forceps and an uncertain object. The distinctive shape of the cupping vessel (similar to Cat. no. 3.49) is clearly and faithfully depicted: a bulbous body,

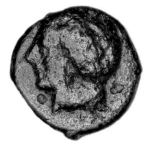

Figure 220 Bronze coin with the head of Apollo, a cupping vessel and a cross-legged forceps, minted in Atrax, Greece, 400–344 BC. British Museum, Cat. no. 6.27

Figure 221 Medallion of the emperor Antoninus Pius, commemorating the arrival of Asklepios in Rome, minted in Rome, AD 140–3. British Museum, Cat. no. 6.28

carinated shoulder, narrow neck, rolled rim and even the suspension ring at the apex of the body.

With the cupping vessel orientated correctly, with the mouth downwards, the forceps is on the right, with its jaws uppermost. The form and proportions of the instrument accord closely to those of a type of iron forceps used for dentistry and bone surgery and, a little less convincingly, to the bronze bivalve instrument used for rectal dilation (see Cat. no. 3.25). Like the cupping vessel the dental/bone forceps was emblematic of ancient medicine, so its identification is more probable than the rectal dilator.

The object to the left of the cupping vessel is less distinct and despite the use of Reflectance Transformation Imaging (RTI) its identity has remained elusive. It does not correspond to any obvious (metal) medical instrument nor does it properly resolve into a human or divine figure or even a snake-entwined staff. It does look rather like a tree or plant, perhaps even a laurel spray to reference Apollo and his healing powers as well as the Delphic oracle. As such it would certainly be a logical choice – drug therapy to complement humoral pathology (the cupping vessel) and surgery (the forceps), all three together representing the principal realms of ancient medicine.

While Thessaly was the legendary birthplace of the paramount healer-deity Asklepios, son of Apollo, Atrax also had a more specific connection to ancient medicine for it was only a few miles distant from Larissa where, according to tradition, the great Hippocrates died in 380 BC. That combination of mortal and divine healers might explain the choice of imagery on this coin that may even have been issued in Hippocrates' lifetime.

400–344 BC.

Gardner and Poole 1883, 14 no. 3.

For another coin with a depiction of a cupping vessel, from Aigiali, Amorgos, of the late 3rd–early 2nd century BC, and references to further examples, from Epidauros and Astakos, see Penn 1994, 141–3; Stampolidis and Tassoulas 2014, 297, no. 166.

6.28. Medallion commemorating the arrival of Asklepios in Rome (1853,0512.238) (Fig. 221)

Minted in Rome

Diameter 38mm; weight 39.4g

Copper-alloy medallion with, on the obverse, the laureate head of Antoninus Pius, to left, inscribed ANTONINVS AVG PIVS PP TR P COS III. The composite scene on the reverse shows at back right the Tiber Island with tree and buildings, at front right the reclining figure of River Tiber facing left to witness at left the arrival of a ship passing under the arch of a bridge with a standing figure at the stern framed by the arch, and a massive sinuous snake, 'centre stage', descending from the ship's prow onto the island. Beneath, in the exergue, the inscription AESCVLAPIVS.

In the 2nd century AD, when this coin was issued, the cult of Asklepios, Roman Aesculapius, was enjoying a renewed vitality, and the priests of the Asklepian sanctuary on Rome's Tiber Island were recording miraculous cures like those inscribed on stelai half a millennium earlier at the great Asklepian sanctuary at Epidauros (see, e.g., Jackson 1988, 11–12, 145–7, 152). The scene on this medallion commemorated the arrival of the cult in Rome in 293 BC, when the city had been held in the grip of plague for three years. Priests consulted the Sybilline Books and determined that the only way to clear the plague was to summon Asklepios from Epidauros. In response to an embassy sent to Epidauros to seek the help of Asklepios, the god made the long sea voyage in the form of a sacred snake. Although Roman suspicion of this foreign deity led to reluctance to accommodate the cult, the snake conveniently disembarked on the Tiber Island, outside the walls of the city, after which the plague abated and the first temple of Asklepios was established at Rome (Ovid, *Metamorphoses* 15.622–744; Krug 1985, 163–5; Nutton 2004, 159–61). In consequence of the mode of arrival of the cult the sides of the Tiber Island were revetted in stone in the form of a galley, a small portion of which still remains in position (Nutton 2004, fig. 11.1).

AD 140–3.

Grueber 1874, 7, no. 4; Stampolidis and Tassoulas 2014, 170–1, no. 52.

6.29. Lamp showing suppliants at a shrine (1893,1114.1) (Fig. 222)

Said to be from the Fayum, Egypt.

Width 170mm; length 100mm

Mould-made rectangular pottery lamp, of a type popular in late Ptolemaic and early Imperial Egypt. It has a raised rectangular base, 10 wick-holes, comic masks at the front corners, and a handle in the form of a reclining lion. The complex scene in the central panel shows suppliants arriving at a healing shrine, possibly to undergo incubation (temple sleep). The pedimented building, with lotus columns and two semi-circular windows in its side wall, may depict a

Figure 222 Pottery lamp showing suppliants arriving at a healing shrine, said to be from the Fayum, Egypt, 1st century AD. British Museum, Cat. no. 6.29

Figure 223 Pottery lamp decorated with images of the two great healing deities, Hygieia and Asklepios, AD 175–225. British Museum, Cat. no. 6.30

hostel rather than the temple itself (probably a temple of Sarapis). Within its entrance at the top of a flight of steps a naked dwarf-like man greets a heavily draped woman who is accompanied by a slave carrying a child. Following on are two draped figures close together, one possibly carrying the other. Nearby is an altar. On the left of the scene a figure leans out of one of the windows, while below, a man in a short tunic stands behind a grazing horse shading his eyes with his right hand.

ist century AD.

Lamps catalogue III, 48–9, 220–1, 241, pl. 37, fig. 58, Q1974.

6.30. Lamp showing Asklepios and Hygieia (1982,0302.4b ex-Wellcome Collection) (Fig. 223)

Provenance unknown.

Length 150mm; width 105mm

Mould-made pottery lamp (Loeschke Type VIII), signed SAECVL, decorated on the discus with a well-modelled representation of Hygieia feeding a sacred snake and Asklepios leaning on his snake-entwined staff.

Made in Italy, by Saeculus, AD 175–225.

Lamps catalogue III, 459, pl. 158, figs 22, 189, Q1384 *bis*.

6.31. Figurine of Asklepios (1868,0110.742 Woodhouse Bequest) (Fig. 224a–b)

From Corfu, Greece.

Height 210mm

A light buff terracotta standing figure of Asklepios on a high rectangular plinth. The god, in characteristic pose, leans on a snake-entwined staff supported under his left arm. He has a full beard and long wavy hair which falls onto his shoulders. He wears an ankle-length cloak which enfolds the lower body and left shoulder but exposes the right shoulder and chest musculature. On the front face of the plinth Asklepios' principal attribute is repeated – a rearing coiled snake motif.

Early ist century AD.

L. Burn, R. Higgins, H.B. Walters, D.M. Bailey (eds) *Catalogue of Terracottas in the British Museum* (London, 1903–2001), C52 and 2239.

6.32. Figurine of Asklepios (1995,0702.1) (Fig. 225)

Found near Chichester, West Sussex.

Height 64.1mm; weight 64.3g

Bronze standing figure of Asklepios. Though small the figurine is well made both in overall form and in the details of face, musculature and drapery. It is complete and in good condition and reveals considerable wear, conceivably from handling by generation after generation of suppliants. The god stands with his weight on his right leg, his face turned slightly to the left. His left leg, lightly flexed, with the foot a little advanced, is supported by a staff held under his left arm, while the right arm is bent at the elbow with hand on hip. The upper torso is bare revealing a finely rendered, strong musculature, as befitted a god of health. From the left shoulder falls the ankle-length traveller's cloak characteristic of Asklepios, its folds of drapery faithfully translated into

Figure 224a–b Terracotta figurine depicting a statue of Asklepios, from Corfu, Greece, early 1st century AD. British Museum, Cat. no. 6.31

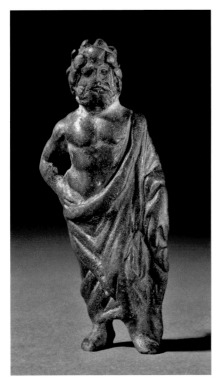

Figure 225 Bronze figurine of Asklepios, from near Chichester, West Sussex, 1st/4th century AD. British Museum, Cat. no. 6.32

Figure 226a–b Bronze figurine of Hygieia, 1st century AD. British Museum, Cat. no. 6.33

bronze. Detailed treatment of the face extends to the pupils in the eyes and individual curls in the full beard, while the hair is crowned by a diadem or wreath.

 1st/4th century AD

 Jackson 1995b; Jackson 2011a, 246–7, pl. 48.

6.33. Figurine of Hygieia (1814,0704.759 Townley Collection) (Fig. 226a–b)

Provenance unknown.

Height 145mm

 Bronze standing figure of Hygieia, looking to her right, her right leg lightly flexed, a *patera* with conical fruit in her left hand and a snake (now lacking its head) coiled round her right arm. Her hair is rolled up each side and knotted at the back, with a curled lock resting on each shoulder. She wears a high tiara-like crown, full-length, long-sleeved *chiton*, *himation* over her left arm and sandals.

 1st century AD.

 Bronzes catalogue, 1431.

6.34. Krater handle showing Asklepios and Hygieia (1905,0710.7) (Fig. 227)

From Egypt.

Height 127mm

 Bronze krater handle with busts of Asklepios and Hygieia, each holding a snake.

 1st century AD.

6.35. Engraved gem of Asklepios (1867,0507.254 Blacas Collection) (Fig. 228)

Height 20mm; width 16mm

Nicolo.

 The gem, set in a modern gold mount, is engraved with an image of Asklepios, standing to front, leaning slightly to

right, with full hair, beard and moustache, draped in a *himation*. His draped left arm rests on his snake-entwined staff. His bare right arm rests on his left wrist.

 1st/3rd century AD.

 Gems catalogue, 1683.

6.36. Engraved gem of Asklepios (1867,0507.252 Blacas Collection) (Fig. 229)

 Height 14mm; width 10mm

 Carnelian

 The gem, set in a modern gold ring, is engraved with a bust of Asklepios in profile to left. A snake-entwined staff stands in the field before him.

 1st/2nd century AD.

 Gems catalogue, 1687.

Figure 227 Bronze vessel handle with busts of Hygieia and Asklepios, from Egypt, 1st century AD. British Museum, Cat. no. 6.34

Figure 228 Nicolo gem engraved with a standing figure of Asklepios, 1st/3rd century AD. British Museum, Cat. no. 6.35

Figure 229 Carnelian gem engraved with a bust of Asklepios, 1st/2nd century AD. British Museum, Cat. no. 6.36

Figure 230 Carnelian gem engraved with a winged and draped figure of Hygieia, 1st/2nd century AD. British Museum, Cat. no. 6.37

6.37. Engraved gem of Hygieia (1867,0507.255 Blacas Collection) (Fig. 230)

Height 23mm; width 13mm
Carnelian.

The gem, set in a modern gold ring, is engraved with the image of a winged and draped Hygieia standing to left, a shield at her feet (a reminiscence of the wheel of Nemesis, or perhaps of the Athena-Hygieia type), holding in her left hand a snake which feeds from a libation bowl supported in her right palm.

1st/2nd century AD.

Gems catalogue, 1694.

6.38. Statue head of Asklepios (1867,0508.115 Blacas Collection) (Fig. 231)

From Melos, Cyclades, Greece. Formerly in the Collection of Louis Charles Pierre Casimir de Blacas d'Aulps, 2nd Duke of Blacas (1815–1866). Found in 1828 buried in a cave

together with inscribed votive relief Cat. no. 6.14 and a number of other votive offerings related to the cult of Asklepios and Hygieia.

Height *c.* 60cm

Parian marble head from a colossal statue of Asklepios. The luxuriant locks and curls of the hair, beard and moustache frame and emphasise the calm expression of the face, and imbue the statue with a sense of great power. The head was constructed from three separately worked pieces of marble, of which two survive. There are drill holes and lead pegs for the attachment of a gold or gilded bronze wreath, now missing.

325–300 BC ('a medium-sized colossus, 3rd or 2nd century BC' – Burn 2004, 163).

Annals of the Roman Institute of Archaeological Correspondence 1829, p. 341; Newton 1867, 32–3; Sculpture catalogue, 550; B. Ashmole, 1951, 'The poise of the Blacas head', *Annual of the British School at Athens* 46, 2–6; Burn 2004, 163.

Figure 231 (far left) Marble head from a colossal statue of Asklepios, from Melos, Greece, 325-300 BC. British Museum, Cat. no. 6.38

Figure 232 (left) Marble head from a statue of Asklepios, from Kos, Greece, 2nd century BC. British Museum, Cat. no. 6.39

Figure 233 Torso from a marble statue of Asklepios, from Epidauros, Greece, 4th century BC. British Museum, Cat. no. 6.40

Figure 234 Marble statue of Hygieia, from Cyrene, Libya, 1st/early 2nd century AD. British Museum, Cat. no. 6.41

Figure 235 Marble statuary group showing Asklepios and Telesphorus, 2nd/3rd century AD. British Museum, Cat. no. 6.42

6.39. Statue head of Asklepios (1868,0620.3) (Fig. 232)

From Kos (previously said to have been found at Ephesus). Height 22.5cm

Marble head from a statue of Asklepios. The head, neck and upper shoulders survive, broken away from a full-length statue. There is damage to the beard, nose and top of the head; the surface is worn and chipped; and at the back the surface has been worn and rounded, perhaps as part of a later reuse. The god, whose lightly upturned face is tilted slightly to the left, has long, thick, curly hair, a full beard and moustache, a bony facial structure and short full lips. A fold of drapery is preserved on his left shoulder.

2nd century BC. Hellenistic.

Sculpture catalogue, 1519.

6.40. Statue of Asklepios (1816,0610.327 Elgin Collection) (Fig. 233)

From Epidauros.

Height 94.5cm

Torso from a Parian marble statue of Asklepios, the head, right arm and lower legs lacking. The god stands with right leg advanced and lightly flexed, leaning gently to his right, originally supported by the now missing lower right arm and staff. The drapery of his cloak enfolds the lower body, left shoulder and left arm leaving only the well-muscled upper chest and right shoulder bare.

400–300 BC.

Sculpture catalogue, 551.

6.41. Statue of Hygieia (1861,1127.25) (Fig. 234)

From the temple of Apollo, Cyrene, Libya. Excavated by Smith and Porcher.

Height 114cm

Marble statue of Hygieia, complete except for her hands. Her drapery is finely rendered and she wears a high decorated diadem. A sacred snake is coiled around her right forearm. Its head is lacking but it was probably feeding from a *patera* held in her extended left hand, now broken. The head may not originally have belonged to the body, but the joining of head and body might still have been an ancient repair.

1st–early 2nd century AD. Roman version of a lost Greek original.

Sculpture catalogue, 1388.

6.42. Statue of Asklepios and Telesphorus (1864,0220.2 Strangford Collection) (Fig. 235)

Provenance unknown.

Height 62.2cm

Parian marble statuary group, on a circular base, comprising Asklepios, leaning on a snake-entwined, knotted staff, flanked by Telesphorus. Asklepios has a full bushy beard and thick curly hair with a diadem or wreath on the crown. His pose is very much that of an elderly and weary traveller, with furrowed brow, downward gaze and forward-sloping bulky upper torso, leaning heavily on his club-like staff. His right hand rests on the left which grasps the top of the staff; his left leg is advanced and strongly flexed while the right is angular and out-turned; and he wears sandals and a large ankle-length cloak which enfolds the lower body and left shoulder but exposes the right shoulder and chest musculature. The head of the entwined snake is broken away, as is the head of Telesphorus, a diminutive figure closely draped in a hooded robe with a square tablet or packet, perhaps an amulet case, hanging from his neck.

Roman, 2nd/3rd century AD, perhaps after a Greek original of the 3rd century BC.

Sculpture catalogue, 1694; *Journal of Hellenic Studies* 3, 1882, 292.

Appendix 1
An Important Group of Roman Surgical Instruments from Italy in the Bristol Museum and Art Gallery

In 1979 the City of Bristol Museum and Art Gallery (now Bristol Museum and Art Gallery) purchased the antiquities from the extensive collection of archaeological and ethnographic objects from Europe, the Far East and the New World amassed by Dr Hugh Alderson Fawcett (1891–1982). Fawcett was a GP and keen antiquarian who, in May 1946, famously alerted the British Museum to the discovery of the Mildenhall Treasure (Hobbs 2008, 377–85). An avid and assiduous collector, Fawcett marked the objects in his collection in white ink with basic information – number, place-name, and his distinctive ligatured *HF* monogram. Amongst the antiquities was a group of four surgical instruments of elaborately decorated form, including one of (at that time) only two known smooth-jawed uvula forceps (*staphylocaustes*) – four are now known (see p. 61).

In 1986, at a time when the present author was preparing a paper on uvula forceps (Jackson 1992), the Bristol City Museum curators of Archaeology and History, Georgina Plowright and Jennifer Stewart, kindly lent him the uvula forceps and the other three instruments – scalpel handle, double sharp hook, double-ended sharp and blunt hook – for detailed recording at the British Museum (**Fig. 236** and nos 1–4 below). The stylistic unity and the distinctive manner of manufacture of the instruments indicated that they had been made in the same workshop, probably as part of a larger set of instruments. It was very disconcerting, therefore, to find that while three of the instruments were marked 'Italy', one, the scalpel handle, was marked 'Palestine'. While Palestine was a feasible provenance, Italy appeared more likely, provoking the thought that the scalpel handle may have been incorrectly marked. Furthermore, in view of the fact that in their own work on the Fawcett antiquities the Bristol City Museum curators had noticed and become concerned about the unusual appearance of the patina of the uvula forceps and the double sharp hook, they agreed that scientific investigation of the four instruments should take place while they were at the British Museum.

The subsequent investigation of the patina of the four instruments by British Museum scientists raised the possibility that two of them might be forgeries with a chemically induced patina (La Niece, BMRL 5525/28676–9. 20/3/1987). As with other antiquities, vigilance is required with surgical instruments, copies of which have sometimes been made by forgers (see e.g. Bliquez 1986; Künzl 1986b). So, with the agreement again of the Bristol City Museum curators, atomic absorption analysis of all four instruments was undertaken. Scientific analysis rarely provides unequivocal results but in this case it did – see **Table 7**. Not only did it demonstrate that all four instruments are brasses of a composition that is consistent with that of other Roman metalwork, but also that the composition of the scalpel handle is so similar to that of the uvula forceps and double sharp hook that there can be no doubt that they were made together (La Niece and Hook, BMRL 5525/28676–9. 2/8/1988). The marking of the scalpel handle with the place-name Palestine should, therefore, be considered a cataloguing or recording error by Fawcett or his supplier; while the unusual appearance of the surface of the uvula forceps and double sharp hook was probably due to over-enthusiastic cleaning followed by some sort of chemical re-

Figure 236 The group of Roman medical instruments from Italy in the Bristol Museum and Art Gallery, inv. nos Ft.1449, Ft.1450, Ft.1452, Ft.1510 – left to right, scalpel handle, double sharp hook, double-ended sharp and blunt hook, uvula forceps. Photo: British Museum

patination at some point before acquisition of Fawcett's antiquities by the City of Bristol Museum and Art Gallery.

Thus, the instruments may be regarded confidently as products of the same workshop. All four are exquisite custom-made precision instruments, providing the most effective operative parts, and all are richly ornamented with mouldings showing a stylised bunch of acanthus leaves while

two also share the same form of lion-head handle finial. The lion-head handle finial is very rarely found on Roman surgical instruments and even though the few known examples are very widespread they may all be products of the same workshop. In addition to the two present examples from Italy, there is one on the handle of a sharp hook in the large set probably from Ephesus (Künzl 2002a, 12–17, A.6,

Table 7 Atomic absorption spectophotometry (AAS) analyses of four surgical instruments in the Bristol Museum and Art Gallery

Notes:
The following elements were also sought but were not found to be present above their respective detection limits:
Au < 0.005, Co < 0.004, Mn < 0.003, Cd < 0.002, Bi < 0.02.
The analyses should have a precision (a measure of reproducibility) of c. ±1-2% relative for copper, c. ±5% for zinc, and c. 10–30% for the remaining elements present at minor/trace levels, deteriorating to ±50% at their respective detection limits.

No.	Lab no.	Description	Other no.	Cu	Sn	Zn	Pb	Ag	Fe	Sb	Ni	As	Total	Sample wt/mg
1	5525-28676-V	Scalpel handle	FT 1510	77.3	<0.2	21.7	0.02	0.044	0.037	<0.02	0.194	<0.05	99.3	5.98
2	5525-28678-R	Double sharp hook	FT 1452	79.1	<0.2	21.7	0.01	0.063	0.045	<0.02	0.083	<0.05	101.0	5.54
3	5525-28677-T	Double-ended sharp and blunt hook	FT 1450	82.8	0.36	16.0	0.26	0.050	0.150	0.12	0.050	0.10	99.9	5.59
4	5525-28679-P	Uvula forceps	FT 1449	76.4	<0.3	22.9	0.02	0.054	0.063	<0.03	0.085	<0.1	99.5	3.18

Figure 237 Lion-head finial at the end of one of the handles of the uvula forceps. Photo: British Museum

Figure 238 Stylised acanthus decoration on the instrument handles – left to right, double-ended sharp and blunt hook, double sharp hook, uvula forceps, scalpel handle. Photo: British Museum

pl. 2), one on the handle of the so far unique suture/ligature needle in the kit of instruments from Cyrene (Jackson 2021, 547–50, fig. 4.7), and one at the end of both handles of another so far unique instrument, a cross-legged, toothed, broad-jawed forceps in the large set said to be from Asia Minor or Syria in the Ashmolean Museum (Jackson 1995a, pl. 2, lower right; Jackson forthcoming). All, like the Fawcett instruments, combine a lion-head finial with a stylised acanthus moulding.

Also distinctive, but more frequently found, though still not common, are instruments with decoration incorporating a stylised bunch of acanthus leaves. In addition to the present four instruments, the motif occurs: on four of the instruments in the small set from the burial group at Aschersleben (Künzl 1983a, 100–1, fig. 80); on two of the instruments in the Cyrene kit (Jackson 2021, 547–50, figs 4.7 and 4.9); on a double-ended blunt hook (Cat. no. no. 3.19) in the British Museum's large set from Italy (Jackson 1986, 124–5, fig. 2.16) and on another unprovenanced example (Cat. no. 3.105); on a combination instrument in the British Museum's small kit (Cat. no. 3.46); on a trivalve vaginal speculum from Pompeii (Bliquez 1994, 188, no. 292) and on another from Mérida, Spain (Künzl 1983a, 102–3, fig. 81); on a stout cross-legged sequestrum forceps from Potaissa/Turda, Hungary (Künzl 1996, 2620–1, fig. 25); and on two more, near-identical, stout, cross-legged forceps (with jaws of uncertain function, though probably for use in bone surgery), one from Allianoi, Turkey (Baykan 2012, 145, no. 296, 205, pl. 17) and the other an unprovenanced example in the London Science Museum (A646736, Wellcome Collection, ex-Gorga Collection). These instruments come from contexts ranging in date from the 1st to 3rd century AD. However, all, including the present four instruments, are exceptionally well made and richly ornamented and may have been products of an individual workshop, using the same master moulds and following established workshop traditions over a protracted period of time (Künzl 1984a, 60). In addition, as

valued instruments, some were probably handed down from generation to generation of medical practitioner and, properly maintained, including replacement of the iron scalpel blade, as necessary, would have been capable of a very long period of use.

In the case of the four instruments formerly in the Fawcett Collection, it is not only the fine design and high quality of manufacture of their operative parts and the choice and stylistic unity of the acanthus and lion-head motifs that unites them but also the form and craftsmanship of all the handles, stems and disc mouldings, and in particular the very distinctive way the layering of leaves in the acanthus mouldings has been emphasised with comparatively crude cut marks (**Figs 237–8**). That manufacturing feature is unique. It has not been discerned on any of the other instruments with stylised acanthus mouldings and it indicates that all four instruments were made by the same hand in the same workshop, as is also indicated by the results of scientific analysis – the instruments were made as a set. Although they were probably part of a once larger set of instruments, they may have belonged to a Roman surgeon who specialised in throat operations. For, even as a small kit, the five operational components – scalpel, sharp hook, double sharp hook, blunt hook and uvula forceps – would have provided a practitioner with the principal instruments required for surgical interventions in the throat, including tonsillectomy and uvulectomy (see pp. 60–1). They would also have been appropriate for many more operations on other parts of the body, including, for example, the removal of varicose veins.

1. Scalpel handle, Type I variant (Bristol Museum and Art Gallery, Ft. 1510) (Figs 236, 238)

Fawcett Collection, 'HF. Palestine. TP.7'
Length 90mm; socket width 7.5mm; weight 14.7g

A small brass scalpel handle with ornate grip. The slender leaf-shaped blunt dissector has a pointed tip and a

Figure 239a–b Uvula forceps, detail of jaws, in plan and profile.
Photo: British Museum

pronounced median ridge on both faces. The grip comprises a baluster with cut stylised acanthus leaf decoration, separated from the dissector by a five-disc cut moulding and from the blade socket by a four-disc cut moulding. The acanthus leaves are neatly shaped and veined but rather rudimentarily layered and truncated. Precisely the same arrangement and techniques are employed on the stylised acanthus mouldings of instruments 2–4. Only the stub of the tang of the iron blade survives, corroded in position in the slender keyhole type socket. The mouth of the socket is noticeably splayed, perhaps forced apart by iron corrosion but more likely a consequence of ancient damage.

BMRL 28676 V.

2. Double sharp hook (Bristol Museum and Art Gallery, Ft. 1452) (Figs 236, 238)

Fawcett Collection, 'HF. Italy. T1.50.x'
Length 205.5mm; length of hooks 38mm; span of hook tips 15mm; weight 19.7g

A highly ornate bifurcated sharp hook of brass, the tip of both hooks broken. The end of one hook is still curved forward in its original position but the other has been distorted and is now a little straighter than it would originally have been. A short and simple crossbar divides the hooks from the stem, which in its lower part is of octagonal (chamfered square) cross-section. The long

slender stem gradually increases in width towards its centre. Beyond a simple disc moulding it is of plain circular cross-section for a short distance until it meets the grip, which comprises a fine series of mouldings: first a baluster with cut acanthus leaf decoration, flanked top and bottom by a triple-disc moulding; next a small waisted and faceted reel, another triple-disc moulding and a long plain baluster; and finally a six-disc moulding topped by a lion-head finial. The craftsmanship is of a very high order, though some of the decorative detail on the acanthus leaf baluster and the lion-head finial is a little coarsely applied. It looks as though the neater engraving on the acanthus leaves – the stem and veining – may have been cast, while the coarser work – gashes to truncate and layer interspersing leaves (one short, one long and layered, one short, one long and layered) – was cold-worked with a punch or small chisel. The intention of the latter work was undoubtedly to give a greater sense of depth. Of the lion-head finial the bordering ruff and muzzle are most prominent, while the eyes are less clear than on the two handle terminals of the uvula forceps.

BMRL 28678 R.

3. Double-ended sharp and blunt hook (Bristol Museum and Art Gallery, Ft. 1450) (Figs 236, 238)

Fawcett Collection, 'Italy. T1.51. HF.'
Length 157.5mm; length of blunt hook 19mm; weight 11.3g

A slender combination instrument of brass, with at one end a sharp hook, at the other end a blunt hook. The sharp hook, small and neatly curved, still has a fine sharp point. The slender tapered stem above is of octagonal (chamfered square) cross-section. It is divided from the grip by a narrow groove followed by a short length of circular-sectioned stem. The grip comprises a slender baluster, with cut, stylised acanthus leaf, decoration, flanked top and bottom by a triple-disc moulding. Beyond is a further short length of circular-sectioned stem followed by a narrow encircling groove, from which point the stem is once more of octagonal (chamfered square) cross-section, tapered, curved and expanded at the end to form the small kite-shaped blunt hook. One edge of the angled end of the hook is now chipped and there is a crack at the neck of the hook. The outer face of the hook has a shallow longitudinal keel while the inner face is flat. The blunt hook is in a slightly different plane to the sharp hook.

BMRL 28677 T.

4. Uvula forceps (staphylocaustes) (Bristol Museum and Art Gallery, Ft. 1449) (Figs 236–9)

Fawcett Collection, 'Italy. T1.47.xx. HF.'
Length 210mm; length of handles (including disc and baluster mouldings) 102mm; length of jaws 40mm; width of jaws 17.5mm; breadth of jaws c. 13mm; weight 55.1g

A highly ornate cross-legged forceps of brass, for applying caustic to the uvula. Each of the hollow jaws is made in one with its respective arm. The only additional component is a small chord-shaped plate, apparently soldered in position, which fills the gap at the back of each jaw. The jaws enclose a capacious, tapered, sub-cylindrical cavity. They are corroded in position, fractionally open. The arms consist of plain, flat, rectangular-sectioned bars, of elongated diamond shape, which cross, and are hinged, at the point of maximum width. A close-fitting rivet, with simple hammered heads, forms the pivot. It is braced on each face by a disc washer with a simple circular engraved design. The arms are divided from the handles by a baluster moulding in the form of a cut stylised acanthus leaf, flanked top and bottom by a triple-disc moulding. The handles are of octagonal (chamfered square) cross-section and terminate in a five-disc moulding surmounted by a lion-head finial. Mane, hair, eyes, muzzle and mouth are schematically rendered.

BMRL 28679 P.

Appendix 2
A Unique Roman Plunger Forceps in the Ashmolean Museum, Oxford

This extraordinary copper-alloy plunger forceps, an ingenious precision instrument of unparalleled form, appeared on the antiquity market in 1992. In the following year an antiquity dealer temporarily lent the instrument to the present author at the British Museum for study purposes. No accompanying information was forthcoming and a rumour that it had been found in Turkey could not be substantiated. With uncertainty as to the future of the instrument a full written record was made together with detailed drawings, photography and scientific investigation before it was returned to the dealer. Subsequently, it was purchased by Gerald and Suzanne Labiner and then, in 1997, donated by them to the Ashmolean Museum (inv. no. 1997.45; Jackson 1997b; Jackson 2007b, 17–19, figs 4–5; Jackson 2014a, 133–4, fig. 18.6).

The forceps (**Figs 240–1**) is intact and in near-perfect condition, with a dark green patina. Quite remarkably, its plunger mechanism is still operative, too. This excellent state of preservation is likely to have been due to burial in anaerobic (probably desiccated) conditions in a secure context, probably a grave. Most simply described as a plunger type slot-slide forceps, the instrument is constructed in three pieces: its slender plunger handle-rod with ornate finial (1) has attached to its lower end a small precisely profiled bracket (2) which slides through corresponding slots in the arms of the forceps (3) and compresses the finely toothed capacious hollow jaws as the handle is pushed. The forceps weighs 41.0g. Its length, with the plunger fully extended, is 240mm; with the plunger fully depressed, 161mm. The capacious hollow jaws measure 28mm × 13mm and have 34 teeth each, which are disposed along the in-turned rim of the long edge and continue round the tip a short distance onto the second edge, a feature that has not been encountered on any other Roman forceps.

The restrained decoration is confined, as normal on Roman surgical instruments, to the non-operative parts, in this case, to crisp mouldings on the handle finial, the upper end of the body of the forceps, and the side-bars of the bracket. Elsewhere the surface of the metal has been immaculately smoothed, especially so on the curved outer face of the jaws in order to avoid accidental damage to internal organs and tissue during surgery. The workmanship of the exquisitely finished mouldings and smooth surface is of the highest quality, as also the tiny teeth on the jaw rims which interlock with complete precision. An oblique line of differential patina just short of the jaws indicates the position of the terminal bracket at the time of deposition of the instrument. Unsurprisingly, the forceps had been left in its most compact and secure form, with the plunger depressed virtually to its fullest extent, in which position the jaws were clamped firmly together.

X-ray fluorescence analysis by British Museum scientists of the two principal parts of the instrument, the plunger handle and the body of the forceps, revealed important results of considerable significance which underlined the exceptional quality of the instrument and its manufacture (Cowell and Hook, BMRL 6416/44420T, 17/5/1993). For, while both were made of leaded bronze, each was found to be of a distinctly different alloy formulation and one that appears to have been carefully selected for the different

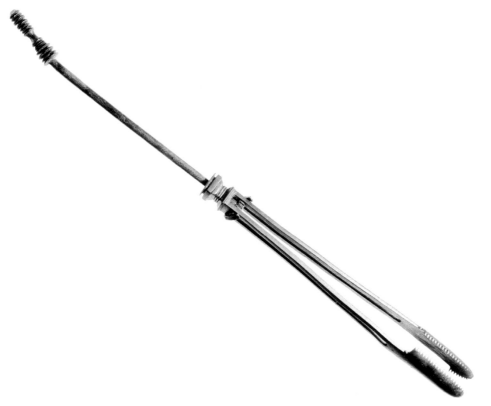

Figure 240 The plunger forceps fully extended. Ashmolean Museum, Oxford, inv. no. 1997.45. Photo: © Ashmolean Museum, University of Oxford

metallurgical properties required of each component. Thus, the body of the forceps, which needed to be springy to facilitate the opening and closing of the jaws by the plunger handle, was found to have an appropriately low lead content, while the plunger handle, which required no such flexibility, was found to have, equally appropriately, a much higher lead content which would have facilitated the casting process.

That sophisticated knowledge and application of metallurgy, together with the application of a unique plunger mechanism to a spring forceps, which was provided with jaws of an equally unique form, must have resulted in an instrument that was not only eminently practical but also novel and ingenious. Its technical virtuosity brings to mind the great rash of technological innovations that blossomed in Hellenistic Alexandria. But it is also a combination that could be taken to suit rather well the requirements of instruments entered for competitions in the annual medical contests at Ephesus (see above p. 13). The Ashmolean plunger forceps is just the sort of instrument we might envisage being entered for that event, a finely designed, accurately crafted, hi-tech, ostentatious tool to impress judges. It was probably not just the judges who were impressed, however. A practitioner's success, beyond his own surgical expertise, would have depended to some degree on winning the confidence of the patient, and while the patient's cooperation and trust may have been obtained by means of a carefully phrased prediction of the likely outcome of his or her disease – prognosis (Nutton 2004, 88–90), confidence may have been gained by the appearance of instrumentation. For, even if not completely credulous, the patient would doubtless often have been impressed and reassured by costly looking equipment, rightly or wrongly

Figure 241 The plunger forceps partly extended. Oxford, Ashmolean Museum, inv. no. 1997.45. Drawing: Ralph Jackson

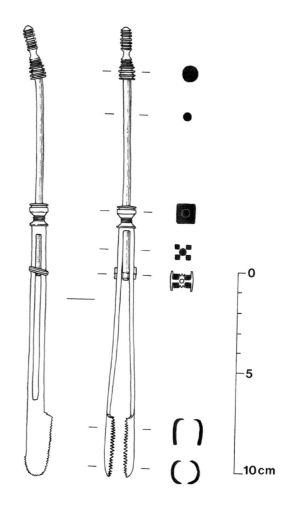

deducing that wealth reflects success, and success implies a competent healer. He or she might have been struck by the sophistication of design, by richly moulded or inlaid decoration or by the sheer quality of manufacture and surface finish, but perhaps the surest way to overawe was to incorporate some novel or ingenious feature, such as the plunger mechanism. Other Roman examples include the application of a screw-thread mechanism to uterine specula (Krause 1995, 41–5) and the adoption of a loose joint for a variety of bone forceps which turned it into a two-in-one instrument (Jackson 2007b, 18–23, figs 8–10).

However, intrinsic evidence suggests the plunger forceps was not just ingenious and impressive but an effective instrument: there is differential wear on the teeth at the tip of the jaws. The form of the jaws is related to that of the distinctive *staphylagra* type of forceps which Greek and Roman medical writers recommended for use principally in operations on the palatine uvula (see pp. 60–1). The application of a plunger mechanism is a refinement hitherto unknown and its very considerable benefit is that by avoiding encumbrances – the pivot of a cross-legged *staphylagra* or the finger and thumb required to move the sliding lock-ring of a spring-type *staphylagra* – it enabled the use of the *staphylagra* type jaw in confined spaces and deep within the body: it was ideally suited to operate in places beyond the reach of other forceps. Indeed, the position of the wear on the teeth at the distal end of the jaws is suggestive of extraction of such things as bone fragments and deeply embedded foreign bodies from wounds; and while it would also have been used to advantage in the operations for amputation of the uvula and for anal fistula, it would very likely have served a range of other roles, too, including, the fixing and removal of various types of growth and tumour and even, perhaps, the removal of calculus from the urinary bladder in cases of lithotomy. The plunger forceps is an example of the highest achievement of those who designed and made Roman surgical instruments.

Concordance of Provenanced Instruments

Location	Catalogue nos
Britain	
Caistor St. Edmund	Cat. no. 3.135
Cirencester	Cat. no. 3.136
Colchester	Cat. nos 3.99, 3.137
Eastry	Cat. no. 3.66
Golden Bridge, Ireland	Cat. no. 3.138
Kenchester	Cat. no. 3.139
Little Burstead	Cat. no. 3.97
London, City	Cat. nos 3.54, 3.77, 3.80, 3.90–3, 3.96, 3.108–9, 3.145
St Albans	Cat. no. 3.140
Sandy/Biggleswade	Cat. no. 3.141
Stonea	Cat. no. 3.67
Cyprus	
Cyprus	Cat. no. 3.151
Egypt	
Gebel Sheikh Embarak	Cat. no. 3.72
France	
Auvergne, probably	Cat. no. 3.134
Lyon	Cat. no. 3.133
Naix-aux-Forges	Cat. nos 3.131–2
Vaison	Cat. nos 3.104, 3.126–7
Greece	
Athens	Cat. no. 3.129
Corfu	Cat. nos 3.49, 3.114, 3.120, 3.130
Italy	
Italy	Cat. no. 3.1–39
Lake Trasimene	Cat. nos 3.71, 3.79, 3.88
Orvieto	Cat. no. 3.123
Rome	Cat. no. 3.68
Ruvo	Cat. no. 3.86
Libya	
Cyrenaica, probably	Cat. no. 3.125
Turkey	
Ephesus	Cat. no. 3.146
Myndos	Cat. no. 3.64
Yortan	Cat. no. 3.124

Bibliography

Abbreviations, short titles

Bronzes catalogue: Walters, H.B. 1899. *Catalogue of the Bronzes, Greek, Roman and Etruscan in the Department of Greek and Roman Antiquities, British Museum*, London.

Chiurazzi – De Angelis Catalogo 1911: *Fonderie Artistiche Riunite, J. Chiurazzi & Fils – S. De Angelis & Fils, Catalogo 1911: Bronzes – Marbres – Argenterie*, Naples 1910.

CIG: *Corpus Inscriptionum Graecarum*, Berlin, 1825–77.

CIL VII: Huebner, A. (ed) 1873. *sigilla medicorum oculariorum*, Corpus Inscriptionum Latinarum 7.85, Berlin, 235–7.

CIL XIII: Espérandieu, E. (ed) 1901. *Inscriptiones trium Galliarum et Germaniarum Latinae. Instrumentum domesticum II, signacula medicorum oculariorum*, Corpus Inscriptionum Latinarum 13, part 3, fascicule 1, Berlin, 558–610.

CMG: *Corpus Medicorum Graecorum*, Berlin, 1946–.

Finger rings catalogue: Marshall, F.H. 1907. *Catalogue of the Finger Rings, Greek, Etruscan and Roman, in the Departments of Antiquities, British Museum*, London (reprint 1968).

Franks List: A.W. Franks, *List of stamps of Roman oculists*, un-dated manuscript (probably about 1880), British Museum.

Gems catalogue: Walters, H.B. 1926. *Catalogue of the Engraved Gems and Cameos, Greek, Etruscan and Roman, in the British Museum*, London.

Guide to Greek and Roman Life 1908: *An Exhibition Illustrating Greek and Roman Life*, British Museum, London.

Guide to the Antiquities of Roman Britain 1964: *Guide to the Antiquities of Roman Britain*, British Museum, London.

IG: *Inscriptiones Graecae*, Berlin, 1873–.

Lamps catalogue II: Bailey, D.M. 1980. *Roman Lamps Made in Italy (A Catalogue of the Lamps in the British Museum*, vol. II), London.

Lamps catalogue III: Bailey, D.M. 1988. *Roman Provincial Lamps (A Catalogue of the Lamps in the British Museum*, vol. III), London.

RIB II: Collingwood, R.G. and Wright, R.P. *The Roman Inscriptions of Britain, Volume II: instrumentum domesticum*, S.S. Frere, and R.S.O. Tomlin (eds), 1990–5, Oxford.

Roman pottery catalogue: Walters, H.B. 1908. *Catalogue of the Roman Pottery in the British Museum*, London.

Sculpture catalogue: Smith, A.H. 1892. A *Catalogue of Sculpture in the Department of Greek and Roman Antiquities, British Museum*, I, London.

Vases catalogue: Walters, H.B. 1896. *Catalogue of the Greek and Etruscan Vases in the British Museum*, London.

Selected ancient sources and translations

Celsus: *Celsus De Medicina*, translated by W.G. Spencer, London/ Cambridge, MA, 1935–8.

Dioscorides: *Pedanius Dioscorides of Anazarbus De materia medica*, translated by Lily Y. Beck, Hildesheim/Zürich/New York, 2011.

Dioscorides: 'The *Preface* of Dioscorides' *Materia Medica*: introduction, translation and commentary', by J. Scarborough and V. Nutton, *Transactions and Studies of the College of Physicians of Philadelphia* new series 4, 1982, 187–227.

Galen: *Galen on Anatomical Procedures*, translated by Charles Singer, London/New York, 1956.

Galen: *Avoiding Distress*, translated by Vivian Nutton, in P.N. Singer ed., *Galen: Psychological Writings*, Cambridge/New York, 2013.

Paul of Aegina: *The Seven Books of Paulus Aegineta*, translated by Francis Adams, London, 1844–7.

Pliny the Elder: *Pliny, Natural History*, translated by H. Rackham, W.H.S. Jones and D. Eichholz, London/Cambridge, MA, vols 1–10, 1938–63.

Pliny the Younger: *The Letters of the Younger Pliny*, translated by Betty Radice, London, 1963.

Soranus of Ephesus: *Soranus' Gynecology*, translated by Owsei Temkin, Baltimore, 1956.

Secondary sources

Adams, F. 1844–7. *The Seven Books of Paulus Aegineta*, vol. 1 (1844), vol. 2 (1846), vol. 3 (1847), London.

Adams, J.N. 1990. 'The *forfex* of the *veterinarius* Virilis (Vindolanda Inv. No. 86/470) and ancient methods of castrating horses', *Britannia* 21, 267–71.

Ali, I.A.K.E. 2018. 'Use of acacia gum in the treatment of skin lesions of two children with Kwashiorkor', in *Gum Arabic*, edited by A.A. Mariod, Cambridge, 221–8.

Allason-Jones, L. 1999. 'Health care in the Roman north', *Britannia* 30, 133–46.

Alphas, E. 2014. 'Terracotta groups', in Stampolidis and Tassoulas (eds) 2014, 267–9.

Andorlini Marcone, I. 1993. 'L'apporto dei papiri alla conoscenza della scienza medica antica', in *Aufstieg und Niedergang der römischen Welt (ANRW)* II, 37.1, edited by W. Haase and H. Temporini, Berlin/New York, 458–562.

Andorlini, I. (ed.) 2001. *Greek Medical Papyri*, vol. 1, Florence.

Anthony Armstrong, N. and Cartwright, A.C. 2020. *A History of the Medicines We Take*, Barnsley.

Antwi, D.K. 2000. 'Roman surgical practice', *Journal of the Royal Society for the Promotion of Health* 120, 188–91.

Apostolov, M. and Atanassova, S. 1974. 'Investigation on the composition of the drugs found in a Roman tomb near by Bansko', *АсКЛеЛИНН/Asklepii* (Sofia) 3, 55.

Arnott, R. 1997. 'Surgical practice in the prehistoric Aegean', *Medizinhistorisches Journal* 32, 249–78.

Arnott, R. (ed.) 2002. *The Archaeology of Medicine* (British Archaeological Reports International Series 1046), Oxford.

Arnott, R., Finger, S. and Smith, C.U.M. (eds) 2003. *Trepanation: History, Discovery, Theory*, Lisse.

Azaroff, L.V. and Buerger, M.J. 1958. *The Powder Method in X-ray Crystallography*. London.

Baader, G. 1967. 'Spezialärzte in der Spätantike', *Medizinhistorisches Journal* 2, 231–8.

Baker, P.A. 2011. 'Collyrium stamps: An indicator of regional practices in Roman Gaul', *European Journal of Archaeology* 14, 158–89.

Baker, P.A. 2013. *The Archaeology of Medicine in the Greco-Roman World*, Cambridge.

Baykan, D. 2012. *Allianoi Tıp Aletleri* (Studia ad Orientem Antiquum 2), Istanbul.

Baykan, D. 2017. 'Medicine in Balkans during the Roman Period', *Balkan Medical Journal* 34, 295–300.

Bayley, J. 1991. 'Alloy nomenclature', in *Dress Accessories c. 1150–c. 1450. Medieval Finds from Excavations in London: 3*, edited by G. Egan and F. Pritchard, London: HMSO, 13–17.

Bayley, J. and Budd, P. 1998. 'The clay moulds', in *Roman Castleford Excavations 1974–85. Volume 1: The Small Finds* (Yorkshire Archaeology 4), edited by H.E.M. Cool and C. Philo, Wakefield, 195–222.

Bayley, J. and Butcher, S. 1981. 'Variations in alloy composition of Roman brooches', *Revue d'Archeometrie*, supplement, 29–36.

Beck, F. 1977. 'Objets gallo-romains découverts à Echevronne (Côte-d'Or)', *Antiquités Nationales* 9, 50–65.

Beck, L.Y. 2011. *Pedanius Dioscorides of Anazarbus De materia medica*, Hildesheim/Zürich/New York.

Bennion, E. 1979. *Antique Medical Instruments*, London.

Berdick, M. 1972. 'The role of fats and oils in cosmetics', *Journal of the American Oil Chemists' Society* 49, 406–9.

Berger, E. 1970. *Das Basler Arztrelief. Studien zum griechischen Grab- und Votivrelief um 500 v. Chr. und zur vorhippokratischen Medizin*, Basel/Mainz.

Biers, J.C. 2004. *A Peaceable Kingdom: Animals in Ancient Art from the Leo Mildenberg Collection*, Mainz.

Bimbenet-Privat, M., Bardiès-Fronty, I. and Walter, P. 2009. *Le bain et le miroir: Soins du corps et cosmetiques de l'antiquite a la renaissance*, Paris.

Bleton, J., Mejanelle, P., Sansoulet, J., Goursaud, S. and Tchapla, A. 1996. 'Characterization of neutral sugars and uronic acids after methanolysis and trimethylsilylation for recognition of plant gums', *Journal of Chromatography A*, 720(1–2), 27–49.

Bliquez, L.J. 1981. 'Greek and Roman medicine', *Archaeology* 34(2), 10–17.

Bliquez, L.J. 1982. 'Roman surgical instruments in the Johns Hopkins University Institute of the History of Medicine', *Bulletin of the History of Medicine* 56, 195–217.

Bliquez, L.J. 1984. 'Two lists of Greek surgical instruments and the state of surgery in Byzantine times', *Dumbarton Oaks Papers* 38, 187–204.

Bliquez, L.J. 1986. 'The Getty instrumentarium. A revised opinion', *Getty Museum Journal* 14, 79–80.

Bliquez, L.J. 1992. 'The Hercules motif on Greco-Roman surgical tools', in Krug 1992a, 35–50.

Bliquez, L.J. 1994. *Roman Surgical Instruments and Other Minor Objects in the National Museum of Naples*, with a catalogue of the surgical instruments in the Antiquarium at Pompeii by Ralph Jackson, Mainz.

Bliquez, L.J. 1995. 'Gynecology in Pompeii', in van der Eijk *et al.* 1995, vol. 1, 209–23.

Bliquez, L.J. 2003. 'Roman surgical spoon probes and their ancient names (*mele, melotis/melotris, specillum*)', *Journal of Roman Archaeology* 16, 322–30.

Bliquez, L.J. 2015. *The Tools of Asclepius. Surgical Instruments in Greek and Roman Times* (Studies in Ancient Medicine 43), Leiden/Boston.

Bliquez, L.J. 2018. 'Greco-Roman surgical instruments: the tools of the trade', Chapter C16 in *Science and Medicine in the Classical World*, edited by P.T. Keyser and J. Scarborough, Oxford, 555–90.

Bliquez, L.J. and Munro, E.J. 2007. '*Paulakion* and *Securicella*: Two hitherto unidentified Greco-Roman veterinary instruments', *Mnemosyne* 60, 490–4.

Bliquez, L.J. and Oleson, J.P. 1994. 'The origins, early history, and applications of the *pyoulkos (syringe)*', in *Science et vie intellectuelle à Alexandrie (Ier–IIIe siècle après J.-C)*, edited by G. Argoud, St Étienne, 83–119.

Bolla, M. 2004. 'La tomba del medico di Verona', *Aquileia Nostra* 75, 193–270.

Bonnet, C. 2018. 'Lipids, a natural raw material at the heart of cosmetics innovation', *Oilseeds & fats Crops and Lipids* 25, D501.

Bonomi, S. 1984. 'Medici in Este romana. 2. La tomba del medico', *Aquileia Nostra* 55, 77–108.

Boon, G.C. 1983. 'Potters, oculists and eye troubles', *Britannia* 14, 1–12.

Botticelli, G.A., Freccero, A. and Matteini, M. 2012. 'Reproduction of pictorial techniques using beeswax, Punic wax, encaustic and other', in *Encausto: Storia, Tecniche e Ricerche (Encaustic: History, Technique and Research)*, edited by S. Omarini, Florence, 141–51.

Boudon-Millot, V. 2008. 'Un traité perdu de Galien miraculeusement retrouvé, le *Sur l'inutilité de se chagriner*: Texte grec et traduction française', in *La science médicale antique: Nouveaux regards. Études en l'honneur de J. Jouanna*, edited by V. Boudon-Millot, A. Guardasole and C. Magdelaine, Paris, 67–118.

Boudon-Millot, V. 2012. *Galien de Pergame. Un médecin grec à Rome*, Paris.

Boudon-Millot, V. and Jouanna, J. 2010. *Galien. Tome IV. Ne pas se chagriner*, Paris.

Bouzakis, K-D., Pantermalis, D., Efstathiou, K., Varitis, E., Michailidis, M., Sagris, D., Mavroudis, I., Vasteli, K., Kastner, J., and Salaberger, D. 2008. 'Design and manufacturing aspects of a vaginal speculum of antiquity, as investigated by computer tomographies', *Journal of Archaeological Science* 35, 633–42.

Bowman, A.K. and Thomas, J.D. 1994. *The Vindolanda Writing-Tablets (Tabulae Vindolandenses II)*, London.

Bowman, A.K. and Thomas, J.D. 2003. *The Vindolanda Writing-Tablets (Tabulae Vindolandenses III)*, London.

Boyer, R., avec Bel, V., Tranoy, L., Grévin, G., Mourey, W., Barrandon, J.-N., Binant, C., Bui-Thi-Mai, M., Girard, M., Gratuze, B., and Guineau, B. 1990. 'Découverte de la tombe d'un oculiste à Lyon (fin du IIe siècle après J.-C.). Instruments et coffret avec collyres', *Gallia* 47, 215–49.

Braadbaart, S. 1994. 'Medical and cosmetic instruments in the collection of the "Rijksmuseum van oudheden" in Leiden, The Netherlands', *Oudheidkundige mededelingen uit het Rijksmuseum van oudheden te Leiden* 74, 163–75.

Bradley, K.R. 1986. 'Wet-nursing at Rome: A study in social relations', in *The Family in Ancient Rome: New Perspectives*, edited by B. Rawson, New York, 201–29.

Breitwieser, R. 2003. 'Celtic trepanations in Austria', in Arnott *et al.* 2003, 147–53.

Brown, P. (ed.) 2001. *British Cutlery. An Illustrated History of Design, Evolution and Use*, London.

Bubb, C. 2022a. 'A new interpretation of the medical competitions at Ephesus (I. Ephesos IV 1161–69)', *Zeitschrift für Papyrologie und Epigraphik* 221, 152–6.

Bubb, C. 2022b. *Dissection in Classical Antiquity: A Social and Medical History*, Cambridge.

Burn, L. 2004. *Hellenistic Art*, London.

Büsing-Kolbe, A. 2001. 'Ein römischer silbertauschierter Skalpellgriff aus Ficarolo', *Archäologisches Korrespondenzblatt* 31, 107–16.

Carson, R.A.G. 1980. *Principal Coins of the Romans, Vol. II: The Principate 31 BC–AD 296*, London.

Caton, R. 1914. 'Notes on a group of medical and surgical instruments, found near Kolophon', *Journal of Hellenic Studies* 34, 114–18.

Caygill, M. and Cherry, J.F. (eds) 1997. *A.W. Franks: Nineteenth-century Collecting and the British Museum*, London.

Chovanec, Z., Rafferty, S. and Swiny, S. 2012. 'Opium for the masses', *Ethnoarchaeology* 4, 5–36.

Chrysostomou, P. 2002. 'Contributions to the history of medicine in ancient Macedonia', *Eulimene* 3, 99–116 (in Greek).

Coccato, A., Jehlicka, J., Moens, L., and Vandenabeele, P. 2015. 'Raman spectroscopy for the investigation of carbon-based black pigments', *Journal of Raman Spectroscopy* 46, 1003–15.

Cociş, S. 1993. 'Instrumente medicale din Dacia Romană', *Apulum* 27–30, 241–9.

Colombini, M.P., Giachi, G., Iozzo, M. and Ribechini, E. 2009. 'An Etruscan ointment from Chiusi (Tuscany, Italy): Its chemical characterization', *Journal of Archaeological Science* 36, 1488–95.

Como, J. 1925. 'Das Grab eines römischen Arztes in Bingen', *Germania* 9, 152–62.

Cook, B.F. 1987. *Greek Inscriptions*, London.

Copley, M.S., Bland, H.A., Rose, P., Horton, M., and Evershed, R.P. 2005. 'Gas chromatographic, mass spectrometric and stable carbon isotopic investigations of organic residues of plant oils and animal fats employed as illuminants in archaeological lamps from Egypt', *Analyst* 130, 860–71.

Cornara, L., Biagi, M., Xiao, J. and Burlando, B. 2017. 'Therapeutic properties of bioactive compounds from different honeybee products', *Frontiers in Pharmacology* 8, 412.

Cotte, M., Dumas, P., Richard, G. Breniaux, R. and Walter, P. 2005. 'New insight on ancient cosmetic preparation by synchrotron-based infrared microscopy', *Analytica Chimica Acta* 553, 105–10.

Cowell, M.R. 1977. 'Energy dispersive X-ray fluorescence analysis of ancient gold alloys', *X-ray Microfluorescence Analysis Applied to Archaeology*, PACT 1, Journal of the European Study Group on Physical, Chemical and Mathematical Techniques Applied to Archaeology (edited by T. Hackens, H. McKerrell and M. Hours), 76–85.

Cowell, M.R. 1998. 'Coin analysis by energy dispersive X-ray fluorescence spectrometry', in *Metallurgy in Numismatics*, vol. 4, edited by W.A. Oddy and M.R. Cowell, Royal Numismatic Society, London, 448–60.

Craddock, P.T. 1978. 'The composition of copper alloys used by the Greek, Etruscan and Roman civilisations 3: The origins and early use of brass', *Journal of Archaeological Science*, 5(1), 1–16.

Craddock, P.T. 1985. 'Three thousand years of copper alloys: From the Bronze Age to the Industrial Revolution', in *Application of Science in Examination of Works of Art*, edited by P.A. England and L. van Zelst, Boston, The Research Laboratory, Museum of Fine Arts, 59–67 (and microfiche).

Craddock, P.T. and Eckstein, K. 2003. 'Production of brass in Antiquity by direct reduction', in *Mining and Metal Production through the Ages*, edited by P.T. Craddock and J. Lang, London, 216–30.

Craddock, P.T. and Giumlia-Mair, A.R. 1993. '*Hśmn-Km*, Corinthian bronze, *shakudo*: Black-patinated bronze in the ancient world', in La Niece and Craddock 1993, 101–27.

Craig, O., Saul, H. and Spiteri, C. 2020. 'Residue analysis', in *Archaeological Science: An Introduction*, edited by M. Richards and K. Britton, Cambridge, 70–98.

Crummy, P., Benfield, S., Crummy, N., Rigby, V. and Shimmin, D. 2007. *Stanway: An Élite Burial Site at Camulodunum* (Britannia Monograph 24), London.

Crummy, P., Crummy, N., Jackson, R. and Schädler, U. 2008. 'Stanway: An élite cemetery at Camulodunum', *British Archaeology* 99 (March/April), 28–33.

Cruse, A. 2004. *Roman Medicine*, Stroud.

Çulha, Z. (ed.) 2009. *Silent Witnesses. From Neolithic Period to the Seljuks*, Istanbul.

Cuvigny, H. 1992. 'La Mort et la Maladie (83–123)', Chapter 5, in *Mons Claudianus: Ostraka Graeca et Latina I (O. Claud. 1 à 190)* (IFAO, Documents de fouilles 29), edited by J. Bingen, A. Bülow-Jacobsen, W.E.H. Cockle, H. Cuvigny, L. Rubinstein, and W. Van Rengen, Cairo, 75–110.

Dasen, V. 2008. 'La petite fille et le médecin. À propos d'une édecins de momie d'Égypte romaine', in *Femmes en Médecine*, edited by V. Boudon-Millot, V. Dasen, and B. Maire, Paris, 39–59.

Dasen, V. 2011a. 'Magic and medicine: Gems and the power of seals', in *'Gems of Heaven'. Recent Research on Engraved Gemstones in Late*

Antiquity, c. AD 200–600, edited by C. Entwistle and N. Adams, London, 69–74.

Dasen, V. (ed.) 2011b. 'La médecine à l'époque romaine', *L'Archéo-Théma* 16, 1–81.

Dasen, V. 2015. *Le sourire d'Omphale : Maternité et petite enfance dans l'Antiquité*, Rennes.

Dasen, V. 2018. 'A uterine amulet from the Roman Empire', Exhibit 7, in *Reproduction: Antiquity to the Present Day*, edited by N. Hopwood, R. Flemming, and L. Kassell, Cambridge.

Davidson, G. 1952. *Corinth, Vol. XII, The Minor Objects*, Princeton, NJ.

De Carolis, S. (ed.) 2009. *Ars medica. I ferri del mestiere. La* domus *'del chirurgo' di Rimini e la chirurgia nell'antica Roma*, Rimini.

De Carolis, S. And Pesaresi, V. (eds) 2009. *Medici e pazienti nell'antica Roma. La medicina romana e la* domus *'del chirurgo' di Rimini*, Rimini.

De Navarro, J.M. 1955. 'A doctor's grave of the middle La Tène period from Bavaria', *Proceedings of the Prehistoric Society* 21, 231–48.

Deneffe, V. 1893. Étude sur la trousse d'un chirurgien gallo-romain du IIIe siècle, Antwerp.

Deppert-Lippitz, B., Schürmann, A., Theune-Grosskopf, B., Krause, R., Würth, R., and Planck, D. 1995. *Die Schraube zwischen Macht und Pracht. Das Gewinde in der Antike* (Katalog Ausstellung Künzelsau-Gaisbach 1995), Sigmaringen.

Deyts, S. 1983. *Les bois sculptés des Sources de la Seine* (Supplément à *Gallia* 42), Paris.

Deyts, S. 1994. *Un peuple de* édecins. *Offrandes de pierre et de bronze des Sources de la Seine* (*Revue Archéologique de l'Est*, Supplément 13), Dijon.

Dieudonné-Glad, N., Feugère, M. and Önal, M. 2013. *Zeugma V : Les Objets* (Travaux de la Maison de l'Orient et de la Méditerranée 64), Lyon.

Dolenz, H., Flügel, Ch., Buora, M., Kûnzl, E., and Gasteiger, S. 2021. 'Gli oggetti di metallo', in *Aquileia. Fondi Cossar : 3.3, – Tomo 2 – L'instrumentum, il materiale vitreo, metallico e gli elementi architettonico-decorativi* (Scavi di Aquileia II), edited by J. Bonetto, S. Mazzocchin, and D. Dobreva, Rome, 681–727.

Draycott, J. and Graham, E.-J. (eds) 2016. *Bodies of Evidence : Ancient Anatomical Votives Past, Present and Future*, London.

Dubois, L.J.-J. 1818. *Catalogue d'antiquités* égyptiennes, grecques, romaines et celtiques: Copies d'antiquités, modèles d'édifices anciens, sculptures modernes, tableaux, dessins, cartes, plans, colonnes, tables et meubles précieux, formant la collection de feu M. le Cte. De Choiseul-Gouffier, Paris.

Dude, L. 2005. 'Extraktionszangen der römischen Kaiserzeit', *Saalburg-Jahrbuch* 55, 5–131.

Eckardt, H. 2018. *Writing and Power in the Roman World: Literacies and Material Culture*, Cambridge.

Eckardt, H. and Crummy, N. 2008. *Styling the Body in Late Iron Age and Roman Britain: A Contextual Approach to Toilet Instruments* (Monographies Instrumentum 36), Montagnac.

Engelmann, H., Knibbe, D., and Merkelbach, R. 1980. *Die Inschriften von Ephesos*. Teil 4 (Inschriften griechischer Städter aus Kleinasiens, Band 14), Bonn.

Eschebach, H. 1984. 'Die Arzthäuser in Pompeji', *Antike Welt* Sondernummer 15, Feldmeilen.

Euskirchen, M. 2018. 'Tombe d'un médecin de Cologne: Chirurgien, interniste et pharmacien', in Verbanck-Pierard *et al.* 2018, 313–15.

Euskirchen, M. 2022. 'Römischer Arztgräber in Köln', *Kölner Jahrbuch* 55, 7–172.

Evershed, R.P. 2008. 'Organic residue analysis in archaeology: The archaeological biomarker revolution', *Archaeometry* 50, 895–924.

Evershed, R.P., Berstan, R., Grew, F., Copley, M.S., Charmant, A.J.H., Barham, E., Mottram, H.R., and Brown, G. 2004. 'Formulation of a Roman cosmetic', *Nature* 432 (4 Nov.), 35–6.

Evershed, R., Vaughan, S., Dudd, S., and Soles, J. 1997. 'Fuel for thought? Beeswax in lamps and conical cups from Late Minoan Crete', *Antiquity* 71, 979–85.

Falder, S., Bennett, R., Alvi, N., and Reeves, N. 2003. 'Following in the footsteps of the pharaohs', *British Journal of Plastic Surgery* 56(2), 196–7.

Faraone, C.A. 2011a. 'Magical and medical approaches to the wandering womb in the ancient Greek world', *Classical Antiquity* 30, 1–32.

Faraone, C.A. 2011b. 'Text, image and medium: The evolution of Graeco-Roman magical gemstones', in *'Gems of Heaven'. Recent Research on Engraved Gemstones in Late Antiquity, c. AD 200–600*, edited by C. Entwistle and N. Adams, London, 50–61.

Faraone, C.A. 2018. *The Transformation of Greek Amulets in Roman Imperial Times*, Philadelphia.

Feugère, M., Künzl, E., and Weisser, U. 1985. 'Les aiguilles à cataracte de Montbellet (Saône-et-Loire). Contribution à l'étude de l'ophtalmologie antique et islamique/Die Starnadeln von Montbellet (Saône-et-Loire). Ein Beitrag zur antiken und islamischen Augenheilkunde', *Jahrbuch des Römisch-Germanischen Zentralmuseums* 32, 436–508.

Feugère, M., Künzl, E., and Weisser, U. 1988. *Les aiguilles à cataracte de Montbellet (Saône-et-Loire). Contribution à l'étude de l'ophtalmologie antique et islamique* (Société des Amis des Arts et des Sciences de Tournus 87), Tournus.

Firmati, M. And Romualdi, A. 1998. 'Il relitto del Pozzino a Baratti', in *Memorie sommerse. Archeologia subacquea in Toscana*, edited by G. Poggesi and P. Rendini, Grosseto, 184–92.

Fischer, K.-D. 1981. 'The first Latin treatise on horse medicine and its author Pelagonius Saloninus', *Medizinhistorisches Journal* 16(3), 215–26.

Fischer, K.-D. 1988. 'Ancient veterinary medicine', *Medizinhistorisches Journal* 23(3–4), 191–209.

Fischer, K.-D. 1997. 'Was ist das δελτάριου in Poxy LIX 4001?', in *'Specimina' per il* Corpus *dei Papiri Greci di Medicina. Atti dell'Incontro di studio*, edited by I. Andorlini, Firenze, 109–13.

Fitzpatrick, A. 1991. 'Ex radice britanica', *Britannia* 22, 143–6.

Flemming, R. 2000. *Medicine and the Making of Roman Women: Gender, Nature and Authority from Celsus to Galen*, Oxford.

Forsén, B. 1996. *Griechische Gliederweihungen. Eine Untersuchung zu ihrer Typologie und ihrer religions- und sozialgeschichlichen Bedeutung*, Helsinki.

Foster, G.V., Kanada, K., and Michaelides, D. 1988. 'A Roman surgeon's tomb from Nea Paphos. Part 2: Ancient medicines: by-products of copper mining in Cyprus', *Report of the Department of Antiquities Cyprus, 1988 (Part 2)*, Nicosia, 229–34.

Foster, G.V. and Kanada, K. 1988. 'The medicines and their analysis', in Foster, Kanada and Michaelides 1988, 229–30.

Fratini, F., Cilia, G., Turchi, B., and Felicioli, A. 2016. 'Beeswax: a minireview of its antimicrobial activity and its application in medicine', *Asian Pacific Journal of Tropical Medicine* 9, 839–43.

Fuentes Dominguez, A. 1987. 'Instrumentos Romanos de Medicina en el Museo de Cuenca', *Archivo Espanol de Arqueologia* 60, 251–74.

Fulcher, K., Stacey. R., Spencer. N. 2020. 'Bitumen from the Dead Sea in Early Iron Age Nubia', *Scientific Reports* 10, 8309 (doi: 10.1038/s41598-020-64209-8).

Garcia-Ballester, L. 1981. 'Galen as a medical practitioner: Problems in diagnosis', in *Galen: Problems and Prospects*, edited by V. Nutton, London, 13–46.

Garcia-Ballester, L. 1994. 'Galen as a clinician: His methods in diagnosis', in *Aufstieg und Niedergang der römischen Welt (ANRW)* II,

37.2, edited by W. Haase and H. Temporini, Berlin/New York, 1636–71.

Gardner, P. and Poole, R.S. (eds) 1883. *Catalogue of Greek Coins: Thessaly to Aetolia*, London.

Garnier, N., Cren-Olivé, C., Rolando, C. and Regert, M. 2002. 'Characterization of archaeological beeswax by electron ionization and electrospray ionization mass spectrometry', *Analytical Chemistry* 74(19), 4868–77 (doi: 10.1021/ac025637a).

Gazzaniga, V. and Marinozzi, S. 2018. 'L'enfant de Fidene', in Verbanck-Pierard *et al.* 2018, 189–93.

Germanà, F. and Fornaciari, G. 1992. *Trapanazioni, craniotomie e trauma cranici in Italia dalla Preistoria all'Età moderna*, Pisa.

Ghiretti, G. 2010. 'Un ambulatorio medico antico: Due libri recenti sul "Chirurgo di Rimini"', *Papyrotheke* 1, 81–96.

Giachi, G., Pallecchi, P., Romualdi, A., Ribechini, E., Lucejko, J.J., Colombini, M.P., and Lippi, M.M. 2013. 'Ingredients of a 2,000–y-old medicine revealed by chemical, mineralogical, and botanical investigations', *Proceedings of the National Academy of Sciences* 110(4), 1193–6.

Gibbins, D. 1988. 'Surgical instruments from a Roman shipwreck off Sicily', *Antiquity* 62, 294–7.

Gibbins, D. 1989. 'The Roman wreck of c. AD 200 at Plemmirio, near Siracusa (Sicily): Second interim report. The domestic assemblage 1: Medical equipment and pottery lamps', *The International Journal of Nautical Archaeology* 18(1), 1–25.

Gibbins, D. 1997. 'More underwater finds of Roman medical equipment', *Antiquity* 71, 457–9.

Gilson, A. 1981. 'A group of Roman surgical and medical instruments from Corbridge', *Saalburg Jahrbuch* 37, 5–9.

Gilson, A. 1983. 'A group of Roman surgical and medical instruments from Cramond, Scotland', *Medizinhistorisches Journal* 18, 384–93.

Gitton-Ripoll, V. 2016. *La trousse du vétérinaire dans l'Antiquité et au Moyen Âge. Instruments et pratiques = Pallas* 101 (Actes du Ive colloque international de médecine vétérinaire antique et médievale, Lyon, 10–12 juin 2014), volume coordonné par Valérie Gitton-Ripoll, Toulouse.

Giumlia-Mair, A. 2000. 'Roman metallurgy: Workshops, alloys, techniques and open questions', in *Ancient Metallurgy between Oriental Alps and Panonian Plain*, edited by A. Giumlia-Mair, Trieste, 107–20.

Giumlia-Mair, A.R. and Craddock, P.T. 1993. '*Corinthium aes*. Das schwarze Gold der Alchimisten', *Antike Welt* 24, 1–62.

Giumlia-Mair, A. and Lucchini, E. 2005. 'Surface analyses on modern and ancient copper based fakes' *Surface Engineering* 21, 406–10.

Gods, Beasts and Men 1991. *Gods, Beasts and Men: Images from Antiquity*, Gerald Peters Gallery/Robert Haber & Company/Artemis Fine Arts Ltd., Santa Fe, New Mexico/Dallas.

González-Minero, F.J. and Bravo-Díaz, L. 2018. 'The use of plants in skin-care products, cosmetics and fragrances: Past and present', *Cosmetics* 5, 50.

Gostenčnik, K. 2001. 'Die Spindelhaken aus Kupferlegierung vom Magdalensberg und aus Virunum in Kärnten', *Archäologisches Korrespondenzblatt* 31, 571–9.

Gostenčnik, K. 2002. 'Agathangelus the bronzesmith: The British finds in their Continental context', *Britannia* 33, 227–56.

Gostenčnik, K. 2004. 'Die medizinische Versorgung in der Stadt auf dem Magdalensburg. Ein Beitrag zum Typenspektrum spätrepublikanisch-frühkaiserzeitlicher medizinischer Instrumente', in *Die Ausgrabungen auf dem Magdalensburg 1986 bis 1990* (Magdalensberg-Grabungsbericht 17), edited by G. Piccottini, Klagenfurt, 357–442.

Gourevitch, D. 1991. 'Biberons romains: Forms et noms', in *Le Latin édecin: La constitution d'un langage scientifique*, edited by G. Sabbah, Centre Jean Palerne Mémoires X, St Étienne, 117–33.

Gourevitch, D. 1998. 'Collyres romains inscrits', *Histoires des Sciences Médicales* 32(4), 365–72.

Gourevitch, D. 2011. *Pour une archéologie de la médecine romaine* (Collection Pathographie 8), Paris.

Gourevitch, D., Moirin, A., and Rouquet, N. 2003. *Maternité et petite enfance dans l'Antiquité romaine. Catalogue de l'exposition Bourges, Muséum d'histoire naturelle 6 novembre 2003 – 28 mars 2004*, Bourges.

Grmek, M.D. and Gourevitch, D. 1998. *Les Maladies dans l'art antique*, Paris.

Grueber, H.A. 1874. *Roman Medallions in the British Museum*, London,

Gui, M. 2011. 'Evidence for medical and personal care in the case of the Roman army in Dacia', *Ephemeris Napocensis* 21, 115–30.

Guineau, B. 1989. 'Étude physico-chimique de la composition de vingt collyres secs d'époque gallo-romaine', *Bulletin de la Société Nationale des Antiquaires de France* 1989, 1991, 132–40.

Guzzo. P.G. 1974. 'Luzzi. Località S. Vito (Cosenza). Necropoli di età romana', *Notizie degli Scavi* 28, 449–84.

Ha, Y.W. and Thomas, R.L. 1988. 'Simultaneous determination of neutral sugars and uronic acids in hydrocolloids', *Journal of Food Science* 53, 574–7.

Hanson, A.E. 1995. 'Uterine amulets and Greek uterine medicine', *Medicina nei Secoli* 7(2), 281–99.

Hanson, A. 2006. 'Roman medicine', in *A Companion to the Roman Empire*, edited by D.S. Potter, Oxford, 492–523.

Hanson, A. 2019. 'The Greek doctor in Ptolemaic, Roman and Byzantine Egypt', in *Greek Medical Papyri: Text, Context, Hypertext* (Archiv für Papyrusforschung Beiheft 40), edited by N. Reggiani, Berlin/Boston, 123–32.

Hauff, E. 1993/1994. 'Die medizinische Versorgung von Carnuntum', *Carnuntum-Jahrbuch 1993/1994*, 89–196.

Al-Hazmi, M.I and Stauffer, K.R. 1986. 'Gas chromatographic determination of hydrolyzed sugars in commercial gums', *Journal of Food Science* 51, 1091–2.

Healy, J.F. 1978. *Mining and Metallurgy in the Greek and Roman World*, London/New York, 245–51.

Heres, H. 1992. 'Ein römisches Arztkästchen aus Kyzikos', in Krug 1992a, 157–65.

Hernandez, E.M. and Kamal-Eldin, A. 2013. *Cosmetic and Pharmaceutical Properties of Fats and Oils. Processing and Nutrition of Fats and Oils*, Chichester.

Heron, C., Nemcek, N., Bonfield, K.M., Dixon, D., and Ottaway, B.S. 1994. 'The chemistry of neolithic beeswax', *Naturwissenschaften* 81, 266–9.

Heymans, H. 1979. 'Eine Hülse mit Arztinstrumenten aus Maaseik (Belgien)', *Archäologisches Korrespondenzblatt* 9, 97–100.

Hibbs, V. 1991. 'Roman surgical and medical instruments from La Cañada Honda (Gandul)', *Archivo Español de Arqueología* 64, 111–34.

Hicks, E.L. 1874. *The Collection of Ancient Greek Inscriptions in the British Museum, I*, Oxford.

Higgs, P. 2014. 'Inscribed votive offering', in Stampolidis and Tassoulas 2014, 230–2.

Hillert, A. 1990. *Antike Ärztedarstellungen* (Marburger Schriften zur Medizingeschichte 25), Frankfurt.

Hillert, A. 2005. 'Stolz darauf, ein Arzt zu sein', *Deutsches Ärzteblatt* 102(37), A2490.

Hirt, M. 2000. 'Les édecins à Avenches', *Bulletin de l'Association Pro Aventico* 42, 93–133.

Hobbs, R. 2008. 'The secret history of the Mildenhall Treasure', *Antiquaries Journal* 88, 376–420.

Hook, D.R. 1988. 'Scientific analysis of the copperbased medals', in *French Medals 1600–1672: A Catalogue of the French Medals in the British Museum*, vol. 2, edited by M. Jones, London, 305–12.

Hook, D.R. 1998. 'Inductivelycoupled plasma atomic emission spectrometry and its role in numismatic studies', in *Metallurgy in Numismatics*, vol. 4, edited by W.A. Oddy and M.R. Cowell, Royal Numismatic Society, London, 237–52.

Hughes, J. 2021. *Votive Body Parts in Greek and Roman Religion*, Cambridge.

Hughes, M.J., Cowell, M.R., and Craddock, P.T. 1976. 'Atomic absorption techniques in archaeology', *Archaeometry*, 18, 19–37.

Hyland, A. 1990. 'Veterinary medicine', in *Equus: the Horse in the Roman World*, A. Hyland, London, 49–60.

Ignatiadou, D. 2015. 'The warrior priest in Derveni grave B was a healer too', *Histoire, Médecine et Santé* 8, 89–113.

Ilani, S., Rosenfeld, A., and Dvorachek, M. 1999. 'Mineralogy and chemistry of a Roman remedy from Judea, Israel', *Journal of Archaeological Science* 26, 1323–6.

Işın, G. 2002. 'Ointment/medicine vessels from Patara: An overview of a simple Hellenistic form in the ancient Mediterranean world', *Archaeologische Anzeiger* 2, 85–96.

Israelowich, I. 2015. *Patients and Healers in the High Roman Empire*, Baltimore, MD.

Jackson, R. 1986. 'A set of Roman medical instruments from Italy', *Britannia* 17, 119–67.

Jackson, R. 1987. 'A set of surgical instruments from Roman Italy', in *Archéologie et Médecine: Actes du colloque 23.24.25 octobre 1986*, VIIèmes Rencontres Internationales d'Archéologie et d'Histoire, Antibes 1986, Juan-les-Pins, 413–28.

Jackson, R. 1988. *Doctors and Diseases in the Roman Empire*, London/Norman, OK.

Jackson, R. 1990a. 'Roman doctors and their instruments: Recent research into ancient practice', *Journal of Roman Archaeology* 3, 5–27.

Jackson, R. 1990b. 'A new collyrium stamp from Cambridge and a corrected reading of the stamp from Caistor-by-Norwich', *Britannia* 21, 275–83.

Jackson, R. 1990c. 'Waters and spas in the Classical world', in *The Medical History of Spas and Waters* (*Medical History* Supplement no. 10), edited by R.S. Porter and W.F. Bynum, 1–13.

Jackson, R. 1991. 'Roman bivalve dilators and Celsus' "instrument like a Greek letter …" (*De Med*. VII, 5, 2B)', in *Le Latin médical: La constitution d'un langage scientifique*, edited by G. Sabbah, Centre Jean Palerne Mémoires X, St Étienne, 101–10.

Jackson, R. 1992. '*Staphylagra*, *staphylocaustes*, uvulectomy and haemorrhoidectomy: The Roman instruments and operations', in Krug 1992a, 167–85.

Jackson, R. 1993. 'Roman medicine: the practitioners and their practices', in *Aufstieg und Niedergang der römischen Welt (ANRW)* II, 37.1, edited by W. Haase and H. Temporini, Berlin/New York, 79–101.

Jackson, R. 1994a. 'The surgical instruments, appliances and equipment in Celsus' *De medicina*', in *La médecine de Celse: Aspects historiques, scientifiques et littéraires* (Centre Jean Palerne Mémoires XIII), edited by G. Sabbah and Ph. Mudry, St Étienne, 167–209.

Jackson, R. 1994b. 'The mouse, the lion and "the crooked one": Two enigmatic Roman handle types', *Antiquaries Journal* 74, 325–32.

Jackson, R. 1994c. 'Medical instruments in the "Antiquarium" at Pompeii', in Bliquez 1994, 200–18.

Jackson, R. 1995a. 'The composition of Roman medical *instrumentaria* as an indicator of medical practice: A provisional assessment', in van der Eijk *et al.* 1995, vol. 1, 189–207.

Jackson, R. 1995b. 'A Roman healer god from Sussex', *British Museum Magazine* 23, 19–21.

Jackson, R. 1996a. 'Eye medicine in the Roman Empire', in *Aufstieg und Niedergang der römischen Welt (ANRW)* II, 37.3, edited by W. Haase and H. Temporini, Berlin/New York, 2228–51.

Jackson, R. 1996b. 'A new collyrium-stamp from Staines and some thoughts on eye medicine in Roman London and Britannia', in *Interpreting Roman London. Papers in Memory of Hugh Chapman*, edited by J. Bird, M. Hassall and H. Sheldon, Oxford, 177–87.

Jackson, R. 1997a. 'Medical instruments in the Roman world', *Medicina nei Secoli* 9(2), 223–48.

Jackson, R. 1997b. 'A novel Roman forceps', *The Ashmolean* 33, 15–16.

Jackson, R. 1997c. 'An ancient British medical kit from Stanway, Essex', *The Lancet* 350, 1471–3.

Jackson, R. 1999. 'Spas, waters and hydrotherapy in the Roman world', in *Roman Baths and Bathing. Part 1: Bathing and Society* (Journal of Roman Archaeology Supplementary Series Number 37), edited by J. DeLaine and D.E. Johnston, Portsmouth, RI, 107–16.

Jackson, R. 2000. 'The medical collections of the British Museum', *Medicina nei Secoli* 12(2), 329–38.

Jackson, R. 2002a. 'Roman surgery: The evidence of the instruments', in Arnott 2002, 87–94.

Jackson, R. 2002b. 'A Roman doctor's house in Rimini', *British Museum Magazine* 44, 20–3.

Jackson, R. 2002c. 'Strumenti e chirurgia ossea nell'Impero Romano', in *La medicina greco-romana: dodici conferenze* (Scienza e Tecnologia nel mondo greco-romano), edited by E. Volterrani and G. Fornaciari, Pisa, 149–66.

Jackson, R. 2003. 'The Domus 'del chirurgo' at Rimini: An interim account of the medical assemblage', *Journal of Roman Archaeology* 16, 312–21.

Jackson, R. 2005a. 'Holding on to health? Bone surgery and instrumentation in the Roman Empire', in King 2005, 97–119.

Jackson, R. 2005b. 'The role of doctors in the city', in *Roman Working Lives and Urban Living*, edited by A. MacMahon and J. Price, Oxford, 202–20.

Jackson, R. 2005c. 'Circumcision, de-circumcision and self-image: Celsus's "operations on the penis"', in *Roman Bodies: Antiquity to the Eighteenth Century*, edited by A. Hopkins and M. Wyke, London, 23–32.

Jackson, R. 2007a. 'The surgical instruments', in Crummy *et al.* 2007, 236–52.

Jackson, R. 2007b. 'Recent important discoveries of Roman surgical instruments', in *Storia della medicina, scienza dell'uomo* (Atti del convegno internazionale Napoli 22–23 ottobre 1998), edited by L. Melillo, Naples, 17–26.

Jackson, R. 2008. 'Imagining health-care in Roman London', in *Londinium and Beyond: Essays on Roman London and Its Hinterland for Harvey Sheldon* (Council for British Archaeology Research Report 156), edited by J. Clark, J. Cotton, J. Hall, R. Sherris and H. Swain, London, 194–200.

Jackson, R. 2009a. 'The role of urban healers in the Roman world', in De Carolis and Pesaresi 2009, 57–104.

Jackson, R. 2009b. 'Lo strumentario chirurgico della *domus* riminese' /'The surgical instrumentation of the Rimini *domus*', in De Carolis 2009, 73–91.

Jackson, R. 2010. 'Cutting for stone: Roman lithotomy instruments in the Museo Nazionale Romano', *Medicina nei Secoli* 22(1–3), 393–418.

Jackson, R. 2011a. 'Medicine and hygiene', in *Artefacts in Roman Britain: Their Purpose and Use*, edited by L. Allason-Jones, Cambridge, 243–68.

Jackson, R. 2011b. 'Scalpel handle', 61–2, in 'The *praetorium* of Edmund Artis: A summary of excavations and surveys of the palatial Roman structure at Castor, Cambridgeshire 1828–2010', by S.G. Upex *et al.*, *Britannia* 42, 23–112.

Jackson, R. 2011c. 'La tombe de Stanway: Un celte romanisé, druide et médecin?', in Dasen 2011, 22–4.

Jackson, R. 2011d. 'Les instruments découverts à Rimini', in Dasen 2011, 25–7.

Jackson, R. 2011e. 'Le chirurgien de Rimini', in Gourevitch 2011, 120–6.

Jackson, R. 2012a. 'Senex, samian and saffron – solution in sight?', in *Dating and Interpreting the Past in the Western Roman Empire: Essays in Honour of Brenda Dickinson*, edited by D. Bird, Oxford, 223–33.

Jackson, R. 2012b. 'Urban healers in the Roman Empire', *Transactions of the Medical Society of London*, 125/126, 2008–9 (2012), 97–116.

Jackson, R. 2012c. 'Roman Colchester at the British Museum', *The Colchester Archaeologist* 25, 16–23.

Jackson, R. 2013. 'De la cosmétique à la cataracte: Les instruments romains pour les soins des yeux', trans. D. Gourevitch, in Pardon-Labonnelie 2013a, 51–61.

Jackson, R. 2014a. 'Back to basics: Surgeon's knives in the Roman world', in Michaelides 2014, 130–44.

Jackson, R. 2014b. 'Tailpiece: Roman mice in art, allegory and actuality', in *Life in the* Limes: *Studies of the People and Objects of the Roman Frontiers*, edited by R. Collins and F. McIntosh, Oxford, 217–31.

Jackson, R. 2014c. Catalogue entries in Stampolidis and Tassoulas 2014, nos 128, 145, 157, 183, 185, 219.

Jackson, R. 2018a. 'Les instruments de Galien', in Verbanck-Pierard *et al.* 2018, 134–47.

Jackson, R. 2018b. 'A Roman embryo hook', Exhibit 6, in *Reproduction: Antiquity to the Present Day*, edited by N. Hopwood, R. Flemming and L. Kassell, Cambridge.

Jackson, R. 2019. 'Just what the doctor ordered!', review of Lawrence J. Bliquez, *The Tools of Asclepius: Surgical Instruments in Greek and Roman Times*, *Journal of Roman Archaeology* 32, 624–7.

Jackson, R. 2021. 'Lost and found: Roman surgical instruments from Cyrene, Libya', in *Des objets et des hommes. Etudes offertes à Michel Feugère* (Monographies Instrumentum 71), edited by C. Léger and S. Raux, Drémil-Lafage, 543–52.

Jackson, R. forthcoming. 'A large set of Roman medical and surgical instruments in the Ashmolean Museum, Oxford'.

Jackson, R. and Leahy, K. 1990. 'A Roman surgical forceps from near Littleborough and a note on the type', *Britannia* 21, 271–4.

Jackson, R.P.J. and Potter, T.W. 1996. *Excavations at Stonea, Cambridgeshire 1980–85*, London.

Jakielski, K.E. and Notis, M.R. 2000. 'The metallurgy of Roman medical instruments', *Materials Characterization* 45, 379–389.

Jocks, I.T. 2020. 'Scribonius Largus' compounding of drugs (Compositiones medicamentorum): Introduction, translation, and medicohistorical comments', PhD thesis, vol. II: Translation with explanatory notes and medico-historical comments (http://theses.gla.ac.uk/82178/; accessed May 2023).

Jokinen, J.J. and Sipponen, A. 2016. 'Refined spruce resin to treat chronic wounds: Rebirth of an old folkloristic therapy', *Advances in Wound Care (New Rochelle)* 5, 198–207.

Kančeva-Ruseva, T., Velkov, K., and Ignatov, V. 1996. *Investigation of Tumuli in the Region of Nova Zagora*, Ruse.

Kanz, F. 2011. 'Le cimetière des gladiateurs d'Éphèse', in Dasen 2011b, 73–5.

Kanz, F. and Grossschmidt, K. 2009. 'Dying in the arena: The osseous evidence from Ephesian gladiators', in *Roman Amphitheatres and Spectacula: A 21st Century Perspective* (British Archaeological Reports International Series 1946), edited by T. Wilmot, Oxford, 211–20.

Karmakar, K. 2016. 'Application of natural gum as a binder in modern drug delivery', *Journal of Analytical and Pharmaceutical Research* 3, 61.

Katsifas, C.S., Ignatiadou, D., Zacharopoulou, A., Kantiranis, N., Karapanagiotis, I., and Zachariadis, G.A. 2018. 'Non-destructive X-ray spectrometric and chromatographic analysis of metal containers and their contents, from Ancient Macedonia', *Separations* 5, 32.

Kidd, D. 1977. 'Charles Roach Smith and his Museum of London Antiquities', *The British Museum Yearbook* 2, 105–36.

King, H. (ed.) 2005. *Health in Antiquity*, London/New York.

Kirkup, J. 2006. *The Evolution of Surgical Instruments. An Illustrated History from Ancient Times to the Twentieth Century*, Novato, CA.

Kirova, N. 2002. 'Specialized medical instruments from Bulgaria in the context of finds from other Roman provinces (I–IV C AD)', *Archaeologia Bulgarica* 6, 73–94.

Kleibrink, M. 1997. 'The style and technique of the engraved gems', in *The Snettisham Roman Jeweller's Hoard*, C. Johns, London, 25–33.

Korać, M. 1986. 'Medicus et chirurgus ocularius iz Viminacijuma', *Starinar* 37, 53–71.

Kornmeier, U. (ed.) 2016. *The Soul is an Octopus: Ancient Ideas of Life and the Body*, Berlin.

Kotansky, R. 1991. 'Incantations and prayers on inscribed Greek amulets', in *Magica Hiera*, edited by C.A. Faraone and D. Obbink, Oxford/New York, 107–37.

Kotansky, R. 1994. *Greek Magical Amulets: The Inscribed Gold, Silver, Copper, and Bronze Lamellae*, Opladen.

Krause, R. 1995. 'Das Gewinde in der Antike', in Deppert-Lippitz *et al.* 1995, 23–54.

Krug, A. 1982. 'Die Gemme eines Arztes', *Medizinhistorisches Journal* 17, 390–2.

Krug, A. 1985 (2nd ed. 1993). *Heilkunst und Heilkult: Medizin in der Antike*, München.

Krug, A. 1987. 'Nero's Augenglas. Realia zu einer Anekdote', in *Archéologie et Médecine: actes du colloque 23.24.25 octobre 1986*, VIIèmes Rencontres Internationales d'Archéologie et d'Histoire, Antibes 1986, Juan-les-Pins, 459–75.

Krug, A. (ed.) 1992a. *From Epidaurus to Salerno: Symposium held at the European University Centre for Cultural Heritage, Ravello, April 1990*, *Journal of the European Study Group on Physical, Chemical, Biological and Mathematical Techniques Applied to Archaeology (PACT)* 34.

Krug, A. 1992b. 'Medizin und Ärztewesen', in *Carnuntum. Das Erbe Roms an der Donau*, edited by W. Jobst, Vienna, 153–61.

Krug, A. 1993. 'Römische Skalpelle: Herstellungstechnische Anmerkungen', *Medizinhistorisches Journal* 28(1), 93–100.

Krug, A. 2008. *Das Berliner Arztrelief* (Winckelmannsprogramm der Archäologischen Gesellschaft zu Berlin, 142), Berlin.

Krug, A. 2011. '*Lege artis* – The rules of the art', *Arqueólogo Portugués* Series V, vol. 1, 543–59.

Künzl, E. 1979/81. 'Medizinische Instrumente aus dem römischen Altertum im städtischen Museum Worms', *Der Wormsgau* 13, 49–63.

Künzl, E. 1982a. '*Ventosae cucurbitae romanae?* Zu einem angeblich antiken Schröpfkopftypus', *Germania* 60, 513–32.

Künzl, E. 1982b. 'Was soll die Maus auf dem chirurgischen Instrument?', in *Antidoron. Festschrift Jürgen Thimme*, edited by D. Metzler, B. Otto and C. Müller-Wirth, Karlsruhe, 111–16.

Künzl, E. 1983a. *Medizinische Instrumente aus Sepulkralfunden der römischen Kaiserzeit* (Kunst und Altertum am Rhein 115, Sonderdruck aus den Bonner Jahrbüchern Band 182, 1982), Köln/Bonn.

Künzl, E. 1983b. 'Eine Spezialität römischer Chirurgen: die Lithotomie', *Archäologisches Korrespondenzblatt* 13, 487–93.

Künzl, E. 1984a. 'Einige Bemerkungen zu den Herstellern der römischen medizinischen Instrumente', *Alba Regia* 21, 59–65.

Künzl, E. 1984b. 'Medizinische Instrumente der Römerzeit aus Trier und Umgebung im Landesmuseum Trier', *Trierer Zeitschrift* 47, 153–237.

Künzl, E. 1985. 'Runde Metallétuis mit Instrumenten aus der Römerzeit', 447–8, 'Datierung anhand von Form und Ornamenten', 448–53, 'Massive und hohle Nadeln', 453–4, 'Die antiken Schriftquellen', 454–64, 'Römische Starnadeln im Rahmen von Instrumentarien aus Kleinasien, Griechenland, Italien und Gallien', 464–8, 'Epigraphische Zeugnisse römischer Augenärzte: Inschriften und Okulistenstempel', 468–77, 'Gallische Augenoperateure', 478–81, = Sections 8–14 in Feugère, Künzl, and Weisser 1985, 447–81.

Künzl, E. 1986a. 'Operationsräume in römischen Thermen. Zu einem chirurgischen Instrumentarium aus der Colonia Ulpia Traiana mit einem Auswahlkatalog römischer medizinischer Instrumente im Rheinischen Landesmuseum Bonn', *Bonner Jahrbücher* 186, 491–509.

Künzl, E. 1986b. 'Eine Serie von Fälschungen römischer medizinischer Instrumentarien. Mit einem Beitrag von Dietrich Ankner', *Archäologisches Korrespondenzblatt* 16, 333–9.

Künzl, E. 1991a. 'La tomba del medico di Obermenzing', in *I Celti*, Milan, 372–3.

Künzl, E. 1991b. 'Die Instrumente aus Ephesos und Kos', in 'Die Antiken der Sammlung Meyer-Steineg in Jena I' (S. Zimmermann and E. Künzl, *Jahrbuch des Römisch-Germanischen Zentralmuseums Mainz* 38), 519–40.

Künzl, E. 1992. 'Spätantike und byzantinische medizinische Instrumente', in Krug 1992a, 201–44.

Künzl, E., 1994a. 'Ein dekoriertes römisches Skalpell des 1. Jahrhunderts n. Chr. aus Vetera I', in *Xantener Berichte* 5, Köln/Bonn, 211–17.

Künzl, E. 1995a. 'Medizin der Kelten. Ein archäologischer Forschungsbericht', in *Mélanges Raymond Chevallier. Vol. 2: Histoire et archéologie*, edited by R. Bedon and P.M. Martin, Tours, 221–39.

Künzl, E. 1995b. Ein archäologisches Problem: Gräber römischer Chirurginnen', in van der Eijk *et al.* 1995, vol. 1, 309–19.

Künzl, E. 1996. 'Forschungsbericht zu den antiken medizinischen Instrumenten', in *Aufstieg und Niedergang der römischen Welt (ANRW)* II, 37.3, edited by W. Haase and H. Temporini, Berlin/New York, 2433–639.

Künzl, E. 1998. 'Instrumentenfunde und Arzthäuser in Pompeji: die medizinische Versorgung einer römischen Stadt des 1. Jahrhunderts n. Chr.', *Sartoniana* 11, 71–152.

Künzl, E. 2001. 'Antike Werbegeschenke: Xenia aus Ephesos', in *Studia Archaeologica et Historica Nicolao Gudea Dicata* (Acta Musei Porolissensis Bibliotheca Musei Porolissensis IV), edited by C. Cosma, D. Tamba and A. Rustoiu, Zalău, 213–18.

Künzl, E. 2002a. *Medizinische Instrumente der römischen Kaiserzeit im Römisch-Germanischen Zentralmuseum* (Kataloge vor- und frühgeschichtlicher Altertümer 28), mit einem Beitrag von Josef Riederer, Mainz.

Künzl, E. 2002b. *Medizin in der Antike: Aus einer Welt ohne Narkose und Aspirin*, Stuttgart.

Künzl, E. 2005. 'Das römische Köln. Die medizinische Versorgung einer grossen römischen Stadt', in *Krank-gesund. 2000 Jahre Krankheit und Gesundheit in Köln*, edited by T. Deres, Köln, 38–53.

Künzl, E. 2011. 'Le décor des instruments', in Gourevitch 2011, 126–32.

Künzl, E. 2013. *Medica: Die Ärztin*, Mainz.

Künzl, E. 2018. 'Was hat die Archäologie zu sagen? Archäologische Beiträge zur Medizingeschichte', in *Medizin und Militär – Surgeons and Soldiers. Beiträge zur Wundversorgung und Verwundetenfürsorge im Altertum* (Archäologischer Park Carnuntum Neue Forschungen 15), edited by R. Breitwieser, F. Humer, E. Pollhammer and R. Arnott, Carnuntum, 15–45, 148–61, 180–1.

Künzl, E. and Feugère, M. 2002. 'Les instruments ophtalmologiques romains: Essai de synthèse', in *Autour de l'oeil dans l'antiquité. Approche pluridisciplinaire, Table ronde de Lons-le-Saunier – Jura – 11–12 février 1994*, Lons-le-Saunier, 115–24.

Künzl, E. and Weber, T. 1991. 'Das spätantike Grab eines Zahnarztes zu Gadara in der Dekapolis', *Damaszener Mitteilungen* 5, 81–118.

Łajtar, A. and Południkiewicz, A. 2017. 'Medicinal vessels from Tell Atrib (Egypt)', *Études et Travaux* XXX, 315–37.

Lambros, K.P.I. 1895. Περί σικυών και σικυάσεως παρά τοίς αρχαίοις, Athens.

La Niece, S. 1986. 'Scientific examination', in Jackson 1986, 161–5.

La Niece, S. and Craddock, P.T. (eds) 1993. *Metal Plating and Patination: Cultural, Technical and Historical Developments*, London.

Langenheim, J. H. 2003. *Plant Resins: Chemistry, Evolution, Ecology and Ethnobotany*, Portland, OR.

Lardos, A., Prieto-Garcia, J. and Heinrich, M. 2011. 'Resins and gums in historical iatrosophia texts from Cyprus – a botanical and medico-pharmacological approach', *Frontiers in Pharmacology* 2, 32.

Leandro, L.F., Cardoso, M.J.O., Silva, S.D.C., Souza, M.G.M., Veneziani, R.C.S., Ambrosio, S.R., and Martins, C.H.G. 2014. 'Antibacterial activity of Pinus elliottii and its major compound, dehydroabietic acid, against multidrug-resistant strains', *Journal of Medical Microbiology* 63, 1649–53.

Leemans, C. 1842. *Romeinse steenen Doodskisten*, Nijhoff's Bijdragen, Arnhem.

Leffler, C.T., Hadi, T.M., Udupa, A., Schwartz, S.G. and Schwartz, D. 2016. 'A medieval fallacy: The crystalline lens in the center of the eye', *Clinical Ophthalmology* 10, 649–62.

Lioux, M. 2016. 'Un garrot dans l'instrumentarium du médecin antique?', *Histoire, médecine et santé*, 8, 69–87.

Longfield-Jones, G.M. 1986. 'A Graeco-Roman speculum in the Wellcome Museum', *Medical History* 30, 81–9.

Longrigg, J. 1988. 'Anatomy in Alexandria in the third century BC', *British Journal for the History of Science* 21, 455–88.

Longrigg, J. 1998. *Greek Medicine from the Heroic to the Hellenistic Age: A Source Book*, London.

Maddoli, G. 1998. 'Il medicamento lykion', *Archeologia Classica* 50, 213–72.

Maiuri, A. 1939. 'Regione I (Latium e Campania). I. Pompei. Scavo della "Grande Palestra" nel quartiere dell'Anfiteatro (a. 1935–1939)', *Notizie degli Scavi* 1939, 165–238.

Majno, G. 1975. *The Healing Hand. Man and Wound in the Ancient World*, Cambridge, MA.

Manning, W.H. 1985. *Catalogue of the Romano-British Iron Tools, Fittings and Weapons in the British Museum*, London.

Marengo, S.M. and Taborelli, L. 2013. 'A proposito dei *Peticii* e il commercio orientale', *Archeologia Classica* 64, 583–9.

Marganne, M.-H. 1994. *L'ophtalmologie dans l'Égypte gréco-romaine d'après les papyrus littéraires grecs* (Studies in Ancient Medicine 8), Leiden.

Marganne, M.-H. 1998. *La chirurgie dans l'Égypte gréco-romaine d'après les papyrus littéraires grecs* (Studies in Ancient Medicine 17), Leiden.

Marganne, M.-H. 2001. 'Une innovation dans la chirurgie hellénistique: L'opération de la cataracte', *Medizinhistorisches Journal* 36, 23–33.

Marganne, M.-H. 2003. 'Le médecin, la trousse et le livre dans le monde gréco-romain', in *Da Ercolano all'Egitto. IV. Ricerche varie di papirologia = Papyrologica Lupiensa* 12, edited by M. Capasso, 117–30.

Marganne, M.-H. 2018. 'Lire Galien dans l'Égypte Romaine et Byzantine: Le témoignage des papyrus', in Verbanck-Pierard *et al.* 2018, 227–33.

Marganne-Mélard, M.-H. 1987. 'Les instruments chirurgicaux de l'Égypte gréco-romaine', in *Archéologie et Médecine: Actes du colloque 23.24.25 octobre 1986* (VIIèmes Rencontres Internationales d'Archéologie et d'Histoire, Antibes 1986), Juan-les-Pins, 403–12.

Marganne-Mélard, M.-H. 1996. 'La médecine dans l'Égypte romaine: Les sources et les méthodes', in *Aufstieg und Niedergang der römischen Welt (ANRW)* II, 37.3, edited by W. Haase and H. Temporini, Berlin/New York, 2709–40.

Mariani-Costantini, R., Catalano, P., di Gennaro, F., di Tota, G., and Angeletti, L.R. 2000. 'New light on cranial surgery in ancient Rome', *The Lancet* 355, 305–7.

Massar, N. 1998. 'Choix d'inscriptions: La profession médicale dans l'épigraphie', in *Au temps d'Hippocrate. Médecine et société en Grèce antique*, edited by A. Verbanck-Piérard, Mariemont, 89–94.

Massar, N. 2005. *Soigner et servir. Histoire sociale et culturelle de la médecine grecque à l'époque hellénistique*, Paris.

Mastrocinque, A. 2011. 'The colours of magical gems', in *'Gems of Heaven'. Recent research on engraved gemstones in Late Antiquity, c. AD 200–600*, edited by C. Entwistle and N. Adams, London, 62–8.

Mattern, S.P. 2013. *The Prince of Medicine. Galen in the Roman Empire*, Oxford.

Matthäus, H. 1989. *Der Arzt in römischer Zeit: Medizinische Instrumente und Arzneien*, Aalen.

Mattingly, H. 1975. *Coins of the Roman Empire in the British Museum, Vol. V: Pertinax to Elagabalus*, London.

McCann, A.M. 1978. *Roman Sarcophagi in the Metropolitan Museum of Art*, New York.

Meiggs, R. 1960. *Roman Ostia*, Oxford.

Meyer-Steineg, T. 1912. *Chirurgische Instrumente des Altertums*, Jena.

Meyer-Steineg, T. and Sudhoff, K. 1921. *Geschichte der Medizin im Überblick mit Abbildungen*, Jena.

Michaelides, D. 1984. 'A Roman surgeon's tomb from Nea Paphos. Part 1', *Report of the Department of Antiquities Cyprus, 1984*, Nicosia, 315–32.

Michaelides, D. 1988. 'Analyses of other ancient medicines' in Foster, Kanada and Michaelides 1988, 230–1.

Michaelides, D. (ed). 2014. *Medicine and Healing in the Ancient Mediterranean World*, Oxford.

Michel, S. 2001. *Die magischen Gemmen im Britischen Museum*, London.

Mills, J.S. and White, R. 1994. *The Organic Chemistry of Museum Objects*, Oxford.

Milne, J.S. 1907. *Surgical Instruments in Greek and Roman Times*, Oxford (repr. Chicago, IL, 1976).

Minchev, A. 1983. 'Roman medicine in Marcianopolis', in *Concilium Eirene XVI. Proceedings of the 16th International Eirene Conference, Prague 31.8. – 4.9. 1982*, vol. 2, edited by P. Oliva and A. Froliková, Prague, 143–8.

Moschakis, C. 2014. 'Grave stele', in Stampolidis and Tassoulas 2014, 347–9.

Nerlich, A.G., Zink, A., Szeimies, U., and Hagedorn, H.G. 2000. 'Ancient Egyptian prosthesis of the big toe', *The Lancet* 356, 2176–9.

Nesměrák, K., Kudláček, K., and Babica, J. 2017. 'Analytical chemistry studying historical pharmaceuticals and health care formulations', *Monatshefte für Chemie* 148, 1557–68.

Newton, C.T. 1867. *A Guide to the Blacas Collection of Antiquities*, London.

Newton, C.T. 1883. *The Collection of Ancient Greek Inscriptions in the British Museum*, Part II, London.

Nielsen, H. 1974. *Ancient Ophthalmological Agents*, Odense.

Nissen, C. 2007. 'Asclépios et les médecins d'aprés les inscriptions grecques: Des relations cultuelles', *Medicina nei Secoli* 19(3), 721–44.

Nuber, H.U. 2004. 'Eine Grablege reicher Landbesitzer in Wehringen', in *Die Römer zwischen Alpen und Nordmeer. Zivilisatorisches Erbe einer europäischen Militärmarkt*, edited by L. Wamser, C. Flügel and B. Ziegaus, Rosenheim, 168–70.

Nutton, V. 1972. 'Roman oculists', *Epigraphica* 34, 16–29.

Nutton V. 1985. 'The drug trade in antiquity', *Journal of the Royal Society of Medicine* 78, 138–45.

Nutton, V. 1992. 'Healers in the medical market place: Towards a social history of Graeco-Roman medicine', in *Medicine in Society*, edited by A. Wear, Cambridge, 1–58.

Nutton, V. 1993. 'Roman medicine: Tradition, confrontation, assimilation', in *Aufstieg und Niedergang der römischen Welt (ANRW)* II, 37.1, edited by W. Haase and H. Temporini, Berlin/New York, 49–78.

Nutton, V. 1995. 'The medical meeting place', in van der Eijk *et al.* 1995, vol. 1, 3–25.

Nutton, V. 2004; 2nd ed. 2013; 3rd ed. 2023. *Ancient Medicine*, London/New York.

Nutton, V. 2013. 'Avoiding distress', in *Galen: Psychological Writings*, edited by P.N. Singer, Cambridge/New York.

Nutton, V. 2014a. Review of D. Baykan, *Allianoi Tıp Aletleri*, in *Medical History*, 58, 122–5.

Nutton, V. 2014b. 'Rhodiapolis and Allianoi: Two missing links in the history of the hospital?', *Early Christianity* 5(3), 371–89.

Olivanti, P. 2014. 'Terracotta relief plaques', in Stampolidis and Tassoulas 2014, 262–3, 269–70.

Ortalli, J. 2000. 'Rimini: la *domus* "del chirurgo"', in *Aemilia. La cultura romana in Emilia Romagna dal III secolo a. C. all'età costantiniana*, edited by M.M. Calvani, Venice, 513–26.

Ortalli, J. 2008. 'Il *medicus* di *Ariminum*: una contestualizzazione archeologica dalla *domus* "del chirurgo"', *Rivista storica dell'antichità* 37 (2007), 101–18.

Ortalli, J. 2009. 'Archeologia e medicina: la casa del "chirurgo" riminese', in De Carolis 2009, 21–45.

Ortalli, J. 2011. 'La *domus* du chirurgien de Rimini', in Dasen 2011b, 30–4.

Ortalli, J. 2018. 'La *domus* du chirurgien à Rimini', in Verbanck-Pierard *et al.* (eds) 2018, 101–9.

Pagano, M. 2003. 'Gli scheletri dei fuggiaschi: l'indagine archeologica dale prime scoperte alle indagini interdisciplinari sui fornici 4 e 12' and 'Fornice 12', in *Storie da un'eruzione: Pompeii, Ercolano, Oplontis*, edited by A. D'Ambrosio, P.G. Guzzo and M. Mastroroberto, Milan, 124–7, 134–6.

Panofka, T.S. 1834. *Antiques du cabinet du Comte de Pourtalés-Gorgier*, Paris.

Pantermalis, D. 1997. 'Η ΑΝΑΣΚΑΦΗ ΤΟΥ ΔΙΟΥ ΚΑΤΑ ΤΟ 1993

ΚΑΙ Η ΧΑΛΚΙΝΗ ΔΙΟΠΤΡΑ', in ΤΟ ΑΡΧΑΙΟΛΟΓΙΚΟ ΕΡΙΤΟ ΣΤΗ ΜΑΚΕΔΟΝΙΑ ΚΑΙ ΘΡΑΚΗ 7, 1993, Thessalonika, 195–8.

Parani, M.G. 2010. 'Byzantine cutlery: An overview', *Deltion tes Christianikes Archaiologikes Hetaireas* 31, 139–64.

Pardon-Labonnelie, M. 2004. 'La *lippitudo* dans la littérature classique: de l'oeil qui dégoutte à l'oeil qui dégoûte', in *Testi Medici Latini Antichi. Le parole della medicina: Lessico e storia*. Atti del VII Convegno Internazionale Trieste, 11-13 ottobre 2001, edited by M. Baldin, M. Cecere and D. Crismani, Bologna, 651–62.

Pardon-Labonnelie, M. 2006. 'La préparation des collyres oculistiques dans le monde romain', in *Pharmacopoles et apothicaires: Les "pharmaciens" de l'Antiquité au Grand Siècle*, edited by F. Collard and E. Samama, Paris, 41–58.

Pardon-Labonnelie, M. 2012. 'Le soin des affections oculaires dans le monde romain: un nouvel inventaire des cachets à collyres', *Revue des Études Latines*, 90, 221–8.

Pardon-Labonnelie, M. (ed.) 2013a. *La coupe d'Hygie: Médecine et chimie dans l'Antiquité*, Dijon.

Pardon-Labonnelie, M. 2013b. 'Du κολλύριου au « collyre »', in Pardon-Labonnelie 2013a, 33–49.

Pardon-Labonnelie, M. 2014. 'Un nouveau regard sur la "tomba del medico" (Morlungo, Vénetié)', *Histoires des Sciences Médicales* 48(1), 107–24.

Pardon-Labonnelie, M. 2021. 'Les couleurs de la vue. Les propriétés thérapeutiques des couleurs dans l'ophtalmologie gréco-romaine', *Pallas* 117, 183–201.

Pardon-Labonnelie, M., Spasić-Durić, D., and Uher, E. 2020. 'Les collyres estampillés de Mésie Supérieure: Un nouveau regard sur la tombe du "médecin et chirurgien oculiste de Viminiacum"', *Histoire des Sciences Médicales* 2, 55–84.

Pastorova, I., van der Berg, K.J., Boon, J.J., and Verhoeven, J.W. 1997. 'Analysis of oxidised diterpenoid acids using thermally assisted methylation with TMAH', *Journal of Analytical and Applied Pyrolysis* 43, 41–57.

Penn, R.G. 1994. *Medicine on Ancient Greek and Roman Coins*, London.

Pérez-Arantegui, J., Paz-Peralta, J.Á., and Ortiz-Palomar, E. 1996. 'Analysis of the products contained in two Roman glass unguentaria from the colony of Celsa (Spain)', *Journal of Archaeological Science* 23, 649–55.

Perk, H. 2012. *Anadolu Antik Dönem Tip Aletleri. Halûk Perk Tip Müzesi Koleksiyonu /Anatolia Ancient Period Medicine Instruments. Halûk Perk Medicine Museum Collection*, Istanbul.

Phillips, E.D. 1973. *Greek Medicine*, London.

Rackham, H. 1961. *Pliny, Natural History*, vol. 4, London/Cambridge, MA.

Radice, B. 1963. *The Letters of the Younger Pliny*, London.

Reeves, N. 1999. 'New light on ancient Egyptian prosthetic medicine', in *Studies in Egyptian Antiquities. A Tribute to T.G.H. James*, edited by W.V. Davies, London, 73–7.

Regert, M., Bland, H.A., Dudd, S.N., Van Bergen, P.F., and Evershed, R.P. 1998a. 'Free and bound fatty acid oxidation products in archaeological ceramic vessels', *Proceedings: Biological Sciences* 265, 2027–32.

Reggiani, A.M. 1988. 'Indagini sui materiali dell'antiquario del Museo Nazionale Romano', *Archeologia Laziale IX (Quaderni del Centro di Studio per l'Archeologia Etrusco-Italica* 16), 455–66.

Ribechini, E., Modugno, F., Colombini, M.P., and Evershed, R.P. 2008. 'Gas chromatographic and mass spectrometric investigations of organic residues from Roman glass unguentaria', *Journal of Chromatography* A 1183, 158–69.

Richter, G.M.A. 1971. *Engraved Gems of the Greeks, Etruscans, and Romans, Part II: Engraved Gems of the Romans,* London.

Rickard, T.A. 1932. 'The nomenclature of copper and its alloys', *The Journal of the Royal Anthropological Institute of Great Britain and Ireland*, 62, 281–90.

Riddle, J.M. 1985. *Dioscorides on Pharmacy and Medicine*, Austin, TX.

Riddle, J.M. 1992. *Contraception and Abortion from the Ancient World to the Renaissance*, Cambridge, MA/London.

Riddle, J.M., Worth Estes, J., and Russell, J.C. 1994. 'Ever since Eve ... Birth control in the ancient world', *Archaeology* (March/April), 29–35.

Riederer, J. 2002. 'Die Metallanalysen der medizinische Geräte', in Künzl 2002a, 54–84.

Riha, E. 1986. *Römisches Toilettgerät und medizinische Instrumente aus Augst und Kaiseraugst* (Forschungen in Augst 6), Augst.

Ritsonis, A. 2014. 'Inscribed grave stele', in Stampolidis and Tassoulas 2014, 344–5.

Roach Smith, C. c.1855. *Collectanea antiqua*, vol. III, printed for the subscribers.

Roberts, P. 2013. *Life and Death in Pompeii and Herculaneum*, London.

Robinson, E.S.G. 1927. *Catalogue of the Greek Coins of Cyrenaica*, London.

Robinson, O.F. 1995. *The Criminal Law of Ancient Rome*, London.

Rocca, J. 2003. 'Galen and the uses of trepanation', in Arnott *et al.* 2003, 253–71.

Romanus, K., Van Neer, W., Marinova, E., Verbeke, K., Luypaerts, A., Accardo, S., Hermans, I., Jacobs, P., De Vos, D., and Waelkens, M. 2008. 'Brassicaceae seed oil identified as illuminant in Nilotic shells from a first millennium AD Coptic church in Bawit, Egypt', *Analytical and Bioanalytical Chemistry* 390, 783–93.

Rouquet, N. 2003. 'Les biberons, les tire-lait ou les tribulations d'une tubulure peu commune...'. in Gourevitch *et al.* 2003, 164–70.

Roy, G.M. 1994. *Activated Carbon Applications in the Food and Pharmaceutical Industries*, Boca Raton, FL.

Salazar, C.F. 2000. *The Treatment of War Wounds in Greco-Roman Antiquity* (Studies in Ancient Medicine 21), Leiden.

Salih, N.K.M. 2018. 'Applications of gum arabic in medical and health benefits', in *Gum Arabic*, edited by A.A. Mariod, Cambridge, MA.

Samama, E. 2003. *Les médecins dans le monde grec: Sources* épigraphiques *sur la naissance d'un corps médical*, Geneva.

Sax, M. 1996, 'Recognition and nomenclature of quartz materials with specific reference to engraved gemstones', *Jewellery Studies* 7, 63–72,

Scarborough, J. 1969. *Roman Medicine*, London.

Scarborough, J. 1996. 'Drugs and medicines in the Roman world', *Expedition* 38(2), 38–51.

Scarborough, J. and Nutton, V. 1982. 'The *Preface* of Dioscorides' *Materia Medica*: Introduction, translation and commentary', *Transactions and Studies of the College of Physicians of Philadelphia* new series 4, 187–227.

Schäfer, P. 1997. *Judeophobia: Attitudes towards the Jews in the Ancient World*, Cambridge, MA/London.

Scultetus, J. 1655. *Armamentarium chirurgicum*, Ulm.

Serpico, M. and White, R. 2000a. 'Resins, amber and bitumen', in *Ancient Egyptian Materials and Technology*, edited by P.T. Nicholson and I. Shaw, Cambridge, 430–74.

Sherlock, D. 2007. 'Roman forks', *Archaeological Journal* 164, 249–67.

Sideras, A. 1977. *Rufi De Renum et Vesicae Morbis (CMG* 3), 1, Berlin.

Sideras, A. 1994. 'Rufus von Ephesos und sein Werk im Rahmen der antiken Medizin', in *Aufstieg und Niedergang der römischen Welt (ANRW)* II, 37.2, edited by W. Haase and H. Temporini, Berlin/ New York, 1077–1253 and 2036–62.

Simpson, G. 1977. 'Early Roman metal objects from the excavations at Neuss', *Bonner Jahrbücher* 38, 562–4.

Simpson, J.Y. 1855. 'On some ancient Greek medical vases for containing Lykion….', *Proceedings of the Society of Antiquaries of Scotland* 1, 47–52.

Singer, C. 1956. *Galen On Anatomical Procedures. Translation of the Surviving Books with Introduction and Notes*, Oxford.

Sjöqvist, E. 1960. 'Morgantina: Hellenistic medicine bottles', *American Journal of Archaeology* 64, 78–83.

Smith, A.H. 1908. *A Guide to the Exhibition Illustrating Greek and Roman Life*, London.

Smith, R.K., Stacey, R.J., Bergström, E., and Thomas-Oates, J. 2018. 'Detection of opium alkaloids in a Cypriot base-ring juglet', *Analyst* 143, 5127–36.

Sobel, H. 1991. 'Römische Arzneikästchen', *Saalburg-Jahrbuch* 46, 121–47.

Sofroniew, A. 2014. 'Ostracon with eye-salve prescriptions', in Stampolidis and Tassoulas 2014, 290–1.

Sorel, P. 1984. 'Une trousse de médecin du IIIe siècle trouvée à Paris', in *Lutèce: Paris de César à Clovis*, Paris, 21–3, 226–32.

Spawforth, A.J.S. 1990. 'Roman medicine from the sea', *Minerva* 1(6), 9–10.

Spencer, W.G. 1935. *Celsus De Medicina*, vol. 1, London/Cambridge (MA).

Spencer, W.G. 1938a. *Celsus De Medicina*, vol. 2, Cambridge (MA)/London.

Spencer, W.G. 1938b. *Celsus De Medicina*, vol. 3, Cambridge (MA)/London.

Spink, M.S. and Lewis, G.L. 1973. *Albucasis on Surgery and Instruments*, London.

Stacey, R.J. 2011. 'The composition of some Roman medicines: Evidence for Pliny's Punic wax?', *Analytical and Bioanalytical Chemistry* 401, 1749.

Stacey, R.J., Dyer, J., Mussell, C., Lluveras-Tenorio, A., Colombini, M.P., Duce, C., La Nasa, J., Cantisani, E., Prati, C., Sciutto, G., Mazzeo, R., Sotiropoulou, S., Rosi, F., Miliani, C., Cartechini, L., Mazurek, J., and Schilling, M. 2018. 'Ancient encaustic: An experimental exploration of technology, ageing behaviour and approaches to analytical investigation', *Microchemical Journal* 138, 472–87.

Stacey, R.J. and Hook, D.R. 2005. 'Analysis of the contents of some Roman and Greek medicine containers', unpublished report, PRO7191, 28 November 2005. Department of Scientific Research, British Museum.

von Staden, H. 1989. *Herophilus: The Art of Medicine in Early Alexandria*, Cambridge/New York.

Stampolidis, N. Chr. and Tassoulas, Y. (eds) 2014. *Hygieia: Health, Illness, Treatment from Homer to Galen*, Athens.

Sternitzke, K. 2012. 'Spatel, Sonde und Skalpell. Medizinische Instrumente im archäologischen Befund', in *Stories of Long Ago. Festschrift für Michael D. Roaf*, edited by H. Baker, K. Kaniuth and A. Otto, 649–66, Münster.

Stettler, A. 1982. 'Der Instrumentenschrank von Kom Ombo', *Antike Welt* 13(3), 48–53.

Strudwick, N. 2006. *Masterpieces of Ancient Egypt*, London.

Sudhoff, K. 1926. *Geschichte der Zahnheilkunde*, Leipzig.

Summerton, N. 2007. *Medicine and Health Care in Roman Britain* (Shire Archaeology 87), Princes Risborough.

Summerton, N. 2021. *Greco-Roman Medicine and What it can Teach us Today*, Barnsley.

Swoboda, E. 1953. *Carnuntum Seine Geschichte und seine Denkmäler*, Vienna.

Tabanelli, M. 1958. *Lo strumento chirurgico e la sua storia*, Forli/Milan.

Taborelli, L. 2012. 'Cachets d'oculistes e contenitori per *medicamenta* tra antiquaria e archeologia', *Latomus* 71, 1026–54.

Taborelli, L. and Marengo, S.M. 1998. 'Il medicamento ΛYKION e i suoi contenitori', *Archeologia Classica* 50, 213–72.

Taborelli, L. and Marengo, S.M. 2010. 'Microcontenitori per *medicamenta* di epoca ellenistica e romana', *Archeologia Classica* 61, 211–42.

Taborelli, L. and Marengo, S.M. 2017. 'Medicine bottles and ointment jars from Morgantina', *Archeologia Classica* LXVIII, 27–51.

Tegethoff, F.W., Rohleder, J., and Kroker, E. 2001. *Calcium Carbonate: From the Cretaceous Period into the 21st Century*, Basel.

Temkin, O. 1956. *Soranus' Gynecology*, Baltimore.

Thackray, C.F. c. 1955. *A Catalogue of Surgical Instruments and Surgical Sundries*, Leeds/London/Johannesburg.

Tomaselli, C. 1983. 'Instrumentum metallico', in *Museo dell'Istituto di Archeologia Materiali, 1*, Fonti er studi per la storia dell'Università di Pavia, edited by R. Invernizzi, C. Tomaselli and M.G. Zezza, Pavia, 55–106, 190–5.

Tomlin, R.S.O. 2008. 'Special Delivery: a Graeco-Roman gold amulet for healthy childbirth', *Zeitschrift für Papyrologie und Epigraphik* 167, 219-24.

Tomlin, R.S.O. 2018. *Britannia Romana. Roman Inscriptions and Roman Britain*, Oxford.

Totelin, L. 2013. 'Sticky eyes or weeping wounds: Trying to interpret the Pozzino tablets', in *The Recipes Project* (http://recipes. hypotheses.org/949; accessed April 2023).

Touwaide, A. 2011. 'L'archéo-pharmacie à la découverte des médicaments anciens', in Dasen 2011b, 54–5.

Toynbee, J.M.C. 1971. *Death and Burial in the Roman World*, London.

Triantafyllos, D. 2014. 'Instrument and medicine case', in Stampolidis and Tassoulas 2014, 314–16.

Tsigarida, B. 2011. 'Le médecin de Pydna' in Dasen 2011b, 14–15.

Tucci, P.L. 2008. 'Galen's storeroom, Rome's libraries, and the fire of A.D. 192', *Journal of Roman Archaeology* 21, 133–49.

Tullo, E. 2010. 'Trepanation and Roman medicine: A comparison of osteoarchaeological remains, material culture and written texts', *Journal of the Royal College of Physicians of Edinburgh* 40, 165–71.

Ullmann, M. 1994. 'Die arabische Überlieferung der Schriften des Rufus von Ephesos', in *Aufstieg und Niedergang der römischen Welt (ANRW)* II, 37.2, edited by W. Haase and H. Temporini, Berlin/New York, 1293–349.

Untracht, O. 1975. *Metal techniques for craftsmen*, New York.

Urban, O.H., Teschler-Nicola, M., and Schultz, M. 1985. 'Die latènezeitlichen Gräberfelder von Katzelsdorf und Guntramsdorf, Niederösterreich', *Archaeologia Austriaca* 69, 13–104.

Uzel, İ. 1995. 'An ancient surgical set in the History of Medicine Museum at the Medical History and Ethics Department at Cerrahpaşa Medical School', *The New History of Medicine Studies*, Istanbul, 133–9 (in Turkish).

Vainio-Kaila, T., Kyyhkynen, A., Rautkari, L., and Siitonen, A. 2015. 'Antibacterial effects of extracts of Pinus sylvestris and Picea abies against Staphylococcus aureus, Enterococcus faecalis, Escherichia coli, and Streptococcus pneumoniae', *BioResources* 10, 7763–71.

Vallance, S.L., Singer, B.W., Hitchen, S.M., and Townsend, J.H. 1998. 'The development and preliminary application of a gas chromatographic method for the characterisation of gum media', *Journal of the American Institute for Conservation* 37, 294–311.

Van der Eijk, P.J., Horstmanshoff, H.F.J., and Schrijvers, P.H. (eds) 1995. *Ancient Medicine in its Socio-cultural Context* (Clio Medica 27/28), Amsterdam/Atlanta, GA.

Vanwalscappel, B., Jackson, R., and Morel, A. 2015. 'Une pince médicale de type "staphylagra" à Sauchy-Lestrée (Pas-de-Calais, F)', *Instrumentum* 41, 38–9.

Vega Avelaira, T. 2017. 'Hallazgos de instrumental medico-quirurgico en el campamento romano de *Aquae Querquennae* (Porto Quintela, Ourense/España)', *Sautuola* 22, 221–32.

Velay, P. (ed.) 1989. *Les bronzes antiques de Paris*, Paris, 405–12.

Verbanck-Pierard, A. (ed.) 1998. *Au Temps d'Hippocrate. Médecine et société en Grèce antique*, Mariemont.

Verbanck-Piérard, A., Boudon-Millot, V., and Gourevitch, D. (eds) 2018. *Au Temps de Galien. Un médecin grec dans l'empire romain*, Mariemont.

Victoria and Albert Museum 1979. *Masterpieces of Cutlery and the Art of Eating*, Victoria and Albert Museum, London.

Voinot, J. 1999. *Les cachets à collyres dans le monde romain* (Monographies Instrumentum 7), Montagnac.

von Moock, D.W. 1998. *Die figürliche Grabstelen Attikas. Studien zur Verbreitung, Chronologie, Typologie und Ikonographie*, Mainz.

von Staden, H. 1989. *Herophilus: the Art of Medicine in Early Alexandria*, Cambridge/New York.

Vulpes, B. 1847. *Illustrazione di tutti gli strumenti chirurgici scavati in Ercolano e in Pompej e che ora conservansi nel Real Museo Borbonico di Napoli compresa in sette memorie lette all'Academia Ercolanese*, Naples.

Walker, R.E. 1973. 'Roman veterinary medicine', in *Animals in Roman Life and Art*, J.M.C. Toynbee, London, 303–43.

Walters, H.B. 1899. *Catalogue of the Bronzes, Greek, Roman and Etruscan in the Department of Greek and Roman Antiquities, British Museum*, London.

Weaver, D.S., Perry, G.H., Macchiarelli, R., and Bondioli, L. 2000. 'A surgical amputation in 2nd century Rome', *The Lancet* 356, 686.

Wells, C.M. 1972. *The German Policy of Augustus. An Examination of the Archaeological Evidence*, Oxford.

Wheeler, R.E.M. 1930. *London in Roman Times*, London.

White, R. 1978. 'The application of gas-chromatography to the identification of waxes', *Studies in Conservation* 23, 57–68.

Wickkiser, B.L. 2008. *Asklepios, Medicine, and the Politics of Healing in Fifth-Century Greece. Between Craft and Cult*, Baltimore, MD.

Wiedemer, H. R. 1962. 'Ausgrabungen Königsfelden 1961', *Jahresbericht der Gesellschaft pro Vindonissa* 1961/1962, 19–43.

Wilson, D.M. 2002. *The British Museum: A History*, London.

Windler, H. 1912. *Chirurgie-Instrumente, Krankenhaus-Möbel, Bandagen, Apparate zur Orthopädie, Sterilisation und Krankenpflege*, Berlin/St Petersburg.

Wright, R.P. 1977. 'A Roman veterinary physician from the Thames Valley', *Britannia* 8, 279–82.

Youtie, L.C. 1976. 'A medical prescription for an eye-salve (P.Princ. III 155)', *Zeitschrift für Papyrologie und Epigraphik* 23, 121–9.

Zachariou-Kaila, E. 2009. 'Personal grooming: Metal objects from Roman Cyprus', *Cahiers du Centre d'Études Chypriotes* 39, 325–46.

Index

Numbers in *italic* denote pages with figures. Numbers in **bold** denote pages with tables.